The French and
Their Revolution

BOOKS BY THE SAME AUTHOR

L'Armée révolutionnaire parisienne à Lyon et dans la région lyonnaise
(Rachais, Lyon, 1952)

Les Armées révolutionnaires du Midi
(Association Marc Bloch, Toulouse, 1955)

*Les Armées révolutionnaires: instrument de la Terreur dans les
Départements, avril 1793–floréal an II*
(2 vols., Mouton, Paris, 1961 & 1963)
translated by Marianne Elliott as
The People's Armies (Yale University Press, 1987)

Terreur et subsistances 1793–1795 (Librairie Clavreuil, Paris, 1965)

A Second Identity: Essays on France and French history (OUP, 1969)

The Police and the People: French popular protest 1789–1820
(OUP, 1970)

Reactions to the French Revolution (OUP, 1972)

Paris and its Provinces 1792–1802 (OUP, 1975)

A Sense of Place (Duckworth, 1975)

Tour de France (Duckworth, 1976)

Death in Paris 1795–1801 (OUP, 1978)

Promenades: A historian's appreciation of modern French literature
(OUP, 1980)

The Streets of Paris (Duckworth, 1980)

*French and Germans, Germans and French: A personal interpretation of
France under two Occupations 1914–1918/1940–1944*
(University Press of New England, 1983)

Still Life: Sketches from a Tunbridge Wells childhood
(Chatto & Windus, 1983)

A Classical Education (Chatto & Windus, 1985)

People and Places (OUP, 1985)

Something To Hold Onto (John Murray, 1988)

The End of the Line (John Murray, 1997)

The French and Their Revolution

RICHARD COBB

*Selected writings
edited and introduced by
David Gilmour*

JOHN MURRAY
Albemarle Street, London

First published in 1998
by John Murray (Publishers) Ltd,
50 Albemarle Street, London W1X 4BD

A catalogue record for this book is available from the British Library

Cased ISBN 0-7195-5467-5
Paperback ISBN 0-7195-5461-6

Typeset in 10.5/12.5 Stempel Garamond by
Servis Filmsetting Ltd, Manchester

Printed and bound in Great Britain by
The University Press, Cambridge

Contents

Abbreviations

AAG	Archives Administratives de la Guerre
AC	Archives communales
AD	Archives départementales
AHG	Archives Historiques de la Guerre
AHRF	*Annales historiques de la Révolution française*
AN	Archives Nationales
APP	Archives de la Préfecture de Police
BL	British Library
BN	Bibliothèque Nationale

Introduction

IN THE COURSE of the 1970s Richard Cobb emerged as a member of that rare breed, a British historian who was also a 'public personality'. Yet he did not attain this status by sacrificing scholarship to journalism or television. Although an Oxford figure of prodigious and flamboyant eccentricity, he remained an inspiring teacher, an obsessive researcher and a productive historian able to combine the writing of stylish and provocative essays with the publication of serious history. Between 1970 and 1978 he published (apart from two volumes of essays) four major works on the social history of the French Revolution, all of them based on archival research he had carried out in France.

French historians were already aware of the man once described by *Le Monde* as '*l'étonnant Cobb*'. By the early seventies their British counterparts had also come to appreciate this emaciated and outspoken don, to welcome the originality of his work and the uniqueness of his angle of vision. Gwynn Williams described him as 'the Goya of our craft', while Sir Raymond Carr called him 'the most illuminating and idiosyncratic' of contemporary historians, a man whose books were 'the work of a poet as much as of a historian'. Honours and appointments accumulated: the Chair of Modern History at Oxford, honorary fellowships at Balliol and Merton, the Wolfson Prize, the Légion d'honneur. In 1983 he published *Still Life*, a delightful evocation of his childhood in Tunbridge Wells, and in the following year he celebrated his retirement with a controversial stint as chairman of the judges of the Booker Prize.

After that his career and reputation fell away. Two further, and slighter, volumes of autobiography appeared, but they were not of the same class as *Still Life*.* Invitations from literary editors (who admittedly found him a rather unreliable contributor) dried up, and Cobb himself was so disgusted by the bicentennial celebrations of the French Revolution that he no longer wanted to write about France. His last years were unhappy and

---

* A charming fourth memoir, *The End of the Line*, has been published since Cobb's death by John Murray.

clouded by illness. Accompanied by his wife and youngest son, he moved to Normandy and then to Whitby before returning to Oxfordshire to live in Abingdon in the summer of 1994. When he died in January 1996, only one of his historical works – a translation from an early book written in French – was still in print. That is the principal reason for this volume.

It is easier to explain the lateness of Cobb's fame than to try to account for its decline. An English historian, whose first book in English does not appear until he has reached the age of fifty-two, is unlikely to receive early acclamation in his own country. Not that he suffered from problems of idleness or unwillingness to write: as a young man, Cobb was simply an unambitious historian who enjoyed working in French archives without thinking of constructing a career. Financing his research by teaching English in Paris, he allowed himself the luxury of deflection, of being directed down unexpected channels, of pausing in his pursuit of the revolutionary armies to linger over the love letters of a *guillotiné* or an eyewitness account of the September Massacres. And even if he resolved to end his research on some matter in 1794, in practice he was unable to resist following it into 1795 or 1800 or even 1820, if the people he was studying had been still alive at that time.

He arrived in Paris in 1935 at the age of seventeen, after leaving Shrewsbury and before going up to Oxford to read History at Merton. The experience of staying with a French family on the Grands Boulevards provided the catalyst for a lifetime's immersion in French life and history. During university vacations he returned to work in the Archives Nationales and in 1938, under the distant supervision of Georges Lefebvre, he began research on François-Nicolas Vincent, an obscure leader of the extremist *hébertiste* faction. For a brief period he was a passionate admirer of Robespierre and Saint-Just, but fortunately this did not last. He later considered them to be the two most repellent figures in French history.

After the war, which he spent in various mundane and not very demanding positions in the British Army, he returned to the Archives Nationales in 1946. Quickly realizing, however, that *hébertisme* was a fruitless subject, he turned to the revolutionary armies sent out from Paris and other cities during the Terror to enforce revolutionary order in the provinces and requisition food supplies for the urban population. For nine years he pursued them through departmental and communal archives, rescuing their obscure members from the dust of innumerable boxes and, through his writing, adding an important and unexpected dimension to the study of the French Revolution. The Archives Nationales, and particularly the papers of the Ministry of Justice, remained at the centre of Cobb's investigations, but he loved provincial research as well, above all in Normandy, Lyon and Lille: many of his early articles were written for journals such as *Annales de Normandie* and *La Revue du Nord*. As he once remarked, his history was not French history, but French provincial history, even if his favourite province was Paris.

During these years of largely anonymous research, Cobb acquired what he later called, in the title of one of his books, 'a second identity', another persona which thought, felt and said different things on the other side of the Channel. The object, he once said, of 'a veritable *conspiration de l'amitié*' in France, he found it easy to make the transference, to acquire that new identity, that 'crossing of the line' which he called 'the most important requisite for the English specialist of the history and culture of a foreign society'. Of course an inability or unwillingness to acquire a second identity has not prevented numerous English scholars from understanding foreign societies, but in Cobb's case the point was fundamental, and he relished it. The compliment he most valued – a French historian's remark that he spoke and thought *comme un titi parisien* – thus sets him apart from other English historians pre-eminent in the studies of another country. No one has ever suggested that Sir Raymond Carr thought like a Madrid teddy-boy or that Denis Mack Smith spoke like *un ragazzo di borgata*.

Cobb's career remained unconventional (in spite of good intentions, he did not manage to acquire a doctorate) until 1955 when, at the age of thirty-eight, he accepted a lectureship at University College in Aberystwyth. This was followed by a research fellowship at Manchester in 1959 and a brief appointment at Leeds before he returned to Oxford as a Fellow and Tutor at Balliol in 1962. Yet for his first fourteen years in England nearly all his work – apart from a handful of anonymous reviews for the *TLS* – was written and published in French. Preceded by books on the revolutionary armies of Lyon and the Midi, *Les Armées révolutionnaires* (translated by Marianne Elliott and published as *The People's Armies* in 1987) appeared in two volumes in 1961 and 1963 and were succeeded in 1965 by *Terreur et subsistances*. *A Second Identity*, consisting mainly of the *TLS* pieces and an autobiographical introduction, did not come out until 1969 and was closely followed by his major works in English, *The Police and the People* (1970), *Reactions to the French Revolution* (1972) and *Paris and its Provinces* (1975). Most of the present volume is taken from these three books.

Cobb's distinctive contributions to an understanding of French history are encapsulated in the titles of these and lesser-known works. *A Second Identity* and *A Sense of Place* indicate his commitment to France and sensitivity to French topography, while *People and Places* and *The Police and the People* suggest his concern with individuals and their relationships with authority and the places they live in. For Cobb, history was not simply a matter of spending long days in the archives: it had to be walked,

observed, smelt, drunk and above all listened to, in cafés, buses, parks and
railway stations. He wrote with such intuition about the poor of revolutionary France because he knew their descendants in the 1940s and '50s:
having spent so much time with peasant farmers, criminals, blackmarket-
eers, legionnaires, sailors and their families, he was naturally more aware
than most historians of their feelings and preoccupations. This too
explains his understanding of human motivation and the great variety of
its sources. He always wrote of people as individuals, not as members of
a class or a crowd or a list of statistics. His revolutionary armies did not,
therefore, consist simply of revolutionary enthusiasts but also of people
who joined up because they liked uniforms, because they were unemployed or bankrupt, or because they were *émigrés* or counter-revolutionaries in need of a disguise: others were bandits enticed by opportunities in
the provinces, or wigmakers who, following the fall in demand of wigs,
relished the idea of plundering a few farmers.

'I have never,' wrote Cobb, 'understood history other than in terms of
human relationships,' a view that set him against Marxists, sociologists,
computer historians and anyone else who tried to 'impose a false sense
of unity and simplicity on a subject which has neither'. How he disliked
historians who were always debating theories or imposing structures
or trying to find a 'grand design' for events that were spontaneous and
chaotic and usually unintended. His approach to the French Revolution
was very much an individual's on individuals, a continuous attempt to get
beyond or under the rhetoric to see how events affected individual lives.
He insisted on looking at the Revolution not through its politics and its
institutions but through human experiences, a process he called 'rediscovering the individual'. Thus in his pages the *sans-culottes* become no
longer a uniform body of people acting out of class considerations but
individuals who did this or that for reasons of family, geography, temperament, habit, selfishness or pure chance. And at the same time the
Revolution itself becomes a little more human, or at any rate less effective
and oppressive. If it did little for the poor, it did not prevent most people
from getting on with their lives without busybodies constantly telling
them what was good for them. In Cobb's books we are made aware of the
irrelevance of the Revolution to most people's needs and interests. What
meaning did it have for poor girls from Lyon – the subject of this volume's
final chapter – who had been seduced and abandoned when pregnant? Of
what possible value were Robespierre's self-righteousness and insistence
on 'virtue' to people who could recognize the 'outriders' of hunger and
knew that famine was on the way? This was surely Cobb's principal
achievement: to have given the Revolution its human proportions, to have
shown us what it meant not for Robespierre and Saint-Just and subsequent generations of revolutionaries but for millions of individuals who

had to endure the events while trying to get on with the business of living their lives and looking after their families.

As Cobb himself put it, he was too much of a *frondeur* to wish to belong to any school of history. At the same time he was too much of an individual and too lacking in self-importance to wish to found one himself. A couple of days before his death, he wrote that, just as he had never been a participant in anyone's cult, 'there could never be a Cobb cult'. He had many pupils, inspired by his teaching and his example, who have become major historians. But they did not become disciples: they knew his genius was unique and inimitable. That is, I think, a partial explanation for the decline of Cobb's reputation after his retirement from Oxford; it needed not only his writing but also his presence – in tutorials, seminars and lectures – to sustain it.

And perhaps also it required some kind of conclusion, some work of synthesis so that later students could pin him down to a coherent, easily remembered viewpoint: 'such and such was Cobb's position, thus it differed from Lefebvre's, thus it contrasted with Soboul's . . .' But that was never Cobb's way. 'My subject is chaotic,' he wrote in his introduction to *The Police and the People*, 'and I may well have written about it chaotically!' Well it was, of course, and he did. Although he never hesitated to make judgements about the French Revolution, its events and its politicians, he was not interested in making an overall judgement, providing a synthesis or producing a textbook of the great saga. Much as he admired Simon Schama's *Citizens: A Chronicle of the French Revolution*, he could never have written such a book himself. Like his angle of vision, his craftsmanship barely altered: the pointillist technique, the armoury of details, the obsession with individual lives – these were as much a part of *Death in Paris* (1978) as they were of his earliest writing.

All Cobb's books have untidy structures, like their subjects, like indeed all history, especially when observed – as in his case – from the level of the street. Thus it is peculiarly difficult to compile a single volume taken from his writings on the French Revolution. The extracts selected here are broadly representative of his work, but a great deal, above all on the revolutionary armies, has necessarily been left out. The core of the book concentrates on *les petites gens*, the main object of Cobb's research, their influence on the Revolution and the Revolution's influence on them, the *sans-culottes*, the counter-revolutionaries, individual activists on different sides, and above all the people he most sympathized with, those on the fringes of the Revolution for whom political events were often irrelevant.

On the style of the opening chapters, two untypically general essays on France and her revolutions, a couple of points should be made. 'The Revolutionary Mentality in France' was Cobb's first article in English, published in 1957 at a time when he was almost exclusively writing (and living) in French. Anyone who compares it with his later work will discern the Gallic influence, the use of concepts and categories and generalizations, which he afterwards pruned from his prose style.

The second essay, 'Revolutionary Situations in France', was written soon after the *événements* of 1968, and the language reflects the author's disgust at the time. It is by any standards a subjective piece, but then Cobb was – and was proud of being – a historian who wrote subjectively. His writing, he once admitted, had been 'conditioned by [his] own experience and prejudices' because he did not believe it 'possible to divorce history from experience'.

David Gilmour
St Antony's College
May 1997

I

*The Revolutionary Mentality in France**

I T MAY BE objected that the title of this article refers to something that has never existed, that there is no such thing as a 'revolutionary mentality' and that in periods of revolution men think and act much as in more normal conditions. This objection may be valid, but is very difficult to put to the test, for if there exists a body of information concerning the behaviour of a certain group of people during the period of the French Revolution, we are much less informed about how they thought and acted in the years before 1789, so that it is not really possible to say how far what we call the revolutionary mentality was a product of the revolutionary situation or how far it was, on the contrary, a continuation of attitudes and prejudices that had already enjoyed a long lease of life during the eighteenth century.

It is possible, on the other hand, to state quite firmly what is *not* meant by this term. The revolutionary mentality is neither a carefully reasoned philosophy of life, nor again a conscious attempt to grapple with all the major problems of the revolutionary period by recourse to a considered body of doctrine. We are concerned here only with the personal attitude of a hypothetical person, called for the sake of convenience the average revolutionary, towards the common events of everyday life in revolutionary France during the high tide of the revolutionary movement, between the summer of 1793 and the late summer of the following year. It is a matter of attitudes, reactions, prejudices, behaviour in the face of given problems and given situations, rather than an ideology derived from any school of thought.

Who is this average revolutionary and how is one to decide on his 'averageness'? Is it not possible that he may in fact be a caricature who, because he makes a great deal of noise and is constantly taking up

---

* From *A Second Identity*, pp. 121–41.

7

attitudes, has left some record behind of his activities and utterances, while the voices of his less ambitious or more moderate colleagues fail altogether to reach the historian? In other words, is not the average revolutionary in reality the professional super-revolutionary, the man who quite deliberately goes about making a career for himself in the revolutionary movement by not only always swimming with the pre-vailing current, but also, whenever possible, a few lengths ahead of it? Or if this is not so, will he not at least be turned in the orthodox mould and constantly looking over his shoulder to make sure that he is still in step? Before attempting to answer these questions, it will be useful first of all to see how others have portrayed what they believed to be the typical revolutionary, and then to discuss what social groups we have in mind in identifying him, and the source material from which our information can be derived.

The most familiar portrait of the revolutionary of the Paris Section or of the small town is that drawn by the enemies of revolutionary France, in the cartoons of Gillray or in the prints issued in Cologne and Verona, representing, let us say, the members of a revolutionary committee at work: empty wine bottles are rolling on the floor, between the legs of scraggy dogs and scrofulous cats, piles of tarnished silver candelabra and gold plate are stacked on chairs or in corners, while the revolutionaries themselves, unshaven, haggard, squinting, or with glazed eyes, sit stu-pidly, under the disapproving gaze of a bust of Marat, some with ladies, gorgeously decked in stolen finery and wearing hats topped with sagging plumes, draped around them like lifebelts; others sleeping loudly with their heads on the table, while watches, necklaces, and jewellery dribble from their pockets. The drunken, villainous, wall-eyed brigand of the Coblenz and the London prints (who, incidentally, bears a strong family likeness to the cadaverous, lank-haired, priest-ridden Frenchman of Hogarth's *Calais Gate*) is, of course, little more than a creation of counter-revolutionary fancy and propaganda. It is hardly necessary to add that it is a portrait inaccurate in almost every detail.

More respectable than these caricatures is the evidence of those who survived to recount their experiences in revolutionary prisons: in these memoirs emphasis is not so much on the depravity of the minor revolu-tionary official, as on his ingratitude. The most ardent revolutionaries, one gathers from this source, were former servants, valets, coachmen, cooks, butlers, ladies' maids, '*valetaille et piédetaille*'. The 'ungrateful servant' thesis does not bear a close examination, however, and there are many more examples of former servants who accompanied their masters into emigration, who remained behind in an attempt to save their property from confiscation or took immense risks in sheltering nobles on the run. The careful analysis of the incidence both of the Terror and of the emigration carried out by the American historian, Donald Greer,[1] suggests that there was a high percentage of former servants and of skilled artisans in the luxury trades – barbers, engravers, fan-makers, and the like – among the victims of the Terror. Revolutionary opinion was extremely suspicious – and not without reason – of all those whose living had depended on the favour or the custom of the *ci-devants*.[2] Could such persons be relied upon to serve faithfully a regime that had brought them loss of custom and grave economic hardship? Many revolutionaries did not think so, but at the same time it was natural that many in this group, thrown out of work by the decline of the luxury trades, should have eagerly sought paid employment under the new revolutionary bureaucracy and should also have attempted to assuage suspicions attaching to their former state by making a great show of revolutionary ardour. Any new regime will bring a host of new possibilities of employment, and posts on revolutionary committees and in other branches of the plethoric revolutionary and wartime bureaucracy created many new openings for people who could show a clean card of political orthodoxy; naturally, there was something of a stampede to get the plums. The *valetaille*, however, never obtained a very considerable share in the distribution of favours.

The average revolutionary is then neither the Gillray wretch with his red cap and squint, nor necessarily the ungrateful servant repaying kindness with plebeian callousness. Politically, he is a member of a Paris Section, in which he might hold revolutionary office, or of the *société populaire* of a town or village, in which he might exercise functions in one of the many committees that came under the control of these revolutionary assemblies. The high-water mark of his active existence as a revolutionary would be between the spring of 1793 and the summer of 1794. We are not concerned here with the administrative importance of this group: it is enough to say that, as an active minority, it fell to them above all to execute the innumerable orders and directives of the huge revolutionary bureaucratic machine.

It is here that there arises the problem of source material. Such men, the humble labourers in the vineyard of the Revolution, are not likely to leave personal records of their activities and to keep diaries recording their day-to-day impressions and intimate convictions. Those who have left us personal reminiscences of their experiences during the Revolution were

---

[1] Donald Greer, *The Incidence of the Terror during the French Revolution* (Cambridge, Mass., 1935), and *The Incidence of the Emigration during the French Revolution* (Cambridge, Mass., 1951).
[2] On the prejudices attaching to former servants and the like in revolutionary circles, see my article 'Le "complot militaire" de ventôse an II. Note sur les rapports entre Versailles et Paris au temps de la Terreur', in *Mémoires de la Société historique de Paris et de l'Île-de-France* (1956), pp. 221–50.

nearly all victims of the new regime, or at least persons who had little sympathy for the revolutionary aims. Possibly some active revolutionaries on the level we are considering may have occasionally recorded their impressions, but if so such records have not come down to the historian. It is only, then, from collective sources (apart from very occasional personal letters) that the historian can draw his material for what must necessarily be a composite and impressionistic portrait of the average urban or rural revolutionary. We can perceive the *sans-culotte révolutionnaire* as part of a group, not as an individual, and we really know nothing of how he behaved in his home on the sixth or seventh floor (in Paris and other big cities social distinctions went not by quarters but by storeys) nor what were his principal thoughts and preoccupations: we can see him mainly in his public and collective capacity, in the midst of those clubs – the *sociétés populaires* – in which the presence of his fellows, as well as of a noisy and censorious public in the galleries, might be expected to impose on him a certain desire to conform at least to the most obvious standards of revolutionary orthodoxy. Source material of this kind will inevitably focus attention not so much on the average revolutionary, for that would imply some possibility of comparison, as on the orthodox *sans-culotte*. As there is a considerable range of collective evidence of this kind, it is quite possible to distinguish between the politically orthodox, the *parfaits sans-culottes révolutionnaires* as they would no doubt have preferred to define themselves, and the genuine rebels, a minority within a minority, most of whom were to suffer the fate reserved for ultra-revolutionaries who, according to official revolutionary logic, were but the other face of the Janus-figure of counter-revolution. But sources of this kind, however widely spread, have very obvious limitations, and the minutes of collective assemblies like the *sociétés populaires*, and even of smaller and more intimate institutions, such as the *comités de surveillance*, give a premium to orthodoxy rather than to sincerity, offering the place of honour to the most vociferous and the most eager revolutionaries, rather than to the average. The picture thus obtained of the collective revolutionary, if not so much of a caricature as the Gillray prints, is nevertheless an oversimplification as well as an exaggeration of certain common traits. In this type of open forum of orthodoxy, pride of place would almost always go to those who slightly overdid the prevailing tendencies. In the choice of material, therefore, I have not deliberately rejected the commonplace in favour of the curious or the fantastic, but have attempted rather to concentrate on those manifestations of revolutionary attitudes that recur the most frequently.

So much for the limitations of a source material that clearly does not allow for precise, mathematical, sociological treatment. What then do we mean by an average revolutionary, one who would have described himself, and been recognized by others as a *bon sans-culotte révolutionnaire*? The *sans-culottes* do not constitute a class but they do represent an identifiable group. They are not drawn from the workers (*ouvriers*), and the lower grades of eighteenth-century wage-earner (*manœuvre, gagne-denier, commissionnaire*, etc.) were seldom admitted as full members to the *sociétés populaires*. They are not necessarily poor, by any standards. Revolutionary terminology is particularly deceptive in this respect for a certain inverted snobbery caused many people to 'democratize' their occupations. Some of those who call themselves artisans, carpenters, joiners, are revealed, when one examines their tax returns, as affluent contractors, employing up to sixty or a hundred labourers, or as comfortable *rentiers* with places in the country bought from confiscated lands.[1] Furthermore, eighteenth-century terminology generally makes no distinction between master and journeyman, between *maître* and *garçon*. From what we do know – thanks primarily to the writings of Soboul, Rudé, Brinton, and others – it can be asserted that the backbone of the *sans-culotte* movement was supplied by master-craftsmen, small employers of labour (in eighteenth-century Paris the average size of a workshop was from four to fourteen *garçons*), small shopkeepers, publicans and *marchands de vin*, the 'better sort of clerks', particularly former *clercs de procureur*, together with a thin sprinkling of professional men – schoolmasters, public letter-writers, *maîtres d'armes*, and, in the countryside, ex-priests and monks and former pastors of the Religion Prétendue Réformée, as well as a few survivors of the luxury trades. Doctors, apothecaries, and barbers are rather rare, popular prejudice against them still being strong; lawyers and notaries rarer still save in the smaller towns; in many places there were even efforts to exclude them *en bloc* from office-holding, along with former priests (though a great many of these got in by the back door as *greffiers*, secretaries, officials of one kind or another, thanks to their superior education), noblemen, and personal servants, as having been the instruments, in one form or another, of the *ancien régime*.[2]

The revolutionary might also be a professional soldier. Indeed it would be hard to overestimate the contribution made by the regular soldier,

---

[1] The case of Jean-Baptiste-Antoine Lefranc, '*charpentier*', commander of the *canonniers* of the Section des Tuileries, in reality a prosperous building-contractor employing at one time over 200 workmen, is an example of this type of verbal deflation. See my *L'Armée révolutionnaire à Lyon* (Lyon, 1952), Appendix H, pp. 117–19.

[2] See for instance AN, D III 78 (470). Comité de Législation, Chartres: comité de surveillance de Chartres à la Convention (18 germinal an II): 'Ne souffrez pas de ces palefreniers de chambre qui croyent avoir beaucoup travaillé quand ils ont éponge ceux qu'ils appellent leurs maîtres, forcez-les de devenir libres, en décrêtant que, hors l'agriculture, il ne pourra y avoir de valets mâles.'

especially the non-commissioned officer of the *ancien régime*, to the revolutionary movement during this period. The Revolution gave these men a brilliant prospect of promotion in the semi-civilian *Garde nationale*, in the new armies, or in civilian revolutionary institutions. The part played by this group in the development of a standard, conformist, revolutionary pattern of behaviour was all the more effective in that the ex-soldiers, unlike their artisan and shopkeeper counterparts, were less parochial in attitude, had fewer local attachments, and, if they were still serving in the Army, or in one of the innumerable organizations that offered posts on the fringes of military life, formed the principal link between the revolutionary movement in Paris or the other big cities and the provinces, and, later, between revolutionary France and the conquered territories. It was people of this type who penetrated the army of Italy and made it into a republican stronghold in which many ardent revolutionaries found a refuge after Thermidor, helping the Italian republicans with their knowledge and experience. Constantly on the move, in many cases a Parisian among provincials, the soldier or semi-civilian played a leading part in the proceedings of provincial *sociétés*.

The average revolutionary is of course, as I have said, in a sense an abstraction. However, the particular group of people with whom we are concerned did think of themselves, as a unit distinct and identifiable, under the expression *sans-culottes*, while their general attitude to life constituted *sans-culottisme*. Both words were used quite consciously and deliberately in 1793 and 1794 to designate the élite of the revolutionary movement. A self-imposed label during the Terror, it became in 1795, in the language of its enemies, a synonym for the *bas peuple*,[1] which, of course, it never was. The sense in which the term was used during the earlier period may be gathered from a few examples. At Auch, a member of the Jacobin Club explains that *sans-culottisme* does not consist in the smallness of one's personal income, but in the sincere cult of equality,[2] that is, it is not an economic, but a moral category. Another definition, from the Lozère, states that 'true *sans-culottes* [are] men who have no other resources on which to live than the work of their hands',[3] which may seem at first to imply an economic definition, if one that was seldom attained, for many of the most ardent revolutionaries would not fit into such a category. More correctly, it reflects the moral preoccupation of the average revolutionary, an article of whose creed was the sanctity of work, particularly of useful manual work. For this reason he had little use for artists, scholars, and other useless people, branded as *oisifs* along with the aristocracy.

---

[1] E.g. Arch. Nièvre. Registre du comité de Corbigny (frimaire an III).
[2] Arch. Gers. L. 694. Société d'Auch (26 ventôse an II).
[3] Arch. Lozère. L. 532. Société de Mende (9 pluviôse an II).

Vingtergnier, a revolutionary professional soldier who ended up by being deported to the Seychelles, similarly stresses the moral factor.

> The *sans-culotte* [he writes] is a man who always goes on foot and who lives simply, with his wife and children ... on the fourth or fifth storey. The *sans-culotte* is useful. He knows how to plough a field, how to hammer and saw, how to cover a roof, make a pair of shoes. And since he works, you are sure not to find him at the Café de Chartres ...[1] In the evening, he goes to the meeting of his Section, not powdered, not scented, nor booted in the hope of being noticed by all the citizenesses in the galleries,[2] but in order to support to the utmost the right sort of resolutions.[3]

An austere, homely man, in fact, for a bachelor cannot be a good revolutionary, it is the duty of a good citizen to raise up children, future '*défenseurs de la patrie*', and bachelorhood is a manifestation of selfish individualism and of a lack of civic sense. The orthodox revolutionary opinion on this subject was no doubt influenced also by current economic theories relating a nation's strength and wealth to the size of its population, and there are plenty of indications that the revolutionaries, citizens of the most populated country in Europe at the time, were conscious of France's demographic strength. Social and moral objections to celibacy are well brought out in a petition, typical of many others, presented to the Convention in the summer of 1794 by the revolutionary society of Sens, in favour of a decree penalizing the bachelor,

> that hideous monster who engenders nothing [and who] is born of luxury ... Virtue will never exist in society so long as there are men who scorn the laws of nature, carrying scandal into society and shame and despair into families; he who does not marry, although normally constituted, cannot in general be virtuous, because, organized like anyone else, he seeks victims everywhere ... he introduces into society the germs of the passions which sooner or later must subvert it.[4]

Sans-culottisme can be defined, then, not so much in terms of wealth as of moral and civic utility. Indeed, in some places the local revolutionaries denounce those who seek to make invidious distinctions between rich and poor and who use the word in a purely economic sense. A member of the

---

[1] The Café de Chartres, in the galleries of the Palais-Royal, was a favourite meeting place of literary men. In 1793 it was reputed to be a rendezvous for Orleanist agents.
[2] For a similar condemnation of 'foppery', see AN, D III 306 (31). Comité de Législation, Yonne, pétition de Héry, 1er pluviôse an III.
[3] Quoted by A. Soboul in 'Problèmes du travail en l'an II', *Journal de Psychologie* (1955), pp. 39–58.
[4] AN, D III 307 (33). Comité de Législation, société révolutionnaire de Sens à la Convention, 6 prairial an III.

society of the small town of Brie-Comte-Robert, on the highroad from Paris to the Brie cornlands, insists on the necessity of

> avoiding those diatribes, those ridiculous attacks against the rich, that base flat-tery of the poor in speaking of the *sans-culottes* ... I cannot see in this town any rich man [adds the speaker, a prosperous farmer]. I see *some* citizens who are better off than others ... and we should hope that their numbers increase as much as possible ... Let us not flatter the poverty of citizens with the honour-able title of *sans-culottes*. We mean by the word *sans-culotte* only a good patriot, a friend of liberty.[1]

This was certainly the definition that would have most appealed to the artisans and shopkeepers who formed the cadres of the revolutionary movement. A *sans-culotte*, we often read, may have a comfortable income provided that it is the recompense of hard work. Property is sacred, so long as it is not excessive. Surplus wealth produces luxury and idleness, and these lead to depravity.

Thus the approach of the revolutionary to the problem of labour is moral rather than social. Every man should engage in some form of useful work, not only because the State needs all hands but because idleness is evil. The *sans-culottes* were particularly severe on those who did their work badly and without enthusiasm. The public executioner of the Orne Department was sent before the revolutionary tribunal for having con-sistently neglected his duties, and, far from keeping his guillotine clean, having allowed it to get into such a filthy condition of rust and dirt that when he was carrying out a public execution in Alençon, it took three attempts to sever the victim's head from his body.[2] A bad workman was a counter-revolutionary in the making, and so was a worker who went on strike or who attempted to leave his workshop; the pressing needs of war production further accentuated the hostility felt by the average revolutionary to all forms of collective labour agitation.

As his name implies, the *sans-culotte* is also distinguishable by his dress. He eschews all the frivolous trappings of the *ancien régime*: powdered wig, scent, silk breeches, silk stockings, bows, buckle shoes, flowered waistcoats, lorgnettes, silver-topped canes, and other such foppish finer-ies.[3] He wears his own hair long, has a simple coat and cotton trousers.

---

[1] Arch. com. Brie-Comte-Robert. Société populaire, 2me registre, séance du 20 germinal an II.

[2] AN, D III 194. Comité de Législation, Alençon, tribunal criminel du Département de l'Orne au Comité de Législation, 5 nivôse an II.

[3] Speaking at the *société populaire* of Tarbes, Monestier du Puy-de-Dôme introduced the members of the club to his colleague Isabeau in the following words: 'Vois, tournes tes regards sur cette société ... tu ne trouveras pas beaucoup de ces têtes artistement coiffées, pas beaucoup des grandes cravates de trois colliers, pas beaucoup des petites bougles [*sic*]

Then there is the vexed question of the moustache. Opinions differ strongly as to whether the moustache is or is not a revolutionary emblem. On the whole, the balance would appear to favour this adjunct when worn *à la gauloise*, that is in the Vercingetorix manner. However, opinion was not unanimous, and country people tended to think of the '*hommes à moustache*' from Paris and the other big cities as bandits, on account of their fearsome appearance,[1] and in the capital itself the long, shaggy moustaches favoured by the officers and soldiers of the civilian *armée révolutionnaire* – as also by General Hanriot and his personal staff – ended by identifying their bearers in the eyes of the general public as partisans of Hébert and his newspaper, the *Père Duchesne*.[2] Beards were definitely proscribed. The Committee of Public Safety allowed the Anabaptists of Alsace and Franche-Comté to retain theirs, but, locally, revolutionary authorities tried to invoke the decree prohibiting all external signs of religious *cultes* as applying to the beards of Anabaptists, rabbis, and Orthodox Jews. Was not a beard, they argued, a '*signe extérieur du culte*' and '*un reste des préjugés gothiques*'? In many places local committees obliged their wearers to remove these '*marques du fanatisme*'.[3]

Simplicity in dress and manner, a proper married status, regular attendance at the local *société populaire*, the execution of guard duties whenever required, and the undertaking of useful productive work were not enough. No man could be a good revolutionary without virtue, and a great deal of the time of *sociétés populaires* is taken up denouncing members who have misbehaved in one way or another. Thus we find Romme, subsequently one of the 'martyrs of Prairial', after delivering a formidable peroration on the standard theme of republican virtue and royalist vice, sending before the revolutionary tribunal an inhabitant of Agen, a revolutionary official, for having attempted to gain the favours of the wife of a prisoner by promising to obtain her husband's release. Such a man, thundered Romme, was a counter-revolutionary, for vice was counter-

---

de gilets cours d'habits pinces, pas beaucoup d'eaux de rose des parfums ... des figures mitonnées, en un mot pas beacoup des *messieurs*, pas beaucoup de muscadins. Notre langage ressemble en tout à notre costume' (Arch. Hautes-Pyrénées L. 1186 bis. Société populaire de Tarbes, 21 prairial an II).

[1] For instance, AN, F7 4774 26 d 4 (Louvet-Dubois, affaire de Thieux, Seine-et-Marne) concerning 'un détachement de l'armée révolutionnaire commandé par un chef à qui l'on donne dans les campagnes le nom du *Général Moustache*'.

[2] AN, F7* 2496 (registre du comité de surveillance de la Section de l'Homme-armé, séance du 27 ventôse an II), 'Le comité arrête que le nommé François Carterait ... se disant brigadier de la gendarmerie seroit conduit à la Conciergerie parce qu'il se disoit porteur d'ordre de couper les moustaches aux canonniers et autres personnes, en conséquence nous paroissant très suspect dans la circonstance critique où nous nous trouvons' (a reference to the arrest of the *hébertiste* leaders three days previously).

[3] For instances of this kind at Montbéliard, see my article 'Les débuts de la déchristianisation à Dieppe', *AHRF* (1956), pp. 191–209.

revolutionary.[1] In most clubs one side of the hall was reserved for women, and often only married couples were allowed to sit together. Women were excluded from some clubs altogether, and the efforts of politically-minded citizenesses to form clubs of their own were eyed with disfavour: the *société républicaine des deux sexes*, known derisively by the Paris *sans-culottes* as the *société hermaphrodite*, was suppressed. A ruthless war was waged on prostitutes, who were held to be counter-revolutionary: the revolutionary authorities particularly attempted to drive them from the garrison towns. The results of this preoccupation with public virtue were strongly resented by such ardent revolutionaries as the soldiers of the so-called *armée révolutionnaire* on their arrival in Lyon.[2]

Obscene literature was hunted down in the book-stores of the Palais-Royal.[3] Betting games, carnivals, fancy dress, billiards, and cards were unsuitable activities for revolutionaries. Betting deprived fathers of the wherewithal to feed little mouths,[4] carnivals and masked balls might permit counter-revolutionaries to escape in disguise, and it was both immoral and unlawful for a man to dress as a woman or a woman as a man.[5] Billiards, besides using up precious candles in a time when grease was needed for war manufacturers, kept revolutionaries away from the clubs in the evening, and it was better not to get the reputation of being lukewarm as far as the meetings were concerned.[6] Cards often led to brawls, and, save on the rare revolutionary packs, bore the figures of kings and queens and other feudal symbols.

The revolutionary was allowed one outlet: it was generally accepted that a good *sans-culotte* was entitled to his drink. Wine was necessary for health,

---

[1] Arch. Lot-et-Garonne, 2me registre de la société d'Agen, 8 messidor an II.

[2] The attacks made on prostitution by revolutionary authorities were not based only on moral and military considerations. *Sans-culotte* opinion was inclined to assimilate prostitutes to the other hangers-on of the *ancien régime*. It was inevitable that *sans-culotte* opinion should eye with such disfavour a group so patently illustrating all the vices of the *ancien régime*, all the faults that were the most hateful to these puritanical shopkeepers.

[3] AN, BB 3 73. Comité de surveillance du département de Paris, 3 pluviôse an II.

[4] AN, D III 177 (23). Comité de Législation, La Charité: société populaire de la Charité-sur-Loire à la Convention, 3me sans-culottide an II: 'Personne n'ignore quels sont les terribles effets de la passion du jeu poussée à l'excès. Le père y oublie sa famille, le magistrat son devoir, le patriote y laisse impunément sonner l'heure de la séance de la société.'

[5] Arch. Marne. Registre (non-inventorié) du comité de surveillance de Sainte-Ménehould. 'Séance du 26 pluviôse ... le comité prend des mesures contre des citoyens qui se disposent à se travestir dans ces jours nommés ci-devant gras. On fera proclamer la loi du 7 août 1793.' One exception was, however, encouraged: that of patriotic girls who dressed up as men to enlist: according to revolutionary propaganda several of these covered themselves with glory on the battlefield.

[6] Arch. Haute-Saône 361 L I. Société populaire de Gray, 21 frimaire an II. 'Un membre a demandé que la société fît une pétition à la municipalité pour défendre toute espèce de danse jusqu'à la paix et pour faire fermer les cabarets à 10 heures du soir.' This was an example of war-time rather than of specifically revolutionary puritanism.

it had nutritive qualities and in time of food-shortage could replace all solid foods save bread; it was a warrior's drink and gave force to the arm of the ploughman.[1] In Normandy similar virtues were claimed for cider. The revolutionary, so severe where some other passions were involved, was unexpectedly tolerant of drunkards, and revolutionary tribunals were extremely indulgent when it could be proved that counter-revolutionary utterances had been made under the influence of wine. The *sociétés populaires* did their best to keep noisy drunkards away from their meetings, but anyone who has consulted many of their minutes gains a very strong impression that much of the noise, disorder, shouting, and quarrelling that so often held up proceedings was due to intoxication. Wine stains, not blood stains, are fairly common on the pages of these minute books, written often in a trembling hand. This is not at all to suggest that the Revolution was a sort of non-stop bacchanalia, but that partial drunkenness was often an important component in a certain type of revolutionary excitability, particularly in meetings or committees. In 1793–4, the urban population was consistently under-nourished and the *sans-culottes* often drank a great deal of wine of the lowest quality – the *vin de Choisy* was notorious for its high chemical content – on an almost empty stomach. The *aubergistes* and the *limonadiers* whose establishments were situated on the great highways played a particularly important part in the political life of the provinces, transmitting the news, ideas, and propaganda brought to them by the soldiers who passed through on the way to the armies on the frontiers.

Civic balls and dances, often in former churches, were given official encouragement, to celebrate great events such as the recapture of Toulon. Civic banquets were another feature of the revolutionary's collective leisure. France being very short of food, and food being rationed, these were often rather dreary affairs, consisting of many speeches and patriotic songs and only one course – the *plat-républicain*. These banquets were also intended as a substitute for the old religious feast-days, revolutionary symbolism taking the place of Christian.[2]

---

[1] Arch. Savoie L. 1770. District de Chambéry, séance du 4 frimaire an II.

[2] These banquets were sometimes rendered more light-hearted by such incidents as that which occurred when sixty citizens and their families of the Section du Bonconseil, in Paris, sat down to table at the *Panier-Fleuri*: no sooner had the plates been served than the guests perceived with horror that each plate bore a feudal emblem: the publican was called for and was asked to remove the offending plates, but this he refused to do, adding that if the citizens were so ticklish in their republican sentiments, they could eat off the table without plates. This they proceeded to do, but not without first smashing 180 of the offending plates, which they later refused to pay for (AN, F7 4774 80 d5, Pottier). A *pâtissier* of the Section des Amis de la Patrie, in order to satisfy popular demand for the *gâteau des rois*, the traditional Epiphany cake dear to all French families, in Nivôse year II, hit upon the simple solution of calling his cakes *gâteaux Marat*, and both his customers and revolutionary orthodoxy were satisfied (AN, F7 4669 d3, Dennevers).

The revolutionaries were optimists; they were convinced that they were in the process of creating not only a new form of society, but also a new revolutionary man, virtuous, serious, patriotic. Hence, in the revolutionary regime, the cult of youth and the idolization of children, seen as the guarantors of the future. Much time was given, in *sociétés populaires*, to the interminable delegations of little citizens and citizenesses, led by their schoolteachers, reciting the Declaration of the Rights of Man and singing patriotic songs. There are a number of instances of small children appearing as witnesses before the revolutionary tribunals and the *comités de surveillance*. At the same time, little mercy was shown towards 'uncivic' children: when two little girls of eight and nine admitted to having pencilled a black moustache on the bust of Marat that stood in the foyer of the theatre at le Havre, the rather sensible Norman revolutionaries took the matter very much to heart.[1] There are plenty of cases of children of fourteen and fifteen being guillotined, particularly in Lyon and Marseille. This, of course, should be attributed to normal eighteenth-century judicial standards which treated children in their teens as responsible adults. Revolutionary justice was indeed more humane in this respect than the judicial system of the *ancien régime*.

In most respects, of course, revolutionary France was a young man's country. It provided new opportunities for the young and looked to the future with unqualified optimism. The ardent patriotism of youth was common to all the revolutionaries. A measure of generosity towards individual foreigners in France, including prisoners of war, was combined with an intense nationalist hatred for all foreign enemies, or supposed enemies. Cosmopolitanism was a crime. Revolutionary centralization, and the attempt to suppress regional differences, especially in language – Jean-Bon-Saint-André and his colleagues complain frequently of the way in which the Breton peasants cling to their 'Gothic jargon' – go along with this.

In their desire to break with the past the revolutionaries also turned their attention to manners. Bowing and scraping and the kissing of hands were branded as decadent, while the *club national* of Bordeaux prohibited clapping, as a form of applause worthy only of slaves. 'Expressions of joy and agreement', decreed a resolution of this club, 'should henceforth be made through the medium of the virile and republican word *bravo*.'[2] A club in the Indre denounced 'the custom of saluting one another with a great sweep of the hat' and recommended a curt sign with the hand.[3]

This preoccupation with a complete break with the past received its

---

[1] Arch. Havre D 2 38. Conseil général de la commune.
[2] Arch. Gironde II L 27. Club national de Bordeaux, séance du 6 brumaire an II.
[3] Arch. Indre L. 1581. Société populaire de Châteauroux, séance du 22 brumaire an II.

most absurd expression in the wave of 'debaptizations' that swept France in the autumn and winter of 1793. Place names were the first to suffer, to be followed by Christian names drawn from the Saints' calendar. After France had become at least nominally peopled with Anacharsises, William Tells, Marats, Gracchi, the more ardent revolutionaries, particularly those of the Midi, fell back on the names of useful plants, trees, fruit, and even fish. The list of the members of the *société populaire* of Perpignan reads like a seedsman's catalogue: *Absinthe* Jalabert, *Haricot* Vidal, *Endive* Pagès, *Érable* Fabre. An inhabitant of Lyon named Février took the first name of *Janvier*.[1]

In the countryside, a certain peasant common sense and inertia acted as a check on the more fantastic forms of revolutionary enthusiasm. Orders were given for the destruction everywhere of wayside crosses: but many rural revolutionaries, anxious not to antagonize their fellows, invoked shortage of labour and the expense of the operation to delay carrying out this and similar orders. By delaying tactics and by the force of rural inertia many village municipalities went through the Terror with the external aspects of rural life largely unchanged. The true *sans-culotte* was essentially a town-dweller.

He seems to have had scant respect for learning and the arts. At Auch, a member 'proposes that no man of letters of this town be received in this club for three years, but that *sans-culottes* be admitted at once', and the club decided that 'those who have received a careful education be excluded'.[2] It should not be inferred from resolutions of this sort that the revolutionaries were resolutely philistine: what they were trying to do at Auch was to exclude from revolutionary office-holding, which was one of the perquisites derived from membership of a club, all those who had enjoyed privileges in the course of the *ancien régime*, and what greater privilege than education?

Anyone who reads for the first time the minutes of local revolutionary

---

[1] Arch. Pyrénées-orientales L. 1454, société populaire de Perpignan. A Parisian, Jean-François Lyon, took the name of *Aristide Lille*: 'le nom de Lyon lui inspirait trop d'horreur' (AN, F7 4774 27 d5). One should add that much *sans-culotte* opinion treated with suspicion this particular type of extravagance, which, it was felt, tended to make the new regime appear ridiculous. It was also suggested that many of those who were so anxious to change their names were in fact people who had something to hide. As in any revolutionary movement, some of those who were the most anxious to prove their revolutionary zeal by exaggerated professions of faith and by ostentatious gestures had a political or criminal past that did not bear too close a scrutiny. There was much foundation for the current suspicion of the more modest *sans-culottes* towards those who *affectaient des principes exagérés*, along with *bonnet rouge*, pipe, moustache, sabre, and all the other paraphernalia of the perfect revolutionary.

[2] Arch. Gers L. 694. Registre de la société populaire d'Auch. Cf. Arch. Isère L. 936, société populaire de Bourgoin, 27 thermidor an II. 'Les hommes qui savoient lire, écrire et avoient de l'esprit étoient fort dangereux à la république' (a remark attributed to Sadet).

clubs and other bodies will be surprised by the almost complete absence of political discussion and by the credulity displayed in accepting the official version of important political changes. Clubs which had subscribed to the *Père Duchesne* and whose members even copied the pungent Parisian slang of which its able demagogic journalist was a master, the moment he had fallen accepted without a murmur the official account representing Hébert as a counter-revolutionary agent of foreign powers, and lost not a day in sending congratulatory addresses to the Convention and to the Committees thanking them for their vigilance in saving the Republic from him. Events such as the execution of Danton or the 9 Thermidor are accepted with the same unquestioning trust, when they receive a mention at all. In a great many minutes the major political events in Paris are passed over in complete silence.

This apparent political supineness was probably not due to fear, to time-serving orthodoxy, or to the desire to be on the right side: plenty of clubs admitted candidly, after the execution of Hébert, that they had been taken in by the *Père Duchesne*, whom they had believed to be a genuine revolutionary patriot. The revolutionaries were extremely naïve politically, they had an almost religious trust in their representatives and in the Convention. Their readiness to believe in even the most fantastic constructions of Fouquier-Tinville's judicial imagination is to some extent explicable by the long series of myths and popular legends about 'famine pacts' and 'foreign plots'. From 1789 onwards, the average revolutionary lived in an almost physical fear of a counter-revolutionary *coup*: moreover, plots and conspiracies were not merely figments of popular imagination and of official propaganda, there *were* plots, there *was* collusion between ultra- and counter-revolutionaries.

Of course, one would hardly expect to find voices of dissent in such public assemblies as the *sociétés populaires*, whatever individual revolutionaries may have thought in their heart of hearts. It would be naïve indeed to expect open discussion of the major political issues of the period in every urban or rural club. But such discussions were impossible primarily because of lack of information. When local revolutionaries were engaged in discussing people or questions that they knew well, they were quite capable of expressing most unorthodox views and of attacking with the greatest bitterness their own local representatives. What was lacking was political discussion on national issues and on the day-to-day Paris scene. And, when all is said and done, most revolutionaries in the provinces were far more interested in concrete problems concerning the food shortage, hoarding, rising prices, and a depreciating currency, than in political events in the capital. Everyday life in small provincial towns during the Terror was far less dramatic than is often imagined, and the realities of life were the queues and the black market rather than the guillotine and the *trompette guerrière*. Local societies showed much more interest in projects for improving communications and for obtaining contracts for local industries than in political discussion, and if they successively celebrated the *Fête de la Raison* and then that of the Supreme Being, if at one time they took in and applauded the *Père Duchesne* and later devoted themselves to somewhat academic discussions on the evils of atheism, if they voted congratulatory addresses to Robespierre and to Collot d'Herbois on their escape from an assassin's bullets and, a few weeks later, were congratulating the Committees on having nipped in the bud the appalling plots of the former, neither official pressure nor open threats ever prevented them from discussing the forbidden and especially dangerous subject of food supplies, so that the only way in the end to ensure that this explosive matter was not dragged into the open was to close the clubs.

Nor were the revolutionaries cowards and time-servers: there were of course a certain proportion of these, especially among those who had been most vociferous and who had made themselves the most conspicuous in taking revolutionary names and in other eccentricities of that type.[1] But, during the period between 1795 and 1816, many of the better-known revolutionaries, both from Paris and the provinces, were to be ruined economically, and a few thousand were to be imprisoned, shot, or deported for the fidelity with which they were prepared to defend, in time of adversity, the political and moral standards that they had so zealously preached in their brief period of power.

---

[1] One of the most conspicuous and successful of these professional revolutionaries, who took part in the revolutionary movement for the material advantages that they could get out of it, was the self-styled patriot Palloy, a wealthy architect with a large house at Sceaux, who hit upon publicizing himself by doing a brisk trade in stones of the Bastille, which he supplied, for payment, to any *société* in France. Palloy never missed an occasion to blow his own patriotic trumpet, and when he was not peddling Bastille reproductions, he was composing odes and patriotic hymns suitable to every revolutionary occasion. At Sceaux he entirely controlled the local *société*, which he later used as an instrument for his own publicity. One is not surprised to find him, at later stages of his career, composing laudatory odes to the Emperor and welcoming Louis XVIII to Sceaux with an adulatory poem.

There were many Palloys in the provinces, but it was above all in the army that one finds some of the most unscrupulous career revolutionaries. The personal dossiers of many high-ranking officers who gained promotion under Bouchotte and who were particularly flamboyant in the display of revolutionary enthusiasm are often most revealing as to the strength of the convictions so loudly – and profitably – expressed. We may thus see former commanders of *armées révolutionnaires*, men who took an active part in the *sociétés populaires* of fortress towns and who did not allow themselves to be outdone by anyone when it was a question of making revolutionary resolutions, humbly and respectfully presenting their claims to a *croix de Saint-Louis* when the time came, in 1814 or 1815, to emphasize their undying respect for the dynasty. The former soldiers of the *ancien régime*, who, as a group, gained more from the Revolution than almost anybody else, were often the first to betray it and to adjust themselves to each regime that followed.

Of course, such revolutionaries as have been considered in this article only represented a tiny minority, just as the *sociétés populaires* themselves accounted for less than 5 per cent of the population of many of the localities in which they existed; and it was their small numbers that were to accentuate their isolation from the mass of the people and greatly to facilitate the task of Fouché's police in the years of repression. Even at its height, however, the revolutionary movement suffered from indifference and public inertia. This was especially true of the rural communities, where the activities of both *comités de surveillance* and clubs were largely seasonal: both might thrive in the autumn and winter months, but the spring sowings put an end to the collective political activities of such rural *sans-culottes* as there were: there are constant references to rural *sociétés* being closed down for lack of attendance, the whole population being engaged in field work. Even in the big urban *sociétés* there recurs a constant and anxious complaint: attendance is slipping dangerously, members are not turning up to meetings, it becomes more and more difficult to form a quorum large enough to carry on business, many 'brothers' only come when there is a *scrutin épuratoire* and once they have obtained a clean bill of revolutionary health, they go off with their *certificat de civisme* in their pocket and are seen no more. Despite threats of permanent expulsion against those who absented themselves from more than three sessions running, the leaders of these *sociétés* were already losing the uphill fight against absenteeism in the spring and summer months of 1794, long before the rigours of the year III, when even the most enthusiastic *sans-culottes* did not feel inclined to sit about in freezing conditions such as had not been experienced since 1709. This decline in political interest and growth of public indifference can be dated from the months of March and April 1794, when, with the fall of the *hébertistes*, the clubs both in Paris and in the provinces found themselves reduced more and more to a passive and congratulatory role: as there was nothing more of interest to talk about, people naturally stopped coming. But even at the height of the revolutionary movement, clubs containing a total membership of five or six hundred very rarely saw more than a hundred and fifty or two hundred at any one session.[1]

The greatest threat, then, to the existence of that artificial, collective man, the *parfait sans-culotte révolutionnaire*, came rather from human nature than from the efforts of the enemies of the Revolution. The *sans-culottes* set too high a standard, their revolutionary man was too perfect to be true, and if from the purely human point of view there existed what might be called a revolutionary temperament, a factor quite as important

---

[1] For attendance figures over a period of a year in an urban club, see my article 'Politique et subsistances en l'an III: l'exemple du Havre', *Annales de Normandie* (1955), pp. 135–59.

in explaining the general comportment of the average *sans-culotte* as any political affiliations, such a temperament could not resist the pressure of time, boredom, fatigue, and laziness. To understand the small minority that remained faithful to their former ideals, one is driven to seek the key to their surprising steadfastness in character and in temperament rather than in social and political background. The general mass of *sans-culottes*, on the other hand, fell away without more than a murmur and disappeared once more into the political limbo of the years 1795–1815.

It may be objected that the purely impressionist portrait I have attempted to give of the average, rather than of the perfect, revolutionary, is as much a caricature as the prints and cartoons of London and Verona. I do not think, however, that to suggest that revolutionaries took themselves very seriously, that they were lacking in irony and flippancy, that they were often unimaginative, prejudiced, and ignorant, is unfair. If the average revolutionary did not belong to any clearly defined sociological category, he did in fact have both the virtues and the limitations of the small tradesman: economically a reactionary fighting against industrial concentration, he was puritanical and even priggish, extremely independent, unimaginative, and prejudiced, an anti-feminist and often a busybody: he was hard-working, a good family man and generally honest. Despite all the efforts of Thermidorian propaganda, the tribunals of the year III were seldom able to substantiate charges of theft and peculation against men who had articles of great value passing continuously through their hands.

The revolutionaries, in short, were enthusiasts; their sincerity was patent, if naïve, and, in some cases, was to be dearly paid for; and just as there is a revolutionary temperament as distinct from an authoritarian temperament, so among historians there will inevitably be those who feel an instinctive sympathy for these enthusiastic, if sometimes misguided, workers in the vineyards of the Revolution, and those who on the contrary will dismiss them as trouble-makers, hooligans, or time-serving followers of a party line.

My portrait of the revolutionary is incomplete in many respects. The whole problem of terrorism, for example, needs separate treatment. I have deliberately limited myself to illustrating some of the more personal traits of the revolutionary mentality, without embarking on a discussion of their rather vague economic aspirations, of the attitude of the *sans-culottes* towards the clergy and towards Catholicism, towards strikes and wage-claims, towards charity and pauperism, of their vague gropings at theories of popular sovereignty. This is only an interim report but I hope that it will correct some illusions and help to give actuality to a group of people that has only recently come into the categories of serious history.

2

Revolutionary Situations in France 1789–1968[*]

FRENCH HISTORY HAS been dominated by the violence of government, ever since the suppression of the great provincial revolts and peasant risings of the seventeenth century and that of the Camisard rising early in the eighteenth. Every succeeding French regime since that of Louis XIV has been based on force (some more than others). Every French government, in a greater or lesser degree, has been a police regime. In every French government in modern times the key ministry has been that of the Interior (or that of Police). France, then, constitutes the ideal 'model' for the study of 'revolutionary situations', if only because there have been so many of them, because government and opposition have so often confronted in crude terms of force, and because one 'revolutionary situation', however ultimately unsuccessful, will eventually create another. It becomes a tradition, a habit, an almost respectable reference back to an accepted past. It has often been said – and rightly – that Paris *sent la poudre*, with each quarter harking back to its hour of heroism and barricade. And what failed on previous occasions may be so improved on as to succeed on another occasion. Failed revolutions, 'revolutionary situations' that have gone wrong, that have gone off half cock, and have been followed by systematic repression and political reaction do not, unfortunately, carry their own lessons. The failure is forgotten, the exhilaration of the first moment of revolt is commemorated and cherished, the martyrs of each failed revolution are remembered (and failed revolutions have the advantage over successful ones in putting out a larger crop of martyrs) and idealized, the cult of anniversaries stimulates vengeance and clothes violence – often empty violence – in the prestigious clothes of history. In 1948 it would have seemed that the unfortunate weight of history had been shed and that the people of France could at last escape from the fruitless and obscene cycle of violence and barricade,

---

[*] From *A Second Identity*, pp. 267–81.

blind destruction and chance death. Twenty years later, a 'revolutionary situation' suddenly emerged, after ten years of Gaullist paternalism and political anaesthesia and exclusive concern for the material comforts of an unquestioning and vulgar pursuit of the new car, the TV, holidays in more and more exotic surroundings, early marriage, a family of manageable size, and the youthful climb up the technocratic ladder, as people, on the road to material success and managerial position, moved further and further out of the city, to live in pseudo-rural 'neighbourhood' estates: riding, swimming-pool, tennis, park, children's playground, patio, whisky, invitations to young married colleagues in the same income group, a limited infidelity (in the same income group), talk of the next car and the next holiday, rapid trips abroad for the firm (discreet infidelity, limited to the Common Market zone), masculinity and violence expressed in terms of horsepower and speed of driving. What strikes one most about the technocracy of the Fifth Republic is its excessive vulgarity: the vulgarity of the close-cropped young executive who, via *Réalités*, has put himself through an express course in fashionable historical interpretations, the vulgarity of his wife, who has mugged up *paella* and *couscous*. It is the France of *Les Stances à Sophie* and *Week-End*, of *franglais* and *manpowerisation*.

The May Revolution was an appeal back to a fraternal past, an attempt to re-create Paris neighbourliness in terms of the quarter and with the memory of the barricades of August 1944 (and of the earlier ones). At first, in the almost universal hatred of the police, it drew on a sufficient consensus to create a revolutionary situation and to keep it going (in order to keep it going), though, even at the start, it had to have recourse to professional strong-arm groups and to semi-gangsters, who later proved an embarrassment. At first, too, before the full effects of the disruption of the public services could be felt, middle-class parents could feel proud of the heroic exploits of their children in the face of the CRS [the Compagnies Républicaines de Sécurité]; the consensus was sufficient too to bring in the younger workers, normally completely out of sympathy with student theorists of revolution (Mao, Fidel, and 'Che' are middle-class icons, teenage pin-ups, it is doubtful if they were ever normally seen in car factories), to split the French working class generationally, and, out of a social climate that had for some time been dormant, produce a general strike of revolutionary implications. At the beginning, there was *accident*, aided by the activities of a tiny group of militants. But, at this stage, the revolutionary situation showed signs of careful *organization*. Everyone had played according to the rules: Charles X had gone, Louis-Philippe had gone, Thiers had gone. De Gaulle – an historian if ever there was one – would go. But he didn't.

So much for the appeal to precedent. Then there was *theory*, mostly empty, nihilistic, and inappropriate, as if a revolution can ever be an end in itself, as if one can ever live on the barricades or in a theatre, as if comfort, sleep, meals, work, routine, leisure can eternally be sacrificed for talk and 'activism', as if Fidel spent his whole political career conquering Cuba, even if he continues to dress as if he did. As if one can become a revolutionary overnight, without study, without preparation; as if a revolution can be created by setting a light to the petrol tank of a car, a belief shared by Cairo crowds. 'Impossibilism' became an end in itself, as it had so often before in the intransigent history of France; and there were once again allusions to the purifying effects of terrorism, to the dreadful beauty of Terror.

And so we have the 'Group of March' and the 'May Revolution' to add to a clutter of dates of days and months. The lesson of the failure has been lost, and only the near-success remembered. The 'activists' are training for the next round, the working class bought off, the government forewarned. There will be no *accidental* revolutionary situation in the near future. But, in the events of the five weeks of May–June, there is much for the historian to ponder on; and he will need to rethink his more distant revolutionary history in terms of accident, organization (especially in the techniques of riot), militancy, and activism, of violence as an end in itself, of destruction and of failure both social and academic.

*

So much work has been concentrated, over the last 170 years, on the long-term causes of the first French Revolution that the time has perhaps come to redress the balance and to examine the more immediate, possibly accidental, physical causes of the advent of a revolutionary crisis. For any theory derived from a view of the 'inevitability' of revolutions is likely to be misleading as an historical interpretation, and, above all, dangerous as a 'model' for future action. There have been many attempts to 'anatomize Revolutions' and to establish a 'standard revolutionary situation' so all-embracing that it will fit any case, at any time, anywhere, so that the student-terrorist of the windy University of Essex can feel himself fully prepared once he has doffed the full kit of the *guerrillero* in the Cuban jungle. The search for an 'anatomy of revolution' is inherent in most Marxist thinking (though Marxist thought, in this respect, can generally be readjusted, with the benefit of hindsight and a re-examination of the Sacred Books, to make allowance for the failure of a potentially revolutionary situation to develop and to explain, in the light of the Iron Laws, why things went wrong when, on a prior analysis, they had appeared to be coming along nicely). And Marxist thought, in recent years, has been able to adjust itself to revolutionary situations that excluded the participation of the industrial working class, military defeat, and mutinies, while assuring that of the mass of the peasantry in a primarily rural, undeveloped economy.

At the other extreme, the search for a 'model', in an effort to predict the advent of a revolutionary situation, and thus to face up to it, either with suitable legislation and social palliatives, or with sufficient repressive force to prevent it from developing, has been the constant preoccupation of American academics in the employment of the CIA. With the various brands of Marxists, it is a matter of proving the superiority of one's own particular theology; and with American academics, to improve the techniques of prevention. Thus in the US both history and sociology have been enlisted in the service of the police and of the forces of repression, in an attempt to categorize, to regiment 'revolutionary situations' into a limited series of 'models' allowing for any situation predictable at least in terms of the past.

Similar, though perhaps less blatant, considerations have governed much of the work on revolutionary history undertaken by American historians in the last twenty years. In his anxiety to establish the existence of a chain or 'cycle' of revolutionary crises for 1760 to 1800, Professor Palmer has undoubtedly been motivated by cold-war assumptions. He is, first of all, anxious to play down both the unique importance and the 'Frenchness' of the revolutionary crisis in France, to the advantage of the preceding American revolution, thus placing the French Revolution in a corset of 'inevitability' almost as narrow as that postulated as dogma by the various Marxist schools; events in Paris in June–July 1789 had to respond to hidden sub-oceanic currents, spreading out from Boston, and including, in a general revolutionary (or *quasi*-revolutionary) seismograph the revolutionary earthquake zone of Euro-America. The waves of his 'Atlantic Revolution' lap the frozen shores of Trondheim, the warmer shores of Smyrna, while this North-Atlantic Gulf Stream spreads even up the Vistula to Warsaw. So, we are told, whether they knew it or not, those who took up arms in July 1789 were acting as units in an historical chain-gang, bound and manacled to what had gone before: Jefferson and Franklin, Wilkes and Liberty, even poor mad Lord George Gordon, Geneva, Amsterdam, and Brabant – people and events of which they were no doubt unaware – it does not matter; bound and manacled too to what was to follow: Babeuf and Buonarroti, on their bicycle made for two, Amsterdamer, Swiss, Piedmontese, Hungarian, Austrian, Polish, and Greek Jacobins, and Jacobin clubs in the Balkans and the Near East, in Edinburgh, Leeds, Sheffield, Dublin, and Bergen. His cycle too is adjustable to failure; when a revolutionary situation does not develop, as it should have done according to the dictates of his cyclical machine, it is dismissed as a *quasi*-revolution. A more recent historian has described the year 1795 as that of England's *abortive* revolution. The Dean of the

Faculty of Arts of Princeton makes, one suspects, the same sort of mistake as the young Régis Debray who believed that the Cuban island 'model' could be applied to the Bolivian uplands. Neither makes much allowance for the particularities of national conditions and for the elements of accident. And Professor Palmer, like Professor Talmon before him, makes enormous claims for theory in the inception of a revolutionary crisis. His approach is political and constitutional, much is made of the magic word 'democracy'; there is no room, in his elegant scheme of things, for thirst, hunger, drought, envy, social resentment, boredom, hatred, malice, distress, failure, poverty, hope, panic, and fear.

Others, Brinton, Arendt, Caute, Stone, have likewise tried each to establish his, or her, own machine of revolutionary situations, no doubt to their own satisfaction, but hardly to the enlightenment of previous crises, though of course so wide is their scope, so comprehensive and, above all, self-evident are most of their premises, that they may, somewhere or another, some time or another, score a bull's-eye in the future. Brinton makes much of militant minorities, and of single parties, bending the most disunited to his commanding will; Caute favours military defeat; Stone constructs six types of revolutionary situation, uses strange words for what historians call social resentment, makes the point that revolutions can only succeed by violence, and the further one that repression works best when it knows what it is looking for. And for those who are shocked by the expression 'revolutionary situation', he tells us that American scientists have proposed to substitute that of 'internal war'. And Stone follows Brinton in proposing as an iron law the progress from Constitutionalism to Girondism, from there to the Revolutionary Government, followed by Reaction, anarchy, near-civil war, and a military dictatorship. They are both following in the path of Alison, the nineteenth-century English historian of the Revolution who was so convinced that it took four years to progress from Constitutionalism to Terror that he went to Paris in 1834 in order to see his theory proved and witness the sudden emergence of the second year II; he did, it is true, get his Terror, but it was that of the government, at the expense of the working class of Lyon. All this makes our history easier, and gives great satisfaction to the American reading public (possibly the most unimaginative, certainly the most ignorant in the world), convinced that it now has the key to any great and violent sedition, past, present, or future. So they can either rest in peace, or order their machine-gun-proof front doors and steel shutters. Yet 'revolutionary situations' have arisen in the absence of military defeat (1789 was one), without a wide consensus between the classes (in 1968, this followed the development of a revolutionary situation, it did not create it), and revolutionary situations have arisen even when the repressive authorities knew only too well whom they were looking for (as in

1789); on this occasion, they had lost the will to repress. And many of Dr Caute's learned arguments boil down to this: revolutionary situations succeed when they have force on their side and when the revolutionaries have the will to use it (the *communards* had force on their side in March 1871, but they did not have the will to use it; and when they had the will – and the discipline – to use force, the Versaillais had had time to recover, and had assembled more force – a lesson that was not lost on Lenin), revolutionary situations fail when the government retains the use of force. It is rather like saying that, in a battle, the stronger side will win. Or that, to keep the people down, you need a reliable police and a well-armed, well-paid, contented army. Thiers knew that.

Ernest Labrousse has proposed a rather more sophisticated formula for the genesis of a revolutionary situation. Such a situation, he observes, will arise when the vast majority of the inhabitants of a country are united in a total rejection of existing society and of the reigning order of things. It is a good formula, because it emphasizes the importance of purely negative polarizations in bringing together, briefly, people of widely different origin, status, temperament, and wealth. A revolutionary situation is, by its nature, brief; it must either develop into rapid success or collapse. In July '89, it was created in forty-eight hours, in March 1871 in twelve, in May '68 it dragged on for five weeks. In the initial stage, a single hate figure is the most effective of all sparks. In July '89 it was provided by Breteuil, in July 1830 by Guizot, in June 1848 by Cavaignac, in March 1871 by Thiers, in May '68 by the CRS. But even such a formula will only cover the actual genesis of a crisis. If a revolutionary situation is prolonged, other fears will arise to divide the ranks of the potential revolutionaries, to devour the moderates (this year, as the crisis dragged on, the Maoists and other young philosophers of neo-terrorism came more and more to the fore), and to frighten to the side of repression those who are alarmed by the spectacle of prolonged and senseless violence, disorder, and damage to property (July 1789 was so successful because it was accomplished, along with the total demolition of the Bastille, which belonged to the State, without the smashing of a single householder's windows).

*

Ultimately, every revolutionary situation is unique and unprecedented. If it were not so, few would ever ripen, for repressive authorities have always known their job better than historians, have indeed themselves always been the best historians at least of habitual and predictable sedition. Few historians love the police and the magistrates. But they would be foolish to underestimate them. Here then is the difference between a habitual sedition, a market riot, weekend rowdiness, feast-day drunkenness, the

Sunday and the Monday brawl, the harvest stabbings, the wedding or baptism rural killings, anti-fiscal arson, the masked assault and robbery of Carnival, the coal-heavers', the tanners', the river-workers' punch-up, the rag-and-bone man's predilection for brutal murder, the well-known dangers of a certain quarter, the anarchy of a laundry-boat, the criminality of a horse-market, the violence and sexuality of the Halles, the Christmas Day anti-Protestant or anti-Jewish man-hunt, the annual violence of anniversaries and thanksgivings, the Monday market riot, the rent-day suicide, year-in year-out infanticide, covered by the complicity of a whole community of the very poor, the known habits and location of abortion, the ancient ties between theft, receiving, prostitution, the old-clothes trade and informing, the post-dance fight, the wine-shop 1 a.m. eruption, the inter-village fracas, the dawn duel, the 4 a.m. suicide, the 2 a.m. wife-slaying, the Breton versus Picard clubbing, the knife-drawing of sailors, the sword-drawing of the *Gardes Françaises* in defence of their regimental honour, the drinking bouts between butchers' apprentices and stonemasons, the eating bouts between Upper and Lower Normans, the antipathy of Rouennais for Havrais, the lack of deference and boastfulness of barbers' apprentices – all matters that the eighteenth-century police of Paris, or of Lyon, or of Marseille, had at their finger-tips, had encountered again and again, would encounter again and again, could always face up to, generally with a minimum of force and ostentation – the difference between all these and a revolutionary situation which by definition, at least the first time it occurs (and there is seldom a second round of play, for the police are ready for the return match), is both unprecedented and mysterious.

For in any such situation, even 1789, and despite all the minute analysis of short-term and long-term causes, despite the *rudéfication* of the Crowd, of the rioter, there still remains a *zone d'ombre* of impenetrable mystery. All is not explained, even when all has apparently been explained, the Mob rehabilitated, its components dressed in the respectable clothes of their respective trades, provided with families, shops, and apprentices, an address, character references, trade, occupational or subsistence motivations (if it is not about bread, which, predictably, it usually is, then it must be about wine, or transport costs, or wages, or recruitment). There is always an explanation for the presence of anybody. The wine merchants and publicans are up in arms over the *barrières*, the builders' labourers have been unemployed since the winter of 1788, the textile workers for two years, the totally unemployed and the seasonal labourers are threatened with imminent expulsion from the city, girls who cannot justify their means of existence and have no fixed address are about to be sent back to their villages (a supreme humiliation, as they have been writing home to impress their parents, sisters, and school-friends with the success they have met in the metropolis), the runaway children are being rounded up in ever large numbers nightly, the soldiers are in arrears of pay and have their feet under the table in the homes of local artisans, into whose families they have married and whose grievances they share, individual members of the *Gardes Françaises* are living off the earnings of prostitution. Everyone can give a good account of himself, his place in a sedition that is becoming a revolution can be explained.

And yet this is not the whole story. Wine merchants and publicans have always been law-breakers, Limousin builders' labourers have always lived on the verge of starvation, the clothing trades have long been over-crowded, seasonal labourers are always being sent home, country girls are always falling, children are always running away from cruel parents, soldiers are seldom in pay, generally marry into their own condition and supplement their income as best they can, neither boredom nor social resentment nor envy waits upon the calendar, the sponger sponges throughout the year, though the summer is a hard time for him every year, the university student becomes increasingly discontented with society as the summer months approach, while some always work hard and others do not, some people are always on the verge of starvation, some trade or other is always going through a bad patch, Kings of France nearly always have brothers and cousins, it is just part of their bad luck, it is often very cold in the winter and very hot in May, fear constantly stalks in the countryside, especially during summer nights, yearly lit up by arson. No riot has ever been completely spontaneous, while, at almost any period, at any time of the year, one trade or another will be conscious of specific grievances, so that counting heads and establishing their occupations will suggest little more than that grave-diggers or shoemakers are almost continuously in a state of agitation. Nor has anyone yet heard of a law-abiding wine merchant or of a virtuous soldier.

Yet, to take July 1789 (or May 1968), the situation was quite unprecedented, it had no parallel in the turbulent, violent history of sixteenth-century Paris (though the massacre of St Bartholomew's Day had, in fact, gone on for nearly a week, the killers had extended from professional Croat or Albanian slaughterers to ordinary Parisians), of the Ligue (a Parisian form of popular anarchism), or of seventeenth-century *frondeur* Paris. In the eighteenth century, save for the pro-Jansenist riots in the parish of Saint-Médard (the poorest quarter of the city, an area much given to excess of mysticism and, during the Revolution, of popular violence, an area too long habituated to the spectacle of violent, dismembered, death, thanks to the presence of the Schools of Anatomy) and the occasional *parlementaire* fracas in front of the statue of Henry IV, the population had been orderly and disciplined.

There existed, of course, 'dangerous classes', 'dangerous quarters', 'dangerous months', and 'dangerous days' as indeed in any other eight-eenth-century city. But the Paris of Restif and of Mercier was in fact much less 'dangerous' than that of Sue and Balzac. The police did not need to be told to keep a wary eye on the river-workers and their women, on pedlars and all those on the move, on locksmiths, gunsmiths, ironmongers, black-smiths, on laundresses and seamstresses and fruit sellers, on scrap mer-chants and old-clothes merchants, on wine merchants, publicans, *logeurs*, and prostitutes. They knew that the inhabitants of the faubourg Saint-Marceau were more violence-prone than any other, and they tended to keep out of that quarter altogether. They were aware too that Paris was surrounded by a circle of anarchical *communes*, neither town nor village, clusters of turbulent carters' inns, of hutments, of cardboard dwellings and even tents, in which dwelt an uncharted, moving population, neither townsman nor villager, but that most alarming of all species, the *faubourien*, that camped, like the Turks outside Vienna, within sight of the golden domes. These were the temporary resting places, the night spots of itinerant crime, and of those who walked, rode, and wandered for their living, of those who did not possess passports and could not be identified. They possessed no priests, no churches, no parishes and lived apart from the normal community. If ever envy, hatred, and violence were to march on the centre of the city and on the affluent quarters of the west, they would recruit their ragged armies from Saint-Marceau, from Saint-Denis, and from the disease-ridden, pestilential places on the fringe. By the end of the century, Paris was surrounded by a bannerless multitude that no doubt dreamt of anarchy, rape, pillage, and arson, and that awaited, with the patience of the utterly brutal, the signal to move, keeping up the fires of hope on the adulterated, fiery wine of the Paris region. This, at least, was what the police would expect; for things in fact appear to have turned out very differently.

There was little that the repressive authorities did not know about the location of potential violence and crime. Paris was an ordered and predict-able city; the hired killer had his place in society, even if he did not actu-ally put up a brass plate or a trade sign. One would know where to go for a professional job of this kind; and one could even take one's choice of methods of dispatch: there were those who stabbed silently, those who strangled, those who suffocated, those who battered with blunt instru-ments, those who drowned, those who pushed out of windows, those who used poison, those who cost a lot and those who did it almost for nothing. They did not figure in the trade almanacs, but they were always perfectly easy to find; they went to their regular cafés, boasted of their prowess, and consorted with women who flattered their brutality. They were brought in every now and then and sent to the galleys.

Paris was then, despite its size, a reassuring city in the eyes of the police.

It contained dangerous elements, but it was easy to keep them in check; and it housed an army of violence, while a second encamped on its fringe. The habitually violent, like the habitually criminal, do not normally constitute a threat to the established order, of which they form a semi-recognized part. Like the police, they have a stake in society. We do not expect to find such people in the armies of revolution and in the ranks of the revolutionists. They are below, or at least outside, the bounds of social resentment; and their conservatism does not readily accept new institutions, unfamiliar authorities, and judges with unknown faces. As far as can be ascertained, few such people participated actively in the revolutionary movement at any stage, though after 1795 quite a lot of them took to the woods in the ranks of counter-revolutionary bands.

It is occasional violence that poses the problem both in contemporary terms and, above all, to the historian. Crime no doubt had its part in the events of June–July 1789, though it seems to have been circumscribed to one glorious night of pillage and rampage; and it was certainly not a student who stabbed a policeman through the heart in the course of the May riots of this year. But there was no faceless Paris underworld *à la Taine*, ready to respond to the call of some unknown Super-Criminal, of some Pied Piper of Saint-Marceau.

There remain, then, several principal problems to the mystery of the breakdown of government – for it is a mystery – and of that very, very fine line that separates a sedition from a revolutionary crisis: that of leadership, of organization, of marching orders, of a hidden élite of militancy, and – who knows? – of financial stimulus, for if a revolutionary situation cannot be bought, be contrived to order, it can certainly be helped on, maintained, encouraged, once it is under way; that of the role of boredom, of an uneasy conscience (for so many militants can be shown to have been able to afford the luxury of full-time militancy, so many of them having been of middle-class origin); that of failure, academic or social, in the genesis of a revolutionary mentality; that of unprecedented violence, of popular savagery; and finally, perhaps the most elusive, the element of accident in the development of a situation resulting in the inability of a government to carry out the primary task of government, that is to maintain order and to keep control over the weapons of repression, army, police, etc.

The problem of leadership must, unfortunately, for ever remain a mystery, at least in the June–July 1789 context (for there is abundant evidence of the predominant part played by militant minorities at the inception of the May crisis). Yet there are plenty of traces of a plan, the soldiers and NCOs of the *Gardes Françaises* were steadily worked upon in the three weeks before 12 July, those who took up arms knew where to look for them and what to do with them; there were points of assembly, people came to the Palais-Royal both for news, for orders, for encouragement, and even for payment. People did not just march anywhere, they went to the place de Grève, the ancient, traditional centre of popular government, they went to the Invalides, attacked the *barrières* and lynched certain officials, concentrated on the Bastille. In any riot, once it is under way, and however chaotically it begins, there is a man or a woman who stands out, pointing the way, holding an emblem, shouting a slogan. No one can identify him or her afterwards, but he or she will be remembered both by participants and onlookers. We must not discount *all* police evidence on the subject of leadership and organization, simply because it is police evidence and because the police nearly always have a thesis to prove.

The element of accident is all-important, as every succeeding revolutionary crisis in France has illustrated. The commonest cause of a riot accidentally developing into a revolutionary situation is either the over-use or the under-use of the repressive powers of government. Force is a delicate weapon needing a very fine element of calculation in its use. The old royal authorities were well aware of this and always endeavoured to make their force as unobtrusive as possible. To deploy a regiment, to call in troops from the frontier was likely to indicate panic and would stimulate popular fears; it was also a back-handed compliment, and therefore an encouragement to the potential rioter, generally a conceited man, as well as an outraged one, and especially subject to indirect flattery of this kind if he sees himself as a full-time student revolutionist. Generally it was safer to wait upon events and, if repression were needed, to use it at night, against a small number of selected individuals. In the morning they had gone, and so had those who had arrested them. Visible force was always dangerous; it might intimidate, but equally it might make people desperate or, worse, foolhardy (especially if they had a female audience to egg them on to prove their masculinity) and when people are foolhardy, then there will be deaths, and then *anything* may happen; the spectacle of a corpse in the streets – or even of a wounded man or woman or, worse, a child, in a pool of blood – is the most fearful and convincing indictment of a regime. Also it is dangerous to identify a regime that is supposed to be mysterious, that relies on awe, mystery, and deference, with a group of soldiers (especially foreign ones, and native ones may not be reliable) or police. Hatred of the police, if not of the *gendarmerie*, is an ancient tradition in France; and the first victims of popular vengeance, at the outset of any revolutionary crisis, have been police and informers.

On the other hand, hesitation, vacillation, the delay in the use of force may simply give riot the time to organize, to move into the vacuum, assume responsibility for order, and administer its own form of terror, through direct democracy, public denunciation, and voting with a show of hands – the favourite political technique both of the *sans-culottes* and of the militants of May '68. In 1789 we have all these phenomena: too much, too visible force, then a withdrawal of force, then a threat of force that failed to materialize, finally the spectacle of the joyful impunity of riot. In July 1830 a few civilian dead brought down Charles X. In February 1848 Guizot and Louis-Philippe were overthrown in the most accidental of revolutions, though it was one that bored intellectuals like Baudelaire had been longing for for years, the greatest crime of the July Monarchy being that it was commonplace and very ordinary, and the crime of Guizot being that he had stayed in power for too long (only eight years, as compared to de Gaulle's ten). In March 1871 the government itself deliberately provoked a revolutionary situation in order the better to repress it (much the same had happened in June 1848). In both cases repression was used on a colossal scale, and to great effect. In May 1968 the government, by deploying too much force too brutally, created a revolutionary situation out of a students' demonstration in its inception no different from hundreds of previous students' demonstrations; and the students, in an effort to create a revolution by prolonging a revolutionary situation, and by challenging violence with violence (often of a sophisticated and well-organized kind that at first took the police by surprise, then increased their brutality), produced an effective counter-revolution, and opened the way to Reaction and to the permitted violence of Committees of Civic Action. Violence, as most of the history of France demonstrates, in the last 170 years, ultimately serves the purpose of government. Many of the *vainqueurs de la Bastille* were shot down on the Champ de Mars, the victors of July 1830 were killed in December 1832, those of February 1848 were killed in June. After the experiment in popular rule and 'direct democracy', Thermidor. After the risings of Germinal and Prairial year III, thirty-five years of repression. After 9–11 May, 31 May. After March 1871, May 1871. Revolutionary situations do not create themselves, nor can they be sustained by the creation of more revolutionary situations; nor do they spring, fully armed, out of theory, nor do they respond to the dictates of a 'model'. Revolutionary situations are accidents, and opportunities, not ends in themselves. To suggest the contrary is to open the dangerous paths of adventurism. And revolutionaries need to do their homework, they may even have to take examinations; Robespierre was a scholarship boy; Billaud-Varenne went to a good school; it took Carnot twenty years to become a revolutionary; Robespierre marinated in over ten years of genteel poverty and social resentment in a small provincial town. By the time they became revolutionaries, most of the leaders were in their late thirties or their forties. Saint-Just was an exception, though one can see why he should have become the idol of generation after generation of *maîtres d'internat*. Vallès must often have dreamed of being a member of a Committee of Public Safety at twenty-six. Perhaps I too am falling into the trap of historical prediction and pattern. But, in France at least, the evidence does seem to suggest that violence as an end in itself generally redounds to the advantage of government, even if the government is a new one. And it would be hard, in historical terms, to point to an instance of a revolutionary situation arising simply by people talking about it.

In all this, there is finally the imponderable element of temperament, personality, youth, generational conflict (generational monopolism, the erection of an age group into a privileged class, the Terror of the Young against the Old constitutes perhaps the most alarming of all Terrors, even more alarming than that so ardently preached, by the steely Saint-Just, of Virtue against Vice, though Saint-Just was working for much the same thing – only the Young were entirely pure and Virtue could only be ensured by the extermination of most of those over twenty-five), personal and social alienation, social resentment, violence as an outlet to boredom and frustration, an uneasy upper-middle-class conscience, left-wing élitism, the contempt for the past, for the common people, for scholarship, for knowledge, arrogance, conceit, and 'impossibilism'. Most of the nineteenth-century French revolutions or revolutionary outbursts were revolts against boredom and complacency, while violence was ardently stimulated by intellectuals in search of ideas and inspiration. M. de Lamartine was not the only person who became a revolutionary *pour se désennuyer*. And in May 1968 predominantly middle-class students, from the west of Paris, revolted against the complacency, the vulgarity, the conformity, and the lack of freedom of a paternalistic regime; their more militant, more theoretical leaders, self-styled *enragés*, misread the past, showing contempt for free discussion, and applying the sub-tropical experience of the present to the tarmac of the boulevard Saint-Michel. Great revolutions spring from a multitude of long-term causes; revolutionary situations can arise out of a misunderstanding, or may be sparked off by professional riot techniques. Their roots are more difficult to perceive because more accidental and faster-developing. Their results, when a revolutionary situation is enjoyed merely for its own sake, are likely to be a reinforcement of authority, with the rallying to the regime of a frightened *bourgeoisie*, of young professional couples, and of those over thirty.

3

The Officers and Men of the Parisian Armée*

T HE UNKNOWNS OF this popular army were the officers, the company or detachment commanders, and the *révolutionnaires* themselves. The few historians who have looked into this most under-investigated institution of the Terror have concentrated exclusively on its general staff. However, the *armée révolutionnaire* was created not to stroll the streets of Paris, or to add to the prestige of certain figures in the rue de Choiseul, but to support a necessarily unpopular programme with threats and terror. It was the task of the artillery and infantry officers as well as the cannoneers and the fusiliers to implement this programme, and the cavalry officers remained apart from the other branches in this respect, as they did also in origin, age, and above all in behaviour. Those other branches were composed of *sectionnaires*; the cavalry for the most part was not.

The Parisian *armée* was an egalitarian force. Little distinguished officer from fusilier or cannoneer, and they were often neighbours with the same social background. The division of the present chapter into two parts reflects, therefore, not a social hierarchy, of which the members of the *armée* would have been unaware, but the different nature of the documentation. Thanks to an abundance of personal dossiers it is possible to construct biographical studies of the officers; for the *révolutionnaires* we can only build a composite portrait from the fragments of rudimentary material.

The *armée révolutionnaire* was not a homogeneous force and possessed little *esprit de corps* in the military sense. It was an army of civilians, whose hero was the *révolutionnaire*, whose rallying point was the Section, and whose essential unity rested on the Sectionary companies. But the absence of complete lists of these companies prohibits any study (usually artificial and impersonal in any case) of its social structure. This chapter therefore is devoted to the individual officers and men of the Parisian *armée*.

---

* From *The People's Armies*, pp. 102–58.

PART I   THE REVOLUTIONARY OFFICER

I   *Cannoneer Officers*

The revolutionary artillery was the élite corps of this popular army. A Parisian and above all a Sectionary corps, its basis was the autonomous company which remained in close contact with the Section in which it had originated. The cannoneers were in the service of their Sections; they were on loan to the *armée révolutionnaire*, and paid little attention to Ronsin and his general staff, whose control over them was weak and transient. They criticised the *représentants* freely, denounced the local authorities at will, and were compliant only towards the *commissaires* of the Committee of General Security, who were frequently members also of the *comités révolutionnaires* in the Sections; for the artillery was not only a Sectionary force, it was linked as well to the *comités révolutionnaires*.

With no superior artillery command, the cannoneer captain was his own master, and his position at the head of a company was much more important than that of a fusilier captain under orders from his *chef de bataillon* and the general staff. Later, during the great crises of Thermidor year II and Germinal and Prairial year III, the attitude of each company would depend above all on that of its captain. As a leading figure in the Section, known to his men as a military commander and even more as a neighbour, owing his elected position to the confidence of his fellow citizens and his acute sense of political reality, his powers of action were considerable. Babeuf, Buonarroti, Germain, Félix Lepeletier and the Police Minister Cochon, all in their different ways experts on these *révolutionnaires*, agreed in according the company captains, as well as the officers and simple cannoneers, a particular importance. They were given by these conspirators a special place in the list of 'men capable of commanding' not only because of their technical expertise, but above all because, as leading *sectionnaires*, they still in the year IV exercised a very real influence over their fellow citizens, who had often served under them in the Parisian terrorist élite. Cochon was to honour these men with a particularly severe surveillance.

They had gained their position in the hierarchy of terror for a number of reasons: they were mature, averaging thirty-five years of age,[1] civilians like the men they commanded, and had a solid footing among the tradespeople and artisans of Paris. Military men were rare in this corps; its members were formed in the image of the militant minority which directed the Sectionary movement, and shopkeepers (often comfortably-

---

[1] Of the 9 officers on whom we have such information, Lefranc was 31, Simon 43, Delacroix 52, Vallantin 38, Poupart 37, Hardy 37, Coppin 47, Suicre 34; Eude, at 25, is out of step with the rest of the group.

off ones), tradesmen and artisans predominated.[1] The cannoneer officers
were Parisians and political men, and everything pointed to them as
commanders of a political army and directors of the revolutionary operation in the departments. In the execution of their duties they were to show
themselves worthy of the confidence placed in them by their fellow *sectionnaires*, and the conduct of certain artillery captains testified to the
sincerity and firmness of their convictions.

If these officers were so important politically, it was not only because
of their activities in connection with a particular instrument of the Terror,
whose life was even shorter than that of the regime and the political
atmosphere which had produced it; they had further claims to be considered notable *révolutionnaires* and their term in the Parisian *armée* was but
one episode in a longer political life. We must also resist the temptation to
view these leading *sectionnaires* as typical representatives of the *armée
révolutionnaire*; they may have formed a political élite within it, but they
were never entirely a part of it. For these experienced terrorists, this spell
in the Parisian *armée* represented the period of their greatest revolutionary activity. But it would convey a false impression of the political understanding of the normal revolutionary officer to take the lives of certain
artillery commanders as representative: the infantry provides more typical
examples of the average officer, while the fusiliers were the Parisian *armée*,
strictly speaking, and their existence terminated with it. The typical
Parisian officer like the typical revolutionary soldier was a fusilier, the
'sans-culotte' of Laukhard's account.

Despite their political importance the cannoneer officers have left little
documentary evidence. Civilians for the most part, they do not figure in
the military archives. Those who played a notable role in Sectionary activity before Thermidor, or participated in the opposition movement after
the year III, may appear in the documentation for the Sections and in the
police records on which it is based. But they were a tiny minority. The 28
companies had more than 80 officers who took part in the activities of the
armée révolutionnaire; but for only 15 of those officers do we know more
than the name and Section – an insufficient body of evidence to permit
reliable generalizations for the whole group. But since this selection was
the product of circumstances as well as police surveillance, we can assume
that these 15 supplied that active and militant minority which came to
dominate and direct every revolutionary institution. Two were notable
révolutionnaires whose political careers continued long after the Terror:
Jean-Louis Eude, captain of the Droits-de-l'Homme Section company,

[1] Among 15 cannoneer officers, there were 2 former soldiers (Diacre and Hardy); 1 building contractor, 1 clockmaker, 1 toymaker, 1 in the shoemaking business, a clerk, a 'worker'
and a farmer. Most were also family men.

and Jean-Baptiste-Antoine Lefranc, who commanded that of the Tuileries. The others need not detain us, except where the chance word or accusation of terrorism tells something of the scope of their actions or their social position.

Eude, the youngest of these cannoneer officers, was born at Saint-Ouen near Paris on 26 August 1768. A master clockmaker, like many artisans involved in the luxury trades he threw himself at an early stage into the revolutionary movement. His brother was a member of the Paris Commune and was to fall victim to the proscription after Thermidor. The two were leading figures in the Droits-de-l'Homme Section, the same Section as Varlet, and one which had a rather unusual social composition because of the number of lodging-houses, with their ragged population of carpenter's apprentices.[1] The Eude brothers did not belong to this class, and politically were far removed from both Varlet and Descombes, another leader of the Section, who was a *commissaire* for subsistences in the Pontoise district and future victim of the *hébertiste* trials. The younger Eude brother, Jean-Louis, was elected company captain on 1 September 1793, before the formation of the Parisian *armée*. We know nothing of this independent artisan's activities in the *armée*, and it was not until after Thermidor, and even more so after Prairial year III, that his resolutely hostile attitude to the new order won him both a place of honour on the list of Babouvists and the attention of the Police Minister, Cochon. Eude was a republican, but it was only in the period of proscription that we find proof of this. Under the Terror he was 'a government man', a 'Robespierrist' *sectionnaire* like his brother, and one whom Soboul places with the Jacobins rather than the *sans-culottes*. However, September 1793 was an important date for this Paris clockmaker; having found a salaried position in the revolutionary institutions he would not return to his trade until after 1814, following a long career in semi-civil, semi-military posts in France and in those parts of Europe occupied by the imperial armies, sometimes as commander of a prisoner-of-war camp, sometimes as a supply officer. For Eude, still a young man in 1793, the *armée révolution-naire* opened the door on a new career, one quite different from his own, and if he gave good service to the Revolution, the Revolution in turn made a personality of him.[2]

---

[1] AN, F 10 450 (Agriculture, workers requisitioned for the harvest, by Section, Thermidor year II).

[2] AAG, Cl. gén. 1308 (Eude) and AHG, Xv f 45. Eude was condemned to transportation at the beginning of year V, after his arrest in the camp de Grenelle affair. But the judgement was quashed and in the year VII he was appointed captain in the 2nd auxiliary battalion of the Côte d'Or. In Brumaire year IX he was serving in the line infantry, 23rd demi-brigade, Army of the Rhine, but was suspended by the Consular decision of 1 Brumaire and was back in Paris by the 5th in his old trade as a clockmaker. He was arrested again with his

Lefranc was a much more important figure than this modest clock-maker, and after a long career in military administration he became commander of a prison camp. A native of Paris, this thirty-one-year-old captain of the Tuileries company was a rich man who called himself a carpenter simply to conform to current taste. He had 'sans-culottized' himself in much the same way as Duplay. But this 'carpenter' was a building contractor and an architect, who carried out important commissions on behalf of the Republic, including the construction of the new powder magazine at Saint-Germain-en-Laye, the conversion of the Ursuline grain warehouse at Saint-Denis, and the repair of the University buildings. It was no simple carpenter to whom Collot and Fouché entrusted the work of rebuilding France's second city, where Lefranc found himself with his company and was made head of public works and member of the General Council by the municipality. At the time of his arrest in the year III he owed 10,000 livres in pay – a token of the numbers in his employ.[1]

But if he was undoubtedly the richest man in the *armée révolutionnaire*, Lefranc's convictions were also the most sincere, his service as a militant *révolutionnaire* the longest and most impressive, and like most energetic *révolutionnaires*, he remained entirely faithful to the Convention after Thermidor.[2] In its service he lost his fortune and liberty, and from the year III until 1816 there was scarcely any republican conspiracy or anti-terrorist proscription in which his name did not figure. In electing him to command their company in October 1793, the *sans-culottes* of the Tuileries Section undoubtedly recognized the kind of man they were dealing with, and from the time of his departure for Lyon onward, Lefranc distinguished himself during long years of service as a masterful adminis-trator of the Terror. Although he never exercised any political function in his Section, apart from commanding its cannoneers, he was to use the methods of an accomplished terrorist en route to Lyon, 'electrifying' the *sociétés populaires*, stimulating the municipalities to pursue economic

---

former sergeant-major, Sormois, during the events of Nivôse year IX, and there is no further trace of him until August 1810 when he was again in service as captain in charge of outfitting draft-dodgers in the 5th depot at Blaye (Gironde). On 22 November 1811 he was appointed commander of the 30th battalion of Spanish prisoners-of-war, and the following year was made commander of seven of these battalions on the Helder. Appointed adjoint in 1813 to the general staff of Mayer, brigadier, he was sent to Naarden to negotiate the sur-render of the Helder forts. On his return to France he re-established himself in his old trade in Bordeaux; having vainly sought another command, from 1816 to 1819 he received a retirement pension of 600 francs. In 1828 he went to live in Sens, and the 1830 revolution revived his hopes of returning to service as a garrison commander. But his requests went unanswered, despite his professions of loyalty to the new dynasty, and he was obliged to take up his old trade, in 1831 establishing himself once again, aged 64, in Paris (342, rue Saint-Jacques).
[1] AN, F 7 4774 12 d 5 (Lefranc).
[2] See *Journal de la Montagne*, nos. 144 and 163.

frauds and 'malveillants', denouncing weakness and negligence where necessary, and commanding the *comités de surveillance* to be more vigilant. He even seems to have instilled this renewed vigilance into the members of his company, chosen out of all the revolutionary units to act as adjoint *commissaires*, to assist – and to watch – the Lyonnais on the *comités révolutionnaires* of the thirty-two Sections.

Not only was Lefranc an exceptional *révolutionnaire* who turned his company into a school for the Terror. Exceptional too was his revolutionary temperament: a well-off man, a Jacobin rather than a *sans-culotte*, he was to become in the year IV an inept and imprudent conspirator; and a conspirator he would remain for the rest of his active life. In the year XII, having just returned from Cayenne, sick and without money, he wrote to Bonaparte from the château of Brest, 'at all events the fever of delirium has gone for ever'. But 'the fever of delirium' took hold of him again in 1816; he became involved in a republican conspiracy and was incarcerated on Mont Saint-Michel.[1] *Révolutionnaire*, French patriot, conspirator, Lefranc was indeed very different from the others, and his experience in repression during the missions of the year II scarcely prepared him for the role of secret conspirator. Given the particular circumstances of the Parisian *armée*, the importance of his career derived not only from his pure temperament and unshakeable fidelity, but even more from the fact that this building contractor was captain of a company of cannoneers. This position, more than his personality, would draw him to the attention of Babeuf, Germain and Buonarroti. Finally, the personal role of Lefranc in the Parisian *armée* was considerable and this militant communicated his zeal, his 'delirium' to all around him. No other member of the *armée* had as great a personal influence on the course of events.

Louis David Sandoz, known as 'Scévola' Sandoz, somewhat resembled Lefranc in his revolutionary service. As a printer and engraver with a shop in the rue de Buci, l'Unité Section, he was, like many militant *sectionnaires*, involved in the luxury trade. He was also a foreigner, born in Geneva. A lieutenant in the l'Unité company of cannoneers, Sandoz remained in Paris when the company was sent to Toulon, occupied with the concerns of his Section, as member of the *comité révolutionnaire* and the Cordeliers, whose sessions he presided over during the crisis of Ventôse–Germinal. He was also the proposer of a motion in favour of mobile guillotines. Like Lefranc and Eude he was part of the republican opposition in the year III, appeared on Babeuf's lists, and was the object of surveillance and arrest on several occasions. On 24 Fructidor year IV

---

[1] AN, F 7 6276 (Lefranc to Bonaparte, 1 Frimaire year XII). He was also suspected of having received assistance from the British Government and made several statements against the French authorities during his captivity in England – accusations which he denied (id., note to the Grand Judge, sent from Brest, 24 Frimaire year XII).

he was arrested near the camp of Grenelle, brought before the military commission of the Temple, condemned to death on 6 Vendémiaire year V, and was shot the same day on the plain of Grenelle. If Sandoz does not quite fit into the category of cannoneer officers, he was nevertheless closely associated with the organization and administration of the *armée révolutionnaire*; he remained one of its most resolute supporters, and his exemplary career as a militant *sectionnaire* deserves a mention among those of the political chiefs of the artillery.[1]

Beside Lefranc, the revolutionary Gil Blas, all the other officers of the revolutionary artillery seem dull. Several were closely involved in the *journées* of the year III, in the Babeuf affair, and in the proscription of the year IX. But during their term in the *armée révolutionnaire* they also distinguished themselves in ways other than as political militants, by their background, by certain attitudes which brought them near the mass of the *sectionnaires*, and by their problems as civilians and fathers. Thus the lieutenant of the Bonne-Nouvelle company[2] was more a leading *section-naire* than an artillery officer at a time when relations were deteriorating between the Sectionary movement and the republican government. Jean-Baptiste Coppin was forty-seven, a Belgian in origin from Ypres who ran a shoe-mending business. As president of his Section's *société populaire* in Pluviôse year II, he demanded the use of the *armée révolutionnaire* against the butchers, whom he accused of favouritism in the distribution of the meagre meat rations. The Jacobin government, always acutely sensitive on matters of food supply, especially meat which was particularly scarce in the spring of 1794, accused him of being 'a disturber of the public peace'. The Bonne-Nouvelle *comité révolutionnaire* for its part, acting as agent for the Committees, and confining him to prison, denounced that 'coali-tion' and that 'esprit de corps' which 'undermined the position of the established authorities' – a condemnation of the claims of a cannoneer company to act independently, by invoking the subsistence laws in favour of the consumer.[3] For the *comité* Coppin's initiative raised the spectre of an independent artillery which might completely escape government control and provide the Sectionary movement with a military wing; and when a cannoneer officer was simultaneously president of the Section's *société*, with his company inactive in Paris and on hand for possible use, such fears were not without foundation. It was only with the disbandment

[1] A.-M. Soboul, *Les Sans-culottes parisiens en l'an II* (La Roche-sur-Yon, 1958), pp. 831–2. See also AN, WIa 138 (denunciation of the terrorists of the l'Unité Section); WIa 138, W 554 (*commission militaire* of the Temple Section); F 7 4276 and 4277 (Babeuf affair).

[2] AHG, Xv 45 (4th co. 2nd bn.): Courmaceul capt., Coppin lieut., Turpin 2nd lieut.

[3] AN, F 7 4653 d 1 (Coppin). Coppin was arrested 14 Pluviôse year II on orders from the *comité* for having said to the *société* 'that we were fifty cannoneers who would not rest until the law was enforced'.

of the *armée* and the return of the cannoneer companies to Paris, that similar examples appear in other Sections of conflict between cannoneers and *commissaires* of the *comités révolutionnaires*.

Delacroix and Dauphinot, captain and lieutenant respectively of the Bon-Conseil company, participated in the first mission of the *armée* to the Gonesse district in September. There, Jean-Louis Delacroix, a fifty-two-year-old basket-maker of the rue Montorgueil, and a native of Conflans-Sainte-Honorine, distinguished himself by his enthusiastic participation in blasphemous processions. He was accused of having decked himself out in a chasuble and of having conducted 'mocking benedictions in the squares', to which he replied: 'I admit that I put on a chasuble, but I don't believe I committed a sacrilege, yes I will say with satisfaction that I watched the baubles of superstition transformed into gold ingots in the republican crucible.' He spent only a short time at the head of this company, obtaining his leave in Brumaire 'to be free to deal with his business affairs'.

Delacroix was replaced by his first lieutenant, Denis Dauphinot, an active *sans-culotte* and *sectionnaire*, and the unflattering portrait of him by the Thermidorian authorities was in effect a tribute to his activities as a *révolutionnaire*. Accused of having deserted a dragoon regiment some years before the Revolution, by 1789 Dauphinot had set himself up as a café-owner in the rue Pavé, his café becoming the haunt of 'libertines and disreputable characters, to whom he served drinks almost all night long in defiance of police rulings'.[1] The Thermidorian mythology in which every *révolutionnaire* was a drunkard and a bad lot merits closer examination. Dauphinot was certainly not as violent as depicted, but his occupation as café-owner lent itself to accusations of this nature. Café-owners and innkeepers occupy a special place in the history of the Terror; they were propagators of revolutionary ideas and at the same time had links with the secret and violent world of crime. A man might derive considerable political importance from such an occupation, since the café-owner was not only in contact with the *sans-culottes*, but also with the floating and wretched population of the garrets, and it was among the latter that someone with political ambitions like Dauphinot might organize a following. This is why the *comités civils* of the year III, and even more the Robespierrist authorities of 1794, so feared the café-owning class.

We know little about the other cannoneer officers. Chevalier, commander of the Section des Marchés company, kept a toy shop in the rue Saint-Denis. Mera, lieutenant in the Gardes-Françaises company, was a haberdasher and draper, and like Delacroix was to request his discharge to

---

[1] AN, F 7 4662 d 5 (Dauphinot), F 7 4666 d 2 (Delacroix), and AHG, Xv 45.

look after his business.[1] Louis Vallantin, captain of the Guillaume-Tell company, born in 1755, the son of a farmer in the Berry, is one of the few to have a dossier in the Archives de la Guerre, for he remained in the army and had a long career in the artillery. His lieutenant, Jean-Michel Suicre, was thirty-four years of age and though a native of Württemberg had lived in Paris since 1775. He is described as an 'artiste' or 'worker', but he must have been a goldsmith, jeweller or clockmaker because he was considered useful in the manufacture of arms and thus escaped the laws against foreigners.[2] He belonged to that same group of foreign artisans working in the luxury trades from which the second-in-command of the Parisian armée, Boulanger, and the chef de bataillon, Halm, had come.

The commander of the Arcis company, Pierre Poupart, a thirty-six-year-old goldsmith, was denounced in Frimaire by one of his men for having squandered the company's effects. The Arcis comité attributed this accusation to personal spite and retained him in his command. But new accusations of a political nature would be made against him in Thermidor when several witnesses claimed to have seen him about to shake the hand of General Hanriot on the night of 9 Thermidor. He was arrested on the 14th, but the comité révolutionnaire came to his defence, claiming that he had mistaken the intentions of the commander-general, and he was released in Fructidor year II.[3] Potemont, a master locksmith, was captain of the Montreuil company and an important sectionnaire of the faubourg and with many other cannoneers he would figure on Babeuf's lists as a possible leader in his conspiracy.[4] The brothers Monvoisin, captain and lieutenant respectively of the Luxembourg company, notable agitators in their Section, and leaders of the republican opposition between 1795 and 1800, were from the same social grouping – one qualifying as an engraver in 1793, the other appearing in police records in the year IX as a clock-maker.[5] The captain of the Arsenal company, Petit, was a tapestry-maker. His name appears on Babeuf's lists (though he is sometimes confused with two others of the same name), and police reports of the year IX credited him with an active role in the journée of 31 May.[6]

Jean Mirau, an officer of the Brutus Section cannoneers, belonged to a

[1] AN, F 7 4646 d 3 (Chevalier); F 7 4774 42 d 3 (Mera).
[2] AAG, Cl. gén. 3822 (Vallantin); AN, F 7 4775 23 d 3 (Suicre).
[3] AN, F 7 4774 81 d 4 (Poupart).
[4] APP, A A/274 (Machine Infernale). In Babeuf's lists Potemont is mentioned as 'good in action, like his company'.
[5] BN, MSS Nouv. acq. fr. 2705 (1 33) – the Monvoisins were members of the Luxembourg Section société. APP, A A/272 (Chevalier-Desforges affair); and see also AN, F 7 4779 (comité révolutionnaire of the l'Unité Section) and F 7 4428 for the brothers' arrest after the journées of Prairial year II, and the liberation of the eldest by order of the Committee of General Security, 27 Vendémiaire year IV.
[6] APP, A A/276 (167) (Machine Infernale).

completely different social group from most of the artillery officers. At the time of his election he was destitute; the armée révolutionnaire was a life-line for him, and thanks to the support of his Section's société, of which he was a member, he secured a position as a checker in the National Treasury's bureau de comptabilité on his discharge. He was one of the few commis among the officers and was also a member of the administrative Council of the 4th battalion. He too would figure in the Babeuf conspiracy.[1] Finally Jean-Louis Hardy, second lieutenant in the Guillaume-Tell company (born at Chantilly in 1765), and Pascal Diacre, commander of the Contrat-Social company, were former soldiers and generally considered as different in this civilian force.[2]

Did these men belong to any 'party'? Can they be described as 'government men' or sans-culotte sectionnaires? Eude and Lefranc belonged to the Jacobin world; Lefranc was even well off, and the 'carpenter' of the rue Thomas-du-Louvre resembles the 'joiner' Duplay of the rue Honoré. But the resemblance stops there; Lefranc would not become a member of the Jacobins until Vendémiaire year III,[3] and far from being a Robespierrist, he gloried in his loyalty to the Convention and was even Thermidorian in outlook. His attitude was that of most of the cannoneer officers, who were attached to the Convention rather than to a man or a particular grouping; Eude alone might be considered a Robespierrist, his brother being a member of the General Council of the Commune. Nor were the others hébertistes, and though Lefranc later became a member of the Jacobins, there are no known Cordeliers in this group. Coppin, the brothers Monvoisin and Mirau were sociétaires who figured prominently in the Sectionary movement, the first by encroaching on the subsistence area, and alienating the Revolutionary Government in the process, the Monvoisins, with their company at Alençon, displaying all the grievances of the Parisians against the 'égoïstes' and 'fanatiques' of the departments. Potemont, the faubourg man, and Petit emerge from political obscurity simply by virtue of their appearance on the lists of the Babouvists and their proscription in the years VII and IX. Vallantin, in behaviour a government man, organized everyone else during his missions. Delacroix was anti-clerical, but no hébertiste for all that.

---

[1] AN, F 7 4774 47 d 1 (Mirau) and C 203 (1099) (Petitions) (List of signatories of the société).
[2] AAG, Cl. gén. 1778 (Hardy); and for Diacre, AHG, Xv 43 (Volontaires nationaux). There are other cannoneer officers of whom we know only the name and Section: Heno, capt., Popincourt co.; Preslot, capt., Champs-Élysées co.; Vincent, capt.; Danneu, lieut.; Charbonnaux, 2nd lieut., 4th co. 3rd bn.; Dupont, capt.; Calippe, lieut., and Gentler, 2nd lieut., l'Indivisibilité co.; Houlier, lieut., and Sanson, 2nd lieut., Faubourg-du-Nord co.; Guérin, capt., 1st co. 3rd bn. These men have left no trace save for their signatures on addresses of congratulations to the Convention, or their names on election lists (AN, C 299 [1951] and AHG, Xv 45 [Cannoneers]).
[3] Journal de la Montagne, no. 163 (3rd ser.) (Jacobins, session 17 Vendémiaire year III).

The War Ministry was not able to place its people in the artillery command, and the decisive influence in the choice of officers was that of the *comités révolutionnaires*. They could err in recommending men like Coppin, who were to prove undisciplined *sectionnaires*, but on the whole they succeeded in gaining the acceptance of popular personalities who were also submissive to the authority of central government. If the need arose – as in the case of Poupart's rescue by the Arcis *comité révolution-naire* – the *comités* would come to the assistance of protégés under attack from the cannoneers or the general body of *sectionnaires*.

The artillery officers were above all men of independent spirit, conscious of their privileged position and feeling themselves superior to their colleagues in the infantry. What is more, they succeeded in establishing this opinion with their own men, with the authorities, and with most of their contemporaries. The artillery officer considered himself the accredited defender of the regime: and expected its gratitude in return.

II *The Fusilier Officers*

We know more of the fusilier officer than his undoubtedly more important colleague in the cannoneers. Since military men were more numerous in the infantry than in the artillery, we have abundant documentation on them in the form of individual dossiers. But such an abundance carries its own dangers, for if it informs us of the military careers of many of these officers, it can also give the appearance of a greater preponderance of military men in this corps than existed in reality. The 'civilian' documentation is also misleading, for it concentrates on 'mauvais sujets' and counter-revolutionaries, or those accused as such, particularly in pre-Thermidorian documentation. This is the drawback of all police-initiated material, for the officer or fusilier who leaves behind a dossier is usually the one who has become embroiled with the police, the *comités révolutionnaires*, or the Committee of General Security. The range widens after Thermidor when all the officers become suspect in the eyes of the authorities of the year III. Always allowing for the style of Thermidorian pronouncements on anything concerning the personnel of the *armée révolutionnaire*, the documentation of the period is nevertheless a rich source of information on the occupations and revolutionary lives of many of the civilians at the head of fusilier companies. The military men on the other hand do not appear in this type of document, for they remained in the army and thus escaped the attention of the *comités civils* and of those responsible for the proscription of these former terrorist units.

Despite these gaps in documentation and the consequent distortions, this material provides information on nearly half the infantry officers (40 out of a total of 81),[1] 24 of whom are military men, the rest civilians. Like the artillery officers they are nearly all aged between thirty and fifty; 5 are over fifty, 3 are less than thirty.[2] While never a veteran corps, the infantry command was nevertheless composed of older men than those on the extraordinary Commissions in the departments. They were the same age as the members of the *comités révolutionnaires* and the militant minority in the Sections, to which most of these officers had belonged. If this sample devotes too much attention to the military men to be truly representative of the corps as a whole, it nevertheless incorporates a wide selection from the Paris Sections (34 out of 48).[3]

(i) THE MILITARY MEN
This group accounted for a number of detachment commanders, some of the most violent. François Briois, lieutenant of the Loude company from the l'Indivisibilité Section, is one example, who, after having served in the Colonial regiment from 1768 to 1790, took part in the repression at Lyon. François Bouveron, captain of the 1st company of the 1st battalion (Sans-culottes?) was a more level-headed person than Briois, with a history of military service just as long, having served continuously from 1773 to 1792. Chuine, another military man, whom Bouveron replaced at Chauny, was to be denounced by his company for his harshness.[4]

The case of Jean-Baptiste Carteron is more complex, because like many second officers under the *ancien régime* this former officer had abandoned his military career to follow one under the Revolution. He was born at Coiffy (Haute-Marne) in 1754, enrolled in the Vintimille regiment in 1771, and transferred in 1776 to the Berry regiment, which he deserted on

---

[1] AHG (*reg. des brevets*, 1793 – year II).
[2] Simon, 54; Réaume, 44; Bouveron, 40; Briois, 42: Carteron, 39; Chamot, 44; Dumany, 51; Gasson, 24; Huel, between 47 and 50; Langlois, 32; Macquart, 34; Edme, 40; Belhomme, Devic, Desjardins, Guénin, Laboria, Pépin, Thévenot and Gayrand, between 38 and 45; Martin, 48; Chaumont, 36; Pudepièce, 60; Joly and Fauveau, 27.
[3] 1 Tuileries (Bourgoin, capt.); 2 Champs-Élysées (Gary, id.); 4 Montagne (Grossin, id.); 6 Lepeletier (Carteron, id.); 7 Mont-Blanc (Garnier, id., and Vitau); 8 Muséum (Dumany, id.); 9 Gardes-Françaises (Collin, id., Keller); 10 Halle-au-Bled (Lecourtier, id.); 11 Contrat-Social (Henry, id., and Lallemant); 12 Guillaume-Tell (Hébert, id.); 14 Bonne-Nouvelle (Réaume and Simon); 15 Amis-de-la-Patrie (Soulet, capt., and Villedieu); 17 Marchés (Langlois); 19 Arcis (Chaussepied, capt.); 20 Faubourg-Montmartre (Chamot, id., and Martin); 21 Poissonnière (Queneuille, id.); 22 Bondy (Chaumont, capt., and Martin); 24 Popincourt (Dagorno, id.; Desjardins); 26 Quinze-Vingts (Dufour); 28 Faubourg-du-Nord (Constant); 29 Réunion (Coste, capt.); 30 Homme-Armé (Huel and Pudepièce); 31 Droits-de-l'Homme (Fouques, capt., and Charbonnier); 32 Maison-Commune (Deslauriers, id., and Thévenin); 33 Indivisibilité (Loude, id., and Briois); 34 Arsenal (Joly); 38 Invalides (Fauveau, capt.; Heusé); 40 Unité (Ruide, id.); 41 Marat (Gasson); 43 Mutius-Scévola (Du Mans, capt.); 44 Chalier (Surbled, id.).
[4] AHG (*reg. d'ordre*), Maubant to Chuine, 22 Ventôse year II, also *reg. des brevets*, 1793 – year II, and see my *L'Armée révolutionnaire à Lyon*.

the significant date of 13 July 1789. The same day he was elected corporal in the Hulin company of the Parisian *garde bourgeoise*, and the following day took part in the capture of the Bastille. As a Vainqueur de la Bastille his revolutionary career was assured, and he quickly passed through all the grades in the National Guard back in his own department. Commencing as commander of the Jussey National Guard in 1792, he was elected sergeant in the grenadiers of the Haute-Saône, 4th battalion, then a gendarme in the 35th division, and his absence without leave in December 1792 still did not prevent his promotion to lieutenant in the 36th demi-brigade. Finding himself once more in Paris – again probably without leave – this man who flitted in and out of public notice was now, in Frimaire year II, elected captain of the Lepeletier Section fusiliers.[1]

Carteron's activities, however, were not limited to the exercise of his command. As an inhabitant of one of the most counter-revolutionary Sections of the capital, he was connected with Fouquier-Tinville and the underground police world. In September 1793, by hiding in a cupboard, he became police informer in a shady case of false non-emigration certificates. On his discharge from the *armée* in Floréal he joined Maillard's hit-men and as a member of the police force of the Parisian general staff carried out a number of arrests in Paris and surrounding areas on behalf of Hanriot.[2] The following month he was again of service to Fouquier as a prison spy in the Burlandeux-Pigasse affair, a complicated business involving both royalists and *hébertistes* (such as the police agent Lafosse) in an attempt to release Marie-Antoinette. Carteron got himself mixed up in the affair, acting from the cover of Mme Bourgoin's house in the rue Grange-Batelière, and finding himself in prison he wrote on 28 Nivôse year II to his patron Fouquier: 'I have just now learnt of your search for those involved in the plan to rescue Capet's widow. I wanted you to know that I discovered this infamous plot and the conspirators had me thrown

---

[1] AN, F 7* 2478, reg. Lepeletier *comité*; J. Durieux, *Les Vainqueurs de la Bastille* (1911), and AHG (*reg. des brevets*).

[2] AN, F 7 4634 d 3 (Carteron), list of his activities under orders of Hanriot and Maillard (25 Floréal year II): '1. at Saint-Germain-en-Laye, case of a conspirator enrolling for the Vendée. 2. at the Palais Infernal when it was blocked. 3. at the Hôtel l'Intendant du Prince Louis, near Clignancourt. 4. rue Saint-Marc, with Maillard. 5. at the Moulin Joli, with Marino, as ordered by General Hanriot and his aides-de-camp. 6. seeking la Tour du Pin ... 7. in the Sans-Culottes Section, with the aides-de-camp, not having been able to find the scoundrel. 8. rue Traversière-Saint-Honoré, three conspirators from Lille. 9. at Argenteuil, arrest of a chevalier and former deputy ... 10. at the château de la Barre with the scoundrel la Barthe, intendant of Monsieur ... with an administrator of the department ... 11. at Mesnil-Simon's for the arrest of Pigasse, who was selling a summons order ... I was sent the following day to Livry by Galquet [*sic*] president of the Committee [of General Security] to bring Richemain in to testify against Dossonville and Pigasse. On my return I was shot at in the Bondy forest and my only recompense was 25 livres to pay for the carriage. Carteron, rue Helvétius ...'

in prison in order to silence me … if you grant me an audience you will be astonished at my revelations.'[1] An inmate of the École Militaire at the time, this hit-man turned informer was a thoroughly nasty piece of work.

Jean Gasson and François Langlois of the revolutionary infantry were also former military men with political associations. The first, at only twenty-five years of age, was the youngest member of this corps; when elected captain of Marat Section company he might even have fallen within the age-range of the first requisition. But he had the backing of the War Ministry, which had a body of supporters in the Section. Gasson was a native of Bordeaux and had served in the Languedoc regiment from 1784 to 1791. He was a volunteer in the 3rd Gironde battalion, and after the destruction of his former company in the Vendée transferred to the 4th regiment of *chasseurs-carabiniers*. Arriving in Paris as a sergeant-major in this corps, he secured permission from the military police to join the *armée révolutionnaire*, and was chosen to command the Marat company. The Marat Section had thus selected someone with all the enthusiasm and imprudence of youth, who would involve his detachment in serious conflict with the local authorities.[2]

Langlois entered the Parisian National Guard in November 1789, after three years in the Lorraine-Infanterie regiment, and at the same time pursued an active revolutionary career in the Marchés Section. At the time of his election as lieutenant in the Marchés company he was a 'herbalist', occasionally a doctor, and a member of the Section's *comité révolution-naire*. He was an active dechristianizer and would later be one of the hard core of ex-terrorists in the years VIII and IX.[3]

François Dumany, who was to command the Melun detachment, possessed all the prudence and calmness in which young Gasson was lacking. Born in Paris in 1742, he was over fifty, and after service of twenty years

---

[1] AN, WIa 184 and W 389 (904) (Pigasse, Mesnil-Simon et Burlandeux affair). Burlandeux, against whom Carteron testified, was condemned to death by the revolutionary tribunal on 29 Prairial year II. It was a ramification of the Batz conspiracy; for this last, see A. de Lestapis, 'Un grand corrupteur: le duc du Châtelet', *AHRF*, nos. 131, 133, 138 (1953–5). Carteron therefore was moving in the most dubious police circles, occupied by Marino, Lafosse and Dossonville. At the same time he was in the service of Hanriot, and yet it seems that he was not bothered after Thermidor, though he undoubtedly continued 'to render service'.

[2] AAG, Cl. gén. 1549 (Gasson) and Arch. Oise, reg. Noyon *comité de surveillance*.

[3] AN, F 7 4774 16 d 3 (Lenoir), denunciation of the Marchés Section terrorists, 30 Germinal year III. See also APP, AA/272 (26) (Chevalier-Desforges affair): interrogation of Bonjour, ex-agent of the Committee of General Security, 14 Nivôse year IX. The police spy accused Langlois of wanting to liquidate the informer Tyraud. The same day a police note said he intended going to the fort at Vincennes to capture the cannon and corrupt the troops. The former revolutionary officer seems to have been a man of action and was already referred to as such on Babeuf's lists for the Marchés Section (AN, F 7 4277).

(1760–80) in the Neustrie regiment, he returned to live near the Louvre in Paris. The Revolution gave him the opportunity of a new military career and he quickly advanced through all the promotion stages in the National Guard of his district, then of his Section, and was second-in-command of the Muséum Section armed force when the *armée révolutionnaire* was formed. Another protégé of the painter David, he became captain of the Muséum fusiliers, and remained with his detachment in the Melun district throughout the existence of the *armée révolutionnaire*. The Melun authorities had so much confidence in the good sense of this Parisian soldier, who knew how to restrain the untimely enterprises of his officers and men, that they appointed him to the *comité de surveillance* of their commune. He was admitted to the Invalides when he came out of the *armée révolutionnaire*, and in the year IV was back in service again in the company of Meaux veterans.[1]

André Chamot, commander of the detachment sent to Montereau and to the Nemours district, was not destined to have the same success as Dumany in his relations with the local authorities. Born in 1749, he too was a former military man, who had served under the surname 'Sans-Souci' in the Chartres-Infanterie regiment from 1768 to 1776. This son of a *charcutier* in Neuilly-lès-Beaune, on the outskirts of Pontoise, set himself up in the rue Montholon in Paris when he left the army. At the time of his arrest at the Grenelle camp in the year IV he was described as a second-hand dealer, a trade which he seems to have pursued from the time of his discharge in 1776 to that of his election as captain of the Faubourg-Montmartre company (the 2nd company, 4th battalion) on 24 Vendémiaire year II.[2] Like many of those former soldiers, Chamot was a militant *sectionnaire* whose loyalty to revolutionary principles explains his involvement in the Grenelle affair.

Charles Loude, captain of the l'Indivisibilité Section company, and later commander of an advance detachment in the Coulommiers region, had spent a decade in the Swiss Guards. His friend Jean Edme, born in 1753, served in the Beaujolais regiment from 1773 to 1790, then in the Parisian National Guard until 1792, and passed into the 102nd infantry regiment on its formation, becoming a lieutenant that same year. Loude and Edme had all the impatience of military men when faced with obstacles raised by the civil authorities, and in the Pontoise district they were to act in a particularly arbitrary manner.[3]

---

[1] AN, F 7 4689 d 5 (Dumany) and AAG, Cl. gén. 1121 (Dumany).
[2] AHG, Xv 45 (Volontaires nationaux – Chamot capt., Masson lieut., Goyot 2nd lieut.), also (Casemates) reg. Chartres-Infanterie, 253. AN, W 554 (camp de Grenelle affair – list of those arrested).
[3] AHG, *reg. des brevets*, Xv 45, for Loude; AAG, Cl. gén. 1280 (Edme). See also my 'L'armée révolutionnaire dans le district de Pontoise'.

Like Maubant, Dumany, Chamot, and, it seems, Loude, Laurent Macquart served for five years in the Chartres-Infanterie regiment before transferring to the National Guard, from which he purchased his discharge after eight years of service. Born at Bar-le-Duc in 1757, the son of a tapestry-maker working in Paris, Macquart also set himself up in Paris in 1786 as a toy dealer and would later take part in the repression of Lyon.[1] Isidore Ruide, captain of the l'Unité Section company (6th of the 3rd battalion), served for two years in the Vexin regiment, secured his discharge in 1783, and took up residence in the rue de Seine in Paris, where he was still living in the year III. This former soldier was a member of the *société populaire* in the l'Unité Section.[2] The final military man of this group was Huel, otherwise known as 'Désiré'. After having served from 1764 to 1777 in the Viennois regiment, he was appointed lieutenant of the l'Homme-Armé company (7th in the 5th battalion) on the formation of the Parisian *armée*. He moved to Lyon with his company and was elected member of the Military Commission and *commissaire* on the *comité de présentation* of the *société populaire*.[3]

The former military men, therefore, these second officers from the Royal Infantry regiments, occupied a very important place in the command structure of the revolutionary infantry. Paradoxical as it may seem, they owed this position not to their technical expertise gained in the *ancien régime* armies or in the officer class of the National Guard, but to the service which they had already rendered the Revolution. Several were important *sectionnaires* or political personalities, all were well known in the quartiers, some as members of their *sociétés sectionnaires*, and Langlois in addition was *commissaire* of his Section's *comité révolutionnaire*. Gasson was supported by the Cordeliers and the *hébertiste* group in the Marat Section; Dumany was also a protégé of David, who placed many such men in the new *armée*. All these military men, therefore, had a solid base in the small-business and artisan world of Paris, whether as toy dealer, herbalist, or tapestry-maker, for all had established themselves there after buying their way out of the army. Most had experienced several years of civilian life before the outbreak of the Revolution. The younger

---

[1] *L'Armée révolutionnaire à Lyon*, p. 91; AAG (Casemates) reg. Chartres-Infanterie, 253 – Macquart joined the same Godeau company in which Maubant was serving in 1781.

[2] AN, F 7 4765 d 2 (Ruide); AHG, *reg. des brevets*; and BL, F 826* (membership list of the l'Unité *société*).

[3] AAG, *reg. des brevets* and my *L'Armée révolutionnaire à Lyon*. The other military men among the infantry officers were Belhomme (Perche-Infanterie 1773–8), Devic (49th régiment d'infanterie 1774–90), Desjardins (Bassigny 1769–77), Fouques (Chasseurs des Pyrénées 1779–87), Gayrand (Vexin 1773–81), Guénin (régiment du Roi 1772–7), Laboria (Gardes-Françaises 1778–82), Pépin (Conty-Infanterie 1777–85), Poisson (Normandie-Infanterie 1757–75), Thévenot (Gardes-Françaises 1778–86), Tramblay (Régiment Royal) (AAG, *reg. des brevets*, 1793 – year II).

ones still serving in the royal armies at the time of the Revolution, took advantage of the event to desert and throw in their lot with the new military authority, the urban National Guard, which was anxious to acquire these former soldiers with their valuable infantry experience.

These military men in fact owed a great deal to the Revolution and on the whole showed themselves grateful to a regime which had offered them so much. The departmental authorities were to find them just as capable of 'revolutionizing' as the civilians. Furthermore, they were responsible for many of the most flagrant abuses of authority such as the arrest of an entire municipal body about to go into session, and the armed invasion of the premises of a *comité de surveillance*. Such acts of authoritarianism, which would so damage the reputation of the Parisian *armée* and incur the displeasure of the Committee of Public Safety, were committed by men who, from their years of service with the King of France, had retained a sense of contempt for civilians and a lack of respect for elected authorities. Whether arranging military quarters in the name of the King or revolutionizing in the name of the Paris Commune and Sections, their mode of action savoured of military despotism. Such brutality might also be directed against the *révolutionnaires*, and to the officers who manhandled the local authorities as though conducting a campaign of military repression, revolutionary style, must be added those who acted like *chiens de quartier* towards their own troops, subjecting them to excessively harsh discipline.

(ii) THE CIVILIANS

Some civilians among the infantry officers played an important part in the history of the Parisian *armée*. Cardinaux, Thunot, Boisgirault of the Panthéon-Français Section; Réaume, Bonne-Nouvelle Section; Chaumont and Martin, Bondy Section; Grossin, Montagne Section; Gary, Champs-Élysées; Collin and Keller, Gardes-Françaises; Fauveau of the Invalides Section: these were the principal organizers of the infantry's revolutionary action in the departments and the main targets of criticism from local authorities. Some were active for only a short period, but Cardinaux, Réaume and Fauveau were seasoned *révolutionnaires* and belonged to the small number of militant terrorists who sought to maintain some cohesion after the disappearance of the Sectionary institutions. Their period in the *armée révolutionnaire* was to be as important for them as for the military men like Lefranc and Eude in the cannoneers, for not only did it leave its mark in terrorist experience gained at first hand, but it reinforced their political leanings and convictions by exposing them to Thermidorian proscription.

In this respect the most instructive career is undoubtedly that of Pierre Cardinaux, lieutenant in the Panthéon company. It was a Section which accounted for three notable personalities in the revolutionary infantry – a reflection of its advanced political consciousness, rather than an accident of documentation. Cardinaux was another of those foreign artisans who had come as young men to seek their fortune in Paris. A native of Neuchâtel in Switzerland, he had been living in the Sainte-Geneviève quartier since 1770, and had set himself up in business as a caterer-restaurateur some years before the Revolution. An active citizen and an elector of 1792, who had been chosen to carry the flag for his Section's armed force the same year, Cardinaux was made a member of the Panthéon-Français *comité révolutionnaire* on its formation in March 1793. With Hû and Jumillard, he quickly established himself as a leading personality in the general assembly and in the *société fraternelle*, playing an active role as the representative of his Section in the *journées* of 31 May and 2 June, and participating in the June–July conflict over plans for the first *armée révolutionnaire*. However, if his career continued into the republican opposition of the years 1795–1801, the cause lay not with Cardinaux himself, an uncultivated and unintelligent man, but in the fact of his wife's acquisition of restaurant premises in a former Génovéfien convent, now national property, during his absence with the *armée*. It was a perilous enterprise at any time, and in Floréal year II a sure road to bankruptcy for Cardinaux, lately returned to civilian life. Despite this setback, however, the restaurateur borrowed the money to open a new establishment on the place de l'Estrapade. The Bal Cardinaux, as it became known, soon acquired a certain notoriety as the meeting place of 'exclusifs' and Babouvists (members of the so-called 'club du Panthéon'), where a number of republican conspiracies were hatched, and in consequence was closely watched by the police authorities. Cardinaux himself was only a poor café-owner, who according to contemporary accounts had succumbed to the occupational hazard of the bottle. Too limited ever to make an effective political leader, he nevertheless found himself at the centre of every plot, from his acquaintance with former terrorists who preferred to drink in his establishment – the tavern for every republican malcontent. As he explained to Fouché on 8 Pluviôse year IX, after his sentence of deportation:

> It is true that I proclaimed myself in favour of the republic . . . to the detriment of my family I acquired some sort of reputation, not out of natural talent, with which I am ill-endowed, and I was never a speaker at any political or public assembly. But I had the misfortune to run a large establishment, where, in conformity with the laws of the time, people gathered to form a political society – my only concern, however, was to sell wine.

Cardinaux seems to have been popular with his Section – 'a good republican', as he was described by the guards of the Panthéon in a police spy's report – and since he was recommended by Parein it does look as if he may have worked for the political police.[1]

The two officers of the Bondy Section company, Chaumont and Martin, come to our attention rather as detachment commanders. Zealous *sans-culottes*, excellent officers, and highly regarded by their men, these Parisian artisans were to become scapegoats, sops to rural vengeance for having acted in a revolutionary manner against the authorities in their anxiety to implement requisitions in the capital's favour. Adrien-Josse Chaumont, captain of the Bondy company, was thirty-six at the time of his election. He was a native of Roigny (Eure), a father of six and a master jeweller at 52, rue du Faubourg-Saint-Martin. His lieutenant, Nicolas Martin, was a forty-eight-year-old Parisian and a market porter. Like Cardinaux, they were the object of quite ridiculous accusations; they were paying the penalty of the excesses committed by the Parisian detachments in the countryside, and even more so for the very principle of supplying the towns through force.[2]

Jean-Étienne Réaume, a native of Acy (Oise), captain of the Bonne-Nouvelle company, was one of the most intelligent and consistent of the militant *sectionnaires* in the *armée*. In 1778, after eight years' service in the Queen's regiment, he set himself up as a toymaker in the rue Saint-Denis, the quarter in which Hébert lived. He was thirty-nine at the time of the Revolution and that December he enrolled in the National Guard. In July 1792 he was made second-in-command of the Section's armed force and in June 1793 became postal *commissaire*. A prime example of the militant *sectionnaire*, this former soldier turned tradesman commanded his company in Lyon, and the almost daily correspondence which he maintained with the *comité révolutionnaire* of the Bonne-Nouvelle Section is particularly instructive on the mentality of a revolutionary officer who had come up from the Sections. Repression he entirely supported, and he adopted all the cruel expressions of his neighbour Hébert to mock Lyonnais condemned to the firing squad and the guillotine. Learning of the arrest of Hébert – one of the celebrities of his Section – and of his chief, Ronsin, Réaume expressed no sense of surprise: 'We must beware of all men,' he observed philosophically, 'and attach ourselves to principles only.'

In his conformism and his severity towards the Lyonnais, Réaume is a

---

[1] AN, F 7 6272; also F 7 4633 d 3 (Cardinaux), F 7 4771 d 1 (Lebois), F 7 4276 (Babeuf affair), F 7 6267 (Chevalier affair), F 7 6271–6276 (déportés, year IX) and APP, A A/272–283 (Machine Infernale). In the year IX Cardinaux wrote reminding Fouché of the services rendered by him, and claiming to have been recommended by Parein.

[2] AN, F 7 4644 d 1 (Chaumont) and D III 5 (298–365) (Comité de législation, Aisne, Laon, criminal tribunal of the department) – trial of Chaumont and Martin; also my 'L'armée révolutionnaire dans l'Aisne'.

good example of a certain type of revolutionary mentality which reflected something of 'Terror bureaucracy'.[1] He had, for example, a tendency towards denunciation, Dossonville, the royalist police agent, who would later take his own revenge, being one of his victims. But he was no coward: a *sociétaire* of the year II, in possession of a membership card from the former Bonne-Nouvelle *société* at the time of his arrest, he was to remain faithful to his convictions; he subscribed to Babeuf's paper, and got himself expelled from the Section's guard in the year III by the Muscadins who detested this prototype terrorist, this 'hero of the Revolution', as one informer called him derisively. He could also be a conspirator when he wanted and would be arrested near the Soleil-d'Or on the night of the Grenelle affair. On this occasion his sentence by the Commission Militaire to three years' detention was reversed because he was not a soldier and not subject to military justice. In Lyon he brought the violence and truculence of the former soldier to the normal activities of this civilian force, and in the year IV his wife initiated divorce proceedings 'on the grounds of cruelty, mistreatment and serious injury'. Another aspect which identifies him with the militant *sectionnaires* was his economic position as a comfortable shop-owner, and despite his reputation as a terrorist, he was chosen by his fellow citizens in the year IV as *commissaire* to assist in the estimates and sale of *biens nationaux*. With the full force of his personality as a militant terrorist, Réaume dominated the officers of his company.[2]

Collin, captain of the Gardes-Françaises company, was a glazier. His lieutenant, Keller, was a zealous denouncer and would later appear on Babeuf's lists as a militant *sectionnaire*. He was detested by the Laon authorities for his provocative insistence on pointing out their every infraction of the *maximum*, and in the year III he was himself denounced as a 'terrorist' by his Section. Toussaint Fouques, captain of the Droits-de-l'Homme fusiliers, was a saddler with a large family. On his discharge from the army he was represented as being unemployed and living in the greatest poverty.[3] Nor had the captain and lieutenant of the Contrat-Social company, Henry and Lallemant respectively, any fixed employment; they

---

[1] R.C. Cobb, 'Quelques aspects de la mentalité révolutionnaire'.

[2] AN, F 7 4774 88 d 2 (Réaume), F 7 4278 (Babeuf affair), W 554-5 (camp de Grenelle affair). He is listed as 'Réum' in the *Dictionnaire des Jacobins vivans* (Hamburg, 1799), 152, with the comment, 'one of the *frères* sent to Lyon to organize massacre and pillage'. The royalist author cites Réaume's letter to the Bonne-Nouvelle *société* or *comité*, and accuses him, incorrectly, of having participated in the *noyades* in the Vendée – he was thus assured a place in the terrorist pantheon. Réaume, with the full force of his militant terrorism, dominated the other officers in his company, of which the lieutenant (Jacques Simon, born 1739) was a journeyman mason, son of another journeyman mason (AHG, Xv 45) (4th co. 2nd bn.).

[3] AHG, Xv 45 (4th co. 2nd bn.): Colin [*sic*], capt.; Keller, lieut.; Vicq, 2nd lieut. AN, F 7 4710 d 4 (Fouques).

were unemployed at the time of their election, and recognized the *armée révolutionnaire* as a way out of their misery, a door on to better times. In Lyon their conduct was so scandalous that they were denounced by their men to the *comité* and *société* of their Section. According to the fusiliers, they were constantly drunk, pursued women and played cards. After their return from such an enjoyable mission the two found themselves again out of work and applied to their Section for employment in the postal service.[1]

Henry and Lallemant were not the only men of this type in the *armée*; their colleagues in the Finistère company, the captain, Doré (aptly so-called), and his lieutenant and acolyte in pleasure, Masson, were of the same breed. We know nothing of the civilian life of the hedonistic Doré. In the *armée* he and Masson devoted themselves entirely to women, cards and cafés, in the limited measure that a small town like Honfleur could accommodate the demands of these two Parisian revellers. Like the two officers from the Contrat-Social Section, Doré and Masson were so little concerned about their men and their military and political duties, that in Germinal they abandoned their company on the road and made their own way back to Paris. They were not *sectionnaires* like their men, and when denounced by the latter to the Lazowski *société populaire* for having preferred the gaming table to the affairs of their company at Honfleur, they simply replied that they had better things to do than listen to constant denunciations and that the Lazowski *société* could 'bugger off'.[2]

There are some officers whose civilian occupations we know, but the information adds little to our understanding of their personalities. The captain of the Montagne company, Grossin, had private means and during his stay in the Compiègne district his men denounced him for his softness towards the farmers. Unlike them he did not seem to see these 'blood-suckers' of the people as the enemies of Paris and the Revolution, seeking rather to spare them the experience of requisitions by force. Despite such accusations, which Grossin claimed to be the retaliatory action of certain *révolutionnaires* whom he punished for indiscipline, he was able to secure a position as instructor at the École de Mars, Sablons camp, when he left the *armée*.[3] Davril, second lieutenant in the 3rd company, 3rd battalion,

---

[1] AN, F 7 4741 d 3 (Henry), and my *L'Armée révolutionnaire à Lyon*.

[2] AN, F 7* 2517 (*comité* of the Finistère Section, session of 4 Floréal year II).

[3] AN, F 7 4734 d 2 (Grossin); see also F 7 4764 d 4 (Lapierre). Lapierre, member of the *société républicaine*, Montagne Section, wrote on 16 Ventôse reproaching Grossin for his supposed indulgence towards the farmers: 'remember . . . that we have declared war on all those blood-suckers of the people, on all *égoïstes*, all aristocrats . . . the soldiers you command complain of your conduct towards these people; they think you have forgotten that you are a *sans-culotte*.' Grossin replied on the 20th denying the charges: 'No, I have not forgotten . . . that I have the honour of being a *sans-culotte*.' Among the former terror-ists banished from Paris in 1813, there was a Grossin, a shoemaker, who in April 1813 was living in Tours (AN, F 7 6586).

was also detested by his men. This young tailor's assistant, like many provisional officers taken from civilian life, had been intoxicated by over-rapid promotion and made himself detestable to his men by his brutality and his pretensions.[1]

Finally, let us look briefly at those other officers whose occupations we know. Constant, captain of the Faubourg-du-Nord company, was a porcelain sculptor, a protégé of Léonard Bourdon, and a member of this Section's *comité révolutionnaire* in Thermidor; as such he played an active part in rallying his Section to the side of the Convention.[2] As a friend of Bourdon's, Constant was a 'government man' by inclination and personal connections. Dufour, first lieutenant of the Quinze-Vingts company, and one of the few faubourg officers of whom we know something, was a day-labourer at the time of his election. Dumany's lieutenant in the Muséum company, Leconte, was a cutler in the rue de l'Arbre-sec.[3] Antoine Pudepièce, at sixty the oldest officer of the corps, was second lieutenant of the l'Homme-Armé Section company and a saddler with his own carriage-hire business in the rue de Braque. On news of his dispatch to Lyon, 'I obtained leave after a month to put my affairs in order, to sell my carriages and lease my house'. His business must have prospered, for he was able to live off the proceeds of the sale and the income from his creditors until his arrest as a former terrorist in 1799. He died in prison in 1800, a delayed retribution for his part in the Lyon expedition.[4] In the year III the former officers and soldiers of the *armée révolutionnaire* were called 'Septembriseurs', but in the year IV, at the time of the mammoth trial of so-called 'massacreurs', only one former officer was named: René Joly, a twenty-seven-year-old shoe-mender, a former *gendarme* and lieutenant in the Arsenal company.[5]

(iii)   THE POLITICAL MEN

For most of the detachment leaders there is no information either on their occupations or on any previous service. Such is the case with Jean Thunot, captain of the Panthéon-Français company, and his lieutenant, Boisgirault, two officers who were much talked about during their mission to Compiègne. There were two Thunots in this Section, one described as a pedlar, the other as a joiner, and our captain was undoubt-

---

[1] AN, WIa 147.
[2] R.C. Cobb, 'La mission de Siblot au Havre-Marat'.
[3] Arch. Seine, D 4 AZ 124, for Dufour; AN, F 7 4774 16 d 3 (Lenoir) (List of terrorists of the Muséum Section) for Leconte.
[4] APP, A A/274 (321); the captain of the l'Homme-Armé company was Jarle, the lieutenant, Moutin. See also id. (Machine Infernale), Pudepièce, defence evidence, 11 Nivôse year IX.
[5] AN, AA 56 (1521) (trial of the Septembriseurs, 23 Floréal year IV; the massacres at La Force).

edly one of them. We know that in June 1793 he was a member of his Section's commission for *certificats de civisme*. Like Boisgirault he was a political militant, and on several occasions denounced reputed suspects and political adversaries like the *juge de paix* Hû (one of the most controversial personalities in the Panthéon-Français Section) to the *comités révolutionnaires* of the Panthéon-Français and Finistère Sections.[1]

Pierre Fauveau, captain of the Invalides company, is another officer with political leanings whose position in civilian life we know nothing about. A friend of Vézien, the battalion commander, and Marcellin, a former inspector of police, he is known to us only by virtue of the many occasions on which he was arrested. He was taken into custody for the first time in Prairial year II under the Robespierrist dictatorship, again as a former terrorist in the year III,[2] and his name was on Babeuf's lists in the year IV. A native of Melun, he was twenty-eight years of age at the time of his election to the *armée révolutionnaire*. But what of the occupations of Lecourtier, captain of the Halle-au-Bled company and such a stern disciplinarian that his men demanded his replacement;[3] or of those known to us only by name, or because of accusations which resulted in their recall to Paris: men like Michel Chaussepied, commander of the Arcis company; Louis Du Mans, captain, Mutius-Scévola company; Edmond, captain, Sans-Culottes company;[4] Queneuille, commander of the Poissonnière company;[5] Gary, who led the Champs-Élysées company to Cluny and Lyon;[6] Bourgoin, commander of the Tuileries armed force, and then captain of its company in the *armée*;[7] Coste, commander of the Réunion company; Surbled, commanding that of Chalier;[8] Villedieu, lieutenant in

---

[1] AN, F 7* 2520 (reg. Panthéon-Français Section *comité*, session 19 June 1793; also denunciation by Thunot, 14 September 1793), and F 7* 2517 (reg. Finistère Section *comité*). See also AN, W 416 (953) (Hû affair), denunciation made by Thunot against the *juge de paix* of the Panthéon-Français Section. For other denunciations made by this decidedly zealous militant, see AN, F 7 4775 30 d 1, and Arch. Seine-et-Marne, L 854 (Provins *comité*).

[2] APP, AA/22 (146) (Committee of General Security), warrant for arrest of Fauveau, 7 Prairial year II; AN, F 7 4703 d 3 (Fauveau).

[3] AN, F 7 4774 10 d 2 (Lecourtier).

[4] Arch. Seine, D4 AZ 124, for Chaussepied; id., D4 AZ 876, for Du Mans; Arch. Honfleur, I 63 (*société populaire*), for Edmond.

[5] AN, F 7 4776 (*comité de surveillance*, 3rd arrondissement), *déclaration de domicile* of Queneuille, 23 Frimaire year III.

[6] AN, F 7 4777 (*comité révolutionnaire*, Champs-Élysées, 4 Floréal year II), and F 7* 2474 (stamp of the *comité* on Gary's *certificat de civisme*, dated 28 Prairial year II).

[7] AN, F 7* 2471 (reg. Tuileries *comité*), session of 23 Vendémiaire, when Bourgoin resigned from the armed force to take up his command of the fusilier company – proof of the importance attached to this new army by the *sectionnaires*.

[8] AN, F 7* 2495 (reg. Réunion *comité révolutionnaire*), and F 7* 2511 (reg. Chalier *comité révolutionnaire*).

the Amis-de-la-Patrie company[1]? These unknowns were clearly neither former soldiers nor leading *sectionnaires*, and the denunciations of the year III, though methodical, did not mention them.

This group of fusilier officers then included leading *sectionnaires*, authentic revolutionaries, disciplinarians from among the former military men, men who spent all their time in the gambling dens, and above all obscure men known only through their declarations of domicile. Nothing distinguishes the latter from the great mass of people in the Sections, whose support had temporarily elevated them to higher things. However, if they forgot their origins and as infantry officers flew their own standard, their men soon recalled them to reality in the year II. Lecourtier was stripped of his command because his disciplinarianism had alienated his entire company. Chuine, a career soldier in command of a detachment sent to Provins, then to Chauny, found himself the object of similar complaints from his men, and on 22 Ventôse Maubant tried to remind him of the realities of such a political command:

> Comrade, after close examination of your claims and those of citizens Tétu, corporal, Prieur, Pierre Seran and the letter signed by the entire company, it seems clear that there is some animosity between you and them. *Since you are a good soldier, and they are also*, these kinds of quarrels must stop between republicans ... You as captain must be a father to these soldiers. When a *révolutionnaire* fails you, you do have a right to punish him ... But to become involved in personal quarrels is beneath the dignity of a true republican ... This affair is not worth all the fuss it has aroused.[2]

Grossin too was denounced to his Section for having forgotten that the object of the *armée* was to feed the Parisian *sans-culottes* and his men considered his indulgence towards the big farmers as some form of criminal *lèse-sans-culotterie*.

These then were the men who – more than the *chefs de bataillon*, few in number and immobilized in garrison towns, more than the artillery commanders whose companies were grouped in the great centres of repression like Lyon and Brest – found themselves in daily contact with the local authorities in the towns and villages. And when one examines the activities of the Parisian *armée* these men, who scarcely figure in the history of the Parisian Sectionary movement, take on new importance. To

---

[1] Villedieu (Jean), lieutenant, was received as a member of the *société sectionnaire*, 23 Ventôse year II (BN, Nouv. acq. fr. 2690 [142]). Among the former terrorists from this Amis-de-la-Patrie Section, disarmed by order of the general assembly on 5 Prairial year III, it is worth noting one, 'Wolff, member of the military commission of Nantes', who may have been with the revolutionary detachment sent to that town (see AN, F 7 4774 53 d 3 [Mothrée]).

[2] AHG (*reg. d'ordre*), 22 Ventôse year II.

them fell the task of making this instrument of the Terror effective in the area for which it was created; they also had to shoulder the responsibilities and frequently the risks which this involved.

III   *The Cavalry Officers*

The peculiar, not to say scandalous, character of the revolutionary cavalry was even more pronounced in its officer corps than in its high command. If most of the *chefs d'escadron* were military men with respectable service records and regular positions in the *armée*, such was not the case with the captains, lieutenants and second lieutenants. Here the *chef de brigade* Mazuel's hasty methods of raising a force made up of all and sundry, and totally dependent on himself, had the most pernicious effects. The officer corps of the cavalry was peopled by favourites over whom Mazuel – the 'Baladin des Brotteaux', as a former friend wickedly called him – had complete control. Mazuel's power derived from the distribution of lieutenancies and second-lieutenancies in 'his' cavalry, and he prided himself on being able to secure confirmation from the War Ministry of all the provisional commissions which he distributed with such abandon to those recommended by the leading figures of the day. 'I was aware ... that the treacherous Mazuel, unable to tolerate anyone who knew all his villainies, sought my undoing,' Borcsat reported to the Committee of General Security; '... on his private initiative he appointed officers, despite the protests of the Corps ... in defiance of the decree which required the appointment of officers from the *scrutin épuratoire*.'[1]

His recruitment methods were a public scandal. Everyone knew that many young men, often within the age-group of the first requisition, found refuge in this corps as lieutenants or second lieutenants.[2] There were also as many deserters in the officer class as in the ranks, and Mazuel gave lieutenancies to foreigners, and well-off young men, whose relatives made pressing requests on their behalf, were also gratified. In this corps Parisians, *sans-culottes* and *sectionnaires* were rare, while men from the provinces, particularly from the south, abounded. In short, the officer class of the cavalry was a caricature of the entire body. 'As far as I can see,' wrote one lieutenant to Mazuel, 'the first squadron is composed of a large number of Prussian deserters and even French deserters from Spain.'[3]

---

[1] AN, WIa 344 (671), Borcsat to the Committee of General Security, 10 Germinal year II. 'Baladin [wandering actor] des Brotteaux [the plaine des Brotteaux where the mass shootings of the Lyonnais took place]' is a take-off on the title of a play in which Mazuel had once acted in Lyon, his home town.

[2] A sample of the ages of these officers will give some idea of the remarkable contrast between the cavalry and the other corps: Richard 21, Steenhouwer 30, Bourgeois 22, Lépine 23, Seran 36, Roman 21, Péré 33, Pérony 32, Menu 57, Machard 46.

[3] Arch. Seine-et-Oise, IV Q 186 (Mazuel papers).

The accuracy of this unfavourable judgement is all too clear from innumerable case histories. Take the French deserters, for example: Romain Richard, a native of Dourdan who was appointed second lieutenant, 1st company 1st squadron, was a twenty-one-year-old deserter from a corps of dragoons.[1] Jean-Baptiste Orhand, the same who had written to Mazuel about the 1st squadron, was a former soldier in the Gardes-Françaises, who had become a fencing master after his discharge, and enlisted in the Beauvais cavalry after having deserted from a corps of chasseurs.[2] Nicolas-Josué Steenhouwer, a Dutch refugee, was also given a position at the request of Cloots. Born in Amsterdam on 7 October 1763, he was a former student cadet in the Dutch navy, who had subsequently transferred to the Hessian Legion. A lieutenant in the Salm cavalry, Steenhouwer had sought refuge in France in 1792 or 1793 and joined the Free Foreign Legion. On his own personal authority Mazuel had him appointed lieutenant in the 1st company of the 4th squadron. It is true that Steenhouwer was soon removed from the corps on ministerial orders, the law on the organization of the *armée révolutionnaire* prohibiting the admission of foreigners, but he was the only foreign officer so expelled.[3] Mazuel respected neither law nor minister and simply recruited as he saw fit. Aigoin wrote to him on behalf of 'a dashing young revolutionary', a Belgian in whom Bastide and Goguet were interested. Clearly this 'dashing young revolutionary' was also furnished with a commission, for Mazuel could refuse nothing to his Montpellier friends.[4] Everyone in the *armée* knew that foreigners could easily secure commissions in the new cavalry, as testified by the letters of request to Mazuel from people like Belair, captain of the 3rd Belgian regiment; from Bouquet, lieutenant in the 1st Hainaut battalion; and from 'Georgius Kenessey', writing in Latin, 'houzard hungarus natus bonus Respublicanus', a deserter 'well-educated, unhappy at the military treatment of his country ... with a liking for the French Republic'.[5]

Hippolyte Bourgeois falls into the second category of well-off young men who, thanks to influential relatives, found positions in a cavalry destined for service in the interior. A lieutenant at little more than twenty years of age in the 2nd company of the 6th squadron, he was the son of a *Conventionnel*, to oblige whom Mazuel kept the young Hippolyte near him, sharing with him the comfortable existence of a *chef d'escadron*, and

---

[1] Arch. Seine-et-Oise, IV Q 187 (Mazuel papers); and Arch. Oise (reg. Chaumont district).

[2] AN, F 7 4774, 59 d 4 (Orhand); and AHG (*reg. d'ordre*), 28 Pluviôse.

[3] Arch. Seine-et-Oise, IV Q 186. Steenhouwer would be shot in 1812 as accomplice to General Malet at the assassination of General Hulin. AN, F 7 6499 (Malet affair).

[4] General Goguet, former commander of the garrison in Brussels in 1792, assassinated 1793, was a native of Montpellier.

[5] Arch. Seine-et-Oise, IV Q 186 (Lamotte to Mazuel, 10 Nivôse year II).

installing him in the Cadran Bleu *auberge* near the park of Versailles. But such favours held their own dangers, and young Bourgeois, with a protector become conspirator and *persona non grata* overnight, was himself arrested along with the two young ladies and the carriage-driver who had accompanied them on their outings to the Trianon. The young Bourgeois paid the price of his gilded existence with several weeks in prison, before his father's pleas to Fouquier-Tinville, the two Committees and to his own colleagues, secured his release. Mazuel was likewise petitioned by Louis Lépine, director of public works with the Paris municipality, to spare his son the horrors of the first requisition.[1]

The case of Pierre-Louis Borcsat is somewhat similar. This twenty-nine-year-old was also a well-off young man. His father was president of the criminal tribunal of the Gex district and a wealthy *notaire* in Ferney-Voltaire, where in 1793 his brother presided over the *société populaire*, in itself a family affair, founded by Jean-Louis. They were all known to Gouly and to Jagot, a member of the Committee of General Security. Borcsat himself joined the light cavalry, but was expelled by the other officers for his attempts to 'republicanize' the ordinary soldiers. Borcsat took his complaint of their 'counter-revolutionary' leanings to the Minister in Paris, and won the ear of the Jacobins, who sent Xavier Audouin and Prosper Sijas to investigate. Audouin secured Borcsat a lieutenancy in the revolutionary cavalry. In this he did Mazuel a disservice, for Borcsat turned out to be a viper in the nest. He found intolerable the insolence and authoritarian spirit of Mazuel, whom he had known for some time, and quarrelled with him from the outset. An element of jealousy undoubtedly underlay the conflict, for the two men were almost the same age; but the republican of Ferney-Voltaire felt he had better revolutionary claims than the silk-embroiderer and playboy from la Croix-Rousse. Mazuel in turn found Borcsat an unwelcome witness to his intrigues, and had him arrested and removed on the pretext of indiscipline. Borcsat remained in detention until the *armée* was disbanded, but triumphed eventually when his old enemy was condemned.[2]

Mazuel's Montpellier friends were the first to commend themselves to the goodwill of their old acquaintance. The former soldier and bailiff from Montpellier, Louis Séran, called 'Mucius', rushed to Paris on learning of

---

[1] For Bourgeois, see AN, W 185 and W 355 (Tribunaux révolutionnaires), and my 'Le "complot militaire" de ventôse an II'; for Lépine, see Arch. Seine-et-Oise, IV Q 186.

[2] AN, WIa 151, Borcsat to Fouquier-Tinville, 26 Pluviôse year II; and WIa 344 (671). Borcsat was imprisoned in La Force on 31 August 1793, 'accused of having used counter-revolutionary language'. On 22 Germinal Jagot wrote in his favour to Fouquier-Tinville; he was interrogated and acquitted the following day, 'since there is no proof against him and he appears to have been arrested simply as a result of the infamous Mazuel's despotic wrath'.

the position occupied by his old companion in misfortune – in 1792 they had been imprisoned together in Montpellier as suspected Maratists. While waiting in the antechamber of his powerful friend's office, Séran scribbled this disconcertingly frank note to him: 'I need a little money to survive for another fortnight [in Paris].' Before that fortnight was up Séran found himself a second lieutenant with the 1st squadron at Beauvais, where he quickly assumed a political role. 'I am going to the *société populaire* with *commissaire* Girard,' he wrote to Mazuel, 'and will do all in my power to fire their patriotism – they need it, for there are no more than 50 Montagnard patriots here, that is to say 50 *révolutionnaires.*' An intriguer and an ambitiously political soldier, Séran presided over the *société populaire* when sent to Lyon, and was denounced by the Lyonnais after Thermidor as a terrorist and agent of the repression.[1] Almost the only cavalry officer to find himself in this position, Séran soon attached to himself a group of other young men from Montpellier, attracted to Paris by the same good news: 'Junius' Fayet, Colombel, Laurent Delpêche (Mazuel's brother-in-law), all alike appointed to second-lieutenancies through their friend's favour.

Besides deserters and 'friends', this corps was composed largely of military men – but military men of a different breed from those who dominated the infantry. The cavalry officers were young men serving in the hussars or the dragoons who had secured their transfer to Mazuel's force thanks to connections in the War Ministry or in the political world. There were also some long-serving soldiers like Paul Péré, a captain in the 2nd squadron who had served in the Gardes-Françaises from 1777 to 1785, then as an army surgeon in the line infantry.[2] Louis Menu was an even more remarkable case – one of those rare veterans with uninterrupted service since 1756, including twenty-two years as adjutant with the Île-de-France regiment. He was also one of the few cavalry officers to be disarmed and denounced as a terrorist in the year III, by the *comité civil* of the Bonne-Nouvelle Section, which places him with the political *sectionnaires* so common among the fusilier and cannoneer officers, but virtually non-existent in the cavalry.[3] But the most typical example of this group

---

[1] Arch. Rhône, 31 L 170 (*comité de surveillance*, Lyon), letter from the Montpellier *comité*, 27 Ventôse year III; and Arch. Seine-et-Oise, IV Q 186, letter Séran to Mazuel, August 1793.

[2] AAG, Cl. gén. 2989 (Péré).

[3] AN, F 7 4774 42 d 2 (Menu). He was rearmed 1 Vendémiaire year IV. In a petition of Messidor year II to the Convention, Menu provided additional information about his life, claiming to have served his country since the age of 17, first with the Aquitaine regiment in Hanover; then, after 1764, as quartermaster, sergeant-major and finally adjutant with the Île de France regiment. After 1787 he claimed to have fought for the Revolution in the capture of the Bastille (though he is not on the lists of Vainqueurs), at Vincennes, at Versailles 5 October, at the Champ de Mars against Lafayette, in the *journées* of 20 June and

was young Hurault from the Contrat-Social Section, who left the Charenton workshops to join the 27th cavalry regiment, moving on to a lieutenancy in the 1st squadron. He was a thankless character who would later denounce Sijas and Mazuel, the two men to whom he owed his new position.[1] In the same way the twenty-one-year-old Jacques Roman moved straight from the 1st regiment of chasseurs to a second-lieutenancy in the 4th squadron, on the recommendation of Xavier Audouin. Roman had arrived in Paris from Grenoble in July 1793. He was soon in trouble with the Guillaume-Tell *comité révolutionnaire*, which suspected him of trying to evade conscription and accused him of scandalous behaviour in his relationship with the wife of a Beauvais *notaire*. On this occasion he was helped by his compatriot, who vouched for his *civisme*.[2] Michel Martin left the dragoons for a second-lieutenancy in the same squadron as Roman, while Chomez made a similar transfer, thanks to help from Duverger, *chef de division* at the War Ministry. Chomez was another of those rare political militants in the cavalry, a member of the Cordeliers club who claimed to have participated in the capture of the Bastille, and a soldier of long standing, having served since the age of eleven both in the Indies and in Europe.[3]

Guignard, a captain in the 1st squadron, had urgent personal reasons for leaving his old corps to seek refuge in the revolutionary cavalry. This former soldier, a native of the Beaujolais, had served under the *ancien régime* in the Gérardmer cavalry. After the Revolution he was appointed to a commission in the Tuileries battalion of the National Guard, moving then to a lieutenant-colonelcy in the 19th infantry regiment. He was well versed in the military practices of the *ancien régime*, and in July 1793 he was denounced by one of his soldiers to the *société populaire* of Mantes 'for shirking his duties' and for having 'cheated the Republic by charging for the clothing of deserters . . . and his soldiers, by taking money from the letters addressed to them'. Guignard took advantage of the August levy to leave his regiment and have himself appointed to the Beauvais cavalry, where he stayed for several months. But even Mazuel's cavalry sometimes had to defer to the wishes of the *sans-culottes* in matters of morality. The Mantes *société* had correspondents in the Lyon *société*: Guignard, unmasked, abandoned by his colleagues, and in every way in an unenviable position, was summoned to explain himself and obliged to tender his

---

10 August – in sum, in every combat where liberty was at stake. 'A founding member of the first *société populaire* of the Republic [though he was not a Jacobin], I am well known, if I may say so myself, as a zealous republican' (AN, AA 74 (1372)). Quite a list of revolutionary achievements, if they can be believed.

[1] AN, F 7 4775 18 d 4 (Sijas).
[2] AN, F 7 4774 98 d 1 (Roman).
[3] Arch. Seine-et-Oise, IV Q 187.

resignation. Claiming a plot against him, he retired to his village in the Saône-et-Loire.[1]

What was the attraction of this new force for these young men? The chance of rapid promotion perhaps? The hope certainly of a milder discipline than in the dragoon corps and less risk than in the light cavalry. Finally, there was the attraction exercised by all newly-formed corps whose cadres had just been organized. A cavalry which was not 'like any other corps' offered perspectives as dazzling as they were vague and roused the ambitions of young officers languishing in dreary and dangerous cantonments far from Paris. Such ambitions were all the more active when candidates were told that they might bypass the *scrutin épuratoire* and election by the company, if supported by someone in the War Ministry, by a *Conventionnel*, by Mazuel or by a juror on the revolutionary tribunal.

In such conditions it is not surprising that civilians and *sectionnaires* were rare. There were nevertheless some: Charles Pérony, a captain in the 5th squadron, also appointed on the recommendation of Prosper Sijas, was a thirty-five-year-old stonecutter living in the Halle-au-Bled Section. This man, who undoubtedly owed much to Mazuel, and would join the other squadron officers in Versailles in signing petitions in support of their commander as a 'persecuted patriot', was nevertheless to give evidence against him which would provide Fouquier-Tinville with the basis for his 'military plot' thesis at the time of the *hébertiste* trials.[2] Mazuel had put together a clientele of 'amis' for nothing. On the day of his arrest these young officers could not dissociate themselves from him quickly enough, and they signed an address congratulating the Convention on its vigilance in having unmasked this 'conspirator' who had succeeded in raising himself to the command of their corps. The 'grandeur mazueliste' (as one 'ami' called it),[3] the personal ascendancy which he exercised over 'his' cavalry, faded with his loss of favour.

But if Pérony thus appears to be an authentic *sectionnaire* in the mould of Bernard Caperon, a lieutenant in the same squadron, there are still some uncertainties about this and a service note of 10 Germinal describes him as being 'an ex-guard of Capet'.[4] As for Delgas, a former adjutant of the Bonne-Nouvelle Section's armed force, then company captain in the revolutionary cavalry, he was highly regarded by the Thermidorian authorities, and would be recommended by his Section to a position on

[1] Arch. Seine-et Oise, IV Q 186–7; and Arch. Mantes, D 38 (*société populaire*, Mantes, session of 11 July 1793).
[2] AN, F 7 4774 67 d 5 (Pérony), and W 355 (739). On leaving the cavalry, the artisan Pérony found employment in a workshop in the Quinze-Vingts Section.
[3] Arch. Seine-et-Oise, IV Q 187, undated letter.
[4] AHG (*reg. d'ordre*), 10 Germinal year II.

the newly-formed *comités de surveillance* of the arrondissement, to which *sans-culottes* were not admitted.[1] Finally, Nicolas Thévenin owed his second-lieutenancy to the recommendation of Brisse, president of the *société populaire* of Nancy and a great friend of Mazuel. Thévenin, who had been a clerk attached to the Moselle Legion, was an active member of his *société*.[2] In contrast, one of the few leading *sectionnaires* in this corps, the forty-six-year-old Jean-Baptiste Edme Machard – first captain of the 1st squadron, formerly second-in-command of the Tuileries Section armed force – seems, like Borcsat, to have been a victim of the despotism of Mazuel, who had him arrested at Beauvais on 21 Vendémiaire year II, and detained in the Sainte-Pélagie. Machard alerted his Section, which rushed to his defence, and denounced Mazuel to the Minister. On 11 Nivôse he was liberated on orders from the Committee of General Security. It was a major defeat for Mazuel, who was already in difficulties by this date. But despite repeated pleas from his Section, Machard never regained his position at the head of the 1st squadron, nor his arrears in pay. He was disarmed at the time of the Thermidorian reaction, but rearmed on 16 Thermidor year III at the request of the *comité civil* of the Tuileries Section, which praised his moderation. With Delgas, Machard had the rare talent among former *révolutionnaires* of being able to please the Thermidorian authorities.[3]

The officers of the revolutionary cavalry, then, had little to recommend them and the corps fully deserved its poor reputation. Parisian opinion was right in thinking it a refuge for adventurers, deserters and suspects, while the Versailles authorities were scandalized by the insolence and drunkenness of these young officers who imitated the scorn their commander had for the civil authorities. They had an *esprit de corps*, these cavalry officers, and it was a detestable one – the basis of a 'military system' in an army which was intended to be democratic, civilian and Sectionary. Nor did these officers have anything to recommend them in their personal behaviour, and the shady dealings of Guignard were not an isolated case. There was also a scandal in the 6th squadron which had extensive ramifications and compromised several officers.[4] Those who

---

[1] AN, F 7 4668 d 1 (Delgas). Delgas was connected with the rich foreign banker de Kock, who played Maecenas to the Bonne-Nouvelle Section, not for any political reason, simply to remain on the good side of the Sectionary authorities. But since his house at Passy thereby became a rendezvous for Hébert, Ronsin, and the officers of the revolutionary cavalry, the banker fell victim to his own hospitality when Fouquier took the opportunity to label him 'hébertiste' (AN, WIa 116 and 117).

[2] Arch. Seine-et-Oise, IV Q 187.

[3] AN, F 7 4774 28 (Machard), F 7* 2741 (Tuileries *comité révolutionnaire*); Arch. Seine-et-Oise, IV Q 187, letters from Blanchet and from Paul, vice-president of the Tuileries *société*, to Mazuel, 13 and 23 Brumaire year II respectively.

[4] AHG (*reg. d'ordre*), Rigaud to Durand, commander 6th squadron, 5 Ventôse year II.

remained idle at Versailles had plenty of time to find yet more ways of discrediting the corps.

*

It is impossible to arrive at any reliable statistical analysis of the social composition of the officer class and the general staff of the Parisian *armée*. In view of the defective nature of the documentary sources, the military men appear more important than they were in reality. Yet, from the tone of those general orders which have survived, the artillery must certainly have been commanded primarily by civilians. The same was probably true for the fusiliers and it was only the cavalry which had an officer corps composed of true military men.

Out of a total of 117 officers from all divisions, for whom we possess occupational information, there were 60 former soldiers, 15 artisans (4 shoemakers, 1 stone-cutter, 1 glazier, 1 market porter, 1 harness-maker, 1 basket-maker, 1 cutler, 1 engraver, 1 apprentice mason, 1 assistant to a tailor, 1 clockmaker, and a fireman); 10 were linked in some way or other with the luxury trades (1 fencing master, 1 drawing master, 1 assistant to a silversmith, 2 assistants to jewellers, 1 porcelain sculptor, 1 decorator, 1 fan merchant, 2 caterer-restaurateurs); 3 or 4 had been in service (2 house servants and a wigmaker); 11 were shop-owners or retailers (2 toyshop-owners, 1 herbalist, 1 stationer, 1 haberdasher-clothier, 1 saddle-seller, 1 second-hand dealer, 1 Rouen 'manufacturer', 2 'merchants', 1 café-owner); there was 1 architect–building contractor (Lefranc), and the actors accounted for 7 (6 of them on the general staff). There were 6 known foreigners, 5 of them in the cavalry (2 Belgians, 1 Dutch, 3 'Germans'), 5 deserters from the cavalry, 2 farmers, 1 day-labourer, 2 clerks or office workers, 2 'without occupation', several 'rich young men', a bailiff, and a man of the law (Parein). The civilian element dominated in the artillery, and undoubtedly, though to a lesser extent, the infantry – though the division between civilian and soldier in the artisan and small-trade world is somewhat artificial, since former soldiers tended to return to such trades after leaving the army. A typical career would be that of the son of an artisan, tradesman or farmer, who joined the army at the outbreak of the Seven Years War, bought his discharge around 1780 and set himself up in a small business in Paris, or, more rarely, as a government clerk. With the Revolution, this former soldier, already well integrated into the life of his quartier, had an advantage over his fellow citizens, and with the formation of the bourgeois National Guard would secure a rank superior to that he held when discharged from the army. In some cases he would have been appointed an officer as early as 1789 or 1790 in virtue of his military expertise, and if promotion came too slowly in the Parisian National Guard, he could always join that of the smaller towns. In any event, the former soldier had been well launched on his new revolutionary career, where, for the less known, a commission in the Parisian artillery or infantry represented the pinnacle of achievement.

Another means of access was by way of the Sectionary institutions, *comités*, *sociétés*, or as reward for participation in the great *journées*. Married men of more mature age tended to dominate the artillery and infantry; the cavalry officers were generally younger and unmarried, and in the eyes of the *sectionnaires*, bachelors in uniform were birds of prey, and objects of scandal.

The motives which lay behind the enrolment of the cavalry officers in the new *armée* are outlined in the foregoing group study. For the artillery and infantry the reasons for joining were the same for the officers as for the men, and will be discussed later. However, there is no doubt that vanity played a greater role in the motives of the former. Election to a captaincy, lieutenancy or second-lieutenancy was not only a kind of political apotheosis, but gave a sense of sweet victory to these small tradesmen, and even more to the former non-commissioned officers, whose wildest dreams were suddenly realized. Commissions were bitterly sought after in the artillery and infantry, and some of those elected succumbed to the temptation to abuse an authority which was more apparent than real. The cavalry was a different case entirely and lieutenancies could be won, without the preliminary of the *scrutin épuratoire*, through personal contacts; and far from being a proof of one's *civisme*, a commission in this branch was more likely to be a cause for suspicion.

These marked political and social differences between the cavalry and the other two branches of the *armée* were reflected also in the behaviour of the different officers. The cavalry officer behaved almost as badly as his men; the cannoneer officer had a political conscience as sharp as that of his men; the fusilier officer held himself apart in an attempt to impose a sense of military values on these civilians – in which attempt he would fail completely.

PART II   THE REVOLUTIONARY SOLDIER

In such a political army the soldier was more important than the officer. The officer was elected and could also be broken by the soldier; the latter considered military hierarchy and military discipline for slaves only, and since he and the officer he elected came from the same social milieu, the haberdasher fusilier addressing his butcher or master-shoemaker neighbour, who happened also to be his captain, did not consider the phrase 'ton égal en droit' ('your rightful equal'), with which the *sans-culottes* liked to conclude letters, an empty formula. He was indeed his officer's equal and if that officer tried to pull rank or impose discipline, he was quickly called to task by the administrative Council, or more likely by the *comité* or *société* of the Section. The *révolutionnaire* had no respect for rank; he was prepared to follow the orders of his officer voluntarily, if that officer seemed to act like a 'revolutionary patriot', but at no time would he abandon his rights as a *sectionnaire*.

It is important to get to know this man, the fusilier or cannoneer, for in the last analysis he *was* the *armée révolutionnaire*. This egalitarian army was not a disciplined force and when the *révolutionnaire* left Paris, the instructions and flattery of the *comités révolutionnaires* would still be ringing in his ears. It was his duty to keep a watchful eye on the 'malveillant', an ear pealed for the malicious word, and above all, 'to watch over the grain supply', and ensure food supplies for his family and his friends. *Force à la loi* was the motto inscribed on his flag, but of that law he was the guardian and interpreter, and if the authorities, however constitutionally established, chose to contest his actions, it was a sign of their ill will towards Paris. In the eyes of the unaccommodating and totally humourless *révolutionnaire*, all opposition to his mission was deemed an act of counter-revolution. Such an attitude augured ill for relations between the detachments and the local authorities, and for the maintenance of even the most elementary discipline.

It is hard to imagine a man as full of his own importance, as touchy and as suspicious as the *révolutionnaire*. Conscious also of the urgency of his mission, and like all *sans-culottes* relentless in its pursuit, his attitude towards the country people, made up of distrust, fear, pride and the desire to punish, was an important element in the conduct of operations. To the country people these Parisians seemed intolerable, which indeed they were. But there were also 'frères' in the departments, less well instructed, less schooled in the Revolution, because not fortunate enough to be Parisians, but *sans-culottes* like himself nevertheless, who must be helped and instructed. Pathologically distrustful of the farmers, Ronsin's soldier was naïve enough to credit the wildest accusations against them, when made by those shrewd enough to represent themselves – often a mere pose – as his rural 'frères'.

The behaviour of the individual was rendered more important by the scattering of the *révolutionnaires* in tiny detachments. It was rare for the *armée* to arrive in force in any given region, save in the case of major missions to suppress revolts. On the whole its image for the country people was that presented by a half-dozen moustached and unkempt men, who swore heartily all the curses and damnations of the *Père Duchesne*, but who were, on the whole, easygoing, unless provoked or fired by the discovery of keys to wine cellars. Above all they were not warlike and were visibly inept in the use of arms. But the countryside was filled with real ex-soldiers, and one can but imagine the cynicism of these 'veterans', obliged to watch the clumsy manoeuvres of these artisans and Paris shopkeepers, disguised as soldiers in their blue and red uniforms. A group of a dozen or so *révolutionnaires* were not at risk when they tried to instil fear into the countryside. But sometimes groups of two or three were sent alone into an area, and it is not surprising that their pose as masters in revolution sometimes exposed them to unfortunate consequences. These faithful apostles of Parisian doctrines, so sure of themselves when they left the metropolis, would be thrashed and half-killed by the villagers leaving church after mass, for having dared to preach the gospel according to *Père Duchesne* to these Thiérache villagers, hostile to innovation and baffled by the presentation of St Joseph as simply an old man. The village on the edge of the wood was not the Sectionary assembly, and traditional religious imagery was far more acceptable than that of the *marchand de fourneaux* – the *Père Duchesne*'s glorification of *sans-culotterie*. The isolated *révolutionnaire* was wrong to place so much confidence in his pipe and moustache; the peasant was not that easily impressed. Thus was the poor Parisian delivered over to the rural populace. Sometimes he was overcome by panic and deserted his post, taking refuge with the nearest *comité de surveillance*; sometimes, prudently, he allowed himself to be 'contaminated'.

The revolutionary soldier has been the subject of so many legends that it is difficult to discover the truth. For some he was simply a brigand in different clothing, one of a 'bande à la Cartouche';[1] for others he was the prototype proletarian, a member of the workers' militia, a man from the faubourgs animated by a sense of class. What kind of man was he in reality? Why did he enrol in the Parisian *armée*? What was his family situation? Was he violent, a man of blood? Before examining him at work, we must first try to understand the man himself. We will try to isolate some characteristics common to the entire corps by studying the individual amidst his fears and suspicions, certainly no longer the pure and flawless *révolutionnaire* of legend, but a small Paris shopkeeper or artisan, thrown into a hostile and dangerous world of small courtyards and vines, of fields and presbyteries with cellars all too well stocked, an expansive countryside, dotted with church steeples and wayside crosses, all alike provocations in his eyes. We must explain rather than judge the man – a task worth the effort, for Ronsin's soldier is a little-understood figure, and yet one whose very ubiquity brought the humbler side of the Paris revolution into many different parts of France. This section we have entitled 'the revolutionary soldier', though he himself would have preferred the term

---

[1] Louis-Dominique Cartouche (?1693–1721), a famous French bandit.

'révolutionnaire' or 'sans-culotte', and one thing he would not have tolerated was being called a 'soldier'.

I   *Portrait of the* Révolutionnaire

The *révolutionnaire* may have sported the moustache, pipe and sabre of Thermidorian imagery, but the resemblance between the real man and the traditional portrait of a Terrorist stops there.[1] Even if the moustache did constitute part of the *révolutionnaire's* attire, it was considered more a sign of virility than anything else, and did not necessarily transform its wearer into a violent brigand. Indeed some authorities made the moustache obligatory, the order of the Limoges *comité de surveillance* for the levy of the Haute-Vienne battalion, for example, referring to the 'moustache, hair worn loose and unpowdered' and the 'sans-culotte uniform' as compulsory attire.[2] 'Nothing equals the frightening display staged for the accused,' wrote Prudhomme of the *révolutionnaires* on duty with the revolutionary tribunal in Brest, 'placed between two gendarmes with sabres unsheathed, before them a soldier of the *armée révolutionnaire* flamboyantly rattling his sword, his face topped by an enormous mat of hair and darkened by a heavy moustache, his bloodthirsty and sparkling eyes barely perceptible.'[3] The moustache was clearly intended as a ferocious accessory, to strike fear into the peasantry. There can be no doubt that they were alarmed by the very sight of these moustached soldiers, whom they considered plunderers and precursors of the *chauffeurs*, to the extent that the country people around Meaux called one leader of a group of *révolutionnaires* 'General Moustache'. For the orthodox *sectionnaire* in the fusiliers or cannoneers, the moustache identified him with the figure from Parisian legend who appeared on the title-page of Hébert's journal. For the country people the same trait symbolized the brigand and the mercenary. The Lyonnais who appeared before the terrible Commission des Sept were struck by the 'ferocious appearance' of Parein, Corchand

---

[1] The very name *révolutionnaire* was designed to inspire terror, and if the Parisian *armée* was called *armée révolutionnaire* rather than *armée centrale* it was for 'terrorist' reasons. On 2 September, when a petition presented to the Convention demanding the formation of an *armée révolutionnaire* was discussed at the Jacobins, one citizen observed that 'the word *révolutionnaire* is not appropriate to the body we wish to establish, and the army should be called *armée centrale*'. Royer (author of the petition) disputed this opinion: 'the word *révolutionnaire* makes the aristocrats tremble, and should be adopted' (*Journal de la Montagne*, no. 95, 5 September 1793).

[2] A. Fray-Fournier, *Les Archives révolutionnaires de la Haute-Vienne: procès-verbaux de la société des Jacobins de Limoges* (Limoges, 1908), p. 100. See also the biography of Dumoustier ('Moustache') in the counter-revolutionary *Dictionnaire des Jacobins vivans*; and see R.C. Cobb, 'The Revolutionary Mentality in France', *History*, October 1957.

[3] L.-M. Prudhomme, *Histoire générale et impartiale des erreurs, des fautes et des crimes commis pendant la Révolution française* (1797), vol. V, p. 489.

and their colleagues, sinister Punch-like figures with their moustaches and huge plumed judge's hats. Likewise the farmers and their wives, roused in the middle of the night by detachments making domiciliary visits, and still half asleep, were terrified by the sight of these strangers with their huge bushy moustaches, rifling the drawers and cupboards.

It was, however, an external ferocity, and far from being a man of war the *révolutionnaire* was simply a family man, of mature years and from a peaceful, small-trading background. Most of Ronsin's soldiers – the cavalry excepted – were, like the officers, aged between thirty and forty-five, a few being fifty to seventy, and some really infirm.[1] Indeed, the *commissaire des guerres* in Paris lamented 'the sexagenarians' among these soldiers 'showing all the decrepitude of their age', and 'others who were so sickly that common sense ought to dictate their non-admission'.[2] Maubant recommended the discharge of one soldier, Mouret (known as 'Sans Dents') 'who is deaf and incontinent'; and the health officers granted leave to many because of hernias, a widespread condition among these middle-aged artisans. But the greatest weakness of these second-rate soldiers was their drunkenness. Old Mouret's case was not an isolated one, and *chef de bataillon* Donville attributed 'the clumsiness of some soldiers in the handling of their arms' largely to their 'drunkenness and slovenliness'.[3] So well established was this reputation of the *révolutionnaire* as a drunkard, that when the *commissaires* of the Finistère Section arrived in a village of the Yonne, at the head of a small detachment, their first act was to seize the key to the *auberge* to prevent the soldiers from ensconcing themselves in it.[4]

In this respect the *révolutionnaires* quickly acquired the habits of real soldiers throughout the ages: those of eating and drinking without paying. Laukhard describes the descent of a detachment bound for Lyon into the Saône valley between Mâcon and Villefranche, a land of plenty the like of which these Parisians had never before seen: 'On several occasions we went into bourgeois homes where people supplied us with free drink,

[1] See AN, F 7* 2478 (Lepeletier *comité*, session of 23 Vendémiaire), for a list of fusiliers of that Section, aged 53, 45, 40, 36 (2), 35, 33, 31, 30, 28 (2) and 27; also F 7* 2517 (Finistère *comité*, 4 Floréal year II) – the fusiliers of the Finistère company were aged 47, 38 and 33.
[2] AHG, B5 75, Paris to Bouchotte, 3 October 1793. There were also some youths: a 16-year-old cannoneer from the Amis-de-la-Patrie Section (AN, F 7 4774 75 d 2 [Pigeon]), the 17-year-old Jean-Louis Gourgot, accepted into the Champs-Élysées cannoneers (id., F 7 4777, Champs-Élysées *comité*). But such cases are rare; the Parisian *armée* was rather a corps of veterans, and in the departments where such youths were recruited, it was into special corps, frequently called *bataillons de l'espérance*, which were entirely separate from the revolutionary forces.
[3] AHG (*reg. d'ordre*), Maubant to Donville, 7 Germinal year II, also his letter to Lefebvre, 2 Germinal.
[4] AN, F 7 4774 52 d 2 (Moroy).

knowing that the *sans-culotte* was not fond of paying.' Further on, having
somehow or other got past Mâcon, 'we stopped for at least half an hour at
every *auberge* en route, drinking heartily, paying rarely'.[1] A wigmaker's
assistant from the Quinze-Vingts Section announced his intention of
joining the *armée révolutionnaire* to a client whom he was about to shave,
adding candidly 'that he expected quite a spree drinking the farmers' wine
and eating their chickens' – a remarkably agreeable method of 'revolutionizing' the countryside and one which the *révolutionnaires* sought to apply
in many areas. At Saint-Brice, in the Gonesse district, they 'allowed themselves to be wined and dined, and consumed about two-thirds of a *demie*
[?] of *vin de pays*'. At Clairoix, near Compiègne, a detachment took two
casks of wine from the mayor's house and did not pay at the *cabarets* for
their drinks.[2] Drunkenness, in fact, was the cause of most of the incidents
between these political soldiers and the regular troops, and the authorities
everywhere ordered the closure of the *auberges* after 9 p.m. to put an end
to such disputes. It also explains much of the throw-away language
employed by the Parisians when talking with the local authorities.
Furthermore, in such remote villages, the *sans-culottes* had little to relieve
their boredom in the evening but the *société populaire*, which met only two
or three times a *décade*, the bed of an obliging *paysanne*, of whom there
were insufficient to go around, or the saloon. Most opted for the latter.
These thirty- or forty-year-olds were long accustomed to supplementing
insufficient diets with vile Choisy wine. And anyway, one could drink more
on a tour of duty than at home: for most *révolutionnaires* such a mission
was a picnic in the countryside (a *partie de campagne*), and later they would
tell of the good time they had then. In the café these bored and nostalgic
Parisians would become more and more violent in their verbal, and often
their physical attacks on a populace which they considered hostile.[3] Then
woe betide those saints in their grottoes and those wayside crosses.

The *révolutionnaire* was usually a family man,[4] with a son at the fron-

---

[1] F.-C. Laukhard, *Un allemand en France sous la Terreur*, trans. W. Bauer (Paris, 1915), pp.
267–8.
[2] AN, F 7 4574 29 d 1 (Magnard) and F 7 4594 d 1 (Benoist); Arch. Oise (district of
Compiègne, reg. deliberations).
[3] Antoine Mouret, a 50-year-old carpenter from the Gravilliers Section, on detachment in
Viarmes, had spent the night drinking in the former abbey of Royaumont at the end of
Ventôse; he then argued with the people of Asnières, a village which he claimed to be
populated with aristocrats, and which ought to be burnt. The net result was that he found
himself accused of being an incendiary, implicated in the *hébertiste* plot, and dragged from
prison to prison, scarcely knowing what had happened to him. (AN, WIa 195 and F 7 4774
54 d 2 [Mouret].)
[4] It is difficult to discover if free unions were common among the *sans-culottes*. Soboul (649)
thinks that *sans-culottes* did indeed live with companions in an unmarried state. In support
of this opinion the case of Chomel, sergeant in the revolutionary cavalry, can be cited:

tier – which made him more than ever conscious of his privileges as a defender of the regime. He had no desire to be used on garrison duty – he had better things to do than march up and down on guard – and when it was proposed to assign them to the defence of the Channel coasts, these Paris shopkeepers refused to leave their cantonments on the grounds that it would constitute 'foreign service'. Their dispatch to Lyon aroused bitter resentment: they had been deceived, they claimed, for they had enlisted on the express condition of serving only near Paris. The *commissaires des guerres* and officers were incensed by this assertive tendency, and if, according to the *commissaire-ordonnateur* Boissay, the *armée* was 'in general worthy of its name', he had to admit to the Minister that there were 'some individuals who spend more time looking for ways of protesting than concentrating on their duties. I am overwhelmed with these complaints from morning till evening ... every day I have 200 or 300 to reply to, which leaves me scarcely any time to do my work.'[1] The 'barrack-room advocate' was a particularly pervasive character in this civilian army. The Parisians intended to derive the maximum benefit from their enrolment and to get everything they considered their due. In the departments they demanded lodging with the locals – preferably the richest – and privileged treatment, with a butcher and baker assigned exclusively to their needs in each locality; as defenders of the regime they had to have white bread. Already overpaid, they demanded, in addition, supplementary wages for serving more than two miles from their cantonments, claiming as justification the right of the *gendarmes* to such payment. Sometimes they had the audacity to make their victims pay for their services by levying 'revolutionary taxes' and pocketing the receipts. Overpaid soldiers, making intolerable demands – the municipalities thought the Republic far too generous.

Moreover, they were full of their own importance. 'I am from the *armée révolutionnaire*, no *commissaire* controls me,' one fusilier from the Réunion company claimed when a member of a *comité révolutionnaire* raised objections to his employment.[2] This happened in Paris. In the provinces the soldiers were worse, and as soon as they arrived in a village they would rush to the tribune of the *société populaire*, uttering threats

'Married in 1779 in Lyon, my wife left me in 1784. I remained alone until 1788', from which time he lived with another woman, whom he wanted to marry in Pluviôse year II. (Arch. Seine-et-Oise, IV Q 187.) For a contrary opinion see *Les Révolutions de Paris*, no. 213 (7 Brumaire), where Prudhomme talks of 'this phalanx of good republicans, most of them family men', and no. 215 (23 Brumaire): 'The women ... may not ... always have praised the stern and uncultivated ways of the *sans-culottes* ... But they reaped the benefit in that regular marriages were the norm among them.'
[1] AHG (*reg. d'ordre*), Boissay to Bouchotte, 18 Ventôse year II.
[2] AN, F 7 4774 II d 1 (Ledoux), Réunion *comité* to Grammont, 24 Frimaire year II.

against the 'malveillants' and words of protection and encouragement for their poor 'frères'. Artisan or small shopkeeper in Paris, launderer, wine-grower, day-labourer, gardener or porter from the city's outlying communes, the *révolutionnaire* shared all the prejudices of the *sectionnaire* against 'les gros': merchants, farmers, corn-factors, entrepreneurs, men of the law. For the merchant, particularly those involved in supplying food, he held a particular hatred. Coppin's attitude towards the butchers of Bonne-Nouvelle was replicated throughout the fusilier and cannoneer corps, not only when they were on mission, but even more in Paris. A *charcutier* in the rue de la Vannerie, Arcis Section, lodged a complaint with the police commissioner against an individual 'in national uniform who claimed to be in the *armée révolutionnaire*', and who, after buying a saveloy costing five sols, 'complained that it was too dear and that all traders were vagabonds and scoundrels who should be guillotined, and if he had any say in it they would all be guillotined on the spot'.[1] Words in the wind, but representative of a feeling widespread among these soldiers.

In the small towns they harassed the *comités de surveillance* – torn between fears of appearing lukewarm and a desire to spare their fellow citizens – with daily denunciations against infractions of the *maximum*. The *révolutionnaires* were not beyond reproach themselves in this respect, and some took advantage of their stay in the country to go from farm to farm buying eggs and butter at giveaway prices. Indeed one butcher from the Tuileries Section actually sent entire carcasses back to his shop there, though this was probably an exceptional case. But always the soldier shared the small consumer's prejudices against the dealer in foodstuffs, small and large alike. Prejudices already well developed in Paris increased apace as they moved away from the capital and these Parisians were convinced that all the merchants in the departments were in league to defraud them.

Suspicious of the merchants and 'les gros', they eagerly received the complaints of the 'poor *sans-culottes*', whether they were comfortable innkeepers or purchasers of *biens nationaux*. The Tuileries cannoneers told Laukhard that nearly all 'the local population [of Mâcon and Lyon] were contemptible merchants who brazenly fleeced the poor craftsmen, workers and labourers of their wages'. 'Those kind of people have nothing better to do than flaunt their wealth and assume airs and graces and don't give a damn for the poverty and distress of the poor devils who toil and

---

[1] APP, A A/60 (Arcis) (commissaire de police), complaint of Bardoux, 9 Brumaire year II. See also AN, F 7 4666 d 4 (Delamare): this cannoneer in the Bon-Conseil company was accused in Prairial year III of having 'repeatedly put forward sanguinary motions, and proclaimed against the merchants and *honnêtes gens*, calling for ... a permanent guillotine'.

sweat for them.'[1] Laukhard, writing in the nineteenth century, was undoubtedly ascribing a sense of class to these *révolutionnaires* which they were far from possessing; nevertheless one recognizes in these words the egalitarianism and puritanism, the moral condemnation of luxury and idleness, which was the essence of *sans-culotte* 'thought', something behavioural rather than doctrinal. It was their mission then to assist the 'poor craftsmen', and in Normandy, in the Gonesse district, in the Yonne and in the Soissonnais, they lent a willing ear to the complaints of the agricultural labourers, the village artisans, the fishermen's wives, the raftsmen, who came to seek their protection against the big farmers, the men of the law, the moderates. The Parisian's self-esteem was flattered by this role as redresser of wrongs, defender of the poor, and he saw himself as something of a *sans-culotte* St Louis. Seated, not under an oak, but in the *auberge*, he listened eagerly to the *aubergiste*, a self-styled 'Mère Duchesne', complaining about 'les gros' of her village. Taking little account of his own ignorance of the people and the ways of the country, the somewhat summary and naïve concern of the *révolutionnaire* for social justice frequently led him to interfere in protracted village disputes.

The 'sixteen commandments of the patriot' stressed vigilance above everything else.[2] The *révolutionnaire* took his instructions about internal enemies extremely seriously, and in village and town was a zealous denouncer, not only of economic offences, but sometimes also of 'mauvais' words. In Lyon one of the victims of the cannoneers' 'denunciation' was a young girl with the charming name of Fanchette, who was courageous enough to say in their presence that she had brought food every day to 'the brave men of Lyon' during the siege, and would do it again if she had to.[3] This was an extreme case, for Fanchette, like so many Lyon people, did not conceal her hatred for the Parisians. The *révolutionnaires* were also quick to condemn any criticism of the regime; they denounced one Vernon man for having stuck his tongue out each time he heard the word 'Republic' uttered in his presence,[4] and pointed 'in horror'

---

[1] Laukhard, op. cit., p. 267. See also the letter addressed by the Finistère detachment in Pont-l'Évêque to their Section, 16 Ventôse, claiming that the rich of the countryside were in league with those of the town, and that 'only the poor *sans-culottes* have difficulty supplying their needs' (AN, BB 3 71). The condemnation of Grammont in this letter is indicative of the same puritan hostility to luxury: 'We want family men to lead us, at least they would see the need of securing bread for their children; instead most of those imposed on us seek only luxuries, while their brothers cannot even find the basic necessities of life.'

[2] Arch. Vaucluse, I VI 12 (*société* of Vaison), 5 September 1793. Twelfth commandment: 'Never inform unjustly, but watch out for the enemies of liberty, and never be afraid of denouncing conspirators, by your silence you would be as guilty as they are' (cited in Cobb, 'Quelques aspects de la mentalité révolutionnaire').

[3] Arch. Rhône, 42 L 149 (Commission Temporaire, Fanchette Mayet).

[4] The denounced man claimed to be afflicted with a kind of nervous tic in his tongue (Arch. Eure, 235 L 89*, *comité* of Vernon).

to those expressing the peculiar desire to 'shit on the Republic' or to 'bugger the nation'. In Paris someone was arrested for having called the *armée révolutionnaire* 'nothing but a pack of informers'.[1] Informers they were not, and as denouncers they were less zealous and certainly less dangerous than the practised experts – the country people, the embittered wives, the concierges, the 'crows' – but like all *sans-culottes*, they attached immense importance to words, and since they were totally lacking in any sense of humour (irony and wit being the prerogative of the former privileged classes), they made no allowances for the linguistic excesses of the ordinary people, particularly the housewife infuriated by the difficulties of everyday life under a beleaguered republic. For them it was all a matter of visible orthodoxy, and they affected an often ridiculous zeal in their effort to locate signs of the *ancien régime* or of 'superstition'. Just as the electors of the Bon-Conseil Section preferred to eat off the table at a fraternal banquet, after having broken some fifty plates bearing the fleurs-de-lis, so the members of the Vernon contingent – and these were the 'purs' – caused considerable anxiety to a cost-conscious municipality by complaining of the floor covering of the Maison-Commune which bore the pattern of the cursed flower.[2] Few local authorities shed any tears over the departure of these wearisome Arguses of the Revolution.

Their iconoclasm, the childish pleasure they took in the destruction of religious objects, were all part of the need to stress a fundamental orthodoxy, and at the same time it symbolized the anticlericalism, even the entrenched anti-Catholicism, of the Parisian *petit peuple*. It would be wrong to think of them as militant atheists; their intervention in religious matters was entirely negative and destructive, as will be seen when the dechristianizing activities of the *armées révolutionnaires* are examined more fully.

The *révolutionnaires* were citizens rather than soldiers; each was conscious of himself as part of the national sovereignty, and when one is a member of the sovereign people, the nagging by commanders is more difficult to endure. 'They called themselves by this name [of *sans-culottes*] or *révolutionnaires*, but they would not be called soldiers or even volunteers,' remarks Laukhard. 'Military discipline meant little to them, and they repeatedly threatened to smash any officer who commanded them to do anything other than march against the aristocrats.'[3] In conflicts with

---

[1] AN, F 7 4583 d 6 (Avenel).
[2] Arch. Vernon, D 1/7 (General Council, session of 1 Frimaire year II).
[3] Laukhard, op. cit., p. 267. Signs of the same sentiment can be found in Collot's address to the Jacobins, 29 Ventôse: 'I know these good Parisian cannoneers, they are above reproach ... In Commune-Affranchie, I heard them say that they were the striking force of the nation, and that their weapons would only be turned against its enemies' (*Journal de la Montagne*, no. 129 [2 Germinal year II]).

their officers, whom they frequently denounced for brutal conduct reminiscent of the *ancien régime*, or even more for having slept with Lyonnaises, they mobilized not only their own Sections, but the departmental *comités* and *sociétés*. The Lyon *sans-culottes*, who destested all Parisians, were delighted at the opportunities thus offered of throwing oil on the fire by actively taking up the defence of some soldiers in the revolutionary garrison, victims of their commanders' 'despotism'. The adjutant-general Grammont tried in vain to rally the captain of the detachment at Provins, who was detested and completely outflanked by his men. 'Without discipline, there can be no strength,' he urged. While Maubant reminded his own troops:

> You cannot be good soldiers if you do not submit to military procedures … You have elected your commanders … You also owe them obedience. Certainly you and they are equals outside the service, but while that service lasts discipline and the most perfect obedience must guide you.[1]

Such efforts were lost on these Parisians. They did not want to listen. If they did not win their cases against the officers they still had the right to resign, and the cannoneers in particular used this way out more and more frequently, citing family or business reasons. If they were refused leave, they took it anyway.

The *révolutionnaires* also found additional reasons in their service records for this ready insolence towards their officers. Survivors of the Champ de Mars, combatants of 10 August, strategists of 31 May did not need to be forced to serve, and Maubant reminded the local authorities that the Parisian soldiers were 'veterans' of the revolutionary movement. It was a way of explaining, if not excusing, their often intolerably arrogant conduct.

As civilians these strange soldiers were not primitive animals. Certainly they wholeheartedly approved of the pitiless repression directed against all the Lyonnais, regardless of their social origin; some soldiers played a direct role in it, others were spectators or guards at the executions. In letters to their Sections, they complacently totted up the daily toll of victims, noting with satisfaction the acceleration of the carnage in vulgar language reminiscent of the black humour of the *Père Duchesne*'s account

---

[1] AHG (*reg. d'ordre*), Maubant to the commander of the detachment at Provins, 22 Ventôse year II. This kind of independent spirit was peculiar to the cannoneers and fusiliers. The cavalrymen were at one and the same time more servile towards their officers and more arrogant towards civilians. Cochet, a cavalier in the 2nd squadron, accused of having threatened a sergeant, declared himself 'as innocent as a new-born babe … you can be sure that a former servant with thirteen years of service knows his place too well to make such threats' (Arch. Seine-et-Oise, IV Q 187). This was the flunkey rather than the *sans-culotte* speaking, and in that Cochet was representative of a good portion of the cavalry.

of the *petite fenêtre* (the guillotine). In this cruel imagery shooting the Lyonnais is translated, 'making the people of this vile town dance the *carmagnole* to the tune of the garrison commander'. But the *révolutionnaire* was no butcher. His violence was largely verbal, part and parcel of the revolutionary orthodoxy, and too much importance must not be attached to it. Indeed there was a kind of demagoguery of verbal violence, with the commanders in particular outdoing each other in its usage and setting the example for the ordinary *révolutionnaires*.[1] But more remarkable perhaps were the number of officers and men in Lyon who pitied the fate of the crucified population to the extent even of protesting against the repression. According to the statements of the Lyonnais in the year III there were some *révolutionnaires* who, at the risk of being condemned as counter-revolutionaries, were prepared to go beyond protests to help the people hide or escape that plagued city.

Conformist rather than naturally cruel, most of these Parisians were honest fellows. And even though temptation was frequently put in their way, particularly when instructed to guard sequestrated property, misappropriation of the caches of money and silver was rare, and these usually ended up in the national crucible after careful inventorying. The soldier had fewer scruples, however, when it came to wine, eau-de-vie and chicken. Everything drinkable and edible was fair game, a kind of *taxe de guerre*, a duty on *incivisme*.

Some cannoneers en route through Avallon proclaimed the doctrine that in 'times of revolution there were no laws, only the people, which was sovereign'. It was occasioned by their report to the *société populaire* of a decision taken by a *juge de paix*.[2] A similar claim appears in the document which Chaumont, a captain of fusiliers, prepared for his defence before the Aisne tribunal; in times of revolution, he argued, it is not always possible to act within the law, and since the *armée révolutionnaire* was instructed to take action against the internal enemies by every means

---

[1] When Parein, just returned from the Vendée, appeared before the Jacobins on 18 Vendémiaire, he declared: 'My colleague Boulanger asks you for a guillotine, I ask for a *second*, and I promise you that the aristocrats and the hoarders will soon be reduced to nothing.' Momoro declared that Parein had already guillotined many aristocrats in the Vendée – which was in fact untrue, for in Parein's time the Commission Parein-Félix was relatively mild (*Journal de la Montagne*, no. 131 [11 October 1793]). Boulanger, the most 'governmental' of the commanders, did not rest there: at the Jacobins on 13 Brumaire, he 'used the occasion of some new betrayals to demand a *mouvement révolutionnaire* to crush all aristocrats, all those who were against the revolution'. Was this not simply another way of demanding legalized massacres? The *société* disregarded it (*Journal de la Montagne*, no. 157). Thus did the commanders, even more than the soldiers, who were a little more humane, rival each other in revolutionary brutality.

[2] R.C. Cobb, 'L'armée révolutionnaire parisienne: composition sociale et politique'. This incident was pointed out to me by my friend, Pierre Tartat, historian of Avallon, who was kind enough to let me see the relevant extract from the communal archives.

possible, it could not always follow laws proclaimed in calmer times. Instead he invoked an alternative law: that of 'revolutionary necessity'. Do these two examples indicate a consciousness of popular sovereignty exercised through the *sociétés populaires* as assemblies of the people? This is perhaps making too much of the tendency of the *révolutionnaire* to favour the local *société* wherever he went, which was largely due to his need to seek allies among the militant minorities in a generally hostile countryside. The *carte de visite* was the Parisian soldier's diploma from his Section's *société populaire*, and his first action on arrival in a new locality was to deposit it with the local *société*. Indeed he would be annoyed if none existed; its absence spoke ill of the patriotic sentiments of the populace, for in his mind, if one was free and republican, one joined a people's organization to read the laws. When a *société* existed the Parisian became a member, and could then leave two diplomas at his next posting, a double testimonial to his *civisme*.

But all this did not amount to any desire for direct democracy or the replacement of the Revolutionary Government and Convention with a new hierarchy of *sociétés*. Such an idea did not occur to the majority of Ronsin's soldiers, who, in their lack of respect for the local authorities, made attachment to the Convention a veritable cult, and the device, *Force à la loi*, an article of faith. Nor was this 'loi' that of the criminal tribunals or the magistrates; it was, rather, the decrees of the Convention, itself the organ of the popular will. When the Convention spoke, the *révolutionnaire* obeyed. In Germinal when it decreed that it no longer needed the *armée révolutionnaire*, the soldiers rushed to resign before the official disbandment, as a sign of their voluntary submission. At no time did they consider resisting a decree of the Convention. 'We are your children, we exist only through you, we will cease to exist on your command,' proclaimed the soldiers in Lyon; and their acceptance of the official version of the 'crimes' of their commanders is one example of such submission. If the Convention said that Ronsin, Mazuel and the Grammonts were conspirators, then it must be true. This was not simply inertia on the soldiers' part, nor even orthodoxy or ignorance; the *révolutionnaire* believed in the Convention.

II *Motives for Enrolment*

The portrait sketched above will help explain why more than 6,000 men in their prime, mostly from Paris or its outskirts, enlisted in the revolutionary artillery or infantry. The extreme case is that of the Quinze-Vingts wigmaker who hoped to 'have a spree' at the expense of the peasantry; belonging to an endangered profession, he had nothing to lose by enlisting and everything to gain from such a highly paid service.

Unemployment or under-employment, high wages, the promise of gas-tronomic spoils, and undoubtedly for the wigmaker the thought of all those farm girls – this was the range of attractions outlined in the account by Taine and indeed in those of many contemporaries. Many *sans-culottes*, scandalized by the gilded idleness of the soldiers left in the École Militaire, asked what purpose this *armée* served except as a leisure pursuit for the idle, the drunken and all the riff-raff attracted by the promise of food and lodging.

These explanations cannot be entirely set aside, but it would be wrong to accept them as generally applicable. Merchants, sometimes well-off ones, or artisans in prosperous trades, did not enlist to escape starvation, but for a number of different motives, which included revolutionary enthusiasm, a taste for adventure, and the vanity of the civilian attracted by a uniform. There was a Tartarin in many of these shopkeepers who dreamed of setting off to impose the law on the provincials. Others thought they could help supply Paris by threatening the greedy farmer with force if he did not send grain voluntarily – an understandable pattern of reasoning when the crisis seemed to have been brought about by the selfishness of the farmers. Then there are the imponderables – such as the violent temperament of some who viewed this instrument of the Terror as an excellent opportunity for action.

These were the stated motives. But the regular soldiers detested the *armée révolutionnaire*, not only because of its high pay, but above all because they considered the *révolutionnaires* cowards, who were afraid of being sent to serve on the frontiers. The laws governing the organization of the Parisian *armée* made it difficult for such men to enlist; but there were ways of evading the law, especially if you were rich and powerful, and several young men subject to conscription managed to gain places in this army designed for domestic service only. But they were the exception; the revolutionary authorities were on the watch for such cases, and most of those of conscription age were eventually ferreted out. It was a ques-tion of the honour – and thereby the efficacity – of the new corps. The presence of well-off young men in its ranks, once it was known to Sectionary opinion, could act as a worm in the fruit. Chance also played its part, for the *armée* recruited wherever it went, and a chance encounter in an *auberge*, a conversation in a barber's shop, might provide an oppor-tunity for the unattached, the itinerant, the pedlar to join. Some of these men who had become attached to the life of the road were former soldiers, and could not fail to be attracted by service in an *armée* which satisfied the desire to be constantly on the move.

'In times of revolution the extremes meet' is a theory of government held by *ultras* and *citras* alike, a way of justifying repression and human sacrifice by the principle of revolution, a theory which has always found favour with 'centralizers' and bureaucrats – a Robespierrist theory, in other words. The theory has some validity when applied to the Parisian *armée*; there were certainly authentic counter-revolutionaries in it, princes and returned *émigrés* badly in need of documents to prove their *civisme*, servants who had accompanied their masters into the Belgian provinces or into Germany, been abandoned by them without pay and made their way back to France clandestinely. Where better to shelter than in the heart of a para-revolutionary institution? Nothing could have been easier. The cavalry was there at Versailles to receive them. Some suspects even managed to get into the infantry. But we only know of those who were discovered. In the disordered state of France in the year II, others must have found a safe shelter far from the eyes of the Sectionary *comités* and the municipalities of their places of origin.

Certain trades were subject to requisition for war work: shoemakers and locksmiths, for example, could be obliged to work for wages set by the *maximum* to supply the needs of the armies. Despite rulings excluding workers in these categories from the *armée révolutionnaire*, many did join, and it took several months – the life-span of the *armée* in fact – to get the locksmiths, shoemakers, iron-workers and engravers out again.

Finally there were the criminals, the bandits, patrons of every new institution. An *armée* whose main task was to make domiciliary visits to peasant households was an excellent screen for banditry, and a number of bandit chiefs operating in the Seine-et-Oise region gained valuable experience there.

But the best way of discovering motives for enrolling is to ask the *révolutionnaires* themselves, always taking into account the date of their explanations. Until Germinal year II they still gloried in what was, until then, seen as a patriotic action. After the disbandment of the *armée*, however, the tone changed and they instead sought excuses for having entered a body already seen as suspect. After Thermidor every explanation was coloured by the need to apologize. It was no longer something to be boasted about, and in the year III the former *révolutionnaires* stressed need above all else; with a large family, they had not thought they could afford to refuse such employment. This was indeed the explanation preferred by their adversaries; yet before Thermidor every *révolutionnaire* had tried to refute the idea that he had been attracted by the high pay.

The explanation put forward by Pierre Prévost of the Contrat-Social Section was undoubtedly that preferred by the *révolutionnaires* and that which they would have liked to see accepted by their fellow citizens. Aged thirty-seven, Prévost was a former soldier, who had served from the age of sixteen to thirty, then worked as a ferryman. He wanted to enrol in the Muséum Section's fusiliers and wrote to the Section's *comité révolutionnaire*:

> Citizen president, wishing to be of use to my country, and with no sense of strain on either my heart or soul, I thought I would present myself to you ... my decision to join this corps comes not from the pay which is higher than any other force ... but because it will allow me to serve my country ... I will go to serve in any department to which I might be sent without asking a sou extra ... the desire to join this corps came only after self-examination, and I said to myself: only known and honest citizens are taken, and that is the truth.

Fine words! But though he may have been an honest fellow, Prévost was clearly carried away by his new authority. Admitted as a fusilier in the Muséum company, he was arrested on 6 Ventôse by the Contrat-Social *comité* for having posed as a police inspector of lodging-houses, and having arrested two women whom he accused of sleeping around. The *comité* accepted his excuse of having acted out of revolutionary patriotism.[1]

Former soldiers jumped at every opportunity for re-enlistment: even the constitutional priest from the Gonesse district, Pontian Gillet – invalided out of the Couronne regiment, and in 1793 acting as curé and public official in Vauderland – petitioned Clémence and Marchand, the *commissaires civiles*, for a place in the new *armée*, assuring them that 'the Republic, protected by the Supreme Being, would be victorious [over] its enemies'.[2] We do not know if the Parisian *armée* took up this offer of service from the padre, with its guarantee of protection by the Supreme Being.

The motives outlined by Pierre Antoine Boudringuin, a locksmith's assistant in the Lepeletier Section, were equally respectable:

> After serving thirteen months in the 2nd Paris battalion and having been wounded near Menin on 27 August 1793, by a *biscayen* in my right thigh, I was moved from hospital to hospital ... finally to one in Paris. On my discharge, 28 Brumaire, the *conseil de santé* gave me living costs for a fortnight. On 14 Frimaire I enrolled in the *armée révolutionnaire* of the Lepeletier Section in the hope of being of use on the arms maintenance side. I was not to be disappointed and was indeed employed in this capacity.[3]

Though only a locksmith's assistant, he was nevertheless liable to requisition, and such enrolment seems to have been a way of avoiding it. Chance

---

[1] AN, F 7 4774 83 d 2 (Prévost).

[2] AN, BB3 75, Gillet to the commanders of the detachment at Luzarches, 30 September 1793.

[3] AN, F 7 4610 d 4 (Boudringuin). After the disbandment of the *armée*, Boudringuin was employed with Colin, a master locksmith, working on the large artillery. Arrested 12 Messidor, for having caused a disturbance among the soldiers, he excused himself by claiming that he had been drinking.

too played a part, and one almanach-seller and travelling pedlar in the Eure was brought by chance into the *armée révolutionnaire*, then crossing the department.[1]

Some enrolments were clearly products of unemployment. Louis Haumann, a seventy-year-old Alsatian living in the rue du Chantre, Gardes-Françaises Section, 'had been a wigmaker until the loss of his acquaintances [the emigration of his clientele], because of the Revolution, forced him to leave, and since then [he] has been serving as a volunteer in the 2nd battalion of the *armée révolutionnaire*'. His was a case of extreme need, and on 13 Messidor he wrote to the Committee explaining that since the disbanding of the *armée* he had been without funds or occupation and asking for relief or work 'that he might be able to supply the needs of his advanced years'.[2] The same reason for enrolling applied to three volunteers from the Tuileries Section, Dubesy, Laporte and Duperret, the first 'a former hairdresser', the other two waiters. Two lieutenants from the Cambrai chasseurs, Berny and Mathon, petitioned the same *comité* on 3 October: 'finding themselves unemployed with the disbandment of their corps', they asked to be allowed into the *armée révolutionnaire* in consideration of 'their former services'.[3] Such cases are multiplied over and over, and despite his proud protestations – 'with our arms we have sworn to crush all the aristocratic, royalist and fanatical vermin which infest the republic' – Hauplond, a volunteer from the Bon-Conseil Section, was also motivated by necessity. When he found himself again unemployed on leaving the *armée* he sought employment in a munitions workshop.[4]

One curious individual, Louis Reguex, a clockmaker's assistant who got himself dismissed from the army for ill conduct, was quite a vagabond, but fairly typical of most *révolutionnaires*. Listen to the recital of his misfortunes: 'My enemies claimed that I was fond of drink, and it is true that it is a weakness, but one can be a drinker without being any the less a republican, so I was dismissed from the Corps on indefinite leave, but I was not discontented, for I could still be useful', and since his service with the *armée* had left him

disgusted at being in a Corps which seemed more burdensome than useful to the Republic ... I returned to my home, and worked at my trade ... even when

---

[1] On 3 August 1793 the Gravilliers *comité* pointed to 'gatherings of locksmiths, nail-makers, etc.', meeting every two weeks in one of the *auberges* of the Section, who had enrolled in several of the corps, even those of the line troops (AN, BB3 73). On a chance enrolment, see id., F 7 4596 d 8 (Berthonier).
[2] AN, F 7 4739 d 3 (Haumann).
[3] AN, F 7* 2472 (Tuileries *comité*, session of 13 Floréal year II), and F 7 4596 d 2 (Berny).
[4] AN, F 7 4739 d 3 (Hauplond).

in the Brie I discovered some false tobacco [this Argus claimed also to have uncovered a cache of silver] ... Now I ask you if such a subject can be a counter-revolutionary ... no, citizens, there is not a Parisian who has a heart like mine and who since the Revolution has not ceased to be vigilant, that is why my enemies worked to secure my dismissal ... They claimed to have heard me say that I had a position with the Sûreté [Committee of General Security, the great police Committee]; but that's a lie for I had had too much to drink, and I can assure you that I probably said to them I had written to the Committee of Public Safety to ask for work.

But the Marchés *comité* was not convinced; it described Reguex as 'un mauvais sujet, errant et vagabond', and had him arrested one morning in a café for having passed himself off as an agent of the revolutionary tribunal and having cursed the traders as thieves and bloodsuckers. His case was aggravated by his desertion from his detachment in the Brie and return to Paris, and he was imprisoned in Thermidor by the revolutionary tribunal.[1] Reguex's story provides a composite portrait of the average Parisian *révolutionnaire*, with his drunkenness, his pride, his desire to return to Paris, and his suspicious nature which caused him to see treasure hidden everywhere. Reguex was above all the unstable wanderer of the *comité*'s portrait. He was bored with his work and sought a change by enrolling in the *armée révolutionnaire*. But when he was sent to the Brie he found service equally boring and granted himself leave to return to Paris. He was not the only soldier to be something of a mythomaniac, with imaginary duties – another product of that intoxicating taste for power so widespread among these Parisian artisans.

Let us move on now to those whose motives are less easy to ascertain. Young Barrau, for instance, a banker's son, a conscript from the Muséum Section, who 'prior to the levy was a shop assistant, then a clerk at the War Ministry, forced into barracks with our young men he soon found means of joining the National Guard: finally, having been sent back from this corps, he thought he could avoid the levy by concealing himself in the cavalry of the *armée révolutionnaire* at Versailles'. But he was soon excluded from this also because he did not meet the height requirements. 'He returned to us therefore and declared that he had been a printer's assistant. A declaration,' observed the Muséum *comité*, 'which we considered ludicrous, since we knew Barrau to have an income of 15,000 to 20,000 livres.'[2] The *armée révolutionnaire* therefore had not worked for this well-off young man. Others were more fortunate: Louis-Hyacinthe

---

[1] AN, W 471.

[2] AN, F 7 4688 d 4 (Deltufo). Deltufo, printer to the Convention, had agreed to employ this young man, Barrau, under his disguise as an apprentice printer. Barrau's father had powerful friends.

Lafrété, for example, a young man of twenty-five, son of the former receiver-general of Lorraine, a banker with correspondents in Madrid, living off his property. Young Lafrété also had been included in the first levy and had taken refuge in Mazuel's cavalry at Beauvais, 'after he had read a decree permitting citizens between the ages of eighteen and forty to join the cavalry of the *armée révolutionnaire*'. But he was reluctant to say much about it to the *comité révolutionnaire* of his Section, which released him from arrest and sent him back to his battalion. His father, who had also been arrested for trying to remove his son from the levy, was named president of the *comité de bienfaisance* of the Mont-Blanc Section in Messidor year II. The reign of the *sans-culottes* was over.[1]

More astonishing still was the case of Jules Guéthenoc, prince of Rohan-Rochefort, who successfully got himself engaged by the cavalry by simply turning up at the gates of the Palace of Versailles. He might, nevertheless, have made an excellent *révolutionnaire*, had he not been discovered the following day talking to a former servant who called him 'Monseigneur' out of habit.[2] The marquis de Baudelaire was more fortunate and remained unnoticed in a squadron for the entire existence of the cavalry. In Ventôse three ex-nobles and two ecclesiastics were expelled from the 6th squadron alone.[3] Indeed, enrolment in the cavalry was the best means for a noble of escaping the attention of the *comités révolutionnaires*.

A similar category was that of servants of *émigrés* who had returned secretly to France. Barré, a cannoneer of the République Section, was a footman who had accompanied his master to Belgium, then left his service in March 1793 when refused a wage rise, and returned through enemy lines to hide himself in the revolutionary artillery.[4] But his case pales into insignificance beside that of Jacques Berteau. This Frenchman living in London, and serving with the English army, had deserted from the Duke of York's forces in Belgium to the French lines near Lille. Having returned to his home town of Boulogne-sur-Mer, and possessing no *certificat de civisme*, he joined an infantry regiment to escape the vigilance of the *comités de surveillance* in the areas through which he passed. Hospitalized

---

[1] AN, F 7 4758 d 2 (Lafrété). See also F 7 4699 d 2 (Duvivier): Siméon Duvivier, native of Passais, Domfront district, aged 24 and a clerk in a business concern, joined the cavalry, and when arrested by the Poissonnière *comité* for having evaded conscription, boasted of having purchased an exemption for 100 écus. His parents, fortunately for them, had abandoned him 'because of his libertinage', and he was described by the *comité* as a 'Muscadin [who] associated with scarcely anyone but women'. He had worked in the office of the artillery's banker, Bouret de Vézelay.
[2] AN, WIa 389 (904). Guéthenoc was condemned to death among the *Chemises rouges*.
[3] Arch. Seine-et-Oise, IV Q 45 (Séquestres, Guillaume de Baudelaire); I am indebted to M. Arnaud de Lestapis for having drawn my attention to this dossier. See also AHG (*reg. d'ordre*).
[4] AN, F 7 4587 d 5 (Barré).

in Saint-Denis (where he claimed to have uncovered a royalist plot) he eventually found his way into the *armée révolutionnaire* in Compiègne. No one asked any questions, and it was only after the disbandment of the *armée*, and his necessary reintegration into civilian life – with all its dangers for one without papers – that his secret was discovered. 'With the *armée révolutionnaire* now disbanded,' he wrote to Fouquier on 2 Floréal, 'I will happily accept the most dangerous posting, for I have long chafed at the inaction of this corps.' Fouquier was to condemn him to permanent inaction by sending him to the guillotine.[1]

A similar case was that of the twenty-five-year-old Prégaux, a former servant and a native of Chaillot, who had served for six years in the Neustrie regiment, deserting in 1790 to enter the service of the marquis de Saint-Clair, colonel of the Belsunce cavalry in Mannheim. After a year he took his leave of the marquis at Breda and entered the service of a Dutchman. On his way through Brussels he became orderly to an officer with the Lille garrison, spent a short time in Paris, returned to Lille, and eventually came to grief as a repairer with a bootmaker in Châlons-sur-Marne. On 30 Brumaire he presented himself to the Champs-Élysées *comité* for enrolment with its company. But instead of accepting this poor illiterate victim of the Revolution, the *comité* had him sent to the Mairie as a returned *émigré*.[2]

There were also less admissible personal motives for joining the *armée*. Nobles, servants of *émigrés*, French cooks in London were all victims of the Revolution. Dourlans, a bankrupt jeweller-enameller, was overjoyed, unlike most of his colleagues, to be sent to Lyon, hoping thereby to place a comfortable distance between himself and his creditors in Paris. Then there is the curious case of the former monk Chandèze, administrator of the Hôpital de la Charité and seducer of a seamstress, who succeeded in having himself elected to head the l'Unité company, doubtless to flee the responsibilities of paternity and the consequences of his amorousness. At the end of September he wrote to his mistress, Victoire Rogay, that he had accepted a captaincy (!) in the *armée révolutionnaire*, claiming to have done so in the belief that she no longer wanted to see him: 'adieu, my heartless love, you are sending me to my death.' But Victoire was having none of this ruse, and on the 28th she wrote to the l'Unité *comité révolutionnaire*:

> I appeal to the law ... I am a young woman who allowed myself to be abused by a man unworthy of my friendship ... But I do not know what to do to rid myself of him; he has threatened to blow my brains out or slit me open if I ever

---

[1] AN, WIa 140.
[2] AN, F 7* 2473 (Champs-Élysées *comité révolutionnaire*, session of 30 Brumaire year II).

leave him ... Furthermore he is a former monk from the Charité ... I am a seamstress and my father gives me a small allowance.[1]

Finally there is the case of François Maillet, a paper-hanger, rue Bourg-l'Abbé, Amis-de-la-Patrie Section, whose motives seem to fit into all the categories cited above: prudent demagogy, need, and patriotism. His Section's *comité révolutionnaire* had him arrested on 29 Brumaire as a suspect, who had defended Lafayette and who had 'tried to assume a mask of patriotism by joining the *armée révolutionnaire*'. His wife, a meat-trader, gave another motive for his thwarted attempt to enrol, in her petition to the Committee of General Security: 'Slackness in his trade and the need to support his wife and children brought about his decision; but he abandoned the attempt and instead accepted a position at 31 sols per day', a more plausible explanation. Maillet himself gave a third: 'Far from having tried to join the *armée révolutionnaire* on his own initiative, he was brought to it by his fellow citizens who knew his zeal; he thought he could refuse it without compromising the Republic, and accept a situation which would also permit him to support his large family.'[2]

There is abundant information on these kinds of men and on the unemployed who approached their Sections or the Committee of Public Safety in an effort to find work again after leaving the *armée*. As always, however, this documentation gives a blighted view of the motives for enrolment, for the small shopkeeper or trader who enrolled on patriotic grounds does not appear. We can conclude that despite the *scrutins épuratoires*, suspects were able to conceal themselves in the *armée révolutionnaire*, particularly if they joined outside Paris. But surveillance by the *comités* did not cease after enrolment and throughout its existence the *armée*, and the cavalry in particular, underwent repeated purges. Take the case of the former wigmaker Lassagne, appointed sergeant of the Bonne-Nouvelle company in October, denounced by his wife as having lived off immoral earnings, and expelled from his company and forced to return to Paris even after he had left for Lyon.[3]

For some, motives were extremely mixed, vanity or material gain, the desire to ensure food supplies to their families, or to undermine 'malveillance', all playing a part. Service in this *armée* was not a vocation, but a

---

[1] AN, F 7 4639 d 1 (Chandèze).

[2] AN, F 7 4774 30 d 4 (Maillet). Maillet remained in prison until 2 Fructidor year II.

[3] AN, F 7 4767 d 2 (Lassagne). For this continued surveillance from the centre see also id., F 7 4777 (reg. Champs-Élysées *comité révolutionnaire*). On 10 Frimaire a cannoneer sergeant, the 32-year-old Bernard from Chaumont-en-Bassigny, was denounced for having an unsigned certificate (he had picked it up in the corridors of the War Ministry). He had also left his post to go to a *cabaret*. This would not be the last occasion on which he was taken to task for insufficient papers or misbehaviour.

privileged position, and the *révolutionnaire* expected respect and reward alike from it. Most had dwelt too long in obscurity not to feel a desire to avenge past humiliations, and in some respects Taine was right to see these humble mortals, having graduated to such heights, imitating their former masters. Under the Terror the shopkeeper was king and with such men vanity always played a greater part than thought of material gain.

III   *Social and Political Composition of the Parisian* armée:
       General Characteristics

In spite of its name the *armée révolutionnaire* was not exclusively Parisian. The cavalry in particular recruited on a first-come, first-served basis with its most dubious recruits coming from the Versailles population of former wigmakers, 'supernumeraries', footmen and coachmen. One squadron was almost entirely composed of farmers, day-labourers and artisans from the Beauvaisis, and if the artillery seemed typically Parisian, recruits from the surrounding communes were attached to the fusilier companies from the outset. All the *sociétés* in the Paris department were circularized by Ronsin and invited to nominate candidates worthy of forming the 'nucleus' of the patriotic army. Some *sociétés* did respond to the invitation, and as early as June the Finistère Section was assailed with demands from the people of Ivry, Gentilly and Choisy. Socially inferior to the Parisians, and worse affected by the food shortages, the people of these communes flocked to take advantage of an institution which offered such desirable employment. Launderers and laundresses from Vaugirard and Vanves came, wine-growers and wine merchants from Issy, Clamart and Meudon, bargemen and dock-workers from Charenton and Carrières, gardeners, market gardeners and small farmers from the Pré-Saint-Gervais and Saint-Mandé, tannery-workers from Saint-Denis, wagoners and 'journeymen workers of every description who pass briefly through our commune' (Montrouge), rabbit breeders from Ivry – in other words a mobile and unstable population camped outside the gates of the capital.[1] It is impossible to calculate the importance of these numbers coming from the area surrounding Paris. The *comités révolutionnaires* in the Sections naturally tended to prefer their fellow citizens, and those from outside Paris had to wait their turn. But the rural or semi-rural element in this urban army does seem to have come from the surrounding communes rather than from the few Sections, such as Bondy, possessing rural populations of their own.[2]

---

[1] Arch. Seine, D L IV 1 (*société populaire* of Sceaux, sessions of 25 Brumaire and 7 Frimaire), in which it was observed that '*sociétaires* [were] for the most part farmers'. Arch. Sèvres, Reg. P (*société populaire* of Sèvres). AN, F 7 4784 (*comité de surveillance* of Franciade, Saint-Denis).
[2] AN, F 10 450 (Agriculture), list of workers by Section, requisitioned for harvest work, Messidor–Thermidor year II.

Moreover, once a detachment had been sent out of Paris it continued to recruit from among the local people or those passing through the area. Take, for example, the pedlar enrolled in the Eure, or the weaver by the detachment in Montereau.[1] Others were recruited in Compiègne, and even the detachment sent to Lyon recruited en route. Ronsin's circular was read to the *société populaire* of Mende; and the Auvergne, which sent so many poor rabbit-skin dealers, impoverished water-carriers and low-wage-earners to Paris, was justly represented in this Parisian *armée* whose composition reflected the diversity of the French population.[2] The cavalry, which contained the most suspect elements of the *armée*, also recruited from among the most poor: *commissionnaires* from Savoy, water-carriers from the Auvergne, lettuce-sellers from the Basse-Normandie, day-labourers and *petit peuple* from the countryside of the Beauvaisis. However, one must not exaggerate the importance of these recruits from the surrounding communes or from the lodging-houses of the most densely populated Sections. The *armée révolutionnaire* was above all a *sans-culotte* institution, and such country people as found their way into it did so only by accident. In no way was it a charity to help the floating population of the capital.

We have very few general guidelines on the social composition of the *armée*. Most of the documentation concentrates rather on the individual and consists largely of police or Committee of General Security papers, and while such individual dossiers may supply a living picture of the persons concerned, and help trace their social mobility, they do not permit any overall statistical analysis. Moreover, it serves no purpose to know that there were a dozen or so shoemakers in the Parisian *armée*, if we cannot discover the total enrolment figure for this trade; and even if that could be established, we would still have to distinguish between master craftsmen and assistants or apprentices. Finally, the recruit described as a

---

[1] Arch. Montereau, D 15 (General Council), session of 13 Frimaire year II. See also AN, F7 4637 d 2 (Chabot). Antoine Chabot, a native of Clermont-Ferrand, lately arrived from Marseille, was accepted by Paris, on the personal recommendation of Ronsin, into the La Montagne company, 17 October 1793.

[2] R.C. Cobb, *Les Armées révolutionnaires du Midi*. See also AN, F 10 450 (Agriculture, workers requisitioned for harvest work). Among the former *révolutionnaires*, it is worth noting Jacques Jouves, born in Puy-de-Dôme; Bizet, a 40-year-old casual labourer; Fougerot, a 32-year-old day-labourer; Doublé, a 35-year-old water-carrier, and Henry, a day-labourer. All were seasonal workers, like Loque, an almanach-seller and pedlar in the Eure, aged 46, who had been a journeyman founder for eighteen years (AN, F 7 4774 25 d 4 [Loque]). See also Arch. Versailles, D 1 24 (General Council, session of 27 Brumaire year II), concerning the brawls after which the cavalrymen Delorme, Lemaître, Francq, Bath, Cerval were arrested. They were all from the Mur-de-Barrez district in the Aveyron, 'speaking Auvergne patois' and scarcely understanding French, according to the claims of the Versailles municipality. The final cavalier arrested on this occasion was Pierre Pez of Issoudun.

shoemaker at the time of his enrolment may very well have followed another trade, or several trades, some years previously.

Such then are the limitations of individual documentation. But it can be supplemented by other sources providing almost complete figures for certain specific groupings: military men, workers in war industries, farmers and weavers, and most of all the 'undesirables'. For administrative reasons, these categories occupy a place in the documentation out of all proportion to their numerical importance in the *armée* itself.

First of all let us examine the snippets of general information available on the overall composition of the artillery and infantry. The detachment in Lyon accounted for more than a third of the effective strength of the entire *armée* and two-thirds of the artillery, and the correspondence of Maubant and the other commanders consequently supplies some valuable insights into the *armée* as a whole. Their letters, for example, refer to the cannoneers' belief that they should be permitted the same privileges in matters of debts owed as any other soldier under arms, particularly since 'they were for the most part small businessmen who had not had sufficient time to put their affairs in order before their sudden departure [from Paris]'. In another letter concerning the ever-growing number of requests for leave, Maubant estimated the number of family men, businessmen or shopkeepers in the Lyon artillery at more than 600. Since there were just over 600 cannoneers altogether in Lyon (627 in Pluviôse if their officers are included), nearly all were small businessmen, if Maubant's figures can be credited.[1] Furthermore, despite the vagueness of this assertion it is confirmed by what we know of the individuals. In the fusiliers the artisan element rivalled that of small business (dominant in the artillery) for pride of place. Both elements tended towards political independence – a point to which we will return. But there was also the matter of individual temperaments, and while one shoemaker might be a militant *sectionnaire*, a born revolutionary, another would never rise above the obscurity of his shop. Finally the farmers, day-labourers, gardeners and weavers held a place of such importance among the fusiliers, that a reminder was issued from headquarters to the effect that since those categories were not subject to requisition for war work, they ought not to be liberated from the *armée*.[2]

---

[1] AHG (*reg. d'ordre*), Maubant to the Committee, 23 and 24 Ventôse. Note, however, a contrary opinion in a letter from the Panthéon-Français cannoneer company to Bouchotte, 28 Vendémiaire year II, stating that it was 'composed mostly of workers and fathers of large families, that none had yet been clothed or equipped . . . the pay of 40 sols . . . is grossly inadequate to defray their expenses' (AHG, Xv 45, Volontaires nationaux, cannoneers of Paris). But this is undoubtedly a case of contradiction, for the word 'worker' (*ouvrier*) could be applied to an independent shopkeeper as well as to a small artisan. See also Arch. Rhône, 1 L 215 (Département).

[2] AHG (*reg. d'ordre*), Ronsin to the Soissons detachment commander, 14 Ventôse year II.

Everybody agreed that the composition of the cavalry was pretty inferior.[1] Besides the 'rural people', the 'seasonal' workers such as the water-carriers,[2] and the domestic servants (and among this group was a black man, a former valet in one of the big houses), its ranks were filled with deserters, French and foreign alike, well-off young men, thoroughly disreputable characters, and even some nobles and former priests. *Sectionnaires* and former soldiers were rare.

Did the *révolutionnaires* belong to any identifiable political groupings? This is largely a question of education, something always very difficult to determine. But the survival of individual dossiers allows us to recognize one fusilier as illiterate, another able to write in phonetic French, and others able to write tolerably well. The cavalry was full of illiterates; some fusiliers could sign congratulatory addresses with a cross; but the majority of the infantry could sign their names. The cannoneers undoubtedly came from a higher social category. Most were members of Sectionary *sociétés populaires*, which required a minimum level of education; as such they were a privileged minority,[3] and if at Lyon it was from the cannoneers that the *commissaires* were chosen for attachment to the thirty-two *comités révolutionnaires*, it was surely because more could read and write then among the infantry. The political militants were the *sociétaires* who were frequently the largest grouping in the artillery, but insufficiently numerous to form a recognizable entity in the fusiliers.

Distinct political groupings such as the Jacobins or Cordeliers were equally rare. In the Contrat-Social company of fusiliers the four Jacobins stand out as an isolated and privileged group, insupportable to their colleagues, and subjected to all kinds of harassment by them.[4] Despite its demagogic pose and opposition to government policy, the Cordeliers was a club exclusively for the officer and the *commissaire civil*. The *révolutionnaires* were too lowly to be admitted (except for the privileged few), and when they denounced their officers to the club, it invariably took the latter's part. Indeed some members even reminded the soldiers to respect their betters. The soldiers soon learnt not to direct their petitions to the

---

[1] Arch. Seine-et-Oise, IV Q 187, Orhand to Mazuel.
[2] *Journal de la Montagne* (1st ser.), no. 119 (session of the Jacobins, 25 September 1793). 'Mazuel proclaimed that several citizens in his corps were water-carriers, with no means of subsistence other than the pay they receive from the nation, the pay for a cavalryman is 16 sous 4 deniers, and their usefulness cannot be achieved with greater economy, for it is impossible to live on less.'
[3] R.C. Cobb, 'L'armée révolutionnaire au Havre-Marat et dans le district de Montivilliers', and BN, MSS Nouv. acq. fr. 2708 (134), Luxembourg *société*.
[4] AN, F 7 4741 d 3 (Henry). 'As Jacobins in this company we are constantly called *clubbists* and denied access to interesting papers ... a complete cabal has been formed ... against us by the command' (undated letter from four fusiliers to the Contrat-Social *comité*, year II).

Cordeliers, who were allies of the clan in the rue de Choiseul.[1] It might be argued that the best-educated of the *révolutionnaires*, like the *section-naires* in nearly all the towns, were eager readers of the *Père Duchesne* and would communicate to their less well-educated colleagues the joys and angers of the *marchand de fourneaux* with whom they liked to identify. Indeed such was their passion for Hébert's paper that at Lyon all their own journals were expressly modelled on it. Admittedly Hébert was a talented journalist who knew how to capture the *sans-culotte* audience. But the reader of the *Père Duchesne* in Paris and Lyon was as indifferent to Hébert himself as he was to his own General – both unfamiliar figures – and showed no trace of *hébertisme* as such.

In sum, the political minority consisted of *sociétaires* with a certain amount of education, who were probably more numerous in the cannon-eers than in the infantry. Finally, the royalists formed another political minority which spanned as many social levels as the 'patriots', and *révo-lutionnaires* condemned to death for counter-revolutionary language were on the whole of humble origin: former servants, wigmakers,[2] and even some artisans with all the social attributes of the *sans-culottes*.

(i)   'ACTIVE MINORITIES': MILITANT *SECTIONNAIRES* AND COUNTER-
       REVOLUTIONARIES

As with the officer corps, certain leading *sectionnaires* can be singled out among the *révolutionnaires*: on the one hand members of the *comités révolutionnaires* and other specialists in repression; on the other, ring-leaders of the *sociétés populaires*, often accused by the Jacobin authorities of being ultra-revolutionaries. One fusilier volunteer belonging to both categories was Louis Mathieu Potel, a joiner and member of the *armée révolutionnaire*, in June and September. This artisan spent but a short time in the *armée*, for in Floréal he was accused of *hébertisme*, and recalled by his *comité*. In the same category, even if 'a government man', was the fifty-year-old marble-cutter, Jean Laurent, member of the Quinze-Vingts Section *comité révolutionnaire*, who remained in the *armée* until its dis-

---

[1] *L'Armée révolutionnaire à Lyon*, pp. 39–43 (the Maubant–Arnaud affair).
[2] On the lack of political consciousness of those in certain sectors of domestic service, and their attachment to the old order of things, see the strange claims of Pierre Millart, a 21-year-old wigmaker from Versailles, enrolled in the 3rd revolutionary squadron, and accused of having referred to the Parisian *armée* as an army of brigands. In his defence Millart claimed 'that he could not be entirely patriotic; for as a wigmaker he had little experience of such and had attended only people who were not themselves patriots and became angry when called citizens' (Arch. Seine-et-Oise, IV Q 186, interrogation of Millart, 15 Brumaire year II). Men like Millart were not true royalists, but as prisoners of their ignorance and their clientele, it was difficult for them to opt for the Revolution. The *sans-culottes* were right to distrust hairdressers, wigmakers and former servants, the rank and file *par excel-lence* of the counter-revolution.

bandment. He then rejoined the *comité* and in the year III was described as one of those responsible for the *journées* of Germinal and Prairial in the faubourg. Parant, a carpenter, Bourse, an engraver, and Baradelle, a bookseller's assistant, all from the Pont-Neuf Section, were members of the Société des Hommes Libres, of which Baradelle was a founding member. Like Potel this young man had already been a candidate for the *armée* in June, while Bourse was a cannoneer.[1]

Combas and Dessirié, sergeant-major and corporal respectively of the Cité Section cannoneers, were both leading *sectionnaires* and specialists in repression in the departments. These two artisans from the Notre-Dame quartier (Dessirié a foreman printer of some thirty years' standing – Combas's occupation we know nothing of) were appointed, with Fourrier, their lieutenant, as temporary jurors on the revolutionary tribunal of Brest, which had been established in Pluviôse year II by an order of the *représentants* in the Finistère. Dessirié was also appointed to the *comité de surveillance* at Brest by an order of Jeanbon Saint-André in Ventôse year II. Combas continued to be involved in republican opposition circles, and in the year IV was a subscriber to Babeuf's paper.[2]

Another specialist in repression was the concierge, Louis, called 'Brutus', a sapper in the Lepeletier Section cannoneers. After serving in Lyon, he moved on to Marseille, where Barras and Fréron, in whom he was to find powerful protectors, appointed him president of the Military Commission.[3] Despite his republican convictions (he was reported in Floréal year IV to have had frequent meetings with Parein and his aide-de-camp Corchand), Barras's support saved him from arrest on several occasions in the year IV, when he served as his secretary. But his turn came

---

[1] AN, W 394 (914) (Potel); and see Soboul, op. cit., pp. 516, 663, 853–4, 961–3. AN, F 7 4768 d 4 (Laurent). BN, MSS Nouv. acq. fr. 2713 (108) (Pont-Neuf Section – its *société* was founded 20 February 1792), and AN, BB3 80.

[2] AN, AF II 102 (750), decision of Tréhouard and Laignelot, 17 Pluviôse; AN, BB3 48 (Brest revolutionary tribunal); and Arch. Finistère, 66 L1 (reg. tribunal). At the end of the year III the three former jurors were sent to Brest and incarcerated in the château, where they remained until Brumaire year IV. For Combas in the year IV see AN, F 7 4278. At this time he lived at 145, rue des Fourreurs.

[3] AN, F 7 4774 26 d 3 (Louis) (Dufils capt., Wicht lieut.). Louis was arrested for the first time in Frimaire year II on the order of the République *comité*. The cannoneers of his Section claimed him back on the 7th of that month, and in Nivôse, the Lepeletier *comité* wrote to that of the République: 'our *comité* has no complaint against him ... on the contrary he is known as a good republican and revolutionary'. He regained his liberty in Pluviôse, when this *comité* spoke of him as being 'on mission by order of the Executive Council'. His dossier (id.) carries the words: 'Louis, called Brutus senior, ex-President of the Military Commission of Marseille'. See also Arch. Bouches-du-Rhône, L 3128 (Commission Militaire). Brutus acquired a particular reputation for brutality; see C. Lourde, *Histoire de la Révolution à Marseille et en Provence depuis 1789 jusqu'au Consulat* (Marseille, 1838), vol. III, p. 352.

eventually in the year IX, when he was deported to Cayenne to die with many other former terrorists.[1]

The forty-six-year-old Pierre Fontaine was another cannoneer who, if the surveillance of the Thermidorian police is anything to go by, must have been a formidably militant *sectionnaire*. He was a goldsmith in the Arcis Section with a workshop employing several assistants near the port Saint-Paul. Suspected of having participated in the September massacres of prisoners between Orléans and Versailles, this independent artisan, like many other Sectionary leaders, was to be accused of 'corrupting' his apprentices with his 'anarchist' ideas. Fontaine seems to have been a 'revolutionary by temperament' whose workshop, like Cardinaux's dance hall, was a school for conspiracy. He too had his place on Babeuf's lists and was another object of police surveillance in the year IV. He too would be deported in the year IX, to die in the Seychelles.[2]

Another cannoneer and leading *sectionnaire*, notably through family connections, was the thirty-eight-year-old shoemaker, Nicolas Duval, brother-in-law to Laurent Burloy, one of the 'ringleaders' of the l'Homme-Armé Section. An inhabitant of the rue des Blancs-Manteaux – departure point for the Chevalier-Desforges conspiracy of the year IX – Duval was one of those 'hommes de liaison' acting as a link between the Parisian Sectionary movement and terrorist circles in the departments. Through his brother-in-law he was connected with the artisan and small-business world of Auxerre and Vermenton, two areas in which the cannoneers of the *armée révolutionnaire* played an important role, and during the years of proscription the police of Cochon and Fouché represented Duval as in contact with the 'anarchists' of the Yonne, a department in which the terrorists remained extremely active.[3]

Julien Hubert, a master carpenter of the Arsenal Section and a fusilier, was a member of the Administrative Council of the Parisian *armée*. With the master mason, Anne Grelêt, and the basket-maker Varet, he was to be accused in the year III of having been one of the main 'proposers of motions' in the Section, while Varet was denounced as an agent of the former *comité révolutionnaire*.[4] These three artisans were consequently both militant *sectionnaires* and leading figures within the *armée*. Bourdin, a fusilier and gas-lighter in the rue Mouffetard, Finistère Section, attracted the attention of Babeuf and his friends as a revolutionary patriot who

---

[1] For Louis's later career see AN, F 7 4278 (Babeuf affair). A police note dated '2e jour complémentaire an VIII' mentions his meetings with a group of enemies of the Police Minister in a café at 25, rue de Rohan, the previous Ventôse (AN, F 7 6276, Police d'État). And see APP, A A/273 (Machine Infernale), also AN, F 7 6271.
[2] APP, A A/275 (232) (Machine Infernale).
[3] APP, A A/273 (542) (Machine Infernale).
[4] APP, A/A70 (Arsenal Section – disarming of terrorists).

commanded the support of the faubourg Marceau workers.[1] Like Fontaine he also employed assistants in his own right.

Petit, a cannoneer and ribbon-maker of the Gravilliers Section, Fouques, a fusilier and fruiterer from the Droits-de-l'Homme Section, Brabant, a box-maker, and Charles Sormois, a former joiner, then jailer at La Grande Force (the last two, cannoneers of the Eude Section company), were likewise leading *sectionnaires* sufficiently well known to figure on Babeuf's lists.[2] The 'Equals' were above all interested in *sectionnaires* who had remained in touch with their colleagues in the terrorist institutions and who had sufficient influence to bring their own adherents with them. Sormois, after a decade and a half of persecution, was to end in 1814 by 'throwing himself at the foot of the throne', this veteran of the Sectionary movement proclaiming his undying loyalty to the Bourbon dynasty![3]

Vainqueurs de la Bastille are not to be found among the rank and file of the *armée*, for their veteran status entitled them to commissions. There were undoubtedly numerous combatants of 10 August, and a former fusilier was to be tried in the year IV as a Septembriseur. Of the former we know little, but two *révolutionnaires* figured on the lists of those wounded during that *journée* and in receipt of pensions from the Republic: those were Joseph Deloutte, a mason from the Gravilliers Section and a witness at the trial of Osselin, and Antoine Guy, a shoe-maker from the l'Unité Section. According to Maubant, many more of these soldiers may have taken part in the capture of the Tuileries.[4] The reputed Septembriseur was a locksmith's assistant from the Droits-de-l'Homme Section, François-Baptiste Joachim Bertrand, a young man of twenty-three and a drum-major of the Parisian *armée*.[5]

---

[1] AN, F 7 4277 (list of 'men capable of commanding').

[2] AN, F 7 4277 and F 7 4615 (Brabant).

[3] APP, A A/282 (398) (Machine Infernale), Charles Sormois to le comte Beugnot, director-general of the royal police, 5 September 1814. Sormois was not the only member of the Eude company to have a bone to pick with the authorities of the year III, his friend, Pierre-François Duclos, being arrested at the same time as he and liberated only on 29 Vendémiaire year IV. Duclos was a militant *sectionnaire*, a wigmaker's assistant aged 24, born in Rouen, who moved to Paris in 1791, where he married the sister of his employer and took over his shop. A member of the *comité* of the Droits-de-l'Homme Section, he resigned in September 1793 to stay in the cannoneers. But after the company was attached to the *armée révolutionnaire*, he left it to remain in Paris. He was appointed to the *comité de bienfaisance*, 15 Ventôse, presided over the general assembly of the Section on the night of 9 Thermidor and went to the Hôtel de Ville where he saw the younger Robespierre (AN, F 7 4684 d 3 [Duclos]). Like Potel, his spell of service in the Parisian *armée* was extremely brief.

[4] AN, F 15 3270 (Secours publics – those wounded in the *journée* of 10 August). AHG (*reg. d'ordre*), Maubant to the Committee of Public Safety, 3 Germinal year II: 'The enemies of the *armée révolutionnaire* should be reminded that it is composed of the men of the revolutionary *journées* who paid with their blood for the affair of the Champ de Mars.'

[5] AN, A A 55 (1521), trial of the Septembriseurs, 23 Floréal year IV.

There were also some leading terrorists who did not belong to the world of the Sections: Brault, a cavalryman in the *armée révolutionnaire*, was one of the permanent agents of the Committee of General Security.[1] The starch-dealer Massé was a Jacobin, aide-de-camp to General Hanriot,[2] and considered the leader of the Saint-Denis ultra-revolutionaries. As early as Brumaire year II the municipal *comité* of this commune denounced him as the author of 'disorganizing proposals' tending to promote civil war between the inhabitants of the commune and those of Paris.[3] Finally, on 4 September, Massé proposed to the Franciade *société* 'cutting the throats of all the inmates of the commune's prisons'.[4] That was the date of the Paris *journée*, which, in its demand for the pitiless pursuit of internal enemies, led to the creation of the Parisian *armée*. Massé was certainly thoroughly informed of the movement which was preparing in the capital. He was later accused of being the instigator of the *journée* of 3 Prairial year III, which broke out in Saint-Denis following the popular risings in Paris.[5] This is not the last we shall hear of this violent and authentic revolutionary, who was in the same mould as the *commissaire des guerres*, Paris. An anonymous note of the year IX to the prefect of police was to point to him as someone worth watching: 'in the *armée révolutionnaire* he committed every possible outrage as a terrorist, anarchist and fanatical Jacobin.' It was Massé who expressed most forcibly those cherished aspirations of the less privileged popular circles, and he had all the qualities necessary to make himself detestable to the conformists of the Jacobin dictatorship.[6]

---

[1] Arch. Seine-et-Oise, IV Q 187 (Mazuel papers).

[2] *Journal de la Montagne*, no. 157 (Jacobins, session of 13 Brumaire). Massé and his friend Créton were both members of the club. See also R.C. Cobb, 'Robespierre und Boulanger', 284.

[3] Arch. Saint-Denis, 1 D 13 (General Council, session of 16 Brumaire), in which Massé and Créton were denounced as organizers of a conspiracy to turn the *sociétés populaires* and the Paris Sections against the Commune, the citizens of Paris against those of Franciade. This is a particularly interesting accusation, for the communes on the outskirts of Paris, like those of the departments, attacked the militant minority in particular, which in turn sought support from the Paris Sections. Appeals from the periphery were often the origin of missions by the *armée révolutionnaire* into the departments bordering Paris, and even more into the Yonne. Local militants of Massé's kind consequently played a major role in the activities of the *armée*. The Parisian *sociétés* and revolutionary *comités*, naturally suspicious of the outlying municipalities, eagerly took up such accusations and used them as an excuse to intervene arbitrarily in the affairs of the rural communes.

[4] AN, F 7 4784 (Franciade *comité de surveillance*).

[5] Arch. Saint-Denis, I D 14 (General Council, session of 4 Prairial year III): 'Massé is recognized as having been the intimate friend of Collot-d'Herbois and aide-de-camp to Hanriot . . . We have reason to believe that the troubles which have erupted in this commune were the result of suggestions by the said Massé and Creton.' As early as 29 Germinal year II, the municipality had refused them *certificats de civisme*.

[6] See APP, A A/281 (294) (Machine Infernale) for the note of the year IX. If the numerous denunciations of the Franciade inhabitants are to be believed, Massé was even a former

The turbulent Étienne Jourdan, protégé of Ronsin and drum-major of the *armée révolutionnaire*, should be placed in the same category. He was thirty-eight years old and had spent sixteen of them in the army. A native of Alès in the Gard, he was to claim relationship with the celebrated 'Coupe-Tête' during the Terror, only to deny it later when it became compromising. In May 1793, while serving in the Vendée with his battalion, despite his illiteracy, he was employed by Ronsin as his aide-de-camp. Even at this date his drunken habits were getting him into trouble with the Tours *comité révolutionnaire*, which demanded his removal after he had caused a number of brawls in the cafés. But despite his bad reputation, Ronsin remembered him when the Parisian *armée* was organized, and secured for him his position of drum-major in the Guillaume-Tell company. On detachment to le Havre he got into more mischief. When he left the *armée* he lived in straitened circumstances and filled in as a replacement in the guard of his Section. In Frimaire year III he was again arrested following disturbances in a café and in the year IV police reports refer to him as at the head of a clandestine meeting of terrorist leaders at the château de Bercy. Jourdan was a primitive, violent and drunken individual; always quick to draw his sword, he had more of the career soldier in him than the militant terrorist of Massé's type, though the two types are frequently found together. But can anyone so completely illiterate really be considered a political militant?[1]

The *armée* did include among its poorest elements a minority of employees and artisans who, before their enlistment, or more often after their discharge, took part in the social agitation caused by government policy on wages. Delamare, a cannoneer and innkeeper from the Droits-de-l'Homme Section, was accused of having taken part in the pillage of the grocery shops after the troubles of February–March 1792; the activities of Chaufourier, a thirty-eight-year-old fusilier from the Mont-Blanc Section, ranged over a wider field. Successively a carter, coalman and navvy in the Rodin quarry, he was arrested in Floréal year II for having taken part in a demonstration of tobacco shredders at the Longueville town hall. At the time of his arrest his destitute wife was requesting relief from the *comité de bienfaisance* of the Section. A similar case is that of Faroux, a cloth-worker and finisher and former fusilier in the Montagne

---

servant, *valet de chambre* of Gouy-d'Arcy, and had killed two horses with sabre blows (AN, F 7* 2, reg. Committee of General Security, 1438).
[1] AN, F 7 4751 d 4 (Jourdan), and Cobb, 'La mission de Siblot au Havre-Marat', 179–80. Questioned about this mission at the Jacobins session, 9–10 Thermidor, Jourdan claimed to know nothing about it, which was probably true. The *Journal de la Montagne*, no. 57 (20 Nivôse), cites a discourse by one Mathieu Jouve Jourdan (former general of the Vaucluse *armée révolutionnaire*) at the bar of the Convention, 11 Nivôse. Was this not perhaps the brother of the drum-major, of whom he had been so proud in 1793 and the year II?

company. On his return from the *armée révolutionnaire* he entered a workshop in the Sans-Culottes Section for the manufacture of bayonets and was arrested during the winter of 1794 'for having been one of the leading participants in the workers' movement'.[1] But such cases were rare for the good reason that the *armée* contained only a small number of wage-earners capable of taking part in any agitation which condemned the *sectionnaires*. The *armée révolutionnaire* itself was charged with the repression of similar movements among the bargemen, raftsmen and workers on the waterways.

Finally, as with all revolutionary institutions, the *armée* contained a minority which opposed the regime, poor miserable wretches, whose sole crime was their open expression of their attachment to the old order of things and to the Catholic religion. With the exception of the journalist Groslay, secretary of the general staff at Lyon and editor of the paper the *Soirée des Campagnes*, none of these unfortunates could be considered as militant royalist supporters.[2] Royalists aside, this militant élite was distributed between the artillery and the infantry. In the cavalry only Brault would qualify for inclusion.

Of the 280 soldiers whose occupations we know, only about 40 were described specifically by the authorities of the years II or III as 'ring-leaders', 'notorious terrorists', leading figures of the *sociétés sectionnaires* or even, by the same token, 'men capable of commanding' in the lists of Buonarotti and Charles Germain. The smallness of the number is not simply due to lack of sources, for the dossiers of the Committee of General Security are in fact a kind of dictionary of the *sans-culotte* élites, and once again they reveal the minority aspect of the Sectionary movement: in the Parisian *armée* as in the wider domain of the Parisian Sections, a distinction must be made between the leader and the general

---

[1] AN, F 7 4644 d 1 (Chaufourier) and F 7 4714 d 3 (Faroux). See also R.C. Cobb and George Rudé, 'Le dernier mouvement populaire de la Révolution à Paris. Les journées de germinal et de prairial an III', *Revue Historique*, octobre–décembre 1955.
[2] Laurent Grison, a cannoneer of the Montagne Section and a ladies' hairdresser, was expelled from the *armée* in Pluviôse for 'counter-revolutionary words'. Vasseur, former servant of Caron, president of the Parlement of Paris, was accused of having said a king was necessary, and condemned to death by the revolutionary tribunal on 3 Prairial year II. He had been a fusilier in the Fontaine-de-Grenelle Section, Savoye, a former soldier and carter, was denounced by the Rozoy-en-Brie *comité* for royalist words, and condemned to death by the same tribunal on 8 Floréal year II. Billoré, a 26-year-old wine merchant of the Lombards Section, accused by his comrades of having used royalist and defeatist words, was more fortunate. He did not appear before the tribunal until after Thermidor and was acquitted 12 Fructidor year II. (AN, F 7 4733 d 4 [Grison], W 354 [734] [Savoye], W 370 [832] [Vasseur], W 442 [62] [Billoré], W 147 [Groslay].) For Groslay see also my *L'Armée révolutionnaire à Lyon*. And see Arch. Seine-et-Oise, IV Q 187 (Hugo to Mazuel, 27 Nivôse year II), for the cavalryman Hugo, arrested on orders from the Mont-Blanc Section and suspected of being the accomplice of Achille Duchâtelet; we do not know his fate.

mass. The militants formed but a tiny minority and for the most part Ronsin's soldiers were obscure individuals, content to follow the tide, and above all anxious not to draw attention to themselves; their political life was coextensive with the terrorist institutions to which they were attached for several months. The militants were less numerous: but each was known to the shopkeepers and artisans of his Section, and their restricted number was not necessarily a sign of weakness. Each of these men could command support from six to ten others, often drawn from among their own employees.

(ii)   UNEMPLOYMENT, BANKRUPTCIES AND OCCUPATIONAL CHANGES

The drawback of making any analysis of occupations on the basis of statistical documentation – lists of enrolments by company, for example, or of the special categories of requisitioned workers – is that such documentation disguises a major social phenomenon, accentuated after 1792, and more so after 1793, by scarcity, the cessation of the exportation and circulation of goods, and the loss of a wealthy clientele. This was the general trend towards salaried employment in the revolutionary administration of people involved in the luxury, food and clothing trades, and to a lesser extent of those artisans most affected by the scarcity of raw materials. Often service in the Parisian *armée* was but the first step towards such a salaried status, artisans, shopkeepers, former *révolutionnaires* seeking positions on their discharge as guards of sequestrated property, clerks, employees in public transportation (the great refuge of shopkeepers and wigmakers short of work), court clerks or prison warders – this last a form of administration which under the Terror experienced a sinister expansion.[1] It is rather in the individual dossier that this phenomenon, so important in the lives of the artisan and shopkeeper under the Terror, can be detected. There we can find examples of the bureaucratization of the artisan and small-business class, a process which restricted the political independence of the *sans-culottes* and at the same time encouraged the trend towards orthodoxy and conformism. An independent shopkeeper might be a 'ringleader', but a guard of sequestrated property or a prison warder was constantly obliged to think of his superiors and the government.

A further disadvantage of such 'lists' is that they fail to distinguish between the small businessman who was still prospering at the time of his enrolment, and those who sought a solution to actual employment. Many who claimed involvement in a trade or business when enrolling in the

---

[1] See R.C. Cobb, 'Quelques conséquences sociales de la Révolution dans un milieu urbain, d'après des documents de la société révolutionnaire de Lille (floréal–messidor an II)', *Revue d'Histoire économique et sociale*, xxxiv, no. 3 (1956), and *Les Armées révolutionnaires du Midi*.

armée, were declaring themselves unemployed by the time of its disbandment, seeking relief for their families and salaried positions for themselves.
The number of actual unemployed enrolled in this army was consequently much higher than suggested by the incomplete statistical
accounts.

Then we have the related problem of the numbers of shopkeepers and
small businessmen who enrolled to escape their creditors. In principle,
bankrupts were debarred from public office, and especially from such a
privileged institution as the *armée révolutionnaire*; they came under the
heading of 'proscribed groups', as did *parlementaires*, *fermiers-généraux*,
nobles, ecclesiastics and lottery officials, and one of the aims of the *scrutins
épuratoires* was to weed them out. However, this precaution was insufficient: bankrupts still succeeded in joining, some even remaining until the
end, while others were expelled after two or three months of service at the
insistence of their Sections.

Occupational instability, unemployment, bankruptcy – these were
typical problems of the period, with the more striking examples being
found in the departmental and communal *armées*, notably those of
Versailles, Lille and Bordeaux. The social composition of the Parisian
armée seems to have been on a higher level, but the papers of the
Committee of General Security provide a number of similar examples
from there too. Galand, a fusilier in the l'Homme-Armé company, a tailor
and porter on his enrolment, was asking his *comité révolutionnaire* for a
position as a guard of sequestrated property in Floréal.[1] The case of
Charles Duser is even more clear-cut: a cabinet-maker in the Gardes-
Françaises Section, he had been unemployed since the first years of the
Revolution. His enrolment only just saved him from destitution and in his
absence his wife had to seek help from the Section. After his discharge, he
approached the *comité de bienfaisance* for temporary assistance to provide
for his wife and children while he sought employment.[2]

Hachet, a forty-three-year-old fruiterer from the Tuileries Section, was
without work when he left the *armée* and requested a position in the
transportation service. Had his business collapsed in his absence, or had
he been obliged to sell up even before his enrolment? This we do not
know. Gaillard of the Gardes-Françaises Section ran a lodging-house and
café in October 1793; in Floréal he was forced to sell up at a loss to avoid
bankruptcy and proceeded to seek employment with the police. The
forty-two-year-old paper merchant Bacot, from the Marchés Section,
joined the *armée révolutionnaire* but was back at his trade in Floréal. A

---

[1] AN, F 7 4714 d 1 (Galand).
[2] AN, F 7 4698 d 1 (Duser). See also AN, F 7 4707 d 3 (Finet), Finet to the Bon-Conseil
Section general assembly, 20 Floréal year II. The assembly returned his request to the *comité
révolutionnaire* with a favourable report.

year later, however, he had abandoned it and tried to enter the *gendarmerie*, only to be rejected because of accusations that he had spoken against the Thermidorian Convention.[1] In such cases it is difficult to determine whether these small businessmen were victims of revolutionary patriotism which had caused them to enrol and neglect their businesses, left under temporary management or in the care of their wives, or whether they sought to forestall threatened bankruptcy and avert the catastrophe of unemployment (all were married with large families) by eagerly accepting the first salaried employment to present itself. There is evidence to support both hypotheses: in Germinal a number of fusiliers would try to have themselves accepted into the artillery,[2] in order to remain in the *armée*; but in the year II, and even more so in the year III, many cannoneers would ask for leave to return to Paris in order to help their wives maintain their shops. A particularly revealing example of this is the case of André-François Dupuis, who enlisted in the fusiliers because he was out of work, and in Germinal succeeded in transferring to the Popincourt company of cannoneers. In Pluviôse year III his wife was demanding his return:

> ... with work of every description difficult to find [she explained], the working class sought to support their families, and my husband ... decided therefore ... as much from republicanism as love of his family [to enrol in his Section's company of fusiliers] ... after its disbandment ... wishing still to be of use to his country, he enrolled in the cannoneers on pay of 42 sols per day.

Having been assured that the pay would remain the same when they were away, he and his colleagues left Paris, 'content in the knowledge that they would be able to continue to support their families'. But the family could not live on the sum of 15 sols to which his pay was reduced, and the wife requested his return to Paris from Tours, where his company was serving.[3] This letter gives an admirable account of the combination of self-interest and patriotism which pushed these artisans and family men to enrol in the highly paid new *armée* and then to abandon the cannoneers at the time of the reform of the year III (a reform which in fact was designed to rid the

---

[1] AN, F 7 4738 d 1 (Hachet); F 7 4714 d 1 (Gaillard); F 7 4584 d 2 (Bacot).
[2] Gilbert Laprat, a hatter's assistant, sought to move from the fusiliers to the cannoneers after the disbanding rather than return to his trade (Arch. Allier, L 851, Moulins *comité*). There were also some former fusiliers who sought to have themselves adopted by the *sociétés* as Jacobin cavalrymen in Floréal and Messidor, when Robespierrist conformism required this of the *sociétés*; see, e.g., the case of Morin, an iron-worker (Arch. Allier, L 901*, Moulins *société*), who was returned to his workshop as a requisitional worker; or the more fortunate cases of Hubert, a former soldier, and Braille, son of a Versailles tapestry-worker, who after leaving the *armée* had themselves accepted as cavaliers by the Sèvres *société* (Arch. Sèvres, *société*, 1st reg.; Arch. Versailles, 1 2 1237, Vertu Sociale *société*).
[3] AHG, Xv 45 (Dupuis's wife to the Committee of Public Safety, 12 Pluviôse year III).

artillery of that very popular element which they represented and which was so suspect to the Thermidorian authorities).

For the wigmaker, the hairdresser, the servants, coachmen and cooks of the great houses, service in the *armée révolutionnaire* offered a deferment of that unemployment which they so dreaded, and on their discharge they once more went in quest of salaried employment. Floquet, former servant to the marquis de Sillery, was doubly fortunate: profiting from his privileged position as a *révolutionnaire*, he denounced his wife as a royalist, had her imprisoned, and having rid himself of her he managed on his discharge from the *armée* to secure a position with military transport. For the seventy-year-old former wigmaker, Haumann, the *armée révolution-naire* was a happy interlude. The jeweller-enameller Dourlans was declared insolvent both in 1788 and again in Lyon, where he was living with the wife of an *émigré*, to the scandal of his colleagues who denounced his conduct to the *comité révolutionnaire* of his Section. He would be denounced again in the year III, but this time as a terrorist.[1]

Finally, there was the problem of unemployment among those formerly employed in administrations which no longer existed. Jean Ferrant, a thirty-eight-year-old fusilier sergeant, had been employed for eleven years with the Ferme Générale. In Messidor, two months after his departure from the *armée révolutionnaire* and still out of work, he asked for a position as assistant in the record office of the Plessis prison. Lavigne, also one of the General Farm's employees and a fusilier from the Guillaume-Tell Section, declared that he was without work at the time of his enrolment. Finally, the fifty-eight-year-old François Guillaume, a sergeant of fusiliers in the Maison-Commune company, and employed with the royal lottery before the Revolution, was again unemployed when he left prison in Messidor year II.[2]

The short and violent career of Claude Nicolas, a fusilier in the Bonnet-Rouge company, underlines the social mobility of those in certain marginal trades – the thin line dividing the honest artisan from the shady dealer – and reminds us of the danger of trusting in appearances. Nicolas, a twenty-five-year-old native of Flavigny, in the Nancy region, posed as a dealer in second-hand goods, a trade which prospered in such times of scarcity. But at the time of enrolment he declared himself to be a launderer. Both trades were in fact screens, for he belonged instead to the world of theft and banditry; his connections were with an itinerant group of horse- and vegetable dealers, pedlars and laundresses in the suburbs, whose real occupation was crime. Nicolas did not remain long in the *armée révolu-*

[1] AN, F 7 4775 32 d 5 (Floquet). On Haumann, see id., F 7 4733 d 4, also p. 85 above, and on Dourlans, id., F 7 4681 d 1, also p. 88 above.
[2] AN, W 174 for Ferrant; F 7 4769 d 4 (Lavigne); W 139, 159 and 168 (tribunaux révolutionnaires) for Guillaume.

tionnaire, but he retained its uniform and promoted himself bandit chief of a fictitious *armée révolutionnaire*, which, under pretext of requisition-ing, pillaged the isolated farms of the Montfort district. This real bandit would be executed in the public square of Versailles with other members of his band in Floréal year II.[1]

(iii) THE CRIMINAL ELEMENT

Claude Nicolas was the only real bandit of this *armée*, one of the only *révolutionnaires* whom we know for certain to have belonged to the crim-inal underworld. Undoubtedly other criminal elements may have entered by subterfuge and escaped the vigilance of the revolutionary authorities. But this seems unlikely given the multiple means of checking available to the *comités révolutionnaires*. Revolutionary vigilance was the order of the day; the police of the year III were very well organized, and along with political suspects and counter-revolutionaries, common criminals were likewise their victims. At no time in the eighteenth century was prostitu-tion attacked with such rigour as during the reign of the virtuous *sans-culottes*, and with Lyon swept of dangerous persons by the municipality and *comités sectionnaires*, the Parisian soldiers there were the first victims of that rigour, and they showed little gratitude for this excessive concern for their virtue.[2] In the interests of virtue and the war effort, Sectionary opinion pursued 'loose women' and men living off immoral earnings with the same severity. Despite the *scrutins*, two or three such men did manage

---

[1] Arch. Seine-et-Oise, 42 L 44 (trial of the Montfort band) and AN, D 11 1282 (437) (Comité de législation, Seine-et-Oise [Versailles]). Son of a weaver of Flavigny, Nicolas at first moved from fair to fair, from Metz to Toul, Lunéville to Reims. His business as a second-hand dealer saw him established – if such a word can be used for a man so difficult to track down – in the rue de Verneuil, Paris, around 1790. He married six weeks before his arrest, and was described in the 'Notice' to the public prosecutor as going under various names and trades. This 'chef de bande' at the time of his arrest had invented a new mode of assassination, with a sledge-hammer made from fire supports. His predecessor as 'chef de bande' had been a former soldier, Bidault, who had deserted 17 July 1789 and lived off theft and crime there-after. He was killed in an attack on a farm near Pontchâtrain, 15 Frimaire year II, and his corpse was described as 'clothed in a sky-blue coat, with waistcoat and trousers striped blue and white, and a pistol with the barrel empty in his left hand'. The other members of the troupe were poor devils like the rabbit-skin dealer, Nicolas Lelièvre, a 40-year-old Parisian serving with military transport at the time of the attack; Guillaume Le Normand, a calico and muslin dealer, aged 41, and a native of Mortagne; Nicolas Rochaux, a second-hand dealer from Paris, aged 26; François-Xavier Gohier, a former servant, then a tailor estab-lished in Paris, aged 31; François Le Blanc, a Versailles locksmith, aged 38; Louis Bûché, a rabbit-skin dealer and tiler, aged 40; Jean-Jacques Loy, called 'Vaudry', a horse dealer living in Paris, aged 24; Jean Langlois, a baker's assistant working in Versailles, aged 32; Toussaint Chambellan, a grocer-haberdasher, living at Versailles, aged 33; Germain Garçon, livestock dealer from the Beauce, aged 39; and Antoine Vidalin, who hired out horses, from the Auvergne, aged 33. All of these men had changed trades and homes frequently, and had only been in Paris a short period. Two at least were deserters. This was 'l'armée du crime'.

[2] *L'Armée révolutionnaire à Lyon*, pp. 9–10.

to enter the *armée*, but these were rare cases.[1] It was more common for the *révolutionnaires* sent on detachment to take along their wives or female companions, referred to as 'lady friends' by the prudish rural *comités révolutionnaires*, or 'hussies' by Taine. On the other hand there was at least one receiver of stolen goods, the wine merchant Busserole, a sergeant in the Gardes-Françaises fusiliers; and when police searched the furnished house of which he was either owner or manager, they found over thirty wallets in the lavatory.[2]

Nicolas and Busserole were the real criminals within the *armée*. Other unsavoury elements were only semi-criminals or criminals by accident, taking advantage of their new situation to make unauthorized requisitions. Beauchant, for example, simply filled out requisition forms on his own behalf and went round the farms in the Compiègne district; for this he was sentenced to two years' detention, in Nivôse year II.[3] Others pretended to be police inspectors and threatened those with guilty consciences[4] – though it is difficult to discover whether this was a form of blackmail, or a product of the kind of mythomania from which the adjutant-general Houssaye suffered, and which certainly existed in all the revolutionary institutions. Then there were the former soldiers who continued the unsavoury practices of the *ancien régime* army, notably that of claiming false stops en route and of misappropriating the company's effects; almost all were sergeants in the cavalry or infantry – a thoroughly dishonest lot in every epoch, without being downright criminals.[5] Finally, there was a small percentage of poor devils found guilty of petty thefts and punished with a pitiless severity out of all proportion to the crime: men like the fusilier Defresne, condemned to four years in irons for having stolen a pistol from a gunsmith's in Provins, or the cavalryman, Rabot, condemned to five years in irons for theft.[6] In Lyon in particular the

---

[1] See the case of Lassagne (AN, F 7 4767 d 2 [Lassagne]). On free unions see above, p. 74, n. 4.

[2] AN, F 7 4627 d 4 (Busserole). He was to be freed by a decision of the Committee of General Security, 21 Vendémiaire year IV (AN, F 7 4428 d 7 [57]).

[3] AN, W 307 (383) (Beauchant).

[4] See, e.g., the case of the brothers Poupart (AN, F 7 4774 81 d 4).

[5] To take but a few examples: Poupart, sgt.-major of the Montagne Section fusiliers – damage caused at Château-Thierry; Lacroix, sgt. – theft of church silver; Jacquemain, sgt. – imprisoned at Versailles for theft; Grenier, sgt., claimed expenses for false stops (AN, F 7 4774 81 d 4 [Poupart], F 7 4756 d 3 [Lacroix], F 7 4732 d 4 [Grenier]; Arch. Rhône, 42 L 2 [Commission Militaire]; AHG [*reg. d'ordre*]; Arch. Seine-et-Oise, IV Q 186–7).

[6] The fusilier Choquet was accused of having stolen 250 eggs in the Provins area. Blondel, another fusilier, had sold military effects, and Artaud, a cavalier, former captain in a battalion of line troops, had stolen the volunteers' advance pay. (AN, F 7 4648 d 2 [Choquet], F 7 4581 d 5 [Artaud], F 7 4603 d 8 [Blondel], D 111 216, D 111 124.) The cavalier Rabot was something of an eclectic, practising thaumaturgy and inventing explosive devices at his home in rue des Prouvaires (AN, D 111 216, Rabot to the Convention, 17 Floréal year II).

Military Commission, comprised of officers and non-commissioned officers from the revolutionary garrison, punished the smallest theft with a harsh sentence of six to ten years, as if the reputation of this *sans-culotte armée* required such pitiless justice. The Lyon terrorists and *révolutionnaires* alike complained of this severity as reminiscent of the dreadful military code of the *ancien régime* army.[1]

Given the nature of the documentation, it is likely that most cases of soldiers found guilty of crimes or offences have been recorded. If so, the numbers are very small: 2 cases of men with indisputable criminal pasts, about 20 of crooked dealings in military supply, 3 or 4 of multiple swindle, in the style of Vidocq, and facilitated by the incredible confusion of the revolutionary and military government, and finally 20 or so charged with petty thefts, largely of clothing, occasioned by extreme poverty. It is difficult to accept Taine's argument, therefore, that the Parisian *armée* was composed largely of anti-social elements, former galley slaves, convicts and members of the mysterious Paris underworld. The civilians who made up the bulk of the *armée* were respectable citizens; Ronsin's *armée* was not a criminal one, and the unsavoury elements came almost entirely from among the former soldiers.

(iv) OCCUPATIONAL ANALYSIS

Of the 280 *révolutionnaires* on whose occupations we have details at the time of their enrolment or the disbandment of the *armée*, there were 118 artisans, 80 small businessmen, 19 soldiers, 11 employees, 10 countrymen, 5 'intellectuals' and 53 'undesirables'. Incomplete as this list may be, it is sufficient to underline the marked differences between the men and the officers. Among the former the military element is less important, and if artisans outnumber small businessmen it is simply an accident of documentation. Within these separate groupings the occupations which recur most frequently are shoemakers, carpenters, locksmiths, café-owners and wigmakers. The figures for the locksmiths are probably complete, thereby giving them a disproportionate importance in the group under consideration. Among the artisans the most important group (22 in all) is that associated with the furniture or building trades: 8 joiners, 2 masons, 2 stone-cutters, a carpenter, a cabinet-maker, a toymaker, a layer of wooden floors, a marble-cutter, a navvy, a glazier, a mattress-maker and a box-maker.[2] Second in importance are those in the clothing trades: 8 shoemakers, 3 tailors, 2 hatters, a button-maker and a ribbon-maker. Shoemakers,

---

[1] *L'Armée révolutionnaire à Lyon*, p. 78.

[2] Certain trades do not fit easily into a rigid classification. In what group would we place toymakers or boxmakers, for instance? The former belong in some ways with the luxury trades, since they manufactured mainly ivory pieces (crucifixes, chessboards, draughts boards) and boxwood articles. Contemporary dictionaries did indeed describe them as

threatened with requisition to make shoes for the army, flocked to take up positions in the various revolutionary bodies. Fifty artisans were involved in trades useful to the war effort: 11 locksmiths, 4 blacksmiths, 4 engravers, 4 clockmakers, 2 assistant metal-casters, 2 boiler-makers, 2 wheelwrights, a metal-gilder, a turner, a gunsmith and 27 'workers in iron' whose precise trades are unspecified. Miscellaneous trades included a journeyman saddler, a fan merchant, a clay-potter and, among the seasonal workers, 5 water-carriers from the Aveyron, 2 *commissionaires*, 2 casual workers. In addition there was a 'machinist' and 3 unspecified 'workers'.

Of the merchants and shopkeepers the food trade accounts for most, and of the 13 soldiers (all cannoneers or fusiliers) 6 were café-owners or wine merchants, 3 fruiterers, 2 caterers, one a seller of roast meats, and one a confectioner. Domestic service also furnishes an important group, 20 in all: 7 wigmakers, 6 former servants (domestic staff, footmen, coachmen), 4 apprentice jewellers and a cook. In the book trade we have a bookshop assistant, two apprentice printers and the foreman of a composing room. Related to these are an instructor, a journalist, a public letter-writer and an actor. From the country come wine-growers, day-labourers, gardeners and market gardeners, all from Paris or its suburbs, 10 in all. Eleven are described as employees: 7 clerks from Parisian government offices, 4 formerly employed with the Fermes Généraux or the lotteries. Of the 19 former soldiers, 12 were NCOs in the *ancien régime* army and 5 gendarmes. Deserters from the first requisition or from foreign armies have not been included in this category, nor those who had been soldiers only since the Revolution.

Fifty-three are listed as 'undesirables' – an impressive figure, seemingly confirming Taine's thesis. Closer examination of the figures, however, shows his exultation to have been unjustified. In the first place this list is certainly more complete than the scraps existing for other groupings and includes all or almost all of those considered 'undesirable' by the authorities of the year II: criminals and degenerates certainly, but even more so those whose origins or previous occupations rendered them suspect. So if the list includes 14 accused of theft, larceny, receiving or embezzling – and most of these were only occasional rather than professional criminals – 2 procurers, 2 adventurers, 2 swindlers, 1 or 2 highway robbers and a blackmailer, there are also 11 deserters from the first levy, 5 or 6 foreign desert-

'turners in ebony and luxury goods'. Such objects, however, were also much sought after by the ordinary people, and the Auvergne and Aveyron pedlars who sold their wares throughout France and at the Spanish fairs specialized in these articles. The trade must certainly have declined after the emigration, but it also had a popular clientele, and it would be incorrect to classify such men with the artisans of the luxury trades, the economic victims of the Revolution. As for the boxmakers, they were little more than packers, makers of cases and boxes, objects for daily use, and belonging therefore to the wood trades rather than the luxury trade.

ers, 6 former nobles, 5 ex-ecclesiastics, 4 well-off young men and 2 who can only be described as inveterate drunkards. Two-thirds of these 'undesirables' were in the cavalry; very few were in the infantry and artillery.[1]

The fragmentary lists nevertheless underline the extreme diversity in the composition of this popular force. It was a diversity reflecting that of the Parisian populace, the *sans-culotterie*, the *menu peuple*, socially so difficult to define because of the fluidity of the line dividing the revolutionary élite and the mass of the *sectionnaires* from the 'Jacobin bourgeoisie'. The Parisian *armée* can be described as *sans-culotte*, but it is difficult to be precise about a social group which brought together an entrepreneur and a master joiner, employing between four assistants and fourteen – and such employers were generally to be found in the ranks[2] – with impoverished and unemployed wigmakers, water-carriers, clerks and even joiners' assistants living in furnished accommodation. It is necessary to add, however, that the latter, the flotsam and jetsam of the Parisian population, were only a tiny percentage of this Sectionary *armée*. Such homeless individuals were unknown to their fellow citizens, who in the elections naturally tended to choose acquaintances, people who frequented the same shops and cafés. It was an *armée* of *sectionnaires*, which meant resident citizens, and it was more difficult for a stranger to enter the ranks of the infantry and artillery than to secure a place on the general staff.[3] To find

---

[1] See AN, F 7 4577–4775 for the individual dossiers on the Parisian *armée* held by the Committee of General Security (listed in my *Les Armées révolutionnaires*, vol. II [1963], Notes bibliographiques, pp. 937–42).

[2] AN, F 7 4648 d 1 (Chompré). Chompré, a cannoneer with the Lepeletier Section, was a locksmith, owning both a shop and a workshop employing four workers. He was denounced by his Section for refusing to return his effects on leaving the *armée*, conduct which the *comité révolutionnaire* found reprehensible in someone they considered as 'well off'.

[3] See, e.g., the decision taken by the Réunion *comité révolutionnaire*, 5 Nivôse (AN, F 7 2494) that 'citizens presenting themselves for the *armée révolutionnaire* ... should enrol only in their own Sections, and be supported by two citizens when they have resided less than six months in that Section'. While not entirely precluding entry to the population of the lodging-houses, it certainly rendered it much more difficult for them. Such precautions also took in deserters who had found refuge in Paris and sought to enlist in the new corps in Sections where they were unknown. (See, e.g., the case of Hocquart, 25, from the Mail Section, who sought to enlist in the Panthéon company; AN, F 7* 2530, Panthéon *comité*.) See also the observations of the Réunion Section *comité révolutionnaire*, 27 Vendémiaire, on the election of the hatter's assistant, Étienne Buisson, as fusilier captain; according to the *commissaire de police* he was unworthy to serve in the *armée*, 'since the said Buisson was someone who had done nothing for the Revolution, had been in possession of a *carte de citoyen* for no more than three months, was certainly a hatter's assistant, but had not worked for more than one month in the past six because no manufacturer would entrust him with merchandise, lives and has always lived in furnished accommodation and has no fixed abode'. The *comité* therefore decided to quash his election and the decision was approved by the assembled company. (AN, F 7 4627 d 1 [Buisson].) A certain Faucheux was rejected by the Bondy Section for similar reasons (AN, F 7 4703 d 2 [Faucheux], the Bondy *comité révolutionnaire* to the Faubourg-Montmartre *comité*, 26 Vendémiaire year II).

any large representation from the lodging-houses in an *armée révolution-naire* one must look instead to the departmental forces outside Paris, notably to that of Lille.

*

What then is the conclusion of this long chapter? Socially, officers and men of the *armée* came principally from the small-business and the artisan world, a world composed above all of resident citizens of several years' standing, known for their *civisme*, their sound morals and their honesty. In addition the infantry command contained a number of former soldiers, who themselves had become artisans or small businessmen and been quickly absorbed into the life of the Parisian districts. The composition of the cavalry was noticeably different, which goes a long way to explaining its behaviour and political indifference, and its obvious defects compromised the entire *armée* in 'patriot' opinion.

The same distinctions can be found in the political affiliations of the three branches. Because of its political indifference, the cavalry might have become a praetorian guard if its squadron leaders had been ambitious: but as prudent men and good soldiers, they avoided such dangers. The artillery was a Sectionary élite, the creature of the Sections and, in the last resort, of the Convention; it would never have risked falling under the control of any one man or group. The state of mind among the infantry was similar, though political consciousness was less developed among the fusiliers and had not reached the same level of instruction as among the cannoneers. As with the fusiliers, however, there was a militant minority among the infantry officers. But despite their independent spirit the fusiliers and cannoneers remained unfaithful to the Convention, and anyone seeking to use the Parisian *armée* against the Convention or the Revolutionary Government, even to replace it with a new system based on the *sociétés populaires*, could not have counted on the support of the officers and men of the revolutionary artillery or infantry.

One could go on indefinitely about the motives which pushed these men to enrol in a political, privileged and grossly overpaid army. Undoubtedly the decisive motives were vanity and material gain. Most of the cannoneers and fusiliers could have done without this new employment and were not dependent on the *armée* for a livelihood. Such relative independence explains their attitude towards a service for which they were not prepared to make too many sacrifices; they expected to remain near Paris and considered their enlistment as some kind of part-time employment.

It was an army of civilians, of shopkeepers and artisans, the marching wing, in the departments, of the Sectionary movement. But if the Sectionary element preserved it from the play of personal ambitions, it was the principal cause of its military weakness. A force of *sectionnaires* constantly looking back to their civilian life, to their shops or workshops, was ill prepared to implement the tasks assigned to them. They were fine when that task was the pursuit of hoarders or concealed grain, the destruction of religious objects or the application of the *maximum*; but ask them to go and conduct the repression of Lyon, Brest or Avranches, and they rebelled, the cannoneers in particular, and the *armée* was bled by increasing requests for leave and by resignations. Throughout its stay in Lyon, 5 to 10 per cent of its effective numbers were absent at any given time, on leave or in hospital rather than in detention,[1] for the sick far outnumbered the unruly and some companies presented a spectacle reminiscent of the Cour des Miracles; and when these cannoneer or fusilier shop- or workshop owners were denied leave to return to Paris, they took it anyway.[2]

All of this went side by side with a lack of respect for the officers and an inaptitude for military exercise and discipline. Former soldiers, in command of the infantry battalions, despaired of such men: the captain was at the mercy of the *révolutionnaires*, negotiating with, rather than commanding, them. There was no sign of any *esprit de corps* developing beyond the autonomy of the Sections, and unity was achieved only at company level. Assisted by time and their distance from Paris (particularly in the case of the huge detachment in Lyon), the loss of the more independent elements through leave, resignation and desertion, the process of proper militarization within the *armée* had unquestionably begun at the time of its disbandment. But it was a temporary development and there was never any question of making real soldiers out of these civilians. The Parisian *armée* was a provisional institution, formed to deal with an exceptional situation. The *révolutionnaires* could be brought to make

---

[1] Arch. Rhône, 1 L 215 (Département, effective number of troops, 20–1 Pluviôse): 2nd bn. – 206 active out of 262 (13 in hospital, 3 on leave, 39 detached on other duties, 1 only in prison); 5th bn. – 426 active out of 476 (21 in hospital, 4 on leave, 20 detached, 5 in prison); 6th bn. – 208 active out of 238 (14 in hospital, 2 on leave, 10 detached, 4 in prison); 7th bn., composed of soldiers from the Allier, Nièvre, and Loire, 339 active out of 366 (11 in hospital, 3 on leave, 11 detached, 2 in prison). For the entire infantry, 1,179 were active out of a total of 1,342, 59 of those absent being in hospital; for the cannoneers, 574 active out of 627 (18 in hospital, 10 on leave, 25 detached, none in prison at this time); for the cavalry, 142 active out of 165 (5 in hospital, 18 detached, none in prison). The sick were more numerous in the infantry and artillery than in the cavalry, composed, as we have seen, of younger men. These figures are the official ones, but if 'individual' absences and desertions are added, the numbers of absentees would be greatly increased.

[2] Peligoux, a cannoneer in the Bon-Conseil company and a dealer in used wood, impudently told his *comité* that when his officers refused his request to return to Paris to put his shop in order, so that his business could be continued by his wife and children, he took leave himself and would return to his company at Alençon when his business was completed. (AN, F 7 4774 65 d 4 [Peligoux].) Leroux, a toymaker from the Gravilliers Section, having enrolled in the artillery 'without sufficient reflection', demanded his discharge, grew impatient, and took it himself in Frimaire (id., F 7 4774 d 19).

certain sacrifices if their patriotism was appealed to; but their enthusiasm did not survive the passage of time. After three months, the cannoneers, claiming that they had been 'deceived', called for their return to Paris and were followed in this demand by many of the fusiliers. Only the cavalry-men grew accustomed to extended service, because all had good reasons for wanting to remain in the squadrons: the young men to avoid service at the frontiers; the ex-nobles and those deprived of certificates of *civisme* or of non-emigration, to avoid prison or the guillotine; the sergeants, former hussars or dragoons, because of the opportunity the marches provided for fraudulent practices; the deserters and foreigners because they found it easier than service with the 'tyrants'.

Here then was an institution which cost the Republic dear, whose members, with their independent and unaccommodating spirit, were sometimes quite intolerable, but who were nevertheless the privileged élite of the regime. The *révolutionnaires* knew how to sell their services dearly; they had precise ideas about their rights and duties and would reject in advance any service which did not fit into the narrow category of the struggle against the 'enemies of the interior'. The Revolutionary Government was accused of having emasculated this instrument of the Terror at the outset. But it was the revolutionary soldier himself who was the main cause of weakness in an institution which ought to have been ter-rifying, and miracles could not have been expected of an *armée* composed largely of Parisian *sectionnaires* who prided themselves precisely on the fact that they were not soldiers.

4

Paris and the Seine
1792–1802*

'Alors les lycéens, dans les salles d'étude, mordillant leur porte-plume ou fourrageant leurs cheveux, suivaient les derniers reflets du jour chassés par la lumière du gaz sur la courbature miroitante des grandes cartes de géographie. Ils voyaient la France tout entière; Paris posé comme une grosse goutte visqueuse sur le quarante-huitième parallèle, et le faisant fléchir sous son poids: ils voyaient Paris bizarrement accroché à son fleuve, arrêté par une boucle, coincé comme une perle sur un fil tordu. On avait envie de détordre le fil, de faire glisser Paris en amont jusqu'au confluent de la Marne, ou en aval, aussi loin que possible vers la mer.'

Jules Romains, *Le 6 octobre*

'Dans la matinée, il ficela avec du fil de fer ses vêtements de femme maculés autour d'un poids de cent livres qu'il laissa tomber dans la Seine, comme il se trouvait seul à l'arrière d'un bateau-mouche.'

Pierre MacOrlan, *La Tradition de minuit*

THE TWO MOST obvious facts concerning Paris and its environment are the forests† and the Seine. The river divided the city, divided even the mentality of the city, provided it with its principal channels of supply, in grain, in wood, in wine, and in coal. The *coches d'eau* also offered the cheapest form of collective human transport between Paris and the towns and villages of the upper and lower Seine valleys, of the Oise, the Aisne, the two Morin, the Marne, the Yonne, the Loing, the Ourcq, the Essonne, and the Bièvre. They made of Auxerre, in mental terms at least, a faubourg of Paris[1] and of Rouen, the foreport of the capital.

---

* From *Paris and its Provinces*, pp. 57–86 ('The Seine').
† The forests around Paris were the subject of the previous chapter in *Paris and its Provinces*.
[1] When, that is, the *coches* actually reached the capital. There seem to have been frequent accidents to this popular form of transport. Thus, on 3 Floréal year III [22 April 1795] the *commissaire de police* of the Section du Muséum, which was situated on the river, reports the discovery of the body of a woman of about 28 which had been recovered from the Seine.

113

The *coches* were also favoured by the humbler sort of seducer, who used the long slow hours of the journey *en aval* to prepare the terrain for the exercise of his verbal and physical talents on arrival in the metropolis. But he might equally fall victim to the apparent naïveté of young girls from the Morvan and the Avallonnais who were seeking to exercise *their* talents on a more promising and varied clientele, after having gained their first experience in the provinces. In such mixed company, it would be hard to distinguish between deceiver and deceived. The police, however, made few such distinctions; the *coches* provided them with an admirable, regular, and entirely predictable opportunity to filter the potentially more doubtful elements of an unsettled population, on arrival or on departure. For they formed a natural trap for the less intelligent malefactor and for the unimaginative deserter. There might, for instance, be nineteen such water-coaches in operation each day between Paris and Rouen, in the early years of the nineteenth century, but there was only one route that they could follow.[1]

In a very different part of the world and at the height of the Counter-Terror, the police authorities of the Directory had succeeded in rounding up the leaders of a dangerous group of highwaymen who, after operating on the mountain roads of the Loire, had decided that the place had become too hot for them and had taken this public form of transport from Lyon to the royalist stronghold of Chalon-sur-Saône: as if further to draw attention to themselves, they had chosen to travel fully armed. They were thus noticed by the navigator, who discreetly denounced them at one of the stops, so that the police were awaiting them at the following one, up river.[2] The *coches*, too, like the Seine itself, would provide a rapid and convenient receptacle for the disposal of compromising objects, including unwanted wives or mistresses.

He concluded that it must have been that of one of the passengers who had been drowned, 18 Ventôse [Sunday 8 March 1795] when the *coche* had capsized near Montereau, always a dangerous spot, especially at the time of the spring high waters, as the point of entry of the fast-flowing Yonne into the more sluggish Seine. Many Sunday travellers seem to have been drowned in this particular disaster (APP, A/A 187, commissaire de police de la Section du Muséum, 3 floréal an III). See also *The Police and the People*, p. 229 (1).

[1] AN, F11 1177, s.d. an IV. 'Les entrepreneurs des Messageries par eau de Rouen à Paris et retour, sous-propriétaires de 19 bateaux, bons et solides en état de faire le service desdites messageries jusqu'à l'an VIII ... sans réparation, à moins de force majeure ...'

[2] *Reactions to the French Revolution*, p. 231. AD, Côte-d'Or L 2658* (comité de surveillance de Dijon, séance du 18 ventôse an III): 'Reçu ... du Comité de sûreté générale ... du 13 ...: "nous vous prévenons ... que Dominique Allier ... vient de partir par le coche et passera vraisemblablement à Dijon ... taille de 5 pieds 6 pouces, visage plat et long, très gravé de petite vérole, habillé en veste chamois usé, un grand chapeau dont l'aile de derrière rabattu, cheveux blonds, sourcils & barbe de même, en marchant tenant toujours la main ouverte, les doigts très écartés ..."' Allier was believed to be the leader of the murder gangs of the Ardèche and the Rhône valley.

It was probably by the Yonne and the Seine and the canal de Briare that the dialect of the Berry had become, by the end of the eighteenth century, the principal component of Paris slang and the provider of much of the secret or semi-secret vocabulary of the argot.[1] It would be impossible, too, to exaggerate the enormous importance of the river network in the provision of the more recent and younger elements of the population of the city. Marie-Chantal Fosseuse had arrived from Nancy by way of the Gare de l'Est.[2] Eighteenth-century Lorraines, Champenoises, and Alsatian girls were to reach Paris by the Aisne, the Seine, the Meuse, and the Marne, and, as Jean Vidalenc has shown in his most recent book, the river network continued to assure the arrival of such recruits to the capital throughout the first half of the nineteenth century, and, indeed, until the construction of the railway network altered the whole balance of recent intake.[3]

It also dictated the calendar of much of the seasonal intake of casual labour or of permanent settlement. The *flotteurs*, for instance, would come down from the woodlands of the Morvan on the high spring waters, in late February or early March; very hot summers would immobilize them in the upper reaches of the smaller, shallower rivers, like the Loing, the Cure, the Essonne, and the Ourcq. By December most river traffic would be interrupted, the Seine freezing hard two or three months most winters, and even longer in the exceptional crisis of 1794 and 1795.

Within Paris, the Seine, from having been a channel of work and supply, would become the principal terrain of winter leisure, with armies of young people and children taking to its frozen surface, to slide and to skate:[4] a poor compensation, but a compensation even so for the terrible hardships caused by such winters, as well as an opportunity for the male-

---

[1] Louis Chevalier, *Les Parisiens* (Paris, 1967), p. 199. The Berrichons were also driven towards Paris by the extreme poverty of the Sologne.

[2] Pierre MacOrlan, *La Tradition de minuit.*

[3] Jean Vidalenc, *La Société française de 1815 à 1848*, II, *Le Peuple des villes et des bourgs* (Paris, 1973). Referring to the origins of Paris prostitution during these years, Jean Vidalenc notes, p. 450: 'L'apport des départements du bassin parisien était ensuite toujours prépondérant, comme si les facilités de transport par voie navigable, sur les radeaux de bois en particulier, avaient constitué un facteur favorable à ces migrations vers la capitale: plus de 300 de l'Oise, de l'Aisne, de la Somme, et aussi du Nord, relié par les canaux et rivières.' The same author states elsewhere, p. 71: 'L'attraction de la capitale ne s'exerçait pas de façon uniforme sur l'ensemble du pays. En fait, la majeure partie des Parisiens de fraîche date venaient de Seine-et-Oise ou des départements qui la bordaient; on trouvait encore un nombre important d'originaires de Normandie, de Bourgogne, des Picards, des gens du Nord et des Lorrains, mais le nombre des provinciaux d'origine plus éloignée devenait vite dérisoire.'

[4] AC, Vernon D1/6 (Conseil général de la commune de Vernon, séance du 11 nivôse an III) and AC, Saint-Germain-en-Laye D 15 (Conseil général de la commune de Saint-Germain, séance du 21 nivôse an II).

factor to avoid the dangerous filter of the bridges and to pass unnoticed by the police and their watchful agents among the crouching artisans who plied on the Pont-Neuf[1] and the Pont-au-Change.

In the hot summer months, it might similarly tempt the imprudent swimmer and bather, taking its toll of the drowned, as well as offering an easy magnet to suicide.[2] It was one of the few open spaces, at least before the Revolution (which created more of these, by opening up to the public the gardens of the Luxembourg and the Tuileries and those of some convents and monasteries, though it did little else for the poor), freely available to the common people. Judging from the almost daily reports, by the *commissaires de police* of the riverside Sections, of bodies fished out of the river during heat waves, bathing, though forbidden, must have been very widespread. In a period when cleanliness was a luxury denied to the general mass of the inhabitants, the river, too, would at least offer a ready form of personal ablution, as well as the means to avoid the expense of recourse to the laundry boats: the frequent repetition of seventeenth-century ordinances forbidding both – and goodness knows what diseases the turgid river must thus have carried in its swirling waters – would suggest that it was in fact widely used for both purposes, especially in the shallow waters just off the quai du Louvre.

Throughout the revolutionary period, the Seine valley was to be the most persistent, often the most rapid, always the most unreliable, channel of news and rumour. There is, in this respect, a constant interchange between Paris and Bray, Paris, Nogent, and Troyes, on the one hand, and between Paris, Vernon, Rouen, and le Havre, on the other. The Parisians did not need to be reminded, by journalists like Hébert, or by the officials of the *Commission des Subsistances*, that the inhabitants of Vernon, or, for that matter, of Pontoise or le Pecq, did not look favourably on the interests of the capital. And one should not really be surprised that a semi-lunatic *poissarde*, from one of the riverside Sections, should have been readily believed, even by quite literate *sans-culotte* militants, when, as a result of overhearing a conversation between grain merchants in a wine-shop near the Halle au bled, she had discovered the entrance of an underground tunnel which ran the whole way, alongside the Seine, from Rouen to le Havre, to enable the enemies of the people to export the grain set

---

[1] Cognacq, the founder of *La Samaritaine*, had started his commercial life as a pedlar on the Pont-Neuf. In 1870, he bought a shop on the quay, at the northern end of the bridge, on what was to be the site of *La Samaritaine*. It was as if he could not bear to be out of sight of the bridge and the river. In his recent book, Dr Theodore Zeldin comments: 'Cognacq really loved the theatre, where declamation recalled to him his own successes as pedlar on the Pont-Neuf': *France 1848–1945*, I, *Ambition, Love, and Politics* (Oxford, 1973), p. 110. Thus eighteenth-century habits and locations persisted well into the late nineteenth century.
[2] *The Police and the People*, p. 158.

aside for Paris, to M. Pitt, on the other side of the Channel. An exactly similar story was given equally wide credence during the Siege of Paris, in the winter of 1870–1.[1]

A slightly more credible version appears in an anonymous report addressed to the Minister of the Interior, some time in the course of the year II:

> Je préviens le C. Ministre qu'il existe encore une autre classe de scélérats au Pecq et à Saint-Germain-en-Laye. Ceux-ci sont des accapareurs de denrées de toutes espèces qui journellement mettent le peuple qui environne ce port de la Seine dans l'impossibilité de se procurer à prix d'argent ce qui lui est de toute nécessité, ils font transporter leurs denrées et ils les emmagasinent. Puis ils les font refouler vers *Triel* où dans cette commune les aristocrates qui les habitent les envoyent dans les départements en insurrection ... Cette commune [Triel] est le séjour de tous les ci-devants Conseillers du Châtelet et de Parlement, de quantité de ci-devant Colonels et capitaines et de toutes les femmes des émigrés, depuis le Pecq et Marly jusqu'à Dieppe, il n'y a pas une maison qui n'en récèle.[2]

This time, it is true, the secret route abandoned the valley of the Seine, at Rouen, to continue overland, via Tôtes, to the port of Dieppe. It was a legend that would at least have suited the much-repeated appeals of the Dieppois in favour of the construction of a canal linking their town to Paris via Forges-les-Eaux and the valley of the Oise. A little later, in the same year, Épone, which had been the ancestral home of the family of Hérault de Séchelles – the *parlementaires* seem to have had a predilection for the Seine valley – was to become an object of as much suspicion in the eyes of various Parisian authorities, including the officers and soldiers of detachments of the Paris Revolutionary Army, as Triel.[3]

In Germinal year III, it was as much the arrival of the *coche* as that of the mail-coach that imposed the date of the popular uprising, two days behind Paris, in Rouen[4] and in Évreux, as well as dictating the times of similar events in Saint-Denis and Saint-Germain-en-Laye.[5] If both the *hébertiste* and the *dantoniste* crises had such immediate repercussions in Troyes, it was not only because both Hébert and Danton were known to have close friends there. The population of Troyes had always looked to Paris, to which it was directly connected by the river life-line.[6] And no 'plot' set in Paris could have been considered complete without its

---

[1] Alistair Horne, *The Fall of Paris* (London, 1965).
[2] AN, W 151 (tribunaux révolutionnaires, Mémoire s.d.).
[3] *Les Armées révolutionnaires*, p. 506.
[4] *Terreur et subsistances*, pp. 257–305.
[5] Ibid., pp. 257–305.
[6] *Les Armées révolutionnaires*, p. 759.

ramifications in Charenton-le-Pont, in Carrières-sous-Charenton,[1] or, for that matter, in Conflans-Sainte-Honorine,[2] or Moret.[3]

The Seine made itself felt at regular intervals, in other ways too. While the right bank had been well protected by the end of the eighteenth century, with the construction of paved quays surmounted by a high stone wall,[4] the riverside areas of the left bank were exposed to seasonal flooding in February–March, the wood and wine ports of Bercy and areas of the faubourg Saint-Marceau being the most affected. The Bièvre, which ran through the Gobelins – indeed, there would have been no Gobelins without it – was a constant source of infection; and the marshland around Saint-Lazare, also annually flooded, prevented urban development in this direction, and long made the quartier Saint-Honoré and the Roule one of the most unhealthy of the city.[5]

It was much worse on the periphery. For the Parisian, the eighteenth century might have been spelled out in terms of the exceptional *crues de la Seine* – a calendar as memorable as and more visible than that of dearth and famine, and one that can still be recalled, in old picture postcards, obtainable from the *bouquinistes*, of the floods of 1910; Restif, by carving with his penknife the dates of successful seductions on the quays of the Île-Saint-Louis was no doubt trying to prove to himself that he really had become a Parisian *à part entière*. But for those living above and below the city, flooding was an annual, though terrible, occurrence, so inevitable, in fact, as scarcely to qualify for a place in the calendar of disaster that, in this great valley, a mental as well as a geographical unit, would weigh so insistently on popular memory, above all in the stark chronicle of the *années disetteuses*.

The valley of the Seine conditioned the lives of the *riverains*, above and below Paris, in less dramatic, but equally dangerous ways. Night fishing

---

[1] Primarily, I suppose, because of its name. Nothing good could be expected of a place that contained a quarry. Charenton itself was very ill-thought of. Furthermore, it was noted that on Sunday 8 December 1793, mass in the church of Carrières was widely attended, not only by the local inhabitants, but also by those of half a dozen neighbouring villages (AN, F7 4782, rapport de la municipalité de Carrières du 19 frimaire an II). Antony enjoyed a similar reputation, partly owing to the existence there of important quarries (AN, F 11 1182, 7 germinal an IV).

[2] 'La justice de paix a été demandée ici ... par rapport à sa grande population & son port qui est le plus considérable des environs de Paris ... servant de point de ralliement & de séjour à tous les bateaux montans, descendans la Haute & Basse-Seine, l'Oise et l'Aisne' (AN, BB 18 831, 9 frimaire an IV).

[3] AC, Moret (Registre IV, séance de la municipalité du 18 frimaire an II): '... que journellement plus de 200 mariniers qui conduisent des marchandises et denrées ... à Paris étaient obligés de se fournir de pain en cette commune.'

[4] Germain Brice, *Description de la ville de Paris et de tout ce qu'elle contient de plus remarquable*, 1752 ed., edited by Pierre Codet (Paris and Geneva, 1972), pp. 117, 518.

[5] Ibid., p. 314.

on the river, with the employment of lights and the use of certain types of tackle, had been specifically forbidden by a series of royal ordinances on the *Eaux & Forêts* dating back to the second decade of the reign of Louis XIV; these were still enforced, like most of the repressive legislation most likely to be directed against the poor and the disinherited, throughout the revolutionary period, though, under the Directory, such regulations were to become increasingly difficult to make into deterrents in any way effective. *Communes* like Gennevilliers, la Briche, Saint-Cloud, Sèvres, Argenteuil, and Colombes, situated in the great bends of the river, were to derive a sense of solidarity, as well as the habit of successfully defying any prohibition that came from Paris, in the massive, collective infractions of these ordinances. As a result, their inhabitants developed the mentality of *fraudeurs*, of people who lived habitually, and with impunity, outside the law. No local *juge de paix* could be expected to act in these cases; he looked the other way, failing even to report such offences.

The Revolution decentralized justice, to the advantage of local, elected authorities, just as it tended to fractionalize the forces of repression, so that the new regime, in this respect at least, tended to make things much better for all those who felt that they had a vested interest in the continuous defiance of the law, whether royal or revolutionary. It might, meanwhile, be objected, that such offences were insignificant and that they were only comparable to the sort of collective law-breaking that one associates with rural *communes*, especially those situated on the borders of two or three Departments and, even more, those placed on the frontiers of the Republic. But these were *not* really rural villages; they were mostly heavily populated with a large proportion of people in real need, even at the best of times.[1] They were *lieux de passages*, some of them actually touching the *barrières* of the capital, and the inhabitants of which had in fact half a foot in Paris itself; for we hear that many of the fishermen of Gennevilliers, for instance, would come to fish in Paris during the day, coming into contact with the *gens de rivière* and with all the most unruly elements of the quayside population, reserving the nights for the more lucrative fishing by lantern offshore from their own *commune*.

The example of their comparative impunity would speak eloquently to many of the fringe elements of the population of the capital. Equally important, from the point of view of the inhabitants of Paris, by fishing throughout the year their activities would naturally greatly reduce the total number of fish spawning in the valley of the lower Seine in its Parisian reaches. What they caught and either ate themselves or sold locally to fishmongers or, more probably, to innkeepers and *restaurateurs*

---

[1] The population of Saint-Denis in 1794 was 6,000; that of Vincennes and Saint-Mande was estimated at 4,000, including only 100 farmers.

catering for the wealthy weekend visitor,[1] was lost to the Paris fish market. This was only a short-term evil; but the habit of illegal night fishing, throughout the year – for even when the river was frozen, we hear that these ingenious people used to fish through holes in the ice – must also have compromised the future, by reducing the total fish population of the river and of its tributaries.

Even during the Terror, the revolutionary authorities never showed themselves so powerless as when attempting to deal with fishermen – whether with those who went to sea, off the Channel coast, or with those who, from Thonon, regularly supplied the Swiss *communes* on the other side of the lake of Geneva, or with those, finally, who made nonsense of more than a century of regulations imposed in the interests of the Lent needs of the population, as well as of the everyday consumption of the Parisian in a foodstuff that was cheaper, more readily available, and less subject to seasonal disasters, than bread or meat. It was above all the nearness to Paris of such *communes* that made such examples of lawlessness dangerous to public order within the city itself.

Riverside communities in the proximity of Paris were subjected to other conflicts and tensions resulting both from the sheer complication of the river and canal networks in the area and from the gigantic needs of the city's bakeries. As most of the mills situated in the Paris area, in the valleys of the upper Seine, the Marne, the Oise and its tributaries, and the many other smaller rivers that connected with them, were operated by water power, constant attention had to be paid to the level of the water used to supply the motive power of the mill wheels. During long, dry summers, milling might be brought to a standstill, while, in the spring and autumn floods of any normal year, many mills would be swept away on the high waters: and, in 1793, the years II and III, conditions were far from normal. The competing needs of neighbouring millers were a source of bitter conflicts, litigation, appeals to the *juges de paix*, and personal violence, often involving whole communities, as one miller attempted to retain the waters for the use of his own mill by constructing a dam that would thus deprive his rival downstream of motive power.

As a collectivity, the interests of the millers would also conflict with the many people like *mariniers*, *gens de rivière*, and *flotteurs* who, by the nature of their livelihood, were concerned to maintain the flow of traffic on rivers

---

[1] '*Le Portier Anglois* a 2 auberges destinées de tout temps aux rendez-vous des ci-devant nobles et qui sont tenues par des hommes égoïstes et regrettant l'ancien régime: *on ne vend plus rien, on ne fait plus rien, le temps passé était bien meilleur*, etc, tels sont leurs discours' (rapport de Rousseville sur Charenton, 16 prairial an II, AN, F7 4746 d 1, Hugot). See also F11 1177 (14 thermidor an IV): 'Certains bouchers de Paris, connus sous la désignation de mercandiers, achètent les bestiaux à mesure qu'ils arrivent sur le marché de Poissy et les revendent avec usure sur les routes et dans les auberges.'

and canals, for, by diverting the course of a stream, they were likely to lower the water level to such an extent that the waterway would no longer be navigable, so that traffic would be interrupted. In the highly-charged atmosphere of 1793–5, millers, at the best of times the objects of ingrained popular hostility on the part of townsmen, were liable to find themselves accused of having plotted to prevent the arrival, at the Paris ports, of much-needed supplies of wood, grain, and coal. The belief that the millers were deliberately exploiting their position in order to hold the inhabitants of the capital to ransom was a major factor in the deep suspicion in which Paris provisioning authorities at this time were to hold both the administrative personnel and the general mass of inhabitants of the District de Corbeil where many of the mills working for the capital were situated. The millers could, of course, reply that they too were doing their best and that the need to keep the mill wheels turning was as imperative as that, so often contradictory, of keeping the channels of communication in working order. It was the sort of conflict to which, in eighteenth-century conditions, there could be no obvious solution. Nor was it a straight conflict between millers and *gens de rivière*: the interests of farmers, carters, and itinerants were also certain to be involved, for, in their efforts to divert the course of waterways, the millers as often as not succeeded in flooding roads and fields, interrupting land communications, and destroying the crops, as well as damaging habitations. There were many complaints of this kind from the riverside *communes* of the District de Grandvilliers, in the Oise, in the course of the summer of 1794[1] and such complaints can undoubtedly witness for many others that have not been recorded, from similar areas.

Let us return a moment to the capital. The Seine had of course dictated the original location of Lutetia, and the city had gradually spread out from the original island site, a fact commemorated pictorially in the coat of arms of the city of Paris. In the eighteenth century, the most important axis of communication within the city was from north to south (rather than, as it is now, from east to west) along the rues des faubourgs Saint-Martin and Saint-Denis, the rues Saint-Martin[2] and Saint-Denis and, on the left bank,

---

[1] AD, Oise 1er registre du directoire du District de Grandvilliers (séance du 18 septembre 1793): 'Les administrateurs ont pris connoissance du mémoire présenté par les officiers municipaux de Thérines ... expositif que la construction du moulin à bled de Jacques Bourdon situé sur la rivière de Thérines vers Épaty, faisant refluer l'eau dans la rue nommée à Cailloux, la seule qui communique du hameau de Montaubert à Thérines, de manière que la communication des gens de pied, de bestiaux et de voitures est interceptée [on décide d'envoyer des commissaires sur place faire l'examen des lieux].'
[2] Saint-Martin 'a donné son nom à un quartier très-peuplé, mais le plus sale peut-être de Paris, & du moins le plus lugubre du côté de la rue Grenéta. Il y a aux environs de Saint-Martin-des-Champs 2 ou 3 marchés très incommodes, qui entretiennent sur le pavé l'humidité & l'infection: une boue noire & fétide ne sèche jamais là, même pendant l'été' (L.-S. Mercier, *Le Tableau de Paris*, X, p. 199).

the rue Saint-Jacques and the rue du Faubourg-Saint-Jacques. This put a maximum strain on three central bridges: the Pont-Neuf, the Pont-au-Change, and the Pont Notre-Dame. Congestion was worsened, at the northern end of the Pont-au-Change, by the sinister medieval bulk of the Grand Châtelet, which narrowed the rue Saint-Denis at the run-up to the bridge.[1] The result was that, at any time of the working day, the three bridges would be the scene of cursing and swearing carters, of endless and violent disputes, of spectacularly horrific accidents, as well as the meeting places of the idle, the ill-intentioned, the prophets of doom, and the mournful dirges of the street-singers, on the irresistible theme of the edifying or unedifying last minutes of such and such a bandit, as he was being broken on the wheel, place de Grève, itself adjacent to the river and within easy reach of the Pont Notre-Dame.

I have suggested elsewhere that it was regarded as a particularly heinous offence *d'avoir parlé sur le Pont-Neuf*[2] (even more, to have *shouted* there). More recently, I came across the case of two girls in their twenties, both of them out of work and starving, in the terrible summer of 1795, who ran into each other while watching a traffic accident on the Pont-au-Change. There they struck up an acquaintance made easier, in this initial stage, by the fact that they were similarly clothed, discovered that they had many grievances in common, were about the same age, and decided to walk north, once it was dark, so as to reach the open fields on the heights of Belleville, where they would steal potatoes for their next meal, and where they were caught, early in the morning, by a municipal *garde-chasse*, who brought them before the *juge de paix* of the *canton rural* of Belleville. As the girls had come from Paris, though it seems that they lived in lodging-houses there, the *juge de paix* was able, for once, to indulge in the luxury of extreme severity, in the interest, of course, of those who had elected him. In the study of the sociability of the poor, of how people establish a relationship, albeit a criminal one, the location of bridges can be a very important indication, as the *point de départ* of so many adventures that ended up happily or, more often, badly. In Lyon I have found that bridges, especially those, more familiar and much shorter, over the Saône, were a favourite point of departure in the simple, ancient, and persistent man-oeuvres of the seducer, full or part-time.[3]

The Seine was not only thus an encouragement to sociability and to petty crime. Its bridges offered a valuable source of information to police spies. An *officier de police*, provided with the detailed description of the personal appearance of a wanted person, would, almost as a first thought,

---

[1] Germain Brice, op. cit., p. 512.
[2] *The Police and the People*, p. 21(4).
[3] See Chapter 10 below.

take up his post on one of these three bridges. Sooner or later, his client, Parisian or stranger, would be forced across, on business or in search of pleasure. The left bank, after all, was not a wilderness, and it contained its own professional skills and specialities.

Finally, as a further, and indeed convincing, tribute to the importance of these bridges, it is worth recalling that army recruiters, *raccoleurs*, those intelligent and eloquent witnesses of popular habit and popular conceits, in fact social historians before their time, were prone to seek out promising material by stationing themselves prominently – and they could not be anything other than that, thanks to the plumes and feathers that they wore in their hats and that gave them something of the appearance of the eighteenth-century vision of the Noble Savage – either on the Pont-Neuf or on the neighbouring quay:

> Un grand nombre, travestis en brillans domestiques, gardaient toutes les avenues de la capitale, et allaient au-devant des rustres inexpérimentés, qui, fuyant les ingrats travaux de la campagne ... venaient chercher un maître opulent... *Le quai de la Féraille* est encore le Champ de Mars où les successeurs de ces *habiles* se promènent avec de hautes plumes sur la tête.[1]

I have never really believed in that hardy annual, the old story about the aged *concierge* in the XVIIIme or the XXme, who told a reporter that, in a lifetime in Paris, she had never seen the Tour Eiffel. Nonsense! In the eighteenth century, in any case, people would be constantly impelled towards the banks of the Seine, by need, by the indulgence of a fantasy, or to watch the fireworks on a royal, religious, or revolutionary state occasion, or, more prosaically, to buy wood, wine, flowers, old clothes, scrap-iron, locks and keys, a canary, a songbird, or a child.

In Lyon, the Rhône acted as a real frontier between the old city on the peninsula, *entre Rhône et Saône*, and the semi-rural badlands of les Brotteaux and la Guillotière, and to cross the pont de la Guillotière, even in pursuit of weekend entertainment and relaxation, was to move into another social unit.[2] The Seine, on the other hand, did not divide Paris at all in the same way.[3] The lower one goes down in the social scale, the more frequent is the transfer from one bank to another. A laundrywoman might live in Grenelle, Vaugirard, or Issy, or in le Gros Caillou, and even work

---

[1] Mercier, op. cit., X, p. 273.
[2] See Chapter 10 below.
[3] At the level of skilled trades, however, the river appears to have remained a frontier between two separate worlds well into the middle of the nineteenth century. Referring to the partial revival of *compagnonnages* during the Restoration, Theodore Zeldin notes: 'Artisans of different orders refused to work together. In Paris the river was a strict dividing line, and rival orders of carpenters, for example, each had a monopoly of employment on the left and right banks': op. cit., p. 214.

there, for these were all places, like Saint-Denis to the north, in which large-scale laundries were heavily concentrated,[1] and yet spend much of the time picking up or delivering packages in the neighbourhood of the Palais-Royal, the Roule, or the Blancs-Manteaux, in the Marais, where both the marché du Temple and the Mont-de-Piété were situated, and which, under any regime, were the object of special attention from the police. It was always as well to put at least the river between the scene of the crime and the temporary disposal of the goods that had been gained from it, thanks to the intervention of an innkeeper, an old-clothes merchant, a *revendeuse*, or some other go-between. A family group, including a mother and her two daughters and her son-in-law, after killing a merchant at dusk, as he was making his way from Paris to Saint-Denis, sold his watch to a publican in the Section des Invalides, while hiding his clothes, kept for eventual sale, in three rooms that they had leased in the same area, and in which as it turned out, they were themselves living, although they had addresses on the right bank.

In revolutionary conditions, the former *noble* faubourg would have obvious attractions to anyone trying to dispose rapidly of stolen goods; not only was it less carefully watched by the police than the Marais or the quartier Saint-Honoré, it was itself the centre of a brisk trade in the furniture, silver, and pictures of the *hôtels particuliers* of *émigrés* and suspects. Equally, those concerned in one of the many murders to have been committed in the bois de Boulogne or anywhere on the highroad from Versailles to Paris would generally have enough imagination not simply to move on into the area of the rue de Vaugirard, the rue Saint-Dominique, or the Gros Caillou, parts of the city that were nearest to the scene of the crime. A much better bet would be to cross the river and try one's luck around the Halles or the Hôtel-de-Ville, or among the numerous lodging-houses of the rue de la Verrerie. At least, there, one would be less likely to be known or recognized; for most of those who operated on the celebrated murder route between the old capital and the new, seem to have come from the western parts of the left bank, or to have moved there from the Versailles region.

Of course, I may be making too much of such obvious, elementary, native cunning. For instance, after committing a murder just beyond the barrière de Vincennes, those who had taken part made the fatal mistake of moving back into the city along the same route. And it is also true that some petty thieves – with one exception, all of them beginners – could display a quite unbelievable lack of imagination, eating, drinking, singing,

---

[1] AC, Saint-Denis 1D 1 4 (séance de la municipalité du 8 brumaire an III). The municipality points out 'que les blanchisseurs de cette commune sont dans l'usage de faire le blanchissage du linge pour les citoyens de la commune de Paris'.

shouting, and generally making themselves seen and heard by as many witnesses as possible, in a restaurant, the owner of which was, no doubt inevitably, a police informer, just around the corner from a house which they had broken into, a few hours earlier and in the course of which one of the thieves had been seen coming downstairs, loaded with stolen hats, whistling and singing, as joyful as a lark. What is more, their meal concluded, the men went back to the lodging-houses of their respective girl friends where, of course, they found a couple of *commissaires de police* waiting for them. Such crass stupidity can often make nonsense of the most carefully contrived theory of the geography of theft and of the disposal of stolen goods. Even so, I think these people cannot really witness for most.

The vital thing was to cross the river, even if one ended up at the nearest, and so most obvious, point on the other bank. Some will recall a Simenon plot at which the vantage point of observation for Maigret was a small café, several feet below the level of the pavement, quai des Grands-Augustins, that, in the 1930s – it no longer exists today[1] – was frequented almost exclusively by Flemish bargees – their boats were moored just below – and that served Stella-Artois, steak, and chips. It was from there that the *commissaire* could observe the lights in his own office, directly opposite, quai des Orfèvres. He could not have been better, or more obviously, placed; in this case, it was his intention to make himself as obvious as possible and his manoeuvre eventually produced the hoped-for results. Simenon's plot can be illustrated in reality in an event that occurred in July 1795. In the early hours of the morning of the 9th of that month [21 Messidor year III], after a very hot night, a lawyer of forty-five, named Tournay-Branchecœur, a man of means, for he owned the apartment in the arcades of the Palais-Royal, no. 23 Maison-Égalité, in which the events occurred, murdered his wife in her bed. The murder must have taken place between four and four-thirty, for, at about five, a neighbour heard the lawyer, whose step he knew, opening the front door on to the arcades, to let himself out. The murder was discovered at about six, Comminges, the *commissaire de police* of the Section de la Butte-des-Moulins, and a doctor, called out in his night-shirt, making an official report on the death at six-forty: the woman had been strangled.

The couple had been living apart for some time and Tournay-Branchecœur had started divorce proceedings, but, for some reason, the husband had decided to spend the night of the 8th to the 9th at his former home. In the course of the night, his wife had been visited by her lover (or by one of her lovers) who, while making love to her – we are not told whether the husband was in the same room or was sleeping in a neigh-

---

[1] It was called *chez Jeff*.

bouring one – had been concerned to emphasize both his presence and his activities by singing, very loudly – some of the neighbours could recall the words – a popular operetta: *Nuit charmante, nuit, sois propice à l'amour*. It is not stated how long this went on for or whether there were repeat performances, but the lover must have eventually departed, for there is no mention of his presence in the morning in the report drawn up by the *commissaire*. For the husband, the night must have been anything but charming, even if he were *en instance de divorce* and might have been supposed inured to his wife's infidelities.

Anyhow, after strangling her – and the neighbours who had been kept awake by the operetta, had heard no sound of a struggle – he opened his bureau and wrote out a note for his father-in-law explaining that he had reached the end of the road and could take no more, and asking him to look after the three children. After leaving the Palais-Royal, he had crossed the river by the nearest bridge – the old Pont-Royal – and had gone straight to a public bathing establishment, *les bains Poitevins*, on the quai d'Orsay, which, like all such places, remained open all night, hiring a *cabine* on the first floor. After he had been in the bath for over an hour, two bath attendants, who were cleaning out the bath in the next box, worried by his silence, looked through the gaps in the wooden slats and noticed that the water in the tub had turned a deep red. This was at eight o'clock, about four hours after the murder; the murderer had been dead for at least an hour, as his blood had darkened the tepid water. *Drame de jalousie*, though it seems unlikely, for the husband was in financial difficulties and may well have decided to kill himself and, only under the extreme provocation afforded by the sultry sociability of a summer night, to have been driven into this extra killing: we cannot know, so it does not really matter. The point about this episode, so worthy of Hitchcock's eager attention, is that it had to be the quai d'Orsay.

It would be inappropriate, at this stage, to discuss the new judicial and administrative units created by the Revolution and to suggest some of their effects on the relationship between Paris, the *communes* on its perimeter, and those placed on the supply lines of the capital. But it is worth emphasizing that the administrative changes thus brought about, both within Paris and in its Department, would greatly have increased the incentive to cross the river, especially if one had anything to hide; and there would be plenty of people who would be anxious to separate themselves from a recent past. Each *commissaire de police*, each *juge de paix* of the forty-eight Sections, enjoyed a considerable margin of freedom and initiative, while being extremely jealous of interference from outside: *commissaires* did, it is true, correspond with one another, even exchanging information, while they were supposed also to keep the *Bureau Central* and the Minister of Justice – and, later, the Minister of Police –

informed of the daily happenings in the restricted areas for which they were responsible. But it is rather rare to find two *commissaires*, even from adjoining Sections, working together on the same case or co-operating in the same *enquête*. The *commissaire*, like the *juge de paix*, liked to be undisturbed in the exercise of his functions. If one were either a resident or a lodger in a given Section, it was often enough, even in the conditions of the Terror, to cross the river in order to begin afresh with a judicial life at least temporarily virgin.

The river did, inevitably, also provide a fairly clear line of differentiation between different types of trades and activities. The position of the Halle aux vins, the wood market, and the horse market confined to the left bank the many activities, legitimate and semi-legitimate, or wholly illegitimate, of those more or less directly attached to these trades and of the even more numerous hangers-on that lived, seasonally or constantly, on their fringes. The adulteration of the wine drunk by the majority of the unfortunate inhabitants of Paris began, of course, at source: that is, in Clamart, Issy, Choisy, Meudon, Suresnes, Puteaux, the chief suppliers of the *vin de Paris*. According to Brice, most of the wine used by Parisians came in either from the south, via the barrière de l'Enfer[1] and the faubourg Saint-Jacques, or, by river, to Bercy; but he had in mind the palatable wines of the well-to-do. Most of the *vin de Paris* would be brought by cart, through Grenelle and Vaugirard and the rue de Vaugirard. A further stage of adulteration was reached thus either *en cours de route*, in the south-western districts of the left bank, or on arrival at the Halle aux vins, in the faubourg Saint-Marceau and Bercy, and the process was completed at the level of each individual *marchand de vin*. Those of the right bank would probably receive wine that had already gone through several stages of adulteration; but this did not prevent them from adding a few more alien elements to what was to be consumed by their customers. Adulteration began outside the city, proceeded in transit within it, and was completed on arrival, on both sides of the river. It might, however, have been considered a speciality of the left bank.[2]

The words horse dealer and horse thief were largely interchangeable and the legislation concerning the purchase and sale of horses at a fair or a market was actually to facilitate the disposal of stolen horses. The horse market was thus to provide the most valuable links between the faubourg Saint-Marceau and the left bank in general and the various bandit groups that operated with such success in the rural *communes* south of Paris, in the neighbourhood of Montlhéry and Arpajon, during the Directory. It had perhaps been a wise move on the part of the *Lieutenant de Police* to

[1] Brice, op. cit., p. 29.
[2] *Reactions to the French Revolution*, pp. 170–2.

have placed the horse market on the very edge of Paris, at a point where
the faubourg bordered on the no-man's-land of the villages of Ivry and
Choisy; at least such a location removed most of those directly concerned
in the trade well away from the centre, though some of the advantages to
be derived from this type of preventative planning must have been obvi-
ated by the fact that stables were spread evenly throughout the city, with
a maximum concentration in the faubourg Saint-Germain, where most of
the riding schools were situated, in the faubourg Saint-Honoré, in the
Palais-Royal area, and in the Marais.[1] Stables also provided a regular
refuge to adolescents and runaway children, as well as to persons who, for
one reason or another, preferred not to risk spending a night in a lodging-
house, or simply could not afford that relative luxury in a world of the
very poor. It was certainly dangerous, as we have seen, to risk bringing a
stolen horse across the river, as there would be plenty of people on the
look out for it on the bridges and their approaches. The physical descriptions of stolen horses recur almost as frequently in the daily reports of the
commissaires de police as those of wanted persons; and they must have
been easier to trace, if only because they were much less numerous. In the
1752 edition of Brice, the *abbé*'s editors calculate the total horse population of Paris at about 100,000, that is, one horse to about seven people[2] (a
proportion made much more familiar as a result of the experience of the
First World War[3]). The number would, of course, have been much less in
time of war.

Stolen horses are constantly used as a means of guiding the police
towards the identification of those who had attempted to dispose of them
within Paris, thanks to the co-operation of blacksmiths and ostlers, who,
like *logeurs* and procurers at the human level, were anxious to keep in with
the authorities, and provided them with a chain of informers spread
throughout the city, but, like the latter, heavily concentrated both in the
faubourg Saint-Marceau and in the neighbourhood of the Palais-Royal. It
will be recalled that, following the attempt on the life of the First Consul,
with the explosion of the Infernal Machine of the rue Nicaise, Fouché had
the remains of the pony that had been blown up, along with the small boy
who had been in charge of the cart, collected and stitched together by a
taxidermist, so that the stuffed animal could be shown to every blacksmith
in Paris; it was by this means that the royalist squires who had bought the
pony from a mews were eventually to be identified.[4]

---

[1] Brice, op. cit., p. 359.
[2] Ibid., p. 30.
[3] *40 Hommes 10 Chevaux*. In England, the proportion was rather more generous to bipeds.
When I began in the army, during the Second World War, we were housed four to a horse-
box, on Chepstow racecourse.
[4] Marcel Le Clère, 'Comment opérait la police de Fouché', *Revue de criminologie et de*

The horse market could then be peripheral; indeed, it was preferable that it should be, for some of the reasons that I have suggested. Horses in any case reached Paris from the south and the west, from the stock-breeding areas of the Perche, so that the trade further contributed to the activities of that dangerous south–north axis, from the barrière de l'Enfer to the faubourg and the rue Saint-Jacques, offering armies of carters, horse dealers, and drovers a last refuge, just before their entry to the city, or on their way back from it, in the numerous inns, taverns, and lodging-houses of the notorious *commune* of Montrouge, not nearly so heavily populated as the alarming plague-spot of Gentilly, its neighbour (which, according to the figures for the year III, had a population of 4,495, as compared to a total of 869 for Montrouge;[1] but both villages would count, in addition, a highly mobile floating population which would remain unaccounted for in any analysis), but certainly quite as dangerous. So the horse market really *had* to be on the left bank.[2]

The grain market, on the other hand, *had* to be central, and *had* to be on the right bank, as the grain port was there, quai du Louvre. The new Halle au bled, so much admired, both for its practical elegance and for its utilitarian distinction, by Arthur Young, had been built very near the Seine, and, one would have thought, in rather dangerous proximity also to the Louvre and the Tuileries, though, of course, neither of these was occupied as a royal residence in the eighteenth century, the Revolution, in this respect, creating a new geography of perils. It was generally possible, in the event of turbulence, to block the bridges across the Seine, between the Pont-au-Change and the Pont Louis XV, as, indeed, was done on the morning of the execution of Louis XVI, place de la Révolution. It was the fact that it had *not* been done, on 10 August, added to the passivity of the moderate battalions of the National Guard from the western districts, that may partly have accounted for the second event.[3]

On a very different occasion, on 6 February 1934, it was thanks to the presence of solid ranks of mounted *gardes mobiles* on the Pont de la

---

police technique, Geneva, January–March 1951. See also my *Terreur et subsistances*, p. 185. Nothing could be done about the small boy, who had literally been blown to pieces by the bomb that he had, unknown to himself, been carrying in the cart that had been hired along with himself and the pony.

[1] AN, F20 19 (Population, recensement de l'an III, Département de Paris, District de Bourg-l'Égalité).

[2] Livestock, too, seem to have been more numerous on the left bank. This one would expect, as the barrière de l'Enfer would be the point of entry of most of the livestock coming from the meat market of Sceaux. For instance, 39 cows are enumerated, in Brumaire year V, in the Division du Panthéon-Français, 15 of them with a single owner, Pévrier, 7, with Sonnet, 6, with Samson. There must have been plenty of fields in this very highly populated quarter (APP, A/A 202, commissaire de police de la Section du Panthéon-Français, 16 brumaire an V [6 November 1796]).

[3] Marcel Reinhard, *La Chute de la royauté: 10 août 1792* (Paris, 1969).

Concorde that finally prevented those participating in this Fascist-motivated riot from storming the Chambre des Députés in the Palais Bourbon. But, just as the prostitutes of the Palais-Royal quarter, if unduly harried by the police, would move *eastwards*, towards the rue des Lombards and the rue de la Verrerie, so riot, in the last ten years of the eighteenth century, would move *westwards*, from behind the Hôtel-de-Ville towards the Tuileries, picking up, as it went on its course, further recruits in the neighbourhood of the cornmarket. The location of the new Halle au bled had not been dictated by considerations of riot control; no one could have foreseen, when it was built, that the royal family would once more be resident in the old royal parish of Saint-Germain-l'Auxerrois. It could not have been put anywhere else. Most of the grain from the Vexin, from the Brie, the Soissonnais, and the Bassigny, as well as the Baltic supplies of dearth years, was brought by water and was unloaded at quai du Louvre. Most of the rest would be brought in by road from the north, from the grain-producing areas of the Pays de France, via the faubourg Saint-Denis and the street of the same name. The cornmarket also had to be near the Halles, in the parish of Saint-Eustache, as the provisioning trade was minutely interrelated. Topographical convenience was probably not, however, the only consideration, though, clearly, the position of the Halle au bled would be likely to impose the location of the cattle and fish markets, the latter placed very near, rue Montorgueil.

All eighteenth-century French authorities, at least at the top level, favoured Paris markets, as opposed to markets held outside the city limits. For one thing, they were easier to watch over; furthermore, being very large and dealing with goods in bulk, they were reassuring (though hardly so in times of dearth) and would thus be likely to produce lower prices. This preference in favour of the capital was an additional grievance of the *communes* of the perimeter, which, with the suppression of the *droits d'entrée*, had at first hoped for much from the Revolution. They were soon to be disappointed, though the new regime did at least maintain Poissy and Sceaux as the two traditional sites for the sale of live-stock, a decision that, in the conditions of the year II and the following year, was to offer dangerous hostages to the interests of the Parisian consumer, as it placed the inhabitants at the mercy of the fat-stock merchants and the authorities of these two *communes*. Either way, in a period of crisis, the provisioning and repressive authorities of the capital were liable to lose out, because the presence *intra muros* of huge, monopoly markets was bound to act as a magnet to riot, by gathering together in one place large numbers of people similarly motivated and often in the same trade.

Both the horse market and the grain market would attract to themselves a myriad of satellite occupations: *traiteurs, restaurateurs, gargotiers, cabaretiers, logeurs,* as well as the armies of prostitutes that plied within visible distance of either; these had to be *visible,* because horse dealers or grain merchants could not be expected to scour Paris in search of them. But they would in fact be different prostitutes, even different types of prostitutes. The *filles du Palais-Royal* did not normally cross the river; it did not occur to them to do so, and, had they done so, their reception at the hands of those in their profession on the south bank would not have been friendly. When pressed, as I have said, they moved in the direction of the east-centre. It required more flair, more refinement, better clothes, a wider vocabulary, to chat up a well-to-do grain merchant or large farmer, from the Vermandois or the Beauvaisis, than to come to terms with some coarse and undemanding horse dealer or carter from the Perche or the Beauce.

Here, for instance, is what happened to three countrymen from the neighbourhood of Senlis, Charles Mercier, miller, Louis Bourée, and Philippe Rougeau, *gardes-moulin,* when they came up to Paris on business, in the course of the winter of 1796. Writing to the Minister of Justice from Brest – they had been condemned to twenty-four years in the galleys – on 11 Germinal year V [3 March 1797], they report:

Dans le fait, nous étant trouvés à Paris, à la halle aux bleds, nous sommes entrés chez un traiteur sans autre intention que d'y prendre notre repas. Nous y fûmes abordés par 3 femmes du monde avec lesquelles nous avons ensuite passé la nuit. Elles nous prenaient certainement pour ce que nous n'étions pas, c'est-à-dire pour des riches fermiers.

En badinant, nous avons promis à chacune d'elles un deshabiller [*sic*]; elles nous ont alors pressés sur cette promesse qu'elles vouloient être effectuée à l'instant, mais nous avons dit que nous [ne] pouvions leur donner qu'après que nous aurions retiré dans un bois du ci-devant prince de Condé un trésor que nous savions y être caché. Elles nous ont tourmenté pour partir sur le champ … En parlant ainsi, nous n'avions d'autre but que de nous retirer de la compagnie de ces 3 femmes et de leur affidé [a man to whom they had been introduced at the inn]; il nous était échappé de dire que notre route étoit par Senlis. A peine le lendemain étions-nous à la barrière du Faubourg Martin et entrés chez un marchand de vin pour y déjeuner que ce nommé Bryngdly [the friend of the three ladies] et 2 autres particuliers nous ont rejoints et ne nous ont point quittés d'un instant, ils ont fait tomber la conversation sur le prétendu trésor, nous leur répondîmes que tout ce que nous en avions dit la veille étoit d'invention purement chimérique. Ils ne nous ont point quittés pour cela.

L'un de nous ayant dit qu'il savoit bien où il y avait de l'argent, mais que c'étoit dans une maison habitée, ils en ont demandé l'endroit & sur l'indication que c'étoit au moulin de Neuilly près Senlis dans un pot de terre … ils ont répondu: *tant mieux, nous allons directement à Senlis, nous savons où il y a une bonne pacotille chez un négotiant, venez avec nous, vous seriez des lâches et des poltrons si vous n'accédiez pas à notre demande.* Enfin ils ont dit qu'ils étoient sûrs de réussir et que d'un coup on en feroit deux, qu'ils sont accoutumés à ce métier et qu'ils en vivoient.

Ils ont payé à boire & nous ont forcés à les conduire à l'endroit indiqué, nous voulions les laisser entrer les premiers et nous esquiver, mais ils nous ont introduits de force, prenant l'un de nous au collet & le poussant dans la maison . . . ils se sont jettés sur le maître de la maison & sur ses enfans, les ont liés et ont demandé où étoit leur argent. Dans le même instant la force armée s'est saisie de nous, laissant libres Bryngdly & ses deux associés.[1]

Clearly their account is not entirely truthful; nor were they as innocent as they would have the Minister believe. But it is very easy to see what happened and not difficult to decide who had been fooling whom. Their business concluded, the miller and his two assistants had headed for a wine-shop within sight of the vast domed building, prepared to see what the city might have in store for them. They did not have long to wait, as is clear from their account, being very soon joined at their table by the three well-dressed ladies who appeared only too willing to make the strangers feel at home and to give them the benefit of their knowledge of Paris. The countrymen were no doubt impressed and wished in their turn to impress, directing their conversation to the subject of the purchase and sale of corn; the ladies were easily convinced, as they were meant to be, that they were in the presence of three important *blatiers* from the grainlands to the north of Paris. Their conversation, their clothing, and their accents – and anyone frequenting the cornmarket would be familiar with the various dialects of the Pays de France, the Soissonnais, the Vermandois, the Vexin, and the Brie – all clearly indicated participation in that lucrative, and, in the conditions of 1796, unbelievably, scandalously profitable, trade.

It was hard to know, at this stage, who was deceiving whom; but the ladies' interest was sharpened by the promise of a complete new set of night clothing for each of them. This would have ensured the travellers of their company for the night. But the men then overplayed their hand, by referring to the hidden treasure; it was probably at this stage that a signal from one of the women brought to their table one of their male accomplices who, like his friends, seems to have believed the story. They also made the even more disastrous mistake of letting it be known to their companions that they would be up and on their way betimes on the following morning, as they needed to be back at their homes near Senlis that same evening. The next day, early, they seem to have been able to shake off the company of those with whom they had no wish at all to

---

[1] AN, BB 18 602 (Ministère de la Justice, Oise, Mercier, Bourée & Rougeau, du bagne de Brest, au Ministre, 11 germinal an V).

travel on the homeward journey. But not only did they, predictably, take the direction of the barrière du faubourg Saint-Martin; worse still, they stopped off for a drink in a wine-shop just outside it and there they had the extremely disagreeable surprise of finding three men awaiting them, including one of their friends of the night before. There was no hope now of shaking them off. Was there not strength in numbers? And what three could do, six could do better? And were they not all men of courage, not cowards who shrank back at the last moment? Did they not know their job as well as they did theirs?

And so, in dismay and outnumbered by their alarming fellow-walkers, self-proclaimed bandits with plenty of experience behind them, they set off, after their own admission that the treasure story was a pure invention had been casually brushed aside; after all, if there were no treasure, there was always money to be taken somewhere or other. For the three country-men, it must have been an extremely gloomy journey, the gloom increasing as Senlis drew nearer. No doubt their discomfort was apparent, for, as we can see, the Parisians were not taking any chances, pushing them into the house ahead of them. It does seem rather unlikely that Mercier and his two companions were on the first operation of this kind; anyhow, it all ended up very badly for them. In the end, the joke was on the Parisians who, if denied the promised treasure, got clear away.

I quote this case at some length, not as an amusing anecdote, though it is not lacking in savour, but because the reasoning of the ladies and of their male friend should also be that of the historian, not so directly involved, not risking, for such a mixture of boastfulness and lack of discretion, a long term in the King's service, but equally concerned to suggest the probable, if not the absolutely self-evident. The ladies, with no doubt a pretty vast experience of grain merchants and their like, knew the many tenuous, yet obvious, links by which the capital was connected with its wide area of supply. When dealing with the Parisian proper, it was a matter of telling where he would be likely to be, judging by his occupation, during working hours or at leisure. When dealing with the visitor, especially if he appeared to be a man of good condition, with a stake in society and a purse full of hard cash, it was reasonable to assume that he would go out by the way he had come in. The miller and his assistants could not have followed a more predictable course in this respect. This is not so much historical guesswork as a matter of observation.

The repressive authorities make similar deductions as to the likeliest route to have been taken by malefactors or murderers, when confronted with two crimes that had been committed, both in 1804, in or on the borders of the Département de Jemappes. Writing on the subject of the first case: the murder of an old woman of seventy and of a girl of ten, in the village of Papignies, about two miles from the small town of Ath, a very important *lieu de passage* on the highroad from Lille to Brussels, at ten in the morning of Boxing Day 1803, during Mass, the Prefect informs the Minister:

> Les premières indications étaient qu'on avait remarqué les pas de deux hommes venant de la maison des personnes assassinées et deux hommes ont été en effet vus vers cette heure, venant du chemin de Tournai ... ces deux hommes ont été vus au faubourg d'Ath, peu éloigné de Papignies, vers dix heures et demi du matin, de là dans un cabaret à Rebaix [at this stage, they must have turned back in their traces] d'où ils sont sortis vers une heure pour se rendre dans un endroit près de Grammont ... ils ont paru émus, quoique s'apitoyant beaucoup sur le sort des victimes.

The two men seem in fact to have done everything humanly possible to draw attention to themselves, spending their money at an inn, going over the ground by which they had come, displaying their knowledge of the murder, and choosing a snowy day to carry out their operation.[1]

The other case is equally routine. Its interest lies in the fact that, on this occasion, the first thought of the police and judicial authorities was to keep a watchful eye on all persons using *des routes détournées et inusitées*, a deduction sensible enough when dealing with a group of people who had just carried out a large-scale robbery in a locality on the borders of a neighbouring Department, and which, in the event, completely paid off.

*

The Seine imposed other distinctions, other differentiations between the activities of north and south banks. I have said that the faubourg Saint-Marceau was especially subjected to seasonal flooding from the Bièvre, which rose even more dramatically every time the Seine rose, leaving its bed and covering wide areas with pestilential mud. It was the principal source of the foul stench of the whole area around the Gobelins. But as the quarter was already malodorous, it might as well become even more so. The Gobelins were a very smelly industry, and the faubourg, which was heavily populated, but both poor and extensive, with plenty of open space for yards and workshops, could attract other trades that were equally stinking. Most of the tanneries were located there, while, on the southern tip of the perimeter, in the very poor and very populous *commune* of Gentilly, an enterprising entrepreneur had set up, in the early years of the Revolution, on a property that he had acquired from the purchase of church lands, a tripe factory (*boyauterie*). Gentilly had, up till

---

[1] AN, BB 18 402 (Préfet de Jemappes au Grand Juge, 21 nivôse an XII). The two men were perhaps not stupid. As it was Boxing Day, they may well have been drunk.

then, been a place for Sunday walks for Parisian families and a village to which the urban artisan came to drink and to dance at weekends. The owners of the local wine-shops, restaurants, and *guinguettes* were repeatedly to complain to the municipality that the tripe manufacturèr was putting them out of business, but as he was a rich man, and they were comparatively poor, they did not succeed in having his establishment removed.[1]

Smells will recruit more smells, and the tripe manufacturerer had not been the first in the field as far as Gentilly was concerned. The village had long been an object of concern to the well-to-do and settled Parisian as the location of the infamous maison de Bicêtre, to which sturdy beggars and children convicted of theft or of other crimes were confined, awaiting their transfer either to the penal settlements on the coast or, in the case of healthy boys under sixteen, to the Navy, as *mousses*. Bicêtre had been extended and largely rebuilt at the end of the seventeenth century, a period prolific in the formation of houses of correction and of lazarettos that were generally plague spots. The stench from the place spread over a wide area and could, in certain climatic conditions, be perceived in the faubourg Saint-Jacques. Nor was this all; for, every month, the *chaîne*, formed of convicted criminals from the various Departments, would arrive there, that from Belgium, Lille, and the north first crossing the whole of Paris, on the north–south axis of the faubourg Saint-Martin to the faubourg Saint-Jacques. This was no doubt alarming enough to the more peaceable and prosperous inhabitants of Gentilly and of its neighbouring *communes*; but what must have rendered the whole of the southern perimeter of the capital an area of intense anxiety and very justified fear was the bi-annual departure, for Brest, Lorient, Rochefort, and Toulon, of the national *chaîne*, formed of all the convicts who had previously arrived in Bicêtre from such centres as Troyes, Reims, Châlons, Évreux, Rouen, Amiens, Lille, Ghent, Brussels, and Antwerp, all plentiful suppliers of criminal talent. The *chaîne* was formed up and left the Paris area each year on 25 May and 10 September,[2] both dates dangerous enough in the normal process of things, especially in a period of real or feared shortage[3] and,

---

[1] AC, Gentilly 1D1/1 (séance de la municipalité du 1er août 1793): 'depuis un mois ou environ il s'est établi sur le hameau de la Maison-blanche un marchand boyautier qui, par la putréfication des matières servant à son commerce est cause d'une exhalaison forte qui se fait sentir non seulement dans les maisons voisines mais encore dans tout le hameau, ce qui nuît extraordinairement à leur commerce en détournant de leurs maisons les chalands et les citoyens qui sortent de Paris pour prendre l'air de la campagne.' There is a further report on his activities on 2 Floréal year II, when a group of local innkeepers 'ont déclaré que ce commerce n'était pas supportable dans un hameau dont le principal commerce consiste à vendre de la viande et du vin et aussi à attirer un grand concours de monde'.

[2] Mercier, op. cit., X, p. 151.

[3] *The Police and the People*, pp. 263–9.

during the Revolution, and more especially during the Terror of the year II, fraught with even more sinister political undertones of panic and uncertainty for the future. We will have occasion later to comment on the *Grande Peur* that swept all the perimeter of Paris, and above all its southern tip, at the time of the Admirat affair, at the beginning of Prairial year II; in that year, the *chaîne* left Bicêtre on 6 Prairial which, to make matters worse, was a Sunday.[1] In the following year, its departure almost coincided with the outbreak of the Prairial Days, their suppression, and the flight of many of those who had taken part in them to the sheltering *communes* to the south.

Each departure must have been a matter of considerable alarm not only to all concerned with the operation itself, but to all those who lived in the villages through which it would pass. The route of the *chaîne* to the three penal establishments situated on the Atlantic coast can hardly have made the highroads from Paris to Orléans, Paris to Dreux, and Paris to Chartres seem more reassuring. But during the Terror and the Thermidorian Reaction, and the anarchical years of the Directory, when escapes from the *chaîne* were extremely frequent,[2] Gentilly must have been the centre of a series of shock waves radiating all over the southern quarters of Paris and the whole of the countryside to the south and the west of the capital. Most quarters of Paris would have witnessed, at one time or another, the passage of groups of manacled and chained men; but the spectacle would be the most familiar to those who lived along the north–south axis. It was no more surprising that Bicêtre and Gentilly should have figured thus so constantly in the preoccupations of all who lived anywhere near the sinister building than that Gentilly should have had the highest mortality rate of any *commune* in the Département de Paris, with 40 births, 32 marriages, and 344 deaths in 1792.[3] One must assume that this was an exceptional year.

It was almost as if successive medical and repressive authorities had followed a deliberate policy in order to make the faubourg Saint-Marceau the most unhealthy, as well as the most alarming, area of Paris. For in the late seventeenth century, the same faubourg had been made the site of the Pitié and the Salpêtrière, the two principal hospitals for the female poor, incurable, and aged. Whether their location had been originally decided upon by the fact that they were far removed from the centres of wealth

---

[1] *Concordance des Calendriers-Grégorien et Républicain* (Paris, 1963). The first departure in the year of *la chaîne* fell again on a Sunday in the years VIII, XI, XII, XIII, and XIV, on a Monday, in the years III, IX, and XV.

[2] *Reactions to the French Revolution.*

[3] AN, F20 19 (Population, recensement de l'an III, Département de Paris, District de Bourg-l'Égalité). The figure is so exceptionally high that it must indicate the existence of a devastating epidemic in the course of 1791 and 1792.

and fashion and that the Seine separated them from the Marais, I do not
know. But their presence can only have further increased the degradation
of this low-lying and underprivileged quarter; it may, of course, also have
helped the task of the medical authorities by hastening these poor women
on the road to death. They were, in any case, in good company. For on the
neighbouring Montagne Sainte-Geneviève, alongside the Faculties of Law
and Theology (the one concerned primarily with death, the other with the
life to come), and the Collèges that gave the Montagne its international
reputation, were situated, in the late eighteenth century, the Schools of
Anatomy. There are frequent complaints, during the Directory and the
Empire, by householders and property-owners of the stench caused by
the rotting and dismembered corpses thrown out in the street or piled up
in open bins in courtyards, after Dupuytren and his assistants had practised their skill on them.[1] As a result, rents tended to be low on the
Montagne, a quarter that people would be inclined to leave, as soon as
they could afford to; but few could, for there were few areas of Paris that
were poorer than Maubert-Mouffetard, and none that counted so many
elderly women, whether spinsters or widows.

The right bank, it is true, was not entirely immune in this respect, owing
to the presence of the municipal garbage heap of the notorious
Montfaucon. At the end of the eighteenth century it was used, along with
the Île des Cygnes, just outside the Paris boundaries, in the middle of the
Seine (hardly a feature likely to improve the river prospect), as the charnel
house of horses and dead animals. Whole areas of eastern Paris were regularly subjected to the stench emanating from the place. The Revolution,
thanks to the tribal violence that it had released among some sections of
the Paris population, had further contributed to these older miasmas; the
authorities of the hôpital de l'Abbaye, in the faubourg Saint-Antoine,
were to complain, in 1797, of the effects on their patients of the proximity of the newly-established cemetery in which many of the less important victims of the September Massacres, slaughtered in the Abbaye, had
been given mass graves in the shallow, sandy soil.[2] There was, in short,

---

[1] APP, A/A 202 (Section du Panthéon-Français, commissaire de police, 4 germinal an VII
[24 March 1799]): 'Un mémoire de plusieurs habitans de la rue des Carmes demandant la
suppression de l'amphithéâtre de dissection y tenu par le C. Bichat, officier de santé démon-
strateur ... pour les motifs de l'insalubrité de l'air, de l'indécence des cadavres de femmes
et d'hommes, exposés nuds aux yeux des jeunes personnes de l'un et de l'autre sexe,
l'horreur qu'inspirent ces cadavres et les dangers qu'ils font courir de la vie aux femmes,
et particulièrement à celles enceintes, enfin sur l'impossibilité des principaux locataires des
maisons voisines dudit amphithéâtre de payer leurs contributions, si leurs maisons restent
vides par un plus long séjour du C. Bichat.'
[2] AN, F15 270 (Fay, économe de l'hospice de l'Est, au Ministre de l'Intérieur, 18 germinal
an IV): 'Je vous ai exposé de vive voix les ... malheurs qui pouvaient résulter du voisinage
du cimetière de l'Abbaye, déjà nous en ressentons les effets. Une odeur cadavérique est

something of a blight on north-eastern and eastern Paris, as well as on south-eastern areas of the city. At that end of the city, both banks had this in common, if little else.

*

So much for the Seine and its numerous tributaries, a river network that so deeply conditioned the attitudes of Parisians, both towards one another, in the context of their own city, and towards a perimeter which, in terms of provisioning, would extend, even in normal years, as far as le Havre, as far as Bray, Troyes, and the valley of the Aube, as far as Montereau, and beyond, to the wood ports of the Yonne and the Cure, and the small towns and villages of the Loing, as far as Château-Thierry, Épernay, and Châlons by the Marne, as far as Soissons[1] and Neufchâtel by the Aisne, as far as Noyon, Chauny, and la Fère by the valley of the Oise, as far as la Ferté-Milon by the Ourcq,[2] and la Ferté-Alais via the Essonne. This river network offered even the most untravelled Parisian an acute awareness of his environment, an environment that extended to the Channel coast, from Dunkirk to the Seine estuary, to Burgundy and Champagne, Artois and Picardy, to the valley of the Loire.

It also imposed fixed *lieux de passage*, localities conveniently placed on the lifelines of Paris, and that would thus form a permanent map of suspicion. *These* categories of suspects, unlike the human ones,[3] did not

---

répandue dans le bâtiment qui l'avoisine, et lorsque les chaleurs vont augmenter, le reste de l'hospice en sera infecté, il est donc urgent d'arrêter sur le champ le transport des citoyens des trois Sections [du faubourg Saint-Antoine], la mortalité étant plus considérable dans ce quartier que dans les autres, vue sa population.'

[1] 'Les moulins des environs de Soissons sont inaccessibles pour les voitures ... La rivière de l'Aisne [?] qui va à Pontoise doit y transporter les grains pour y être moulus ... Les routes de Château-Thierry, de Reims, de Laon et de Paris ont des chemins ferrés ou pavés, mais il y a peu de moulins sur ces routes' (AN, F11 1177, Gilbert, commissaire à Soissons, au Ministre de l'Intérieur, 20 frimaire an IV).

[2] 'Les grains des magasins de Villers-Cotterets devront être dirigés par terre sur la Ferté-Milon où ils seront chargés sur des bateaux' (AN, F11 1177, rapport du 29 prairial an IV). See also AN, F11 1185 (s.d. prairial an IV): '... à une lieue de Mary, lieu d'embarcation pour Paris de tout ce qui descend la rivière d'Ourcq sur laquelle est située la Ferté-Milon.' Mary is opposite the port of Lizy-sur-Ourcq.

[3] And, of course, not only in 1793 and the year II. Pierre MacOrlan wrote his novel, *La Tradition de minuit*, in 1929. It centres on a *bal musette, le Bal des Papillons*, situated near the quai de Versailles, near the viaduc d'Auteuil, 'petite boutique qui sentait le port d'eau douce et les kermesses de mariniers ... le soleil animait gaiement une bande de Kabyles qui sortaient de chez un boulanger, les poches pleines de croissants chauds.' The plot centres round the murder of the owner of the bar, Noël *le Caïd*; in the course of the investigation, one of the characters, clearly au fait with the ingrained habits of the Paris police, makes the following comment: 'La police d'ailleurs est assez silencieuse. Elle prend le vent ... On va faire des rafles sur les quais et dans toutes les boîtes de Javel. Les uns pensent que l'assassin est un Kabyle ou un Chinois, et les autres pensent que c'est un affranchi du quartier.'

change: river ports like Vernon, Mantes, Meulan, Pontoise, Beaumont, Pont-Saint-Maxence, Bray, Montereau, Moret, Chauny, Meaux, Lagny, Épernay, la Fère, Soissons, and, nearer still, Gennevilliers, Argenteuil, and Saint-Germain, occupied a permanent place in the demonology of the Parisian, as he anxiously scrutinized the *mercuriales* or the height of his river.

5

'Popular Movements', Popular Protest, and Repression in France 1793–1818[*]

PART ONE   THE PATTERN OF POPULAR PROTEST 1795–1815

'A la Révolution il faut du sang.'

Attributed to a terrorist from Salon

I.   *Popular Violence*

To some extent at least, any revolution is likely to be a popular revolution; for it is impossible to overthrow an existing order – and most orders destroyed by revolutions have been repressive – by force, without at least the physical participation of a section of the common people, whether as a rebellious crowd or as a group of mutinous soldiers. Revolutions are opened – and closed – by violence. The violence is mostly provided, at least to begin with, by the common people of the towns, or by the rural poor; later, as new repressive organizations are formed to replace those swept away or dissolved, the violence may become more controlled, and may be put into the service of government and even used against those who provided the initial force to topple the previous order of things. But, as long as the exercise of government remains a matter of dispute between various groups, the opportunity and the temptation for recourse to popular violence will remain. It is likely always to take some time to push or ease the people out of a revolutionary situation once they are no longer needed. They may, it is true, be temporarily dismissed, but if the revolution is prolonged and runs into such emergencies as war, defeat, invasion, and rebellion, they are likely to come back, angrier, more vengeful, and in larger numbers. For their bodies are needed, either on the frontiers and in the armies to defend the regime and push back the forces of counter-

---

[*] From *The Police and the People*, pp. 85–211.

revolution, or at home to protect the capital and the other cities against hidden and open enemies. As the tempo of violence and terror increases, the role of the people will increase correspondingly. But, if the pace of the revolution can be slackened and the new regime stabilized at home and abroad, the people can be disbanded and sent back home, the need for violence will decrease, and what violence is retained can be exercised by specialists.

The principal weapon of the people, then, is collective violence, or the threat of it – more often the threat than the thing itself. But violence, though popular-operated, may not necessarily be used in the interest of the people, though they will always provide the physical force. A riot, once started, can be canalized by politicians into directions that suit their own purposes and that may have little relation to popular grievances. The people are indispensable, but they can be deceived: violence can be mobilized, enlisted, by the government, or by factions; through the medium of the press, journalists can designate to popular violence specific enemies who are not especially dangerous to the popular cause, while leaving unchanged general conditions that weigh most heavily on the urban poor. Violence can so often be the alibi for the absence of any coherent policy. It will always have a popular appeal which will become more insistent the longer the revolutionary crisis lasts and the more enemies of the people the crisis raises up, month by month: a number of skilful journalists and ambitious demagogues raised themselves up on the shoulders of violence and made their careers out of it; some of them – many thought rather suitably – were later destroyed by it.

Of course, violence was not the only weapon of the common people. But the threat of it was always present, not only in the crudest form of popular discontent, the riot or the demonstration, when the people surrounded the Convention, as they did confusingly often – so many *journées*, so many quasi-*journées*, that did not quite come off, or only half occurred, though they still get a date – pointing their guns on the building, even if they did not actually light their fuses. Perhaps they never intended to; but this is not the kind of question that the same legislator is ever likely to put to the test. For the eyewitness, as for the historian after him, the prudent course was to suppose that people who were pointing guns were likely to fire them if they did not get what they wanted; the best thing was to keep them waiting as long as possible, so that they went home to dinner, taking their guns with them.

Even in the most sophisticated forms of popular political activism – *le mouvement sans-culotte, le mouvement sectionnaire* – violence was always just under the surface. There were frequent hints at *la juste colère du peuple*; orthodoxy was enforced by fear, thanks to the system of voting by show of hand; the forty-eight Paris Sections, if sufficiently pushed, might combine, on some specific issue – they were always talking about it – to force the hand of the Revolutionary Government; the *sectionnaires* were constantly asking for more terror and more repression, believing that violence held the cure for most evils. The Sections themselves were powerful, even dangerous, because they controlled the artillery companies and could give the orders to trundle out the cannon *pour sauver encore une fois la République* (there was a lot of this) as a final argument when all else failed. They could do so, but at the height of their political effectiveness they very seldom did; for the *sectionnaires* ultimately showed considerable reluctance to use force against the *représentation nationale* – to do so seemed an act of political cannibalism – as long as anything was expected of it. They still preferred persuasion, though the persuading might be brutally worded. Even in the year III, they hesitated when the balance of force was still wholly on their side. We cannot then speak of crude violence, at least when dealing with the more organized political manifestations of the popular movement. It was violence tempered with unstated conventions and with a considerable respect for revolutionary legality; for such a thing existed and the *sans-culottes* really believed in it.[1]

Both contemporaries and several generations of liberal or reactionary historians were shocked by the spectacle of popular violence during the French Revolution. Contemporaries feared that these new, unexpected, and unpredictable forms of violence might be used against property-holders and respectable people, rather than against poachers and lawbreakers. In fact, what seems to have shocked contemporaries and historians alike is that the violence should have been popular (and, by implication, lawless, brutish, chaotic, undirected). Mercier, in 1797, frequently refers to the violent language of the common people, rich in incitation to murder, varied too in cannibalistic metaphor – 'j'aimerais te manger le foie', 'j'aimerais t'ouvrir le ventre et te manger les tripes', 'je voudrais manger la tête d'un bourgeois', 'mangeons une bonne fressure d'aristocrate', and so on – and he describes the evolution of this popular violence in its verbal expressions: 'Les mots *carnage, sang, mort, vengeance*, cet ABC de l'idiome jacobite [*vengeance*, in fact, belongs by right to the Thermidorian period, even on the admission of the Thermidorian local authorities] est répété, crié, hurlé ... par la *Huaille*. La *Huaille* a régné pendant près de quinze mois, a despotisé la ville.' Referring to the verb *lanterner*, he observes: 'Ce mot signifioit autrefois perdre son tems à ne rien faire ... au commencement de la révolution, il

---

[1] See the very pertinent remarks of M. Sydenham, *The French Revolution* (1965), on the subject of the popular respect for the Convention and for the recognized rules of 'revolutionary legality'.

signifioit pendre un homme à une lanterne. *Guillotiner* et *guillotine* ont pris un tel ascendant que ces mots ont totalement effacé ceux de *lanterne* et de *lanterner*.'

> J'ai entendu [he claims to recollect] crier à mon oreille: 'Que les Français périssent, pourvu que la liberté triomphe!' J'en ai entendu un autre s'écrier dans une section: 'Oui, je prendrois ma tête par les cheveux, je la couperois, et l'offrant au despote, je lui dirois: Tyran, voici l'action d'un homme libre.' Ce sublime de l'extravagance étoit composé pour les classes populacières, il a été entendu, il a réussi . . .

We may recall the women of the people, as depicted by *la Lanterne Magique*, eating the 'corps nuds et palpitans de leurs victimes'; and this was the language which, in the year III, changed sides, to be used by former terrorists when describing the horrors of the White Terror; in Pluviôse of that year, the survivors of the first wave of massacres in Nîmes – and the future victims of the next – describe the scene: 'Chacun de ces infortunés a souffert mille morts avant d'expirer, on les mutila, et les assassins couverts de sang portoient et élevoient en trophées les membres encore palpitans qu'ils venoient de couper.' There is by then a standard vocabulary of massacre. A jeweller from the Section des Lombards is accused, in a Thermidorian report, 'de s'être flatté d'avoir coupé dix-huit têtes' in September 1792, and, whatever we make of this popular boastfulness, there is no doubt as to the intentions of the man who made the report. They are as clear as those of Mercier and the lantern slide lecturer. All conveniently forgot the violence of others – of the old royal government, of the old royal army, and of *la Royale*, with its barbarous punishments; of the old penal system and the *bagne*, with its ball and chain and similar refinements; of the old police ordinances and the language of the old administration, which, when addressed to the common people, could express itself only in threats and in the promise of retribution; of the treatment of Protestant children, especially in the Généralité de Rouen; of the old ruling class, and of their servants; of the Parlements, and of the *basoche*; of the cavalier of the *maréchaussée*; of the *garde française*, so proud of his proficiency in killing quickly and hardly admissible into the inner sanctum of regimental solidarity until he had a corpse or two to his credit; of the hussar and the dragoon; of the sailor, and of the *guet* – just as everyone often tends to ignore the violence of 1795 and the years following and to forget that Terror could be White as well as Blue. Nor do they ask themselves how else the people could exercise their will and get their grievances seen to.

   Certainly an enraged crowd, a group of rioters in full cry, the repeated invitation of *A mort!* screamed like a litany, the bestiality of massacre and lynching, the near-cannibalism of some women and a very few male rioters, are repellent, dreadful, hideous, and above all depressing, just as the corpses that are strewn so copiously in every print, patriotic or counter-revolutionary, of the great revolutionary *journées* or of the great massacres are absolutely inadmissible, whatever their clothing, whichever their uniform, just as severed heads and headless bodies cry out endlessly against the Revolution and all its works.

Certainly, too, what is so often clothed over and 'historicized' as something called the 'popular movement' (how much is the historian's terminology dominated by thought of syllabus or by the search for a chapter heading?) was frequently cruel and cowardly, base and vengeful, barbaric and not at all pretty to watch. Professor Rudé's Crowd is somehow altogether too respectable; one hesitates to credit all these worthy shopkeepers and all these honest apprentices, family men too, with such horrors, and, in identifying the assailants, one is in danger of leaving the assailed out of the picture. Any honest historian of popular movements – and especially those of the French Revolution – must at times be seized with doubts. Is he not attempting to steer away from a violence that, on close inspection, becomes unbearable? Is he not trying to find excuses for brutality and murder? Is he not taking refuge in the convenient jargon of collective behaviourism to explain, to rationalize, massacre? Is there not something indecent, obscene, on his part, thus to pause, for so long, among yellowed sheets that describe, in the stilted language of French law, the details of a village lynching, or of a Christmas Day brawl ending in bloodshed? Is he not trying to get it both ways – the exhilaration of riot, experienced in the safety of a record office? Is he not making his *homme révolutionnaire* gentler, kinder, more tolerant, more whimsical, than he really was? Is he not trying to take the sting out of the *massacreur* by emphasizing the conceit, the naïveté, and the credulity of the *sans-culotte*, even if the one is not, in a particular instance, the other? Should not he, who, in fact, would never march behind the banner, would always stay at home, or who would be the first to run at the sound of firing, keep away from popular protest altogether and take refuge in the History of Parliament? Most historians of the French Revolution must have asked some of these questions, at one time or another, and especially in moments when they have been glutted with horror. And it would of course be both dishonest and misleading to represent the 'popular movement' as a study in rumbustious good fellowship, enthusiasm, generosity, fraternity, and hope, or as an early groping towards various forms of socialism, while leaving out of account the violence.

Yet this violence is not so odious and inadmissible as that of war or of diplomacy; it was never gratuitous, nor was it ever exclusive to any one class – or any one party: all classes, all parties were enthusiastic advocates of violence when there was a good chance of using it against their immediate enemies, though they tended to discover the advantages of mercy when they looked like being on the losing side. Just as riot is never an exclusive occupation (at least in Europe), just as the crowd is an evanescent, fleeting thing, so violence, in its physical form, is only incidental in a revolutionary movement rich in every possible element. The *septembriseur* was active for, at most, three days; but he had a lifetime as a shoemaker, a butcher, a shopkeeper. The blacksmith's hammer, which beat away so insistently and with such clangour that smithies had to be in backyards, from 5 a.m. to 8 p.m. in summer, from 7 a.m. to 6 p.m. in winter (no wonder the *sans-culotte* movement had the best run for its money in the autumn and winter months!), might be used once in a century on a human skull; and the butchers' apprentices, who so constantly wielded the axe, the chopper, and the knife, and whose appearance was so fearful, are said to have been the gentlest of souls, save when, rarely, roused. Violence is never excusable; but it is the job of the revolutionary historian to make it understandable – and this is perhaps already half-way to an excuse – to understand it himself, watch it rise and fall, and to keep it in its proper place, which is not on the dust-cover of a book concerned with the common people.

A much greater problem than these personal and moral ones is to estimate which types of violence were considered permissible, and which were not, in popular and in revolutionary terms. For violence was not born fully armed *tous crocs dehors* in 1789; nor did it go out of revolutionary France in 1794 or in 1799. It is always there, it always, unfortunately, has to be lived with, and it is always changing its forms. In the period under consideration, it ranged from the drunken and verbal, from fear and panic, from calculated incitement to murder, from clueless mad rumour, from carefully phrased threats, to the bloodless violence of most *journées*, to the bloody holocaust of the Tuileries, to prison blood-baths, to rural lynchings, rigged trials, and judicial murders, the death labels so generously enlarged upon by Saint-Just and Robespierre, the language of Thermidorian class vengeance, individual murders that had nothing at all to do with the Revolution (though they tended rather to be put out of business by the collective violence of the period), to private suicides (that had a lot to do with the Revolution), to religious savagery and anti-religious atrocity. Its victims were, at least by modern standards, limited in number, and, as far as the violence of the common people was concerned, were more often wood and stone, glass and china, than flesh and blood.

We must not make too much of violence, at least in its crudest form: like the Terror, like meat, it was a rare luxury, a weekend affair, or the accident of Feast Days and anniversaries. (The Revolution attempted, vainly, to cut down on the former, but multiplied the latter, the anniversary of past violence becoming the pretext for new violence.) It was much more talked about than done, and it is its comparative rarity, not its frequency, that makes it so mysterious. And the common people were not altogether to blame: they had been brought up in a bad school by the old rural police; and they were taught in a worse one by the Revolutionary Government of the year II. Later, in 1795, they had violence forced upon them; there was no other weapon left. And once the faubourg – all the faubourgs – had been disarmed, the only hope was the Infernal Machine, though this was a form of violence favoured by individual enthusiasts. It was not in the popular tradition, and came from abroad, probably from Italy. Violence and riot are one aspect – the most hopeless – of the popular movement. But as the popular movement was itself largely hopeless, they must figure large in the history of this period.

2.   Urban and Rural Riot

The history of the popular movement, in its most elemental, crudest, and most visible form, is that of the crowd, or riot, both urban and rural, though it may well be objected that a series of disconnected riots, spread over a period of six or seven years and in response to immediate and gener-ally unrelated stimuli, can hardly be described as a 'movement'. The difficulty here is that without riot there is very little left to write about. Save for a brief period of effective political activism in 1793–4, the 'popular movement' could only express itself either through the food riot or through attempted 'coalitions'. As these were illegal, they were con-sidered by the authorities as 'riotous assemblies' and so also eventually took the form of riot, or else of monster petitions that, since they brought many petitioners together in one place, would again be considered as 'assemblies' and would end, if not in riot, then in massacre. The history of the crowd, at least for Paris, has been so well covered by George Rudé that it would be both superfluous and impudent to embark on a further analysis of the various riots and *journées* which marked the history of the capital – and, in many cases, of France – between April 1789 and Vendémiaire year IV. It would in any case be difficult to pursue this par-ticular subject beyond that date; for the types of urban riot that Rudé deals with disappear entirely, at least from the Paris scene – though there are urban riots of a similar nature elsewhere in 1810–12 – for reasons that will become apparent. Rural disorders, on the other hand, scarcely ever cease; they are endemic in the period 1790–2,[1] during most of the Directory, and they were extensive at least in the north-east in 1801–2, and again in 1812–14.

The difficulty here is to distinguish between agrarian disturbances

---

[1] Michel Vovelle, 'De la mendicité au brigandage: les errants en Beauce sous la Révolution française' (Actes du 86me Congrès national des Sociétés savantes, Montpellier, 1961).

arising out of attempts to preserve seigneurial rights and so on, traditional law-breaking like smuggling and poaching, and, especially after 1795, sheer banditry. For during the Directory banditry was never purely criminal; it always took on political undertones, even in the north of France; and in the south-east it is inextricably bound up with the activities of the various murder gangs in the movements of the White Terror, so that it is impossible, in this instance, to draw a clear line between criminal violence and gang operations that are politically orientated. The operations of the *chauffeurs* may be doubtful; but they do surely represent one form at least of popular commitment and in many areas the only form, for the *chauffeurs* do not emerge on a large scale till 1795, when banditry might be the one opening left to the popular protester. The activities of the various *Compagnies*, however, quite clearly qualify for inclusion in any study of popular movements. For the White Terror was a movement which, if not led by those of popular origin, drew for its rank and file on much the same elements as Rudé's Crowd and the Paris *sans-culotterie*. It is important to remember that, on a regional basis, one of the most effective and persistent 'popular movements' during the revolutionary period was counter-revolutionary, ultra-royalist, and, to some extent, anti-urban.

3.   *Desertion and* Insoumission *1793–Year VII*

Apart from riot, early attempts at 'coalitions' (where the transport workers proved particularly effective), banditry, and White terrorism, popular protest would eventually be likely to take the form of desertion, or of *insoumission*, since a man can hardly desert from a corps he has never joined. Both are of double interest to the historian of popular protest: first of all, in their own right, as an example of increasing war-weariness and of the alienation of important sections of the common people from a regime in which they no longer felt any stake and with whose declared aims they had become increasingly out of sympathy. For, save in certain particular rural areas, desertion was not a popular phenomenon in the year II; *la resquille* was, on the contrary, one of the favourite themes of Sectionary denunciation during the period of popular militancy, and in the minutes of *sociétés populaires* and *comités de surveillance* there are frequent hints that the sons, nephews, and relatives of the well-to-do and the well-connected were less likely to end up on the frontiers or in the Vendée than those of poor artisans and shopkeepers. There are repeated popular complaints too about the readiness with which the army transport and supply services – *charrois militaires*, *habillement*, and so on – welcomed in suitably recommended *fils de famille*. We hear of the *gentilshommes charretiers*[1] and of a

---

[1] Arnaud de Lestapis, 'Gentilshommes charretiers', *Revue des deux mondes*, September 1953.

mass of *garçons perruquiers* safely employed in the *charrois* or in the hospital services, of a *fils de Conventionnel* who managed to get himself attached to the headquarters of the Revolutionary Cavalry in Versailles,[1] and of a banker's son who, though he had never set his hand to a printer's block in his life, succeeded in being taken on as a compositor at the *imprimerie des lois*.[2]

Many of these complaints, like those concerning meals in restaurants or prisons or the distribution of meat, may no doubt be attributed to jealousy, the *sans-culottes* wanting those fairly safe jobs to be reserved for their own children or even for themselves, or arguing that, if they were not to have them, then no one should, a dog-in-the-manger attitude characteristic of the popular movement throughout the French Revolution. And *sans-culotte* militants were better placed than *fils de Conventionnels* to be noisily virtuous on the subject of the patriotic 'blood tax', because most of them would not be called upon to pay it, being either over twenty-five or mobilized in skilled crafts for war production. Even so, the sense of indignation, however noisy, appears genuine; it accounts for *sans-culotte* suspicions of people like Mazuel, who, as a captain in the *fédérés* after the *10 août*, had taken such a very long time to leave Paris for Nancy (there was so much *chose publique* to be saved in Paris before he could safely deprive the capital of his vigilance), and who, as one of the leaders of the *cavalerie révolutionnaire* in the year II, managed to find excuse after excuse not to leave Versailles for Lyon, or elsewhere (a reluctance that was to cost him his head).[3] Of his staff, rather gaudy young men, mostly actors, it was likewise felt that they spent too much time consorting with courtesans and attending plays when they had no business to be in Paris at all. *Insoumission* and *la resquille* were viewed then in class terms, while desertion was, quite rightly, taken as characteristic of counter-revolutionary commitment. It could hardly have been otherwise; for deserters, being outside the law, would, like the *prêtres réfractaires*, and often with their encouragement, be driven into banditry and armed resistance. Much of the time and effort of *comités de surveillance* was taken up in 1793–4 with tracking down deserters to their village, forest, or mountain hide-outs; and much of the hostility felt by the *sans-culottes* to the farmers drew its strength from the belief that they were harbouring deserters and were even encouraging their children and their farm hands to evade military service, out of selfishness as well as out of hatred for the townsman's Republic. Even though most deserters at this stage of the Revolution were probably men of the people – the *fils de famille* did

---

[1] *Les Armées révolutionnaires*, pp. 175–6, 819.

[2] Ibid., p. 198.

[3] Ibid., pp. 131–9, and *L'Armée révolutionnaire parisienne à Lyon et dans la région lyonnaise*, p. 26.

not have to desert, because they were able to find themselves safe jobs in the cities or in the rear areas – those who encouraged them to take to the woods were not. In the year II, desertion is definitely not a form of popular protest.

The position changes already in the year III. The *sans-culottes* – or their sons – were prepared to fight for their own regime, even for that of the Jacobins; they were less enthusiastic about fighting for the Thermidorians, especially when they began to realize from letters received from their wives that, while they were revolutionizing Europe, their families were being allowed to starve at home. No doubt the main offenders were the *jeunesse dorée*, but they were *embusqués* rather than deserters, while the neo-terrorists still counted on army support. But the first *bandes* date from this period (we hear of them already, in the woods of Monville, behind Dieppe, in Brumaire year III). In the years that follow, desertion takes on the magnitude of a 'popular movement'. In the year IV volunteers and conscripts no longer desert in driblets but in large groups, *avec armes et bagages*, avoiding the bridges and commandeering boats to cross the rivers in their path westwards. In the course of that year we hear of a whole company of soldiers, in uniform, with their regimental numbers on their collars, walking from Sarrelouis, the length of half a dozen Departments, to reach the outskirts of Melun (they were from the Seine-et-Marne), without at any stage being challenged.[1] In Frimaire year IV, the Dieppe authorities hear reports of bodies of deserters, supplied with artillery and a baggage train, robbing and killing in the forests of the cantons of Envermeu and Longueville.[2] The enormous extension of desertion in the year IV and the year V – probably the peak – is the most striking testimony to the powerlessness of the Directory almost anywhere outside Paris.[3] From the year V to the year VII there are increasingly frequent reports, from a variety of Departments: Somme, Oise, Seine-et-Marne, Seine-Inférieure, Calvados, Tarn,[4] Basses-Alpes, Allier, Aisne, Gard, Vaucluse, Bouches-du-Rhône, Ardèche, Lozère – of every con-

---

[1] AN, F9 316 (Ministre de la Guerre au Ministre de l'Intérieur, 23 nivôse an IV).

[2] Arch. Seine-Maritime L 5240 (administration municipale d'Envermeu, à celle de Dieppe, s.d. frimaire an IV).

[3] A *commissaire* from Lautrec was convinced that desertion had a political origin. 'Il est persuadé que l'Angleterre, qui épie tous nos mouvements et à qui les crimes ne coûtent rien, entretient des agens dans chaque département pour rembourser aux parens les frais des garnisaires' (AN, F9 316, administration du Tarn au Ministre, 11 messidor an VII).

[4] 'Des émissaires du royalisme placés sur la route qui conduit à l'armée d'Italie depuis Saint-Pons jusqu'à Nîmes … s'emparent de nos réquisitionnaires et conscrits et après leur avoir dépeint le dénuement vrai ou faux où se trouvent nos armées et les dangers inévitables qu'ils courent en s'y rendant, les font rétrograder sur leurs foyers ou leur procurent des contre-feuilles … au moyen desquelles, côtoyant les montagnes qui entourent le levant bordant le septentrion de notre département, ils se rendent … dans quelques lieux de la ci-devant Gascogne' (AN, F9 386).

script from a given canton having returned home and living there unmo-
lested. Better still, many of them did not return home: they had never left
it in the first place. There is something splendid about defiance of government on such an impudent scale. In the year VII too the severed fingers of
right hands – the commonest form of self-mutilation – begin to witness
statistically to the strength of what might be described as a vast movement
of collective complicity, involving the family, the parish, the local authorities, whole *cantons*. The man who was out of step by then was the unfortunate *commissaire du directoire* who found himself, in small town or
village, attempting to resist the general trend. They did their best – one of
them came out with the suggestion that the young men who had cut off
their fingers should be made to parade, in women's bonnets, on the *fêtes
décadaires*. It might, he argued, revive popular interest in these ill-
attended occasions, as the common people could always be drawn by the
spectacle of someone's public humiliation or discomfort (particularly
someone known by name), and it would also shame the offenders in the
eyes of the younger female population.[1] The government also employed
such desperate remedies as the *colonnes mobiles*, garrisoning, collective
fines, the arrest of relatives, the repetition of which suggests that they were
hardly effective. Even the Empire, with a vastly more numerous and more
reliable rural police, did not succeed in more than temporarily slowing
down the speed of the haemorrhage which, from 1810, and above all from
1812, once more reached catastrophic proportions. There could have been
no more eloquent referendum on the universal unpopularity of an oppressive regime; and there is no more encouraging spectacle for a historian
than a people that has decided it will no longer fight and that, without fuss,
returns home. Prefects and Sub-Prefects did what they could to keep
desertion figures secret; but no one, not even a Napoleonic official, could
make deserters invisible. They tried at least to prevent them from crossing
back into the French part of the Empire. The common people, at least in
this respect, had their fair share in bringing down France's most appalling
regime.

4.   The Regional Incidence of Desertion

But the study of desertion and *insoumission* has another, less direct
interest in retrospective regional terms. Just as lists of subscribers to

---

[1] AN, F9 316 (Désertion, Tarn) (juge de paix du canton de Lautrec, au Ministre, 9 brumaire
an VII): 'Si l'on ne croit pas pouvoir les rendre utiles dans les armées ... ils pourroient être
condamnés à marcher le décadi à la suite de la municipalité, au milieu de quatre femmes et
portant comme elles une quenouille et une coiffe ... En punissant ainsi la lâcheté par la
honte ... on auroit l'avantage certain d'attirer aux fêtes décadaires ce public encore si indif-
férent pour les institutions républicaines mais toujours si avide de ce plaisir malin qu'on
trouve dans l'embarras d'autrui.'

Lebois and to Babeuf enable the historian to take a general count of surviving militancy two years after the collapse of *la sans-culotterie*, the study of the regional incidence of desertion offers a valuable indication of the strength or weakness of surviving Jacobinism and, for that matter, of popular militancy (by that time, largely indistinguishable) from one region to another, three or four years after the experiment in popular government. For the *sans-culotte* movement was patriotic, and long after the *sans-culottes* had disappeared as an effective, collective political force, the indignation inspired by desertion would represent one of the more characteristic attitudes of the *exclusifs* and of other surviving elements of popular militancy. By the same token, the scale of desertion, in the year V or the year VII, would offer at least a good indication of the lack of revolutionary enthusiasm of a locality, a *canton*, or an *arrondissement*, in the year II. In other words, the study of the relative incidence of desertion, like that of the reopening of churches to public worship, offers not only a crude means of measuring republican commitment at the time of the inquiry, but also an indication of the degree of revolutionary fervour of the same area three or four years previously. It would be reasonable to assume, for instance, that a *commune* which had been constantly behind on its *réquisitions*, that had given proof of stubborn ill will towards Paris or another neighbouring city, and in which the *maximum* had been evaded and the urban food commissioners and *apôtres* had been molested, would be likely to have a particularly high rate of desertion in the year VII. It could also be assumed that the rural authorities that had displayed a marked hostility to the urban consumer in the year II would be likely to give shelter to deserters in the year V.

Desertion would in any case be more widespread in the countryside than in the towns, not only because the countryside was less patriotic, less revolutionary, but also because it was easier to hide and to obtain food there. Thus the scale of desertion will further illustrate one of the central themes of the year II: the conflict between town and country. Ideally, a complete map of desertion and *insoumission*, Department by Department, *canton* by *canton*, would present a retrospective guide to local and regional attitudes to terror and repression and to the whole system of the year II.

Unfortunately, there is not sufficient material to make such a map possible on a national scale. The best we can do is a sketch map drawn from scattered areas. Even if the material existed, the figures would need to be interpreted with caution. A Department that has a very high desertion rate is not necessarily very unpatriotic and strongly opposed to the Republic. It may merely be very wild and easy to hide in. One must expect more deserters to be noted in the Nord, the Ardennes, the Moselle, the Bas-Rhin, the Somme, the Meuse, the Marne, or the Seine-Inférieure, all within easy walking distances of the various army zones, than in the Haute-Vienne or the Creuse. And the same could be said of the different regions within a Department; the authorities of the Tarn, in the year VII, complain that the northern part of the Department lends itself to desertion, owing to its inaccessibility, and we have similar complaints from the Cantal in the year IV.[1] For the deserters stated to be present in a given Department are not necessarily from that Department; on the contrary, they are almost certainly from somewhere else, for deserters, like other outlaws, are likely to be frequently on the move. In Floréal year VII, the authorities of the Oise complain of the stream of deserters passing through the Department towards the neighbouring Somme;[2] a month later, those of the Somme make similar complaints, except that the stream is now said to be towards the Oise.[3]

There are also a number of accidental factors the importance of which it is hard to calculate: the presence, in a given town, of a doctor who is known to be obliging, of a *conseil de santé* that has the reputation of being easy-going, will attract recruits from a wide area beyond the Department or the *canton*. Again, to quote the authorities of the Oise, this was why Amiens became something of a Mecca to the potential *embusqué* of the year VII. Yet at all periods the Somme had been an intensely revolutionary bastion. Much, too, will depend on the degree of zeal displayed by the local *gendarmerie*, a zeal which, the *gendarmes* being *du pays*, will be related to the general attitudes of the local population. The same could be said of rural *maires* and of local municipal authorities. It was with desertion as it had been with the *maximum*, the *recensements*, and the *réquisitions* of the year II: local officials followed the general consensus of opinion of their *administrés*, they seldom attempted to lead it; they were much more concerned first of all in gauging it, then with not colliding with it head-on, than with attempting to change it. Local officials were not heroes; and a *maire* who went out of his way to track down deserters would soon have the whole rural community on his back – to arrest a deserter was to aggress against a whole family – one had to make one's choice, it would be unwise thus to antagonize the family of a well-to-do farmer, and if one deserter was to be tolerated, then all had to be, all, at least, from the circle of wealthy property-holders. A *maire* could display

---

[1] AN, F9 316 (commissaire du Directoire dans le Tarn au Ministre, 11 prairial an VII): 'Il est d'autres cantons très ——? très populeux, qui n'en fournissent pas un seul (tant l'influence des prêtres réfractaires y est grande) et où les fuyards de tout le département sont sûrs de trouver un asile ... Les colonnes mobiles ne peuvent rien dans un pays de montagnes et de forêts', and *Les Armées révolutionnaires*, II, p. 590.

[2] AN, F9 316 (Désertion, commissaire du Directoire dans l'Oise au Ministre, 27 floréal an VII).

[3] Ibid. (commissaire du Directoire dans la Somme au Ministre, 13 prairial an VII).

his zeal on the cheap at the expense of the family of some poor woodcut-
ter or day-labourer. There was not much point in earning the congratulations of a distant *commissaire du Directoire*, of an *agent de recrutement*
with an office in the *chef-lieu*, if, before they arrived, one was to be shot
in the back from behind a hedge. So the attitudes of local authorities –
there were some exceptions, a few officials prepared to risk their lives for
the rather shabby Republic of the year IV, even in the countryside – would
reflect those of the areas in which they had to live.

It was, for instance, characteristic that, ordered by the *agent national* of
Avignon to arrest a deserter in his own home, in Thermidor year III, a
lieutenant de gendarmerie should have reported

> que ses gendarmes avoient été insultés et que cela les décourageoit beaucoup . . .
> le lendemain ledit lieutenant est venu me prévenir qu'il étoit impossible de saisir
> l'homme en question dans sa maison à cause de son immensité et la grande
> quantité d'avenues dans des jardins immenses, (qu')au surplus ses gendarmes ne
> vouloient plus lui obéir . . . qu'il étoit plus prudent d'attendre de le voir passer
> dans les rues que d'aller dans sa maison . . .

The young man had little to fear, for he belonged to one of the wealthiest
families of the city.[1] The same official had reported, a month earlier, 28
Messidor year III:

> Dans le département de Vaucluse il s'y trouve à présent environ 5 à 6,000 déser-
> teurs ou de la première réquisition . . . ils ne craignent pas de dire publiquement
> qu'ils ne veulent pas partir, et si on employoit contre eux une force médiocre,
> il est à présumer qu'il arriveroit les plus grands malheurs. Les municipalités ne
> veulent ou n'osent pas faire la moindre démarche.[2]

In the papal city, deserters from the bourgeoisie lived openly at home
throughout the Thermidorian Reaction; and in Prairial year III, they
flocked to arms, when called to put down the neo-terrorist rising in
Toulon. Fortunately, they did not have to leave, as the rising collapsed
before they had been enrolled. It was only in the *Carreterie* that it was
possible to find women whose husbands were serving in the armies.[3]

Avignon is typical both of a region notoriously hostile to the
Revolution, and of a class which, after Thermidor, preferred to fight its

---

[1] Arch. Vaucluse 3 L 26* (agent national du district d'Avignon au représentant Boursault,
15 thermidor an III). The young man, Carrière *cadet*, is denounced by the local neo-
terrorists as one of the leaders of the White Terror murder gangs in the year IV.
[2] Ibid. (agent national du district d'Avignon au représentant Réaz, 28 messidor an III).
[3] Ibid. 3 L 34* (agent national d'Avignon, au représentant Goupilleau de Montaigu, 6 prairial an III) and *Les Républicains avignonnais traduits devant le tribunal criminel de la
Drôme, au peuple français* (Valence, 24 Floréal an V).

own battles at home, in the streets of Paris and of other towns, against its class enemies, in the ranks of the *jeunesse dorée*, to revolutionizing the rest of Europe in a threadbare uniform. Duval makes no bones about having been an *embusqué*. In the northern cities, desertion was primarily a class affair, at least until the year IV, and many of the women who are stated to have taken a leading part in the *journées* of Germinal and Prairial had husbands in the armies; the fishermen's wives who led the Dieppe riots of Floréal and Prairial complained that it was particularly heartless to allow their children and themselves to starve standing up while their husbands served the Republic in the navy.[1] But the husbands were not slow to draw their own conclusions; and, as we have seen, by the year IV desertion was no longer confined to one class.

It flourished most, however, in the areas that had been the worst disposed towards the urban revolution of 1793–4. It is without surprise that one reads, in a report dated 14 Ventôse year V from the *commissaire du Directoire* at Villeneuve-la-Guyard in the Yonne, that 'nulle part la désertion n'a fait plus de progrès que dans ce canton; il y a plus de 120 déserteurs qui se refusent au départ, il y en a 16 à Villeblevin, commune qu'habite le commissaire [Lorillon], dont deux portent son nom'.[2] For this Lorillon had, in the year II, been *agent national* of the District de Sens, as well as a fervent enemy both of Paris and of the *sans-culotte* municipality of Villeblevin, which he had eventually succeeded in having removed.[3] One is not surprised to hear what a *commissaire* in the Tarn has to say in a letter of 11 Prairial year VI: 'Je ne dois pas vous dissimuler ... que les quatre détachements que nous avons fournis ne proviennent que des cantons qui ont constamment marché dans la ligne de la Révolution.'[4] In the Allier, the centre of trouble the same year is in the canton of Bourbon-l'Archambault; in the village of Ygrande 'de 23 conscrits qui sont partis, 22 sont revenus et restent tranquillement dans leurs foyers'.[5] In the year II, this *canton* had been denounced by the energetic revolutionary authorities of Moulins, Montluçon, and Gannat as a *foyer de fanatisme*, and had been subjected to the noisy attention of revolutionary battalions.[6] One is not surprised to hear the complaints of a former *commissaire* in the *canton* of Cœuvres in the Aisne, in a letter dated 20 Nivôse year V:

---

[1] Arch. Dieppe D 1 6 (séances de la municipalité des 14 et 16 prairial et du 19 messidor an III).

[2] AN, F1b II Yonne I (commissaire du Directoire près l'administration cantonale de Villeneuve-la-Guyard, au Ministre, 14 ventôse an V).

[3] *Les Armées révolutionnaires*, II, pp. 517, 521, 523–6.

[4] AN, F9 316 (administration du Tarn, au Directoire, 7 thermidor an VI).

[5] AN, F9 301 (l'agent national forestier de Cérilly, au Directoire, 7 messidor an VII).

[6] *Les Armées révolutionnaires*, II, p. 630.

Tout à coup, dès le moment que l'on a su ma destitution, on sonne les cloches avec affectation … Plus de deux tiers peut-être des volontaires partis dans le tems pour l'armée sont de retour dans leurs foyers où ils restent paisiblement. On a, par de fausses attestations complaisamment apostillées par les anti-républicains en place, fait obtenir depuis plusieurs mois des congés ou exemptions de service à plus de 20 fuyards les plus sains et les plus vigoureux de ce canton … Maintenant ils se montrent avec insolence … ils narguent impunément les parens de ceux qui sont à leurs postes.[1]

For both this Department and this District (Soissons) had shown exceptional hostility to the food commissioners of the year II, and, apart from the District de Provins and that of Sens, no place in the Paris provisioning zone had been more unpopular with the *sans-culottes* of the capital.

When, in Fructidor year VII, the administration of the Department of the Basses-Alpes sighs: 'Depuis longtems l'esprit public est nul dans ce Département',[2] it might have been echoing the denunciations of the *apôtres* from Valence and from Marseille who had been sent to evangelize the place in the autumn of 1793. In Thermidor year VII, recruiting riots break out in the canton of Goderville which, five years previously, had been repeatedly denounced for its unwillingness to carry out the requisitions in favour of the Rouen, le Havre, and Dieppe markets;[3] while, already in Messidor year II, the Dieppe authorities draw attention to the collusion between the municipality of Biville-la-Rivière and the deserters living openly in the village;[4] only a few weeks previously a group of farmers from this village had been called to Dieppe to explain why they had not supplied an eighth of the grain required of them for the market of the port. The map of desertion, at least seen through these few fragments, coincides again and again with *la carte de la mauvaise volonté* with reference to the provisioning policies of the year II. It would probably coincide also with that of open resistance to *déchristianisation*. But, in the present state of research, it is impossible to do more than suggest that such parallels may exist elsewhere between revolutionary ill will and apathy in the year II and the extent and acceptance of desertion in the year V, the year VI, and the year VII.

---

[1] AN, F9 301 (Louis Baudet, ex-commissaire dans le canton de Cœuvres, au Ministre, 20 nivôse an V) and R.C. Cobb, 'L'Armée révolutionnaire dans l'Aisne', *Revue du Nord*, pp. 132, 133, 134.
[2] AN, F9 301 (administration des Basses-Alpes, au Ministre, 9 fructidor an VII) and *Les Armées révolutionnaires*, II, pp. 561, 570.
[3] Arch. Seine-Maritime L 5340 (comité de Dieppe à l'agent national du district, s.d. messidor an II).
[4] AN, F9 316 (Désertion, Seine-Inférieure, arrêté de l'administration centrale du département du 21 thermidor an VII) and R.C. Cobb, 'La mission de Siblot au Havre-Marat' and 'L'armée révolutionnaire parisienne au Havre-Marat et dans le district de Montivilliers', *Annales de Normandie*, May and October–December 1953.

It is a parallel that would be well worth pursuing more thoroughly in a number of similar areas, previously ill noted by the Paris or other city authorities of the *sans-culotte* period: the District de Provins, the District de Beauvais, the District de Pontoise, the District de Compiègne, to quote some of the more notorious examples. In local and regional terms, the polarizations of the year II are likely to be those of the year VI or VII and, in many instances, those who, in the year II, had discharged their functions to the maximum interest of their *sans-culotte* brothers back in Paris or Toulouse were those who, when they had survived – for many were murdered in between – were denouncing the tacit acceptance of desertion from the year V onwards.

Desertion not only reflects regional and class attitudes; when it is very widely accepted it represents an important, if negative, attitude on the part of the common people. It is then what might be described as a 'popular movement by default', like the non-participation of so many *sans-culottes* in the *journée du 9 thermidor*. Popular militancy should not be defined only in its positive forms; people must be allowed to opt out of a system or of a commitment if they feel so inclined. This is why desertion is an integral part of our subject, especially in a period when the common people had few other means of openly expressing their hostility to a regime which had repressed and impoverished them in a heartless and systematic manner.

5. *Beggars and Vagrants: the* Bandes *of 1811–12*

The police, as the previous section shows, had their own ideas about the 'popular movement' and their own priorities with regard to potential sedition. They were above all obsessed by the dangers of all sorts presented by large groups of people on the move; and their principal concern was to control, when they could not prevent, the movement of population. Highest on their list came *oisifs*, 'sturdy beggars', urban and rural vagrants who, in time of dearth, during the winter months and even more in the spring, at the opening of the *période de la soudure*, roamed the countryside, sometimes, in periods of extreme hardship, in armed bands, ranging from farm to farm and demanding food and shelter as a right (one such band insisted on supper, a bed, and a good breakfast, for twenty or thirty companions), using threatening language, hinting at a return visit in even greater force, with the reminder that barns, thatched roofs, crops, and fodder burn easily even in winter when suitably helped.

The imperial police in particular harried vagrants. A series of ferocious *arrêtés* of 1806–12 virtually made the genuine vagrant who absented himself from the workhouse an outlaw. Any such association of even two vagrants on the move, unless they were husband and wife, father and son, or mother and daughter, was treated as a seditious turbulence, instantly punishable before a summary court by deportation. Any movement of vagrants in the countryside after dusk was subject to similar punishment.

The imperial authorities were likewise concerned to make vagrants the responsibility of the *communes* from which they came – this was another way of keeping them off the roads. And, in times of distress, rather than give them material relief in money or in food – which, it was felt, they would then sell to obtain drink – the favourite solution was to organize public works that would keep them occupied in one place and under the local authorities. The Napoleonic police went on the assumption that a beggar was not dangerous as long as he was in his own community; it was when he ganged up with others – especially with other townsmen – and then, under the anonymity of a mask, proceeded to comb a wide neighbourhood, that he became a potential outlaw and a danger to order and property. So the first concern of the authorities, once such *attroupements* were stated to be on the march, was to have them rounded up by the *gendarmerie* or the army, and sent back to their towns of origin. (They were not particularly afraid of the rural vagrant; for, they argued, he was known, had a name, and, being identifiable, would stop short of such extreme acts as arson or begging while armed.)

The danger was real enough. During the winter of 1811 and the first three months of 1812, the Prefects speak of enormous armies of beggars on the move in the countryside. Most of them, they suggest, are 'foreigners', who have come from the neighbouring Department – a characteristic reflex both of police and of public authorities when faced with violence or disorder on an unaccustomed scale. As usual, the Seine-Inférieure appears to have been the most disturbed Department; the Prefect, in a letter dated 8 April 1812, when the crisis was at its height, notes: 'le désœuvrement est toujours à craindre surtout parmi le peuple... Les mendians se multiplient chaque jour.'[1] In July, referring to the previous spring, he writes: 'Des troupes de plus de 500 mendians assiégeoient les portes des propriétaires, des cultivateurs, des marchands',[2] and, in September, in his general report on the dearth, he produces much more alarming figures, for two other traditional centres of extreme hardship in time of dearth: the regions of le Havre and Dieppe:

Dans l'arrondissement du Havre, la mendicité s'étoit accrue à un tel point dès l'hiver de 1811 que des troupes de plus de 1,200 individus se répandoient à certains jours de la semaine [Mondays and Tuesdays] dans les communes et demandoient des aumônes qu'il eût été souvent dangereux de leur refuser...

---

[1] AN, F 11 718 (Préfet de la Seine-Inférieure au Ministre, 8 avril 1812).
[2] Ibid. (Préfet de la Seine-Inférieure au Ministre, 31 juillet 1812).

Dans l'arrondissement de Dieppe il s'en formoit des attroupemens de 1,800 à 2,000.[1]

The Prefect of the neighbouring Department of the Somme was to report on 24 June that 'les indigens ... sans exagérer ... alloient mendier au nombre de plus de 60,000'.[2] The authorities of Amiens, in 1795, give a similar figure for vagrants combing the district in March–April of that terrible year;[3] in view of the overpopulation of the Somme, his estimate does not appear to have been exaggerated. The Prefects of the Finistère and the Cher refer, more modestly, to groups of from twenty to forty as operating in the countryside;[4] despite their small numbers, their methods seem to have been equally alarming. The Prefect of the Cher, in a letter dated 19 March, at the height of popular panic and alarm, explains:

> Voici comment s'exerce cette mendicité. Pendant le cours de la journée les mendians (dont le nombre excède toute croyance) marchent isolément et vont de porte en porte; l'usage est de donner à chacun un morceau de pain, et l'on n'oseroit les refuser, crainte du feu dont ils menacent; à l'entrée de la nuit, et au nombre de 20, quelquefois 30, ils se présentent dans une ferme isolée (comme elles le sont pour la plupart dans ce département), alors, ils ne mendient plus, il faut leur donner à souper, à coucher, puis à déjeuner ... les forces manquent pour les arrêter, les prisons manquent pour les enfermer.[5]

The Prefect of the Finistère has a similar story to tell: 'La mendicité faisoit des progrès effrayans,' he writes, in August, of the previous winter, 'les mendians se réunissoient par bandes de trente à quarante pour aller au loin lever l'impôt de leur subsistance sur le travail d'autrui; et leur audace croissante étoit déjà parvenue au point qu'ils n'étoient point fâchés d'être redoutés.'[6] The Prefect of the Oise believes that the groups of beggars passing through certain areas of the Department, in the spring of 1812, have come from the neighbouring *communes* of the Somme and the Eure. 'Dans le canton de Chaumont', he states, in a letter dated 24 March to the Minister of the Interior, 'qui avoisine le Département de l'Eure, les pauvres vont la nuit, en assez grand nombre, et quelquefois masqués, frapper chez les fermiers et les sommer de leur livrer en dehors de leur habitation du pain et de se retirer afin qu'ils ne puissent pas les reconnoître',[7] but, a

---

[1] Ibid. (Préfet de la Seine-Inférieure au Ministre, 8 septembre 1812).
[2] AN, F 11 718 (Préfet de la Somme au Ministre, 24 juin 1812).
[3] Arch. Somme Lc 1433 (district d'Amiens, prairial an III) and AN, D §1 9 (mission de Duport dans le district d'Abbeville, messidor an III).
[4] AN, F 11 708 (Préfet du Cher au Ministre, 19 mars 1812) and AN, F 11 710 (Préfet du Finistère au Ministre, 26 août 1812).
[5] AN, F 11 708 (as above).
[6] AN, F 11 710 (as above).
[7] AN, F 11 715 (Préfet de l'Oise au Ministre, 24 mars).

fortnight later, he expresses the opinion that many of them are in fact locals: 'Les sous-préfets et les maires ... sont persuadés que plusieurs des gens qui vont quêter avec le visage masqué sont de leurs voisins qui ont du bled chez eux.'[1]

Several Prefects attribute the insurrectionary character of some of these *attroupements* to the presence in the ranks of beggars of large numbers of townsmen. 'Si, dans le fort de la disette, il a été commis quelques excès, dans les campagnes,' said the Prefect of the Orne, 'les habitans des villes qui s'y répandoient en troupe nombreuse en ont été presque les seuls auteurs.'[2] The Prefect of Rennes complains that the weavers of the *chef-lieu* have left their workshops, to scour the countryside in large groups.[3] In March 1812 the Prefect of the Loir-et-Cher is told of the presence of armed bands of beggars in the communes of Moisy, Semerville, and Ouzouer-le-Doyen, in the neighbourhood of Blois.[4] In the Eure-et-Loir, 'au 1er janvier 1812, les campagnes étoient couvertes de mendians, qui, voyageant en troupes, visitoient les fermes & les moulins, demandoient insolemment du pain'.[5] But elsewhere rural vagrants invaded the towns: Parthenay, in the Deux-Sèvres, 'à été infesté de mendians'. The Prefect adds the comment:

> On a remarqué ... la maladresse du curé; prêchant sur l'aumône, il lança des reproches violens contre les riches qui ne donnoient pas assez, et sembla les désigner à la haine du peuple. Les habitans aisés accusèrent le curé d'avoir prêché la loi agraire; j'eus occasion de lui faire quelques remontrances, et pour prouver qu'il avoit mal interprété ses intentions, il prêcha le jour suivant sur les devoirs des pauvres, avec si peu de mesure que les riches durent à leur tour le protéger contre l'animadversion des indigens.[6]

In the Sarthe, the pattern is more familiar: 'La misère étoit extrême [in the spring of 1812]. Des mendians, rassemblés par troupes plus ou moins nombreuses, parcouroient les campagnes, jetoient l'alarme ...'[7]

As always, when it is a matter of extensive vagrancy and rural disorder on a semi-insurrectionary scale, the Norman Departments, the Somme, and the Eure-et-Loir – in the year IV, the area of the notorious *bande*

---

[1] Ibid. (7 avril).
[2] Ibid. (29 avril).
[3] AN, F 11 711 (Préfet de l'Ille-et-Vilaine, 14 juin).
[4] AN, F 11 712 (Préfet du Loir-et-Cher, 24 mars).
[5] AN, F 11 709 (Préfet de l'Eure-et-Loir, 4 juin). Referring to the small town of Nogent-le-Rotrou, the Prefect writes in November 1812: 'Sur une population de 7,000 âmes, il en est 2,400 qui se livrent à la mendicité et qui se répandent dans les campagnes environnantes.'
[6] AN, F 11 718 (Préfet des Deux-Sèvres, 10 août).
[7] AN, F 11 716 (Préfet de la Sarthe, 12 août).

d'Orgères, and, thanks to the immense forest of Orléans, with the Loiret, a traditional centre of rural banditry – top the list. Girardin, the Prefect of Rouen, refers to vagrancy as entrenched in the Seine-Inférieure 'from time immemorial'.[1] But some of the Breton and western Departments were also affected. There are no reports of vagrancy in the south; and the Aube, which the Prefect describes, with some exaggeration, as 'the poorest Department in the Empire' (there would have been plenty of other candidates for that much-disputed title, from the Ardennes to the Lozère, the Ardèche, the Aveyron, or the Cantal), while undergoing extreme hardship – the mortality was exceptionally heavy in the winter of 1811 and the spring of 1812 – seems to have been preserved from the operations of large-scale vagrancy, despite an enormous forested region round Ervy; the Department was, however, like that of the Marne, heavily garrisoned. It is possibly for the same reason that there are no reports of beggar groups in the Nord, the traditional terrain of the *chauffeur* and the smuggler; the Nord was also particularly well placed, at least in this particular crisis, to receive early relief, with the massive import of grain from the Dutch and Rhenish Departments. There is nothing surprising, then, either about the location of the beggars' armies or about their methods, reflecting as they do the old hostility of the townsman for the well-to-do farmer and for the country population as a whole that one encounters, especially in the Norman Departments and the Somme, in the course of the year III and the year IV.

What is surprising, given the repressive conditions of the Empire, as far as the common people were concerned, is the relative permissiveness both of local authorities – naturally prudent, as they were, in the immediate path of these 'invasions' – and of the Prefects and Sub-Prefects, who, when faced with disorder on this scale, preferred to use persuasion rather than the *gendarmerie*, enticing the vagrants back to their towns with the promise of the free distribution of food (*les soupes à la Rumfort*) and with the organization of relief in the form of public works. It was a measure of their success that outbreaks of actual rioting were few, despite the gravity of a situation where dearth and disease were accompanied by explosive political undertones and, in many places, the most alarming rumours. Certainly, it would be wrong to suggest that the common people had been schooled, since 1795, in the habit of obedience – there is nothing deferential about the behaviour of the beggars as described in these reports, and there is no doubt about their extreme hostility to the urban and rural well-to-do; rather it would seem that, as a result of the May Decrees, the urban consumer was readily convinced of the good intentions of the Imperial Government.

---

[1] AN, F 11 718 (Préfet de la Seine-Inférieure, 11 septembre).

6. *The Barometer of Popular Protest and Disaster 1795–1812*

Let us briefly consider the fortunes and misfortunes of the common people between the Thermidorian Reaction and the end of the Empire. White terrorism, one of the most effective weapons against the former *sans-culotte* militants and their masters, was already on the decline by 1803, after eight anarchical and sanguinary years in the south-east and the Rhône Valley. The great murder year was 1795; but there appear to have been almost as many murders in the year IV, and in the following year the activities of the *compagnies* became even bolder. Political assassinations were frequent throughout the year VII (there is little evidence for the year VI), with a cluster of murders in the Vaucluse in September 1799. There was a further spate of murders in and around Lyon in the year VIII and the year IX. But by 1802, the movement had exhausted itself, though there are eleven political murders recorded for the Rhône in 1803 and 1804. Lyon was no doubt exceptional in this respect, even in the south-east. This was not, however, the end of the story; for the movement was to revive, often under the same leadership and with the same *sabreurs*, in the favourable circumstances of the summer of 1815, when it re-emerged in much the same areas, even in the same villages, as in 1795 onwards, and sought out much the same sort of victims, now doubly suspect. Indeed, a number of people were murdered in the Gard, the Bouches-du-Rhône, the Vaucluse, and the Lozère in 1815 mainly because their near-relatives had been murdered in the previous White Terror. A number of the murderers, too, on both occasions, had lost parents to one or another of the Revolutionary Terrors. For any assessment of the two White Terrors, it is essential to keep in view this succession of events.[1]

There was a general flare-up of the traditional hunger riot in 1795, when there were spring and summer riots in all the principal towns of the north (Paris, Saint-Germain-en-Laye, Versailles, Mantes, Rouen, Sotteville, Darnétal, le Havre, Dieppe, Fécamp, Saint-Valéry-en-Caux, Saint-Valéry-sur-Somme, Honfleur, Caen, Lisieux, Pont-l'Évêque, Alençon, Amiens, Abbeville, Calais, Arras, Lille, Dunkirk, Péronne, Troyes, to mention some of the more serious outbreaks), and even in such places as Bordeaux. Popular violence rose to two peaks, first in Ventôse–Germinal, then in Floréal–Prairial – there is a remarkable concordance between the dates of riots in the whole area of the Lower Seine, a concordance that led some of the higher authorities to refer to the spread of disorder as 'an electrical shock'.

But this kind of riot disappeared in the year IV; the situation was by

---

[1] 'The White Terror', in the *Times Literary Supplement*, 10 August 1967. For the White Terror in the south see below, pp. 180–96.

then so fearful that the potential rioter was either dead or dying, busy pawning his remaining possessions, including his bedding, queuing for bourgeois charity, roaming the countryside in search of food, or enlisting in the *bandes* of *chauffeurs*. A great many potential rioters took the extreme remedy of committing suicide – in Paris, the suicide figures had never been so high, even in the year III. The only urban disturbances in the year IV were led by women. On previous less desperate occasions they had always managed to bring out the men, but this time they failed to do so. There followed a series of good harvests in 1796, 1797, and 1798, and this for the time being delivered the Directory from this traditional danger. The regime was fortunate in this respect at least, if in no other – for no other French government has had to contend with open defiance and disobedience and an administrative strike on quite such a scale. Regional disturbances occurred once more in the Nord, the Pas-de-Calais, and the Somme in the crisis of 1801–2; the former Prefect of the Pas-de-Calais was to attribute them to the machinations of 'English agents', who had come over to drive up the price of grain by massive secret purchases, and thus provoke an artificial crisis and arouse popular fears. These were followed by nearly ten years of peace on the markets – one of the longest breaks ever allowed to a French government in eighteenth- or early nineteenth-century conditions.

But if dearth, and its usual accompaniments of grain riots, *arrêts*, and panic, receded for a decade, the diseases of the poor knew no remission throughout these years, but increased in virulence with each added year of war in the first fifteen years of the century.[1] Dysentery and typhus were particularly prevalent in a series of villages in the Seine-et-Marne, along the military highroads to the east, almost without interruption from 1806 to 1815, as well as in the *communes* on the eastern periphery of Paris, again the point of entry of troops from the Rhine. In the former region the epidemics reached their height in two waves, from the winter of 1811 to the end of the summer of 1812, and from the winter of 1814 to the end of the summer of 1815. Both waves coincided with massive French or allied troop movements.

The principal sources of infection were the villages of Vaudoy-en-Brie, an important centre on the high road from Paris to Bar-le-Duc; Champdeuil, on the road from Melun to Meaux; and a cluster of localities on the edge of the Forêt de Fontainebleau, south of Melun and on or near the road from Gien and the Gâtinais: Guercheville, Amponville,

---

[1] Asked to explain the causes of these diseases – mostly typhus and various forms of dysentery – medical officers from Melun and Nemours were to report: 'C'est ... dans la continuité de la guerre qu'il faut chercher la cause de cette dépopulation.' 'L'état continuel des guerres dans lequel la France a été plongée depuis vingt-quatre ans en est la cause principale' (AN, F8 79, Épidémies, Seine-et-Marne, 1806–1815).

Jacqueville, Achères-la-Forêt, Ury, Dormelles, and Noisy-sur-École; in all, there was heavy mortality between 1810 and 1812.

The second outbreak occurred in the small towns of Château-Landon, Moret, and Montigny-sur-Loing, and in the neighbouring village of Écuelles, again all localities situated on or near the military highroads from the south-east and from the centre to the capital, from 1814 to 1815. The epidemics also lapped the eastern fringes of Paris; Pantin was the centre of a series of disasters – cholera, dysentery, typhus – that were endemic from 1808 to 1812 and were attributed by the medical authorities to the extreme poverty of the inhabitants of the *commune*.[1] In 1812 the area of infection spread to Bondy, Bobigny, Noisy-le-Sec, la Villette, and Fontenay-sous-Bois. 'C'est la misère profonde de la plupart des habitans,' says a report of this last *commune*,[2] while in Saint-Denis there were annual bouts of typhus, during the summer months, from 1805 to 1812.[3] In 1806 and 1807 there were two recurrent outbreaks of typhus, this time south of Paris, in the vicinity of Sceaux: Créteil, Bonneuil, and Maisons.[4] Thus, by 1810 to 1812, the capital was lapped by diseases of the poor to the north, east, and south, while the disasters in the east of Europe were further aggravated by extremely destructive outbreaks in localities in which troops had been garrisoned, during the three successive years, along the roads of the Seine-et-Marne. By some miracle, Paris itself remained free from infection.

The year 1812 not only saw a massive deployment of vagrants and heavy mortality among the poor to the east of Paris, but also witnessed a resumption of the traditional market riot. The worst occurred in Caen, on 2 March 1812, a Monday:

le lundi est toujours un jour difficile [observed the Prefect of the Calvados, in his report for 7 April], malgré l'extrême misère, les ouvriers le passent dans l'oisiveté et [dans] toute la débauche à laquelle ils peuvent se livrer ... La halle étoit fort agitée, des femmes furieuses vouloient acheter les grains à un prix arbitraire et réclamoient la taxe ... Dès que je fus sur la place, une foule considérable me suivit en criant *Du pain et l'ouvrage* ...

A mill and a grain store were attacked and pillaged, the house of a grain merchant was sacked and set on fire, the grain barges in the port were unloaded by a crowd of several thousand, among which women from the

---

[1] 'C'est la classe indigente qui est particulièrement attaquée ... tous les ans, dans les mois d'été les habitans ... sont attaqués ... de fièvres bileuses ... de choléra, de dysenterie ... les gens riches n'ont aucune communication avec les pauvres' (AN, F8 77, Épidémies, Seine).
[2] AN, F8 77 (Épidémies, Seine).
[3] Ibid.
[4] Ibid.

faubourg of Vaucelles – textile workers and laundresses – appear to have been the leading spirits and the most vociferous in incitement. The rioters were soon joined by a group of conscripts, who were due to leave the town on the following day; the Prefect, the magistrates, and the police were insulted.

The riot also had serious political undercurrents; for it was rumoured among the crowd that the Emperor had died in Moscow and that a Council of Regency had been proclaimed; and the rumours persisted for the next month, coinciding with the worst period of the dearth crisis, which, as always, was almost as severe in this Department as in the Seine-Inférieure. On 14 April the Prefect was to inform the Minister of the Interior: 'On répand ici la nouvelle de séditions très graves à Amiens [there had been a minor disturbance there a week before, on the 7th] et à Lyon; dans cette dernière ville, le peuple auroit désarmé la troupe et tiré le canon sur elle' – a further tribute to the reputation enjoyed by the Second City even among the common people, as well as among the repressive authorities, for, in fact, the rumour was completely unfounded, and Lyon and the Rhône were one of the quietest areas throughout the crisis; on 19 April, the Prefect reports further:

> on vint me rapporter qu'à l'instant même . . . une femme, épuisée de faim, avait lancé ses deux enfans du pont de Vaucelles dans l'Orne, & s'y étoit précipitée après eux . . . Ce bruit avoit causé une vive et dangereuse impression; il étoit le sujet de l'entretien des groupes qui environnoient la halle; je ne savois moi-même qu'en penser, lorsque les recherches les plus exactes me donnèrent la conviction que ce récit étoit faux, & conséquemment l'œuvre de la malveillance . . . Hier un homme atteint de la démence s'est avisé de traverser une partie du faubourg de Vaucelles, & de se jeter dans la rivière; il a été de suite transformé en un homme que la faim avoit réduit aux derniers excès du désespoir. Il a été sauvé & est maintenant à Beaulieu dans une loge de fou.

Two days later, the wretched man informed the Minister:

> On fait circuler sur les bords de la mer les bruits les plus absurdes et les plus fâcheux. Des étrangers bien vêtus ont été remarqués parcourant la côte et se plaisant à donner les nouvelles les plus alarmantes. La révolte de Lyon est toujours mise en avant; on ajoute que . . . l'Ambassadeur de Russie a pris la fuite, que l'Impératrice elle-même s'est retirée en Allemagne.

On 26 April, he writes:

> Il faut que je dise à V. E. encore que la publicité donnée aux désordres qui affligent l'Angleterre à raison de la cherté des grains, loin de prouver que ce fléau est commun à toute l'Europe, qu'il est le résultat nécessaire d'une mauvaise récolte, et d'encourager à la patience, provoque les séditieux; le peuple cite ces

détails dans tous ses entretiens et s'en autorise dans ses projects de troubles. Les briseurs de métiers de Manchester et de Nottingham sont à la veille de trouver des imitateurs dans l'arrondissement de Vire. Déjà un fabricant (M. Triel), qui emploie un grand nombre d'ouvriers, a reçu une lettre anonyme menaçante.

No wonder the Napoleonic Prefects feared food riots more than any other form of public protest, for it would be hard to discover a more characteristic example of the relationship between dearth, rumour, and panic than these reports from Caen.

The imperial authorities had been seriously disturbed by the extent of a riot that they thought no longer possible under the repressive conditions of 1812 ('disorders of this kind,' states another Prefect in the course of the same crisis, 'which were possible under the previous regime, can no longer be seriously feared, thanks to the reverence and fear inspired by the person of His Majesty'). Like most of their predecessors in the year III, they attributed it to the intervention of contrived sedition. The Prefect was blamed for his lack of foresight, and, within a week of the riot, after the garrison had been strongly reinforced, a court martial was set up to try the ringleaders. Its verdict was exceptionally severe; on 14 March eight persons were condemned to death: Lhonneur, *maître d'écriture*, Samson, *excoriateur*, Barbanche, *marin*, fille Goujeon, *fileuse*, femme Prévost, *dentellière*, Vesdy, *blanchisseur*, fille Tilly, *rentière*, femme Retour, *filassière*; nine more were sentenced to eight years' hard labour, and a further nine to five years' imprisonment. Most of those convicted were women textile workers from Vaucelles, as well as day-labourers, porters, and *badestamiers*.[1]

Much of the severity of the military judges can be attributed to what they regarded as the many and dangerous parallels between the March 1812 riot and events in Caen in 1789 and during the Revolution. On the day of the riot, women had been heard evoking the fate of M. de Belsunce, a young army officer lynched in July 1789 when he had attempted to disperse a riotous crowd; and there had been ugly reminders of the attachment of the *petit peuple* to the *maximum*. A little later, in April, when the news of the March Decrees reached Caen, it was at once rumoured that the government, following the example of the Prefect of the Seine-et-Marne, had decided to establish a *maximum* 'et de taxer le bled à f. 33 l'hectolitre. Des blanchisseuses ont quitté leurs bateaux et se sont mises à danser en rond presque sous les fenêtres de la Préfecture.' This was the sort of thing that the imperial authorities most wanted to avoid. The

---

[1] A few days later the local wits placarded up in the town: 'Le Préfet a perdu l'appétit, le Maire a perdu l'honneur, et ils ont mis la France aux fers.' Samson's *nom de guerre* was *L'Appétit*, and one of the women condemned to a heavy prison sentence was named Lafrance. Even the Empire had not entirely destroyed the irreverence of popular humour.

Prefects, a number of whom had served under the old regime, in positions of repressive authority, were well aware of the strength of rumour and of the remarkable persistence of popular memory. Throughout the 1812 crisis there are constant evocations of the *maximum*, although authorities at all levels are extremely careful never to use the word in public (they use it often enough, and with horror, in their reports to the Minister) and to point out that the March and May Decrees did not constitute anything of the sort. In such circumstances the *petit peuple* was its own best historian.

Caen was the most serious outbreak of popular disorder in 1812, owing to its political implications. There were market disturbances, as there had been in the spring and summer of 1795, in the Pays d'Auge, at Honfleur, Pont-l'Évêque, and Lisieux, all places extremely sensitive to shortage or to the threat of it. Apart from in the Calvados, the most serious threat to public order occurred at Issoudun on 25, 26, 27, 28, and 29 April; it was, in fact, mostly talk, various inhabitants of the faubourg Saint-Paterne threatening to set fire to the houses of the rich, two women being accused of having said 'qu'elles mettroient le feu aux quatre coins de la ville', and the *maire* being in receipt of anonymous threats of arson; there was also an attack on the office of the *droits réunis*. On the last day, 29 April, however, a huge granary belonging to Heurlant-Dumez, the richest land-owner in the area, went up in flames. Again repression was vigorous; and again most of those sentenced were women. There were disorders at the end of January in Rennes and in Fougères; on 10 March the Prefect of the Indre-et-Loire refers to a crime wave that he attributes to poverty: 'les voleurs et les assassins ont attaqué particulièrement des porteurs de bleds ...' On 16 March in the course of a market riot in Beaune, the *maire* was knocked down. There was a riot in Elbeuf in the same month; and, after a series of arrests in the Eure, ninety offenders were sent to Rouen for trial. On 7 April, a group of women attempted to prevent a grain convoy from leaving Amiens for Abbeville.

On the whole the regime got off lightly. The Napoleonic order did not intend to place itself at the mercy of a grain riot; the Prefects, a vastly improved police, the regulations concerning 'associations' and 'assemblies', saw to that. A few poor *dentellières* were no match for such a concentration of bureaucratic repression, especially when they had no programme other than *Nous ne voulons pas mourir de faim debout*, no organization to fall back on, and little to encourage them other than the memory of the realities of the year II and the slogans of the year III. In all the riots of 1812, they seem to have enjoyed only a minimum of masculine support. The Empire also had a much wider provisioning area to draw on than had been available either to the old royal government or to revolutionary France, when, in times of shortage, Paris food commissioners would poach on the provisioning areas of Rouen, Amiens, Lille, Metz,

Troyes, Dijon, and even Lyon, thus driving up the price of grain. In 1812 Paris, the stricken Norman Departments, the Somme, and the Nord received massive supplies fairly rapidly – the situation in Rouen was beginning to improve in the second half of July – over land or by waterway from the Ruhr and other Rhineland Departments, as well as from Holland. Lyon and Rhône were similarly saved from the full effects of the dearth by imports from Swabia and the Palatinate.

At home, in the meantime, the sting was taken out of riot and the people were eventually kept quiet – there were no riots after the end of April – by a massive mobilization of private charity on the part of the Prefects and Sub-Prefects to finance the soup kitchens in the cities. At the end of the year those that had contributed most to the organization of the *soupes à la Rumfort* received a shower of decorations – the *Ordre de la Réunion* was the great stand-by – graded in gold and silver medals; they had earned them; for they had soon reduced the potential rioter to the humble recipient of *notables'* charity. In some Departments, Rolls of Honour were drawn up, with the amounts contributed by each person, for display at the *mairie* or the *sous-préfecture* (in le Havre, the Hombergs and the other inhabitants of the Grand Quai top the list, with the masonic lodge of *L'Aménité* a close second; in the Norman countryside, Protestant landowners, by their generosity, were to earn the rather grudging thanks of the Prefect, Girardin). The pulpit was likewise mobilized – the *curés* cannot all have been as stupid as the over-zealous incumbent of Parthenay – to preach submission, patience, and gratitude. Napoleon's regime was thus made safe from the grain riot, not only by repressive legislation and the use of troops, but also by a combination of the charity bazaar, the pillage economy of conquest, and by the existence of a European market in grain that stretched without barriers from the Atlantic to the Ems, from the Channel to the Adriatic. Belgian and Swiss intermediaries, Dutch and Rhenish corn-factors, and the suppliers of the armies in Spain (largely grain-merchants from the Lauragais) did very well indeed out of a crisis that had been solved by the spring of 1813 (though with a considerable increase in mortality in Rouen,[1] in the Eure,[2] in the Gers,[3] in the Ille-et-Vilaine,[4] and in the Indre-et-Loire[5]) when the restrictive decrees and regulations were withdrawn.

---

[1] AN, F 11 718: Prefect to Minister, 8 September 1812: 'Dans la ville de Rouen ... il y a eu beaucoup plus de décès pendant les sept premiers mois de 1812 que pendant les mois correspondants de 1811.'

[2] AN, F 11 709: 'Car c'est une vérité, un grand nombre a péri surtout dans la classe des vieillards et des enfants' (lettre du directeur de l'hospice de Bourg-Achard, 22 décembre 1812).

[3] AN, F 11 710 (Préfet du Gers au Ministre, 29 juillet 1812): 'L'année dernière les décès ont surpassé les naissances de près de 2,000.'

[4] AN, F 11 711 (Préfet de l'Ille-et-Vilaine au Ministre, 18 avril 1812).

[5] Ibid. (Préfet de l'Indre-et-Loire au Ministre, 1er juin 1812).

There was even as a result of the March and May Decrees, widely identified in the popular mind with the *recensements* and the *maximum* of the year II, some return of popular confidence in a regime that, up till then, had appeared uniquely repressive and heartless in its dealings with the common people. The laundrywomen of Caen were not the only ones to dance for joy when the first garbled versions of the decrees began to seep through the curtain of official secrecy. Prefects' reports state that, while well-to-do circles regarded the decrees with deep dismay as a return to 'the deplorable system of eighteen years ago' – requisitioning, billeting, and garrisoning, the employment of force against the rural landowner[1] – the Emperor had never been so adulated by the poor. It must have been very embarrassing for him. But by the spring of 1812 it was possible to withdraw the decrees and to return to normal. It was typical of the regime that their withdrawal should have been accompanied by the banishment of former *sans-culotte* militants from Paris and from some other cities. The best way to remove the unpleasant impression left with the *honnêtes gens* by this brief return to the economy of the Terror was thus to demonstrate that the government was still as repressive as ever as far as the *classes populacières* were concerned.

PART TWO   THE POPULAR MOVEMENT IN DECLINE
(1795–1818) AND THE NATURE OF *SANS-CULOTTE*
MILITANCY

'Ils sont au plus 60 hommes et autant de femmes et à cette petite minorité ils voudroient mener la Section qui est de 8 à 9,000 hommes. Je n'accuse pas la totalité de la société, mais bien 6 ou 8 particuliers.'

An inhabitant of the Section du Panthéon

7. 'A la recherche du sans-culotte'

In the previous section we have attempted to give a brief account of the forms and of the chronology of popular protest between the fall of Robespierre and the collapse of the Empire. Our concern has been to outline what happened to the 'popular movement' during these years and even to question whether such a thing could be said to have existed at all. In the present section, if we except the brief period of popular militancy that has been described as 'direct democracy' or as *le mouvement sans-culotte*, the scope of our subject is limited to the various more traditional

---

[1] One infuriated Norman gentleman was to complain to his Sub-Prefect: 'Monsieur, ma maison, mes basses-cours, tous mes bâtimens enfin ont été visités, et la gendarmerie a fini par s'emparer de ma personne. Nous voilà donc revenus en '93' (AN, F 11 718).

forms of popular agitation, the ways in which it might impinge on higher authority, and the general course of 'popular movements' in their cruder, more spontaneous forms between 1795 and 1815. What happened after the short period of popular rule may help to explain both why that rule was so short-lived and why popular protest was, on the whole, so ineffective. For it is in the post-Terror period, particularly in the year III, that a key to the proper understanding of the *sans-culotte* movement of the year II may best be sought. In other words, the movement itself should not be studied in isolation in the purely year II context. There is as much to be learnt from the long years of failure and disenchantment as from the highly dramatic, and largely accidental, experiment in popular democracy, itself soon tempered by revolutionary bureaucracy and centralization. The whole 'problem', if there be a problem at all, can most effectively be ventilated by thus working back from 1795, from 1796, and from the next nineteen years, to the conditions of 1793 to 1794.

First of all, then, we have to deal with the *sans-culotte* as such – that is to say, with a person not as he was, let us say, in 1792, or as he would have become in 1795 or in 1796, but as he was for a brief period from 1793 to 1794. For the life and death of the *sans-culotte* can be circumscribed within a period running more or less from April 1793 to April 1794, allowing for a possible overlap up to Thermidor year II or even to Brumaire year III. It would certainly be stretching the species too far to describe, as a Norwegian historian has done,[1] the course of the popular movement during the year III as *la défaite des sans-culottes*, for, from the second month (Brumaire) at latest of that year, there was nothing left to be defeated; the *sans-culotte*, no doubt, was unaware of this at the time, just as he had previously been unaware that he was, first, being used by the Revolutionary Government, and was then being dismissed with scant thanks by the same government, once his services were no longer required. Having once exercised a little power, at least at the level of the *commune*, the *sans-culotte* could not easily acclimatize himself to a situation in which he was excluded from even the humblest office. And it was largely his enormous self-confidence and self-righteousness, his conviction so often and so unwisely expressed in cafés and public places that *le règne des sans-culottes reviendrait* and that then the *honnêtes gens* would have to look to it, that was to precipitate his political destruction and often his personal ruin in the course of the year III. What he so blandly hoped for, others feared more than anything else; and they were in a position to see that his ill-advisedly expressed hopes would not be realized, if necessary by killing the man himself, his physical being, after destroying what had been a political reality. Certainly, by a mixture of

---

[1] Kåre Tønnesson, *La Défaite des sans-culottes* (Oslo, 1959).

imprudent threats and boastfulness, by the frequent evocation of a Terror, bigger and better than ever – and his remarks, so easily seized upon by Thermidorian magistrates or *comités*, would generally be further inflated *en cours de route* – he directly contributed to his own destruction.

The *sans-culotte* is not an individual with an independent life of his own. It could not be said of him 'once a *sans-culotte*, always a *sans-culotte*'; for, apart from the difficulties of an exact definition of this status, discussed briefly in the previous section, he exists at all only as a unit within a collectivity, which itself exists only in virtue of certain specific, unusual, and temporary institutions: once the sectionary institutions have been destroyed, or tamed, the *sans-culotte* too disappears; in his place, there is what there had been before – a shoemaker, a hatter, a tailor, a tanner, a wine merchant, a clerk, a carpenter, a cabinet-maker, an engraver, a miniaturist, a fan-maker, a fencing-master, a teacher. There is nothing left save perhaps the memory of militancy and a hankering after Brave Times, that appear all the braver when remembered under very hard ones. The *sans-culotte* then is not a social or economic being; he is a political accident. So are the institutions that gave the *sans-culottes* their brief opportunity for collective expression. We shall return to this accident of history when we consider, in more detail, the much-disputed question of the relationship between the *sans-culotte* movement and the Revolutionary Government, between *la sans-culotterie* and *la bourgeoisie jacobine*, or more simply, to invert the order (for how could anyone put him second?), between Robespierre and the popular movement.

*

Most historians are now familiar with Albert Soboul's rather formalized account of the relations between the classes – especially the urban classes – in the course of the revolutionary period, both from his *Précis*[1] and from his even shorter *Que sais-je?*[2] A *pas de deux* or sometimes a *pas de trois*, that might be set to music as a historical ballet. Opening scene: bourgeoisie and people, hand in hand, dancing on the prone figure of Privilege. Scene Two: (the people having done their stuff) bourgeoisie and monarchy, hand in hand, dancing on the prone figure of the people. Scene Three: bourgeoisie and people, hand in hand, dancing on the prone body of monarchy. Scene Four: an intermezzo between bourgeoisie and people, only occasionally hand in hand, more often hands vainly extended, both playing hard to get. Scene Five: bourgeoisie dancing alone, on the prone bodies of people and monarchy. One knew it would turn out like this all

---

[1] Albert Soboul, *Précis d'histoire de la Révolution française* (Paris, 1962).
[2] Albert Soboul, *La Révolution française (Que sais-je?)* (Paris, 1963).

along, for that is the rule of a particularly rigorous choreography that will not allow a step to be taken out of place (and, if necessary, the *sans-culotte* may have to be nudged and reminded of his part: 'Get back into line, you are part of the Popular Movement'; the bourgeois, too, forgetting that he is either a Girondin, or Jacobin, or Montagnard, or Thermidorian, may have to be recalled rather roughly to realities, and not be allowed to wander off on his own to look at the shops or enjoy a walk in the country). It is admirably done, the actors know their parts, sink to the ground on the appropriate note, rise again when summoned. The prompter is very discreet and hardly at all in evidence.

Yet one has doubts; it all seems too well rehearsed. And the doubts are confirmed by the same author's definitive account of the *mouvement sectionnaire* in Paris and of its relations with the Revolutionary Government. For in this great work[1] the ballet steps are only briefly remembered, as a matter of form, at the opening and closing of chapters that in their massive middle disclose a much more confusing scene: uncertainties of contour, difficulties of definition, lack of clear objectives, shifting loyalties, internal contradictions, personal squabbles, the role of personalities and of militant minorities, preliminary committee work, the 'fixing' of an agenda, passion, confusion, credulity, myth, anarchy, noise. It is not even certain whether the two tentative partners are, at all times, aware of each other's existence, and there is much more groping and shuffling and searching and back-turning than anything like an ordered movement. This, in its always complicated, detailed narrative, looks much more like the real thing. Soboul's great merit is to have explored that narrative, re-created it, and put it end to end, so that, in the long-drawn-out and complicated process of gradual divorce between a very varied, highly decentralized *mouvement sectionnaire* and a Revolutionary Government that contains a wide range of revolutionary fervour, one is guided by a day-to-day chronology.

8. *The Role of Militant Minorities*

Albert Soboul is describing a mass movement that operated, for a limited period, through certain institutions. The movement did not create the institutions, but the institutions, which already existed, created the movement and imposed upon it certain inbred structural weaknesses. These weaknesses necessitated forms of organization that were tentative and strongly federalist, and that in turn involved a great deal of preliminary negotiation. It is often stated that the popular movement during the French Revolution tended towards extreme forms of decentralization, and Soboul's Paris *sectionnaire* is taken as the obvious example. But the

---

[1] Albert Soboul, *Les Sans-culottes parisiens et le mouvement sectionnaire* (Paris, 1958).

sectionnaire is federalist because the Section is; thus the institutions model the movement, and the Section forms the *sectionnaire*. The Section was an urban village, the Quarter, a world to itself. Of course, when confronted with threats from outside, the Sections would seek to work together, and to impose a common programme. But the peril had to be very great; and much time and energy were taken up by quarrels between different Sections and by personal bids for power within the Section itself. The movement, all forty-eight Sections lumped together as a *mouvement sans-culotte*, may reasonably be described as a mass one comprising some two hundred thousand Parisians; but within each Section, effective power is exercised by small minorities of revolutionary militants – twelve or twenty men at the most,[1] who, thanks to their skill, to the strength of their vocal organs, to their physique,[2] to the time they are prepared to devote to militancy, to their own prestige, to their own patronage (for a number were important employers of labour), are able to manipulate the pro-ceedings of the large assemblies *en petit comité* and push through their proposals well in advance. (Later their opponents made much of this, in their efforts to isolate the *dominateurs*, the *aboyeurs*, from the general mass of *sectionnaires*, and suggested that the experiment in 'direct demo-cracy' disguised what was in fact the workings of a 'secret committee' manipulated by a handful of men. This is a constant theme in Thermidorian *enquêtes* and propaganda, and all the more convincing in that it corresponded to a certain degree with the reality, as recalled by people of many shades of opinion, a year later.)

Soboul's own account shows that a great deal of preliminary work went into preparing Sectionary business, that there was often a lot of lobbying, that matters were seldom left to the chance of a free vote, and that the *sans-culotte* movement could hardly be described as spontaneous or even as particularly democratic unless we admit that there existed a degree of super-*sans-culottisme* which placed some *sectionnaires* over their fellow citizens, in a category apart, élitist and unassailable. For there existed, at least in the *bureaux*, an inner ring of self-taught militants who, though political amateurs, were soon learning how to manipulate an assembly and prepare business from within a *comité*. In time, they would have become

---

[1] Mercereau, an *officier de paix* of the Section du Panthéon-Français, comments on the manner in which the *société sectionnaire* was run: 'Je déclare que la société est le germe de toutes les haines, ils sont au plus 60 hommes et autant de femmes et à cette petite minorité ils voudroient mener la Section qui est de 8 à 9,000 hommes. Je n'accuse pas la totalité de la société, mais bien 6 ou 8 particuliers' (AN, F7 4774 d 3 (Mercereau)).

[2] One *meneur*, who is also an *inspecteur*, is accused, in the year III, of having terrorized his fellow *sectionnaires* by attending all the meetings of the *assemblée générale* and of the *société*, accompanied by an enormous and very fierce dog (Cobb and Rudé, 'Le dernier mouvement populaire de la Révolution à Paris', *Revue Historique*, October–December 1955).

professionals. Already, by the first months of the year III, when in *commune* after *commune* they were dislodged from their entrenched positions, generally by the outside intervention of a *Représentant en mission* – it would take nothing less to prise them out of their hold on a *comité* or a municipality – they had acquired a professional mentality, considering themselves indispensable to the forward march of the Revolution and to the particular interests of their own town or village. So much was this the case that, right up to the summer of 1795, their one thought was that they would soon get back, as their fellow citizens were bound to realize, sooner or later, that they could not do without their valuable services. But they were, of course, removable, even in the circumstances of the year II, and many of the bitter personal squabbles that take up so much space in Sectionary minutes – sometimes for weeks on end, to the exclusion of all else – arose out of attempts to dislodge the reigning clan that had, for one reason or another, made itself generally intolerable – and most of these *meneurs* were loud-mouthed, arrogant, intolerant, some of them were impossible little tyrants, constantly boasting of how they disposed of the power of life and death, gaily talking of the heads that would fall and taking an obvious enjoyment in sending shudders down the backs of those whom they were seeking to impress or to cow – and to replace it by people who were popular in the assemblies or in the *sociétés*, areas in which the virtues of the proverbial 'good committee man' were likely to be less appreciated.

Even at this level, there were bound to be conflicts between the general mass of *sectionnaires*, for whom politics could only be very much of a part-time evening occupation, and the small groups of committed men, who claimed to do their thinking for them. Sectionary politics are full of clans, and so are those of provincial *sociétés*; for these were mostly people who knew each other well – that is to say, who knew much that was damaging about one another – and posts in the *bureaux*, especially those which raised their holders to a prominent position, above most of their fellows, on a *tribune* or in the president's high chair, were objects of as much envy and back-biting as an officer or non-commissioned rank in the *Garde nationale*. The butcher, the grocer, the shoemaker of the quarter or of the *bourg* are bound to live in conceit. Their wives lived even more so and it was because of the corroding influence of feminine jealousies that some popular assemblies sought to exclude women, even as onlookers. The greatest glory was that which was visible to the whole street, to the whole village. The soldier decorated for gallantry and the scholarship boy will hurry home to exhibit themselves. And, though women did not vote in the assemblies, they did much to blow on the furnaces of neighbourly discord if they felt that their husbands or companions were not getting the recognition that they deserved for their patriotism and long service to the

Revolution. If the *patriotes de 93* were in control, then the whole syndicate of the *patriotes de 89* – and the *sans-culottes* could generally muster a few of these – would be grumbling in the wings about newcomers, demagogues, and so on, in sulky deprivation. Revolutionary patriotism, they suggested, should be calculated in terms of length of service to the Cause.

To this the newcomers might reply that the first in the field had fallen by the wayside, having compromised themselves on one of the many occasions between July 1789 and May–June 1793 when it was possible to plump for the wrong side. There was much to be said, in the conditions of the year II, for having been out of public life till 1793. It might, in fact, more often be a conflict between the April men and the September men, for not a great many *sans-culottes* could show service much before 1792, and the great internal revolutions within the Sections occurred between the spring and the late summer of 1793. Many *meneurs* (*aboyeurs* as the Thermidorians were to call them) made themselves intolerable by their insolent bearing, and, at the beginning of the year III, there was a genuine and very widespread revulsion against the former *dominateurs*. They had at best been meddlesome, 'superior', and impatient of criticism, at worst tyrannical, heartless, brutal, and insufferable. Militancy is not likely to breed fraternal love; the militant had few friends and many toadies; and in the year III such people would have no friends at all, those whom they had once obliged or protected being the first to keep their distances. But already in the year II it is possible to distinguish between a minority of activists and the general mass of good, middling, or indifferent *sans-culottes*. As popular institutions everywhere declined, after Floréal, this distinction would already have become more marked, with a vast increase in this last category, so that the militants would become members of a tiny *cénacle*, devoted to keeping going a 'movement' that no longer existed – an act of revolutionary piety that was to be the principal concern of those who survived for the next twenty years.

Perhaps one of the greatest weaknesses of the popular movement of the year II was this reliance on very small groups of individuals, easily isolated and immediately identifiable, who through imprudence, conceit, or the foolish notion that their power would endure for ever, had made themselves and the movement with which they had become identified (and Thermidorian propaganda was devoted to 'personalizing' *la sans-culotterie* in a handful of names and character sketches) thoroughly disliked by a wide section of the community that included many people of their own condition. The hatred so often shown to them in the conditions of the year III cannot only have been the result of intelligent vilification; in some cases at least, particularly in Lyon and the Midi, they were hated because they had been hateful. Nothing very terrible happened to the former terrorists of the Upper Norman Departments. The most surprising thing about these zealous servitors of Terror and Repression was that they should have taken so many risks and offered themselves up so completely as hostages to the future. For few of their victims, real or potential, ever made the mistake of calculating that the Terror and the 'popular movement' would go on for ever, or that they could be anything other than temporary and accidental. Perhaps the enjoyment of power and genuine revolutionary patriotism were stronger inducements than common prudence. If one is to judge at all from Thermidorian reports – and these are, of course, heavily loaded – it is amazing how suicidal many of these militants had been, though more in speech than in action. Many of them were to pay with their lives for words uttered as boasts, to demonstrate that there was nothing that they could not, or would not, do.

In principle, Soboul is writing about a mass movement – this is his own approach – but in fact his celebrated thesis is mostly concerned with the role of élites and the methods employed by individual militants. He does name the militants, but he does not give any of them the benefit of a personality. The result is that we can see how they operated, but we gain virtually no impression of what they were like, whether they were sincere or were time-servers, whether they were out for publicity or for the fruits of office, whether they had sound sense or were crackpots. We just have to accept that they were militants and that something, whether ambition or sincerity, distinguished them from the general mass of their neighbours. He introduces us to *les sectionnaires* – that small core of six or seven hundred, sometimes even fewer, twenty or thirty in places like le Havre or Dieppe, ten or fifteen in small towns like Salon or Martigues – upon whom was to fall the weight of future successive proscriptions; but we do not meet *le sectionnaire*, the man himself, swimming in the history of the Revolution, fighting to keep his head above tormented and fast-flowing waters.

This is partly the author's own choice, for he is dealing with so large a team that, in a study of this kind, there could hardly be room for portraits of individuals. It might be objected too that recourse to personal 'case histories' puts too great a burden on the historian's imagination or on his powers of selection, that such a method is 'unscientific', and even borders on the anecdotal.[1] Even so, the impression remains that there is an element missing: Soboul has lived with his *sans-culottes*, but, perhaps, not very intimately – they are there to serve a purpose, and can then be dismissed. He gives only a cursory glance at their domestic arrangements and makes little attempt to track them down into non-political leisure; and, after

---

[1] The present author has been criticized for having, in his *Armées*, allowed certain of his characters too long an audience, simply because they had a lot to say for themselves, or because they were attractive, or amusing, or curious. See the review article by Hr. Kåre Tønnesson, in *Past & Present*, No. 1, 1964.

1795, they enter the night of time – unless they are lucky enough to have attracted the approving attention of Babeuf and his Revolutionary Selection Board.

This is a pity. The *sans-culottes*, particularly the more extravagant figures who, especially in small towns far from Paris, emerged at the head of them for a few months, were often intense individualists. They regarded the revolutionary movement as their own personal property and were unwilling to take orders from any man, however high placed and however covered in sash and ribbon. It is quite possible to add that further dimension by extending the time limit of research, as far as the Paris *sans-culottes* are concerned – hence the interest of following the 'popular movement' in Paris into the Slough of Despond from 1795 to 1816 or beyond, not so much to discover why the popular movement failed as to discover what happened to its leaders after the year III. The scope of research can also be extended by, for instance, investigating the 'pauperization' of the former *sans-culotte* cadres in the years IV and V, through petitions to the *Commission des Secours*, in order to justify indigence and so qualify for relief, at least in the form of free bread.[1]

Another method is to choose a smaller canvas and to study the *sans-culotte* milieu and certain dominant traits of the 'revolutionary temperament' in a provincial setting. For the real terrain of 'ultra-revolutionism' – a 'movement', if the term can be used for anything so individualistic and anarchical, far more extreme and less calculating than that of the Paris *sectionnaires* – was not in the capital, for the Parisians had the Revolutionary Government on their doorsteps and could not make a move without provoking threatening rumblings from the Committee of General Security. The opportunity for the 'ultra-revolutionary', a man who might be described, according to tastes, as *le révolutionnaire intégral*, as *un grand exaspéré*, or as *un grand naïf* and a fool of suicidal proportions, was in the Departments. There was a geography of 'ultracism' and revolutionary extremism. It extended in a vast half-moon, whose open end faced south, from Perpignan and Toulouse, via the valley of the Garonne (Moissac and Tonneins), to Libourne, thence to the Creuse and the Haute-Vienne. Parts of the Loiret and the Nièvre were at the top of the curve, which then sweeps down the valleys of the Loire and the Allier to include this last Department, thence via Mâcon to fan out into the present economic area of Rhône–Saône, from the Monts du Forez to the Swiss frontier, with Lyon as its capital[2] – and finally down the valley of the Rhône to the Mediterranean.

---

[1] See below, pp. 201, 204–5.
[2] 'La Commission temporaire de commune affranchie', in *Terreur et subsistances*, pp. 55–94; *L'Armée révolutionnaire parisienne à Lyon et dans la région lyonnaise*.

These, and certain garrison towns elsewhere, are the places where the ultra-revolutionary may be encountered in his untrammelled splendour and where the full implications of the *mouvement sectionnaire*, often only hinted at in the constricting circumstances of Paris, are developed, although briefly, to a full flowering of anarchical freedom. This too was the terrain of revolutionary experimentalism in every direction – popular justice, popular fiscality, dechristianization and popular cults, popular armed forces.[1] In some instances this experimentalism was the work of locals; but more often those who carried out the experiments were strangers, sometimes Parisians, generally townsmen, with strong contingents of talent from such places as Moulins and Nevers, Mâcon, Toulouse, Valence, Vienne, Grenoble. Such men, for a time, had no one on their backs and were not restrained by the influences of family or community.[2] We do not need Kropotkin to remind us that 'communalism' could have a better run for its money in the *commune* of Crémieu,[3] in that of Heyrieu,[4] in that of Tonneins-la-Montagne,[5] than in the *commune* of Paris.

The Committees were themselves well aware that the Sectionary movement was much more dangerous in the Departments than in Paris. This is what they meant when they asserted that *hébertisme* was a provincial phenomenon (it was). When they spoke of *l'ébauche d'un nouveau fédéralisme populaire*, they had in mind what was happening in Valence, Avignon, Marseille, and Montpellier, rather than what was going on under their noses in the capital. And, in the purges of the winter of 1793 and the spring of 1794, most of the arrests were in provincial towns, the nearest of which to the capital was Troyes; very few ultras were arrested in Paris itself, but a number of Parisians were arrested in Lyon, Bordeaux, Perpignan, Nice, Lille, and so on, along with their local helpers.[6] Again, as a result of the purges of the year III provincial ultras sought refuge in large numbers in Paris, which thus became, for the first time, the true capital of impenitent ultracism; their presence there did much to radicalize the surviving revolutionary movement, impelling it into channels never previously explored by the cautious, if vociferous, traditionalist,

---

[1] *Les Armées révolutionnaires*, II, pp. 425–63, 545–96, 618–33, 672–94, 707–40.

[2] Ibid., II, pp. 618–33.

[3] Contamin, the future *babouviste*, had been *agent national* of this small town in the Isère (see *L'Armée révolutionnaire à Lyon*, etc.).

[4] The *agent national* of the commune of Heyrieu, in the Isère, Dorzat, was guillotined in Paris in Messidor year II as an 'ultra-revolutionary'.

[5] Tonneins-la-Montagne was one of the few *communes* to have petitioned the Convention for the appointment of a *Grand Juge* and to have given active support to the *hébertiste* programme of more repression and of militarism (*Les Armées révolutionnaires*, II, pp. 814–15).

[6] Ibid., II, pp. 767–75.

and generally backward-looking Paris *sectionnaires*. Ultra-revolutionism, like its antithesis, ultra-royalism, flourishes fastest and most furiously far, far from Paris. This may have been an accident of temperament or it may have had something to do with local traditions (dechristianization did); but it was certainly largely due to the fact that the further one was away from Paris, the more one could get away with. Like so many other aspects of the popular movement during the revolutionary period, ultra-revolutionism owed much to immediate, accidental causes: distance, a power vacuum, the urgent exigencies of repression (and repression, in the autumn of 1793, had to be regionalized), local peculiarities. It is for this reason that, like any other branch of French social history, it can only properly be studied at a local or regional level. We have in fact to adopt the angle of vision of the average ultra-revolutionist, whose horizon rarely extended very far beyond what he could see.

9.   The Sans-Culotte *and the Outside World*

A problem that has much exercised present-day historians is why the popular movement in France went into a long decline from 1795, for twenty years or more, at the very time when, in England, the working-class movement was beginning to take shape – for Edward Thompson, 1795 is the year of England's 'abortive revolution' – and to tread, however timidly, the dangerous paths of sedition and armed revolt. If the course of the popular movement in England may have been influenced by what was happening in France, the contrary was certainly not the case, at least before the 1820s. The *sans-culottes* were supremely unaware of what was happening anywhere; for a long time they daily expected to hear that a mob had stormed St James's and the Tower, that George III had been overthrown, and that a similar fate had overtaken Charles IV, the Emperor, the Empress, the Sultan, the King of Portugal, *le roi sarde*, *le tyran de Naples*, and so on (they were delighted to hear of the assassination of one of the club, Gustavus III). The *sans-culottes* of Lorient even deluded themselves into believing in the imminence of a mighty nationalist rising on the part of *le pauvre Hindou, doux et timide* (a further illustration of just how wrong the *sans-culottes* could be) – a tempting belief, for it might have been the salvation of that decaying port. When none of these things happened, when foreign oppressed peoples failed to oblige, the *sans-culottes* hardened their hearts and developed a revolutionary chauvinism not very far removed from militarism and expansionism, while at the same time turning inwards, with the result that there was a revulsion at both popular and government levels in the early months of 1794 against the 'cosmopolitans' in Cloots's circus of professional, national-costumed refugees. By the summer of 1794 the surviving *sans-*

culottes had become as wildly, madly xenophobic as Robespierre, Saint-Just, and Barère.

The sans-culottes could afford to be noisily bellicose and demonstratively patriotic. They were mostly beyond military age and in little danger, unless they belonged to skilled trades of use to national defence, of being sent away from home, much less to the frontiers. They certainly were patriotic and they wanted to win the war, but from a distance (the place to win it was Tonneins-la-Montagne). Sans-culottisme also had a vested interest in war. But unlike Jacobinism it was not outward-looking or exportable (after all, the frontiers of sans-culottisme were so often confined to a single commune and it was very difficult to link up the efforts of sectionnaires even in two neighbouring towns). It is not surprising that it did not have an international audience. Indeed, Counter-Revolutionary Europe made no distinction between sans-culottisme and Jacobinism. Everyone, as far as Reeves or Playfair was concerned, was a 'Jacobin rascal', all were banditti. The sans-culottes might never have existed. No wonder they were to be kept out of the history books till 1958.

The popular movement during the Revolution was not only narrowly French but narrowly provincial. This is why, despite the occasional violence (and much of that violence was provincial also, the Revolt of Lyon in particular being both popular and anti-Parisian), it is reassuring. Later, no doubt, under the Directory, with the popular movement narrowed down to a tiny group of irreconcilables, to a conspiratorial élite, well described in the contemporary word exclusifs, and with the influx of Italian refugees and conspirators, a change does come about. No Infernal Machine would have been complete without its accompanying Italian. And many former sans-culottes discovered the world not only beyond the hill, but beyond France, in the supply services of the French armies of occupation. But this was after sans-culottisme had disappeared, at a time when there was little or no hope at home and when the popular movement, hitherto open, public, and persuasive, had developed new, secret, conspiratorial forms that had nothing in common with le mouvement sans-culotte. We can then dispose without much difficulty of the fact that while something was happening in France, something very different was happening in England. There was no reason why it should have been otherwise; the English public too was hopelessly misinformed about the pace of events in revolutionary France and was always at least two chapters behind. By 1795 it had just about reached the Girondin phase; and although Austrian, Hungarian, Greek, or German democrats, after 1795, called themselves 'Jacobins', and were called 'Jacobins' by the repressive authorities of their respective countries or empires, they were in reality much more like Girondins.

10.   *Causes and Consequences of the Failure of the 'Popular Movement'*
from 1795 to 1815

(i)   THE WHITE TERROR

Perhaps too much is made also of that other 'problem': the absence of an
effective popular movement in France during the period 1795 to 1815 (or
later). There is no great mystery about this as far as Paris and the other
cities are concerned. Once the popular movement had been defeated, in
Prairial year III, and the people disarmed, not only in Paris but in every
town in France – even rural *communes* would have their dozen or so *désarmés* – then clearly the *sans-culottes* could no longer impinge on events
by violence. An unarmed *sans-culotte* was politically a non-being. Two
recent French historians have suggested that the attachment felt by the
sectionnaire to his pike could be explained in sexual terms; certainly, once
deprived of it, he lost his sense of citizenship along with the visible emblem
of militancy. Just to make sure, the Thermidorian authorities did not stop
at disarmament. More often than not it was the first qualification for
arrest, and in every town more than half the *désarmés* were to spend anything up to six months in prison, the last of them being released at the time
of the amnesty of Brumaire year IV. In Paris as many as five thousand
people may thus have been arrested and deprived of their livelihood. The
total number of arrests for the whole country has never been worked out.
It must have amounted to more than eighty or ninety thousand, for even
in a smallish town like le Havre, with a population of twenty thousand,
between fifteen and twenty so-called *meneurs* were sent to prison,[1] and
their absence from work would no doubt affect the existence of some fifty
or sixty dependants. In Ingouville, with two thousand inhabitants, eight
poor artisans were arrested as partisans of the former *maire*, Musquinet-
Lapagne.[2] In both places, the arrests took place within a month of the fall
of Robespierre. There do not appear to have been any arrests in Dieppe;
but in the late spring and summer of 1795 about twenty former terrorists
were expelled from the *Garde nationale*, were asked to be available to give
an account of themselves at any moment, and were subjected to minor
humiliations; in Dieppe and le Havre they had their windows broken in
a series of weekend rowdinesses in the summer of 1795.[3] Many more

---

[1] *Terreur et subsistances*, pp. 221–55.
[2] AN, F1b II Seine-Inférieure I (Membres de l'administration d'Ingouville, Graville,
Sanvic, Lheure, Sainte-Adresse, Blesville, Saint-Jouin, destitués depuis le 10 thermidor, s.d.
an III).
[3] Arch. Dieppe D 1 6 (municipalité, séances des 28 germinal, 4 et 23 floréal et 19 messidor
an III). See also AN, D III 269 d 48 (Comité de législation, Seine-Inférieure, Dieppe,
commissaire national près le tribunal du district de Dieppe, au comité de législation,
1er pluviôse an III).

such people left their towns of origin to escape arrest, taking refuge with friends in Paris, where a small colony of Havrais was established in the year III and the year IV, as the subscription lists to Babeuf's paper reveal.

Many Lyonnais attempted to hide out in the countryside of the Forez, where their appearance, their clothes, and their accents caused them to be rapidly detected. A few of the more fortunate *mathevons* managed to reach Paris or Marseille, where they were immediate objects of suspicion, as the nuclei of groups of neo-terrorists. Mâconnais, inhabitants of a town that had given enthusiastic service to Terror and repression – partly, no doubt, out of hostility to Chalon, subjected to moderate influences – headed likewise for Paris, where they were at least physically safe; one, however, was ill inspired enough to show himself in Lyon in the year V. He was at once recognized, beaten to death, and thrown into the Saône. Very few managed to escape attention altogether if they remained in France; the Thermidorian authorities at District and *commune* levels showed considerable zeal in tracking down each other's refugees and in sending them back to their places of origin, which in the south-east often meant sending them back to a messy, battered death by rural lynching or by massacre in an urban prison.

The commonest opportunity for individual killing was when a former militant was escorted from the prison of the *chef-lieu* by a small posse of unenthusiastic *Gardes nationales* in order to be interrogated by the *juge de paix* of his former place of residence. That thoughtful official would have taken care to announce the day and time of his arrival several days in advance, so that the villagers could look forward to a killing with much the same excitement as they might await a *corrida* or a gathering of *boulistes*. The progress of the prisoner would be announced by word of mouth, several kilometres ahead of him. He would enter the village as he might a bull-ring, between two lines of shrieking women and children, excited by the prospect of blood. Sometimes the *juge de paix* was even obliging enough to see that the prisoner's arrival coincided with meal time. In several cases the prisoner was dispatched there and then on the main square or even at the entry to the *commune*. In any case it was only a matter of waiting; for, in other instances, he was butchered in prison, at nightfall, in the rather naïve belief that darkness would make the murderers less easy to recognize. In the Loire, the favourite killing time was *à l'heure du souper*, between nine and ten, when men were sure to be at home – a few, however, under cover of darkness, were able to reach their attics and escape over the roofs.[1] In Lyon, in the favourable conditions of

---

[1] For the murders in the Montbrison area, between Germinal and Thermidor year III, and in Germinal year V, see AN, BB 18 690.

the years III and V, *on assassinait en plein jour*, a fact that the authorities take as a clear sign of the collective responsibility of the inhabitants. There are similar reports from the Loire and the Haute-Loire. Equally, urban terrorists would be in constant danger from the moment they were transferred from the prison of their home town till they reached the town in which they were to be judged. Many never reached the courts at all. Here again the judges facilitated the work of potential murderers by informing their colleagues well in advance of the route to be taken by the prisoners. There is nothing mysterious about the geography of the White Terror and the many roadside and riverside murders of the years III, IV, V, and VII. Any road leading to Lyon was dangerous and there were two or three hundred convenient sites for slaughter between Lyon and Grenoble, Mâcon and Lyon, Lyon and Moulins, Montbrison and Lyon, Montbrison and Feurs, Montbrison and Boën, Saint-Étienne and le Puy, Yssangeaux and le Puy (a road on which many soldiers and *gendarmes* were also killed, mostly in the year IV), between Saint-Anthème and le Puy, Langeac and le Puy, Pradelles and le Puy, Craponne and le Puy, between Mâcon and Bourg, between Avignon and Marseille, Nîmes and Aix, Toulon and Marseille, Sisteron and Aix, between Pamiers, Ax, Tarascon, and Saverdun.

For there is no denying the effectiveness of the White Terror as a deterrent to popular militancy in an area that represents about a third of the national territory, nor is there any doubt about its essentially anti-popular character, even if a number of victims were wealthy farmers or high-ranking officials and many of the killers men of the people. In crudest terms, the White Terror accounted for perhaps as many as 2,000 popular militants in the area between the Swiss frontier and the Mediterranean, from Chalon-sur-Saône to Marseille and from the Monts du Forez and the Massif Central to the Alpilles. Bouvier, in the *Cinq-Cents*, reckoned that 1,500 had been murdered in the Vaucluse alone, in the killing grounds of the Haut-Comtat, between the year III and the year VII.[1] This may be something of a guess, and in Paris the extent of the White Terror was often deliberately exaggerated by authorities like Barras, Fréron, and Goupilleau de Montaigu, and by the press, in order to get repressive legislation introduced, while under the Directory, particularly in the year V, local garrison commanders, concerned to protect their own soldiers, no doubt tended to inflate the number of murders, so as to obtain full powers over the civil authorities with the introduction of a state of siege. The figures quoted for Lyon in particular, for the period year III–year VII,

---

[1] *Conseil des 500. Motion d'ordre faite par Bouvier* (séance du 26 fructidor an VII): 'Le nombre des brigans est de 1,000 à 1,200. Ils auroient commis 1,500 assassinats. Ces bandes sont composées principalement de réquisitionnaires.'

varied wildly according to whether the informant was hostile or favourable to the capital of the south. But detailed examination of the judicial records of the Bouches-du-Rhône for the last five years of the century provides a definitive minimal figure. Eight hundred persons of both sexes were murdered between Brumaire year III (the date of the first murder of the White Terror proper, though already in October 1793 a *patriote* had been shot and left dead by the roadside at Saint-Ambroix, in the District d'Alès (Gard), and there had been previous murders in the Bouches-du-Rhône in 1792 and 1793)[1] and the end of Fructidor year VIII. Four hundred and twenty-eight of these were killed in the Bouches-du-Rhône; the remaining 372 identified victims were killed in the Vaucluse,[2] the Gard (where there were about 20 victims in the year III alone),[3] the Lozère (with attacks on Protestant farmers), the Ardèche (the point of departure of many of the murder operations in the Haute-Loire in the year IV), the Drôme (a Department relatively immune),[4] the Basses-Alpes (where over 50 murders had been reported by the beginning of the year VI, most of them committed in the years IV and V),[5] the Loire, with 16 identified victims in the last four months of the year III,[6] the Haute-Loire, with 32

---

[1] AN, F1b II Gard I (Département au Ministre de l'Intérieur, 1er octobre 1793). The victim, Servier-Labadier, had incurred the hatred of the municipal authorities of the *commune* of Saint-Jean-de-Valérsilse by showing an alarming zeal in rounding up deserters.

[2] Tissot and Blaze, in their address to the Convention, dated 14 Thermidor year III, mention a further twenty-five murders committed up to that date in the Vaucluse, principally in the communes of l'Isle-sur-Sorgue and Mondragon.

[3] Of these, nine were murdered in Nîmes. These included the former *maire*, Courbis, and two members of the former Revolutionary Tribunal. The other murders identified took place in Beaucaire and Pont-Saint-Esprit.

[4] 'Vous ignorez peut-être que le Département de la Drôme, entouré des Départements de Rhône, de Vaucluse, et de l'Ardèche, foyers de contre-révolution, où l'assassinat des républicains étoit à l'ordre du jour depuis le 9 thermidor, s'est conservé sain dans la corruption générale' (AN, F1b II Drôme I, commissaire du Directoire au Ministre, 18 frimaire an IV).

[5] AN, F1b II Basses-Alpes I (les patriotes fugitifs des Basses-Alpes, actuellement à Paris, au Conseil des 500, 19 vendémiaire an VI). On 27 Frimaire, the Ministre de la Police wrote to his colleague of the Intérieur: 'Une longue continuité d'assassinats en a souillé depuis plus de deux ans le sol infortuné … il y a trois semaines qu'on assassinait encore aux portes de Digne, à Sisteron, à Manosque, à Oraison et dans quelques autres communes … Les patriotes exilés depuis plus de trois ans n'y rentrent qu'en frémissant.' A report later the same year states: 'Les assassinats se multiplient d'une manière effrayante dans le département des Basses-Alpes … C'est contre les républicains, les acquéreurs des biens nationaux que sont dirigés ces actes de brigandage.'

[6] AN, BB 18 690. The known victims of the murders of Germinal–Thermidor year III are: Giron, *tisserand*; Bouarde; Clément, *greffier*; Perraud, *vigneron-jardinier*; Poche, *chapelier*; Paley, *officier de santé*; Bard, *maçon*; *l'abbé* Bouchet; Reprennant, a refugee from Lyon; Mari, *officier municipal* of Saint-Étienne; Magnien, *imprimeur*; Drouillet; two inhabitants of Saint-Étienne; Jay; Grison's brother. A further twenty-five inhabitants of Montbrison left the Loire in order to escape assassination, returning only in the early months of the year IV.

named victims, most of them killed in the spring of the year IV,[1] the
Rhône, with a minimum of 87 murders for the period year III–year XII
(1795–1804) over and above the 109 named victims of the three prison
massacres of the year III (this too is a minimal figure).[2] Four or five people
may have been killed in the Tarn in the year IV[3] and there were five victims
of a single foray in Clermont-Ferrand.[4] There appear to have been many
murders in the Ariège (three victims are known by name); and we know
of eight victims in the Ain, of three in the Var, and of one in the Gironde.
But this figure of 846 is far from representing the total number of political assassinations – our calculations do not include private vendettas,
family poisonings, murder with robbery, all common in the south-east
during these years – in these Departments.

Many murders remained unreported and never reached the ears of the

---

[1] AN, F1b II Haute-Loire I. These included Samon, *négotiant*, of Yssangeaux; Géry, *culti-vateur*, of Montgevin; Durand, *laboureur*, of la Gaillarde; Dusny, *tisserand*, of Tixe; Pamelier, *greffier*, of Yssangeaux; Bonfils, *aubergiste*, of Craponne; Pouviane, *cultivateur*, of Saint-Just; Charitat, *cultivateur et riche propriétaire*, *officier municipal* of Négraval; Fayolle, *lieutenant dans le 6me bataillon des côtes maritimes*, of Retournac; Sollilhac, *ex-gendarme*, of Beauzac; Cartlet, of Vergues; and a score of *gendarmes* killed in operations against the *compagnies*.
[2] These include an *agent de police*, a refugee from Mâcon, two inhabitants of Saint-Genis, three terrorists from the Croix-Rousse, three former *officiers municipaux*, a refugee from Feurs, several soldiers, some of whom seem to have been killed in brawls with royalist-inclined hussars, others the victims of the Lyon *crocheteurs*; a refugee from Chasselay; two former *officiers municipaux* of Neuville, and several unidentified people whose bodies were found in the Rhône or the Saône (Arch. Rhône I L 208, 209, 382, 383, 393, Département, assassinats ans III–VII, and 2 L 53+.93+.96+, District de Lyon-Ville, an III). Other identi-fied victims include a Lyon hatter, a Lyon jeweller, the wife of a stonemason, a prostitute, a night-watchman, a wine merchant and his wife, all from Lyon, three children from la Guillotière, a wealthy landowner from Beaujeu, several *gendarmes* from Vaugneray, Thizy, and Tarare (AN, BB 18, 685–6–7–8, Ministère de la Justice, Rhône, ans III–XII) (Arch. Rhône 8d.1*, 18d.10*–11*, 21d.1*–2*–3*–4*–5*, 12d.3*). Among those identified as Lyon *égorgeurs* and against whom legal proceedings were started were ten people in the drink trade – *aubergistes*, *marchands de vin*, etc. – 5 *crocheteurs*, 4 river-workers, 3 hairdressers, 2 butchers, 2 bakers, 2 *notaires*, 2 porters, 2 old-clothes merchants, 4 silk-workers (AN, BB 18 690).
[3] AN, F1b II Tarn I: 'Il y a eu 4 à 5 assassinats de patriotes, entr'autres à Semalens, à Teillet, à Saint-Gervais, &ca, et le commissaire n'a rien dit' (*Journal des Hommes libres*, No. 97, 22 nivôse an V). The *commissaire*, Terral, admitted that a man had been murdered at Saint-Gervais, in Prairial year IV, but claimed that his murderers had been tried and condemned to death.
[4] AN, F1b Puy-de-Dôme I. This was a particularly cold-blooded massacre. On Sunday, 21 Messidor year V, the members of a *cercle constitutionnel* organized a picnic in the Bois-du-Cros, outside Clermont-Ferrand. Their meeting was authorized by the authorities; but, in the course of the afternoon, a company of the *Garde nationale* surrounded the wood and fired at random into the Sunday crowd. Five were killed instantly, thirty-three were severely wounded, several of whom died in the next few weeks. The massacre was carefully planned and was carried out with obvious enjoyment by the *Garde nationale* and their female supporters.

higher authorities. The *accusateur public* of the Gard had the greatest difficulty, on taking up his post in Brumaire year IV, in obtaining even the scantiest information about the murders committed in this unhappy Department during the previous year. An unknown number of those who had been severely wounded in pistol or sabre attacks died within a matter of weeks or months in the places of refuge to which their relatives had moved them (in the Ariège, one victim lingered on for three months). The figures extant for the Var are quite unrepresentative of the scale of the White Terror there both in the year III (following the Toulon rising) and in the year IV. And there were pockets of murder in the Isère,[1] frequent murders in the Ain,[2] and isolated affairs in the Mont-Blanc, the Jura, and the Saône-et-Loire.[3] In the Rhône, as many as 350 people may have been killed, though a number of these were soldiers and other strangers to the city; several were killed in duels between rival corps, a few may have floated down from localities upstream on the Rhône and on the Saône, while some were undoubtedly the victims of criminal gangs.[4] Individual murders were almost a daily occurrence in Lyon itself and in the *communes* of its periphery (in Messidor year V, when the Second City was put under a state of siege, this was extended to Vaise, la Croix-Rousse, and la Guillotière)[5] from Pluviôse year III to the end of the summer of

---

[1] AN, F1b II Isère I (Burdet, ex-juge de paix de Vienne, au Directoire, 30 fructidor an V).

[2] AN, F1b II Ain I (Paté fils, de Bourg, à Gauthier de l'Ain, 28 brumaire an V).

[3] AN, F1b II Saône-et-Loire I (extrait du procès-verbal de l'administration municipale de Mâcon, 9 prairial an V): 'A Pont-de-Vaux, la semaine dernière, trois hommes ont été assassinés, point de témoins, il m'a été dit que deux sont morts, au faubourg de la Barre la semaine dernière deux citoyens ont été assassinés, ils sont morts ... j'ai des soupçons que les assassinats sont organisés, les soupçons viennent de ce qu'ils ont tous le même caractère ... Notre commune a été tranquille ... pendant 15 mois, un seul homme avoit été assassiné et tué en messidor [an IV] par des chanteurs du *Réveil du peuple*.'

[4] Arch. Rhône I L 283. On 24 Messidor year V, a group of dragoons, associated with a prostitute called *Suissesse*, who was also a thief and who had been the mistress of a bandit, condemned to death in the year III for murder and highway robbery, attacked a *gendarme* outside the Caserne des Augustins. In many other cases, the Lyon authorities attempt to argue that the murders reported to the Directory are the work of small groups of professional criminals, themselves strangers to the city. Certainly the dragoons appear to have been deeply involved in theft.

[5] Arch. Rhône 1 L 383. Lyon and its three *communes* were placed *en état de siège*, under the authority of General Kellermann, by the Directory, on 24 Messidor year V and again on 14 Pluviôse year VI. The local authorities, bitterly hostile to Canuel, the *commandant de place*, and to his troops, attempted to have the garrison removed and civil authority re-established, in the interest, so they said, of the city's trade. Their real objection to the presence of the troops was, no doubt, that it limited the activities of the murder gangs, the municipal officers being good friends of the *compagnie de Jésus*, and because the soldiers were Parisians or Dauphinois who hated the Lyonnais. It was for this reason that they consistently argued that the bodies seen floating in one of the two rivers must have been killed upstream, north of Lyon, and why they so persistently attempted to play down the constant repetition of political murders.

the year V, and seven known murders can be listed for the period Pluviôse–Germinal year III, before the prison massacres of Floréal and Prairial of that year.

The big murder year was the year III, with a minimum 420 victims for the three Departments of the Bouches-du-Rhône, the Gard, and the Vaucluse. A hundred and fifty people were killed the same year in the Rhône and the Loire. There were forty-five known murders in the former area, and twenty in the Rhône and the Haute-Loire, in the year IV. In that year, killings may have actually increased, when many former terrorists returned to public office, as a result of the amnesty of Brumaire year IV (though, in the Lyon area at least, there was a drop in the number of victims, thanks no doubt to the presence in the Loire of Reverchon). Thus Saurel, whose son had been assassinated in Frimaire year IV, was appointed *commissaire du Directoire* for the canton of Malemort-du-Comtat, in the former District de Carpentras, in the following Pluviôse but was unable to take up the appointment, as he knew that if he returned to his village those who had killed his son would not hesitate to kill him too. (This is what they meant when they said they would give him *le pouvoir exécutif*.)[1]

Thirty-three murders are recorded in the Gard, the Bouches-du-Rhône, and the Vaucluse, for the year V, when conditions were especially favourable to the *égorgeurs* in the Midi – it was perhaps their best year – thanks to the presence of General Willot in Marseille and the return of many royalists to Department or municipal office. (One of them, Vincent, a member of the municipal administration of Marseille, was a leader of a murder gang in that and the following year.) In the year V, too, there were at least seven murders in the Saône-et-Loire at the time of the *assemblées primaires*; the murders appear to have been connived at by the members of the Departmental administration, who, in Mâcon, gave orders for the military not to be called out at the request of the municipality, whose members still showed some concern to protect the lives of leading republicans in the town.[2] If this was the position in Mâcon, it is not surprising

---

[1] AN, F1b II Vaucluse I (Notes de Saurel, sur les propos des habitants de Mallemort). On 6 Brumaire year IV, a large crowd gathered outside his house, shouting: 'Descend, coquin de Saurel Robespierre et nous te ferons ton compte ... nous voulons avoir ta vie, boire ton sang et manger ton foie.' His son, a member of the *comité* of the year II, was murdered at six in the morning of 5 Frimaire year IV on the road to Pierre Blanche, by a baker nick-named *le capucin* and Barthélemy Gras, *dit le coupeur*. Saurel took refuge in Carpentras, 7 Pluviôse following. A year previously, 9 Frimaire year III, another terrorist, Antoine Mus, had been assassinated by the same group; his body was left outside for two days.

[2] AN, F1b II Saône-et-Loire I (Rubat, commissaire du Directoire à Mâcon, à Roberjot, le 9 prairial an V; Dutroncy à Reverchon, le 13 prairial; Genty le jeune à Reverchon, le 13 prairial; lettre de Genty le jeune, de Mâcon, le 15 prairial; Genty le jeune à Reubell, le 19 prairial; Genty le jeune à Reverchon, le 28 prairial).

that the year V – especially the summer months – should have been an exceptionally good period for the activities of the *compagnies* in Lyon, which the military authorities rightly described, in Messidor and in Fructidor, as the *centre d'impulsion* of the White Terror in the South;[1] there were twenty-one murders in and around the city between Nivôse and Fructidor, resulting in the death of at least thirty-one persons (the military authorities were to put the figure as high as sixty-seven); and there were some dozen murders or attempted murders in the Loire – mostly in Montbrison, in Germinal, at the time of the *assemblées primaires*.[2] As in the year III, these murders appear to have been carried out on orders from Lyon.

There is sparse documentation for the nine murders – three in the Bouches-du-Rhône, five in the Rhône, one in the Var[3] – committed in the year VI, and for the twenty-five of the year VII. But, with the exception of the Bouches-du-Rhône and possibly the Loire, these figures for the whole period year III–year VII (two murders in the Rhône, a department in which nine people were killed in the year VIII, five in the year IX, one in the year X, two in the year XI, and seven in the year XII) certainly do not represent even a quarter of the incidence of the White Terror in these south-eastern and south-central Departments; and to obtain anything like an over-all picture of this carefully planned and well-organized system of extermination, it would be necessary to extend the investigation to the Hérault, to the Cantal (where murders are stated to have been frequent),[4] and to the Ardèche, all places in which the *compagnies* controlled considerable areas, especially in inaccessible mountain fastnesses, the paradise of bandit and deserter. For the Haute-Loire we have figures only up to the end of the year IV. It is established too that there were isolated murders, at least in the year V, in Dijon. It would certainly not be unreasonable to suggest that as many persons were murdered in the south-east and the west between 1795 and 1803 as perished during the Terror of the year II. If only in terms of numbers, the White Terror was brutally effective.

It was even more so in the quality of its victims; for the movement was neither blind, nor anarchical, nor spontaneous. In this respect, it differed

---

[1] 'Nous avons encore demandé au Bureau Central s'il existe dans Lyon une compagnie d'assassins à gages, organisée sous des chefs, et à laquelle on donne le nom de compagnie de Jésus ... Le général Canuel ... nous a assuré ... que c'étoit à 11 brigands vivant dans Lyon et épargnés par la police qu'étaient dûs les meurtres' (Arch. Rhône I L 283, rapport du Département du 27 messidor an V) (AN, BB 18 685–6).

[2] AN, BB 18 690.

[3] Arch. Rhône I L 283 and AN, F1b II Var I. The murder in the latter Department took place at Hyères on 12 Nivôse, New Year's Day.

[4] AN, F1b II Saône-et-Loire I (Dutroncy le jeune à Reverchon, 17 prairial an V).

significantly from the ultra-revolutionary movements that had flourished in much the same areas in the autumn of 1793. Witnesses report that groups of *égorgeurs* wore identifiable uniforms – blue jackets with red woollen epaulettes. Their leaders were generally widely known – often local squires, back from abroad; north of Lyon, the *gens à cadenettes* and the *oreilles de chien* are identified by name, as local royalists, either from Lyon itself, or from Chalon, and their victims were chosen with discrimination. They represented the *fine fleur* of *sans-culotte* militancy in places like Lyon, Marseille, Aix, Arles, Salon, Martigues, Tarascon, Beaucaire, Nîmes, Bagnols, Pont-Saint-Esprit, Bourg, Lons, Mâcon, Pont-de-Vaux, Privas, Montbrison, Feurs, Boën, Chazelles, Givors, Saint-Genis-Laval, Neuville, Oullins, Condrieu, Yssangeaux, le Puy, Langeac; in rural *communes* and *bourgs* – Auriol, Aubagne, Noves, Lambesc, Sénas, Orgon, Graveson, Mallemort, and the equally sanguinary Mallemort in the Vaucluse, Saint-Chamas, Istres, Eyragues, Barbentane, Pélissanne, Gémenos, L'Isle, Mondragon, Morières, Hyères, Saint-Maximin-la-Sainte-Baume, Rians, Porrières, Tourves, Saint-Just-en-Bas, Chalmazel, Pralong, Champdieu, Magneux-Haute-Rive, Moingt, Vaugneray, Mornant, Allègre, Saint-Paulien, Félines, Jullianges, Retournac, Craponne, Beauzac – they were the artisans and the *journaliers* who, in the year II, had established contacts with the urban *sectionnaires* and had sacked the local churches.[1] Members of *comités de surveillance* and of *comités sectionnaires*, of regional *tribunaux révolutionnaires* and *commissions révolutionnaires*, are picked up for massacre first. Several former *maires* – including those of Nîmes, Martigues, and Port-Chamas – and *commandants de la garde nationale*, as well as leading *sociétaires*, are killed. Three *agents nationaux de district* of the year II, including that of Marseille, were murdered in this area, for the White Terror of the year III was as much directed against former Jacobins as against *sans-culotte* militants.

In social terms, however, the *sans-culotte* composition of the *égorgés* is so strikingly apparent – much more than that of many of the popular institutions of the previous year – that one might well ask whether the White Terror was not as much directed against a class, for being what it was, as against groups of officials, for being what they had been, though most of the murderers were people of similar origin. In a number of

---

[1] On 7 Ventôse year III, the *comité* of Salon wrote to the municipality of Mallemort: 'Nous avons reçu l'extrait des différentes déclarations ... faites relativement à la dévastation de l'église de votre commune et nous avons partagé votre indignation.' The same day they wrote to the *agent national* of Martigues: 'Il est venu à notre connaissance que les églises de ta commune avoient été dévastées sous l'infernal régime de Robespierre par les sans-culottes de ton pays.' In both *communes*, those who were murdered later in the year III or in the year IV had been denounced as the *dévastateurs des églises*.

instances, the widows or daughters *se déclarent réduites à l'indigence la plus extrême* as the result of the murder of the bread-winner. In one case, in Lambesc, all the male members of the family, a father and his two sons, were killed and the surviving womenfolk had to sell the family land. Many of the victims had large families of young children, who would grow up, with vengeance in their hearts, among their parents' murderers and would sometimes themselves be struck down twenty years later, as people with an inconvenient memory. The White Terror was socially and economically effective as an instrument of the anti-popular offensive that began in earnest in the spring of the year III.

But it also struck higher up. At least ten *commissaires du Directoire* – most of them former militants – were assassinated. More than forty claim to have been shot at in the street, in a café, or while sitting at their windows. A *commissaire* in Aix complains in the year VI that the *sabreurs* are in the habit of leaving the corpses of their victims on his front doorstep. In the Marseille area, Lyon, and the Haute-Loire, army officers and *volontaires* from urban battalions are frequently done to death, generally by stabbing or shooting, when caught out alone or in pairs. (The *sabreurs*, many of them deserters, rightly regarded the army as the most effective surviving citadel of neo-terrorism.) A number of unfortunate *gendarmes* were likewise slaughtered on their country rounds; but in the Saône-et-Loire it is claimed by republican sympathizers that the local *gendarmerie* is hand in glove with the *oreilles de chien* based on Chalon and on Lyon. In the Bouches-du-Rhône, the Gard, the Vaucluse, and the Lozère, the victims of some of the most appalling massacres are wealthy farmers (Protestants in the Lozère), killed at night, along with their families and servants, in their *bastides*; their bodies are hung from cypress trees at the entry to their farms. They were all *acquéreurs de biens nationaux*. We hear of similar victims in the Basses-Alpes. Other victims include a *receveur*, a chief inspector of police, an official concerned with recruitment, a tax collector. Near Mâcon, a *compagnie*, sent to kill a *commissaire* on his country estate, finding him absent, murders his *vigneron* instead.[1] Those who directed the White Terror were not content to kill off the survivors of the popular movement or to frighten its remaining potential leaders out of the area (there are references to a whole colony of Mâconnais in Paris, in the year V, headed by Roberjot and Reverchon; in their letters to these high-ranking refugees, the local *patriotes* urge them

---

[1] AN, F1b II Saône-et-Loire I (Tableau actuel du département de Saône-et-Loire, s.d. prairial an V): 'On croit votre commissaire près le Département (Rubat) à sa campagne à une demie-lieue de Mâcon, une compagnie d'égorgeurs s'y rend dans la nuit et après (avoir) examiné partout chez son vigneron et ne trouvant pas Rubat, ils assassinent ce malheureux vigneron et sa fille, ces scélérats n'étoient pas des voleurs, mais des égorgeurs qui en vouloient au commissaire Rubat.'

on no account to return). They also sought to make the republican government unworkable and to demonstrate its incapacity to protect life or property.[1]

The calendar of the White Terror reflects, though often in caricature, the general course of the political reaction in Thermidorian and Directorial France. There are only a few isolated murders in the winter months of 1794–5 (one in Brumaire, one in Frimaire, two in Nivôse year III). The killing season opens, but still spasmodically, in Pluviôse (three murders). By Ventôse, the *sabreurs* are beginning to exact a regular toll – on the 16th, in the Lyon *comité*, 'un membre a dit: des assassinats se commettent journellement'. The anti-terrorist legislation of that month gave direct encouragement to the White Terror by placing its potential victims within easy reach of local gangs. There are more murders in Germinal than in Ventôse, more still, including some of the big prison massacres, in Floréal. But the movement does not acquire its full intensity until Prairial, when it was spurred on by news from Paris, by the intensification of anti-terrorist legislation, and, above all, by the report of the neo-Jacobin rising in Toulon. All over the south-east there was a genuine fear that, following the example of Toulon, the terrorists were everywhere about to return to power and to active terrorizing. In Marseille there were murders on the 1st, 2nd, 3rd, 10th, 13th, 14th, 17th, and 27th, some of them committed by *Gardes nationales* on their return from Toulon. Other killings took place in Tarascon on the 6th; in Pont-Saint-Esprit on the 8th, 10th, and 13th, when groups of prisoners, in transit from the Vaucluse to the Gard, were crossing the very long bridge over the Rhône (a monument as important in the geography of the White Terror as the celebrated bridge at Avignon or the bridge between the Saône-et-Loire and the Ain at Mâcon); in Pélissanne on the 12th; in Salon on the 16th; in Sénas on the 27th; and in Nîmes on the 28th. Prairial year III was the first really good month for the *sabreurs*. The momentum was maintained throughout the rest of the summer – murders in Tarascon, Entraigues, Salon, and Morières on 3 Messidor (a Sunday), in Saumane-de-Vaucluse on the 7th; in Avignon on the 8th; in Aubagne on the 9th; in Beaucaire on the 17th; and in Eyragues on the 21st; eight murders for Thermidor and Fructidor.[2] The pattern is

---

[1] Arch. Bouches-du-Rhône L 174* (lettre du Département au Ministre de la Police, 3 germinal an IV): 'Cette impunité (des sabreurs) atterre les Républicains. Le peuple, qui ne juge des choses que par les effets, croit que les assassins eurent raison d'égorger les républicains ... On lui fait croire que tel est le sort réservé aux imprudens qui se mêlent des révolutions; que le triomphe du républicanisme n'est qu'éphémère ... le Peuple le croira, et aura raison de le croire, tant que les assassins resteront impunis.'

[2] There are murders in Montbrison on 1er Prairial, and again on the 4th (Ascension Day), in Geneva on the 7th (a pan-French affair), in Lyon on the 8th, in Montbrison on the 13th (a Monday), in Lyon and in Montbrison on the 25th (a Saturday); in Montbrison on 6 Messidor (the eve of the Saint-Jean), and on the 11th (Monday, the eve of the Saint-Pierre);

similar for the year IV: fourteen murders for the winter months (Vendémiaire to Nivôse), seventeen *sorties* for the summer.[1] In the year V and the year VII, Messidor, Thermidor, and Fructidor top the list; but in the Saône-et-Loire the murder month in the year V is, as in the year III in so many other places, Prairial. The total score gives twenty-seven massacres or murders for Prairial (mostly in the special circumstances of the year III), sixteen for Messidor (nine in the year III), ten each for Thermidor, Fructidor, and Floréal – that is, in all, seventy-two massacres or murders between 20 April and 21 September, twenty-six for other seasons. While killing in this part of the world went on all the year round, it reached its maximum intensity in summer violence, mid-June to mid-September being the height of the season, as it was that of the epidemics that, in the north of France, swept off the urban and rural poor in the years III and IV.

The course of the White Terror also reflects, with remarkable fidelity, the habits of rural and urban riot and turbulence. Predictably, then, Sunday heads the list, with twenty-nine murders or massacres; there are fourteen for Monday, twelve for Saturday, and eleven for Friday.[2] Fifty-six, out of a total of ninety-four *sorties*, are weekend affairs; thirty-nine take place mid-week, most on Tuesday and Thursday, favourite days for markets and court proceedings. There are three murders on successive Christmas Days (after midnight Mass), two on successive New Year's Days, four on successive 9 Thermidor. 28 Thermidor (15 August in the years III, IV, and V), Ascension Day, Palm Sunday, Whitsun Eve, Midsummer Night, and St Bartholomew's Day are other favourites.[3]

Forty-two of the affairs summarized take place in Lyon and its satellite *communes*, eighteen in Marseille, fourteen in or near Montbrison, five in Arles, five in Tarascon, four in Noves, four in Aix, eight in the small town of Graveson, three in Nîmes, three in Pont-Saint-Esprit, five in Avignon, five in Mâcon, four in Lambesc, with scattered murders in twenty or thirty other places in the Bouches-du-Rhône, the Gard, the Vaucluse, the Rhône, the Loire, and the Haute-Loire. Three areas particularly notorious for vio-

---

in Pamiers on the 26th (Sunday). There are murders in Saverdun (Ariège) on 29 and 30 Thermidor (Saturday and Sunday).

[1] The year IV is the principal murder year in the Haute-Loire, whereas in the Lyon area the *sabreurs* seem to have gone underground. Murders in the Haute-Loire occur on 4 Brumaire (Monday), 3–4 Nivôse (Christmas Day), 6 Nivôse (Sunday), 15 Nivôse, 2–3 Pluviôse, 11 Germinal, 21 and 22 Germinal (Sunday and Monday). There are only three murders in the Lyon region for this year: 28 Nivôse (Givors), 26 Ventôse (Charney), 4 Prairial (Lyon).

[2] In the Lyon area, the score is: Sunday 16, Saturday 13, Monday 17, Wednesday 17, Friday 14, Tuesday 9, Thursday 11: in other words, 42 for the weekend, 51 mid-week, including Friday.

[3] In the Lyon area, Christmas scores two murders, 1 January two murders; Ascension Day, 9 Thermidor, Palm Sunday, Whitsun eve, Carnival, the eve of St John, the eve of St Peter, and, suitably, St Bartholomew's Day, one each.

lence and for gang rule were the countryside round Bagnols on the Rhône opposite to the Vaucluse, the canton of Saint-Paul-Trois-Châteaux, in the south of the Drôme, again bordering the Vaucluse, and mountain areas of the Haute-Loire bordering the Loire and the Ardèche (the inhabitants of the Haute-Loire had the reputation with their neighbours of being particularly uncouth and ferocious). The persistence of violence in such places as Noves, Barbentane (where murders had been going on ever since 1792), Graveson, and Montbrison is indicative of the organization and impunity of the local gangs – some of them really popular, their exploits the affectionate pride of whole communities. It also shows the bitterness of personal, political, and religious feuds in small towns and villages. (Many of the victims of the White Terror in the Lozère and the Ariège were well-to-do Protestant farmers or city artisans, and some in the Carpentras area were Jews.) Like the Terror of the year II, the White Terror of 1795–9 reached its ugliest proportions in small communities, *entre gens de connaissance*. Most of the murderers were well known to their victims – some, a few hours before dying of their wounds, identified them: 'C'est le fils Fabre', 'Ce sont *les Gros Yeux* et son frère *l'Effrayant*'. Sometimes the customers of one inn go to the inn on the other side of the square and proceed to kill all those who are drinking there. And just as *on assassinait en famille*, whole families were assassinated. Many women were killed – generally, republican reports would have it, while clutching babies to their breasts. A number of children were also bayoneted to death; while, in Salon, Saint-Chamas, Noves, Eyragues, children are reported at the head of the *égorgeurs*. Even in Marseille the murderers insult their victims by name before finishing them off; in Nîmes and Pont-Saint-Esprit, the victims were public figures, well known to the whole population. Finally, both in rural and urban incidents, women are revealed as particularly ferocious. They provide the incitement: 'Sabrez, sabrez, mes amis, n'en laissons aucun, aucune, si vous êtes des hommes, tuez-les tous, jusqu'aux femmes et aux enfants, et toi, petite Montagnarde, tu le regrettes bien, ton maximum' is the litany of *la femme Colon*, an Arlésienne, as she attempts to enlist a group of *sabreurs* against some *sans-culotte* neighbours (she also wanted to push a mother and daughter into the *Vieux Port*). Not only do they revel in a cannibalistic vocabulary, but they actually take part in murder. They dismember the bodies of victims – in Eyragues women drag a body along by the hair, and tip it over the ramparts – and they boast about their ability to kill (*c'est moi qui . . .*).[1] It

---

[1] '*Voici le beau Durand, le sansculotte*, la femme Tourette a dit à une voisine: *Je lui en ai bien foutu, j'ai de son sang au bout de mon bâton.*' A witness adds the detail: 'Sur les remparts, plusieurs enfans attroupés jetoient des pierres contre led. cadavre' (Assassinat de Claude Durand, ex-commandant de la garde nationale d'Eyragues, à Eyragues, 21 messidor an III) (Arch. Bouches-du-Rhône L 3072).

was not always mere boasts: in Lyon, Roux, a member of the municipality of the year II, was recognized in the street, 29 Germinal year III (a Saturday), by a group of women, who stoned him to death and tore the body to pieces, scattering the bits into the Saône.[1]

Most of the victims of the White Terror – especially in the countryside – are poor people who cannot afford the luxury of exile in a distant town and are tied to their work by debt, by family, or by easy credit. Some, it is true, took refuge with relatives in villages a few miles away, in a neighbouring Department or District; but this did not put them out of reach of the gangs, who came to get them in the course of a day's outing. The result was that a number of rural or semi-rural terrorists from the Bouches-du-Rhône were murdered just over the border of the Vaucluse, in some instances just on the far bank of the Durance, like that carpenter's wife from Châteaurenard whose headless body, half-eaten by wolves, was discovered at the riverside. There was also a considerable amount of exchange of information between judicial and local authorities as well as between the gangs themselves, who appear to have kept in close touch between one Department and another, at least in the whole area from Lyon to the sea, and from Chalon and Montbrison to Lyon. (It was not unreasonable to see in Lyon the headquarters of a vast movement that covered the whole of the Rhône–Saône valley and the Monts du Forez; Lyonnais killers are reported in Mâcon, Bourg, Montbrison, Lons, Oullins, Neuville, Saint-Genis, and Yssangeaux, as well as in Marseille and Avignon, while killers from Montbrison boast of how they have lent a hand to the Lyon killers in the prison massacres.)[2]

The judges and the *juges de paix* were the most effective auxiliaries of the *sabreurs*, who would soon have been rendered harmless had the judiciary made the smallest attempt to carry out government instructions. They saw to it that their potential victims should be made conveniently available, and that the murderers should have nothing to fear from the law. Persecuted *sans-culottes*, on the other hand, were unable to have their

---

[1] Arch. Rhône 31 L 164* (29 germinal an III). We hear too of a group of Avignonnaises, 'les nommées Thérèse, veuve de Baignet … porteur de chaise, et la femme du nommé Bergin, devuideuse, et la fille de ladite Baignet', who, after a former terrorist has been assassinated in the street, pick up the body: '*Prenez avec la Bergin chacune par un pied chacune et moi qui suis plus forte je le prendrai par la tête*, ce qu'elles firent … et le transportèrent en le laissant aller avec rudesse, au milieu de la ruelle, en outre la Bergin se saisit d'une grosse pierre, la lança sur ledit Fanton …' (Arch. Bouches-du-Rhône L 3082, par devant le juge de paix du 1er arrondissement du canton d'Avignon, 9 thermidor an V).

[2] The Thermidorian *comité* of Salon writes, on various occasions, in Nivôse, Pluviôse, and Ventôse, to the *comités* of Apt, Auriol, Marseille, Toulon, Sénas, Istres, and Martigues, in an effort to trace down the *terroristes salonnais* who had taken refuge in these *communes* and requesting that, if found, they should be returned forthwith to Salon (Arch. Bouches-du-Rhône L 1858, comité de Salon, an III).

complaints registered with the *juges de paix*, who also failed to notify the higher authorities – *agents nationaux, commissaires du Directoire* – of the murders and acts of violence committed within the areas of their jurisdiction. This is one reason why it is difficult to obtain an over-all picture; indeed, in some rural areas, the families of victims were afraid to declare their dead to the *état civil*. If really pressed, the *juges de paix* and the judges of the *tribunaux criminels* – in the year V, royalist almost without exception in the south-east – would warn *sabreurs*, some of whom were their close relatives, well in advance that a warrant was on the way. It was hardly surprising that most of the known murderers were declared in flight when their trials came up; a number of them are stated to be absent in Lyon *pour leurs affaires*.

In the south-east, distance offered no guarantee of security, and a *mathevon* was no safer in the Bouches-du-Rhône, the Gard, or the Vaucluse, than he would have been if he had sought refuge in the countryside of the Rhône and the Loire; Lyonnais perished in the prison massacres of Aix, Marseille, and Nîmes, Foréziens and Bressois in those of Lyon; a Mâconnais and a Forézien were lynched in Lyon in the year V, and *assommeurs* went out from Lyon to kill their own people in the Loire, the Haute-Loire, the Jura, the Isère, the Saône-et-Loire, and the Drôme. Only the Puy-de-Dôme seems to have offered a comparatively safe refuge to the artisan from Lyon or from Montbrison during the dangerous months of Germinal year III to Brumaire year IV. Despite strong local ties, the gangs appear to have had some sort of centralized command: in the Haute-Loire, their activities seem to have been directed from the Ardèche and the Gard, and there is talk there, in Floréal year III, of a concerted military action involving the *compagnies* from Marseille, Montpellier, Pont-Saint-Esprit, and Montbrison.[1] White terrorists were certainly far more successful at co-operation between neighbouring Departments, towns, or villages than the much more locally orientated *sans-culottes* had been. They also possessed a far more efficient network of escape and refuge. A carpenter from Lyon might hope to receive help from those in his trade in Marseille; but it was easy to look for him among other carpenters. The *sabreurs*, like the *chauffeurs* at the other end of the country, enjoyed the support of a chain of innkeepers, so that, their operations completed in the Bouches-du-Rhône, they could lie low for a time in Nîmes or in Montpellier. The high road from Lyon to Montbrison and that from Lyon to le Puy contained more welcoming *étapes* at the disposal of the *sabreurs* than they did official ones for troops on the march.[2]

---

[1] AN, F1b II Haute-Loire I (rapports de germinal an IV).

[2] The Lyon *sabreurs* appear to have had stopping-places in such convenient localities as Chazelles, Mâcon, Yssangeaux, Craponne; and one of the leading *assommeurs* of Montbrison is an innkeeper (AN, BB 18 690 and F1b II Haute-Loire I).

After the year III, save in a few Departments like the Nièvre where they continued to enjoy massive support at least from the urban poor, the former terrorists were above all the victims of their isolation within the communities in which they had to live. The *sabreurs*, on the other hand, could count on the complicity of virtually the whole rural population.

Murder was the most effective and dramatic weapon of anti-terrorism. Even in the north, individual terrorists were murdered by highwaymen or were driven in fear to live in the woods, 'comme les bêtes sauvages, hommes chassés, signalés et incarcérés', comments, with delectation, the *agent national* of the District d'Avignon, in his report for 21–30 Germinal year III. 'Voilà le sort de ceux de ces scélérats qui ont l'effronterie de paraître encore parmi nous. Les autres demeurent cachés, errans et vagabonds dans les bois avec les bêtes féroces, mais encore moins féroces qu'eux.' Reduced thus to animal status, they could be hunted down, like the wolves and the hyenas and the *tigres d'Afrique* they are so often called in standard Thermidorian vocabulary. Near Lambesc the three Martins, father and two sons, are hunted across half a dozen fields, by a group of *sabreurs* armed with shotguns, before being finally shot down. Afterwards the huntsmen return to the *auberge* to celebrate their outing and display their kill.[1] In the Ardennes, the coldest Department in the country, in the middle of the fearful winter of the year III, the wife of a hatter from Sedan, after being driven out of her house in the night, gave birth to a child, which at once died, in the mighty forest of the frontier region.

Two reports to the authorities in Dieppe, both for Frimaire year IV, tell much the same story: in the *canton* of Longueville 'on tue et on brûle ... Les crimes restent impunis', while the *juge de paix* of Envermeu writes 'que ce canton commençoit à être inquiété des brigans et que récemment un homme avoit été tué d'un coup de feu dans la forêt d'Arques et dépouillé de tout ce qu'il avoit sur le corps'.[2] This, perhaps, was the main difference between the White Terror of the south and the banditry of elsewhere. In the south, people were killed deliberately, for political reasons, because they were known, had occupied certain offices. But their corpses

---

[1] The culinary theme is repeated in a remark attributed to the young murderers from Montbrison: 'Il y a encore de ces coquins de mathevons à Montbrison, *il faut que nous ayons leurs foies.*' These operations, carried out mostly in Floréal and Prairial, prove to be thirsty; Magnien asks for a drink, his captors tell him he will get one on arrival, and then kill him at the roadside. They then go to an inn and ask for meat and wine; the landlord can only oblige with milk and eggs. And with this spartan meal they slake their thirst and appetite, while boasting of their exploit. After the Bois-de-Cros massacre, the murderers finish off the wine and food left by the dead or fleeing picnickers.

[2] Arch. Dieppe, Grand Registre de la municipalité, frimaire an IV.

were not rifled and they were left with their clothes;[1] in the north, people might be killed because they happened to be passing along a path in the forest, and their bodies were left naked.

(ii) MORAL AND ECONOMIC BOYCOTT

Murder was the extreme form of anti-terrorism. There were other less dramatic but equally effective methods of dealing with the former militants. First of all, there was the 'climate' of the year III, the terrible moral and even physical isolation of the militant minorities of the previous year. 'Guerre à mort à ces monstres est le cri général de tous nos administrés,' notes, with his usual satisfaction, the Thermidorian agent national of the District d'Avignon, 1–9 Floréal year III, 'et le seul qui plane avec prépondérance sur l'horizon de ce district. L'isolement dans lequel se sont placés les restes impurs des partisans sanguinaires de cet affreux système, le mépris qui les couvre, l'horreur qui les environne, le désespoir qui les tourmente ... tous ces motifs ne servent pas peu à maintenir la tranquillité.'[2] No wonder that, in the cities of the south, the surviving cadres of terrorism were in the habit of seeking out each other's company, huddling together in cafés and inns kept by their partisans where, in a hostile environment, they were a sitting target for a murderous mob as well as a constant source of information for the police.

But there were more practical ways of expressing this sense of moral banishment. The first time that Jacques Chérest, the head of the Chérest family, returned to the small town of Tonnerre, the scene of his domination during the period of revolutionary government ('depuis près de deux mois ses adhérans annonçoient son arrivée, et devenoient plus insolens, plus audacieux, à mesure qu'ils la croyoient plus prochaine'), on 10 Floréal year III, the situation rapidly got out of hand. On the 11th, the municipality sent a courier to Auxerre to ask for troops. The procureur syndic suggested that in the meantime the Garde nationale take up positions in his house, in order to protect him and his family from an increasingly ugly mob, 'mais la garde nationale a déclaré nettement qu'elle se croiroit déshonorée d'être mise en faction chez un scélérat, un

---

[1] This was not always the case, however, in the south-east and south-centre, where the activities of the compagnies sometimes appear to have been indistinguishable from banditry. In the Loire, the body of the printer Magnien was left naked in a ditch. Near Allègre, in the Haute-Loire, a gang, having broken into the farm of the agent national of the village of Neyraval, tortured the owner in an effort to discover his treasure. Having shot him outside his farm, they went off with six bulls and cows and a hundred and twenty-five sheep. The farmer, Charitat, was a very rich man. In a visit to a farm at Talhac, canton de Saint-Paulien, the murderers warn the farmer and his son: 'Vous avez encore du numéraire et des assignats, il nous les faut' (AN, BB 18 690 and F1b II Haute-Loire I).

[2] Arch. Vaucluse 3 L 48* (rapports décadaires de l'agent national du district d'Avignon, 1–10 floréal an III).

terroriste, un buveur de sang'. In the evening, according to Chérest's own account,

> au moment où il se mettoit à table avec sa femme, ses deux enfants et une ouvrière, sont entrés chez lui environ vingt citoyens tous armés qui lui ont dit de les suivre sur le champ ... plusieurs l'ont pris au collet, l'un d'eux par le milieu du corps, et l'ont conduit jusques sur la porte de la rue ... ils l'ont laissé libre au milieu d'eux ... il étoit injurié et menacé par les uns ... les autres engageoient au silence ... ajoute que sa femme a été aussi maltraitée chez lui ...

Hearing of his plight, the municipality sent an escort of *gendarmes* to bring him to the prison, where he was shut up for the night. Early next morning, the Chérests, who were well-to-do people, took the hint and left for Saint-Florentin. They returned, however, a year later, as a result of the amnesty of Brumaire year IV. This time, on three successive nights (23–25 Prairial, Saturday, Sunday, and Monday), two of their barns and most of their crops went up in flames. The head of the family went to the *juge de paix*; the case, on eventually coming up before the local court, was dismissed. Chérest was told that he could seek redress before the *tribunal de police correctionnelle*, 'pour fait de simple police'. A month later their windows were broken, and some of their livestock were poisoned. The Chérests, however, saw out the storm; they were big employers of labour and time was on their side.[1]

It was much the same with the leading terrorists of Moulins and Nevers; on 5 Fructidor year III (a Saturday) Delan, the former mayor of Moulins and a well-known doctor, Verd, Perrotin, and Agar were taken out of prison, for transfer to Grenoble; a threatening crowd at once collected and they were only saved from lynching by the prompt action of the *agent national* in having them reincarcerated. An imperative order from the Committee of General Security forbade their transfer to the Isère; they would quite certainly have been assassinated on their way through Lyon. (This had indeed been the intention of the Moulins judicial authorities, who had ordered the *gendarmerie* to route them through the Second City.) By the middle of the year IV, after varying terms of imprisonment, they were all back in office in the Departmental or municipal administration.[2] But, like the Chérests, these were fairly comfortable people – even

---

[1] AN, F1b II Yonne (1) (procureur syndic du district de Tonnerre, au comité de legislation, 13 floréal an III) and ibid. (commissaire du Directoire dans l'Yonne, au Ministre, 8 vendémiaire an V): 'A Tonnerre on proscrit, on désigne à la fureur de quelques scélérats la famille Chérest, trois fois on attente à leurs jours.'

[2] AN, F1b II Nièvre I (Discours de Rouyer, du 15 brumaire an IV) and F1b Allier I (Rouyer, au Directoire, 5 germinal).

Marat Chaix, the ultra-revolutionist of Corbigny, was a *propriétaire* and some of his devoted supporters were his employees.[1]

If such people could escape lynching or prison massacre, they could expect eventually to resume their ordinary activities and even public office. Others were less fortunate; the wives and families of rural *sansculottes* – *tonneliers*, *bourreliers*, *galochiers*, *sabotiers*, blacksmiths – were subjected to an economic boycott, being unable to obtain bread or dairy produce in their own villages; when their wives or daughters went to the fountain or the *lavoir*, the village women drew together, pushed over their pails, trod on their washing; and on the way back home dirt and stones were thrown at them.[2] Their children had to be taken away from school. Their families walked in the village with *propos* and looks constantly in their backs. The local authorities refused to pay relief to the wives of soldiers – and a husband or a son in the army was an additional sign of guilt – but, of course, turned a blind eye to deserters, living comfortably at home.

Nastiness could be the most effective in a small community; and rural nastiness was the worst of all, the most persistent and the most chiselling. The *comité* of Aix, in a letter to Maignet dated 9 Ventôse year II, has some comments that might well be generalized:

> Tu nous demandes, citoyen représentant, des renseignemens sur les principaux agitateurs de la commune de Berre; les divisions de ce pays ne nous sont point parfaitement connues, mais elles ne nous sont point tellement étrangères que nous ne puissions te communiquer quelques réfléxions, non seulement sur cette commune, mais sur la généralité des petites communes de notre Département. Dans ce pays les citoyens se trouvent depuis longtems divisés par des motifs absolument étrangers à la cause que nous défendons. La Révolution les a trouvés dans cet état d'opposition & sous le prétexte de la servir, les chefs des différens partis en ont abusé pour venger leur ressentiment & alimenter les haines particulières.[3]

Even as near Paris as Suresnes, the former militant was not safe from rural persecution; early in Ventôse year III, Dessirier, a former cook who had been a member of the *Commission Temporaire* in Lyon during the

---

[1] Ibid. (Chaix, de Lormes, au Directoire) (19 frimaire an IV). Also *Les Armées révolutionnaires*, II, pp. 619–22.
[2] In Montbrison, wives or widows of terrorists have their skirts pulled up and are then beaten by young men belonging to the murder gangs. Others are made to kneel in the street and ask to be forgiven for their past errors. A witness 'vit près de chez lui quantité d'individus qui tenoient la femme du C. Frioux, que pendant que les uns levoient ses jupes … Legrand dit *le Bourru* lui donnoit des coups sur les cuisses toutes nues avec des cravaches' (AN, BB 18 690).
[3] Arch. Bouches-du-Rhône L 1707* (comité de surveillance d'Aix, an III).

previous year, was out walking in the main street of the village with his wife and children when all at once they were pursued by a crowd of sixty or seventy screaming inhabitants – mostly women and children – including the schoolmates of the younger Dessirier, shouting for the death of the *buveur de sang*, the *buveuse de sang*, and of the *petits buveurs de sang*. The family managed to reach their cottage without more damage than having their clothes torn; but, for the next three days, they were barricaded in their home by a mob that kept up an incessant vigil and prevented the children from sleeping by maintaining a hubbub throughout the night. If the municipality did nothing to encourage this cruel sport, they did nothing to put an end to it, denying to the *sans-culotte* family the protection of the *Garde nationale*. Eventually some friends of the former militant among the village artisans were able to contact the Committee of General Security in Paris, informing it of the family's plight; they returned with a *commissaire* of the Committee, and an *arrêté* dated 4 Ventôse: 'instruit que des citoyens de Suresnes, égarés sans doute, ont employé la violence contre la famille du C. Dessirier [le Comité] charge la municipalité de Suresnes de prendre toutes les précautions nécessaires pour maintenir le calme'.[1]

Dessirier was fortunate in living near enough to Paris to be able to attract the attention of a Committee that was to save many former militants from the effects of persecution. *Sans-culottes* even as near as the Yonne could not easily invoke such an august protector. In Sens, for instance, the local militants were subjected, throughout the year IV, to nightly concerts, organized by the *jeunesse dorée*, with rattles, French horns, drums, and trumpets, the firing of crackers, and the repeated singing of the *Réveil du peuple* until three or four in the morning. The wives of former *meneurs* were refused the assistance of midwives. Doctors, on the other hand, so many of whom had occupied positions of power during the Terror, were better placed than anyone else to ride such storms of rural and small-town nastiness. For even the most convinced royalists might need their services; and they held one of the most effective means of escape from military service. It was not the same for the artisan. No wonder Paris – or the nearest big city – seemed to the harassed *sans-culotte* a golden land, in which it was possible to live in peace, protected by anonymity and indifference. In the year IV, four hatters from the Forez, with one suit of clothes between them, were to explain that they preferred thus to live in one room – with a single bed and one blanket – than to remain subjected to the constant nagging hatred of their neighbours. No wonder some of these unfortunates walked to Paris, from as far away as the Ardennes or the Puy-de-Dôme or Mâcon.

---

[1] AN, F7 4675 d 1 (Dessirier).

(iii)   THE COST OF MILITANCY

The Thermidorian Government added to the distress of the former *sans-culottes* by legislation directed both against their collective means of self-expression and their private livelihood. A law of 25 Vendémiaire year III prohibited all efforts at collective action on the part of *sociétés populaires* – the Thermidorians were only completing what the Jacobins had begun in the Law of 14 Frimaire – at the same time making the publication of membership lists compulsory. (This was later to be the most valuable source for the organization of collective purges.) A particularly mean law – dated 13 Frimaire year III – required former members of *comités de sur-veillance* and *comités révolutionnaires* to reimburse the *Trésor* for the sums that they had received as salary in 1793–4. As most of these officials had been in office for at least a year, this might amount to a lot of money, which small tradesmen and artisans who had abandoned their shops or trades to take up full-time employment under the Terror would hardly be in a position to pay back in the year III, when they were attempting to recover what was left of a family business, compromised by long absence. The former *commissaires* of Dieppe stated flatly that they were unable to pay the State back what the State had given them for devoting all their time and energy to the service of the Republic and to the pursuit of English agents. 'Sa composition' – they stated of the *comité*, when it first came under fire in the last days of the year II – 'fut de tous citoyens laborieux, la plupart sans fortune et chargés de nombreuse famille ... leurs commerces respectifs ont été totalement abandonnés ... la plupart ont été obligés de contracter des dettes.'[1] In this instance, that was the end of it. But the Dieppois showed little inclination to make life impossible for their former terrorists – the ex-*commissaires* were merely disarmed and excluded from the *Garde nationale*, while disparaging references were made, every now and then, to their mean background – and, as in other Upper Norman towns, both the Terror and the Reaction were remarkably mild, at least from the political point of view. It is not known how the law was applied elsewhere; but there can be no doubt that those who drew it up intended further to penalize the *sans-culottes* by economic sanctions just when they were least able to face up to them. (Only a month later, the *maximum* was abolished.) Militancy henceforth was indeed a luxury that former *sans-culottes* could ill afford. This is, in fact, the gist of an imaginary conversation between two *exclusifs*, reported for Ventôse year IV:

---

[1] Arch. Seine-Maritime L 5529 (comité de Dieppe, les anciens membres des comités sectionnaires à l'agent national du district, 9 ventôse an III) (Dumès à l'agent national, 11 ventôse an III) (Guillaume Selle, tailleur d'habits, ex-membre du comité de la section Marat, à l'agent national, 12 ventôse an III) (Desmarquet à l'agent national, 16 ventôse an III).

S. Est-il vrai que D*** a donné sa démission et que vous n'êtes plus que deux de cette Section?

C. Cela est vrai, D*** a refusé, étant obligé de donner tous ses momens au rétablissement de son commerce qu'il avoit négligé depuis trois ans pour servir la chose publique, comme vous savez; de sorte qu'étant seul avec sa femme, il ne pourroit pas donner le tems nécessaire aux fonctions qu'il avoit à remplir.[1]

By the year IV, the majority of former militants would find themselves in the position of the imaginary D***; and those erstwhile terrorists who returned to public office after Vendémiaire year IV, especially in Departments like the Nièvre and the Allier, where they were to monopolize the Departmental and municipal administrations, were people well able to afford public office. Most of the former members of the *Commission Temporaire* from these two Departments were wealthy men of law, property-holders, or journalists. In such conditions, one would need to be an Antonelle or a Félix Lepeletier to be able to accept public office or to indulge in the luxury of conspiratorial militancy.

(iv) PAUPERIZATION

Equally effective deterrents to the survival of the *sans-culotte* political class were the long periods of detention which, combined with the famine of the year III and the collapse of the *assignat* and a winter without fuel (which meant unemployment for a great many artisans, unable to light their stoves or furnaces), spelt economic ruin for *sans-culottes* dependent on their work to keep themselves and their families alive. Many were thus reduced to the status of paupers; 's'il lui falloit acheter du pain,' writes a father of seven, in Germinal year IV, 'ses forces & son courage ne pourroient y suffire et la misère auroit bientôt détruit sa famille malheureuse.'[2] 'Il y a neuf mois,' reports another, at the same period, 'j'étois garçon perruquier, mon état a tombé par la révolution ... j'ai vendu ma montre ... avec les boucles d'oreille de ma femme et d'autres effets pour louer une petite boutique pour vendre de la friperie, mais malheureusement je n'ai pas fait mes affaires.'[3] A year earlier, of a former *commissaire*, Section de Brutus, it is reported: 'Il est pauvre ... Pour faire honneur à ses créanciers, il a été obligé de louer sa boutique [de pâtissier] et de vendre tous les ustensiles concernant son état.'[4] The wife of an artisan from Mouzon gives a dramatic account of the plight of the former *sans-culotte* milieu, in a petition to the Commission des Secours dated Prairial year III: 'Nous sommes régalés à sept personnes que nous sommes avec cette livre de pain [de la

---

[1] AN, F7 3054 (rapport de police du 5 ventôse an IV, dialogue entre deux 'exclusifs') (rapporté par Charvin, officier municipal du 3ème arrondissement).
[2] AN, F II 1812 (Pierre Hudelle à la Commission des Secours, 5 germinal an IV).
[3] AN, F II 1814 (pétition à la Commission, s.d. germinal an IV).
[4] AN, F7 4775 25 d 4 (Jacques Tavet).

ration] ... ma pauvre famille qui, remplie de talens, meurt de besoins, n'ayant pas un point d'ouvrage, vu la grande misère, car tout le pays est affamé, il n'y a que les impériaux qui ne manquent de rien, car ils ont notre pain', and she goes on to refer to 'les spectres de Mouzon, ces anatomies vivantes', complaining that 'la municipalité ... les gens aisés voient toutes ces misères du plus grand sang-froid'.[1] A former *frère de l'École chrétienne*, in a letter from Sens in Messidor year III, when the crisis was at its height, offers an even more apocalyptic picture of prevailing conditions, in a language suggestive of a clerical background: 'On laisse le malheureux dans ses fers et au milieu des épines tandis que l'on sème des fleurs sur le passage des riches', adding philosophically a judgement on the end of hope and on the general mood of apathy:

> Les aristocrates nous diront sûrement que l'histoire des révolutions, des empires, nous apprend que toutes les républiques n'ont eu qu'un temps de prospérité et qu'elles ont fini par se dissoudre ... A ceci je dis qu'il est malheureux pour les français que les cœurs se partagent ... La France devient aujourd'hui le théâtre de victoires au-dehors et des fléaux les plus violens au-dedans ... C'est un martyre bien douloureux d'avoir faim et de ne pas avoir du pain pour de l'argent ... tous les jours l'on est obligé de vendre ses effets pour avoir du pain ... les français sont fous, il n'y a plus de raison en France.[2]

A former *sans-culotte* who in these conditions petitioned the Commission for entry into a workhouse or asked to be considered for the receipt of the bread of the *douzième secteur*, reserved for the totally destitute (even *indigence* seems to have been a privilege hard to come by officially in those hard times: 'il faut apparemment être au rang des gens dans le besoin, être dans la crasse, couvert de haillons, hurlant et jurant dans les rues,' complains an inhabitant of Compiègne, an unsuccessful petitioner, in a letter dated 25 Messidor year III)[3] and distributed free, was not likely to give the government any trouble. He would become, in effect, a pensioner of the government, dependent on official favour to obtain the daily loaf; his position would be no more independent than that of a former militant, described in a police report of Germinal year IV: 'Potemont et Moreaux sont de mauvais citoyens; je ne parle pas de Diochet, depuis que la police le fait vivre, il n'est plus à lui, il est *vendu* ...'[4] And many other poor *sans-culottes* were reduced to a state similar to that of Diochet.

---

[1] AN, F15 2820 (Jeanne-Catherine Hervez, femme Christophe, de Mouzon, à la Commission des Secours, 1er prairial an III).
[2] Ibid. ('Le modeste Pierre Doyen, tenant ci-devant les petites écoles chrétiennes [à Sens] ... ancien maître serrurier, entrepreneur en bâtiment à la Convention, 26 messidor an III).
[3] Ibid.
[4] AN, F7 3054 (rapport de police du 5 germinal an VI).

(v) THE DISEASES OF THE POOR

What was not achieved by political proscription, detention, persecution, exile, murder, extreme hardship, withdrawal from France, was often completed by disease, the companion of dearth, pauperization, hopelessness, and apathy; in many towns of the north of France – Rouen, Dieppe, le Havre, and in their suburbs, in the overpopulated countryside round Amiens, in Valenciennes, Fumay, in the Vosges, in a number of villages in the Orne and the Sarthe – the poorer sort of *sans-culottes* and their families were wiped out in a series of sweeping epidemics that struck, two summers running, in September (Fructidor) 1795 and 1796, following two intensely cold winters and two droughts that, while sparing the well-to-do, decimated the population of the poorer quarters and the faubourgs. In fact, there could hardly have been a greater concentration of misfortunes to have fallen on the heads of the urban and rural poor.

(vi) SUICIDE

It was altogether too much for some of these underprivileged, including a few former militants. There are reports of frequent suicides, both from Paris (where, according to Duval, whole families disappeared in the waters of the Seine) and Saint-Denis, particularly among the women of the people, throughout the year III. There are thirteen such reports, for three Paris Sections, between the middle of Brumaire year III and the first month of the year IV. A carpenter of the Faubourg, who had been a leading militant of the Section de Popincourt and a member of the *comité révolutionnaire*, threatened just after the Prairial Days with further imprisonment, decided that life had become completely intolerable for people of his condition and with his past. (His neighbours, who were very much afraid of him, describing him as a man given to violence and his household as one frequently punctuated by screams and blows, said he was a *septembriseur*; he had boasted about it and displayed his sabre in several cafés. He had been arrested a first time on 9 Thermidor year II, on the orders of the *robespierriste comité*, with whose members he had had a series of violent quarrels, and had been released on 12 Frimaire year III. After the Prairial Days, he had good reason to believe that he would once more be proscribed; he had also been told by a friend, an innkeeper, and like any good *sans-culotte* he was ready to credit anything that came from such an impeccable source, that the authorities were about to place the Duke of York on the throne of France: *vu l'horreur*, he comments, *qu'il avoit du nom d'un Roy*, this was too much for him.) He first of all attempted to poison himself, his wife, and three daughters, with an omelette containing verdigris; when this failed, he tried to gas his family with the fumes of the stove, but was no more successful. He then fetched an axe from his tool set, and slaughtered his wife and two of the girls, aged three and four, while they slept, during the night of 9–10 Prairial, after having taken the eldest to be cared for by a neighbour. Finally he had attempted once more to gas himself. He was eventually traced to the Hôtel-Dieu, after a week, when his landlord discovered the holocaust. On his recovery, he was interrogated in Messidor. The Committee of General Security was interested in his role in the Germinal Days and in those of Prairial. His defence was that, after falling out with the committee of his Section in the year II, 'convaincu qu'il n'étoit pas propre à se mêler des affaires politiques, il ne s'en est occupé en aucune manière'. He was tried and condemned to death by the Seine criminal court, on 2 Thermidor year III, and was executed on the same day, just a year after the fall of Robespierre. He was clearly a very stupid, very naïve, very violent man, the prototype of many poor *sans-culottes* both of his condition and of his Section – a victim of his past and of circumstances that were beyond his control and that he did not fully understand. He did understand, though, that in the conditions of the year III, people like himself would lose, whatever they did, whether they kept out of politics altogether, or whether they once more took up arms, as he had been accused of doing, as in Germinal and Prairial. His utter desperation was symptomatic of the state of mind of a whole section of the *petit peuple*, in the terrible circumstances of Prairial year III, after the Faubourg had been disarmed and reduced to a funereal silence.

It is not known whether Denis Denelle had many imitators. There were a number of brutal murders in Paris, in the three Sections with which we have been mainly concerned, in the following months.[1] Already in the previous autumn the municipality of Saint-Denis, 'instruite des assassinats qui se réitèrent depuis quelque tems sur les routes de Paris et de Gonesse', had decided to increase the number and size of night patrols along the highroad to the Pays de France.[2] None of these murders appears to have had any political significance, except insofar as they represented the increasing violence of a cruel period in which the law-abiding poor had little prospect, other than a lingering death from cold and starvation.

(vii)   THE YEAR IV

It is not at all difficult to understand why, after the appalling experience of *Nonante-cinq*, the common people of Paris and of the other cities of the

---

[1] APP, A/A 95–8 and A/A 187–8. In the Section du Muséum there were two murders of *filles de confiance* of goldsmiths, on 30 Brumaire and 8 Pluviôse year III. In the Section de la Butte des Moulins there were three murders, one on 20 Vendémiaire, two on 21 and 22 Messidor, the same year. All three victims were women. The third murder was a matter of vengeance, the woman having been killed by an ex-lover.
[2] Arch. Saint-Denis I D 1 6 (séance du 12 nivôse an III de la municipalité de Franciade).

north had had enough of militancy and lay low and kept very quiet. In Rouen that year there were a number of disturbances, provoked by hungry women, but this time they were unable to shame their men into action.[1] In Paris former militants were often reduced to begging for bourgeois charity in dramatic petitions to the *Commission des Secours*, while others in desperation left the city in the hope of finding survival conditions in the Departments. *Nonante-six* was rather worse, with even higher mortality rates in the cities, even less bread, less food and less prospect of employment; there was much murmuring, but more apathy.[2] The prediction made by a counter-revolutionary in March 1793 in a letter addressed to London and intercepted by the Dieppe committee, had at last come true.[3] In the year IV many women of the people returned to the old remedies of religion; others, according to Duval, used the Seine, in numbers even greater than in the previous year.[4]

(viii)   EXILE

The great mass of the former *sans-culottes* thus suffered at home. They were murdered, they died, they committed suicide, or just succeeded in keeping above water during the two terrible years of crisis until good harvests and high wages improved their economic position if not their political status. Those better placed economically took refuge in Paris, or at least left the scene of their former activities. The wisest of all did not wait for the anti-terrorist legislation of Ventôse, Germinal and Prairial, Messidor and Thermidor of the same year, to draw their own conclusions. Some took refuge in the reassuring anonymity of military bureaucracy – army transport, military hospitals, supplies – which kept them on the move, in France, always one or two steps ahead of the arrest warrant and just out of reach of the *accusateur public* of their home Department or of that in which they had been active in the service of the Terror.

In the year III, the French armies themselves were on the move, pouring

---

[1] *Terreur et subsistances*, pp. 307–42.

[2] 'En vérité, le peuple, la classe ouvrière, des citoyens, meurent de faim au sein de l'abondance,' write the authorities of Lapalisse, in Brumaire. In Prairial of the same year, a former lawyer petitions the Commission: 'Je voudrois bien ne pas imiter ce juge du tribunal civil du Palais, mort, il y a 12 jours, d'inanition chez lui ... Comme cet exemple trop fréquent de mourir de faim n'est pas bon à suivre pour un ci-devant Procureur du feu Roi et qui ne peut mendier, je me recommande à vous' (AN, F1b II Allier I, and F II 1182, subsistances an IV).

[3] 'Ce qu'il y a de triste, c'est que ce malheureux peuple ne reconnoît pas assez la main de dieu qui s'appesantit sur nous et il lui faudroit une famine pour crier miséricorde' (Arch. Seine-Maritime L 5328, comité de Dieppe).

[4] Georges Duval, *Souvenirs thermidoriens* (Paris, 1843): 'Cet état de choses poussa au désespoir une foule de malheureux, qui aimèrent mieux se donner la mort que de mourir dans les angoisses de la faim. Des familles entières prirent ce parti extrême, et les flots de la Seine en ont su quelque chose.'

into Sardinia, Catalonia, the Austrian Netherlands, and the Rhineland, and a number of ex-terrorists followed in their wake in similar employment. The *armée d'Italie* – and more particularly the entourage of the *adjudant-général* Brune – was said to have been a favourite refuge for people with a revolutionary past. Most of these were to occupy, for the next twelve or fifteen years, comfortable and even profitable jobs in or on the fringes of military government in distant parts of Europe. From popular militants and revolutionary bureaucrats, they were thus often easily transformed into repressors.

It was not so much a matter of inclination as of circumstance, though the *sans-culotte* leaders had always tended to authoritarianism and had at all times been impatient of opposition, which, like Robespierre, they regarded as wicked and, therefore, counter-revolutionary. In many parts of Europe, especially in the Flemish areas of Belgium, the old town versus country conflict of the year II was translated, in much more dangerous terms, into one between French occupiers and foreign resistants. Former *apôtres civiques*, one-time *commissaires civils*, former commanders of people's armies now found themselves once more lording it over the peasantry, levying requisitions, carrying out house searches, applying price controls, billeting troops, blaspheming from Italian or Flemish pulpits.

This time, however, it was not a matter of Parisians or Bourbonnais making themselves felt at the expense of Briards, Lyonnais, Foréziens, or Dauphinois, but of Frenchmen making life hell for Flemings, Piedmontese, Catalans, and Rhinelanders. Thus some of these erstwhile *sans-culottes* – already in the year II displaying a marked class hostility to cosmopolitanism – closed in even more on themselves, ignorant of the language, complaining of the food, contemptuous of the dirt and of the 'superstition' of their *administrés*, acquiring a colonialist mentality, and themselves actively contributing to the repression of popular revolt. It is true that they could persuade themselves that such popular revolt as they encountered was clerically inspired, counter-revolutionary, and 'fanatical'. They were none the less carrying out the functions of police and were contributing to the solidity of a military regime in which they held the important stake of their own posts and their own salaries. No doubt they often had their families with them too, and these would increase the mental gulf between them and the locals.

Much has been made, it is true, of the revolutionary role of these semi-civilians in northern Italy. But these *commissaires des guerres* would have been former Jacobins and a cut above the ex-*sans-culotte préposé à l'habillement militaire*. There were few Stendhals at this level. Commanding a Spanish prisoner-of-war camp in Holland – the task that fell to one of the more active political officers of the old Paris Revolutionary Army –

was not the best school for militancy; and the man cursed his luck when he had to give up his camp and return to France in 1813. For every Lefranc, so resilient in deportation and exile as to become the medical adviser and architect of the Sultan of Zanzibar and the protégé of a French *émigré* family in Batavia, there would be nine former *sans-culottes* confirmed in their instinctive *poujadisme* and *esprit de quartier*, as a result of contact with the Balkans, Egypt, or Poland. The comforts of occupation made them lazy as well as repressive, corrupt as well as unfraternal. By the time they were forced back to France in 1813 or 1814 there would not be much militancy left in them. They were of course bitterly disappointed because they had lost their jobs, blamed the new regime for the faults of the previous one, and grumbled as much as the *demi-soldes* they so much resembled. But long absence and a totally unfamiliar way of life had cut them off from the *petit peuple*. They came back as strangers and were thought of as such by their remaining relatives; and a number of them were so unhappy that, rather than remain in Paris, or wherever they had previously lived, they set up in trade with their savings in some unfamiliar place, in partnership with a fellow ex-bureaucrat of Occupation, and tried to prolong into civilian life the comradeship of a semi-military society. After selling up his affairs in Paris, the former commandant of the prisoner-of-war camp went off to Bordeaux, settling there as an oculist. They were by then completely lost as *sans-culottes* and more or less as civilians.

No one has attempted to assess the size of the French Occupation bureaucracy. It had already been very large when the armies were still at home in the year II and had formed the cement that had held together, for as long as the patronage lasted, the so-called *hébertiste* party. It gave that group representatives in every garrison town and provided it with an interested rank-and-file of eight or nine thousand *commissaires*. Nor has an attempt been made to analyse its composition, other than to follow up a few score *meneurs* to their deaths from the plague, from typhus, from cholera, in Egypt, Dalmatia, and Poland, or to their murder in a brawl in Geneva. But the transformation of many of them into allies of repression must have had some effect on the collapse of popular militancy, for the army took some of the best of the old Sectionary leaders and some of the most enthusiastic of the provincial ultra-revolutionists. By the time the survivors came back, at best they might make good *bonapartistes*. A few of course retained their convictions, evangelizing Poles and Illyrians. But a Lyonnais militant in Illyria was a militant lost to Lyon.

The actual number of people thus lost to popular protest in France may have been trifling; but their quality often made up for this. Many of them had sought posts in the army in 1795 because they could not bear the spectacle of political reaction and of the persecution of the *patriotes* in

Thermidorian France. These were not the sort of people who could move with the times, taking refuge in the obscurity of their *arrière-boutique* and divesting themselves hastily of the compromising emblems of popular sovereignty, throwing themselves at the feet of Thermidorian charity, as so many poor *sans-culottes* with large families were forced to do. Lefranc, Eude, Paris, Gourgonnier, and their kind – to name a few of these exiles – were bachelors, men with few ties, of the roving sort (some of them had been members of the famous *commissions ambulantes* of the year II), the sort of servants of Terror that have been described so felicitously by Professor Godechot as the *hommes de liaison*, the very stuff in fact of militancy and ultra-revolutionism.[1]

Exiles of this calibre represented then a net loss to France in terms of militancy and of experience in repression, terror, anti-rural economics, anti-religious and egalitarian evangelizing. Many others of the rank and file of popular protest were lost before they even started. As militarism made increasing inroads into the younger *classes*, during the Directory and Empire (how many Brutuses, how many Émiles, how many Gracchuses, born to militant parents in 1793 and the year II, disappeared in the snows of Russia in 1812!), a great many potential rioters were swallowed up in the army itself. They might of course desert, but they deserted outside France, and preyed upon German farmers, not French ones. The army was a great centre of lawlessness and banditry, but at least till 1812–13 these were primarily at the expense of foreigners. The principal concern of the *gendarmerie* and of the *prévôté* was to prevent deserters from getting back into France and a watch was kept for them along the old frontiers.

But these various categories were in any case taken out of the main stream of popular history. One can only guess at the possible effects of their removal from France, of their conversion from individualistic militancy to colonialistic administration. And to use war as a means of removing *mauvaises têtes* from the scene of danger – that is, home – is an ancient device of repressive regimes, just as they have, again and again, provoked war in order to keep the people down. In France, it is true, war was at first the *sans-culottes'* opportunity; but in the long run, it was also their undoing, the means of their enslavement. The Thermidorians were the first to discover the army as a weapon of anti-popular repression, and military commissions as a discreet and expeditious form of anti-popular justice. The Directory and the Empire did not need to carve out an African empire in order to create their *Biribi*. Occupied Europe would do. All these, however, are purely negative factors.

---

[1] Most of the material for this section has been derived from *Les Armées révolutionnaires*, II, Epilogue, pp. 877–93.

(ix)   REPRESSION

What is much more important is the positive achievement at home. The Directory saw an enormous improvement in the police powers of government, at least within the urban context, and as far as the northern *sans-culottes* were concerned (the southern ones did not matter all that much). Under the Jacobin dictatorship, there had existed in Paris a dozen rival police organizations – each Committee had one of its own, the Commune had one, the Minister of the Interior had one, the Department had one, the Sections had one, the *Mairie* had one – mainly devoted to denouncing one another and sending their employers the sort of information that they wished to hear. The Thermidorians, too, had to contend with a similar *embarras de polices*, of the most varied political affiliations – the *inspecteurs*, oddly enough, tended to be neo-terrorists and to display most of their energy in the pursuit of royalists. Now, however, the police had a Ministry, a centralized direction, a *Légion*, regular pay, an increasing army of informers (with fewer and fewer people to inform on). It was getting better at its job, and it found allies in popular apathy, hopelessness, and humiliation.

A section at least of the popular movement, the one previously dominated by women, now turned in despair to the age-old remedies of loyalism, deference, and religion. Already in the hunger riots of the spring of 1795, if in Paris the slogan had been *du pain et la Constitution de 1793*, in Rouen in a similar riot, on the day the news of the Paris rising had reached the Norman capital with the postal coach, it had been *du pain et vive Louis XVII*. A great many women of the people came to prefer the rule of *notre bon Roy*, whoever he might be, to that of the Thermidorian Rump.

What had much helped the task of the police already in the year III was the revulsion very widely felt among the mass of *sans-culottes* for the former *dominateurs*, no longer feared, their excesses denounced in hundreds of reports and in all the papers, now distrusted as having used popular grievances to further their own ambitions, considered too, by their professional colleagues, as 'bad for trade'. So many shoemakers had been denounced up and down the country in 1795 as archetypal terrorists that the corporation must have cursed those compromising fellows who gave the whole trade a bad name. Repression carries its own lesson; there must have been something wrong with these people for them to have been so direly and so frequently punished. Repression, when intelligently directed, isolates, especially when combined with leniency towards the mass of the common people. The history of the period 1795–9 suggests above all that repression can be effective if applied intelligently and discreetly against a limited number of people, always the same. The Directory had the good sense to avoid political trials; unlike the Jacobin dictatorship, it did not need to persuade or to convince, for it did not rely on popular support, but on popular apathy.

The only affair that the new regime deliberately sought to publicize was that of the *babouvistes*, and for this it had every reason. It had caught the lot – it was the sort of inept conspiracy that any regime, authoritarian or weak, must dream of. The publicity would amply demonstrate the intelligence and vigilance of the authorities, frighten property-holders, and illustrate the isolation of the *babouvistes* from the common people. Finally the conspirators had obligingly left lists of some three thousand names, the *fine fleur* of revolutionary militancy all over France, ten to twenty for each Department, several hundred for Paris. Thus the Directory had a weapon with which to threaten the hard core of *meneurs* for the rest of their days. The lists were used repeatedly, both for arrests and for deportations. Never perhaps in history have conspirators rendered such a magnificent service to the police – and to historians. Not that most of these unfortunate men were even *babouvistes*; most of them were people whom, because of their past record, Germain and Buonarroti thought they could use. How these people must have cursed the honour thus rendered them by the idiotic *Égaux*.

Deportations, unlike the guillotine, did not make martyrs, though the effect was much the same. Few ever returned from the Seychelles or Cayenne. Only three out of seventy-nine deported under the *Sénatus-Consulte* of Nivôse year IX ever got back to France, and these were at once hustled away from Paris to be confined to hot and sleepy little towns in the Aude and the Hérault.

(x)　*RÉSIDENCE SURVEILLÉE*

The time-honoured French system of *résidence surveillée*, much favoured by the Ministry of Police of the Directory and by the Prefects of the Empire, was likewise an effective and unobtrusive method of isolating militant minorities, a condition being, of course, that it was to a place of confinement at a considerable distance from the previous area of militancy. It would have been silly to send Parisians to Pontoise or to Chartres (though Chartres is still the main centre for *interdits de séjour*). It was much more effective to send them, as Lefranc and Sormois were sent, to Lunel, or like Carlo Levi, who was from Turin, to Eboli. It was important, too, not to send all the militants to the same place, the surest way of creating a new *foyer de sédition* and of forming a University of Exile. To be effective *résidence surveillée* required a police numerous and efficient enough to prevent the *consignés* from returning secretly to their old stamping-grounds with the additional prestige of semi-outlawry. Nor would it do to confine former militants to places well known as disaffected and as centres of neo-terrorism and neo-Jacobinism, such as Lorient,

Auxerre, Moulins, Nevers, Toulouse, Grenoble, Lons-le-Saulnier, Dijon, or Montbéliard. In the big 1813 round-up, the Napoleonic police took care to choose towns reputedly harmless, like Sens or Niort, small enough for the *consignés* to be at all times prominent and visible, yet not homogeneous enough for them to capture a following in a predominant trade or profession. Industrial centres and towns with a single, specialized craft (the Avignon *taffetassiers*, the Moulins hatters, the Cholet weavers, the Lyon silk-workers, etc.) were thus unsuited for this purpose. If it had not been so near the frontiers, Alsace would have been ideal; the interior of the Breton Departments was also well suited to isolate the lonely militant in unfamiliar, even hostile surroundings. In this respect, as in most others, the imperial police showed a very fine scale of discretion – not to say a humour of a cruel sort – in its allocation of *consignés*, condemning Parisians to places like Niort, Issoudun, or le Puy. The Fourth Republic did even worse and confined Joanovici to Mende and the King of Morocco to Corsica.

(xi) THE AGE OF MILITANCY

Finally, there is the matter of the generations. The average age of militancy for revolutionary leaders at assembly level was between thirty and forty – a great many were born, like Robespierre, in the 1750s – and that of the humbler *sans-culotte* militants, less well fed and much worse housed, was somewhat higher: thirty-eight to forty-five.[1] Country militants tend to be older than the urban *frères et amis*. The average age of the Dijon committee of the year II is forty-six.[2] On these figures, by 1815 most of the former popular leaders would be dying out or too old, too isolated, too lonely, too out of touch, too incapacitated, for effective militancy. A half-blind watchmaker like Eude is no longer much good for any movement; and *conciliabules nocturnes* – something that, like *signes de ralliement*, haunts the suspicious vigilance of successive French police organizations – are hardly dangerous when only attended by a handful of old decrepit men, come together to evoke the memory of better times. Many too, as we have seen, as a result of police persecution or economic boycott or unpleasantness from neighbours, or a combination of all these things, decided in 1795 or in the two following years to leave the towns in which they had played a

---

[1] These calculations are based on the ages of members of *comités*, though these may be slightly higher, owing to the popular respect for age and the belief that vigilance could best be entrusted to those with considerable experience of life, than those of less privileged *sans-culottes*. With this reservation, out of 98 members of Paris committees whose ages are given, the average age emerges as 46. In Dieppe, the average age of the *commissaires* is 38, exceptionally low; for in the neighbouring *communes* it is 44 for Bacqueville, 46 for Eu. In the neighbourhood of le Havre, the average is: Ingouville, 40; Lheure, 49; Sanvic, 49; Sainte-Adresse, 48; Blesville, 42; and Saint-Jouin, a more rural community, 51 (AN, Série Alphabétique F7, Arch. Seine-Maritime L 5239, and AN, F1b II Seine-Maritime I).
[2] Arch. Côte-d'Or L 2658*.

revolutionary role, and set up in places where they might hope not to attract attention. The militants of the south and of Lyon came in large numbers to Paris; those of Paris, a great many of whom had not been Parisians very long, returned to their places of origin and lived out the Directory and Empire in Rouen, Amiens, Beauvais, Roye, Abbeville, le Havre, Alençon, Nogent-le-Rotrou, Sens, Auxerre, Melun, Pontoise, Orléans, Montargis, Gien, Pithiviers, Évreux, or in the neighbouring countryside, if they still had relatives there. In either case this voluntary exile was an admission of defeat and powerlessness; if there had been any hope at all they would have stayed on and prepared for the next round of *journées*.

(xii)   THE SECOND GENERATION
In a few exceptional cases, however, death, exile, martyrdom, persecution helped rather than impeded the survival of militancy, by developing the conditions favourable to the creation of a family cult. Widows of *guillot-inés*, *fusillés*, and *déportés* were, by the nature of things, the most eager thus to carry on the flame and to transmit it to the next generation; it was a role almost forced upon them, for what other claim could they make on people's interest and sympathy? They would be the last to admit that their husbands, or companions, had died in vain. The sensible ones – Anne Levêque, the widow of Ronsin – did get remarried, and, in her case, married even better. (Her new husband was a proper General, and was sent under the Empire as Ambassador to the United States.)[1] The irre-concilables nourished the coming generation on a mixed diet of reverence, revenge, romantic republicanism, and the purifying beauties of violence. They were, in fact – these professional widows, draped night and day in their weeds – the first to contribute to that long and disastrous tradition of historicism that, for over a hundred and fifty years, has been the bane of French popular movements. *La veuve* Sijas,[2] *la veuve* Loÿs,[3] *la veuve* Babeuf, *la veuve* Le Bas,[4] saw to it that their sons never forgot: Émile,

---

[1] *Les Armées révolutionnaires*, pp. 98–102. She married Turreau, who had fought in the Vendée.

[2] 'La femme de Sijas court, s'agite, intrigue, prêche les ouvriers, et veut absolument venger la mort de son mari' (rapport de police du 5 nivôse an V, AN, F7 3054).

[3] 'Notre commune renferme actuellement ... quelques anarchistes, vieux partisans de Robespierre ... agens et amis secrets de Babeuf ... Nous avons vu paroître dans notre commune le C. Vial, membre du club de l'hôtel de Noailles, les nommés Olivier et Poicelot, anciens membres du comité révolutionnaire de la section du Bonnet-rouge ... Nous savons qu'ils s'assemblent dans la maison de la veuve d'un nommé Loys, de Loys qui étoit secré-taire des jacobins le 9 thermidor et qui, arrêté à Marseille, s'est pendu dans sa prison' (administration municipale de Fontainebleau au Ministre, le 6 messidor an IV, AN, F1b II Seine-et-Marne I).

[4] *La veuve* Le Bas, along with Buonarroti, might be described as the originator of the Robespierriste myth and the founder of the cult of Saint-Maximilien. Worse still, she spoke of the coldly sanguinary Saint-Just as if he had been a saint.

Babeuf's son, later known as Robert, and his daughter-in-law were early schooled as Avengers.[1] If there were no sons, daughters would do. They were often even worse, more passionate, more single-minded, devoted, intransigent priestesses at revolutionary shrines; a number of them, logically enough, retained of Jacobinism its militaristic chauvinism, and ended up as convinced Bonapartists. At a lower level, there was a strong group of faithful – the wives of *sans-culotte* leaders who had been deported to Cayenne and the Seychelles and who, in the former Section du Panthéon and among the hutments of the Gros Caillou, in the former Section des Invalides, an area closely watched by the police from the year IV to 1818 and considered especially dangerous, because it contained in close proximity the very rich and the very poor, attempted to keep people together, with meetings, always known to the police, in cellars and cafés. Women like *la femme* Marcellin, a laundress, seem to have shamed a few men back into momentary activity; there are references to them at the time of the 'discovery' of the Infernal Machine of the rue des Blancs Manteaux, and again with reference to the *affaire* Aréna.[2] Their activities were pitifully unsuccessful, but they gave the police something to report on.

Militancy was thus transmitted via widows or sons or daughters into the next generation, well into the nineteenth century. In 1830, 1848, and 1871 the militant would be acting the same old play over and over again, publishing the same old newspapers, taking over the same old titles, and many of the *insurgés* of the *Trois Glorieuses* had a second go in the June Days, many of the women of the Commune were the wives or the widows of the *proscrits de juin*.[3] It therefore becomes important to follow individual careers, to trace the family descent of terrorism and to describe the survival of a mentality feeding on violence and on a romantic desire to compete with the past, to be 'worthy of the past'. The worst thing about the popular movement of the year II was that it gave three generations of revolutionists something to live up to, to merit, to imitate, to re-enact, in conditions that were not remotely connected with those of 1793–4 and when the repressive powers of governments and armies had been vastly improved. It was a tradition that drove several generations of popular protest into empty, hopeless violence, into building barricades easily toppled by colonial generals back from Algeria, into provocations that gave narrowly bourgeois governments the pretext that they were seeking

---

[1] '*Babœuf-Robert*, libraire, prévenu d'avoir vendu le *Nain Tricolore*' (rapport de police du 26 février 1818); '*Finet, femme Babœuf* (Catherine), libraire, prévenue de complicité dans la vente du *Nain Tricolore*' (rapport de police du 1er mars 1818) (AN, F7 3029). It is characteristic that the younger Babeuf should have been engaged in promoting Bonapartist propaganda.

[2] *Les Armées révolutionnaires*, II, p. 892.

[3] Edith Thomas, *Les Pétroleuses* (Paris, 1964).

for solving the problem of poverty by the extermination of the urban working class. It was a tradition that drove a section of the revolutionary movement into the pathless politics of hate and massacre, producing, at each generation, a new Hébert – a Vallès,[1] a Rochefort, a Darien,[2] a Baudelaire – *exaspérés* whose policies began and ended with the evocation of a gigantic Red Dawn in the course of which the *petit peuple* and the factory workers would settle accounts with the French bourgeoisie. It was a tradition which also resulted in polonomania and *Marchons sur Varsovie*, belgophobia, anglophobia, neo-Jacobin war-mongering, the belief in the purifying effects of an international blood-bath, the assumption that an international war was the likeliest opportunity for revolution at home, and many other similar ineptitudes that were to dog the French Left throughout the nineteenth century and even through part of the twentieth. It was a tradition rich in a constantly renovated martyrology, evocative of *fusillades* and *murs*, barricades and mutinies. One thing at least that the popular movement of the year II was to ensure for France was a plentiful supply of revolutionary dead, a regiment of tombs in the Père Lachaise and the Cimetière du Montparnasse, multiple occasions for bringing out the red banners and looking steadfastly backwards into an anachronistic *sans-culotte* past. The *sans-culottes* hardly deserved this, for at least they had used violence, or more often the threat of violence, to some purpose, and for a time with some success. Another heritage was the Babeuf Plot, which has never ceased to plague and bore historians right up to the present day.

PART THREE   THE POPULAR MOVEMENT IN ITS PRIME: THE *SANS-CULOTTES* OF THE YEAR II

> 'L'oppression et la tyrannie les avoit tirés de leur nullité sociale. La justice et l'humanité les y a replongés, sans doute à jamais . . .'
>
> A Thermidorian judge on the Dieppois terrorists

11.   *Thermidorian Language and Assumptions*

Thermidor was widely depicted by its early apologists as a return to normal. People were told that with the *retour au règne des lois* there would be an end to fear and judicial violence and that things would settle down. This was partly wishful thinking on the part of the new rulers; for the regime, as we have seen, especially in the south-east, very soon lapsed into

---

[1] *TLS*, 4 (1965). (*Courc*, article on Vallès.)
[2] *A Second Identity*, pp. 342–55.

violence and anarchy, with the active encouragement of such eminent Thermidorians as Cadroy, Isnard, and Boisset, the heralds of the White Terror, even if other equally representative *éminences* of a divided governing class, such as Barras, Fréron, and Goupilleau de Montaigu, did their best to keep the reaction within legal bounds and to re-establish the authority of Paris by putting an end to killing and violence. At first, at least, there was something in the claim, for it was an achievement in itself to have brought to an end a self-perpetuating bureaucracy of repression, purged the revolutionary tribunal, and protected the population from the implications of the tentacular and hideous law of 22 Prairial. Immediately after Thermidor, the *bourgeois* and the *notables* were not the only people to begin to sleep soundly at night, without fear of a nocturnal house search; the relief was felt quite as strongly among the *petit peuple*, equally threatened by the spread of a bureaucratic Terror tied to the realization of the concept of unanimity, if necessary by the extermination of the whole male population over the age of thirty. It was not only Thermidorian pamphleteers who were to confine *l'Ombre de Robespierre* so joyfully *aux enfers*; there was at first plenty of popular literature on the same theme. The end of Terror seemed a positive gain to the nation as a whole; and it took several months and the experience of famine to convert what Mercier and Duval call the *classes populacières* back to terror and to repression.

Of course, these hopes rapidly proved unfounded and the universal feeling of relief soon gave way to dismay and alarm as, even in the first weeks of the regime, demands for vengeance became increasingly vocal and the political reaction proceeded at a speed more and more difficult to control. Certainly in the year III there would be no end to fear, but rather a beginning of it, as far as a great many humble people and a number of *Montagnard* leaders were concerned. But what the Thermidorians also meant by a return to normal was that France should henceforth be ruled by the *honnêtes gens* and that the common people should be sent back – maybe with a grudging reference, when it could be proved that they had been 'misled', but with no reference at all when they had played a leading part in the affairs of the year II – to their proper place in society, one in which they could not meddle in politics or play at revolution. The time had come to end such nonsense. The Thermidorian view of the natural order of society – what contemporaries describe, in the language of the year III, as *une saine harmonie sociale*[1] – and of the family, is expressed baldly in a number of reports, pamphlets, and printed denunciations concerning the *dominateurs* of the previous year.

---

[1] Certainly not the same *Harmonie Sociale* as that suggested by a *société sectionnaire* of the same name in the year II!

It is a view clearly stated by a judge, that eminent stand-by of Thermidorian 'order' (the judicature had, after all, been fully reinstated, and was henceforth guaranteed against competition from 'people's courts' and similar horrors), the *commissaire national près le tribunal criminel* of Dieppe, in a report on the members of the former *comité*, dated 1st Prairial year III, when the anti-terrorist tide was at its height: 'L'oppression et la tyrannie,' he observes, on the subject of the eleven former *commissaires* (the twelfth[1] had defied the Reaction by dying in Pluviôse of the same year) 'les avoit tirés de leur *nullité sociale*. La justice et l'humanité les y a replongés, sans doute à jamais.'[2] One could not hope for a clearer announcement of the Thermidorian programme for the future of the common people. For who were these people so properly confined once more to their *nullité sociale*? Apart from the usual shoemakers and innkeepers, and urban artisans, there was a brewer, described as *vivant de son bien*, an *officier de santé*, and finally a doctor. It was in fact the archetypal composition of a *comité* in a town, even to the doctor, so often the butt of Thermidorian denunciation for having betrayed his class and abused his influence with the poor by allowing himself to be carried to positions of power. (It was easier to explain away the presence of *officiers de santé* in committees, for these were merely an inferior sort of doctor, constantly snubbed by the old *Académies*, and easily written off as *aigris*. The Thermidorians, like Anouilh, were much given to *Bitos*-like theses on the subject of revolutionary militancy.)

Equally revealing is the comment on some of the leading terrorists of the Allier, accused in a document of Pluviôse year IV of having preached 'le mépris des autorités constituées, en consultant les valets d'écurie et le cuisinier d'une auberge sur ceux des fonctionnaires qu'il falloit destituer.'[3] Of a member of the *comité* of Gannat in the same Department, it was claimed in Vendémiaire of the same year that he had 'contraint les domestiques dudit Reclesne [a wealthy landowner of Gannat] à se mettre à table avec lui, leur disant de profiter du moment, que c'étoit la dernière fois qu'ils y mangeroient, leur défendant de servir davantage à table, qu'ils étoient autant que leur maître, qui n'étoit plus rien.'[4] Marcillat too, a former priest and another well-known terrorist from the Bourbonnais – he had been a member of the *Commission Temporaire* of Lyon[5] – had similarly disgusting eating companions: 'Il mangeoit familièrement avec l'exécuteur de la justice, dont il prenoit des

---

[1] Michel Godeby, who had died on 12 Pluviôse.
[2] AN, D III 269 d 48 (Comité de législation, Seine-Inférieure, Dieppe, commissaire national au comité).
[3] AN, F1b II Allier I (rapport du 1er pluviôse an IV sur les terroristes de l'Allier).
[4] Ibid. (tribunal correctionnel de Gannat, 12 vendémiaire an IV).
[5] *Terreur et subsistances*, p. 68.

leçons.'[1] The Thermidorians were particularly sensitive to what had so often been a deliberate effort on the part of the roving *commissaire* to illustrate, in as dramatic and enjoyable a manner as possible, the new *sans-culotte* order of things. The *commissaires* would get their victims to cook them copious meals, which they then had to serve standing up, while the *commissaires* themselves sat down with the local *gendarmes* and the artisan members of the local *comité* – a Passion Play in food egalitarianism that was performed over and over again in the areas subjected to ultra-revolutionism.

On Laporte, a *commissaire* from Moulins, there is the comment: 'son état d'aubergiste n'a pu lui procurer aucune des connoissances nécessaires pour la place importante qu'il remplit dans une commune de 15,000 âmes.'[2] (He had been a member of the highly popular municipality of the year II.) *Bias* Parent, a former priest, and later *agent national* of the very revolutionary District de Clamecy, is stated to have 'démoralisé le peuple' in giving them false illusions about their political and social importance.[3] Nor was this all; not only had they preached and practised the subversion of the social order, they had also – it is still the same group of Bourbonnais – encouraged 'la dépravation des mœurs en traitant de despotisme la sollicitude d'un père pour ses enfants, de jalousie, le tendre intérêt d'un mari pour la réputation de son épouse, en disant à la tribune de la société populaire qu'une fille à 21 ans, une femme mariée, n'étoient plus soumises à aucune autorité'.[4] (It is characteristic of Thermidorian views of society that the very liberal laws of the revolutionary period in favour of bastard children and younger sons and daughters should have been withdrawn, in the course of the year III, in favour of legislation re-establishing *l'autorité*

---

[1] AN, F1b II Allier I (*Tableau des crimes du comité révolutionnaire de Moulins*, Imprimé, s.d. an IV). He is also accused – and this again is characteristic – of having said 'qu'il mettoit les femmes en réquisition pour ses menus plaisirs'. This is a very common accusation in Thermidorian documents; the point, once more, is that the awful crime of these people was not to have commandeered just any girl – there would be no fuss about a *fille d'auberge* – but the daughters of *notables* and big farmers. In the denunciations made against the former *concierge* of the Salon prison, the girl Cadenet is above all scandalized that such a wretch should have had the impudence to suggest that he would like to kiss her and sleep with her, as she was pretty; on her own admission he did not succeed in doing either. But what effrontery! (Arch. Bouches-du-Rhône L 1862, dénonciation de la fille Cadenet, 17 ventôse an III). There is every probability that, just as they commandeered meals, many *commissaires* may thus have commandeered girls, especially the daughters of the well-to-do and of *ci-devants*. It was a matter of combining business with pleasure, and there could be no more dramatic way of expressing the new *sans-culotte* hierarchy. It was also one of the military aspects of Terror and Repression; and in any war or revolution the soldier might see himself as one of the eighty, 'Dans le lit de la Marquise'.

[2] AN, F1b II Allier I (la députation de l'Allier au Directoire, 25 floréal an IV).

[3] AN, F1b II Nièvre I (tableau des fonctionnaires amnistiés de la Nièvre, 20 frimaire an V).

[4] AN, F1b II Allier I (Mangenest, de Montluçon, au Directoire, 1er pluviôse an IV).

paternelle and the legal rights of the eldest male child as established in some local *coutumes*.)

In the various accusations directed against the terrorists of the Allier and the Nièvre – probably the most advanced people of the ultra-revolutionary period – while there are few references to their cruelty and brutality, there is a constant harping on the company that they kept, on their own origins, on their stated views on society. To have eaten with an executioner, when one was an educated man, a former priest, and a *propriétaire*, that was what was scandalous, that was what represented a state of affairs which could not be allowed to continue a moment longer and that must never occur again. (The Thermidorians were confident that they could see to that.) People who behaved in this way were accused by them of having *démoralisé le peuple*. What they meant by this was that they had not kept them in their place, had given them dangerous and false ideas of grandeur, and had encouraged them in habits of laziness.

In this sense at least, Thermidor did represent a return to normal conditions, for what was most abnormal, as well as most intolerable, was that a 'popular movement' should ever have existed at all, in its own right, should have developed its own institutions and forms of political expression, and should have been politically effective – in combination, it is true, with other forces – for so long, especially in a country so devoid of representative institutions as eighteenth-century France where, up to the Revolution, the only form of popular protest had been the traditional market riot or bursts of wild and hopeless violence. In the words of Professor Reinhard, 'ce fut la guerre qui révolutionna la Révolution'; and it was war that gave the *sans-culottes* their opportunity. It was understandable, with the example of 1793 behind them, that so many nineteenth-century neo-Jacobin and neo-*sans-culotte* leaders should have looked to war as the best means of achieving Vallès's longed-for *la Sociale*.[1]

12. War and Terror (1793–1794)

The Thermidorians were right to affect such amazement, even if their indignation was somewhat self-interested. For the development of the *sans-culotte* movement during 1793 was entirely accidental and arose from the convenient pretext of total mobilization and emergency. The *sans-culotte* movement was as much a product of the war as the *maximum*, the *réquisitions*, the law on hoarding, the economic controls, and 'dechristianization'. Six months before the Thermidorians, the *dantonistes* had drawn the right conclusions: to dismiss the Terror, to put an end to repression, to send the people's judges back to the obscurity of their shops and

---

[1] *La République Sociale.*

basements, to rule in the absence of meddlesome *sans-culottes*, and to deprive the revolutionary dictatorship of its alibi, it was necessary to put an end to the war. But they had come six months too early: the war had yet to be won, the government still needed popular support, *sans-culotte* bellicosity was still something to be reckoned with, while the *dantonistes* put their heads in the noose by attempting to conduct an independent foreign policy in time of war, so that they could readily be branded as traitors. The Thermidorians, some of whom represented *la queue de Danton*, could keep the war and dismiss the popular movement, because the bulk of the armies was outside France, because victories gave the promise of a pillage economy, and because 'dechristianization' provided them with a treasure-chest of furniture and pictures that could be exchanged for grain through Swiss or other neutral intermediaries.

Until the outbreak of war, successive revolutionary authorities had proved themselves quite capable of keeping the people down both in town and in the countryside: indeed, the bourgeois *Garde nationale* was much better at it, more ruthless, and also more interested, than the old royal troops had been. If rural disorder was persistent and widespread throughout 1790 and 1791, it was also remarkably unsuccessful, bringing on brutal and effective class repression. It did not matter to Lafayette and Bailly, as long as the country was at peace, that the *habits bleus* were loathed by the common people of Paris. They had done what was expected of them at the Champ de Mars, and, outside Paris, in Étampes, Angers, Nîmes, and elsewhere; and they were to do it again and again, firing on rioters, who were often just petitioners, and showing none of the hesitation in the use of force and musketry characteristic of the old royal authorities.

The first opportunity for the emergence of *sans-culotte* militancy came with the opening in July 1792 of the *Garde nationale* to the *citoyens passifs*, though it took them more than a year to displace the previous officers and to gain control of the all-important artillery companies (*canonniers*), the object of bitter conflicts between moderate and plebeian Sections in June–July 1793.[1] The opportunity was created by mobilization and invasion; but it followed that the *sans-culotterie* as an effective force could last only as long as the emergency lasted, and that, like Terror and repression, its influence could only be transient. Indeed, it was not to last even as long as the emergency; for by the spring of 1794 the government had discovered that it could not only run the Terror without popular support, but also use it against the popular militants. So that war, once the people's opportunity, could also be a pretext, when centralization had been firmly established, in the period December 1793–March 1794, for dealing with the so-called 'ultra-revolutionaries', creators and

---

[1] *Les Armées révolutionnaires*, I, pp. 40–8.

commanders of people's armies, who were inconvenient and expendable because they stood in the way of an increasingly invasive revolutionary government. At the same time, the war was used even more directly as a means of removing from Paris – and from other cities – the *sans-culotte*-controlled artillery companies, by sending them to the frontiers or to the west, where they were painlessly incorporated into the ranks of the army proper.

This process was not a straight conflict in class terms between a predominantly middle-class Jacobin dictatorship and a socially distinctive 'popular movement' drawing its support primarily from that alliance to small shopkeepers and artisans known as *la sans-culotterie*. There may have been elements of such a conflict. Many of the popular militants, however, were themselves people of middle-class origin, some of them *notables*, and quite a number of the 'ultra-revolutionaries' were professional men or ex-soldiers. It was much more a conflict over the exercise of power. The *sans-culottes* – or whatever we choose to call them – claimed to exercise sovereign power in the name of 'direct democracy': the deputies were merely their mandatories, and answerable to them as such. This claim they proceeded to substantiate by actually exercising power and 'legislating' through institutions of their own creation that were not responsible to the central government or to the subordinate authorities. Thus police powers and the control of armed forces fell to *sociétés populaires*, that is to the militant minorities that controlled these completely unrepresentative bodies, dominated, in most instances, by very small groups of *meneurs*, allied as much by friendship or common hatreds as by ties of trade or craft. For, as in the case of the Paris Sections, it would be difficult to identify the provincial *sociétés* with any particular class or social group. Their composition varied enormously and was never quite the same from one town to the next; if, generally speaking, they represented a good cross-section of professional and trade life in any given town, in many places they allowed little place to the lower ranks of urban society. Thus, in le Havre, membership ranged from sea captains, merchants, tradesmen, artisans, schoolmasters, to former priests and clerks; the *Grand Quai* was absent – many of its inhabitants were in prison in the year II – but so were the shipyard workers, the fishermen, and ordinary sailors.[1] In Lyon, the hard core, both in May 1793 and again in Floréal year II, consisted of a selection of the more skilled trades – printers, compositors, goldsmiths, and so on – municipal officials, including the director of the post office, and the middle ranks of the silk industry: *négotiants* and *fabricants en soie*, rather than *ouvriers en soie*.[2] It was perhaps not sur-

---

[1] *Terreur et subsistances*, pp. 99–105 ('La société havraise').
[2] *L'Armée révolutionnaire à Lyon*, p. 50.

prising that in the crisis of 29 May 1793 the club should have backed the Jacobin municipality, while the Sections went over bag and baggage to federalism; there was no doubt on which side the common people of Lyon stood. The membership of the *société révolutionnaire* of Lille is even more surprising, for it included some of the richest cotton manufacturers in the place, together with wealthy property-holders and investors in national lands, along with the usual rank and file of tradesmen and textile workers, most of the latter *fabricants* in their own right.[1] Membership of a *société* might have a plebeian look about it, and certainly some *sociétés* fell into the hands of genuinely artisan and shopkeeper elements, but very often – just how often it would be the object of further local research to prove – it was a convenient disguise under cover of which the old *notables* of 1790 or of 1792 continued to exercise their influence. Of course, they were prepared to make concessions, as long as they were able to retain positions of power; and some of them were in the forefront of *sans-culotte* revolutionizing. In 1793 the *société* was more important than the municipality. It was a sort of revolutionary *syndicat d'initiative*, devoted above all to the promotion of local interests; and, on this platform, there would be a wide consensus of agreements. Its first aim, then, was to attempt to control municipal government. This was easy, for the *société* held the decisive weapon of the delivery of *certificats de civisme*; in other words, it could control appointments and remove even elected officials who met with its disapproval.

From the vantage point of municipal government, the *sociétés* then proceeded to establish alliances, private treaties, exchange of information, and 'federations' with their neighbours in other cities. This resulted in endless fractionalization of authority and the establishment, especially in the south of France, of hundreds of 'municipalist' republics, within which the more dramatic forms of revolutionary action could be pursued without let or hindrance, while at the same time the particular interests of a given area were promoted. 'Communalism' has been described as one of the most characteristic traits of the popular movement and, if it can be taken to mean a tendency to anarchism, this is certainly true. But it could be put to other, more disguised, uses, and very often 'communalism' is simply the rebirth of regionalism or municipalism, in a more respectable, apparently revolutionary, form. It might serve the interests of a *République du Midi*, but it is questionable whether it would have done those of the One and Indivisible. The 'federations' of September–November 1793 were in fact the revolutionary equivalent of the duc d'Angoulême's Kingdom of the South of the summer of 1815; they even covered very much the same areas of the south-east and south-centre.

---

[1] *Terreur et subsistances*, pp. 151–78.

There were several of these 'federations' in existence – one grouping seventy-seven *sociétés* of the Midi, with permanent headquarters in Marseille; another in Alsace; a third in Upper Normandy – when the Jacobin dictatorship intervened, in the winter of 1793, no doubt to avert what might have been the next stage in the organization of a sort of counter-government, or at least of a parallel government (and there had been plenty of foolish talk to the effect that 'les sociétés populaires sont souveraines, elles sont donc au-dessus de la loi', in the course of the autumn) on a national level. The Revolutionary Government chose to think so, as an excuse for intervention against a process that it described as 'l'ébauche d'un nouveau fédéralisme populaire'. It is, however, unlikely that anything of the sort would ever have happened; it is hard to imagine Paris *sectionnaires*, Lyonnais or Marseillais *sociétaires* being prepared to co-operate with anyone else, other than in terms of the total subjection of their partners to the municipal interests of their own cities. (This was particularly true of the role of the *sociétés* as instruments of enforced provisioning in the normal supply areas around their cities.) There was much more danger of anarchy – especially when the 'federations' had started to raise their own armed forces, composed exclusively of *sociétaires* – than of the formation of a national rival to the Revolutionary Government.

13.   *'Communalism' and the Popular Movement (Autumn and Winter of 1793)*

In the Departments this movement was largely spontaneous, insofar as it represented the traditional desire of each city, each town, each village to be left alone and not to be interfered with by strangers from Paris. It was truly a form of 'popular federalism', but it would bring in many other elements as well. For, being so anarchical and undisciplined, it also attracted men of a certain type, instead of men of a certain social condition: it attracted revolutionary optimists, zealots, and wild men, the 'perfectionists' of the revolutionary period, who believed in taking on everything and everybody at once and who, in the government's view, 'did not know where to stop'. It also, of course, drew patent demagogues, adventurers out for a good time or an opportunity to make up for a compromising past by some singular extravagance, all manner of crackpots, and a few men of blood who were out for pillage and vengeance and who equated revolutionary action with beating up.

All these categories were easy to compromise; some had pasts that would not look good when trotted out by government prosecutors, always prone to judge what people were by what they had been – a tactic used persistently by Robespierre and Fouquier-Tinville against poor Jacques Roux. All of them, by their intransigence and single-mindedness, were sure to have ranged against themselves a maximum of powerful and respectable enemies. Their verbal extravagance and impudence made them open to every sort of misinterpretation. Their conceit, their posturing, their arrogance, and their constant self-dramatization rendered them ideal subjects for official indictments as counter-revolutionaries, *exagérés*, *anarchistes*, and other bad things. They had done, and above all had said, so many silly and so many violent things, that their words and actions could be put to almost any interpretation. Nor were they the sort of people *qui pensaient au lendemain*. The government men, on the other hand, did, seeing to it that many of these imprudent enthusiasts were denied one altogether.

On this provincial level at least, it was much more a conflict of tempera- ments than of class or even of policies. For how to force an *exagéré*, a revolutionary individualist, into a class categorization? And the conflict was quite inevitable, both in human and in political terms. The govern- ment men had time on their side, and knew it; it was only a matter of waiting for the wild men to hang themselves in the coils of their exagger- ated promises and threats and to make themselves so intolerable to so many people for their downfall to become a matter of urgent necessity. The *exagérés*, it is true, enjoyed a certain amount of popular support, and each one, in his own 'parish', possessed his select band of devoted parti- sans. But the support for them was too personal to be effective when it was decided they had had a good run for their money and it was time to bring them in. There was no wide movement of protest in their favour; in any case most of their supporters were too humble to matter. (What could *Marat* Chaix do with his little band of rural *galochiers*, *savetiers*, and so on, when the word went out against him from the people in Nevers?) Unlike the Paris *sectionnaires*, who could mobilize a considerable army of solid master-craftsmen and shopkeepers, the provincial ultra-revolution- ists could count ultimately only on poor village artisans and on the lower ranks of urban wage-earners. Many of their supporters were not even *domiciliés*, being drawn from the itinerant trades, from the rural poor, and from those who lived in lodging-houses.

Most of these provincial militants were incapable of seeing beyond the limits of their own town or District. They were anxious to exercise power, but once they had conquered it at the municipal level, by placing their adherents in the *mairie*, in the *société*, and in the *comité* (almost always the higher authority of the District escaped them and it was generally from the District that their eventual undoing would come), they felt that they had achieved their main objectives; it was then only a matter of holding on and laying the foundations of the social republic within their own parish. Neither they nor their supporters were prepared to think in national terms. So when it came to a contest for power with the 'government men', they were at an enormous disadvantage; they were not even prepared to consider a conflict on such terms. They were not interested in what might happen or was happening in Paris or who exercised power there, so long as they themselves were not interfered with. This put them in an impossible situation; for they would in any case have the District against them, and the District would have access to the *députation*. Their only hope would have been for them also to have someone in Paris to whom they could appeal for support and succour: the Cordeliers, a deputy, a Sectionary committee, the *Commission des Subsistances*. But they were generally too ignorant of Parisian affairs and of the various hierarchies of revolutionary power in the capital and too wrapped up in parish-pump revolutionism to think of looking for outside support; at best they might attempt to call in one of the regional commissions of summary justice. It was only in the District de Gonesse, and in other areas on the periphery of the capital, that such local ultra-revolutionaries were able to enlist support from a deputy, from a Section, or from one of the Ministries. Here they had the advantage of access to the many rival centres of power. Most of the wild men were much further away from the centre of political life than that; their very distance from the capital had often been their opportunity. So they were removed without much difficulty by *Représentants en mission*, backed by armed force, and by *commissaires* bearing arrest warrants.

Indeed one can hardly speak of a conflict at all, at least in political terms, for the local militants never at any time thought of power in national spheres. Nor, for that matter, did the far more politically sophisticated Paris *sans-culottes*. These at least possessed the force and the institutions which could have made the conquest of power quite possible. Yet they only used their force to persuade the Convention, never to drive it out and replace it. Ultimately, they did not question the sovereignty of the Convention, even if they did challenge the legitimacy of the Revolutionary Government.

14. Hébertisme

So much for popular militancy in its most spontaneous and decentralized form. There existed, however, a more serious political challenge to the Revolutionary Government from a group of Paris politicians who, while claiming to represent the popular movement and while imitating most effectively the popular language, were seeking power for themselves. Here the conflict was even more one of persons than of principles, the principal objection of the so-called *hébertistes* to the Revolutionary Government being that they were not in it. They were 'outs' who sought to use the popular movement in order to become 'ins'; their programme did not amount to much more than the fulfilment of rather limited personal ambitions. It is not even certain whether they were out to seize power, if necessary by force, since the Revolutionary Government did not give them a chance to show what their intentions might have been; but they could probably have been bought off cheaply enough: Hébert with the Ministry of the Interior, Vincent with that of War, Ronsin with the *Marine*, a strange choice for a former sergeant-major. Or they might have even been contented with the *Contributions Directes* or the *Postes*. The government would not bargain on that basis and, as the *hébertistes* too were committed to war, the great provider for their numerous protégés, and yet publicly called for the end of a wartime emergency government, they became tied up in the fatal contradiction of all wartime oppositions and were easily disposed of, so far as the public were concerned, on a charge of treason. They had no alternative programme to propose, but only an alternative government. They did not even intend to end the revolutionary dictatorship, but merely to exercise it on their own account.

15.   Sans-culottes *and Jacobins*

The conflict between the Jacobin dictatorship and the popular movement, the parting of the ways between the *robespierristes* and the *sans-culottes*, was much more straightforward than has often been suggested. Programme played little part in this divorce, nor can any 'inevitability' of conflict be discovered in terms of class. The two sides represented forms of government (un-government might be a better term to describe the communalism of the popular militants) that could not co-exist for more than a few months. It took the central government some time to realize what was going on in the Departments – it was uninformed or misinformed – and a good deal longer to make its will felt and to put an end to the administrative anarchy that had resulted from the various experiments in popular government. No government can tolerate anarchy indefinitely, and that of the year II had both the will and the means of putting an end to it and of subjecting France to a single central impulse.

The destruction of the popular movement was carried out long before Thermidor; the first steps were taken in September 1793, the chains of centralization were forged in December, the first purge of 'ultras' occurred in January 1794, and the destruction of the popular institutions and the arrest of the militants followed in March–April. By May, though the common people remained armed, they no longer had any weapon save arms, or any way of putting pressure on the Revolutionary Government, or of making their opinion felt, than by force. There was no longer such a thing as popular opinion to be reckoned with, and all that was left to the *sans-culotte* was either armed revolt or a sulky apathy.

In other words, one has seen the last of *la sans-culotterie*, of *le sans-culottisme*, if not of individual *sans-culottes*, and one is back with the crowd; and even that failed to materialize and come to the rescue of the Revolutionary Government on 9–10 Thermidor. Popular protest was henceforth reduced to its purely physical expression: the *journée*, the riot, the leaderless uprising. After the fall of Robespierre, some popular institutions revived briefly, soon to be decisively checked. The revolts of Germinal and Prairial were hopeless, unprepared, almost leaderless, and without any clear programme; on both occasions the rioters had the Convention and the Thermidorian Government in their power, but they could not make up their minds what to do next, and eventually marched back to their quarters. They had lost the habit of political discussion and they were without the militant minorities of the previous year. But although these had not taken part in the uprising, being mostly not the sort of people to come out into the street at any time, they were dealt with later by the Thermidorian Government which then set about systematically destroying them economically.

In short, anything sufficiently organized to merit the description 'the popular movement' was only of very short duration and politically effective for only a few months, in the whole five years of the revolutionary crisis: March–April 1793 to March–April 1794, with September, October, November, and December representing the height of unrestrained 'communalism' in certain Departments. 'Communalism' was for a time possible, because nothing was done to check it. It had, too, its regional strongholds, inaccessible to rapid centralization, far from Paris, and drawing on village or regional loyalties that had little to do with the Revolution. Ultra-revolutionism not only had a regionalist appeal; it appealed to certain types of persons. Just as 'municipalist' republics could in the last resort be no match for the Committee of Public Safety, so these *naïfs* were no match for the 'government men' who were thinking more in terms of France and Europe than of Crémieu and the rural poor. The temporary importance of the popular movement was an accident that was rapidly put right. The government bought off some of the best militants, 'bureaucratized' some of the most effective popular institutions – there was no doubt an agreeable irony in getting the militants to do the government's dirty work and in transforming former *tribuns* into policemen. Militancy was, in the long run, a luxury that an artisan or an innkeeper could ill afford; but, once the militant accepted a salary, he became a government official. A few temporary concessions were made to popular demands, most of them spectacular but harmless. The irreconcilables were arrested and a number destroyed in the spring of 1794. Their fate was enough to discourage their disciples.

The Revolutionary Government had decided to govern; as soon as it did that, there was an end to the 'popular movement'. It is true that the Jacobin dictatorship itself suffered in the process, becoming anaemic for lack of popular support and increasing isolation; but that is another matter. We are concerned here to explain why the popular movement collapsed in the spring of 1794, and why, despite various attempts to revive it and to give it a new purpose, it henceforth never achieved anything other than blind revolt that provided the pretext for ruthless and effective repression, not to explain why *robespierrisme* failed.

Albert Soboul is right to emphasize that, in the long run, the *sans-culotte* movement could not possibly succeed; but he puts too much stress on its inner conflicts in terms of class and social content, on the class barriers that divided it from Jacobinism. Many of these are *vues d'esprit* of a historian aware of the course taken by European movements of popular protest in the nineteenth century. In year II terms, it was a choice between anarchy on a truly magnificent scale and rigorous, ordered government. As the country was at war, there is nothing surprising about the fact that after a period of vacillation and governmental indecision, after a few rounds of rather inconsequential scuffling, during which neither side seems to have been very clear about its objectives (indeed the popular movement was at no time clear about these, except that it wanted to act as a sort of permanent, luxurious, irresponsible opposition at ground level), the government should have won.

Perhaps the word 'conflict' is itself misleading for a situation that was never clear-cut in terms of programme or even of power. The popular movement was never totally opposed to the Revolutionary Government. The *sectionnaires* were content to criticize certain aspects of it; but, in a number of important ways, they were prepared enthusiastically to second its efforts and to act, in fact, as an unofficial government agency. Both wanted to win the war and defeat counter-revolution at home, though they might differ as to how these objectives might best be achieved. The militants, for instance, thought that the war could never be won till the army, the navy, the Ministries, the Commissions, and the police had been completely purged of all their more professional elements, suspect because they had served the previous regime. They believed, like the Jacksonians, that a sound heart, patriotism, revolutionary conviction, and unpretentiousness could in all circumstances replace professional skill and that there was no job that *un bon patriote révolutionnaire* could not undertake with confidence. They thought, in fact, that patriotic amateurs could always do better than uncommitted professionals, and their ideal general was the goldsmith's apprentice, Jean Rossignol, or the *suisse* from Saint-Eustache, Sépher, even though each in his sector had made a fearful hash of his campaign. They encouraged the election of officers by the lower deck in the navy. They succeeded in obtaining the head of the *général-comte* Custine, because he was a Count and had been insolent to his Minister of War, and despite the fact that he was an able commander. And they made sure that the *commissaires de police* were elected by the Sections (with the result that this was probably the only time in French history when the police were popular).

Yet, while they called for the employment at every level of amateurs, they also wanted endlessly to extend the sphere of governmental interference and make it embrace every productive or commercial activity. Food commissioners and *réquisitionnaires* – amateurs too – should be let loose on the farmers, should tell them what they could and what they could not cultivate; and *apôtres civiques*, some of whom were, in a sense, professionals, for, as former priests, they had learnt to preach before the Revolution, should be sent into the countryside to eradicate religion as a necessary preliminary to winning the war. (What would be the point of winning if one were still left with 'superstition' and 'old druids'?) The Committees had other priorities. They believed in employing talent where it existed, and strongly opposed hard-and-fast rules that would have minimized the freedom of choice they considered to be the prerogative of any government. They had no intention of letting such high appointments be dictated to them by ignorant artisans and semi-literate shopkeepers. They did not think that the war could best be won by raising against the Republic the maximum number of enemies both at home and abroad, by outraging Catholic opinion in the countryside, and by alienating the few remaining neutral powers. And in the thirst for information which they shared with the previous regime, they preferred professionals – informers, members of the old police, innkeepers, procurers, prostitutes – to amateur zealots. They listened more closely to the reports of *agents nationaux*, who were government appointees, than to those of *sociétaires*, the self-appointed Arguses of revolutionary orthodoxy. They were even prepared to do a bit of spying, to plant informers in prisons, to encourage the long tongues of portresses and *concierges*, to accumulate secret *dossiers* that might come in useful one day, as a means of combating the enemy within, rather than rely on denunciations made in open assembly. (The *sans-culottes*, it is true, went in for a great deal of delation, but they wanted to hold a monopoly of the trade.) They were quite ready to muffle the revolutionary war trumpet for Swiss, Dutch, Danish, or American ears, and they did not believe that every foreign refugee was a patriot by nature and right of birth and the ideal counsellor on foreign affairs.

The quarrel was about means, not about fundamentals. The militants were revolutionary perfectionists, and the members of the Committees were 'possibilists'. Both were right according to their own lights. The real dilemma was that neither side could get along without the other. The government needed the help of the *sans-culottes* to carry out its policies of food procurement and, since there was no single monolithic party, the Committees had to rely on the *sociétés populaires* to publicize official news and diffuse government instructions. In the absence of a centrally operated, political, secret police (not even its embryo existed in the year II), the Committee of General Security had to entrust the actual running of Terror and repression, surveillance, vigilance, denunciation, the control of lodging-houses, and the checking of passports to local men: printers, shoemakers, tailors, tinkers, gunsmiths, innkeepers, and clerks – with local prejudices and local axes to grind. The Terror itself had thus to be delegated and run at several removes. (There is an endless multiplication of *délégations* in the Departments during the year II, with an almost limitless laying on of hands to produce such sieved end-products of popular sovereignty as a *délégué d'un délégué d'un délégué d'un Représentant du peuple*, to such an extent that the government had to intervene, in December 1793, to put an official limit to the *délégation des pouvoirs*.) This was not a matter of choice: there were not enough professionals to go round, especially in the Departments. In this respect, the government was much more prisoner of the *sans-culottes* than the latter, even when they became its salaried officials, were the prisoners of the Committee of General Security. The local men knew what was going on, and they told the Committees as much, or as little, as suited their own purposes. The Terror was administered on a national putting-out basis, and the local men generally had the last word.

The popular militants were patriotic before they were revolutionary. And they were quick to suspect sinister motives when the Committees sought to moderate their ardour. If the Committees condemned the collective denunciation of all foreigners, the local zealots at once smelt an attempt to make a deal with the Allies and to sell out their Revolution for a compromise peace. If the Committees condemned, on grounds of political expediency, root and branch dechristianization, local 'ultras' became convinced that a deal with the Pope was in the offing. The *sans-culottes* were patriots; they were super-patriots, their patriotism was of the jealous, suspicious, and exclusive kind; they were the only patriots; and they alone, by their constant vigilance and civic devotion, were frustrating Pitt's plans to set fire to Châteauroux, to burn down the mills of Corbeil, to destroy the crops of the Pays de Caux, to deliver up Narbonne to the King of Spain, to subvert the *société populaire* of Bonnet-la-Montagne (Saint-Bonnet-le-Château), and to destroy, by calumny, *les bons bougres révolutionnaires* of Crémieu.

Everywhere the finger in the hole in the dyke that held back the flood waters of counter-revolution was that of a local *sans-culotte*. Each member of the *comité* of a small town in the south-west was well aware that Pitt had sent his hired assassins across France to remove his arch-enemy in Moissac or Tonneins. All the talk about dying at one's desk, of springing into the breach, of holding the bridge pierced by a thousand lances, of drinking the hemlock, and a lot else besides, was not just talk. They really believed in dangers that could not but flatter their self-importance. This was a patriotism so farouche as to be difficult to work with. There was no lack of patriotic response, on the part of the common people of the towns, to government appeals for co-operation. The trouble arose because the *sans-culottes* wanted that co-operation to be on their own terms. At the local level – that of enforcement – the Committees had little protection against côteries, family feuds, regional antagonisms, and local bully-boys. It was always possible, of course, for a *Représentant*, or a delegate of one of the Committees, to remove authorities that had clearly become obnoxious and intolerable; but this might bring in another gang and release the flood-tide of vengeance. And purges carried out at too frequent intervals would make administration impossible and might produce an administrative strike. Public office under the Terror could be dangerous and it was always compromising. Indeed, it is surprising how readily people accepted it, and how eagerly they clung to it once they had obtained it. There were compensations. Some of them were material and *patriotes* used the Terror to have a very good time: such an opportunity was unlikely ever to recur again in a single lifetime. But most of the compensations were in terms of pride and conceit; for the sort of people the Revolutionary Government had to work with, humour, encourage, and praise, were mostly not people who had ever previously been in a position of power. In short, there had to be some sort of pact between the government and the minorities of local militants, if the government was to be at all effective outside Paris. In this respect the Committees had to reckon, if not with the 'popular movement', at least with militant élites.

The government had, of course, advantages too, in its relations with these local minorities. It had prestige: the voice of Barère was heard afar, the name 'Robespierre' might produce the hush of respect – or of dotty fervour – in small towns in the Gers or the Tarn. It inspired awe: the roving *Représentant* arrived in a clatter of majesty, with the dust of an escort and to the sound of trumpets, that left the villager gaping and made the urban tailor anxious to be seen at the table of the great man. The *satrape* kept people waiting and ate his meals in public, while reports and petitions were read to him. He agreed condescendingly to spare a few precious moments to visit the local *société* and give them the Good Word and the honour of setting eyes on a portion of national sovereignty. The government had a monopoly of official news and could always count on the twin pillars of popular credulity and popular orthodoxy. Local *patriotes* believed what they were told about events in Paris; a former Friend of the People was an Agent of Pitt, if the *Représentant* or the *Bulletin* said so.

This readiness to accept the official version was also an indication of a considerable degree of local indifference about what was happening in the capital. Up to the spring of 1794, it is true, there were other sources of information – including half a dozen *Pères Duchesne* in various provincial towns. The news they gave was Cordelier-orientated, while Cordelier groups managed to obtain a hold over *sociétés* in garrison towns, thanks to the presence of *commissaires du Pouvoir Exécutif*; but only for a time. Once the *Représentant* had spoken, orthodoxy was re-established. But the *Représentants* themselves spoke with many voices, and quarrels among rival teams of *proconsuls*, sent to the same areas, often gave local minorities the opportunity to stay in power or to topple their rivals. The *Représentants* had prestige, but they differed violently about appointments to local offices, so that the system of sending them up into the Departments, far from increasing centralization and putting a premium on orthodoxy, often exacerbated local quarrels and multiplied local clienteles.

Orthodoxy then might speak with many different voices. The inhabitants of the District de Gonesse, visited by three rival groups in rapid succession, and sometimes together, learnt to distinguish between them and soon found out which group would favour which interest. It was in this manner that the political rivalries of the capital reached down into *bourg* and village. Ultimately, people were not enormously interested in what happened in Paris. Their chief concern was how to put distant events in the capital to local use: to renew a *comité*, to score off a political rival. So everyone would discover his or her own *hébertiste* or *dantoniste* at the right moment.

Finally, the government had money, the power of appointment and dismissal, of arrest, disgrace, imprisonment, and execution. A number of local 'ultras' were guillotined, in the summer of 1794, because they had been too impudent, too enthusiastic, too independent, too drunken, and too lecherous. Others were killed because they had had the wrong protectors; this is why there was a certain mortality among the agents of the *Pouvoir Exécutif*. Several people were arrested at this time because they had been seen talking to one of the roving *commissaires* who had turned out to be a *complice d'Hébert*. Thus many paid heavily for their pride in high company, or for the manner in which they had originally been appointed.

Nevertheless, in the conditions of the year II, the government was dependent to a considerable extent on the goodwill of *sans-culotte* minorities, on the patriotism and enthusiasm of the urban *petit peuple*. It could do without both and still govern, rather more effectively, since it no longer had popular opinion to consider, in a bureaucratic vacuum, with a stream of orders pouring down and a stream of echoes pouring up. This was what happened to the government in the summer of 1794. It gave a great impression of monolithic orthodoxy and of almost religious unanimity. In fact, both barely covered apathy and indifference, the deadliest of diseases for an embattled revolutionary regime – what Albert Soboul describes as 'l'usure morale du petit peuple' – disillusionment and boredom. Having destroyed their institutions, prohibited the free expression of popular opinion on such key issues as rationing and provisioning, religion and épuration, the government then turned to the emasculated militant and appealed to him: 'do not go away, we still need you', 'do not ease up', 'do not absent yourself from the club, the fight is still on'. It might well be, but the heart of the sans-culotte was no longer in it, he did not feel needed. People did not care any more; they had had enough of militancy and, if the government no longer had any use for the 'popular movement', the militants of the 'popular movement' felt it was time to return to private life, to the shop, to the family, and to billiards.

The government itself set about destroying the most effective popular institutions (sociétés sectionnaires, etc.), though these had served the dictatorship well. The others collapsed under the weight of indifference, from want of attendance, during the summer of 1794, the Summer of Disenchantment. The 'popular movement', having served its purpose, was dismissed. But it did not do the government any good. Administration had never been so efficient, but, as Saint-Just lamented, la République s'est glacée. However difficult the relations between the Jacobin dictatorship and the militants had been, the experience of Ventôse–Thermidor year II proved that the two were interdependent. The power struggle had at last been solved, at the expense of the popular militants. The amateurs had been replaced by the professionals – or at least by ex-amateurs who had been bought into bureaucracy as a result of full-time employment. Robespierre and his friends disappeared, leaving an endless trail of historical bubbles to mark the spot and to plague us ever since. They were soon followed by the whole paraphernalia of Revolutionary Government, which collapsed in bits, from the top downwards.

The people for a time rejoiced, so completely divorced had they become from a government with which they no longer felt personally associated and the rigour of which, victory having come, they could no longer justify. Why should there have been more Terror, more repression, more government, and more bureaucrats once the emergency was past and the danger over? The sans-culotte militants had been terrorists; and at one time they had actually been demanding more Terror, more repression, as a solution to every problem, and they had suspected the Revolutionary Government of moderation, of wishing to protect the rich and the greedy, when their demands had not been met. But, after Floréal, even the *sans-culottes* lost their faith in Terror and were converted away from repression – both of which they had envisaged only as a form of popular justice and as an exercise of popular vengeance. For one thing, both weapons were now being used against their own kind. But, above all, they could not see the purpose of a Terror that had become anonymous, bureaucratic, secretive, that no longer attempted to explain and to persuade – and a great deal of the people's Terror had been verbal exaggeration, blustering, bluff, and blood-and-thunder talk – and that struck out, with apparent blindness, at all sorts and conditions.

The degree to which the *sans-culottes* had become alienated from the government can best be gauged by the fact that, like the future Thermidorians, like Babeuf, they rejoiced at the end of fear, at the cessation of the *système de la dépopulation*, and pursued, in the wake of the Thermidorian hack writers, Maximilien Robespierre into an imaginary hell, there to torment him with his authoritarian tendencies. For had he not aimed at dictatorship, using the broad back of the common people as steps to the throne? The *sans-culottes*, like the *honnêtes gens*, were prepared to believe this, at least in the early weeks of the new regime. (When they later changed their minds, their judgement had become impaired by historical hindsight and nostalgia, and Robespierre and the much-evoked 'popular movement' had entered the realm of myth.)

The committees of government disappeared. Most *Représentants* were recalled. The *sans-culottes* were driven out of the *comités de surveillance*, one of the few places in which they had been allowed to remain, as servants of a government Terror, after Floréal. They were replaced by men of wealth, when the *comités* were not suppressed altogether. (They were maintained only in largish towns, a sure indication that what was left of the Terror was to be directed against the urban *petit peuple*, and that the country population could breathe again, sure of total impunity.) But many of the *agents nationaux* remained, and what survived of the Jacobin dictatorship was what had caused it to dry up and had isolated it: an invasive, self-interested, self-perpetuating bureaucracy, concerned only to continue.

If the Thermidorian regime eventually became almost as centralized as its predecessor, it was under pressure from a bureaucracy that it was unable to remove. But the Thermidorians were under pressure from many other lobbies as well. Far from acting with efficiency in a political vacuum once most potential sources of opposition had been removed or silenced, they had to satisfy a motley collection of contending interests – none of them popular: *députations*, now all-powerful both in Paris and in their fiefs; a reinstated judiciary, impatient to punish those impudent *sans-culottes* who had presumed to take the administration of justice out of the hands of the professionals (judges, magistrates, and *juges de paix* were the most ardent exponents of the anti-popular Terror of the year III, and without their help, encouragement, and complicity the White terrorists would have been unable to administer their own rougher, parallel Terror); a gilded youth of *embusqués*, anxious to revenge themselves for the frequent jeers and occasional blows that they had received from *sans-culottes*, by attacking anyone who was not dressed like themselves, and in revolt against the austerity of the previous regime; speculators and contractors who dictated to the government; the amoral, the licentious, and the pleasure-loving; officers avid for promotion and fame (any battlefield would do, especially the streets of Paris, where laurels could be won against hastily erected barricades and where the *repos du guerrier* – the victor over the poor and the hungry – could be assured the same night); ladies of the new court, with their *salons* and their young protégés to promote. The Thermidorian Government was indeed so much a regime of lobbies that it was often difficult to distinguish the regime from its solicitants and to see where lobbies ended and government began. What was worst in the Jacobin dictatorship remained, soon to be joined by many elements worse still. The one thing that was effectively silenced was *vox populi*.

16. Conclusion

The expression 'popular movement' is a thesis in itself. When used by historians and examiners (and it is a great favourite with both) it implies a considerable degree of organization, leadership, the existence of a minimum agreed programme, and above all the realization by those who take part in it that they are taking part in it, and their awareness of a collective identity, both in relation to their 'brothers', and against certain other groups in society and politics. For the period of a little over twenty years that has been the object of this study, a 'popular movement' might be allowed some claim to existence for at most a single year (from April 1793 to April 1794). It might also be argued that the White Terror in the south-east, which enjoyed very wide popular support and employed *sabreurs* of popular origin, might be likewise described as a primitive 'popular movement'; the argument against this would be that the White Terror was not autonomous and that it was being used and manipulated by others, from outside, for political aims that had nothing to do with the popular cause. The other forms of popular protest are either too individualistic (suicide, murder, the cult of the dead, vengeance) or too transient (market riots, *bandes* of vagrants) to qualify as a 'movement', though desertion on a sufficiently large scale might so qualify, in a very negative sense. *Babouvisme* was a 'movement', no doubt, but with the people left out, and only a hypothetical following, in the form of a list of a few thousand names, left obligingly for the information of the police. There was nothing 'popular' about it, though Babeuf and his fellow *clubistes* were graciously prepared to use the people as cannon fodder in order to win, in a bloody coup, a revolutionary dictatorship which would have kept the People informed of what was best for it.

So we have used 'popular movement' with extreme caution and with reference only to *le mouvement sans-culotte*, or rather *les mouvements sans-culotte*; for each town, each *commune*, was to produce its own brand of *sans-culottisme*. It is doubtful, too, whether the *sans-culottes* ever had a clear idea of themselves as an entity, save to distinguish themselves from those whom they disliked: bourgeois, farmers, wholesalers, entrepreneurs, *hommes de loi* and *hommes d'esprit*, painters, and artists. (Common dislikes, it is true, are an effective binding force, as long as the common hate-figures are much in evidence.) And it is only in the year III, with the memory of lost militancy, and in an effort to revive flagging hopes and rouse failing spirits, that we hear the slogan *Vive les sans-culottes*, although already it was shouted along with *Vive la Montagne, Vive les jacobins*. As the *sans-culottes* were so uncertain what they were, what their 'movement' was, whether they were in it or not, it is not surprising that historians should have some hesitation in allowing them a distinctive identity and in asserting the exact nature of their movement.

By concentrating first on popular militancy in decline, we have attempted at the outset to illustrate the generally disorganized, transient, and ultimately hopeless character of protest in a period during which Authority could, with each succeeding year, meet force with yet more force, uncontrolled violence with swift, effective, and, at the same time, discreet, unobtrusive violence, and when the repressive powers of government were constantly improving. During the twenty years between 1795 and 1815, such purely negative factors as disease, hardship, old age, exile, apathy, hopelessness, are even more important perhaps than the positive achievements of repression. It is the combination of the two that makes the position of the common people so desperate.

Our second purpose in thus putting last first is to explore, from the vantage point of 1795 (and beyond), the built-in weaknesses of the so-called *sans-culotte* movement even in its prime, during the year II. It is impossible to appreciate the true nature of the Terror of 1793–4 without taking into account the Counter-Terror of the year III (and, unlike 'movement', Counter-Terror is not a word invented by historians and then foisted on their helpless forebears, but an expression used most aptly to describe at the time something that was exactly that) which was a sort of collective reprisal for the excesses, threats, brutalities, humiliations, and enthusiasms of the previous year. In the same way, one would obtain quite a false impression of the energy and autonomy of *le mouvement sans-culotte*, examined in isolation in the year II context, if one did not move on to discover how rapidly and completely that movement collapsed in the very different circumstances of the year III. It is a matter of placing the two years back to back, in order to bring out both the basic contrasts, the prevailing consideration of vengeance (and vengeance is necessarily backward-looking; the ferocity of vengeance in the years III and IV is due to the fact that it did not have to look back very far), and also the comparative continuity of government policy (for the Jacobins finished off the 'popular movement'; the Thermidorians merely had to mop up individual militants, crush spontaneous protest, and disarm the people, and were in a much stronger position to do this than their predecessors). The year III is not just an epilogue to the year II, not just the year One After Robespierre (though some historians would suggest that this was its most important feature). It should be seen rather as the explanation of the year II.

The year 1795, from every point of view, is the decisive year of the whole revolutionary period, for it was basically the Thermidorian Settlement that survived into the *Restauration*. The one problem that the Thermidorians did not solve was that of government, but this was because they were themselves deeply divided. They did succeed in rendering the common people politically ineffective for the next thirty-five years, even if they left to the Directory a country in a state of advanced anarchy, profitable only to the royalist, the White Terrorist, and the bandit. Their successors merely had to clear up the pieces, using the printed lists drawn up by the Thermidorians, and every year, from 1796 at least to 1810, made the government stronger and the people weaker. The most formidable shackles and leg-irons to be applied to individual men of the people, the most ferocious legislation affecting the gathering together of more than two persons, were manufactured in the early years of that oppressive regime, between 1805 and 1808. In 1812 there was a timid renewal of popular protest, at once repressed with extreme ferocity. It is doubtful if the common people had much to do with the collapse of the Empire and the dispersal of the gangster dynasty.

One should not make too much of the contrast between the year II and the year III. Even if it sounds foolish, it is as well to remember that the year III came after the year II, and that the Thermidorians inherited from the Revolutionary Government most of the pre-conditions of the famine crisis of 1795–6, as well as a redoubtable legacy of hatred, envy, and the thirst for vengeance. To recall this is not to lessen the responsibilities of the Thermidorian governing class, nor to blacken their predecessors. It is only after six months or so of Thermidorian rule that the common people reacquired at least a negative self-awareness, out of hatred for the new ruling class, and began to idealize in contrast a dead Robespierre and Jacobin rule. The fact that they then began to look back on the year II as a lost Golden Age did not make the year II into a real Golden Age; the *sans-culotte* of the year II was a better judge of Robespierre than the same man a year later. It was just that in 1795 things were so much worse, so that, in retrospect, even former *sans-culottes* might begin to make the mistake of identifying the Jacobin dictatorship with a people's government. Things being worse still in the year IV, this tendency to myth-make about 1793–4 increased still more.

From whatever angle one wishes to approach French popular history during this period, 1795 is the ideal vantage point for looking back. There had been no disaster on this scale for eighty-five years, that is within living memory; and, as far as the common people were concerned, there would never be anything like it later. June 1848 and May 1871 were man-made blood-baths, and they affected only the urban working class; 1795 was both man-made and a disaster of nature. Apart from this, the Thermidorians, as we have seen, are the first, the most systematic, and the best informed, if not the most unprejudiced, historians of the previous 'popular movement', not only in Paris, but in every town and *bourg* in France. We should mistrust their evidence, but we certainly cannot do without it. It is also a much less 'orthodox' period than that of the Revolutionary Dictatorship. In the summer of 1794 we are so deafened by *les cris unanimes* (or rather by *le cri unanime*, for only one voice was needed) that we cannot hear any individual voice at all, at any level. Throughout the Thermidorian period, on the contrary, there is a veritable hubbub of confused shouting, vituperation, denunciation, and screams for vengeance, self-justification, and abuse. Nothing could be less *unanime* than Thermidorian France and, whatever faults may be attributed to the regime, it cannot be accused of having prevented the statement of unorthodox opinions. (It did not, in any case, have the force or the will to do so.) The neo-terrorists, furious at the turn of events, enraged by deprivation of office, stung by persecution, hit back in kind. They are not afraid to wake up towns with shouts of 'Vive la Terreur, vive les sans-culottes, la guillotine en permanence', and so on. At least up to Prairial they are almost suicidal in their outspokenness,[1] and with the amnesty of Brumaire year IV to encourage them their militants rush once more into print and into speech. Nor, as we have seen, did the *sabreur* go about his

---

[1] Jean Lafond, *vigneron*, is reported to have stated, in a café in Montbrison, on the eve of the Feast of Saint-John (16 Floréal year III), 'que c'étoit une horreur de voir les massacres qui se commettoient journellement dans Montbrison, mais que cela ne dureroit pas, et qu'on risquoit fort de voir une seconde fois la Montagne, que le nommé Tillon père, de Saint-Galmier ... lui dit *tu es un scélérat de parler de la sorte et tu en mériterois autant que ceux qu'on a assommés*' (AN, BB 18 690, déposition de Jean Lafond, 10 nivôse an VI).

work quietly; he talked before, during, and after a killing. And if witnesses speak of the 'silence of the grave' with reference to the Faubourg, it was a silence that only lasted a few weeks, under the stunned impact of defeat and disarmament, at the time when Denelle, feeling that there was nothing more to be done or said, took up his tools and killed his family. We have to wait for the year IV to see *vox populi* reduced to a pitiful whining for bread or for a place in a *hospice*. La Montagne, despite its name, does not command anything like the view offered from the level of the Thermidorian Plain.

If one thus makes a stand on the year III, and attempts, like the police, to see individuals *dans la durée*, rather than merely in the dramatic, hieratical attitudes of Soboul's *Ballet de l'An II*, then the perspectives become radically different from those offered by a day-to-day account of the courtship, honeymoon, rows, and divorce of naïve Popular Movement and cunning, calculating Revolutionary Government. And the former, instead of being a person in her own right, is revealed as an accident of a chance encounter, a hasty, shameful, furtive affair, *entre deux rames de métro*, that was never meant to happen. In this perspective the questions usually put by historians both of French and of comparative popular movements seem largely irrelevant or, at least, clumsy and slightly off the target: 'Why did the Revolutionary Government turn on the Popular Movement?'; 'Why did the Popular Movement decline in France at the very moment it was gathering force in England?'; 'What did the Popular Movement owe to *rousseauisme*?' (a poor question, as it can be answered in one word); 'What was the influence of Babeuf on the survival of the Popular Movement?' (same comment); and so on. The real question – and it is one that puzzled, astonished, and shocked the Thermidorians – to be asked would be: 'How did a popular movement ever come into being in the first place?' and not so much why it failed, but by what miracle it ever succeeded at all, however partially and however briefly. There is no doubt about the causes of its decline; but any assessment of the *sans-culotte* movement even at its height, in the autumn and winter of 1793, must bring out its accidental character, its fragility, its incoherence, and its endless fractionalization. How could the *sans-culotte*, himself a freak of nature, more a state of mind than a social, political, or economic entity, with his parish-pump outlook, ever have been the slightest threat to government? Certainly, he never thought of competing with it, much less of taking it over. (This was the fatal miscalculation of the *hébertistes*.)

The expression *le mouvement sans-culotte* is itself misleading, in another way, when applied to a series of attitudes that have in common only extreme individualism, regionalism, and a strong dose of anarchy. Before the Revolutionary Government took over, the Republic was in the process of disappearing in a welter of popular 'communalism'. And, just as *le mouvement sans-culotte* is a historical abstraction, the conflict between it and the Revolutionary Government has been greatly over-stated and over-simplified, whether in terms of class, of political methods, or of programme. The *sans-culotte* himself, an individualist, aware only of sharing a certain number of basic attitudes with people of his own kind and Quarter, did not know that he was engaged in such a conflict; hence his genuine surprise and indignation when, early in 1794 or later in the spring of that year, he found himself subjected to official persecution as an ultra-revolutionary and as an embarrassing enthusiast whose initiatives on many fronts at once had, by comparison, made the government appear unenthusiastic, moderate, and timid. He was only trying to be helpful.

This may seem to reduce the *sans-culotte* movement to such derisory proportions that, like the *peau de chagrin*, it eventually disappears alto-gether. But the argument is not that there was no such movement; rather that the movement was not nearly so coherent and single-minded as has often been suggested, and that there were movements very varied both in composition and in aims, rather than a single movement. In Lyon, for instance, the movement, almost by accident – and accident is our domin-ant theme throughout this section – became identified with 'federalism'; or, rather, the Parisian authorities, both *sans-culotte* and Jacobin (it would take Lyon to make them agree), said that it had. But the Lyonnais did not think of themselves as 'federalists', 'royalists', 'counter-revolutionaries', and so on. In their own view, they represented the very essence of *sans-culottisme*. For they were defending Sectionary autonomy against the incursion of an arrogant and dominating Jacobin municipality, and were upholding the position of their own city as Capital of the South, a posi-tion that was being challenged, as usual, from Paris. It was equally natural for the inhabitants of Vienne-la-Patriote to feel that they were acting as true *sans-culottes* when, in response to the traditional anti-Lyon senti-ments of the inhabitants of the former metropolitan see, they resisted the Lyon 'federalists', and co-operated with the armies. In Marseille the *sans-culottes* could not make head or tail of the situation but, so long as their Sections assured them that the best way of defending the Republic was to follow the example of the 'federalist' municipality and central committee, they did what the Sectionary leaders told them; for the Section could never be wrong, being the quintessence of *sans-culottisme*.

Sans-culotte was a new word, but it covered a clutter of ancient atti-tudes, traditional loyalties, and prejudices. What was new was the word itself, the institutions with which it was associated (and the institutions existed before the word), and, above all, the opportunity of the spring and summer of 1793. And the *sans-culottes* are uniquely important, in the history of the French Revolution, because they at once seized this oppor-tunity and carried out, at least at municipal level, and intermittently in certain areas of the countryside, the first experiment in people's government. It was an experience so extraordinary, so unique, that it was never forgotten, either by the *sans-culottes*, who had enjoyed every minute of it, or by those who were briefly subjected to popular rule. In immediate terms, *sans-culotte* co-operation made Terror and Repression more or less effective, in proportion to the relative zeal or lack of zeal of the local militants, and ensured the success of the more important economic controls; but it was even more important as an example to the future.

It was not, however, an experiment carried out in a vacuum. There were few occasions and few places, even at the level of the commune, where *sans-culotte* militants could enjoy undisputed power. There was nearly always somebody else to be reckoned with: a municipality, an *agent national*, a District, a roving *proconsul*, a government spy, the Committee of General Security, which had eyes in so many places and a much clearer view of what was happening in the Departments than the more august Committee of Public Safety. The *sans-culottes* could not exist politically on their own; had they been given an opportunity to do so, France would have fallen apart. They were partners on a tandem; they did much of the footwork, but they did not steer and could not see where they were going. So one is obliged to describe once more the relations between *sans-culottes* and Jacobins, and to run through the rather sad history of the divorce between the 'popular movement' and the Revolutionary Government.

Our purpose has been to reassess the *sans-culotte* movement and to render it in its contemporary proportions. One way of doing this has been to emphasize the role of militant minorities. It was not a *mouvement de masse*, the masses did not respond, they were not even invited. It was much more a matter of clans and coteries – in some towns in the Landes it was little more than a family concern. The *sans-culottes*, who liked to keep their club small, *entre gens de connaissance*, did not attempt to bring in the population of the *garnis*, or the general mass of wage-earners – this possibly is one reason why wages figure so little in *sans-culotte* demands – for whom their programme would have little appeal.

At the same time, they would have been clueless and incoherent without their militants, their *dominateurs* (for they 'dominated' the *sans-culottes* as well as the bourgeois). Perhaps some of these may have emerged here in colours too black. We have not attempted to idealize them, and it is difficult to escape the impression that they were generally intolerable and occasionally brutal and cruel. But they were also enthusiastic, moderately disinterested, and undoubtedly patriotic. As we have compared Terror and Counter-Terror, the popular movement and the Revolutionary Government, so we should compare their servitors; and the *sans-culottes* were certainly preferable to the steely bureaucrats of *robespierriste* unanimity, or to the vindictive judges and heartless bourgeois of the Thermidorian regime. They were individualists sometimes to the point of eccentricity and anarchy; this was to be their undoing. They did not stand a chance in any case, and may even have been dimly aware of this; for, in their bluster, their precipitation, and their noise, there is a hint of desperation, as though they were engaged in a race against time. Equally they may have been blind to the dangers threatening them from the very first moment of militancy, for they were so self-satisfied, so convinced of their own indispensability for 'la marche en avant de la Révolution', that they could hardly believe that the Republic could be 'saved' without their vigilance and devotion. Even at the height of the Thermidorian Reaction they were looking forward to a return to power and revolutionizing – or talked as if they were; this may merely have been to keep up morale, or their talk may have been inflated by Thermidorian eavesdroppers to frighten middle-class opinion with the bogy of 'le retour au règne de la Terreur'.

They were probably not very intelligent, at least in their political methods. For they attempted to maintain their hold on an assembly or a *commune* more by bludgeoning opinion than by persuading it, though a great many people would not be open to their persuasion. They were deliberately rude and unnecessarily vulgar, as though they had taken a leaf out of the *Père Duchesne* – being polite was unrevolutionary – and they probably made many more enemies, both for themselves and for the *sans-culotte* Republic, than they need have done. But they were administering a medicine unpleasant to most, and it was difficult to be an effective terror-ist and, at the same time, to be loved by many, for, in one form or another, the Terror was likely to indispose most people. It was both brave and dis-interested of them to have taken on such a job in the first place, since it brought few profits, save in terms of pride, and many dangers. They were remarkably patient with those less educated than themselves, spending much time and energy explaining the meaning of words and commenting on events. (This concern was, of course, also another means of racing against *la force des choses* and of prolonging their own power.) Most, too, were quick to spot the revolutionary fraud, the demagogue, and to censure selfishness and personal misconduct. For people with no previous experience of administration and of authority of any kind they did not do so badly. The minutes of popular assemblies and committees, if erratic in spelling, are reasonably well kept and clear. They were both efficient and effective (which the Thermidorians found hard to forgive). Whatever their virtues or failings, the system of the Terror, as well as the so-called 'popular movement', had to go along with them.

Hence the importance of individual behaviour, of temperament; hence, too, the prime necessity of approaching the year II in terms of the *histoire des mentalités*. It is an approach that, unlike the statistical analysis of collectivities: crowds, assemblies, armies – which has its own rather frozen and, for a 'movement' dominated by minorities, largely irrelevant, rewards – must leave many vital questions unanswered. We did not meet these people after all, have either their own word for themselves, or that of their enemies, and we must place a considerable premium on imagination, selection, and surmise. Any attempt to reconstruct *l'homme révolutionnaire*, rediscover *la mentalité sans-culotte*, must in fact owe as much to the historian as to the evidence derived from his documentation. He is engaged on a work of invention, and it is up to him to persuade the reader that his selection has been representative, and not influenced by presupposition. Certainly it would be impossible to reconstruct a complete robot-revolutionary, a prototype of the local terrorist, to witness for the whole kind. All the historian can do is to indicate, from a wide selection of case histories and from long habit of these people, certain common traits, and at the same time constantly to reiterate the endless variety of the species. Just as the Terror in, let us say, the Seine-Inférieure, bore no resemblance to the Terror in the Gard, the Bouches-du-Rhône, or in the Département de Vaucluse, so the terrorist might in one place be a mild *attentiste*, anxious primarily to keep in with everybody, making a display of zeal for the benefit of his superiors and at the same time taking the sting out of terrorist legislation in order to spare his *administrés* hardship and persecution, and, in another, might be a man of blood, the personification of the Thermidorian *buveur de sang*, enjoying bloodshed and violence and the fear in which he was held, cultivating the image of his own ferocity. (Much would depend on the latitude.) No account of the Terror would be complete without the presence of a few people of this last kind; for, if most ultra-revolutionaries were wild merely in word and in gesture, some *dominateurs* appear to have used the Terror to murder or to have murdered their enemies and rape their daughters. Such people were more numerous on the other side, among the White terrorists, but the White Terror came after that of the year II, and some at least of the *sabreurs* had victims to avenge. Whether these had been killed *révolutionnairement*, that is to say by judgement of some commission of summary justice, or had been simply murdered in the street or hanged from a tree, would not make much difference to their relatives or friends. The important fact was that they had been killed with violence. To many Moulinois in upper circles, the revolutionary authorities of that town who had sent thirty-two *notables* before the *Commission des Sept* in Lyon, which had condemned them all to death, were not revolutionary *patriotes*, but murderers; and so it seemed permissible to murder them (there were several attempts to do so) if the opportunity arose.

Any discussion on this period of the Revolution will begin and end with violence. Some may find excuses for the terrorists of the year II because they put violence to the service of a beleaguered Republic and of a state of emergency; and this is how the terrorists themselves were to argue when under attack, adding rather oddly that they had not been influenced by personal considerations and that they bore their victims no ill will. But, in the south at least, where there was a long tradition of vendettas, violence in the service of family vengeance would appear equally legitimate and unavoidable. And if one were to kill to preserve *la République une et indivisible*, why not kill for *Christ et Roi* (even if the former would not have approved and the latter, who was a child, dead or dying, had not been consulted)? 'Il faut du sang à la Révolution' was the one point of agreement between terrorist and *sabreur*. Many *sans-culottes* believed that blood would even solve the problem of dearth, while, in the year III, the urban *petit peuple*, faced with famine, were to argue: 'du tems de la Terreur, quand fonctionnoit la guillotine, le pain étoit en abondance; maintenant qu'il n'y a point de guillotine, le pain manque, pour avoir du pain, il faut la guillotine en permanence, pour ne pas mourir de faim, il faut du sang.' And they were right, in the sense that the *maximum* without the guillotine behind it would have been a flop. The southern royalists used blood to assert their authority, and to demonstrate the powerlessness of a Republic unable to protect even its own officials and wealthy property-owners. At both ends of the political spectrum, particularly at popular level, there was a wide consensus of opinion that the Revolution could survive only on blood, that the comte d'Antraigues' 'Kingdom of the South' could be constructed only on blood. (His own stated ambition was that 'he would like to be the Marat of the Counter-Revolution'.) The historian does not have to decide between the two programmes; the best he can do is to put in the dock the men of blood from both sides and let them argue it out in their own abrupt way. What he cannot do is to leave blood out when dealing with popular movements and popular protest.

It will be objected that our account does omit something called 'Popular Thought' and that we have not made obeisance to Rousseau and to *rousseauisme*, to the Man and the Message. We have discovered attitudes, prejudices, hopes, mentalities, violence, credulity, and orthodoxy, but of 'Popular Thought' not a trace. An attachment to 'municipalism', the much-repeated statement that 'les sociétés populaires sont souveraines', demands for an upper limit on property, on income, do indicate a basic political programme; the passionate insistence on equality in everything, including such visible things as food and clothing, does reflect moral attitudes, but it is hard to see what they owe to a system of thought. Rousseau, it is true, is frequently and reverently evoked, along with Robespierre, Marat, Brutus, William Tell, and Algernon Sydney, in the proceedings of popular assemblies; but this is merely a formal statement of orthodoxy, a sans-culotte 'For what we are about to receive', to be got through before proceeding to serious business (food problems, the defence of local interests, denunciations, scrutins épuratoires). The sans-culottes were rough-and-ready people, engaged in a struggle to gain control of local administration, they possessed neither a national nor a world vision, and they were not political theorists. They voted with a show of hands or par acclamation not in homage to some abstract concept of unanimity, but in order to cow possible opponents. Rousseau is as irrelevant to an understanding of the sans-culotte movement as Babeuf.

What, it may be further objected, do murder, suicide, disease, mortality, desertion, the White Terror, prostitution, vagrancy, chauffage, pauperization, epidemics, have to do with the development or the decline of popular movements and popular protest? Are we not merely stringing together themes that are related only because we put them on end, one after the other? Will not the historian always find what he is looking for? In order to illustrate the dramatic, apocalyptic character of the crisis of the year III and the year IV, it is of course easy to levy an army of suicides, count up the murders, collect the corpses, and produce scattered reports of epidemics, up and down the country. But do not these phenomena always exist? Were there no suicides in the year II? Did not people die in the year I? Were there no murders during the Revolutionary Dictatorship? Are there not always deserters in time of war? Were there no serious epidemics between 1789 and the summer of 1794? The answer is: of course they do, of course there were, of course they did. It is a matter of scale, of extent, as well as of content and repetition.

For Paris, we have used the papers of the commissaires de police for 1793 and the year II; we were looking, it is true, for the Paris Revolutionary Army, and not for suicidés, assassins, and fallen girls; but we noted these too, en passant. Suicides were rare, and they were not women of the people, but generally elderly ci-devants, abandoned by their children, who had emigrated. Suicide, in the year II, witnesses to quite a different form of distress from that of the years III and IV. Murders, private murders, were rare during the Jacobin dictatorship, at least in the towns of the north. (They were no doubt numerous in the south.) Prostitution, relentlessly harried by zealous sans-culottes, was on the decline. The poor are always with us, but in the year IV they are poorer than ever, and there are many 'new poor' as well; whereas in the year II many of the latter had managed to keep their heads above water and to maintain their families in bread and themselves in employment, even if it were only as gardes-scellés. Desertion became a national problem in the year III, and it was closely connected with White terrorism, which recruited extensively among réquisitionnaires, and, right up to the year IX, it represented a conscious political protest, a vote of no confidence in the republican regime.

Mortality rates began to rise in the last two months of the Jacobin dictatorship, as a sort of mute accompaniment to Robespierre's fearful *journées* of Prairial and Messidor, as though disease was attempting to keep up with the quickening pace of Terror. But, in the year III and the year IV, they were double or treble the average in towns like Dieppe, le Havre, and Rouen.

Who died? Primarily, the women and the small children of the urban *petit peuple*, of the *faubouriens*, and of village artisans, weavers, and shipwrights. Many urban artisans and elderly *indigents* also died; the rich did not die. And, unlike the cholera of 1832, the epidemics of the years III and IV (and those of 1812) were respecters of class. No leading Thermidorian died; indeed, Benjamin Constant and Madame de Staël returned eagerly to Paris, to see the fuming remains of Revolution, once it was all over and the danger was past, and to throw themselves avidly into the social round, in the middle of a famine of which they were no doubt unaware.

There were epidemics at the end of every summer, year in year out, but in comparative terms the revolutionary years had been healthy ones. The Revolution opened in 1789 and closed in the summer of the year II and the two following summers with waves of epidemics on a scale that was at once noted by the health authorities and that necessitated the sending of army doctors to the stricken areas. The second wave, from 1794 to 1796, the health authorities attribute to malnutrition, despair, and moral fatigue. There is no doubt in their mind about the connection between this sudden offensive of diseases of the poor and the contemporary political situation. They may, of course, have been wrong; but even if they were, these epidemics killed off a number of former *sans-culottes*, and increased the economic ruin of a great many more, as a result of long periods of unemployment and absence from work.

Prostitution, too, vastly increased in the year III, not so much because vice had come back to its own, with Madame Tallien on her sofa and Madame Récamier in her draperies, but because its recruiting agent was hunger, its recruits girls of the people. *Chauffage*, too, was a form of protest, as well as a source of revenue, directed against the *sans-culottes'* principal enemy, the big farmer. Some *chauffeurs* came from trades and occupations similar to those of the *sans-culottes*. Denelle's crime was a political one, and has a direct bearing on the events of Prairial in the Faubourg. And the increase of banditry and highway robbery is both a product of famine conditions and an indication of the alienation of a section of the common people from a bourgeois Republic that had nothing to offer them; one seldom hears of either in the year II. The suicide of the poor *Bourguignon* is a political gesture, as he makes clear in the letter pinned to his clothes.

Finally, the White Terror is even more directly relevant, for not only did it spring out of the previous Terror, it also killed off large numbers of very carefully selected militants (in this respect, more effective than epidemics that made no distinction between leaders and led) and drove many more to seek safety out of their Departments and away from the places where they enjoyed political influence. The White terrorists were in origins and temperament the same sort of people as the ultra-revolutionaries and terrorists of the year II.[1] Sometimes – we have at least two instances – they were the same people. In 1793–4 they had killed for the Republic; in the year III and later they hired themselves out to other masters. They had, after all, only one speciality. Not that such instances can be taken as characteristic; but it is interesting that such a transference should have been possible at all. White Terror and 'ultra-revolutionism' are opposite ends of the same phenomenon, and they occupy very much the same terrain.

All these phenomena, especially when taken together, had a direct, if often negative, bearing on the popular movement and its decline. Momentarily, it is true, under the impact of persecution and disaster, there may have been more unity among a common people reduced to a general bottom level of famine and impoverishment than had existed in the year II, when relative well-being, or at least sufficiency, isolated the politically, and often economically, privileged *sans-culottes* from the mass of wage-earners and *habitants de garnis*. In the year III, they were all engulfed together in the same catastrophe, but it was a unity in despair and in death, not one that would lend any strength to popular indignation. Of course, our figures are not complete, they do not include all the murders, all the suicides, or even a small proportion of the prostitutes; and our mortality rates are derived from half a dozen towns only, and the figures for entries to *hospices*, for about the same number. This is not a definitive study of the total impact of the crisis of years III and IV, any more than it is a definitive study of the *sans-culottes*. Such a study would in any case be impossible on a national scale, and it will be a long time before we have exhaustive studies of them even in a dozen towns. We are merely suggesting certain hypotheses, certain possible lines of research, and laying out a number of road signs: 'Work in Progress' – but, scrappy and scattered, they are indicative of the proportions of a crisis that, as a deterrent to popular militancy, was even more effective than the White Terror and years of repression. Vagrancy and armed begging and the formation of *bandes* constitute alternative forms of protest, when more sophisticated types of political protest are denied the common people. Protest is driven

---

[1] AN, BB 18 689, for the Lyon assassins. Those accused of having taken part in the Marseille prison massacres include five *perruquiers*, two *boulangers*, a *chapelier*, a *cultivateur*, a *maçon*, a *portefaix*, an *emballeur*, a *tabletier*, a *fabricant de savon*, a *maître-ès-arts* (an interesting use of a university education), a *commis*, and an *armurier* (AN, BB 18 174).

into these increasingly primitive and ultimately hopeless forms, as a result of the destruction of the popular movement and the disappearance of *la sans-culotterie* as a collectivity capable of political expression.

The common people were back where they had started; they were in fact much worse off, for they were now faced with a much more efficient and ruthless apparatus of repression than that of the *ancien régime*, and they had, besides, to carry the additional burden of failure and lost hopes; they had been in the High Seats – or at least they had seemed high to them – and they had been driven out of them, oppressed, insulted, humiliated. All they had gained was a strange religio-revolutionary mish-mash, the Cult of Robespierre, and a lot of good that would do them. It is a sad story.

*

Here then is the *sans-culotte*, as a political animal dead and buried. But, and some may regret it, that is not quite the end of him. It has often been pointed out that the Revolution left no permanent monuments in brick, stone, and marble – unless perhaps the strange *monument Sec*, in Aix-en-Provence – but only constructed in cardboard and papier-mâché. The *sans-culotte*, however, left a monument of another kind which survived at least right through the nineteenth century, leaving, to each successive generation, the example of the Revolutionary Passion Play. People remarkably like *sans-culottes* emerged during the *Trois Glorieuses*, their names are on the *colonne de Juillet*; and there are only eighteen years from the July Days to the June ones. During the Commune, there were pseudo-Héberts, pseudo-Chaumettes, pseudo-Robespierres, the *communards* had discovered *hébertisme*, they had not rediscovered *sans-culottisme*; but, among the *fédérés*, there were many who preached the old *sans-culotte* remedies on the subject of dearth and hoarding, and believed too in the same myths. In the spring and summer of 1848 and in the spring of 1871 'direct democracy' flourished noisily and at great verbal length, clubs multiplied in former churches. In Paray-le-Monial, in April 1848, the *clubistes* dug out of the *mairie* the minute book of the old *société* of the year II, and used it to note down the sessions of the year LVI of the Republic. All through the period popular protest recruited, too, its quota of crackpots, of men with empty, violent minds, of people dreaming only of blood, of bored intellectuals, the nineteenth-century equivalent of Jean-Luc Godard and his admirers, who awaited the coming of a great and bloody Revolution *pour se désennuyer*. The most permanent memorial to the poor *sans-culottes* was the evocation and the habit of violence. It was as if future generations had taken them literally, when they had spoken with threats and bluster. Yet there had been much more to them than that, more than a lot of windy, bilious violence *à la Vallès*, of avid appetite for decomposition and carnage *à la Baudelaire*. They deserved better of history. But they had to wait till 1958 for their definitive Paris Pantheon, and even in that they might feel rather ill at ease; they would have preferred something more modest, less grandiose, more in the spirit of the Quarter.

6

*The Sources of Counter-Revolutionary or Counter-Terrorist Commitment**

'Il faut observer que ce prévenu ne marchait jamais qu'armé d'un fusil double, d'un pistolet et d'un couteau, il ne parlait que de tirer ou de saigner quand on l'arrêterait, il avait même osé dire au président et au commissaire près l'administration municipale ... qu'il tuerait le premier gendarme qui l'arrêterait, il est prouvé que les deux prévenus, au moment de leur arrestation, avaient chacun leur fusil double sur la table ...'

> AN, BB 18 125, L.R. Duval, chef du 44me escadron
> de la gendarmerie nationale, de Valence,
> au Ministre, le 3 germinal an VII[1]

Historians of individuality, not to say of crankiness and of the extremes of eccentricity, will be much better off with the Counter-Terror than with the bureaucratic Terror of the summer of 1794. For here at least there is no bleak concept of unanimity, no standard model, no striving after an indivisibility that would eventually engulf all personal *traits* in the regimented prissiness of the Republic of Virtues or in the military totalitarianism of Saint-Just's hideous cardboard Sparta. There were almost as many Counter-Terrors as there were counter-terrorists, and for almost as many motives: personal, regional, visceral, respectable, criminal, or tribal. And as these latter were so often thrown on their own devices, whether to continue the struggle in the rocky fastnesses of south-central France, or to attack mail coaches, government couriers, and army pay convoys (this was, after all, another and most effective form of carrying on the same struggle), or

---

* From *Reactions to the French Revolution*, pp. 19–43.
[1] Dubois, of the village of Vaisseaux, had been killed, shot by a *garde nationale* while trying to escape, when he was being escorted to prison by the *gendarmes*, on 3 Germinal year VII (23 March 1799). Duval prudently sent the *gendarmes* away into the Drôme 'pour attendre la tournure que prendront les choses'.

to wage an economic war against the Republic – or what was left of it[1] – from the urban or suburban retreat of a counterfeiter's roomy house, or to eke out unlikely employment in unpleasant parts of Europe, or even in America,[2] their commitment took the most extreme form of personal self-expression. The genuine counter-revolutionary, concerned to promote the cause of the Princes, was more likely to emigrate; but he might return, in order to direct operations. The counter-terrorist, whose attitude was generally more negative – for various reasons he was opposed to the existing regime, without necessarily wishing to put a King in its place – was more likely to stay behind, and fight out his lonely battles in a terrain with which he was familiar and to which he was devoted. In any case, this sort of man would be left largely to his own devices, so that his personality was much more important than whatever confused positive programme he might enunciate. And he had the advantage, in terms of individual commitment, of proposing solutions that were also almost entirely negative. He and his motley followers knew at least what they were *against*; they shared identifiable and named hate-figures; and they were agreed how they were to deal with these. They objected to most that had happened in their own region since 1792, more often since 1793, sometimes only since 1795. Few would have rejected the Revolution out of hand. That is why it would be dangerous totally to assimilate the counter-terrorist and the much more positive counter-revolutionary. The latter often had a rural background and were animated by grievances against towns and townsmen. But we should not make too much of this. For, as we shall see, in certain parts of France, they were to enjoy plenty of urban support. Generally speaking, they do not appear to have been particularly motivated by religion, though religion could on occasion be a useful pretext.

The Revolutionary Government bureaucratized death in the pursuit of a programme of virtue; death was not given names, it might embrace 90 per cent of the male population of France over the age of fourteen – it was generally understood that thirteen and a half was too young to qualify for the guillotine, save perhaps in areas of civil war.[3] The Counter-Terror

---

[1] 'On paroît vouloir se retrancher sur les craintes de la guerre civile. Mais par qui et contre qui cette guerre aurait-elle lieu? Les conventionnels forment heureusement une trop mince faction dans l'état, leur parti est bien celui des *solitaires*. Ils ont [pu?] indisposer tous les citoyens contr'eux; les gens de bien, par les crimes affreux auxquels ils ont co-opéré, ou qu'ils ont commis; les républicains, par l'assassinat de Brissot et des 22 glorieux fondateurs de la liberté républicaine, les royalistes, par la mort de Louis XVI, les terroristes par la punition de Robespierre, et par les journées de Germinal et de Prairial' (brouillon de notes de l'écriture de Marchéna, s.d., an IV, AN, BB 18 739, Ministère de la Justice, Seine).

[2] Jean Vidalenc, *Les Émigrés français, 1789–1825* (Caen, 1963).

[3] It has often been argued, by Georges Lefebvre among others, that the terrible Law of 22

went for individuals, and it had to make do with small, loose-knit bodies of armed men, concerned with individual vengeance, decentralized lynching, and exemplary murder.

> Ces Brigands s'organisèrent en colonnes mobiles, sous le commandement des La Mothe, des Dominique Allier, des Chabert et autres. Dans la nuit, ils se rassemblaient, faisoient des marches forcées, se rendoient dans les maisons pour égorger ... Le jour, ils revenoient dans leurs demeures et à leur travail, de façon qu'il a été commis plusieurs crimes pendant quelques tems sans en connaître les auteurs.[1]

In the year VII, a year after this report concerning the southern tip of the Ardèche, a judicial official from Marseille was to tell the Minister that the members of the murder gangs that operated in the mountainous country that lay behind the port lived, slept, ate at home, emerging briefly at dusk or in the early hours of darkness, to slaughter republicans as they went by or to kill them in their own homes.

The counsel for two acknowledged participants in the activities of a *bande* of counter-terrorists, again in the southern part of the Ardèche, further outlines the tactics forced upon their members:

Prairial year II [10 June 1794] was designed to try unobtrusively and to dispose, with the minimum of fuss, of such members of the Convention as might appear dangerous to the Committees of Government. But, in fact, its provisions were far wider than those needed to meet such limited or preventative purposes, for, by introducing extensive moral definitions of what constituted an 'enemy of the people', the Law could expose any individual convicted of some slight moral failing – ill-treating his father, political indifference, political absenteeism, calling in question official statements, immoral conduct, the persistence in bachelorhood, a public display of lack of enthusiasm, non-attendance at a boring official function – and, under Robespierre's papacy, all such functions were boring – over-indulgence, physical or architectural ostentation, the use of outdated formulas of politeness, raised eyebrows, the use of the eyeglass or the lorgnette in a manner suggesting contempt, etc. – to the risk of outlawry and to the death sentence on simple proof of identity. By the Law, citizenship was given a moral content; it followed that citizens who lacked Virtue, were in fact non-citizens, being politically dead, and could thus be physically eliminated as well, as an operation of moral regeneration. It followed also that individuals might only become aware of their moral turpitude at the precise moment that they found themselves precipitated from a perpendicular to a horizontal position under the cutting edge of the guillotine. Their presence there was proof in itself, just as the presence of a number of heads in one basket could be taken as proof of the existence of a conspiratorial group, even if the heads, while still unsevered, had never met in real life. See also AN, BB 18 739 (papiers de Marchéna, an IV): 'Des sycophantes ont ensanglanté pendant 18 mois le sol français pour nous donner, disaient-ils, le bonheur des Spartiates; ils instituaient des fêtes au malheur dont ils étaient les auteurs ... Ils avaient arrêté l'élan de l'esprit humain qui s'était frayé des routes nouvelles.'
[1] AN, BB 18 124 (commissaire près le tribunal de Largentière au Ministre, 6 fructidor an VI).

La Chouannerie est un nouveau genre de guerre qui avait été inconnu jusqu'à présent dans les nations policées; c'est une guerre de sauvages où chaque individu isolément cherche son ennemi, le tue et le pille partout où il se trouve. Les Rebelles furent appellés Brigands parce que dans la vérité ils se conduisoient dans leur genre de guerre comme les brigands qui étoient dispersés par petites bandes de 3, de 6 ou de 8, qu'ils égorgeoient et pilloient leurs ennemis partout où ils les trouvoient et isolément parce qu'ils n'étoient pas assez forts pour attaquer un corps considérable.[1]

By the summer of 1794, the Revolutionary Government had taken to killing by stealth; but a counter-terrorist murder had to be as public as possible, in order for its message to get home – hence, for instance, the advantage of a lynching on a bridge, or on the main square, or the hanging of a southern farmer on a cypress tree at the entrance to his recently purchased farm, a former *bien national*; hence too the habit followed especially in the rural *communes* of the Lyon region of leaving notes attached to the bodies of former republican officials, both to identify them and to emphasize the reasons for their murder.[2] In an underpopulated Department like the Ardèche, composed of isolated, scattered hamlets of thirty houses or so – such as the celebrated murder village of Montréal, just south of Largentière – such added guides were hardly necessary. Everyone would know the rare, isolated republicans, and neo-Jacobins; and no one would hear their screams or their cries for help. In one instance, involving the murder of a well-to-do *commissaire du Directoire*, over twenty armed men arrived in a village, in broad daylight, knocked at the door of a well-known inhabitant, stayed with him for a night and a day, noisily feasting and singing, setting out early on the second day on their mission. Having killed the man in his country seat and mutilated his body, and leaving his housekeeper tied up, walking still as a body, their faces uncovered, they are met by an inhabitant, who greets them: *bonjour citoyens*. They are in no hurry to pass unnoticed, stop and remonstrate with the man: *apprends que nous ne sommes pas venus de si loin pour nous entendre traiter de citoyens*. It was a question of wanting to be heard as well as seen. And, although the victim, when suddenly confronted with his murderers, rang a bell attached to the roof of his house – he had been expecting something of the kind – no one in the neighbouring village was prepared to admit that he had heard this private *tocsin*.[3]

---

[1] Ibid. (Plaidoyer pour Boutières et Chabrolin, de la commune de Chassiers, Ardèche, s.d., an IX).

[2] *The Police and the People*, p. 345.

[3] This was the murder of Louis Blachère-Laprade, a well-to-do inhabitant of Montréal, who lived in a *bastide* within sight of the centre of the village. At the time of his murder he was *commissaire du Directoire* of this canton. He was killed in his farmhouse on the night of 4–5 Fructidor year V (Monday–Tuesday, 21–22 August 1797) at the height of the

The methods of the Counter-Terror were anarchical and violent, and highly personalized; and its leaders were amateur enthusiasts whose methods reflected their generally strong sense of individuality.[1] All were motivated above all by the military virtues of personal honour,[2] family pride, and physical courage;[3] most of them were lacking in any form of common sense. Some rejected the Revolution and all its works; others, however, like the comte d'Antraigues, were prepared to look back to the golden days of 1789 as to a period in which the lost liberties of the provincial squire had been triumphantly reasserted and in which ancient, engrained habits of subordination had been replaced by local initiative

---

royalist Counter-Terror. The murderers, in a group of at least twenty, later attempted to set fire to the genitals of their victim. The authorship of this particular murder, which had repercussions throughout the Department and even in Paris, and which resulted in a series of lawsuits that dragged on during the following three years, is a matter of dispute. Some judicial authorities assert that it was carried out by the Chevalier de la Mothe and Roudilhes Lavermalethe, at the head of a group of *égorgeurs* whom they had brought over from the village of Joannas. Another, rather more persistent, version designated two inhabitants of Montréal, Boutières and Chabrolin, as the assassins. The defence counsel of the latter was to admit that his two clients had indeed committed political murders in the course of the Counter-Terror; but the father of Boutières was to claim that, whatever his son may have done, he had not in fact killed Blachère. For a more detailed account of this much-quoted murder, see footnote 1, below, and *Reactions to the French Revolution*, pp. 216–17, 224–7.

[1] AN, BB 18 124 (Plaidoyer pour Boutières et Chabrolin, s.d., an IX). This interesting document represents one of the fullest expressions of the sources of commitment and of the personal attitudes of these two well-known leaders of a southern murder gang from the southern end of the Ardèche. Accused of having committed a number of political murders in the Department in the course of the year V, they claimed the benefits of the amnesty of the year VIII. 'Il n'y a point de Révolution sans fanatisme, parce que sans un vif enthousiasme toujours bien voisin du fanatisme, il ne serait pas donné aux hommes d'entreprendre et de consommer ni les grands maux, ni les grands biens que les révolutions opèrent . . . Or je demande . . . qui osera au milieu de l'effervescence révolutionnaire, dans le croisement de toutes les impulsions, dans cette bouillonnante Atmosphère où le peuple français fut plongé durant 4 années; qui osera distinguer, calculer, assigner ce qui est le fruit d'une perversité intime et ce qu'il convient d'attribuer à l'ignorance, aux préjugés, à la crainte, à tous les genres de séductions et d'entraînements? Qui osera faire en un mot la part du crime et celle du malheur?'

[2] Ibid. 'Quelle cruelle dérision que de soutenir que les prévenus ne sont point seulement brigands, mais encore voleurs et assassins de grands chemins . . . Je vais prouver qu'ils ont été forcés de se jeter dans la chouannerie, que, de tous les chouans amnistiés, c'étaient ceux qui avaient la meilleure réputation.'

[3] 'Ils ont assassiné l'adjoint de la commune de Prunet, sur la grande route de Jaujac, enfin . . . ils ont enlevé de vive force à la gendarmerie des prisonniers sur la grande route d'Aubenas; Granier [Chabrolin], en tirant sur la gendarmerie dans cette affaire, eut la pouce emportée et une grande balafre à la joue, par l'explosion de son tremblon qui creva . . . C'est à eux deux que nous devons nos malheurs, ayant été les premiers à organiser le brigandage dans ce pays . . . Ce sont deux bêtes féroces qui ne respirent que carnage, je connais leur audace et leur férocité' (AN, BB 18 124, commissaire du gouvernement à Fouché, 25 pluviôse an IX).

and proud independence of authority.[1] Some found an outlet in secret inks, in the exciting and flattering paraphernalia of conspiracy; others favoured weekend sorties in which individual terrorists or simply officials of the Republic currently existing would be the quarry (for the counter-terrorist needed his terrorist, and a great many of those who were killed in the badlands of the south-east had no doubt never been terrorists at all, any more than their murderers, their crime was more probably to have survived the Thermidorian regime or the Directory in its early years). Unlike their victims, the counter-terrorists were released from the stultifying, and, in the conditions of the years III to VIII, it must be admitted, dangerous, burden of a *public* life, so that, in the south-east at least, their political activities would be an outcome of temperament, as well as of private interest and were but an extension of their private lives and of their family circle, which, in the Rhône valley, was particularly wide, wide enough in fact to take in whole communities, a whole clan, half a village, a whole village, a quarter of a canton, and to include distant cousins and relations by marriage. Many *sabreurs* had brothers, parents, or cousins to avenge – or at least that was often to be their claim, though one suspects it may often have been a pretext – and they often accompanied a killing with such comments addressed to the victim, as: *prend ça pour mon frère, et encore ça pour mon père*.[2] The Counter-Terror was also an extension of the wider obligations of employment, patronage, kinship, and regional loyalties and antipathies. When, in the south-east, the Counter-Terror expressed itself in the crudest, physical terms of the local murder gang – Company of Jesus, Company of Jehu, Company of the Sun – it owed its relative success or failure to the influence of local squires, to their ability to express themselves in terms of physical audacity and verbal incitement,[3] to their hold over their tenants, and to those who, for a variety of

---

[1] 'Nous n'avons pas oublié sans doute quels ont été jusqu'à l'immortelle époque de l'Abolition de la Royauté les bienfaits de ce patriotique enthousiasme, les divers soutiens de la tyrannie monarchique graduellement ébranlés, ses crimes découverts, ses espérances confondues ... les privilèges anéantis, le sentiment de la Liberté éveillé dans toutes les âmes, un esprit public créé ... une activité salutaire substituée aux mornes habitudes de l'esclavage, l'Aristocratie elle-même et plus souvent défendue contre les attentats inconsidérés de la vengeance ... l'Armée nationale régénérée, accrue sans mesure par le patriotisme à la victoire; voilà les souvenirs touchants que vous rappellent les beaux jours de la Révolution' (Plaidoyer, pour Boutières et Chabrolin).

[2] *The Police and the People*, pp. 352, 359 (3C).

[3] As well as of impudence. The *sabreurs*, according to many reports, made no attempt to act surreptitiously; they not only boasted of their prowess, they even proudly displayed various badges and insignia indicating their commitment. Being in fact a minority movement, save in certain places like Lyon or in Departments like the Ardèche, they had every interest in publicizing their adherence to the cause of Christ & King. Antigeon, an inhabitant of Pont-Saint-Esprit, writes to a friend, André, *homme de loi*: 'Ma plume se refuse à te crayonner Lyon, elle ne peut que te dire que la presque totalité des habitans applaudit au

personal reasons, were drawn to the wild ways and to individual acts of bloodshed and violence.

A sortie of a southern murder gang began in the *auberge* and ended in the château, with long pauses between killings in other wayside inns or urban wine-shops of the kind frequented by men from a single locality or from an identifiable trade. So the ranks of the counter-revolutionary squire could be expected to draw upon those who lived habitually on the border of crime and violence: the poacher, the smuggler, the horse-dealer, the carter, the carrier, the river-worker (especially the *flotteur*, though he might equally be attracted to the violent ranks of the Ultra-Revolution),[1] the *crocheteur*, a vigorous man, armed with a heavy stick, who worked with his muscles, lifting immense weights, at the riverside or not far off,[2] the cattle-dealer who, like Chavannes, was constantly on the move, had an excuse to be anywhere at any time, at least within the radius of a canton, would be well acquainted with a score of innkeepers and their assistants and would, like the blacksmith, have an excellent pretext to enter farms and private houses and scout out their interior layout, the old-clothes merchant,[3] the junk merchant, the blacksmith, the sailor, the docker, the hairdresser, the former servant, the ex-soldier (especially, no doubt, from such regiments as that of Auvergne, Royal-Piémont, Lyonnais, and the household troops), the fencing-master (generally himself a former NCO), the innkeeper, the locksmith, the counterfeiter,[4] and his necessary allies, the jeweller, the coppersmith, the engraver, and the *notaire*, so often himself a specialist in forgery, and a member of a profession that, in the eighteenth, nineteenth, and twentieth centuries, seems to have been highly accident-prone, and, in the south-west at least, the former *parlementaire* (though he would generally remain behind the scenes, furnishing money, encouragement, hospitality, and, possibly, a hiding-place, but unwilling, unlike the squire, actually to take part in operations; many of the *parlementaires* of Toulouse were, in any case, too old, by the late 1790s, for such vigorous and uncomfortable forays that often entailed several hours' march over scrubby, difficult country, at night or in the early hours after dawn). Indeed, in such a *negative* polarization, the appeal would extend

massacre des patriotes et abhorre les Républicains. Les assassins s'y promènent audacieusement, portant une ganse blanche croisée formant un 8, tous les patriotes ont été obligés de fuir cette ville et n'osent plus y rentrer' (7 frimaire an IV [27 November 1797]).

[1] See below, pp. 299–316, the section concerning Guénot.
[2] On the Lyon *crocheteurs*, of the port Saint-Vincent, see *The Police and the People*, p. 339 (O).
[3] On the importance of the old-clothes merchant as a link in any criminal or terrorist organization, see *Reactions to the French Revolution*, pp. 180–215, the section concerning the *bande d'Orgères*.
[4] On the subject of the counterfeiter, see below, pp. 279–81, the note concerning Galle, engraver.

far beyond class or condition, sometimes to include virtually a whole community which, as the result of the accidents of geography and of the political and administrative history of the Revolution, had collectively invested in the defeat of the Republic (of all the Republics) and in the prolongation of any form of violent anarchy that might weaken the existing regime in Paris.

The Counter-Revolution and the Counter-Terror tended to keep to the hills, occasionally descending into the plains on some marauding mission of pillage and vengeance. Its strongholds were the semi-fortified hill villages of the Massif Central and the Lubéron, of the Ardèche, the Lozère, the Haute-Loire, and parts of the Aveyron; and so, in collective terms, it often expressed itself as the vengeance of the mountaineer on the republican plainsman. It also thrived in the thick chestnut woods so abundant on the borders of the Ardèche and the Haute-Loire and in most of the Lozère, drawing to its ranks an anarchical, wild army of woodcutters, foresters, charcoal burners, and *scieurs de long*. Its appeal and even its emblems had much to offer *l'homme des bois*. But, in the Rhône valley at least, it also possessed its urban strongholds. The facts of geography were aided, in this respect, by the accidents of revolutionary history. A town that had been rejected as *chef-lieu* by the *comité de division*, was likely to feel unsympathetic to the new regime, especially if, under the Civil Constitution, it had lost its diocese and its ecclesiastical courts as well. It would have been surprising if Lyon, deprived at one time of its very name, cut off from its hinterland to the west, and reduced to the rump of a Department, following its surrender in October 1793, could have thereafter felt any sympathy for rule from Paris and for the Republic either of the year II or of the year III.

In short, the Counter-Terror became a way of life, the expression of an individual mentality and the affirmation of a strongly-held sense of regional loyalty, most clearly expressed in the form of hostility to Paris, to everything that emanated from the capital, and to any form of violent political change that Paris attempted to impose on the rest of France. In this respect, the Counter-Terror was able to unite ancient history and historical memory with the experience of the recent past and with present political facts. Professor Reinhard, in his perceptive study of the 10 Août, emphasizes again and again the persistence of attitudes hostile to Paris, from the time of the Flight to Varennes to the varied reactions displayed towards the most prepared, most expected, and yet the most unexpectedly violent of revolutionary days.[1] The map of non-acceptance, or of acceptance with misgivings and many restrictions, is quite remarkably persistent

---

[1] Marcel Reinhard, *La Chute de la royauté: 10 août 1792* (Trente journées qui ont fait la France, XVIII, N.R.F., Paris, 1969).

in the period from May 1791 to August 1792; and it was to represent, at least as far as the Rhône valley was concerned, that of the White Terror during the Directory and the early years of the Consulate and the Empire. Commitment to some form of Counter-Terror dated back, at the very latest, to the events of 1790, though, in Departments like the Ardèche, the Lozère, the Gard, and the Haute-Loire, it could almost certainly be traced back further still, to personal feuds, regional disputes, inter-village violence, and recurrent outbreaks of disorder, social conflict, and banditry, to the 1770s and 1780s; more detailed regional studies of the phenomenon would almost certainly reveal the continuity of this process, over a period of fifteen or twenty years; and if the Counter-Revolution could survive a whole generation, to re-emerge, in much the same areas, in the summer and autumn of 1815, in the form of the second White Terror, its inner strength may well be accounted for by an appeal back to a generation that preceded that which emerged in open militancy in the course of the revolutionary crisis. In areas where family relationships were particularly strong and binding – among the *brigands* of the Ardèche who had been brought to justice by the end of 1801, there were several groups of three or four people with the same surname – and where family quarrels easily took the form of persistent and bloody vendettas, the Counter-Revolution could look back to its corps of grandfathers and fathers, to the prestige of aged heroes, as well as having a firm stake in the present, and, indeed, in the future.

For, save no doubt in the west, while enlistment in its ranks carried an undoubted *panache*, agreeably tickling masculine vanity, in the conditions prevailing in the Rhône valley and throughout the south-east during the Directory and even the Consulate, generally speaking it did not carry many very grave risks. Very few *égorgeurs* were ever killed in these parts; in the Ardèche, we hear of about twenty bandits *tués, se défendant les armes à la main*, in the last two years of the Directory, while a further forty were condemned to death by military commissions or special courts, and this probably represented a higher percentage of risk than in some of the neighbouring Departments. A number of counterfeiters were, it is true, guillotined – they had, after all, committed a worse crime than that of killing a republican or his family. But, on the whole, there seems to have been a good chance of survival; the Counter-Revolution would not have lasted so long otherwise; it is significant, in this respect, that the amnesty proclaimed at the beginning of the Consulate had little effect in checking the activities of the *bandes* in the north and south of the Ardèche, despite the hopes placed in clemency by the local garrison commanders.[1] It

---

[1] 'Il serait essentiel peut-être encore de rapprocher de cet arrondissement un des Conseils de guerre de la 9me division. Ces tribunaux en sont trop éloignés. La mort d'un coupable

stretched forward into the years to come, as well as being able to show a respectable line of descent.

In respect of continuity, it could thus look to the same advantages as those enjoyed by some of the most celebrated bandit groups that, after surviving in semi-clandestine and sporadic activities for a matter of years, came out into the open, engaging in highway and rural banditry from 1795 and throughout the Directory. Several of the older members of the *bande d'Orgères* are said to have seen previous service in the *bande Hullin*. And, unlike these groups of highwaymen, the Counter-Revolution could generally count on the complacency or even the active complicity of the judiciary.[1] It had the *past* on its side[2] and it was able to put even genealogical knowledge (genealogy was as much an obsession as killing republicans with many counter-revolutionary squires, especially in the proud but poor highlands of Languedoc or Provence, in the Vivarais, the Vellay, and the Rouergue) to practical use; and this mattered, especially in the rural context, and at a time when the *present* was either Robespierre or Thermidorian class selfishness or Directorial incoherence, military rule, and courts martial. For most of the period of the White Terror, nearly all the towns in the Rhône valley and the whole of the Ardèche, the Lozère, and the Haute-Loire were declared *en état de siège*, their municipalities subjected to the orders of *commandants de place*, generally strangers to the area – a situation both humiliating, especially to a proud city like Lyon,

---

exécuté à Montpellier n'est point une leçon pour ceux qui sont tentés de l'imiter dans l'Ardèche … L'esprit contre-révolutionnaire enfanta les premiers crimes des brigands, la crainte du supplice, les désespoirs servent à les perpétuer, le pardon pourrait y mettre un terme. Quand la douceur ne parviendroit qu'à diminuer le nombre des brigands, quand elle n'aboutirait qu'à prévenir quelques assassinats, qui pourrait dire qu'elle eût été mal à propos employée? … Le désordre s'accroît sans cesse, chaque jour est marqué par un nouvel attentat … Challemel.' (AN, BB 18 125, Challemel, au Ministre, 24 pluviôse an VIII).

[1] AN, BB 18 125 (commissaire près le département de l'Ardèche, au Ministre, 18 thermidor an IV): 'Cette quinzaine remarquable par les prévenus qui ont été jugés m'a convaincu que la moralité est à deux doigts de sa perte, le tribunal a jugé un fils qui a assassiné son père, le juré a déclaré que le père, mort sur la place, n'était pas mort des coups que lui avait donnés son fils, une femme qui a été accusée d'avoir tué son enfant, a été déclarée non-convaincue.'

[2] The comte d'Antraigues, who had Protestant ancestors and was proud of the fact, is a good example of the hold of the past and the weight of history – bad history – on the attitude of an obstinate, unruly nobleman from Villeneuve-de-Berg in the Vivarais. He admired the sixteenth-century Huguenots, because he saw in them people like himself: independent provincial squires who had taken up arms to defend the liberties of their province against 'ministerial despotism'. But he was equally convinced that the French Revolution had originated in a Protestant 'plot', so that, in exile, he spent the revolutionary years re-fighting the Wars of Religion in imagination in his own Vivarais, and on both sides! This did not prevent him from making a very considerable personal profit from his role as *conseiller-ès-contre-révolution* to most of the Allied Courts, once he had secured the patronage of that of Lisbon. See Jacqueline Chaumié, *Le Réseau d'Antraigues et la Contre-Révolution 1791–93* (Paris, 1965), and my 'The Comte d'Antraigues and the Counter-Revolutionary Mentality' in *A Second Identity*, p. 177.

and, in practice, quite remarkably ineffective: the garrison commanders often themselves paid the price, as illustrious victims of the White Terror, and the generals are constantly complaining, in the latter years of the Directory, of shortage of troops in areas in which the terrorists knew the terrain and operated in small elusive groups. The Counter-Revolution, in the conditions of 1795–1802 or so, for these were the years in which it made itself physically the most effective, at least in the Rhône valley, would have an undoubted pull on all those who, for one reason or another, had never loved the *sergent de la maréchaussée* and did not love any better his successor, the *sergeant de la gendarmerie nationale*.

The appeal might come from many different and conflicting sources. The womanizers, at both the top and bottom levels of society, might feel the pull in that direction, for the type of lady who offered rewards in the form of the *repos du guerrier*, and who admired the military virtues of a prickly sense of honour and of ability to kill, would be more drawn to Christ & King than to the collective *trompette guerrière* of a depersonalized Sovereign People. It was the squire*ss* who sent the squire out on such violent and dangerous missions, as much as it was the *marquise* who shamed the *marquis* into emigration and into enlistment in the *armée des Princes*;[1] once enlisted, the newly-arrived *émigré* would be further exposed to a wave of feminine scorn. Those who had left in July 1789 could hold their heads high, those who had followed in August and September might still be asked to take chocolate at the *lever* of the maréchale de Castries, those who had come in December might be received into the antechamber of a lady-in-waiting; but those who had waited till 1790, till 1791, till the 10 Août would be lucky if they got a civil word even from a lady's maid. The scorn and hatred felt for the *monarchiens* were fanned by female *émigrées* who felt that they had let the side down, had *pactisé avec l'ennemi*, and who, in exile, sought to keep standards up. There is no one more punctilious than an *émigré*, save possibly an *émigrée*.[2]

---

[1] *A Second Identity*, p. 64, essay on Restif de la Bretonne, *Les Nuits de Paris*. See also his *Tableaux de la vie et des mœurs du XVIIIme siècle*. 'Je n'ai jamais pu supporter que, dans les tems de chevalerie, des Belles excitâssent aux combats sanglans; ni que du nôtre elles encouragent les guerriers et les chasseurs.'

[2] Of course, it might work the other way. Madame de la Tour du Pin, who emerges quite definitely as the senior partner, was able to persuade her husband, by working on his military sense of honour and by reminding him of his personal duties to Louis XVI, that it was incumbent on him to remain in France, at least till 10 August, in order both to protect the King and to preserve the Army from total decomposition. In her opinion, and it is a perfectly respectable one, coming from a woman who was a member of an old Irish military family (Dillon), those Army officers who had emigrated in the early months of the Revolution were in fact deserters who had hastened the rot within the Army. Later, she protected her husband, when he went into hiding near Bordeaux, during the Terror; later still, she was able to obtain passage for the whole family on an American frigate bound for Charleston (*Memoirs of Madame de la Tour du Pin*, London, 1969).

At the other end of the scale, there is a Greek choir of raucous feminine incitement, provoking, stimulating, accompanying the more spectacular activities of the murder gang; while, at the end of the foray, once the men had slaked their thirst and satisfied appetites stimulated by brutal and battering lynchings, there will be women of the lowest condition: prostitutes, *blanchisseuses, revendeuses, brodeuses, crieuses, repasseuses, bouquetières, empailleuses de chaises, fileuses, marchandes d'aiguilles, colporteuses*, and so on – the proletariate of female urban employment and seasonal labour, awaiting the returning heroes, at an inn frequented by habitués (inn-keepers were deeply committed to the politics of exaggeration and violence, whether of the Counter-Revolution or of the Ultra-Revolution), or in some discreet house in a faubourg (Vaise, la Guillotière), or in a gambling establishment, or in a house of ill-fame,[1] ready to congratulate them, to hear a first-hand account of their operations and to drink to their prowess, to the death of the Republic, of republicans, *mathevons*, puritans, law-makers, law-enforcers, and to the success of the next outing.

The Counter-Revolution would not have amounted to very much without its women[2] and without its boisterous, noisy, and quite open round of pleasures; and this is what the Revolution, at least in its *robespierriste* phase, had so much lacked. For the Revolution in fact lasted only five years and the Jacobin dictatorship only eighteen months, whereas the Counter-Revolution, in one form or another, always highly fragmented and regionalistic, always closely identified with local loyalties and antipathies, lasted nearly twelve years. So important is it to have pleasure, women, drink, gambling, romance, and boastfulness on one's side. Christ & King was not an empty formula. It had quite a lot to offer, even in terms of hard cash, at least up to 1799, when Wickham was paying out huge sums of secret service money, especially to organizations in the Lyon region and to those operating nearer the Swiss frontier, in the garrison towns of the Doubs and the Jura.[3] Even as late as mid-February 1800, a report from the Ardèche on the subject of the *bandes* still active at the southern tip of the Department, and particularly in the notorious arrondissement of

---

[1] AN, BB 687 (commissaire près le tribunal correctionnel, à celui du Département, 10 prairial an VIII): 'Dans l'intérieur de la ville, et dans ses faubourgs, les maisons de prostitution n'y recèlent pas seulement des filles sans vertu, mais le plus souvent des objets volés et les auteurs des crimes. Les maisons de jeu leur servent encore de point de réunion, c'est là même qu'ils recrutent, en offrant au joueur malheureux qu'ils ont dépouillé les moyens de regagner ce qu'ils ont perdu en s'associant à eux.'
[2] 'Des femmes connues sous le nom de *Dames de la Miséricorde* font ... tout ce qui est en leur pouvoir ... pour faire évader les prêtres contre-révolutionnaires et les assassins connus sous le nom de Compagnie de Jésus' (AN, BB 18 394, commissaire près le tribunal criminel de Grenoble, au Ministre, 10 pluviôse an VI).
[3] Harvey Mitchell, *The Underground War against Revolutionary France. The Missions of William Wickham, 1794–1800* (London, 1965).

Largentière, was to state: 'On voit des étrangers venir dans l'Ardèche pour les renforcer ... Ils promettaient dans un temps à ceux qu'ils voulaient enrôler 30 sols par jour, une bonne nourriture, de bons habits, et la part au butin.'[1] This last would have been a considerable inducement in a Department in which successful attacks on army pay convoys, on travelling tax collectors, military paymasters, and on government stage-coaches were almost monthly occurrences at any time between 1795 and 1801, tending even to become more frequent in 1798–1801. The profits must have been enormous, and they would not have been limited to the groups operating in the Ardèche, and there is plenty of evidence to suggest that they were linked up with similar bodies active in the Haute-Loire, the Gard, and the Lozère.[2] Of Dumas, one of the Lyon leaders of the *compagnie*, it was said that he obtained a house out of the profits of his participation in the activities of the *bandes*.[3] So there was no lack of material inducements, as well as the comforts associated with the *repos du guerrier*.

It was not surprising that one could live inside the Counter-Revolution, in a way in which it had proved impossible to live inside the Terror, or even the Revolution as a whole. To employ a contemporary phrase, *on pouvait s'installer dans la Contre-Révolution*; and the move might prove a comfortable one, the house, solid and welcoming. Such a man as Froment in the Gard and no doubt many of those who were to lead the Counter-Revolution in the Ardèche, from 1792 or so until the early years of the Consulate, and who had suffered personally from the early economic reforms of the Revolution might thus set up house in their bandits' 'Kingdom of the South' for anything up to ten or fifteen years. A few –

---

[1] AN, BB 18 125 (Ardèche, directeur du jury de l'arrondissement de Largentière, au Ministre, 24 pluviôse an VIII). An earlier report, from the year VI, states: 'Depuis quelque temps il affluait dans ce Département une multitude de Brigands la plupart émigrés ou prêtres réfractaires, ils y avaient été attirés par l'avantage d'une retraite facile dans les bois et dans les montagnes dont notre Département est couvert ... Ils abondaient surtout dans les cantons de Béage, de Burzet, des Vans, de Joyeuse, Banne, Largentière et une partie de Bourg-Saint-Andéol. Ils s'étaient adjoints tous les malfaiteurs, ils avaient des relations et des créatures dans un très grand nombre de communes, ils séduisaient la plupart des habitants par des motifs de religion' (commissaire près le tribunal de Largentière au Ministre, 6 fructidor an VI, AN, BB 18 124).
[2] See below, p. 263 (3).
[3] 'Je suis informé que Dumas, chef d'une des compagnies de la Compagnie de Jésus, et peut-être chef principal de la Compagnie a été arrêté à Lyon ... Dumas était à Lausanne en août de l'an IV ... Il revint à Lyon recommencer ses brigandages, dont il se procurait l'impunité par les sommes qu'il recevait de *Vikam* [Wickham], avec lesquelles il payait la contre-police de la Compagnie de Jésus plus avantageusement que ne l'était la police du Gouvernement. Il a été adjudant de Précy, peseur de foin, mercure et escroc; avant la Révolution, il mourrait de faim, depuis le 9 thermidor il a vécu dans l'abondance, il a constamment eu un cheval de main, il a entretenu des femmes et a acheté une maison à Lyon, rue des Augustins' (lettre anonyme au Ministre de la Police générale, 12 fructidor an VI, AN, BB 18 690, Rhône).

perhaps they were the lucky ones – might even come out the other end and take part in the second White Terror of the summer of 1815, in the services of the duc d'Angoulême, and in another 'Kingdom of the South'. This was, however, more likely to happen in the Gard than in the adjacent Departments of the Ardèche, the Lozère, and the Haute-Loire. It must have seemed to many that, in this part of the world, the Counter-Revolution had time itself on its side and that it was only a matter of seeing it out, in basalt gorge, deep chestnut valleys, in hilly forest land, and in a honeycomb of caves and ravines.

> C'est au nom de la justice et de l'humanité, que ces scélérats, en troupes, fils de négotiants, gens d'affaires, prêtres, ci-devant nobles, commis bureaucrates, déserteurs de la réquisition, etc., appelés *honnêtes gens* par les royalistes massacroient ceux qu'ils avoient en liste, courroient dans vos maisons, le sabre nud, le pistolet armé, fouilloient dans vos papiers, buvoient et mangeoient chez vous après avoir égorgé vos pères, et chargeoient ensuite leurs chevaux de jambons, saucissons, etc.[1]

This of a Lyon group – no doubt a description characteristic enough of methods and impudence, but certainly giving too narrow a class interpretation of composition. For the *bandes* had a far wider appeal than that. A multitude of former *gardes du corps*, horse-dealers, cattle-merchants, former adventurers, river-workers, engravers, market porters, pedlars, ex-priests, ex-soldiers, clerks and officials from administrations that had been suppressed – *fermes, loteries*, ecclesiastical and Admiralty courts, and so on – for whom the Counter-Revolution offered the chance to make a second start in life – artisans from villages that had been declining economically during the twenty or thirty last years of the old regime, indeed, the majority of the inhabitants of certain cantons of the Ardèche, the Haute-Loire, and the Lozère might decide thus to invest in the Counter-Revolution, perhaps as much for economic reasons as for personal or family motivations.[2] In places like Vallon, Largentière, Joyeuse, Villeneuve-de-Berg, in the south of the Ardèche, Barjac, and Saint-Ambroix, just over the border, in the Gard, or equally in Saint-Bonnet-le-Froid, at the northern tip of the Ardèche where it abuts on the Haute-Loire, it would have taken a great deal of courage any time between 1795 and 1802 to have been anything other than at least an accomplice of the *bandes*. In this part of the world, it was the republicans who were

---

[1] AN, BB 18 685 (Rhône, *Jean Durif, ex-juge de paix, à ses concitoyens*, affiche imprimée, 8 pluviôse an IV).
[2] 'Ce brigandage est formé, soutenu & dirigé par des hommes à qui la Révolution a ravi quelques privilèges ... ils enrôlent dans leurs bandes assassines beaucoup de déserteurs' (AN, BB 18 125, directeur du jury de Largentière au Ministre, 24 pluviôse an VIII).

almost suicidally brave.[1] The members of the *bandes* were constantly bolstered by a comforting sense of local solidarity; whole communities were on their side, every village, every house, every cottage, every farm was a natural and willing refuge. In short, *ils prenaient la couleur du paysage.* Military operations were to a large extent illusory, in such conditions, though they were frequently and extensively carried out in the last years of the Directory and even during the Consulate. Some military authorities thought that an amnesty would be more effective than the deployment of large forces against elusive groups that were quickly swallowed up by the craggy terrain. But, when an amnesty was actually proclaimed, at the beginning of the Consulate, it does not seem to have met with any more success than the previous policy of collective fines on *communes* convicted of having given support and refuge to known assassins and bandits, a policy pursued in virtue of a law of Vendémiaire year IV.[2] The main effect of the amnesty was to give local judicial authorities an excuse to refuse to reopen charges against murderers acquitted one or two years previously. One should perhaps not generalize too much from the particularly dramatic example of the Ardèche. But very similar conditions existed in much of the Rhône valley, including some of the towns; the Ardèche was not an isolated terrain, a Principality of Banditry; the movements there were closely linked up with Lyon, Nîmes, and possibly Marseille.[3]

---

[1] Ibid. (Notes sur l'assassinat de Michel Duchamp, de la Viole, par le nommé Aubet, dit *Galliot*, de Marols, 1er fructidor an VI): 'Il est constant que le 4 floréal dernier [an VI, 24 April 1798] Michel Duchamp, de la Viole, commune d'Antraigues, fut assassiné d'un coup de poignard par Jean-Pierre Aubet, dit Galliot, de Marols, dans la maison du C. Serres, à Mézillac. Ce fut la suite d'une chanson républicaine que led. Aubet donna la mort à Duchamp après avoir dit à haute voix *au diable la République, qu'elle s'aille faire foutre.*' While the assassin was being escorted to the prison in Antraigues, a group of villagers, fully armed, attempted to rescue him. In the ensuing mêlée, Joseph Duchamp, the brother of the victim, killed the murderer, when he was about to be rescued. Naturally, for once the judicial authorities showed an unaccustomed zeal in bringing to justice Duchamp. 'Pourquoi poursuît-on cette affaire avec autant de châleur? Parce qu'il s'agit de vexer 30 républicains?' But, after several interventions from the Minister, Duchamp was finally acquitted by the Privas tribunal, 5 Pluviôse year VII (24 January 1799). He was unusually fortunate.

[2] The law of 10 Vendémiaire year IV (2 October 1795). The localities most frequently sought out for collective punishment in the Ardèche were the *communes* of Montréal (canton de Largentière), Mézilhac, Malbos, Saint-André-de-Lachamp, Bessas, Uzer, Vallon, Mayrel, Baume, Vessiaux, Ruoms, Pradon, Saint-Sauveur-de-Cruzières.

[3] 'Ces compagnies maintiennent entr'elles une correspondance suivie ... Elles correspondent encore avec les Brigands des autres départements et même avec les rebelles de la Vendée' (AN, BB 18 125, directeur du jury de Largentière au Ministre, 24 pluviôse an VIII). 'Il est comme assuré que la colonne des brigands qui était à Villefort s'est divisée. Une partie a passé dans le département de l'Aveyron, une partie dans celui de la Haute-Loire, et l'autre partie est rentrée dans celui de l'Ardèche. Leur but est, dit-on, de s'y recruter ... Une correspondance très active qui traverse le nord de ce département entretient leur communication dans les départements de l'Aveyron, de la Haute-Loire, de l'Ardèche, même de Lyon' (ibid., commissaire près les tribunaux de la Lozère au Ministre, 17 floréal an VIII).

In other words, apart from material inducements – and these no doubt declined after 1802 or so – in wide areas of the Rhône, the Haute-Loire, the Ardèche, and the Lozère, to opt for the Counter-Revolution was the easier option. It might not even represent a conscious decision at all; it was more a matter of slipping from one form of law-breaking to another, perhaps slightly more dramatic one. It did not represent any hiatus in a form of life and it might even have habit on its side. Certainly, in financial terms, it would be a declining investment during the Empire. And the rewards would be very small indeed in those of honours, after 1814–15. Even so, in these Departments, even after the Restoration and the end of the second White Terror (which brought a last, often conclusive, round of killing, and also frightened large numbers of suspected republicans, Bonapartists, and neo-Jacobins out of the area altogether, to take refuge in the larger cities), those who had enlisted for so long in the disparate ranks of the Counter-Revolution would undoubtedly have thought that the years spent lurking on twisting mountain roads, hiding behind crude stone walls, at dusk or in the early light, or huddling round camp fires in almost inaccessible caves, or walking, at night, through the rocky escarpments of the borderland between the Ardèche and the Haute-Loire, in the bitter cold (Saint-Bonnet-le-Froid was not a euphemism) had been worth it, both in terms of personal pride, family obligations, and of actual enjoyment. At one end of the scale, commitment to Counter-Revolution would have afforded many agreeable opportunities both to the very strong[1] and to the very cruel. (One should think of this part of the world in terms of Montenegro, at the turn of the century, as described by Djilas, rather than as part of revolutionary or eighteenth-century France.) And the better-educated, once it was all over, might switch over to Walter Scott, or genealogy, or both.[2]

Nor was this all, by any means; for pleasure-seekers could find their way through any regime, even the pleasure-hating one of the Incorruptible. The anarchical Terror of the autumn and winter of 1793 had as much to offer as the White Terror of 1795–1802 (or the Counter-Terror as it has sometimes, and most aptly, been described) to the simple,

---

[1] 'Il fallut leur faire la guerre comme aux renards; on employa en conséquence, à cet effet, le bois, la paille et le soufre ... ils se rendirent ... on distinguait parmi eux un assassin de l'Agent de la Commune de Saint-Remèze, le nommé Platon; ce brigand était connu par sa férocité et sa force colossale; il fut tué avec un de ses compagnons, comme on les transférait dans les prisons de Largentière'(AN, BB 18 125, rapport de l'adjudant-général Nivet, commandant dans l'Ardèche et dans la Lozère, au Ministre, 7 pluviôse an VIII). (Nivet himself had been an energetic and effective terrorist and a committed Jacobin soldier, both in Brussels and in Lille. He was the sort of man whom the Directory could trust to be completely ruthless when in charge of the repression of White terrorism. See my *Les Armées révolutionnaires*, pp. 244, 673, 768.)

[2] *A Second Identity*, pp. 177–82.

resourceful man out for a good time, concerned with the satisfaction of the baser needs and with any occasion for self-dramatization. Indeed, both Terrors were likely to appeal to the same sort of people, at least at ground-level activism; and, sometimes, the same sort of people, even the same people, served both in succession. There was nothing very remarkable about that.

> Le nommé Lambert, garçon perruquier, de Carpentras, l'un des principaux agens de la réaction royale, et terroriste forcené en 1793 et 94, avoit été arrêté à Grenoble comme prévenu d'être complice de la conspiration qui éclata ici les 1er et 2 brumaire [an VI] [22 and 23 October 1797] ... Pendant sa traduction en cette commune, son évasion a été favorisée sur la route. Cet individu s'est rendu à Lyon, et de là il a écrit au juge de paix de Carpentras, une lettre menaçante, datée du 1er février 1798 ...

The letter is characteristic of the man himself and of the conceit of a great many former ultra-revolutionaries, who, rather than return to obscurity, enrolled subsequently in the *compagnies* or in the *bandes*, in order to satisfy their taste for ostentation, self-dramatization, and violence. In this particular case – and it is no doubt representative of many counter-terrorists from the south – there is also a touching concern for his family: 'do not touch my father, leave him alone', 'let my brother come home', and so on – which makes his magnificently impudent letter doubly interesting, as a commentary on a certain mentality, especially in view of the extreme rarity of documents of this kind:

> Je t'écris la présente [writes Lambert from his hiding-place in Lyon], pour te faire savoir que la personne dont tu avais si bien recommandé par un mandat d'arrêt aux autorités constituées de Grenoble, te conseille de quitter ta place plutôt que de faire une seconde folie pareille à celle que tu as faite envers moi, parce que tu animerois les esprits contre toi, et tu pourrois t'en repentir par les suites du tems; quant à moi, je te pardonne, toi et tous ceux qui peuvent m'avoir dénoncé, c'est-à-dire tout autant que tu laisseras mon père tranquille chez lui, et que vous rappellerez mon frère aîné dans son pays pour qu'il puisse y jouir d'une parfaite tranquillité, ou sinon – je tiendrois compte des injustices que vous avez commises envers nous, je ne t'en dis pas davantage, je suis L'IMPÉRISSABLE A. LAMBERT.

The Counter-Revolution was, however, much more closely identified with crime, and with the criminally-inclined, than had been any of the forms of the republican Terror.[1] For one thing, it offered, for a time, an

---

[1] Commissaire près le tribunal de Carpentras, au Ministre, 29 pluviôse an VI, AN, BB 18 394, Isère. This did not, of course, prevent ingenious and resourceful men from using characteristic institutions of the Terror for their own criminal purposes, especially in the chaotic conditions of the autumn and early winter of 1793. All that was often needed to

escape and a refuge, as well as a sort of respectability,[1] to desperate men who were on the run. A person who had but recently escaped from *la chaîne* – an operation of quite outstanding simplicity, pretty well all over France throughout the Directory; the Directorial *chaîne*, like the Directorial prisons, seems to have been specifically designed to escape from, and thus to afford, at regular intervals, the Counter-Terror and the Counter-Revolution a steady supply of recruits,[2] and, even in Paris, the Minister, the judiciary, and the police are constantly faced with the intractable problem of establishing the true identity of escaped convicts – could find comradeship, food and drink, the admiration of a certain kind of woman, and an opportunity to display his physical strength and daring within the only semi-secret confines of a royalist murder gang or of a rural anti-terrorist group. His enlistment would then give new meaning to his persecution at the hands of a society made up of administrators, tax collectors, garrison commanders, *commissaires du Directoire* (of whom a phenomenal number were sought out for assassination, especially in the Ardèche), agents of the *Ministère de la Police générale*, jumped-up property-holders, purchasers of church lands, and parvenus. For he would not have much to fear from judges and juries, especially in the south-east, at least up to the time of the *coup d'état* of Fructidor year V (September 1797). But, from the beginning of the year VI, as a result of the massive purge of judges, jurors, *directeurs de jurys d'accusation*, and so on, a purge which was especially thorough in most of the Departments of the Rhône valley, and the establishment of military courts in most of the internal *divisions militaires*, he would be likely to find that crimes which could be

---

carry out requisitions in foodstuffs or precious metals was a tricolour sash, a piece of paper with a suitable heading, the ready and, preferably, loud use of the phrase *Au nom de la loi*, and a great deal of impudence. There are many instances, up and down the country, of false *armées révolutionnaires*, constituted by bandits, terrorizing farms and carrying out requisitions ostensibly for the benefit of the Republic. Several of them operated north and west of Lyon; we hear of them in the Beaujolais and, perhaps significantly, at l'Île-Barbe! See my *Armées révolutionnaires*, pp. 217 (239), 695–734.

[1] 'Ces bandes sont encore grossies par une foule de scélérats couverts de toute sorte de forfait, à qui la Révolution ne fournit pas de prétexte, mais qui cherchent l'impunité dans leur association avec de nouveaux coupables' (AN, BB 18 125, Ardèche, directeur du jury de l'arrondissement de Largentière, au Ministre, 24 pluviôse an VIII).

[2] 'Quelle existence peuvent avoir des hommes flétris et qui fuient la chaîne? Ils craignent de se livrer paisiblement au travail ... ils n'ont donc plus de ressources que dans le vagabondage, et ces hommes, condamnés souvent pour simples vols, deviennent assassins, parce que le crime va toujours par gradation, et que ne pouvant plus rôder pour des escroqueries, ils sont forcés de ne paroître que la nuit et d'employer la violence. Et ce qui les favorise, c'est qu'ils reviennent toujours en nombre des bagnes, qu'ils forment bandes et s'associent' (AN, BB 18 687, commissaire près le tribunal correctionnel de Lyon, à celui du Département, 10 prairial an VI). There are many references in BB 18 682–93 to the dilapidated state of the Lyon prisons. A number of the members of the *bande d'Orgères* had escaped from half a dozen prisons before their trial and execution.

dressed up as political gestures, even if in fact they responded merely to private and purely criminal motivations, could no longer be committed with such a complete assurance of impunity. In Paris at least, there was a sharp decline in crimes of violence, breakings-in, and petty theft from the early months of that year, while, in the neighbourhood of the capital, *chauffage* and banditry appear to have received their first serious challenge from the repressive authorities. This was the turning point, too, in the fortunes of the southern murder gangs. Executions by courts martial rose steeply from Nivôse year VI (January 1798), when further powers were given to the military authorities in the execution of summary justice.

Furthermore, ordinary criminals, both professional and occasional, appear to have been among the principal victims of the political and economic Terror of 1793 and the year II, that is at a time when even the most minor theft, such as that of a couple of logs of wood, displayed on the wood port of the Jardin des Plantes, or of scrap-iron on the quays, objects *exposés sur la foi publique* (a fact which made theft much easier but which brought correspondingly greater penalties than theft committed in closed premises as a result of breaking-in), was regarded as a crime against the Republic and was liable to be punished as such. Criminals at all levels, but especially petty criminals, such as servant girls, seamstresses, shop assistants, and children between the ages of ten and sixteen, were thus unlikely to feel any attachment to the system of the year II, either at the time or in retrospect, because both the ordinary courts and political bodies such as *comités de surveillance*, had displayed quite unprecedented ferocity in the delivery of sentences and a greatly increased effectiveness in the pursuit of repression. The year II had been a very bad time indeed for both the urban and the rural poor, for, even in the smallest *communes*, the task of the normal judicial authorities – *juges de paix*, *directeurs de jury*, and so on, officials relatively harmless and inactive, at least when dealing with local law-breakers – had been shared by local militants and busybodies who had used the extensive powers conferred on the revolutionary committees to mete out a brutal class justice in defence of private property and public order. Under the Directory, there are many references, in the correspondence of the Minister of Justice, to the almost personal vindictiveness both of the ordinary judicial authorities, of the *commissaires de police*, and of the various political watchdogs: *commissaires révolutionnaires*, and so on, especially when dealing with cases of theft, particularly of articles likely to be of use to the war effort, of counterfeiting – another form of 'crime against the Republic' (even when it consisted of filing down gold coins bearing the effigy of Louis XV or of Louis XVI), *faux en écriture* – nearly always a political offence, since it would be designed to enable those who were politically suspect to slip through the net of the numerous paper checks: *certificats de domicile, certificats de non-émigration, certificats de civisme* established to keep a constant check on persons on the move, to certify beyond dispute individual identities and to ensure political orthodoxy.

In the petitions addressed to the Minister between 1796 and 1799, those awaiting trial frequently refer to the 'système despotique et barbare de l'an II', while making flattering references to the clemency, humanity, and sense of legality of the Directorial courts. Such remarks may of course have been little more than an *exercice de style*, an effort to curry favour with the existing authorities; but they did also correspond to the reality of the Terror, at least in the towns. For it is indisputable that the Terror had weighed the most heavily on the poor, especially on poor women and runaway children, who constituted the readiest and most numerous recruits both to professional and occasional crime. By treating almost all types of habitual crime as potentially counter-revolutionary, the Revolutionary Government may have achieved some temporary success in its repressive functions and in the defence of both public and private property. Murders, for instance, were extremely rare in the Paris region in the course of the year II, while there are few instances, at least in that area, of rural banditry. But it had also driven the politically uncommitted, the apolitical, and the indifferent into securing a vested interest, if not in Counter-Revolution – that would have been too positive a commitment – at least in the Counter-Terror. The result was that, even as late as the year VII, the Republic, in the eyes of the criminal, would remain eternally that of the year II. And, in any case, someone who had been mouldering in prison, awaiting trial, for two or three years, would be unlikely to make any clear distinction between the year II and the years that followed. Seen from *la Grande Force* or from Bicêtre, from Saint-Joseph, or Roanne (the Lyon prisons), all the revolutionary years would appear equally colourless and equally drab. The Revolutionary Government had been almost too successful in its repressive attitudes; and it had thus raised up against itself, even more against its successors, a host of irreducible enemies, of humble people not normally given to any form of political commitment.

With the invisible passport of the password, the counter-terrorist, the man on the run, would move from town to town, from inn to inn, from trade to trade, from village to village, as along the lines of an escape route of the 1940s. There would be at each stage someone to take him in, to take care of him, to keep him fed and warm, mend his clothes, repair his boots, and to send him on his way, with a verbal introduction, to the next staging-post, and with a word too of encouragement.[1] Fraternity was on all the

---

[1] See, for instance, Arch. Vaucluse L 28* (agent national du district d'Avignon au juge de paix de Pujaut, 29 nivôse an III, on the subject of the murder of seven persons near Tavel): 'J'ai découvert que led. Olivier Payen restoit à Avignon en germinal an II ... et qu'il est

battle flags of the Republic. But it was a reality with the Counter-Terror; it was forced upon it as a means of survival. The Counter-Terror organized its travel better, because it had to meet vigilance with more vigilance, because it had to be constantly on the move, and so prepare its hidden posting-houses and stopping places, what could be called, in modern slang, its *clandés*.[1] But also, with magnificent impudence, it put to its own use the official channels of communication of the Republic; the attacks on the Lyon to Paris mail are innumerable between the year IV and the year VII, and nearly always at the same spots, just outside the former city. But so they were on the Lyon to Grenoble, the Lyon to Marseille, the Marseille to Toulon, the Lyon to le Puy, the le Puy to Privas, the le Puy to Aubenas, the Privas to Valence, and the Privas to Nîmes coaches. Indeed, in the Ardèche, no public highway was in any way safe, even for army pay convoys. And, with equal impudence, bandits, counter-terrorists, *chouans*, and *chauffeurs* often appropriated to their own criminal and violent purposes the official government couriers. We hear of these being used, in the south-east, as emissaries of the Princes and as *agents de liaison* of different groups of *compagnies*,[2] while, in the Alençon region, they regularly deliver up their dispatches, pay packets, and valuables to groups of bandits awaiting, with watches in their hands, their passage through a thickly forested area, a few miles from the town, just over the border, in the Mayenne.[3]

A *perruquier* from the south, who had been engaged in highway robbery and who was travelling under a series of identities and with a pocketful of passports, as he moved from Marseille to Avignon, from there to Valence, thence to Aubenas, le Puy, and back to Vienne, thence to Grenoble, Lyon, Chalon, Dijon, Auxerre, Paris, and Rouen, being careful generally to avoid small towns – save very safe ones like Aubenas or Largentière – would seek out each time another *perruquier*. It was easier

---

actuellement à Montpellier avec sa femme. C'est un homme de 40 à 45 ans, il a un bras plus court que l'autre, c'est une espèce de marchand du Piedmont ou du Dauphiné . . . Je te dirai encore qu'il y a une espèce de compagnie ou société de ces espèces de gens qui, sous prétexte de commerce, volent et assassinent tant qu'ils peuvent . . . Je te dirai encore qu'à Nîmes il y a un nommé Barbien, aubergiste, qui a été longems lié avec eux.'

[1] For a modern instance of a change of *clandés*, see Albertine Sarrazin, *L'Astragale*. Mlle Sarrazin was brought up in reform schools, was later involved in organized crime, received several prison sentences, broke her leg while escaping from prison, so that she had to be put up in a safe place while her leg set. She eventually married a long-service prisoner, wrote three autobiographical novels, and died in her early thirties. Her novels are moving and compassionate as well as humorous.

[2] 'Je suis informé . . . que les couriers du Gouvernement se permettent de colporter et de distribuer dans les courses qu'ils font dans les départements des feuilles et journaux antirépublicains et qu'ils les remettent particulièrement aux militaires qu'ils rencontrent' (AN, BB 18 449, Ministre de la Police générale au Ministre, 5 vendémiaire an V).

[3] AN, BB 18 762 (substitut près le tribunal d'Alençon au Ministre, 28 ventôse an VII).

still for all those who travelled for their business: horse-dealers,[1] cattle-merchants, river-workers, tinsmiths, pedlars, carriers and carters, commercial travellers (*courtiers en soie*, who so often needed to go from Lyon to Paris, and who were so difficult to bring to trial – they were always absent *pour leurs affaires* – proved most effective links in the network of the murder gangs), jugglers and street musicians, people who worked in fairs, told fortunes, itinerant magicians, wrestlers, artificial savages, the ubiquitous old-clothes merchant (we find some of these from as far away as Lyon, Marseille, and Nantes in groups of thieves operating within the Paris boundaries during the Directory), and so on, for they had an excuse to be anywhere at any time. In the course of years, they could have worked out the most elaborate chains of complicity and clandestinity, with close contacts with *logeurs* known to be safe, with girls who did not work for the police, with receivers, more static old-clothes merchants (in Paris, those who operated from the faubourg Saint-Germain were thought to be safer than those, longer established, who plied their trade in the neighbourhood of the Mont-de-Piété, marché du Temple), locksmiths and junk merchants who were members of the confraternity, and whose help could frequently be required. The Counter-Revolution, like crime, tended to move by water; but it had its own private itineraries, as well as the public posting routes of the Republic, it travelled too along deep, high-hedged tracks, it had its own ferries and its own ferrymen,[2] its many hidden *points de chute*, in large, shuttered houses, on the fringe of towns, in the faubourgs, just outside the city limits, beyond the jurisdiction of the more zealous urban magistrates and the inquiring *commissaires* of Sections, spacious houses, with large walled gardens, and many exits.

---

[1] 'Le tribunal criminel, par jugement du III ... a condamné à la déportation ... Louis-Julien Marie, âgé de 30 ans, natif de Nonant, département de l'Orne, marchand de chevaux et piqueur, demeurant à Rouen ... convaincu ... d'avoir méchamment ... provoqué au rétablissement de la royauté' (AN, BB 18 808, Ministère de la Justice, Seine-Inférieure, commissaire près le tribunal de Rouen, au Ministre, 13 nivôse an VI).

[2] 'D'ailleurs, sur les quais du Rhône, près de Vienne, on arrête, on vole, on tire des coups de pistolet, on menace du sabre. Ce sont 3, 4 ou 5 personnes. Elles sont inconnues, changent de vêtements, se cachent on ne sait où ... personne ne les connoît, personne ne sait leur repaire' (juge de paix de Villette-Serpaise au Ministre, 5 messidor an VI, AN, BB 18 394, Isère). See also BB 18 686 (Burdet, juge de paix de l'arrondissement de Vienne, au juge de paix de l'arrondissement du Midi à Lyon, 2 pluviôse an V): 'Il m'est revenu un peu trop tard pour les faire arrêter que 4 individus très suspects, dirigeant leur marche de Lyon à Avignon, avoient annoncé en passant à Vienne et dans l'auberge où ils étoient logés qu'une horde d'assommeurs venant de Lyon se disposoient à se rendre par eau dans le département de Vaucluse à l'effet d'y organiser les massacres qui ont eu lieu dans différentes communes de la République, et qu'en passant à Condrieu ils devaient opérer celui de tous les amis de l'ordre.'

7

Counter-Revolution and Environment: The Example of Lyon*

'Il ne faut pas confondre cette Ville, dans l'état où elle se trouve, avec plusieurs autres. Ses clôtures ont été abattues, et les brigands peuvent par tous les points rentrer pendant la nuit dans leurs repaires, ou en sortir. Il existe même des ouvertures qui conduisent dans les caves des anciens bastions démolis qui servent de retraite aux effets volés, ou aux cadavres des assassinés ou aux assassins. Cette circonstance doit rendre la police extrêmement difficile à Lyon.'

> Commissaire près le tribunal criminel du Rhône,
> au Ministre de la Justice,
> le 10 prairial an VIII (30 May 1800)

THE COUNTER-REVOLUTION had, above all, its great *capital*, the most important centre of communication between Switzerland, Piedmont, and the Rhône valley, the link between the Midi and Burgundy, between the Massif Central and the Forez, and Dauphiné, a city proud of its tradition of resistance to Paris (or to Versailles), of its independence of authority, and, more recently, of its daily feats of violence. This was Lyon, after 1793, and any time up to 1803: the twin centre of Counter-Revolution and crime.

It was a town ideally organized for escape, for robbery, for hiding, and for murder, in whatever cause, and, during these years, *any* murder could be passed off as an act of political vengeance and as a blow for the absent King, so much had the Jacobin and terrorist minority been detested in the city. Nature had provided two rivers, both deep, one fast-flowing; man had provided a score of bridges and several kilometres of quays. It is not known just how many people were thus tipped into the Rhône or Saône, their bodies often to re-emerge as far down as Valence, between the end

---

* From *Reactions to the French Revolution*, pp. 44–62.

of 1794 and the early years of the Empire; it would certainly run into four figures.[1] What is fairly certain is that few were supporters of Christ & King, that most had, in one form or another, been involved in the repressive bureaucracy of the year II; and, even when they had not been, it would be said that they had.[2]

Indeed, Lyon was such a good place to murder people in, that people came from a long way off to do it. The provincial specializations of the inns and eating houses helped; *Au rendez-vous des Ardèchois* meant what it said (and still does). It was reasonable for an avenger from Montbrison or from Feurs to look out for a former terrorist from his town in a lodging-house called *l'hôtel des Foréziens*, or at the horse market or in a café near it, so many Foréziens being *maquignons* or blacksmiths. A Mâconnais ex-terrorist, on a two-day visit to Lyon for his business, was recognized and murdered by another Mâconnais while crossing the pont la Feuillée.[3] The localization within the city of people of specified provincial origin, as well as the specialization of certain trades by people from certain villages, in Lyon conditions at least, greatly aided the counter-revolutionary and the law-breaker.

Furthermore, the city was on the very edge of its bizarre, amputated Department.[4] A five-minute walk across the pont de la Guillotière would bring the man on the run into the Isère and to a faubourg notorious for its violence and its anarchy and for the number of its carters' inns. *La Guille*, momentarily reincluded in the Rhône under the Directory, to be re-attached to the Isère in the early years of the Empire, was an ancient and respected centre of crime;[5] it was also on the route from the *bagne* of Toulon to that of Rochefort. The manacles, balls, and handcuffs of those condemned to the galleys who went through the place, in both directions, twice a year, had a habit of falling off or breaking while in la Guillotière, as if they had been children's toys. The neighbouring *communes* of les Brotteaux and Villeurbanne, attached throughout this

---

[1] For an estimate of those murdered in Lyon and its faubourgs between the year III and the year XII, see *The Police and the People*, p. 140.

[2] Ibid., p. 338: the murder, in Lyon, of Bigot, a horse-dealer from Roanne, wrongly accused by his murderers of having been a former member of the Commission de Feurs.

[3] Revillon fils, commis au Département de Saône-et-Loire, and a friend of the former *conventionnel* Reverchon, was recognized in Lyon at the beginning of Prairial year V (May 1797); his body was thrown into the Saône from the pont la Feuillée (*The Police and the People*, p. 337 (L)).

[4] 'Cette ville ... doit plus particulièrement fixer l'attention du Gouvernement ... par ... la situation d'une ville placée à l'extrémité du Département et limitrophe de ceux de l'Isère et de l'Ain, à tel point que, dans moins d'un quart d'heure, le coupable échappe à l'action de la police, en passant rapidement d'une juridiction dans une autre' (AN, BB 18 687, commissaire près le tribunal correctionnel, au juge du tribunal criminel de Lyon, 30 brumaire an IX).

[5] *The Police and the People*, p. 334.

period to the judicial arrondissement of Vienne, in the Isère, and thus out of range of the military authorities that held Lyon in a state of siege and, in most cases, proved very vigorous in the pursuit of political crime and banditry within the city and its faubourgs, further constituted ideal hiding-places for fugitives from justice; les Brotteaux, near the pont Morand, the old killing ground of the *mitraillades*, dotted with *guinguettes* and *cabarets*, with its numerous ponds and dense under-growth, was a favourite rendez-vous for bandits returning from night forays into the Isère, and also formed an excellent repository for the corpses of former *mathevons*. In the anarchical conditions of the Directory, there was little co-operation between the military authorities of Lyon and the *gendarmerie* of Vienne. On the other side of Lyon, at its northern exit, on the road to Paris, brigands, bandits, highwaymen, counterfeiters, and political murderers could be assured of a safe refuge in the *commune* of Vaise, which further specialized in attacks on the Paris–Lyon mail-coach. From the north-east end of the city, a quarter of an hour's walk would take the law-breaker into the Ain.

The city itself was almost equally well organized for clandestinity, escape, and unobtrusive murder. The network of *traboules* enabled the criminal or the assassin to move underground, cutting through high blocks of ochre-coloured seven-storey houses, without ever emerging at street level, almost from one end of the peninsula to the other. After the long siege of 1793, the town was partly in ruins, its walls down, its forts dismantled and unroofed, many of its houses falling down, and a multi-tude of locks and keys, of every size, displayed on the junk market (*marché aux fers*) of the quays.[1] A report of Prairial year VIII (May 1800) brings the point home in no uncertain terms: 'Il ne faut pas confondre cette Ville, dans l'état où elle se trouve, avec plusieurs autres,' writes the *commissaire près le tribunal criminel*. 'Ses clôtures ont été abattues, et les brigands peuvent par tous les points rentrer pendant la nuit dans leurs repaires, ou en sortir. Il existe même des ouvertures qui conduisent dans les caves des anciens bastions démolis qui servent de retraite aux effets volés, ou aux cadavres des assassinés ou aux assassins. Cette circonstance doit rendre la police extrêmement difficile à Lyon.'[2] A year later, the body of the director of the *hospice des vieillards*, who had been murdered by

---

[1] 'Il s'est opéré dans cette commune une quantité majeure de démolitions ... il s'est vendu à cette occasion, ou volé, beaucoup de serrures et de clefs superflues. Ces objets ont été achetés par des marchands de vieux fers qui les revendent au premier venu; le malfaiteur n'a qu'à prendre l'empreinte de la serrure d'un domicile, il est moralement sûr de trouver chez ces marchands en détail plusieurs clefs assorties' (AN, BB 18 687, commissaire près le tribunal criminel au Ministre, 18 nivôse an VIII).

[2] AN, BB 18 687 (commissaire près le tribunal correctionnel, au Ministre, 10 prairial an VIII).

one of the inmates, remained in the cellar of the building without being discovered for a month.[1] Many bodies were found, their throats slit, among the ruins of the old fortifications. It was a décor worthy of Sue or of *Fantomas*. The extraordinarily steep streets of la Grande Côte, la Croix-Rousse, Vaise, and Fourvière offered a further invitation to argument and violence following the multiplicity of accidents provoked by runaway handcarts and barrows.[2] Finally, Lyon possessed the almost unique privilege in having no *concierges*, no portresses, and few *cochers de fiacre*[3] (defeated by the gradients), the usual auxiliaries of the political and criminal police and the most profitable source of information both about residents and strangers. (In Paris, the Terror would have been powerless without them.) It was, therefore, difficult to establish the comings and goings of inmates, the arrival or departure of unfamiliar faces, the postmarks on letters received, the size and shape of parcels carried out furtively at night or brazenly at midday, chance remarks murmured or shouted in the night, the usual stock in trade of that unpleasant female animal in Paris. Something was done, however, to remedy this situation in the year III, when, in order to facilitate the progress of the White Terror and to point out to the *sabreurs* of the murder gangs their potential victims, the Thermidorian municipal authorities ordered that lists of residents should be displayed, at eye level (*à une hauteur commode*) at the entrance to each block of dwellings; many former *mathevons* were thus traced and murdered, while similar lists, printed in Lausanne in 1795, were widely circulated in the city.[4]

But the *mathevon* was in any case a terribly isolated individual who, unlike the criminal or the *égorgeur*, did not enjoy the active or tacit complicity of a whole quarter, of a whole community. Individual members of former revolutionary committees of the Lyon Sections and of its faubourgs were, for one thing, generally householders, and so prisoners of their addresses and of their employment. It is significant, for instance,

---

[1] AN, BB 18 688 (commissaire général de police de Lyon, au Grand Juge, 5 fructidor an IX). The *directeur*, Joyeux, had disappeared on 8 Thermidor year IX (27 July 1801). His body was discovered in the cellar, under four feet of earth, on 4 Fructidor (22 August).

[2] AN, BB 18 688 (le général divisionnaire Duchesne, commandant la 19me division militaire, au Ministre, 15 pluviôse an X): 'Un assassinat horrible s'est commis dans la ville de Lyon le 10 du pt. [30 January 1802] sur la personne d'un père de famille; ce délit s'est fait en plein jour, dans une rue passagère, et les prévenus, arrêtés en flagrant délit, sont trois carabiniers de la 21me brigade ... L'individu tué conduisoit une voiture à bras qui dans une pente rapide [à Vaise] heurta l'un des militaires; celui-ci donna un soufflet au conducteur de la voiture qui le frappa à son tour, alors il fut percé d'un coup de sabre et mourut.'

[3] On the role of *cochers de fiacre* as informers, see below, p. 302, the section on Nicolas Guénot.

[4] *The Police and the People*, p. 34.

that the score or so of Lyonnais *abonnés* to the papers of Lebois and Babeuf were living at the same addresses and were in the same trades as they had occupied during their period of power.[1] Far from being covered by a whole community, such people were frequently sought out for public lynching, often within a few yards of their homes or place of work and with their neighbours as an enthusiastic, pitiless audience.[2] Any time between the year III and the year XII, it proved quite impossible to find witnesses prepared to testify about a murder or to gather together a jury willing to condemn a notorious assassin. Even if the witnesses had come forward, it is unlikely that the judicial authorities – *juges de paix* or the judges in the higher courts – would have shown any inclination to listen to them, much less to follow up their testimony with anything more than a purely token effort to bring the criminals to justice. It was not so much that the *juges de paix* and the other subordinate law-enforcement officers were afraid of people whom they knew very well to be members of the *compagnie de Jésus* or of similar secret societies – fears of this kind certainly existed in smaller towns and had a similarly paralysing effect on the execution of justice – in Lyon, they generally approved of what they were doing, were prepared to look the other way, or even to warn individuals who had come to the notice of the military authorities, who were genuinely anxious to re-establish order and to see that justice was done, to go into hiding or to leave the city.

The extent of official complicity of this kind was such that it has been suggested that the gaolers of the Lyon prisons issued false declarations of release or imprisonment, altering the dates, according to need, in order to cover the movements between France, Piedmont, and Switzerland, or within France, of the more active *émigrés*. Boissonnet, the energetic *accusateur public* of the Grenoble tribunal, a man constantly concerned to stamp out White terrorism, imported into his Department from across the river, had few illusions on the subject of his Lyon colleagues, and it was always with alarm and misgiving that he saw a criminal case from his Department being referred to one of the tribunals of the Rhône. For he knew very well from an experience drearily repetitive in the course of the years IV, V, and VI that such a transfer was the surest way of securing the acquittal of even the most notorious assassin, whose activities had been witnessed by a hundred-odd countrymen on the other bank of the river. He was also well aware that, however much he might harry the Lyon authorities at all levels, denouncing them for their dilatoriness to the

---

[1] Ibid., p. 71.
[2] Godefroy and Gallimard, after being exposed, were murdered in the presence of an enormous crowd, canton de l'Hôtel-Dieu, on their way back to prison, 15 Floréal year V (4 May 1797) (AN 686).

Minister of Justice, or even to that of *Police générale*, his efforts, combined with those of both Ministers, and with the additional support, on occasion, of the whole *députation* of the Isère, acting through one of the assemblies, would have singularly little effect, other than to sharpen the hostility felt by Lyonnais of all conditions at the spectacle of what they regarded as impudent interference on the part of meddling Dauphinois and the usual bullying to be expected of Paris. If a man who had committed a murder or a series of murders in the Isère, succeeded in reaching Lyon, there was little chance of the authorities there ever succeeding in laying their hands on him, even if, as no doubt they generally did, they knew perfectly well where he was staying. The *Bureau Central* of Paris was equally sceptical as to the effectiveness and the zeal of its own opposite number, the *Bureau Central* of Lyon. In a characteristic affair in which a *commissaire du Directoire* and his brother-in-law had been murdered in the Isère, their assassins had crossed the river, reached the Loire, and had eventually taken refuge with the father of one of them, a well-known silk manufacturer, in Lyon; two were never discovered, the third was acquitted. It was hardly surprising, in such circumstances, that the numerous relatives of the two victims should have threatened to take the law into their own hands and to carry out reprisals against those – a doctor, a *juge de paix*, and a *fils de famille* who was also, predictably, a deserter: a pretty trio indeed of *égorgeurs*, the doctor using his skills to hack to pieces the corpse of his victim – whom they had actually seen shooting or stabbing their relatives. We do not know whether they ever actually followed up these threats[1] – if they did, we can be sure that they would have been brought to justice, and, if they had the misfortune to have been brought before a Rhône court, that they would have been punished with the full severity of the law.

Lyon was thus a sort of *zone franche* not only for those who had committed crimes within its ill-guarded and crumbling walls but also for those who had gone out into the neighbouring Departments, to exercise political murder or to carry out private vengeance, or both, in the Isère, the Loire, the Saône-et-Loire, the Ain, and the Ardèche. The facility offered to the accused to appeal to a court outside the Department in which the

---

[1] There were plenty of instances of crimes of vengeance of just such a kind in the sanguinary southern tip of the Ardèche. See above, p. 263 (1). See also AN, BB 18 124 (Ministre de la Justice au commissaire près le tribunal du Département, 7 nivôse an V): 'Dans la nuit du 29 au 30 brumaire [an V, 19–20 November 1796] il se commit un assassinat à Saint-André-de-Bourlenc, en la personne de Jean Maurin; on n'a pas ouï-dire que les amis de l'assassiné eussent vengé sa mort par un autre assassinat . . . il a été fait des poursuites contre les meurtriers de Jean Maurin . . . il n'est que trop vrai qu'il se commet des assassinats dans le département comme partout ailleurs. C'est un malheur qui a sa source dans l'immoralité' – rather a lame explanation for the vicious tribalism of the inhabitants of the canton of Largentière!

crime had been committed proved, in the conditions of the period of the Directory, one of the best guarantees of impunity. The Rhône was no doubt the great favourite in this respect; but the courts of the Ardèche and the Haute-Loire were likewise much in demand with the White terrorist from Lyon, from the Loire, or from the Gard. The notorious complaisance of the ordinary Lyon courts, rather like the area of the White Terror itself, *faisait tâche d'encre*, to include most of the judicial area of the right bank of the Rhône. Indeed, after the *coup d'état* of Fructidor, the Directorial authorities gave implicit recognition to the fact that nothing was to be expected of the local courts and of the local magistrature, by placing most of the *communes* in the area *en état de siège*,[1] that is, under military rule, and by setting up military commissions that deliberated *in camera* and that dispensed with juries, in Avignon and Montpellier, and, for a time, in Privas. The fact that a certain number of self-avowed White terrorists were eventually condemned to death and shot or guillotined[2] was almost entirely due to the zeal of these military judges, though some of the leaders of the movement managed to elude even that redoubtable net, with the help of their counsel.[3] The left bank was a different matter; but these were the courts to be avoided at all costs. We do not hear of Lyon *sabreurs* or of Ardèchois gentlemen-assassins being transferred to the jurisdiction of the Isère or the Drôme.

So the Lyonnais were lucky in many ways; furthermore they knew they were, and tended to stick to their city or at least to remain in the area that comprised the principal zone of activity of the White Terror, from Mâcon to Marseille and including the Departments on the right bank of the Saône

---

[1] AN, BB 18 124 (commissaire près le tribunal du canton de Largentière, au Ministre, vendémiaire an VII): 'Je vous préviens que d'après un arrêté du Directoire Exécutif en date du 4 ce mois [4 vendémiaire an VII, 25 September 1798] la commune de Largentière, ainsi que celles de Joyeuse, Bannes, Burzet, Concouron, Jaujac, Montpezat, Thueyts &ca ... viennent d'être mis en état de siège.'

[2] One of the murderers of Blachère-Laprade (brother-in-law of Saint-Martin, of the 500), *commissaire du Directoire près l'administration municipale du canton de Largentière*, killed in his country seat at la Prade, near Montréal, on the night of 4–5 Fructidor year V (21–22 August 1797), is said to have been a returned *émigré*, Fabre-Vernon, condemned to death by the *commission militaire* of Lyon – which, of course, was not composed of Lyonnais – on 24 Floréal year VI (13 May 1798), and shot the same day.

[3] This is what happened in the interminable affair of Boutières and Chabrolin, dit *Garnier*, both of the *commune* of Chassiers, accused of having participated in three murders, including those of Blachère and another *commissaire du Directoire*, Brun, in the course of the year V. When they were eventually brought before a special court in the Ardèche five years later, in the course of the year X, their counsel objected to the presence among the judges of the *chef de bataillon* Heyraud, second-in-command to the *adjudant-général* Ruby, and of Saint-Prix, a former member of the 500, whose brother had been murdered. Heyraud had shown too much zeal in the repression of brigandage – as had his chief. As a result of these objections, the trial appears to have been held up indefinitely (AN, BB 18 124, Ardèche).

and the Rhône. We do not find many of them in Paris,[1] though, when they
did come there, they brought with them their noisy quarrels, their interminable vendettas – the 29 Mai, it would seem, would *never* be forgotten,
it had a much greater force of polarization than any of the national dates
that had marked the course of the history of the Revolution – another
example no doubt of Lyonnais particularism – fighting out the everlasting
war between *honnêtes gens* and *mathevons* on the uncomprehending and,
even in Thermidorian conditions, unsympathetic Paris scene. It was not
surprising that Lyon and its inhabitants should have enjoyed such a
detestable reputation with the Paris press as a whole – not merely with
that of the neo-Jacobins – from 1795 to 1799, the Paris journalists depict-
ing them, along with the Marseillais, the Avignonnais, the Nîmois, as
cannibals and savages, covered in blood from head to foot, perpetually
foaming at the mouth, with a dagger or a stiletto in one hand, a pistol in
the other. The Lyonnais tended to take this sort of thing as merely another
expression of Parisian arrogance; and, if they moved, it was more likely to
be southwards, to Marseille, following the course of the Rhône[2] – perhaps
it was as well for the 'cannibals' to stick together – just as the Auxerrois,
the inhabitants of Vermenton, and those who lived by the lac des Settons
in the Morvan, tended to be orientated, via the Cure, the Yonne, and the
Seine, to Paris, and its wood ports.[3]

They were secretive people, their town contained many secret places,
underground passages, concealed doors, cellar rooms papered in old rose
or scarlet and crammed with gold plate, comfortable houses enclosed by
high walls, plane trees, and cypresses, large enough and discreet enough
to contain an army of counterfeiters (one of the unofficial local industries
and a further activity in which Counter-Revolution and crime could feed
upon one another's skills[4]), with hidden back rooms of difficult approach

---

[1] Restif, returning on foot to Paris in 1759, comes up with two Lyonnaises, a middle-aged
woman and her alleged daughter, on the road through Burgundy. The so-called mother
intends to sell the girl to a *matrulle* of the Palais-Royal; Restif contrives to separate them,
the older woman continues on her way, the girl, whom Restif cannot marry, promises to
return to Lyon (*Monsieur Nicolas*, V, p. 2440). Lyonnais in Paris tended to be *crocheteurs*
and sedan chair carriers.
[2] *The Police and the People*, p. 31.
[3] 'Elle sourit, comme pour se moquer de mon adieu éternel en allant à Paris, a 45 lieues et dont,
au moyen de la rivière, notre Ville n'est qu'un Fauxbourg' (*Monsieur Nicolas*, IV, p. 1808).
[4] AN, BB 18 685 (commissaire près le tribunal correctionnel, au Ministre, 10 frimaire an V):
'Les vols se sont multipliés, les prévenus de l'assassinat d'Istria ont été portés en triomphe
aux cris de *vivent les honnêtes gens, à bas les mathevons*, les fabricateurs de faux papiers-
monnoie ont été acquittés.' See also *Rapport au Ministre*, s.d. an V: 'Des rescriptions
falsifiées ont été saisies en grand nombre, chez Cognet fils, négociant à Lyon. Le vérificateur
les a déclarées fausses. Tous les instrumens du crime placés dans l'atelier de Cognet attestoi-
ent contre lui et 5 ou 6 complices. Mais Cognet est connu pour un *compagnon de Jésus*; il
en étoit, dit-on, le *monnoieur*, quels que soient leurs crimes' (ibid.).

and giving the promise of a society apart and of secret itineraries connecting up with inns up river, towards l'Île-Barbe and Collonges, and with other similar roomy houses in the faubourgs.

There is, in the papers of the Minister of Justice, a telling description of just such a house, to which had been brought, after a series of stops elsewhere, a Lyonnais engraver called Galle. In a statement to the *commissaire*, dated 29 Prairial year IV (17 June 1796) and which, more than anything else, gives the no doubt authentic flavour of polite, almost gentlemanly, crime and banditry and the ever-present threat of sudden violence beneath the agreeable veneer of sociability and good manners, he describes his adventures:

> ... Qu'un jour, revenant des Brotteaux, il est accosté de 2 citoyens très bien vêtus qui lui disent le bien connaître, qu'ils ont quelque-chose à lui communiquer, et le conduisent chez Michaud, aux Brotteaux, où il y avait un goûter tout prêt, des vins étrangers, &ca. Il déclare être sorti de là un peu pris de vin; de là il fut conduit à un appartement tenant à un jardin qu'il croit être rue Bourgneuf, maison du cheval verd, c'est l'appartement le plus reculé dans ladite maison. Il se trouva pareillement dans ledit appartement un souper tout prêt et des femmes que l'on qualifioit de *madame une telle*, &ca, mais qu'il a bien reconnu ces dames pour les avoir vues chez la Dervieux, tenant maison publique de filles, qu'il a été retenu dans cet endroit deux jours à faire ce qu'on appelle la ribote et qu'ensuite, toujours entouré des mêmes personnages, il a été conduit à la Croix-Rousse, Grande Rue du Faubourg, dans une maison qui est située près d'un café, dans cette maison il a remarqué qu'il y avait une branlière, que l'on y danse ordinairement le dimanche et que les particuliers dont il est question y occupent une chambre, que c'est un traiteur qui est reputé l'homme le plus fort dans ladite commune, qui est venu le servir à table; de cette maison, il a été conduit à l'Île-Barbe à côté de l'église, dans une maison assez vaste, il y a une belle treille à l'entrée, là il a été conduit dans une chambre où on lui a dit *n'ayez pas peur* [the *tutoiement* is out of favour in this milieu], et de suite il a vu garnir le plateau de la cheminée d'une quantité de pistolets que sortaient de leurs poches ceux qui allaient et venaient dans cet endroit, on lui a proposé de faire une gravure pour un timbre-sec, pour servir à la fabrication de fausses promesses de mandat, il lui a été en même tems offert une grande quantité d'outils propres à la gravure, des loupes, &ca., il a vu qu'on affectait de lui faire voir beaucoup et pour le rassurer, on lui a offert cent louis d'or. Il a été retenu dans cet endroit pendant huit jours, d'où il n'a pu sortir qu'en disant que la crainte l'empêchait de travailler à un objet si délicat ... Dans l'intervalle des douze jours qu'il a été retenu, il a vu paraître à peu près cent visages différents, toujours bonne table, et c'est Tisey, dit *Jean de la Voute*, qui a servi ordinairement, on avait indiqué au déposant Carillon, boutonnier, rue Ferrandière, No 49, au 3me étage, comme étant celui qui devait faire la planche, en conséquence, revenant à Lyon, il est allé chez ledit Carillon où il a déposé les outils qu'il avait apportés de l'Île-Barbe ... Il a bien reconnu le nommé Laurencin pour un des chefs, mais qu'il n'a entendu nommer personne que par des sobriquets, on lui donnait celui de *Monsieur de la*

Canardière, et il a cru s'apercevoir qu'effectivement on voulait l'envoyer à l'eau. Il a remarqué un grand bel homme … ayant ordinairement avec lui un chien danois moucheté, un jeune homme qui doit avoir le bras gauche plus court que le droit, et un autre très gros homme gêné dans sa marche, qu'il croit monter très souvent à cheval [the engraver is a sharp observer and would have done well in the police], gravé de petite vérole, âgé d'environ 24 ans, et il croit que son nom est Cuiseux [another local name], il est instruit que ceux qui sont dans le complot se rendent souvent au café du cheval blanc, rue Grenette, au 1er étage. Depuis son évasion, et qu'il se cache, il sait qu'on est allé le demander chez ses connaissances … Le nommé Marjouillat, bijoutier aux halles de la Grenette, doît connaître la majeure partie de cette société, car il assure que c'est ce Marjouillat qui l'a indiqué comme étant en état d'entreprendre une pareille opération.[1]

The engraver, one feels, was lucky to have survived, after acquiring such dangerous knowledge, having been entertained so joyously, in such alarming, but apparently agreeable, mixed company, having been treated both so politely and so generously, and having, like a man partially blinded, been guided through the various stopping places on a journey both mysterious, unpredictable and yet faintly recognizable, thanks to the numerous clues, including the company, not entirely unknown, the horse-man who appeared to walk with difficulty, the large dog, and the pretty trellis work outside the large house, near the church, at l'Île-Barbe, a place, like the establishment *chez la Dervieux*, that would be likely to be known to a skilled artisan who lived near la Grande Côte, at the northern end of Lyon. Had fear not prevented him from completing his delicate work, it is more than likely that Galle would have earned his nickname and that his body would eventually have been found somewhere in the Saône, between the pont de Collonges and la Mulatière. We can at least be grate-ful to the trembling engraver for having survived, on this occasion at least – for it seems unlikely that he can have been allowed to retain for long such detailed evidence, even though he had taken the precaution of not return-ing to his home; there were, as he says, people 'asking after him' – and for having given us this dramatic account of the semi-hidden world of White terrorism and crime, confined within its own characteristic itinerary of friendly inns, back rooms of big houses, top rooms of apartment houses,

---

[1] AN, BB 18 685. Laurencin and his friends appear to have had powerful protectors. According to the *Bureau Central*, Sibil, *juge de paix* of la Croix-Rousse, warned Laurencin of the statement that Galle had made to the *commissaire général*, so that he – and no doubt many of the hundred-odd other persons that the engraver claims to have seen in the course of his alarming, but not uncomfortable, fortnight in the country or in quiet inns – had time to leave the city, keep well away from l'Île-Barbe, and go into hiding in some other hospitable house, either in the neighbouring countryside, or, further afield, in some wretched mountain inn or bleak *mas*, in the rugged Ardèche, a building with a wide view, commanding every possible approach for miles around.

and large country houses in the valley of the Saône and within walking distance of the river: confined too within the semi-secret code of nick-name, slang, and allusive, but polite conversation, as well as within shared pleasures and shared missions and political assumptions. His story has all the strange fascination of a rendezvous given by a Resistance organization, in the same hidden city and its surroundings, in the 1940s, or that of a secret society planning an *attentat*, with the help of Piedmontese or Dauphinois technicians of infernal machines in the 1820s and 1830s. Lyon, one feels, even in the pre-romantic age of the Directory, was already both deeply romantic and, if at least one belonged to such a confraternity, enjoyably mysterious. Clearly, the engraver's hosts, like most counter-revolutionists in this part of the world, were able to combine loyalty with pleasure and to enjoy themselves, with the help of 'foreign wines' and ladies who used polite formulas, while serving Christ & King.

The other ingredients were chapels of strange cults down dark alley-ways, narrow streets lacking in lighting, an icy wind to blow out the lantern of the passing night-watch, a constant coming and going over the twenty-odd bridges and footbridges, on the ferries and along the quays,[1] peninsular bottle-neck through which all going from east to west would be forced, a young wine, constantly, cheaply, and plentifully available (Lyon's 'third river'), a language rich in impenetrable slang, as well as in threats and in incitement, an availability of weapons of all descriptions[2] (Lyon, although it in no way belonged to a largely alien Midi, save, perhaps, through some of the 'fringe' elements of its more unsettled population, was sufficiently far south to be in the stiletto and stabbing country), and the habit of carrying them resulting in the nickname of a heavy stick as a *juge de paix*[3] (certainly more effective at least than those enervated individuals who, far from being officers of peace, were those of war and vengeance), the prevalence of drunkenness, gambling, and

---

[1] According to one report, in Lyon *Le Réveil du Peuple* had couplets appropriate to the geography of the city:

'Frappons donc, mes amis / Ces coquins de mathevons,
        Assommons, jetons du pont en bas,
    Noyons donc / ces brigans de mathevons . . .'

(commissaire près le tribunal correctionnel, au Ministre, 10 frimaire an V, AN, BB 18 685).
[2] 'Il avoit fait venir, dans le même tems, de Lyon à Condrieu, le nommé Pain, l'un des plus fameux égorgeurs de Lyon, l'assassin d'Istria, Corse, poignardé dans son lit à l'hôpital ... Ils s'étoient promenés tous les deux, le pistolet à la main, dans les rues, places publiques et cafés' (AN, BB 18 686, Pierre X. Montblanc, au Ministre, 9 germinal an VI). A report by the Lyon *juges de paix*, hardly the most zealous upholders of law and order, dated 11 Floréal year IV (30 April 1796), refers to Lyon as a town 'où une foule de brigans marchent tou-jours armés et commettent dans les campagnes environnantes et dans la ville les crimes les plus horribles et les plus multipliés' (AN, BB 18 685).
[3] *The Police and the People*, p. 325.

whoring, the beauty of the local women. These were the ingredients of a collective mentality, of a way of life as distinctive as *Guignol* and *Gnafron*, and, in the exceptional and terribly violent circumstances of the revolutionary period, of intransigent, vengeful political commitment.

In Lyon, perhaps more than anywhere, the borders between private life and political militancy were less apparent, running into one another in a city in which people lived on top of one another, in a crowded peninsula, and in which they sought air and breathing space on the broader confines of the long, double waterfront. Thus counter-revolutionary commitment could be dictated as much by trade, by geography, by the patterns of work and leisure, by the friendships and lasting enmities of the dark, towering street, as by the experience of an immediate and bitterly painful political past that called out for revenge. In Lyon, after 1793, there was no frontier between private vengeance and collective vengeance, while any murder was political, or, at least, would at once be taken as so. Here then perhaps is the extreme example of the interaction of private life and of political intransigence.

Lyon was, of course, wholly exceptional, from every point of view. There was, and is, no other city remotely like it. Its geographical situation was unique, the city having as yet little room to expand eastwards, towards Villeurbanne, les Brotteaux, and la Guillotière, an expansion, at first sight so apparently natural, even desirable, that was checked by artificial administrative frontiers; nor could it expand westwards, the cliffs of Fourvière and of Saint-Just acting as a natural, insuperable barrier. And so it had to build upwards, higher than any other eighteenth-century town, making its streets deeper, darker, more sinister (the dank rue Écorche-Bœuf amply merited its name, in terms of human slaughter too), and its society more 'perpendicular' than any in Paris or in Marseille. Its gradients likewise emphasized the importance of the pedestrian, slowing or completely interrupting any other form of traffic, driving the potential victim down his pre-ordained and predictable course, to a lynching near a bridge or on one of the tiny pocket-handkerchief squares that balanced precariously, diminutive enclosures of horizontal repose, confined theatres, as much suited to *les boules* (and, in this respect, at least, and it is an important one, Lyon was already part of the Midi, representing, in habits of leisure, like those too of *les joutes*, a way of life altogether distinct from the France that lay north of Mâcon) as to the other free spectacle offered by noisy abuse, between neighbours, in that slow, lazy, unique drawl that distinguishes the speech of the Lyonnais even from that of the Dauphinois that it most resembles, and by intimate aggressions, fisticuffs, and even killings, in daylight, *entre gens de connaissance* – it was difficult to kill on the slope – while providing the assassins with a headlong escape route down the steep steps, to the next level, that of a different quarter, almost of a different world.

For in Lyon, apart from the formidable frontiers imposed by the wide, fast-flowing, and dangerous Rhône – the former border between the old Kingdom and the Empire and one that still, as we have seen, had a very real meaning, in terms of violence and law-breaking, in the late eighteenth century – and that, equally real in human terms, between the left bank and the underprivileged right bank of the Saône, and those imposed by la Croix-Rousse and Fourvière and by the tip of the peninsula, south of Ainay and Perrache, each level drew to itself the life of a quarter, distinctive, exclusive, and mutually intolerant. Perhaps the most characteristic square in the whole city is that of the present *mairie du 1er arrondissement*, as much the centre of a village as the place du Tertre, before it became a tourist attraction, a place of human proportions (unlike the cold, pretentious Bellecour), reached, like everything else in Lyon, by steps, protected, in this case, by two bored, comatose Louis-Philippard lions, in jet-black stone, a meeting place as natural, and as civilized as that, high up hill, almost impregnable, attained only at great physical effort, of the Grand'Place of la Croix-Rousse, a meeting place, a market, a potential centre of sedition, the headquarters of the *canuts*, who, from their heights, could dominate the whole city, with the exception of Fourvière, and who owed much of their independence to the fact that they lived at a level the puffing bourgeois would scarcely care to approach and the approach to which, in case of need, could be rendered extremely difficult to anyone coming from below. So, to all the other distinctions – *rive gauche*, *rive droite*, *entre Saône et Rhône*, *Ainay*, *Perrache*, the city added those that divided, physically and morally, the inhabitants of the heights from those whose horizon was confined by the high yellow houses, down in the peninsula below. In Lyon, as in le Havre, as in nineteenth-century Paris, there would be trouble when those from the heights decided to come down into the city spread below them. *Le Gros Caillou* was as much a monument to the proud exclusiveness of the *Croix-Roussiens*, at the time of the Revolution still inhabitants of an independent *commune*, as the cannons of *la Butte* were to the artisans of north-eastern Paris. It was a city that could inspire intense loyalties around each tiny *place*, while the steps that cascaded down, like so many streams, into the entrails of the city, were merely means of escape, connecting links that loosely bound together this strange huddle of quarters.

It was a geography that would enmesh the soldier, the stranger, with sudden cul-de-sacs, exitless courtyards, the springing curtain of a blind ochre wall climbing to the sky, while giving every possible advantage to the aggressor, the local inhabitants, the malefactor, in possession of the secret network of the *traboules*, and further favoured by unguarded bridges and gates – the authorities seem to have been particularly lax about keeping them manned during the night hours, especially during the

Directory, as though they were anxious to make things easier for those who roamed outside the city, in the nominal service of Christ & King, returning to their hidden places of rest in the early hours – and by the endless variety of ruins, underground passages that channelled through the steep hillsides, and that enabled counterfeiters or Companions of the Sun, at the slightest warning, to emerge from the various exits of large walled gardens of properties, one at quay level, another half-way up Fourvière and connecting directly on to a *montée*, yet another, on the further side of the hill, facing towards the Monts du Lyonnais and the billowing, wild open country. La Croix-Rousse too possessed gardens that thus spilled over both towards the Terreaux, to the terraced market gardens facing over the narrow gorges of the Saône, as it turned southwards, or towards the widening fan of the countryside, in the direction of Cuire and Caluire, where General Delestraint, Jean Moulin, and a full session of the *Conseil National de la Résistance* were surprised, in a doctor's house with green shutters, not unlike that, no doubt, of the counterfeiter's, as described by the engraver from la Croix-Rousse, in 1943: more than a fluke, in such a topography, and that can only be accounted for by an imprudence or a denunciation.[1] Further still beyond the Croix-Rousse lie the innumerable properties of the Mont-d'Or, in the valley of the Saône, the anarchical freedom of such places as l'Île-Barbe and Collonges, frequently described, like Vaise, as the regular headquarters of bandits and highwaymen, thieves and conspirators.

Between 1940 and 1945, Lyon became the capital of the Resistance, not only by default and because Paris was occupied from the start, not only because many Parisians found themselves swept there, perching in furnished rooms on the slopes, with no mail and no news of their relatives and faced with unexpected leisure and a totally unfamiliar mode of existence, when the floods of the *Exode* had at last receded, leaving people in unexpected places and, sometimes, in unhoped for situations – the mad of the Paris asylums briefly enjoying unprecedented freedom and even power, on one occasion exercised with extreme efficiency, long-term convicts from Clairvaux discovering the liberty of the open road as their gaolers fled ahead of the German columns, a *professeur de philo* at the Collège de Montargis who walked off westwards with a seventeen-year-old female pupil, leaving behind wife and family, and embarking on a five-year holiday – all interesting and encouraging lessons on the theme of

---

[1] It was widely believed at the time that the arrests at Caluire had been due to the imprudence or to the treason of René Hardy, an engineer and a member of the CNR, who had been captured by the Gestapo, tortured, and who claimed to have jumped from a train, while being escorted from one prison to another. He later turned up in Lyon and resumed contact with General Delestraint. The *affaire Hardy* gave rise to prolonged legal proceedings after the Liberation, and Hardy published his own account in a book.

public disaster and private opportunity, a theme that is of course very central to the study of any revolutionary period in terms of individuals[1] – not only for all these reasons, but primarily because it was still such a secret place and because, despite the expansion into la Guillotière and Villeurbanne and les Brotteaux, and the construction of wide avenues along the quays of the Rhône and through the centre of the peninsula, its recalcitrant terrain still naturally favoured the escaper and slowed down the pursuer, whether motorized or on foot, just as, fifteen or more years later, it was to favour the activities of local groups of the OAS. The disasters of 1940 enabled many Parisians, who had never previously thought of stopping there, in their headlong rush towards the sun and the beaches of the Mediterranean, to discover Lyon; none of those who survived is likely to forget the experience; and most would recognize a certain artistic suitability in the fact that the most dramatic, most dangerous, and most secretive period of their lives should have had as a predatory daily background the extraordinarily scenic, piled up, tiered terraces of that strange city, its tall houses staring out through long black windows, as through the gaping holes of nineteenth-century cannon fire – curling puffs of cotton-wool – or exploded infernal machines, their rectangles outlined bizarrely with the shattered relics of shutters, thousands and thousands of blind eyes, revealing nothing, like the space at the bottom of stone staircases, with the cluster of letter boxes, revealing only the names of tenants.[2] To destroy the diversity and the secrecy of Lyon, it would be necessary to blow it up, quarter by quarter, *montée par montée*, just as the German military authorities blew up the *Vieux-Port* of Marseille, destroying in the process *Marius* and *Olive*, the *pastis*-soaked world of Marcel Pagnol and the beloved sunny squares and secret places of the *bourlingueur*, at last, briefly, back in port, Blaise Cendrars.

It would be hard to think of any other city in Europe the inhabitants of which had been so completely conditioned by environment. This is why Lyon affords such an admirable example for the exploration of the

---

[1] Some of the more bizarre consequences of the *Exode*, in human terms, are recounted in Jean Vidalenc's excellent *L'Exode* (Paris, 1959). There are many eloquent accounts of the experience of life in Lyon during the Occupation, by refugees and *résistants* from Paris. The best is probably to be found in the admirably imaginative and beautifully written memoirs of the late Emmanuel Astier de la Vigerie, for whom, as for so many other Parisians, Lyon was a literary, as well as a deeply moving human, experience.

[2] Lyon has been surprisingly neglected by film producers; but the dramatic, intimate, and topsy-turvy qualities of the jumble of quarters and of the steep gradients have been very well rendered in two French films of great visual beauty: *Thérèse Raquin* – set in Lyon, quartier Saint-Paul, an admirable initiative on the part of the producer and a perfect background to that sordid story – and Jean-Pierre Fréville's sober, dignified, and utterly convincing *L'Armée des ombres*, with particular reference to the scene of the arrest in the restaurant.

relationship between public and private life, between public disaster and
private profit, between the public calendar of collective memory and collective vengeance, and the private calendar of love, seduction, and nostalgia. Lyon, unfortunately, but no doubt characteristically, was to throw up
no *Promeneur solitaire*, no *Hibou nocturne*, no Restif de la Bretonne, to
witness the violent events of the present and to record private anniversaries with his pocket-knife, in the stone of bridges and quays. And so we
have to grope our way, almost as blindly as the unfortunate garrison
commanders and the even more unfortunate troops, who felt themselves
ostracized by the generally silent and contemptuous inhabitants – even the
local prostitutes often would have nothing to do with them – and for
whom garrison duty in the Second City was the most fearful, most
dreaded imposition. Looks were enough. No wonder morale went
rapidly, drunkenness increased, no wonder garrisons had frequently to be
relieved![1] Lyon is, of course, an extreme example; and, from 1793 to 1803,
it might be said to have indulged in an 'occupation complex'. It was not
and is not the sort of place to reveal its carefully kept secrets, its mysterious cults, to the stranger, especially perhaps if he is a Parisian. One
Englishman at least, in recent times, has succeeded in crossing the
borderline and in gaining full admission to the club – *Lyonnais de part
entière* – and to be admitted to such a sanctum of regional patriotism
as *l'Académie des Pierres Plantées*. But it took him over forty years of
gargantuan eating to do so; the final result, however, was as convincing
as the transformation effect by Edouard Herriot, once he had likewise
been adopted.[2] Henri Béraud, as a member of the *Club des Cent Kilos*, as
well as a native of les Terreaux, was unusually well placed to observe
and to describe the beloved city of his childhood.[3] In such a situation, the
historian can only guess at what lay behind the violence and brutality of
word and deed. There remains for him, when confronted with this strange
city, a very great element of mystery.

But even in more settled places, like Rouen and its neighbourhood,
Dieppe and its hinterland, le Havre and its surrounding *communes*, there
are plenty of examples of a similar identification between public and
private crime, especially in the case of murder. The period of the
Directory, by throwing the electorate into an annual paroxysm of political intransigence at the time of the yearly convocation of the *assemblées
primaires* – themselves dangerously close to the always uneasy, rumour-
ridden period that immediately preceded the harvest and that, in times of

---

[1] *L'Armée révolutionnaire parisienne à Lyon et dans la région lyonnaise.*
[2] Sir Reginald Parr, British Consul-General at Lyon for over thirty years and personal friend
of Edouard Herriot.
[3] Henri Béraud, *La Gerbe d'or* and *Le Martyre de l'obèse.*

political uncertainty, would be further strained by reports, whether true or false, of arson, the burning of crops, and so on[1] – gave a further, artificial, constitutional stimulus to the politics of public and private vengeance. Each year, from 1796 to 1799, the meeting of the electoral assemblies is heralded, a few weeks ahead, and accompanied, by a sudden rise in the murder rates; and this is as true of the scattered and much less dramatic murders of Upper Normandy as of the more organized acts of collective vengeance of the Rhône and of its neighbouring Departments. The difference is mainly one of proportion; the figures, let us say, for the Seine-Inférieure, are too small to be really eloquent or to illustrate a recurrent cycle of violence; and, in this part of France, as in the Eure-et-Loir, the distinction between public and private crime is much more difficult to make than in the clear-cut repetition of murder in the south. It exists none the less, though in an attenuated form; and no doubt one should not make too much of the distinction between the criminal, and apparently apolitical, activities of the *chauffeurs* in most areas of northern France, and the flamboyantly displayed political violence of southern gangs and southern bandits.[2] The victims, at least, would not have been over-concerned with such distinctions; and perhaps they should be allowed the last word.

---

[1] Marcel Reinhard, *La Chute de la royauté*, pp. 71, 76. The author makes two further points, on the subject of the yearly calendar of fear. The Flight to Varennes took place between Easter and the *Fête-Dieu* and on the eve of elections. One could not have imagined a worse combination.

[2] In *The Police and the People*, p. 150, I have made too much of the distinction between the purely criminal, apolitical, character of *chauffage* in the north of France, and the purely political aims of the *bandes* in the south. Both were forms of political protest, and both contained criminal elements. Some of the *sabreurs* were not above pillaging their victims.

8

*The Biographical Approach and the Personal Case History**

'... & là étant à nue tête et à genoux, dire & déclarer à haute et intelligible voix que méchamment & témérairement il a commis rébellion à la justice & tué d'un coup de pistolet ledit Berthault ... qu'il s'en repent & en demande pardon à Dieu, au Roy & à Justice, ce fait, le condamnons à être rompu vif sur un échafaud qui sera à cet effet dressé sur la place publique des halles ...'

> Extrait d'un jugement rendu par la sénéchaussée criminelle d'Angers le 9 avril 1778

'J'ai vécu sous le poignard 18 mois, on est venu chez moi pour m'assassiner, j'ai reçu un coup de fusil au milieu de la nuit, rien ne m'a effrayé ...'

> Musquinet-Lapagne à son frère, le 22 pluviôse an II (10 February 1794)

'Il en résulte que ledit Musquinet est un de ces hommes profondément scélérats, lesquels, cachés sous le masque du patriotisme, ne s'occupent qu'à ourdir les trames les plus funestes au salut du peuple ... on les voit se remuer en tous sens pour égarer et tromper les bons citoyens, et les amener à s'entre-égorger et par ce moyen faire détruire le peuple par le peuple.'

> Acte d'accusation contre Musquinet-Lapagne devant le tribunal révolutionnaire de Paris, dressé le 26 ventôse an II (16 March 1794), jour de sa condamnation à mort et de son exécution

(The three extracts concern the same man.)

THERE WAS, THEN, a fusion between the public and the private life of the counter-revolutionary. There existed, too, no doubt, a continuity, a natural gradation between his pre-revolutionary existence and his political militancy and semi-criminal activity of the revolutionary period. It was normal for a *faux saunier* to enlist as a *sabreur*, for a smug-

---

* From *Reactions to the French Revolution*, pp. 63–126.

gler to seek a new vocation as a counterfeiter or as a distributor of *faux assignats* or *faux mandats*. Many case histories illustrate the ease and naturalness of such transformations – perhaps too strong a word to describe processes as a result of which people slipped, almost imperceptibly, from one form of semi-criminal activity to another, from private violence, to public and collective violence – as well as emphasizing the importance of accident and chance opportunity in the development of a completely new activity.

Revolutionary periods are, of course, particularly rich in both accident and chance, and thus offer a tempting premium to all those for whom, in the normal course of events, the promise of sudden change, promotion, enrichment, excitement, had seemed definitely excluded. This is another way of saying that a revolutionary crisis, in any of its constantly changing and rapidly developing phases, offered not just one, but a series, of chances to those who had done badly in life or who had been done badly by life, to better themselves. For some – the more elevated, the better-educated, the chance would come in 1789, the time when the call came for Robespierre and his like, provincial lawyers, barristers, obscure law officers, provided with an excellent education that had, nevertheless, resulted in fifteen or twenty years of social frustration, personal humiliation, and professional marination in towns that, further, had little in the way of intellectual stimulus or excitement to offer. A few, like Brissot, had come up to the capital a few years earlier. But the fate of a Brissot or a Hébert, in the four or five years before the Revolution, was not likely to encourage others to emulate them. Brissot had eked out a wretched, undignified existence as a hack-pamphleteer, having to sing for his supper, doing the scorned rounds of the professional sponger. His chance came too with the arrival of so many provincials in 1789; he could at least offer to introduce them to the right people. Hébert had to sit in the box office of a theatre; and he was ignominiously dismissed even from that paltry job.

Most would have to wait till 1792, 1793, or 1794. For the crudest, most primitive, the opportunity would probably only come in 1795 or 1796. Each year, almost each month, in the revolutionary crisis, demanded its own particular skills, and recruited its own most appropriate temperament. Generally speaking, 1789 had less to offer, in terms of chance, to the majority of French males, than 1792 or later. 1789 had an appeal above all to *notables*; it enabled many of them to move almost overnight, from provincial, honourable obscurity, to prominence on the national, Parisian scene. War and Terror multiplied the need for privileged and militant minorities, especially in the extending bureaucracy of delation and surveillance. But they had little to offer, other than death or outlawry, to the younger age groups. In 1793 and in the year II, the obscure, frustrated, rancid thirty-five-year-old might at last find his feet and climb into a position of temporary power; they were years of opportunity for the townsman, at least as far down as the householder level. In 1795 and in the five years that followed, the provincial, especially the southerner, might expect some reward for previous frustration or even persecution. It was a good time for vengeance, and, by then, there were a great many avengers, potential, or actively engaged. It was also, to some extent, a period of anarchical freedom and opportunity, at least in violence, for the younger generations.

But before attempting thus to assess the impact of the revolutionary period in terms of individual opportunity and of personal and private life, before seeking to explore the slow, subterranean, perhaps unsuspected emergence of a terrorist mentality over a period of gestation, the historian like the police and the other repressive authorities before him, when contending with people at the lower and lowest levels of society, is confronted by the enormous problem, especially after five years of revolutionary upheaval, of establishing a given person's true identity. These people are not faceless; far from that, in the wake of police and judiciary, we know almost too much about their faces, and, indeed, about their physical appearance in general. Every scar has been counted, located, minutely described – from the middle of the left cheek down to the level of the right nipple – origins attributed: knife wound, sabre cut, agricultural accident, the marks left by a wild beast – marks of burns mapped, their causes suggested: gunshot, pistol, fire, cooking accident, hot iron, scalding. Traces of smallpox are monotonously depicted, freckles counted. There is an eager assessment of missing fingers, toes, stumps, hands, forearms, arms, feet, legs to the knees, whole legs, armies of one-eyed men and women are raised up, the origins of dislocated shoulders speculated about: an effect of one of the carrying trades, a building accident. Hernias and *descentes* are divined, by an ungainly manner of walk, through the privacy of clothing, their origins again suggested: the lifting of weights beyond the capacity of the human frame. A deformed leg may suggest a criminal past, a leg badly set, after a jump from some mouldering, medieval jail, *l'astragale*. Hunchbacks, semi-hunchbacks, those who lean forward while walking, those who cannot walk straight, those who tremble, those who are subject to epilepsy, those who cannot shut their mouths, are lined up, apparently every man, every woman in three, they appear so numerous. The noseless, a rarer breed, are noted *en passant*. Teeth are counted, their absence remarked upon; the appearances of those who have lost half their hair, through some nutritional deficiency, is carefully described. Colour of hair, colour of eyes, stance are bread-and-butter affairs, one would have thought hardly worth recording. But they seek to penetrate deeper: after the colour of the eyes, their expression: *le regard crâne, le regard impudent, le regard sournois, le regard inquiet, le regard franc, le regard timide, le regard changeant, les yeux exorbités, le regard noir, le regard doux* – eyes for every occasion, every temperament, every character, every mood. There must have been some past military experience here, for the manner of holding oneself is not forgotten: *marchant d'un pas leste, la démarche souple*. The pallor of disease, *signe avant-coureur de la mort*, is eagerly scrutinized, its causes guessed at: consumption, typhus, adulterated food. The very fat and the very thin are enumerated. The redness of a face may indicate a violent temperament, employment in a wine-shop or in the markets, Norman or Breton origins, an over-abundance of blood.

When the possibilities of the human body, with all its varied deficiencies, damages, abnormalities, and insufficiencies have been exhausted, attention is turned to artificial distinguishing marks, many of them provided by the object of so much scrutiny, perhaps too stupid, too unimaginative, or possibly too proud, to pause and think that he or she was thus writing his or her own *portrait parlé*. Tattoo marks are sought out and recorded with obvious eagerness; it is felt that they may reveal aspects of a past best forgotten but the memory of which had at one time been carefully cherished and thus preserved for posterity. They could be invaluable signposts to trade, provincial origin, army or naval service, travels, and frequentations. Other, more obvious marks had been provided gratis by a vigilant State: *V, VV, G*, branded on the shoulder. There is always a rapid inventory of garments, from hat to shoes, and with room for at least one complete change of clothing. If there are no shoes, bare feet, *sabots*, or slippers are indicated. The colour, quality, and material of clothing are minutely analysed; one is faced with a population dressed in coats and garments of many colours, the patchwork of poverty, theft, or charity, ill-stitched together, rather than the result of any aesthetic choice, the variety of hue increasing as one descended the social scale, especially among itinerants, for the peasant grandchildren and great-grandchildren of *le Lorrain* still affected the russet hue, the colour of earth. Jewellery is doubly indicative; it is easily described: golden hearts on a velvet band round the neck, silver cross on a metal chain, a gold medallion on a gold chain, double, triple pendants, ear-rings (male and female), bangles, ankle rings, striking watches worn at the side or round the neck. It is often suggestive of a form of employment, of provincial origin, or of association with crime. And naturally aesthetic judgements are mobilized, not in the interest of beauty – though, when dealing with the face, there is always an assessment of looks: good, medium, poor, bad, hideous, repulsive – but in that of calculation of means of existence, legitimate or illegitimate. A well-dressed female pedlar is likely to be a more dangerous person than one clothed in rags. A female itinerant, *ayant l'air d'une fermière, d'une marchande*, is probably up to no good, and has dangerous, desperate associates.

The repressive authorities were doing their best for themselves, if not for historians, for their *portraits parlés* tell us perhaps more about the police and the *gendarmes* than about those to whom these visible passports were so painstakingly fixed. In their avidity to accumulate distinguishing marks of every known kind – and they used their ears as well as their eyes, indeed were highly sensitive to the enormous variety of accents that might give so much away: *se disant beauceron, mais parlant comme les Auvergnats, se prétendant Parisien, mais ayant le parler normand, se disant Picard, mais parlant comme un provençal* – they no doubt ended up by creating a new category of collective identity which, because it was so generalized, would hardly be of much help as an aid to recognition. It was as if they had filled the highroads and the markets of France with a bizarre multitude of semi-cripples, a population of hunchbacks, of one-eyed men and women, of land-bound pirates, of legless, misshapen creatures, the denizens of a thousand *Cours des Miracles*, suddenly released by some cataclysm of nature from their dark, dank courtyards, to terrify the respectable, the healthy, the fully-formed. If, as the saying goes, *au royaume des aveugles, les borgnes sont rois*, there must have been more kings than subjects in late eighteenth-century France. The loss of an eye, a disfigurement, a scar on the cheek were not so much use as aids to identification, if every other person had lost an eye, was disfigured, or had a scar. It was, in any case, the disfigured, the maimed, and the crippled who were the most likely to be seen on the roads, in strategic positions outside churches, well to the fore in the path of processions, or to shock the unaccustomed traveller outside his posting-house or at the entrance to a great fair, vagrancy, itself so closely allied to crime and to every simple form of deception, putting a premium on all the more visible, dramatic forms of disease, illness, and maiming. No accomplished *errant vagabond* could set forth without a small suite of hobbling children, purportedly his own, though they seldom would be, were in fact more likely to have been borrowed, from the usual village stock of gnomes, idiots, small epileptics, and foamers-at-the-mouth. They were as much part of his stock in trade as the performing bear and the violin of the wandering Savoyard.

Nicknames, it is true, might be a useful supplement to the insufficiencies or the mysteries of an ill-kept or even deliberately falsified *état-civil*. It would seem unlikely, at least at first sight, that a bandit who was described as *les Gros Yeux*, had small ones, or that *l'Effrayant* had a reassuring, prepossessing appearance. A man who was described as *Pierre le Charpentier* was no doubt generally something of the kind – and dressed accordingly, or at least was seen ostensibly to carry around some of the characteristic tools of his trade – or had been at some stage of his career. *Le Provençal* might not be strictly accurate, especially when bestowed on someone who was at the time living in Paris or anywhere else north of the Loire. But even that was of some help; it indicated that, owing to his accent or to the colour of his hair, he stood out from the general mass of the inhabitants, just as much as the filthy matted hair and the stench of his clothing would indicate to all in the north a pedlar child from Savoy. Nicknames thus could be useful; or so we might suppose, as their use was encouraged by the military authorities of the old royal Army, as a guide to rapid identification and thus as a check on desertion. But things were not always what they seemed to be. In criminal or semi-criminal circles, nicknames were used as much deliberately to confuse the authorities, to send them off on false scents, or as the expression of a peculiar form of private humour, much appreciated among those who lived outside the social order, as an accurate description of appearance, origin, temperament, or trade. Thus, in the *bande Hullin, les Gros Yeux* often meant just the opposite, while the *Petit Beauceron* was more likely to be a giant from somewhere else. The key to such *noms de plaine* were closely kept secrets; under torture, a bandit would be more likely to reveal his own name, which, in the conditions of the eighteenth century, would probably be of little use to the authorities when applied to a man who had spent years wandering all over the kingdom, than his nickname, under which he had operated and by which he might be known to members of his own or other *bandes*, and through which he might be connected, in the eyes of groping and under-staffed repressive authorities – the countryside, both under the *ancien régime* and during the Directory, was terribly under-policed, though this was certainly not the case in the Terror years, when members of revolutionary committees gave much of their energy to the pursuit of the vagrant, the wanderer, and the very poor – with their activities in widely scattered parts of the country. One of the leading members of the *bande d'Orgères, le Rouge d'Auneau*, was to lay claim to several names – these could be had almost for the asking, at least under the *ancien régime*, when local *curés* and parishes would often be generous and remarkably undemanding with the issue of unofficial passports (under the Revolution, passports were better prepared and were granted much less readily; but they were easy to forge and no doubt easy to steal) – but there may in fact have been more than one *Rouge d'Auneau*, each answering proudly to that name and laying claim to some of the glory that might be attached to it. So that, in this particular milieu, nicknames might be a positive source of confusion to the authorities. Several persons might masquerade under the same surname; but, equally, several more might operate under the same nickname, all of them red-haired, none coming from Auneau. Charles Hullin himself is almost entirely enveloped in mystery;

he shunned publicity and was seldom seen by members even of his own gang, and then only in very small groups. Bandits were often foolish braggarts and drunkards, especially in female company; and when they lay claim, in their nicknames, to the virile or military virtues, they may be believed. But they were not entirely stupid and were, therefore, unlikely to use their nicknames as signposts to the police and the informer. Or rather they were signposts often designed to send both off on the wrong track.[1]

Such a constant preoccupation with deformities, distinguishing marks, and clothing nevertheless indicates the very real difficulty of establishing a person's true identity, especially at the lower levels of society and in a population composed largely of itinerants, including hordes of wandering children, some of whom had long since run away from home, others of whom had been sent out on the roads to beg or to peddle boxes of needles, pins, or matches by their parents.[2] Even at the height of the Terror, with the introduction of a multitude of paper checks and the formation, technically at least, of a *comité de surveillance* in every *commune* in the Republic – in mountain areas and in regions of poor communications, probably only one village in four ever actually possessed such an institution – and an unceasing check on travellers and on lodging-houses, it was always possible for the man on the run, for the ingenious adventurer, or the refractory priest, to pass through the net, especially if he had friends

---

[1] For much of the preceding passage on the subject of nicknames in use among bandits, and more especially among the members of the *bande Hullin*, a celebrated, amorphous group of highwaymen, robbers, and receivers that operated in the 1780s in the Beauce, in much the same areas as the later *bande d'Orgères*, I am greatly indebted to Dr Olwen Hufton, of the University of Reading, who has completed a detailed study of poverty and vagrancy and forms of crime in late eighteenth-century France. I have in particular much profited from her observations on the subject of nicknames in use in this *bande* and of the danger of taking them too literally. I would also like to express my thanks to her for her information on the subject of the use of deformed children in the pursuit of the more refined forms of begging and vagrancy. No student of the fringe elements of French society and of rural poverty can afford to neglect her admirably sensitive, imaginative, and compassionate work in these and related fields. Her method of research is an admirable example of the intelligent and telling use of the 'personal case history', especially in the instance of some of the more ingenious vagrants who sponged off whole communities – often comparatively poor ones – sometimes for a matter of days, by a liberal use of relics and medallions.

On the subject of military nicknames, see Robert Dauvergne, 'Les prénoms militaires en France sous l'ancien régime', *Mémoires, Paris et Île-de-France*, 1952. See also AN, BB 18 757 (commissaire près le tribunal d'Aix-en-Provence, au Ministre, 16 floréal an VI): 'depuis le peu de tems que je remplis les fonctions de commissaire ... j'ai été témoin que la nommée Bouchard femme Pegne, dite *la chiqueuse*, poissarde de cette commune d'Aix, prévenue de complicité des assassinats commis sur les détenus de la maison d'arrêt d'Aix, mise en accusation, a bien opté pour un autre tribunal que celui d'Aix.'

[2] Olwen Hufton, 'The Life of the Very Poor in the Eighteenth Century', in *The Eighteenth Century*, ed. A. Cobban (London, 1969).

or accomplices. In the much more anarchical conditions of the Directory, the assumption of several identities or the total loss of any identity other than the very vague clue afforded by a nickname was not a particularly difficult operation. Most of the members of the *bande d'Orgères* were in the habit of travelling with a pocketful of passports which they used indiscriminately in turn.[1]

An illustration of the enormous difficulties facing the judicial or police authorities, in their efforts to establish the true identity of a suspect, and thus to bring him to justice – for to try a man under a name other than his own would invite a case of *cassation* if it were discovered – is afforded in a report made by the commander of the Lyon garrison, dated 2 Pluviôse year VIII (22 January 1800), to the Minister of Justice. The report concerns a person describing himself as Louis Beau, '30 ans, natif de Rouen, doreur sur bois', suspected of desertion, highway robbery, theft, and murder. On cross-examination, Beau, 'prévenu ... d'assassinats, de massacres et de l'arrestation des malles ... jusqu'alors a dit avoir été baptisé dans l'église de Saint-Maclou de Rouen, dans le mois d'août 1770 ou 1771, ce qui a été reconnu faux' – the Lyon military authorities had got in touch with Rouen, the municipality of which replied that no such person existed on the parish registers for August of either year. On this occasion, the man had to be released, despite the heavy charges against him (he was said to be 'étroitement lié avec des voleurs redoutés, l'un nommé Maréchal, qui a été condamné à mort à Grenoble, et un autre nommé Bouchartat, évadé des prisons'). He was presumably re-arrested, for a few months later, in Fructidor, he claims to be Claude Cavaillon-Pinaud, native of Novalaise, in the Mont-Blanc, adding that he had left the village in 1793, at the age of twenty-three – he had probably been caught by conscription. This time, the Lyon judicial authorities were taking no chances; they had him escorted to his second alleged birthplace by a *posse* of *gendarmes*. Having got to Novalaise, he 'n'a pas su indiquer les noms des villages avoisinans Novaleize, ni les voisins de son prétendu père, ni le nom du Pasteur qui étoit à Novaleize lors de son départ, ni son signalement; il ne se souvient pas s'il y avoit des maisons en face de l'église, il ne se rappelle ni le nombre des cabarets, ni le nom des cabaretiers de l'endroit', this, one feels, was probably the test question, the one that clearly revealed his imposture – 'il ne connoît pas l'âge de son père ni de sa mère ... il ne connoissoit point le nom du hameau où demeuroient ses prétendus père et mère; il ne se rappelle point les noms de ses parrain et marraine.' He had not done very well, in the course of his excursion to Novalaise; he could not even remember the number of inns

---

[1] *Reactions to the French Revolution*, pp. 181–211. [Editorial note: For reasons of space it was impossible to include Cobb's chapter on the *bande d'Orgères* in the present volume.]

and the names of the innkeepers; he might be presumed, in the course of seven years – and much had happened in those seven years – to have forgotten the name and the appearance of the parish priest, or those of his godparents. However, 'contre tant de témoignages, il se trouve celui de la femme de Joseph Cavaillon qui le reconnoit pour son fils.'[1] It was a big step from Rouen to a small village in the arrondissement of Chambéry and it was clearly impossible to establish this man's true identity. We do not know what the Lyon authorities eventually did with him. But it would have been difficult to bring to trial a person with no past, or one with two conflicting pasts.

The case of Beau, or whatever his name may have been, is by no means rare. In Paris, the *Bureau Central* was daily faced with similar problems, in the course of the Directory. On 17 Floréal year VI (6 May 1798), the *Bureau* informs the Minister:

> Le nommé Bertrand, dit *la mouche* ... a été arrêté comme prévenu d'être évadé des fers et d'avoir changé de nom, ainsi que le font tous ceux qui parviennent à s'évader des bagnes. N'ayant plus aucun moyen de reconnaissance depuis que la marque a été abolie par les nouvelles lois nous avons envoyé ledit Bertrand à Bicêtre pour voir s'il n'y seroit pas reconnu par quelques forçats aussi évadés; plusieurs ont affirmé le reconnaître, mais ils n'ont pu se rappeller le nom sous lequel il a été condamné. Nous l'avons en conséquent fait ramener à la chambre de dépôt.[2]

The *Bureau* was more successful in its efforts to re-establish the past of two other *forçats*. On 26 Vendémiaire year VII (17 October 1798), the Minister is informed:

> Nous avons fait arrêter un nommé Claude-Denis Coisset, natif de Paris, âgé de 32 à 35 ans, de la taille d'un mètre 62 c., ayant les cheveux et sourcils noirs, le front petit, le nez gros, les yeux bruns, la bouche moyenne, le menton pointu, le visage oval, ayant une cicatrice au-dessus du sourcil, et une autre qui lui partage le sourcil gauche, comme prévenu de s'être évadé des fers, et connu pour être un fameux voleur, qui a subi plusieurs procès criminels. Cet individu nous ayant justifié de son congé de forçat de la peine de 2 années de fers qu'il avoit subie depuis l'an IV, nous étions sur le point de la relaxer, lorsque de nouveaux renseignemens nous sont parvenus sur son compte ... le nommé Claude-Denis Coisset, dit *l'enfant*, exerçant la profession de fondeur, doreur, et acheveur, nous est indiqué comme ayant été condamné à Paris en 1792, par un premier jugement à la peine de 24 années de fers, et par un second jugement à la peine de mort, auxquelles peines il s'étoit soustrait, parce que les brigands

---

[1] AN, BB 18 687 (rapport au commandant militaire de Lyon, 2 pluviôse an VIII; commissaire près le tribunal criminel du Rhône au Ministre, 3 fructidor an VIII).
[2] AN, BB 18 757 (Bureau Central au Ministre, 17 floréal an VI).

qui présidoient aux massacres du 2 septembre à … la Force l'avoient mis en liberté.[1]

A startling instance of a public catastrophe being put to private advantage. Coisset had been identified *in extremis*.

Even more indicative of the methods employed by the police and the judicial authorities when faced with this intractable problem is the cross-examination, by the same *Bureau*, on 25 Ventôse year VII (15 March 1799) of a suspect from the Yonne:

> Germain-Vincent Boulot … 32 ans à 33 ans, natif d'Irancy [Yonne] … marchand colporteur, demeurant à Paris, rue de la Verrerie, No 112 …
> D. Depuis quand êtes-vous à Paris?
> R. Depuis 29 ans passés … j'ai été absent de Paris en 1787 …
> D. N'êtes-vous pas connu aussi sous le surnom de *Le Moine*?
> R. Non, Citoyen.
> D. N'avez-vous pas été condamné à Paris le 18 juillet 1787 à la peine de mort par la Cour des Monnoies pour distribution de faux écus? Cette peine n'a-t-elle pas été commuée en celle des galères à vie dans le mois d'août suivant et ne vous êtes point évadé de la frégate *La Sybille* le 10 juin 1790?
> R. Non, Citoyen.
> A lui observé que l'individu dont il s'agit avoit une cicatrice à la dernière phalange de la main droite et du côté droit. Sommé de nous représenter cette main pour vérifier si la marque s'y trouve … nous y avons trouvé cette cicatrice à la phalange indiquée …
> D. Avez-vous déjà été arrêté?
> R. J'ai été arrêté en l'an III, pour le même motif qu'aujourd'hui … [The report continues:] Il est connu parmi les voleurs comme évadé des fers, et parmi les citoyens honnêtes comme un mauvais sujet … un dernier motif sur lequel il s'appuie pour prouver sa non-identité est de ce que n'ayant point été flétri, il ne pouvoit être considéré comme étant celui recherché pour cause d'evasion des fers, puisque sous l'ancien régime les condamnés aux fers étoient marqués *GAL*; mais que cette dernière objection est facile à refuter au moyen de ce que la flétrissure ne pouvoit avoir lieu qu'en vertu d'un jugement, et que celui rendu … contre Boulot … avoit prononcé la peine de mort … et qu'on ne pouvoit lui faire appliquer le fouet ni la marque en pareilles circonstances.

Although given away by the scar on his small finger, Boulot continued to fight back, in defence of his 'non-identity'. In a letter to the Minister, addressed from Bicêtre, he argued:

---

[1] AN, BB 18 760 (Bureau Central de la police de Paris au Ministre, 26 vendémiaire an VII). See also AN, BB 18 753 (Desmaisons, chef du Bureau Central de la Police de Paris, au Ministre, 8 fructidor an V): 'D'après les renseignemens que j'ai pris relativement au nommé *François Joubert* … il paroît que cet individu n'est autre que le nommé *Louis Carpentier*, condamné le 17 décembre 1792, à 24 ans de fers, par le tribunal de l'Eure, puis évadé du port de Brest le 13 vendémiaire an III [4 October 1794].'

... ma taille est portée à 5 pieds 3 pouces; maintenant, quoique je n'aie aucune infirmité, je n'ai que 5 pieds 8 lignes ... les yeux du condamné [of 1787] étoient roux, les miens sont gris bruns, son visage est porté rond, et le mien est absolument oval, il avoit le front bas, et j'ai le front très haut ... le véritable condamné ne s'est évadé qu'en 1790 ... à l'époque de ce jugement j'étois à Irancy, lieu de ma naissance, d'où je ne suis parti que vers la mi-novembre.

Despite the obvious discrepancies between the two *portraits parlés*, the one drawn up in 1787, the other either in 1795 or, more likely, in 1799 – and Boulot was the first to point out that he could hardly have grown shorter in the course of these ten years and that it would have been a freak of nature if his eyes had changed colour – Desmaisons, in charge of the *Bureau Central*, remained unconvinced by his disclaimers. 'Vous reconnoîtrez aisément,' he wrote to the Minister, on 18 Germinal year VII (7 April 1799), 'malgré les dénégations hardies de cet individu, qu'il n'est autre que le forçat du même nom [The weakness of Boulot's position was that he could not deny being Germain Vincent Boulot, though he claimed that he was not the same Germain Vincent Boulot as had escaped from the galleys; by some extraordinary coincidence, there had been two people, with the same name and Christian names, both from Irancy and both of an age.] qui s'est évadé des fers, et que par conséquent, ladite administration a fait sagement de le réintégrer à Bicêtre, en attendant qu'il soit reconduit au bagne de Brest.'[1] That was no doubt the end of the matter so far as poor Boulot was concerned. Perhaps, in view of the obvious contradictions between the two descriptions of what was claimed to be the same man over a period of ten years, an element of doubt remains. But the affair emphasizes above all the inaccuracies of checks on identity that were likely to be both wildly inaccurate and heavily repetitive. Even the scar on the right small finger may not have been a serious indication.

In greatly increasing mobility, in producing a hiatus between the old

---

[1] AN, BB 18 762 (Desmaisons au Ministre, 18 germinal an VII). The difficulty of establishing a true identity and of proving a valid past could, in certain circumstances, also work against the interests of former convicts. A case in point is that of Caste, who writes to the Minister, 10 Thermidor year V (28 July 1797): 'Jean-Jacques Caste, natif d'Étiolles près Paris, vous expose que, condamné par arrêt du Parlement de Paris, en date du 20 mars 1789, aux galères perpétuelles pour vol, avec effractions, cette peine a, suivant le vœu de la loi du 3 septembre 1791, été commuée en celle de 10 années de fers. Jean-Jacques Caste ignore à quelle époque précise, et par quel tribunal, cette commutation fut prononcée. Tout ce qui s'offre à sa mémoire c'est que ce fut en 1793. C'est peu après qu'ayant trouvé les moyens de s'évader Caste fut rendu quelque tems à la liberté. Aujourd'hui que de nouveaux fers l'ont enchaîné ... il est pour lui de la plus grande importance ... que le jugement de commutation arrive en même tems que lui au bureau des chiourmes du port où il sera conduit. Faute de cette précaution, Caste serait exposé à subir la peine que lui inflige l'arrêt du Parlement, ou tout au moins la plus forte que prononce le Code pénal, celle de 24 années de fers' (BB 18 753).

judicial and criminal personnel and that of the new courts, in abolishing branding and the only physical checks on a criminal past provided by the old penal code, and in putting a premium on every form of imposture and on the assumption not only of false identities, but also of false functions, the revolutionary period and that which followed both increased the possible range of fraud and facilitated escape from justice. Beau was certainly no exception in this part of the world. Whole areas appear to have contrived to have existed quite outside the chartered dictates of the *enregistrement*; and in a Department where all the local authorities were in the habit, no doubt ingrained over the years, but further stimulated by the demands of conscription, of falsifying or simply leaving blank – they could always be filled in later with false entries – the registers of the *état-civil*, a very large section of the population would escape altogether such written regimentation, living under fictitious names with equally fictitious wives.

In a Department like the Ardèche, there seem to have been no limits to the impudent ingenuity of the local community, happy collectively to defy the trying demands of authorities optimistic enough to attempt to pinpoint identity, age, and family status. It was not surprising that this wild place enjoyed such a persistent reputation for banditry, White terrorism, and law evasion when, even as late as 1801, it still remained very difficult to prove a given person's marital status or true surname and where, often with the open connivance of the local authorities, men were prepared to dress up as women in order to assume marriages with other men. Administrative anarchy on such a scale must defy even a regime as meticulous as the Consulate. It was not surprising that, throughout the Revolution and under the Directory, the Ardèche as a whole, with the possible exception of a few urban oases such as Privas, Tournon, and Annonay – but certainly not Aubenas or Largentière – contrived to live largely outside established law and to ignore the dictates of orthodoxy, much as if this recalcitrant country, with its appalling communications, had constituted an independent principality of banditry and ultra-royalism.

THE RISE AND FALL OF A PROVINCIAL TERRORIST

Bearing in mind the limitations imposed by fraud, guile, or collective administrative complicity on the extensive use of the personal case history, people like Beau and Departments like the Ardèche being as recalcitrant to historical documentation as to the demands of justice, a technique involving recourse to the biographical approach could be fruitfully applied to the exploration of a terrorist mentality and to the sources of revolutionary commitment. Terrorists were not born overnight, and as the average age of the committed militant was from thirty to forty-five,[1] the key to his commitment must be sought, when such evidence exists about people not given to writing up their personal recollections, in a life of hardship, deprivation, and brutality during the decade preceding the revolutionary outbreak. In other words, it is necessary to extend to the humbler levels of society the benefits of the 'long view', exploited with great success by such talented biographers as Marcel Reinhard or Leo Gershoy, in their studies of Carnot and Barère.[2] After so many years devoted to the investigation of 'social structures', it would be reasonable to insist upon the urgency of returning to the more conventional bio-graphical approach, while, of course, still taking into account the collect-ive assumptions of a trade, of a certain province, or of a given town or quarter, when attempting to assess the motivations of revolutionary militancy.

There is an admirable illustration of this theme in a recent biography of a middle-ranking terrorist,[3] previously only known to history as the sub-ordinate agent of the Committee of General Security who had carried out the arrest of André Chénier – a purely anecdotal claim to fame – in which the author proposes as his aim – and it is one that should be that of any specialist of the revolutionary period – 'de remonter à un passé tout proche ... et d'examiner la structure rigide et désespérante des cadres [de l'ancienne société], la dureté générale des conditions de vie'. And of the

---

[1] These calculations have been made on the basis of the average age of members of *comités de surveillance* in a number of towns and villages of Upper Normandy and Burgundy. They represent, therefore, a bureaucratic type of militant, rather than the spontaneous, anarch-ical, ultra-revolutionary individualist, though, from the little we know about this last type, he would fall into much the same age group. See *The Police and the People*, p. 168 (I) (2). See also my *Les Armées révolutionnaires*, I, pp. 314–29, and II, pp. 547–54, 619–22.

[2] Marcel Reinhard, *Le Grand Carnot*, 2 vols. (Paris, 1950); Leo Gershoy, *Bertrand Barère, A Reluctant Terrorist* (Princeton, 1962).

[3] Claude Hohl, *Un agent du Comité de sûreté générale: Nicolas Guénot. Contribution à l'Histoire de la Terreur* (Commission d'Histoire économique et sociale de la Révolution française, Mémoires et Documents, XXII, Paris, Bibliothèque Nationale, 1968). M. Hohl is at present *Directeur du service des Archives départementales de l'Yonne*. Much of his material is derived from the judicial and police series of the *dépôt* in Auxerre; but he has also used the F7 and BB 18 series in the *Archives Nationales*. His biography is a model of research method, indicating as it does the full possibilities of work at this level in the *Archives départementales*, and, indeed, in the *Archives communales*, which he uses to great effect for Voutenay, Guénot's birthplace, and the combination of research on local and Parisian levels. Guénot, it is true, is a particularly good case, as he obligingly divided his career between the Yonne and Paris, thus offering the historian many glimpses both of the public and the private aspects of his very long career – for he further obliged the historian by living on into his late seventies.

For a further example of the use of a number of personal case histories, see my articles: 'La commission temporaire de Commune-affranchie' and 'Quelques conséquences sociales de la Révolution dans un milieu urbain d'après des documents de la société révolutionnaire de Lille', in *Terreur et subsistances*, pp. 55–94, 151–78.

pre-revolutionary career of his subject, the same author writes: 'La période de sa vie qui précède la Terreur prend rétrospectivement l'allure d'un temps de préparation au rôle que cet individu allait tenir.'

Nicolas Guénot, in fact, offers an almost ideal case history of the emergence of a terrorist mentality and of the progressive commitment, in individual terms, to the politics of violence. It so happened that he plumped for the Jacobin Terror; he might equally well have become a member of a royalist murder gang, a *sabreur* in the service of Christ & King. The important thing about him was that his place of birth, his trade, the terrible hardships that he had suffered in the fifteen years before the outbreak of the revolutionary crisis had predestined him to the politics of intransigence and vengeance. For Guénot, as for so many archetypal terrorist militants, the Revolution, and more especially the exceptional circumstances of 1793 and the year II, afforded the opportunity to get even with a cruel society and to take it out on his former exploiters: in this case, the rich and powerful timber merchants of the valleys of the Yonne and the Cure, on the edge of the lakes and forests of the brutal and wild Morvan.[1]

Guénot was born in April 1754 – four years earlier than Robespierre – in the small *bourg* of Voutenay, in the Yonne (Upper Burgundy), a place numbering a little over three hundred inhabitants at the beginning of the century, on the Cure, a few miles south of the great timber port of Vermenton, where, at about this time, in the 1750s, Restif's cousins were so successfully engaged in the wood trade for the provisioning of the Paris fuel ports.[2] He was the second son, and had a younger brother and a sister. He died in May 1832, aged seventy-eight, probably as the result of the cholera epidemic that swept France, England, Italy, and Russia in the course of that and the two following years. In his quite exceptional longevity, he was no doubt untypical of the average terrorist militant, a great many of whom were never even to see the Restoration; but it was only in this respect that he was untypical of the common run of the more enthusiastic acolytes of terror and repression, delation, and denunciation.

His life too might be taken as an illustration of that theme so much favoured by eighteenth-century novelists, so strongly condemned by the physiocrates: *la montée à Paris, les dangers de la ville*, the corrupting influence of the capital of luxury and vice. Only ten years earlier, *Monsieur Nicolas* – the *Edmond* of *Le Paysan perverti* – the printer's apprentice from nearby Auxerre – had come up to Paris, on the *coche d'eau*, to seek out his fortune. Guénot, too, it might be said, likewise became contaminated, though he had never had the chance that Restif had had of a well-

---

[1] Jean Vidalenc, *Le Peuple des campagnes* (Paris, 1969), p. 94: 'Les querelles des flotteurs de bois de Clamecy avec leurs employeurs alimentèrent souvent la chronique judiciaire.'
[2] Restif, *Monsieur Nicolas*, II, p. 1018, III, p. 1605, quoted in *The Police and the People*, p. 229 (I).

to-do, patriarchal family background, an education with the Jansenists of
Bicêtre, the constant care for his welfare of an elder brother who was a
priest, and a network of family relationships provided for him when he
first went to Auxerre. His father was a river-worker, like most of the
inhabitants of this large village, situated in the thick woodlands of the
southern tip of the Yonne. Guénot himself was naturally, inevitably,
drawn to the trade of *flotteur* – the men, mostly from the Morvan and the
Avallonnais, who floated the *trains de bois* down the Cure and the Yonne,
into the Seine at Montereau, thence to the wood ports of Paris at
Charenton and quai du Louvre. Like most dangerous trades – the men
often had to wade up to their necks, in icy and fast-flowing waters, in
order to retrieve runaway logs that had broken away from the rafts – the
flotteurs constituted an intensely proud corporation, famous for their
solidarity and feared for their readiness to brawl. They were ruthlessly
exploited and ill-paid by the timber merchants. No trade could have been
more readily orientated towards Paris, the *flotteurs* sometimes doing the
journey a dozen or twenty times a year. Many of them stayed in the
capital, whether in winter employment, when the river traffic was interrupted till the March floods had subsided, or, in a desperate endeavour to
escape from the servitude of the river altogether, in some other following,
inland from the quays, but always within striking distance of them, as
if the river even then exercised over them some sort of fascination, as a
lifeline connecting them with a hard, rough childhood, with home and
origin, and with their visible reminder, the *coche d'eau*, which brought up
to Paris its daily contingent of Bourguignons and Bourguignonnes, of
Morvandiaux and Morvandielles, as if indeed they preferred the proximity of known exploiters, of the timber merchants, to that of complete
strangers plying trades that had no connection with the river.

Guénot made his first journey to Paris on a *train de bois*, at seventeen,
in 1771. But he had had the independence – or perhaps the good sense –
for Voutenay could offer him nothing better than this dangerous and
physically demanding trade – to stay on in the capital, working, as far as
one can make out, first of all on the quays of the timber port of the
Louvre, as a docker or a porter – he was clearly a man of enormous physical strength, as indeed the *flotteurs* and the *gens de rivière* had to be – but
before long, he moved slightly inland, to the vicinity of the Halle au bled,
that is still within reach of the river world, its inns and its wild personnel.
He was engaged for a time as a temporary *cocher de fiacre*, and, though
he did not possess a *patente*, which was required from the *Lieutenant
criminel* to exercise this important trade – for the *cochers* were liable to
come by a great deal of random information that might be of interest to
the government, whether it was a matter of abducting a girl to the discreet
house of a man of high connections, of transporting stolen goods, or of

getting out of the city, to a safe hiding-place, any person who needed to escape the attentions of the authorities with a maximum of speed and discretion – he seems to have established, in the course of the first half of the 1770s, some useful connections with the police, as well as with the underworld. It was difficult to be a *cocher* without being both a part-time informer and an occasional auxiliary of the underworld. Both connections were well worth keeping up for a man without means, and with only the minimum of education – Guénot could in fact read and write, but his spelling needs to be read out loud for his prose to be understandable – anxious to make his way in the world; and, unlike many other Bourguignons who had come up to the capital, he possessed no relatives in the city.

At twenty-one, in 1775, he enlisted in the *Gardes Françaises* – a choice that tells us a lot about the young man, for they were about the most brutal, violent, and undisciplined regiment of the old army.[1] They were intensely proud of their ability to kill, rapidly and silently, in defence of their regimental honour; and they were consequently very dangerous people to drink with, even more dangerous people to take on in a round of toasts or in a series of bets. As the result of a very long stay in Paris – they were attached to palace service in Versailles – they had come to establish close links both with the underworld and with the police. It was generally understood that the lowest sort of prostitutes reverted to them by right – the next grade belonged, by a similar understanding, to the better-placed informers.[2] So, for the second time, Guénot was moving in an underworld of uncertain frontiers, but in which the police, the soldiery, and the criminal could meet on their own terms. In the course of seven years' service – all of it apparently spent in Paris – he was almost constantly in trouble with the magistrates and the *commissaires*, mostly for assault and for other acts of violence committed both on civilians and on soldiers of other corps in the course of weekend dances or in cafés. He was also court-martialled more than once for indiscipline and insolence and, on one occasion, for having attacked an NCO (who had apparently provoked him, for otherwise he would have been punished far more severely – he got away with a flogging). He was in and out of prison throughout his service; and in one of the brawls in which he was involved and in which

---

[1] *The Police and the People*, p. 325.

[2] *Monsieur Nicolas*, IV, 1757, p. 1957: 'Nous trouvâmes un jour, rue Beaurepaire, une jeune fille, prostituée de la veille elle avait tous les symptômes de la fraîcheur et du non-usage. Un soldat-aux-gardes, qui en eut vent, par le Monsieur de cette maison, disputait, quand nous entrâmes, pour l'avoir gratis, attendu que c'était le droit des Militaires, des Espions (disait-il), d'avoir la fleur des filles. On portait alors l'épée. J'en avais une longue et plate . . . Gaudet n'avait qu'un couteau de chasse; il apprenait à faire les armes depuis notre vie libertine; il se jeta sur mon épée et provoqua le soldat.'

sabres were drawn, he was severely wounded in the left arm, the use of which he never fully recovered. At twenty-nine, in 1783, after the peace, he was dishonourably discharged, and found himself, for the first time, *sur le pavé de Paris*. He was either expelled, or threatened with Bicêtre; or he may even have made the decision to return to Voutenay.

In any case, he went back there in 1783. But, with an arm almost entirely out of action, he could not go back to his original trade. For a few months, he acted as a farm labourer in the employment of his younger brother, who had made a success of his *vignoble*. But this must have been intolerably humiliating to the former *garde française*; and he was soon dismissed by his brother, after a further assault. In 1784, he took to the woods and was never seen without his rifle, clutched in his valid arm. He was now homeless, sleeping at night in huts of stolen logs, thatch and straw, roaming the woods by day and living off random poaching and the theft of wood. By 1785, he was once more in trouble, this time with the *maréchaussée*, following an assault on a farmer whom he suspected of having denounced him for poaching and whom he had shot at; he was also accused of having attempted to set fire to his farm. He was in prison in Vermenton for some time, and had become an object of fear to most of his compatriots, including the members of his own family.

It is not known when he returned to Paris. But he had had enough of Voutenay. All we know is that he was back in the capital at the beginning of 1789, and that he was once more exercising the trade of *cocher de fiacre*, this time with a proper *patente*. He had, it seems, also re-established useful contacts with *les mouches* – that myriad of informers employed by the *Lieutenant de Police* – and was almost certainly himself putting in occasional and appreciated work in this capacity. At this stage, public catastrophe and private fortune blended, in this particular instance to give to this man's mediocre, unprepossessing, and generally unsuccessful career the impetus and acceleration of outside events.

If he had not been born in the 1750s, Guénot would no doubt have been of little interest to the social historian. He was no exception to the general run of the *flotteurs* of the Avallonnais and the Morvan, among the most truly savage people in France – urban witnesses earlier in the century, at about the time of Guénot's birth, had described these rivermen as Hottentots, and it is true that the much-vaunted Enlightenment would not have meant very much to people who looked to the river for their living; Voutenay was an exceptionally brutal community, in which the timber merchants exploited to the full an abundant local labour force of landless rivermen, for as long as they were strong enough to carry out their herculean task. (They might be good for fifteen years or so, from the time of their first employment at adolescence – fifteen or sixteen – if, in the meantime, they had had the good fortune not to have been drowned or permanently maimed, or had not died of consumption or of some other disease of the lungs to which their watery calling naturally exposed them, especially at the time of the great spring floodwater, after the long interruption of the winter months, when the logs could go hurtling towards Paris – a period naturally favoured by the wood merchants, as prices would then be almost as high as in the late autumn.) There was not much future for the retired *flotteur* unless, like Restif's sober cousins, he could become a minor entrepreneur in his own right, in charge of the *trains de bois* for the profit of a company.[1]

But Guénot was a man to whom the Revolution came almost exactly at the right moment, considering his age and his condition, as an opportunity to better himself, as well as a last chance to escape from a life previously marked by consistent failure. It is, of course, easy to blame him for his own misfortunes. Yet it is difficult to see how a more patient, more docile man could have bettered himself, at the level at which he had been forced to live. His violence was as much the result of rage and frustration at an unjust order of things, as a product of temperament and a result of long periods of heavy drinking in braggart military company. So the Revolution came as his big, unique chance. And, up and down the country, there must have been tens of thousands of men like him, of whom we know little or nothing. His military experience served him at last in enabling him to cut some sort of a figure in the quarter in which he had set up; he had had the good sense, for a man with a past that could be embarrassing, on returning to Paris, to establish residence in a District that he had not formerly inhabited, so that his escapades in the *Gardes Françaises* could be conveniently forgotten, while his value as an instructor to the newly constituted *Garde nationale* would gain him a certain prestige among his new neighbours. Former NCOs and soldiers were among the chief beneficiaries of the early years of the Revolution and, indeed, of the Revolution as a whole. Only actors stood to profit so much from the violent hiatus in society.

His new residence, perhaps not untypically, was near the Palais-Royal, in what was to become the Section de la Butte-des-Moulins, or Section de la Montagne. Guénot was thus near the principal centres of gambling, prostitution, and receiving. By 1791, he had been promoted to the position of unofficial auxiliary to the *commissaire de police* of that District. The same year, along with another *cocher de fiacre* and a laundryman, he

---

[1] *Monsieur Nicolas*, III, 1755, p. 1605: 'Mes deux cousins, par leur mérite personnel, s'étoient élevés à l'emploi de facteurs, ce qui les avoit tirés de la classe des tricoteurs qu'ils commandoient: leurs voyages étoient payés comme pour un trayeur, à chacun des dix trains descendans à Paris, qui étoient sous leur inspection, et ils faisoient bien leurs affaires. Ils savaient en outre parfaitement travailler à la vigne, et on les estimoit beaucoup à Vermenton, en qualité de vignerons.'

was rewarded by the municipal authorities for having uncovered and denounced a group of counterfeiters, associated with a counter-revolutionary, the sieur de Coligny; but the significant fact about this incident was that he warned some members of the gang of their impending arrest, so that they were able to make their escape. It seems probable that he may have had a share in their profits. In June 1792, he briefly entered the prison service, as turnkey in Sainte-Pélagie, while at the same time acting as a regular informer. After the September Massacres, we find him helping the *commissaire* of the place Vendôme, with particular responsibility for the lodging-houses, numerous in a quarter contiguous to the Palais-Royal. This was a further opportunity for him to exploit his specialized knowledge of the personnel of prostitution, and no doubt brought further profits. At about the same period, he carried out an unauthorized house search in the Section de la Halle au Bled, and was momentarily suspended from his rather vague functions in the neighbouring Section.

Early in 1793, he was transferred to the service of the *commissaire* of the Section des Piques – still near the Palais-Royal, which seems to have been his lodestar – and with special responsibility for the surveillance of the prostitutes, lodging-house keepers, speculators, deserters, and runaway noblemen – a profitable combination in its potentialities for graft. In February, he was involved in the uncovering of a gang of receivers, led by an old-clothes merchant who had been attached to the administration of the Mont-de-Piété. As on a previous occasion, Guénot was accused of having given some members of the gang, including its chief, the tip, so that the most important were able to escape. One of his colleagues was sentenced, as a result of this act of collusion, to twelve years in the galleys, but Guénot was acquitted by a Paris criminal court; he seems at this time to have enjoyed the protection of the *Commune*.

He was now given a roving commission to keep an eye on the *garnis*, the Mont-de-Piété, and prostitution – the trinity of escape, receiving, and vice. He was also once more carrying out house searches, armed with a pistol and a sabre and wearing an official sash. In March–April 1793, his beat was extended to include the Champs-Élysées; this brought him in a more extensive clientele of conjurors, magicians, jugglers, sword-swallowers, tightrope walkers, palmists, artificial savages, and hucksters, who plied in the booths and tents that thrived in this frontier zone of the capital, in the gardens and undergrowth off the wide avenues – a paradise for pickpockets and a trap for the gaping provincial.

By the autumn of 1793, he had graduated further to the position of accredited agent of the *comité de surveillance du Département de Paris*,[1]

---

[1] Henri Calvet, *Un instrument de la Terreur à Paris: le Comité de salut public ou de surveillance du Département de Paris* (Paris, 1941).

carrying out on its behalf repressive missions and arrests in the neighbour-hood of Paris. But his greatest opportunity came at the end of that year – he was then thirty-nine – when he began to be employed as a full-time agent of the Committee of General Security,[1] while still retaining his rather ill-defined post in the Section des Piques – the double award of a persistent and zealous informer. It was in this capacity that, on 17 Ventôse year II (7 March 1794), he carried out the arrest of André Chénier, in Auteuil, perhaps his principal claim to fame with most historians, but not the most significant event in his career as a terrorist.

More characteristic was his denunciation of a group of timber mer-chants from his own village, whom he chanced upon in a café near the Seine and whom he had the great satisfaction both of denouncing, as having evaded the *maximum*, and subsequently arresting. Among his other catches in the course of the spring and early summer of 1794 were Vergennes, several members of the Loménie de Brienne family, and the baron de Grimaldi – quite a distinguished bag, in fact. While on these repressive missions in the District de Sens, in his own Department, he also arrested several timber merchants and large farmers. He was also to be involved in one of the most controversial missions, to the village of Viarmes, in the bitterly quarrelsome District de Gonesse.[2]

There is no doubt that he immensely enjoyed this opportunity to turn the tables on his class enemies, as well as the exercise of power, even at this modest, purely executive level (Guénot was in fact rather more than a mere *porteur d'ordre* who carried out arrest warrants, for he was sufficiently in the confidence of the police Committee to initiate arrests at his own discretion). We can see him entering houses in the course of a night search, armed with pistol and sabre, and proudly displaying his badge of office, and girt with a tricolour ribbon, in an effort to emulate the prestigious *Représentants en mission*. When he delivered a warrant, he accompanied his action with a crude commentary, deriving great satisfac-tion from blood-curdling threats against the rich. Meanwhile, his ill-spelt letters flowed in unabated to the Committees and to Fouquier. He enjoyed the Terror, had reached the high spot of his career at forty, was in it for what he could get out of it, and had the further satisfaction no doubt of feeling that the enemies of the Republic were also his own. Many of those whom he arrested he had known before the Revolution. He was undoubtedly partly motivated by considerations of vengeance; but, in view of his subsequent career, this is not a reason to doubt his sincerity as a terrorist. He certainly used the Terror to carry out his own private war against the rich; but some at least of these may well have sinned against *la*

[1] This Committee employed a large number of agents all over France.
[2] *Les Armées révolutionnaires*, II, pp. 486, 532, 612, 798.

sainte loi du maximum. He was to have a very long time to reflect on his role as a terrorist; for his iron constitution played on him the cruel trick of keeping him alive for another thirty-eight years.

However, in Floréal year II (April–May 1794), he appears to have been dismissed, on a charge of embezzlement, in one of those extremely complicated affairs, involving the threat of arrest as a form of blackmail that so often deepens the history of the Terror. In any case, he seems to have fallen foul of Le Bas, the *robespierriste* member of the police Committee and, one might think, a dangerous person to quarrel with at this stage. He kept away from the Committee for the rest of the summer and even failed to draw his full pay. His disgrace was bound to have come about sooner or later; but, as far as Guénot was concerned, it had happened at a most fortunate time and through the agency of just the right person. He was still in disgrace, possibly even in prison, at the time of 9 Thermidor, a circumstance that enabled him to pass as a *victime des triumvirs*, as well as of Le Bas and Duplay, thus securing his full clearance early in the year III and preserving him from the more bitter effects of the Thermidorian reaction. After being formally acquitted on the embezzlement charge, in Frimaire year III (November–December 1794), he seems to have been reinstated in the police, though in what capacity it is not clear. It is suggested that he took part in the *journée* of 12 Germinal, and, both for this reason and as a result of his terrorist activities, he was denounced by his Section, after the Prairial Days; the *assemblée générale* called both for his disarmament and his arrest.[1] Guénot was too much of a marked man to have escaped lightly on this occasion, and, unlike many ex-terrorists, he was not immediately released as a result of the amnesty of Brumaire year IV (October–November 1795). Towards the end of the month, his wife petitioned the Minister of Justice in his favour. The Minister, while referring the matter to the *juge de paix* of the Section de la place Vendôme, wrote in the margin of the petition that Guénot was to be held in prison

---

[1] AN, BB 18 739 (Ministère de la Justice, Seine, extrait du procès-verbal des délibérations de l'assemblée générale de la Section de la place Vendôme, 5 prairial an III): 'Appert ... que divers membres de l'assemblée générale accusent *Nicolas Guénot* de plusieurs délits, tant dans la journée du 12 germinal que pendant l'époque de la terreur, accusé d'avoir coupé les traits de la voiture des députés condamnés à la déportation, d'avoir dit qu'il avoit fait ce jour-là une bonne œuvre et qu'il ne donneroit pas sa journée pour 500 livres.

10. d'avoir été dénonciateur à gages dans la Section ainsi qu'il appert par les pièces qui sont au comité révolutionnaire de l'arrondissement.

20. d'avoir dans les Départements fait violence à une femme enceinte, de l'avoir arrachée de son lit, desquelles violences elle est morte.

L'assemblée générale avoit d'abord arrêté qu'il seroit désarmé, mais par suite elle ordonne son arrestation.' The accusation of having ill-treated a pregnant woman is very much *monnaie courante* in Thermidorian literature on the subject of the ex-terrorists. In Guénot's case, however, it may have been more than an empty formula.

pending criminal proceedings.[1] We do not know what the outcome of these may have been; but he was undoubtedly released by the beginning of the year V. There are few references to him during the next five years. Throughout the rest of the Directory, he appears to have carried out rather obscure duties as an *inspecteur de police*, while maintaining fruitful connections with the underworld, then at the height of its manifold activities. A man with a semi-criminal past and with at least one foot inside the Paris police system would probably have little to fear in a period when the collusion that always exists between the police and their clientele was unusually close and effective; and Guénot, it may be recalled, already had some experience in dealing both with counterfeiters, prostitutes, receivers, and returned *émigrés*, all high priorities with the *Bureau Central* of the Directory years.

In this respect at least his career is unrepresentative of that of most middle-ranking terrorists who, especially in provincial France, found themselves exposed, during the years 1795 to 1799, though with varying fortunes during that chaotic period – many of them, for instance, returned briefly to public office in 1797, generally to be evicted once more a year later[2] – to the full effects of the White Terror in the south-east and of the appropriately named Counter-Terror everywhere else. Guénot was in fact probably saved by his connections with the criminal world. He was above all lucky in being able to stay on in Paris, where any ex-terrorist could be reasonably safe and where he had not carried out his more dramatic repressive missions. He continued to enjoy protection from the police authorities and was possibly employed, in a subordinate position, by the newly-formed *Ministère de la Police générale*.

His luck ran out, however, in 1800, when he was dismissed, following a further charge of embezzlement. Soon after being caught begging near the Palais-Royal, he was confined to Bicêtre as a vagrant; and, in 1801, a police order sent him back to Voutenay, *en résidence surveillée*. This was

---

[1] AN, BB 18 739 (ibid., Marmouzet, juge de paix de la Section de la place Vendôme, au Ministre de la Justice, 1er frimaire an IV): 'En réponse à la lettre que vous m'avez adressée en date du 24 brumaire dernier [15 November 1795] où étoit joint un mémoire de la citoyenne Guénot, qui demande la liberté de son mari, détenu à la maison du Plessis, je vous adresse copie de l'extrait du procès-verbal de l'assemblée générale ... du 5 prairial dernier [24 May 1795], c'est tous les renseignemens que j'ai pu me procurer concernant le C. Guénot.' [The *juge de paix* was either a newcomer, or remarkably bad at his job, or an ally of Guénot, for this to have been the only information on the subject of a figure so notorious in his Section to have come his way!] There is a note in the Minister's hand at the bottom of this document: 'R. au B. central pour joindre le dossier de cette affaire et remettre le tout à la division des tribunaux criminels, 14 frimaire 4.'

M. Hohl, in his biography, has not used the two documents in BB 18 739.
[2] Isser Woloch, *Jacobin Legacy: the Democratic Movement under the Directory* (Princeton, 1970).

the cruellest fate that could befall any ex-terrorist who had ever been active on the local scene; in the conditions of 1795 to 1800, such an order was often to send the victim to an absolutely certain lynching. Guénot was at least fortunate that this had not happened to him six years sooner. Even as it was, no homecoming could have been more dreadful, for, in the course of the previous seven years, much of his activities as a terrorist, especially in the Yonne, had filtered back to his compatriots; there was a natural river grapevine between Paris and Voutenay, and no Department could have been better informed about the affairs of the capital than the Yonne, with, of course, the Seine-et-Oise and the Seine-et-Marne, equally closely linked to Paris by road and river. This was why, in the course of the nineteenth century, the Yonne was so often the first to feel the *contre-coup* of the violent events of Parisian *journées*, though no doubt, the P.L.M. having bypassed the river valley, to take in Montbard and Dijon, this was less true after the 1850s.

The Napoleonic municipality was dominated by *notables* and headed by one of the leading timber merchants, the *maire*, Bourgeois. The leading local ex-terrorist was, embarrassingly, a *notaire*, who had undergone a fraudulent bankruptcy – something, in fact, right out of the Thermidorian case-book.[1] Guénot was guaranteed poor company. Harried by the almost universal loathing of the villagers, the poorer of whom had no doubt been jealous of Guénot's undoubted successes on the Paris scene – village communities do not easily forgive those of their members who go away and send back good reports – Guénot once more took to the woods, where he lived, on and off, for the next two years, clad in skins and stinking rags, his feet wrapped in sacking, leading a hermit-like existence in a hide-out made of branches and ferns, suffering agonies in the bitterly cold winters of Burgundy from his old wound, a prisoner of the heartless horrors of rural poverty and from the very real and constant terror that Bourgeois, his friends, and the Napoleonic *Garde nationale* exercised over the whole community, sending regular reports to the Prefect, the Sub-Prefect, and the Minister of Police, on the subject of seditious remarks, drunkenness, village brawls, poaching, vagrancy, and any other threat to the established order. (Voutenay was no exception, in this respect, to the sort of administrative terror that was the common lot of French rural *communes* under the imperial regime – a terror all the more pitiless in that it was invariably exercised by the well-to-do against the very poor.) It was not misanthropy alone, then, that induced Guénot to keep to the sheltering cover of the woods during the daytime. He knew that he could expect no mercy from Bourgeois. At night, he ventured out of his woodland retreat to the edge of the village, where some charitable

---

[1] *The Police and the People*, pp. 45–8.

soul – a poor carpenter, who had occupied minor office during the Terror – in this brutal and vindictive rural community, was in the habit of putting out food for him outside his cottage.

On one such occasion, on 30 December 1802, emboldened perhaps by previous impunity and driven from his hut by the intensity of the cold, Guénot accepted the hospitality of his well-wisher, whose cottage was on the very edge of the forest. At dawn, his presence having been reported by the eager spies of the *maire*, who had been waiting for months for just such an opportunity to settle accounts with *l'homme des bois*, he was ambushed in the cottage by a company of the *Garde nationale*, commanded by Bourgeois himself, as he was about to return to the forest, with a basket of food and a bottle of wine. He managed to climb into the attic, as the men broke down the door of the single room, closing the trapdoor after him, and hurling insults through it at his tormentors; but later, the *maire* having secured the help of a carpenter, he climbed out through a skylight and emerged in full view of the baying rustics, on the roof, holding on to a chimney with his valid arm, and shouting barely distinguishable imprecations at his hunters (in the course of his time in the forest, he seems to have forgotten how to form coherent sentences) who had surrounded the cottage. Encouraged by Bourgeois, five members of the force took repeated shots at him, one from his kitchen, resting his rifle on the sink and exclaiming joyfully to his wife, each time he scored a direct hit: *je l'ai touché, je l'ai touché, j'ai touché le corbeau*. He received at least a dozen wounds, and after an hour and a half of random firing, bleeding copiously, he released his grip from the chimney and fell from the roof to the ground, breaking a leg and several ribs, and, while lying on the ground, daring his enemies to finish him off. He was, however, saved from certain lynching by the providential arrival of a *gendarme*, whom he knew and who was not from Voutenay. Guénot appealed to him to take him in charge; the *maire* claimed that he was quite well enough to walk the ten miles to the nearest prison, at Vermenton. But the *gendarme* obtained a cart and had him carried there. After a few days in Vermenton, he was transferred to Auxerre, convicted of vagrancy, and sentenced to the galleys. He was, therefore, escorted, on foot, to Rouen, where the *chaîne* was being formed for Rochefort. The garrison commander, a general, however – evidently a man who did not quite come up to the standard of callousness expected of the Napoleonic civilian official – decided that a semi-cripple, scarcely able to walk, deprived of the use of an arm, and weakened by loss of blood and by the long journey on foot from Burgundy to Upper Normandy, would never be able to reach Rochefort and would not be much use in the galleys even if, by some miracle, he did. He therefore ordered that he be sent back, by public transport, to Voutenay.

312 The Biographical Approach

He was back in the village in March 1803. Shortly after, in a final and pathetic attempt to escape from his dreadful environment, he nevertheless took to the roads again, begging on his way, to reach Pithiviers, where he had a niece, who promptly turned him over to the *gendarmes*. He was once more escorted back to Voutenay, on an administrative order from the Prefect of the Yonne. This was his third, and final, return to his unloved and unlovely birthplace. He then resumed his existence as *un homme des bois*, devoting what energies he had left – and he must have been a prodigiously strong man, both physically and morally – to persistent efforts to bring his would-be assassins to justice. There was no justice for poor men in Napoleonic France; however, he did encounter some measure of success with the public prosecutor of Avallon, who ordered criminal proceedings to be started against the *maire* and his accomplices. Higher authority would have none of this – Napoleonic officials put authority before justice – the proceedings were quashed and the prosecutor blamed for his untimely zeal; shortly afterwards, he was removed. It had taken the combined efforts of the Minister of Police and the Prefect, in a series of urgent representations to the *Grand Juge*, to bring a halt to the wheels of justice.

As far as Guénot was concerned, the White Terror was to continue for the next eleven years, under a regime for which it has been claimed that it brought internal peace and order to France. Increasingly embittered and isolated, half mad and now well on into his fifties, addressing himself to the birds and the trees, muttering curses and obscenities, his hide-out perceptible half a mile off from the stink of excrement, and throwing stones at the village children when they taunted him: *père Guénot, père Guénot, tu ne nous fais pas peur, hou! hou!* imitating the hoot of an owl.

Like other ex-terrorists,[1] he welcomed the Restoration as an opportunity at least to get even with his tormentors. The flow of his semi-literate denunciations once more began, addressed this time to Decazes, whom he assured of his devotion to the Bourbon house, a house which he had loyally served in the *Gardes Françaises* – he did not mention the manner in which he had left that corps; he may even have been sincere in these expressions of devotion, for his persecutors had all loyally served the Empire. The letters and petitions continued through 1816 and 1817. But they remained unanswered; the *gendarmerie royale*, as had been the *gendarmerie impériale*, was even instructed to keep an eye on the wild man of the woods, as he ploughed through the undergrowth, in his Crusoe-like clothing, clutching with his valid arm the only friend he had left: his

---

[1] Jean-Baptiste Antoine Lefranc, *Les Infortunes de plusieurs victimes de Napoléon Bonaparte ou Tableau des malheurs des 71 François déportés sans jugement aux îles Séchelles, à l'occasion de la machine infernale du 3 nivôse an IX* ... (veuve Le Petit, Paris, 1816).

inseparable rifle. At this stage we lose sight of him. His iron constitution and perhaps, too, an open-air existence preserved him throughout the two Restoration reigns; his death is recorded, at the age of seventy-eight, in May 1832. He had married at some stage of the Revolution, and, by 1795, had five children; but these he abandoned in Paris on his enforced return to Voutenay. He never saw them again; during the Empire, he occasionally consorted, at nightfall, with one or two village artisans, possibly as eccentric as himself, perhaps, too, like himself, former terrorists, though in a less exalted, local sphere.

There is no doubt that Guénot enjoyed the Terror. But it is difficult to know what he thought of the Revolution, for such a man does not confine his thoughts to memoirs. It is likely that Robespierre, Virtue, and the Supreme Being passed him by. What recollections would he have of the year II, his *annus mirabilis*? Probably, in his utter isolation in the woods, his mind became confused, so that he could no longer distinguish the year II from what went before or what came after. But there is no doubt about his courage, about the intensity of some rudimentary convictions, even if they were derived largely from hatred and from the desire for vengeance. He was almost pathologically violent; but so were his fellow-villagers. Balzac's *Les Paysans*, the author reminds us, came from the Avallonnais. It was his extreme good fortune that the strange chances of the Revolution should have enabled him to put his private violence to public use. There were no doubt many more terrorists like him, though less discoverable (the historian is well served with Guénot, for it is possible to follow much of his career, especially under the Empire, through the judicial records, a happy archival accident, though hardly so for the chief personage concerned), and certainly less corrupt, than he.

This harrowing story of rural brutality and nastiness is perhaps most indicative of the emergence of a terrorist vocation. But it also illustrates, horribly, the persistence of the polarizations of the revolutionary period, of how these too grew from those of the old order, and the everlasting memories of rural vengeance.

It is, too, a commentary on the much-played theme of *la montée à Paris* – a commentary all the more striking in that Guénot, like Restif and Restif's characters, reached the capital by the *coche d'eau*. But poor Guénot was no Dick Whittington; in lieu of a cat, he had to make do with the beasts with whom he shared the forest and whom he sometimes ate: stoats, weasels, foxes, adders, rabbits, and badgers – and, in his case, *la montée* was followed by a bitter return, *une descente aux enfers*, the cruelty and the sheer length of which was too great a punishment even for a man who, briefly, had shown himself singularly merciless, harsh, vengeful, and unscrupulous in the pursuit of his enemies. It is not a pretty tale, but it illustrates perhaps better than anything that has been written over the last twenty years or more, the whole history of the Revolution, through the life and experiences of one man, and a man who had never read Jean-Jacques or anything else very much other than the catechism and, later no doubt, the *Père Duchesne* (the *Grandes Colères*, if not the *Grandes Joies*, of which would have been very much his style; Hébert knew his Guénots). M. Hohl's book is a startling contribution to the neglected, but so important, history of mentalities. Guénot is the Terrorist Rediscovered and Re-created.

Of course, one must not make too much of Guénot as a sort of archetype. We know a great deal about his life before, during, and after the Revolution, because he was seldom out of court and was on the criminal fringe. It would be too easy to write off most forms of revolutionary commitment to the baser instincts, to envy, malice, and cruelty, as well as to the desire to make material gain out of an exceptional situation rich in opportunities for graft and for other forms of profit in kind (for it seems likely that Guénot, like most informers and policemen, may have forced prostitutes to supply him with their dangerous services *gratis*[1]). It is an unfortunate accident of history that we are likely only to be fully informed about that minority of terrorists that, for one reason or another, had come up against the law and had been involved in litigation and subjected to various forms of administrative *surveillance*. One is well informed, for instance, about the pre-revolutionary career of Jean-Marie Lapalus, one of Javogues' principal agents;[2] but one is not so well served on the subject of his master. There is nothing in Javogues' career in the ten years before the Revolution that would give any hint of the intensity of his intransigence, of his violence, and of his temerity as a *proconsul*. Perhaps the year II created Javogues in a new image; certainly, after his recall, he seems to have subsided into obscure mildness; and, even when the object of frequent denunciation during the Thermidorian reaction, he appears to have kept strangely quiet, as if he had spent all his energy, all his violence and all his enthusiasm in the course of a few chaotic, noisy months, displaying himself, like an angry comet, to his bewildered compatriots.[3] But his death represented a return to what one would expect of

---

[1] *Monsieur Nicolas*, IV, 1759, p. 2221: 'La Police (dit Nanette) a sans doute ses raisons pour nous rendre la vie la plus dure qu'elle peut; hôpital toujours à craindre, rançonnemens de l'Inspecteur, vexation et tyrannie des Locateurs, avanies des Passans, tapage et brisemens des boucaneurs, arrestations arbitraires du Guet. Mais le pis, c'est le fait-chanter des Espions. Aussi plusieurs s'abonnent-elles à l'Inspecteur, pour n'en point avoir. Mais quand une Fille en a, il couche avec elle quand il veut, vérolé ou non ... Maret, notre Inspecteur, Chesnon, notre Commissaire, sont dans l'usage de donner toujours raison aux Espions.'

[2] Colin Lucas, 'La brève carrière du terroriste de Jean-Marie Lapalus', *Annales historiques de la Révolution française*, no. 194, October–December 1968.

[3] See the same author's *The Structure of the Terror: the Case of Javogues and the Loire* (1973).

him. Carrier, as we are so often told, was a great lover of children and had been regarded, in his native Cantal, as a shy, retiring, mild, and gentle person. In this respect, Marcel Reinhard's life of Carnot and a recent biography of the unattractive Cochon, the second Minister of Police, have more to offer on this subject of the contrast between the quietude, the mildness, and the drab predictability of a provincial career in the fifteen or twenty years before the Revolution, and the vigour of repressive activity in the course of a mission in the year II.

In a way, *Guénot* is such a good book because it is good almost by accident, by default. The author does not always realize just what a gold mine he has dug out, he is unwilling to obtrude on a personality sufficiently remarkable as a study in his own right, and perhaps we should be grateful to him for having been hesitant to bring out the pointers. But it is also clear that he is not always aware of the value of his short book as an example of the exploration of a personal case history and its application to our general understanding of the history of the Terror and the Counter-Terror. He clearly thinks of his subject as a semi-monster, and he frequently chides him for his cruelty, his violence, and his thirst for vengeance. Perhaps he does not, in the end, sufficiently relate the violence of the man to that of his background; and, in this respect, he is both less generous and less perceptive than Babeuf when, horrified by the lynchings of the first few days of the Revolution, by the sickening spectacle of the sudden tribalism displayed by the hitherto mild, peaceable, ironic Parisians, he reflected that the common people had been brought up in a bad, brutal school and that popular violence had derived much from the impunity of the violence, the provocativeness, and the sheer insolence of *les Grands*, in their relations with the lower orders, and, more especially, with their womenfolk, as well as from the savagery of a government that did not hesitate to employ terror against the rural law-breaker. When first in Paris, in 1759, as a young printer's apprentice, Restif goes for a walk, with a girl on his arm, along the still untended, semi-wild avenues off the Champs-Élysées. After a time, he is caught up with by two elegant young men in silk jackets and carrying swords, who begin to walk at the same level as the couple, stopping when they do, keeping pace with them, jostling the young man and his girl, closing in more and more on Restif, persistently jogging his arm, tripping him with their feet, to the insistent accompaniment of the phrase: *que faut-il pour fâcher Monsieur?* The young Bourguignon looks stolidly ahead, refusing to be provoked. After a few more yards of this scene, with the four still walking abreast, one of the young men, after placing his swagger stick in some dirt on the road, holds it up to Restif's nose: *et ça, est-ce que ça va fâcher Monsieur?* Restif has had enough; breaking away from the girl, he picks up a piece of building material – a plank or a long piece of wood, lying by the path – and sets about the pair with it, to such effect that his aggressors, after a thorough trouncing, take to their heels. But the scene has been observed, and, immediately, the apprentice is set upon by a group of big Picard servants, in livery. At the same time, a horseman of the *maréchaussée*, riding by, pulls in his horse. The two young men, returning to the scene, ask him to take Restif in charge. He is soon brought before the *commissaire* of Chaillot and is about to be confined, before appearing in front of a magistrate, when the poor girl breaks down and starts weeping. The young men, perhaps moved, and anxious to make at least a token display of gallantry, tell the *commissaire* that the whole thing had been a joke and that they wish to withdraw the charge; they then take their leave, followed by the servants. The *commissaire* tells Restif that he has been fortunate, asking at the same time if he had recognized the livery of the servants; the apprentice, a newcomer to the capital, states that he has not. *C'est la livrée des d'Orléans*, comments the *commissaire*. Restif was to recall the incident in 1784, when he was writing that section of *Monsieur Nicolas* that dealt with his early life in Paris. 'Such is the tyranny of les Grands,' he then observes. But, ten years later, when he was completing the printing of this vast book, and having experienced the year II, he went on to add: '*La tyrannie des petits, des jaloux, des incapables, est pis encore.*' A great many people of all ranks had had similar experiences in the years before the Revolution, and had no doubt remembered them as vividly as Restif had this characteristic display of provocative and totally gratuitous insolence, nearly thirty years after it had occurred. This was, after all, the reality of life – or one of the realities of life – in *ancien régime* France. Guénot, too, was the product of a society, of a place, and of a trade. He did not need to have experienced the insolence of *les Grands*. It would have been surprising had he been anything other than violent, rancorous, and uncouth.

THE CAREER OF A GOVERNMENT TERRORIST

In this respect, the distance between private life and public terrorism seems far more dramatic when applied to people of a very different social origin. Let us take the case of Cochon de Lapparent, the subject of a recent biography by one of his descendants, Paul Boucher, who has had access to the family papers. In his pre-revolutionary career, Cochon is indistinguishable from five hundred other *conventionnels*: born in 1750, a law degree from a provincial university in the early seventies, the third generation in a provincial family that had remained in the same geographical area for nearly a hundred years, the purchase for him by his father of a comfortable and unexacting law office – in this instance in Fontenay-le-Comte – a marriage into a legal family of equivalent wealth, the acquisition both of more land and of some urban property, in the fifteen years before the Revolution, a slight instance of luck – a lawsuit won against the Duke of Orléans, who had attempted to assert his right as an *apanagiste* to drain and put under cultivation a section of the *marais poitevin*, thus threatening with ruin a whole class of people who lived off the produce of the marshland – and hence a certain popularity. Cochon was a dull, utterly typical, member of the professional legal class. He was elected to the Estates-General, but only as a *suppléant*. A death made him a full deputy. During his first stay in Paris, he surrounded himself with people from his home town, sharing a hotel with Goupilleau de Fontenay, and always taking care to protect his rear by maintaining a regular correspondence with the leading inhabitants of his home town. Disenfranchised under the Legislative Assembly, he returned to his province, this time as a judge in one of the new courts. He was, one feels almost inevitably, elected to the Convention.

But it is at this stage that the career of this unattractive and unexceptional man takes an unexpected turn. In January 1793, he had no hesitation in voting the King's death. In March of the same year, under pressure from the war emergency, he showed unexpected physical courage, as well as a sort of steely ruthlessness that nothing in the previously unrippled life of this calculating provincial would have hinted at. He was sent to Valenciennes at the height of the military crisis, in March 1793, arriving in the town a little before it was completely invested by the imperial armies. Faced with a population driven desperate by the bombardment and by municipal authorities anxious at all costs to reduce damage to property, if necessary by capitulating to the besiegers, he showed rather more energy than any of the military commanders, threatening some of the leading *notables* with courts martial and the firing squad if they did not carry out his orders. He was himself physically assaulted by a group of panic-stricken householders.

On the fall of Valenciennes, he returned to the obscurity of the middling benches of the Convention, taking no part at all in the faction fights of 1793 and the year II, but busying himself with various technical matters. In the year III, he was entrusted with an important diplomatic mission to the Dutch Estates-General; in his dealings with their High Mightinesses, he gave further proof of ruthlessness. In the following year, he became second Minister of Police. In the course of his tenure of that important Ministry, he sent Babeuf and some of his fellow-conspirators to the guillotine, and, a year later, had Javogues and the other so-called 'Grenelliens' shot. Their death does not seem to have worried him; it was merely a piece of routine business.

Cochon too was a terrorist, but, unlike Guénot, one by calculation, rather than by temperament or predisposition. With him, it was a matter of turning terror on or off, as from a tap, according to the circumstances. He was the sort of man who should have been made a Napoleonic Prefect, as he could always be relied upon to defend, if necessary, ruthlessly, established authority. So he was made Prefect of Antwerp. Here, very soon, he found himself with a large-scale peasant revolt, inspired by the Flemish rural clergy, on his hands. Once more, the provincial lawyer and the family man resorted to measures of intimidation and terror. He was rewarded with the Prefecture of Poitiers, and, towards the end of the Hundred Days, he was given Rouen. Waterloo caught him in the process of moving into his new Prefecture. He promptly offered his services to the Bourbons, and seemed surprised when they were refused. It does not seem to have occurred to him that Louis XVIII might feel scruples about employing a man who had voted his brother's death. He was apparently quite prepared to serve any regime that could find a use for his administrative and repressive abilities.

As it was, he had to go into exile, setting up house once more with Goupilleau de Fontenay, in Louvain. But he had influence, and in 1819, almost alone among the exiled regicides, he was able to secure his return to France. As with Guénot, it was not, however, a happy homecoming, though the persecution of Cochon on the part of the local authorities took on a less dramatic form. A former Prefect was unlikely to be physically assaulted; but he was ostracized, had to crouch in a narrowing circle of family friends, and was subjected to endless vexations on the part of the public prosecutor. In Fontenay, too, memories went back a long way, and, in this bitterly divided Department, the *bleus*, of whom Cochon is no doubt a rather typical personality, were the object of a particular loathing on the part of the local squirearchy. Cochon died in 1825; even his funeral and his obituary in the local paper were the subjects of bitter polemics that went on long after this dull man's death.

There are certain parallels between these two very different careers. Both men were policemen, both informers, though they informed at quite opposite levels. Guénot would have heard of Cochon – he was, very indirectly, employed by him – but it is unlikely that the Minister was ever aware of the existence of his subordinate. Both were of the same generation; for Cochon, the opportunity came at thirty-nine, in 1789; for Guénot, at thirty-nine, in 1793. Cochon lasted out much longer in public life, but was eventually subjected to persecution within his own community. Neither seems ever to have been able entirely to escape from the circle of provincialism, though Guénot tried his best to do so, on a number of occasions, being driven back, like an unlucky player in a children's game, to base: in his case, his awful village, whether by pressure of poverty or by administrative order, whereas Cochon never seems to have been really happy anywhere else. In Guénot's case, too, the terror was used against his compatriots, villagers, and farmers from the Yonne, while Cochon preferred to terrorize foreigners and strangers, and to oblige people from his own part of the world. Cochon wanted above all to cut a figure in Fontenay, to be accepted there as a notability, Guénot asked for nothing better than to be forgotten for ever in Voutenay. But one should not take the parallel or the contrasts any further. Guénot was an unusual, even interesting, monster; Cochon is a boring, very ordinary administrator. It is also likely that Cochon did not particularly enjoy the Terror for its own sake or for what he could get out of it. He was scrupulous and unimaginative. But he was, of course, a much more effective terrorist than the poor *flotteur*. Yet he did not inspire quite the same subsequent resentment; for Cochon was a man of substance, he had a sort of pre-emptive right to exercise authority, even if it meant, when the public circumstances demanded it, becoming a terrorist. It was impossible to single him out for a persecution, because so many other people of his condition were in a similar position. A whole section of the revolutionary provincial and legal class had had blood on its hands. Cochon was thus cushioned both by his condition and by a political past shared with many others. Guénot was entirely expendable; he had also been presumptuous, or so it would have seemed both to the *notables* of Voutenay and to his fellow-villagers.

Terrorists like Cochon were not individualists – there were perhaps a few such among them, wild, raving eccentrics like Javogues or even Carrier – they were administrators and they belonged to an administrative class. The career of Cochon can be repeated over and over again, with due allowance for regional variations. It would be as impossible to reconstruct the mentality of a Cochon as that of a Carnot. Both could be terrorists when it suited them and moderates when circumstances required. Both were accused, at much the same time, of royalism. They were the sort of people who were capable of adjusting themselves to the passage of time. They are, therefore, dull and predictable and deserve to figure in that French historical Madame Tussaud's, *le Dictionnaire des Girouettes*. There is perhaps no inherent merit in consistency; but, in the case of Guénot, there was no convenient, comfortable line of retreat, no possibility of retirement, no chance of forgiveness or forgetfulness. This sort of terrorist could not quietly retire.

THE PROFITEER OF TERROR

A similar blending between public emergency, the great events of the revolutionary period, and private advantage, both in personal, financial, and career terms, is revealed in a case that came before the *tribunal crim-*

inel de la Seine in the course of the year IV.[1] It concerns Pierre-Alexandre Chartrey, who was forty-two at the time of this, apparently his first, encounter with the Paris courts, and whose revolutionary career offers certain parellels with those of Guénot – Chartrey operated, however, at a level altogether higher than the former *flotteur* – and of Cochon, for, like Cochon, this man was to owe his greatest opportunity to the extensive, and little controlled, bureaucracy of a temporary Occupation regime, in a capacity conveniently, because vaguely, situated on the frontier zone between military and civilian responsibilities.

Chartrey's chance came in 1792, as a result of the Revolution of 10 Août, that is, at the age of thirty-eight. Unlike Guénot and Cochon, he was a native-born Parisian who, before the Revolution – presumably for a number of years – had exercised the unremunerative and extremely humble trade of public letter-writer (*écrivain public*), in a tiny shop, passage du Saumon, cul-de-sac du Coq. It would have been hard to have fallen lower, in the hierarchy of occupations open to the literate or the barely literate; a public writer was little better than a private tutor or an usher, though the position would give its holder a certain notoriety in his quarter, as he would have a very wide circle of acquaintances and clientele, mostly drawn from the humbler walks of life, especially in their relations with the public authorities, the law, and one another. The *écrivain* would no doubt be expected to provide advice, as well as expert penmanship, and, if he were intelligent and patient and well prepared to listen, he might act as a less prestigious, but consequently more approachable, *juge de paix*, though, presumably, he would have less time to devote to his customers (he did, after all, earn his living by the line).

Such a man could also be of great use to the police (who, in any case, had a hold over him, as he was a *patenté*); and, in a revolutionary situation, the extent and the variety of his clientele among the very poor and the very humble, especially among the variegated population of the *garnis* (but even among the more established *sans-culottes*, many of whom, sometimes even the most affluent, were likely to be in need of his services at least on the most important occasions of their lives) might stand him in very good stead in the politics of a Section and as the mouthpiece of the *citoyens passifs*. The public writer was well placed to claim the position of a pocket, parish Solomon. It was certainly a job that can have offered little reward financially; indeed, when questioned by a prosecutor clearly determined to suggest that Chartrey, at the outbreak of the Revolution, had been living only just above the barest subsistence level, with his single *échoppe*, in a dark alley-way, he was at once at pains to prove that, at the

---

[1] AN, BB 18 741 (Ministère de la Justice, Seine, extrait du greffe du tribunal criminel, 13 pluviôse an IV).

time, he had other sources of income; he employed, he was to claim, several subordinate writers as clerks, and had had establishments – though, in the year IV, he was unable to name any of them – in other parts of Paris. Pressed further, he was to add, almost as an afterthought, and rather grandly, that he had derived further profits from the 'exercices chimiques auxquelles il se livrait de tems en tems'. We are not told the nature of these. The prosecutor was not convinced and, in 1796, in the indictment, he is described as 'écrivain sans fortune avant la Révolution … accusé de dilapidations, de concussions, pillages des biens d'émigrés &ca'.

When cross-examined, in 1796, on the subject of the origins of his visible affluence, he was further to describe himself as 'un patriote des premiers jours de la Révolution, un homme de 89'; he may indeed have been both, though it does not seem very likely. He was, very definitely, 'un homme de 92' (just as much as Guénot could be described as 'un homme de 93'). He was elected to the *Commune* on 11 August of that year; and, the same day, he was appointed to the newly-formed *comité de surveillance du Département*. Shortly afterwards, he was appointed one of Roland's *commissaires du pouvoir exécutif*, at the time of the first Terror, when it was urgent to reassure the Departments on the subject of what had recently happened in Paris. He left Paris on 3 September, on the second day of the Massacres, and spent a month as a roving propagandist and revolutionary commissioner, visiting the Seine-et-Oise, the Yonne (like Guénot, in a humbler capacity, eighteen months later), the Saône-et-Loire, the Rhône-et-Loire, and the Ain, returning to Paris on 3 October. For part of his mission, he was accompanied by Michel, *marchand de vin*, and a member of the Cordelier club. While in Auxerre, he is said to have set up the first revolutionary committee to have been established in the Yonne; he was to deny this in 1796, but, pressed, later admitted that he had indeed formed a temporary committee to deal with suspects. By October, in fact, Chartrey had emerged as a fully-fledged terrorist; he may even have been a *septembriseur* – he was questioned on this in 1796, and pointed out that, having left Paris on 3 September, he could hardly have taken part in most of the Massacres.

The next stage of the steady progress of his revolutionary career is equally characteristic. No doubt he had joined the Cordeliers. In any case, on 9 December 1792, on the recommendation apparently of his friend Sijas, he was appointed by the War Minister, Pache, *commissaire extraordinaire des guerres* with the *armée du Nord*. He left for Belgium on the following day, reporting to Ronsin, a man not unlike himself – he had been an unsuccessful regular soldier, an irregular actor, and an unsuccessful playwright who wrote little better than an *écrivain public* – the *commissaire ordonnateur*, who, on the orders of Dumouriez, had set up his headquarters in Liège, possibly to keep him well away from Brussels; Dumouriez did not like Ronsin, regarding him as the personal spy of the Minister and of the Cordeliers. On Ronsin's orders, Chartrey was transferred to Brussels on 21 December – this too may have been a move in the conflict with the General – and arrived there on Christmas Day. His task in the former capital of the Austrian Netherlands was a very important one; he was to carry out the sale of all *émigré* property in the city, including that of the former Governor, the Archduchess Marie-Christine, who had had to flee from her palace in the clothes in which she stood up, owing to the speed of the French advance, and of the leading members of her court. The former public writer was thus to dispose of the town houses, furniture, pictures, plate, and jewellery of the great princely families – de Cröy, de Mérode, de Ligne, d'Ursel – and of the Brabant nobility and merchants. A vast amount of clothing, jewellery, art treasures, and furniture must have come under his control and under that of his two immediate subordinates, Delorme, a former employee of the *Contrôle-général*, and Lamotte, his secretary. It is not known in what conditions the confiscations and sales were carried out; but Chartrey was his own master and was subject to no immediate scrutiny on the spot. Much of the plate and furniture seems to have been stored in the former palace in which he had his offices and residence. With the defeat of Neerwinden, in March 1793, he prepared to organize the transfer to France of a convoy of wagons containing much of the jewellery and furniture of the Archduchess's court. According to his own account, two wagon-loads were held up and pillaged, on the road from Ghent to Brussels, at Alost, by a group of peasants, who attacked and drove away the military escort. Two more got away. In the general conditions of chaos then prevailing, Chartrey was able to move most of his treasure convoy from Brussels to Lille, thence to Paris – no mean achievement in itself and a tribute to his talent for improvisation. According to his former subordinate, Delorme, far from sending the wagons to the *Domaines* or the *Garde-Meuble*, he had several of them unloaded in the courtyards of the houses occupied by Danton, Lacroix, and Ronsin, who personally supervised the operation. Delorme was to add that, in April 1793, he had shown him various objects bearing the Austrian arms.

His next assignment was as *commissaire des guerres* in Montpellier, where he seems to have spent 1794 and part of 1795. He took Delorme with him; but the latter was to state, in 1796, that growing suspicious at the grand style of living affected by his superior, he had left Montpellier after a few months, returning to Paris, where he was to obtain a post in the *Contributions directes*. Towards the end of the year III, in Fructidor (August–September 1795), for reasons that are far from clear – perhaps he had been dismissed – Chartrey, his wife, and daughter left Montpellier for

Dijon, where he lingered for some six weeks; from there, he came up to Paris, leaving his family in a Dijon inn, apparently in the hope of obtaining an appointment with the Committee of General Security. He was likely to have formed useful connections at least with the subordinate levels of the political police. But the move to Paris was a mistake, although he seems to have taken the elementary precaution of keeping his real address concealed; on arrival, he registered at one lodging-house, where he left his bags, and sent to stay in another. For, within a few days of his arrival, he was recognized in the street, as he came out of his real lodgings, by his former subordinate, Delorme. The meeting seems to have been most unwelcome, Chartrey doing his best to shake off his inquiring friend and suggesting that they meet later, *à tête reposée*, in a restaurant nearer to his home. Delorme would have none of this and, though they parted company, he had no difficulty, by hanging about for the rest of the day in the neighbourhood, in tracing Chartrey down to his real address. He may have acted in self-protection, or he may have felt that his former employer had done him out of his share of the Brussels loot, or he may simply have been motivated by jealousy. In any case, he went to the police, to whom he denounced Chartrey as a *dilapidateur des biens de la République*. Chartrey was arrested early in the year IV, on a warrant issued by the *Bureau Central*, and was incarcerated in the Force. He was questioned for the first time, by the *directeur du jury d'accusation*, on 29 Brumaire (20 November 1795). He came up for trial on 13 Pluviôse (2 February 1796).

At the trial, before the *tribunal criminel de la Seine*, Delorme was the principal, and, indeed, the only, witness for the prosecution. Chartrey had not only taken care to conceal his Paris address from anyone who might have known him during his pre-Revolution days; he had not left any forwarding address with his family in Dijon, merely telling them that he would be back in a few days. When the prosecution wished to hear his alleged wife and her mother as witnesses in the trial, they were unable to trace them down to any inn in the *chef-lieu* of the Côte-d'Or. Delorme was himself convinced – or so he claimed – that, out of the proceeds of the Brussels haul, Chartrey had bought a property, in the name of his mother-in-law, somewhere in the neighbourhood of Dijon, where neither he nor his family was likely to be known. This may have been one of the reasons why Chartrey had been so anxious to conceal the details of his movements, both from possible acquaintances in Paris, and from his family, who, it might be supposed, on his departure from Dijon, after receiving the expected signal from him, had paid the bill and moved off to the concealment of the hidden *domaine*. In any case, despite prolonged inquiries ordered by the court, they could not be traced.

The main charge made by Delorme against his former employer was then that he had appropriated for his own uses property belonging to the

Republic, including the personal effects of Marie-Christine, among which there was said to have been a clock given to her by her sister, Marie-Antoinette. Chartrey was closely questioned, both about the origins of his personal fortune, his political career and his private life which, judging from the transcripts from his trial, had likewise contained considerable zones of mystery and deviousness. The investigating magistrate was to show particular interest both in the origins and present status of Chartrey's second wife, for that was how he described her, though there are suggestions that he had been already married and had never obtained a divorce. She appears to have been a young country girl, aged sixteen or seventeen at the time when Chartrey had first met her, then a *fille de salle* in an inn at Évres, a village in the Pas-de-Calais, on the highroad to Lille, near Boulogne-sur-Mer; their encounter no doubt took place when Chartrey was on his way to Belgium. In any case, once established, no doubt in considerable splendour, in Brussels, the *commissaire*'s first thought was to send for her to join him there, accompanying his invitation, so it is claimed, with a trunk containing magnificent brocaded clothing, as a token of his intentions and of his wealth. The girl must have been dazzled by the style of her uniformed thirty-nine-year-old lover's way of life, in the former archducal palace of Charles de Lorraine. Delorme, who may well have witnessed their first encounter, was to state at the trial, with his usual cattiness, that, on this occasion, she had been 'tellement dans la misère que le C. Chartrey, en l'envoyant chercher de Bruxelles, lui envoya des vêtemens pour se couvrir,' adding, to bring out the dramatic contrast in her condition:

> ... aujourd'hui il seroit assez impossible de trouver une femme aussi bien étoffée qu'elle l'est; elle l'est à profusion, c'est assez en dire, elle a jusqu'à une layette de point de France d'une beauté épouvantable, venant sans doute de Bruxelles, du palais de Marie-Christine ... elle étoit née de parens pauvres et infortunés ... elle alloit dans son jeune âge avec sa mère journellement à la forêt y faire chacune un sac de bois qu'elles vendoient pour se procurer leurs subsistances ...

Delorme was evidently particularly pleased with this tableau of rural misery, for he returned to it on a number of occasions, always to contrast it with the present spectacular affluence of the so-called Madame Chartrey.

He further claimed that, on his return to Paris in March 1793, after Neerwinden, Chartrey had shown him a number of clocks, jewels, plate, table objects, silverware, and tapestries, all bearing the Austrian arms:

> qu'il a vu un jour dans la cour du C. Ronsin ... 2 voitures de meubles et effets mobiliers arrivant de la Belgique et au-devant desquelles voitures étoit allé le C.

Lamotte l'aîne, que le C. Chartrey avoit eu pour secrétaire à Bruxelles ... que les meubles étoient destinés à être partagés entre Danton, Lacroix et Ronsin, ainsi que Chartrey l'a annoncé.

The court was to attach considerable importance to this matter, observing: 'il faut savoir ce que sont devenus les effets mobiliers de Ronsin, Danton et Lacroix après leurs décès. Les domaines nationaux ont dû s'en emparer, mais les a-t-on vendus, les a-t-on rendus aux veuves et héritiers? Dans ces deux cas, il doit y avoir eu des inventaires et des procès-verbaux.' Inquiries, however, with the Ministry of Finance, drew a blank, the Minister stating that the French, after Neerwinden, had had to withdraw from Belgium in such conditions of chaos that they would hardly have had the time to draw up detailed inventories of the articles that had been confiscated. Chartrey was himself questioned:

à lui demandé si pendant son séjour à Paris ou à Bruxelles il a eu connoissance de ce qui étoit devenue la pendule envoyée par la ci-devant Reine de France à l'archiduchesse sa sœur. A répondu qu'à la vérité à Bruxelles il a été vendu une quantité de pendules à différens citoyens et que celle dont [on] nous parloit doit être comprise dans cette vente ...

It seems that the prosecution was unable to make out a case against Chartrey, in the absence of any concrete evidence, though the presiding judge pressed him on the conditions in which he had undertaken his journey from Dijon to Paris. Why had he left his wife – or alleged wife – and daughter, in the Burgundian capital, staying at an inn, and why, having come from Montpellier to Dijon by public stage-coach, producing his passport and those of his family, had he taken the immensely expensive course of hiring a private cabriolet to take him from Dijon to Paris? Why had he come alone? Why, on his arrival, had he taken the precaution of obtaining two addresses? How had he communicated, from Paris, with his wife? Why had he told her to leave the inn? Chartrey was evasive on all these subjects, but it could not be proved that he had sent written instructions to his wife, and he argued convincingly that he had to take the most rapid form of transport from Dijon to Paris, as he had had an urgent appointment with the Committee of General Security (as that body no longer existed, it was not possible to obtain any clarification on this point, though, presumably, the court could have approached one of the former members, as it did, for instance, in the case of Villambre, an agent of Puisaye, arrested near Rennes, on the subject of whom the Minister wrote to Rovère[1]). He also questioned him on the subject of the

---

[1] There is a considerable dossier on Charles Villambre in AN, BB 18 741.

September Massacres, in which Chartrey denied having taken any part, since he had left Paris very early on 3 September, an argument not entirely convincing, since he could have been a *massacreur* on the 2nd and during the night of the 2nd to the 3rd, and still have been on his way to the Seine-et-Oise. Perhaps he was attempting to establish a criminal charge against the former *commissaire des guerres* as a *septembriseur*, should the accusations of peculation fail to materialize. It was, in any case, the current practice of the courts, during the Thermidorian reaction and the early years of the Directory, to insinuate that *any* former terrorist had not only been a thief and a drunkard, a libertine and an adventurer, but also, possibly, a murderer. Chartrey, with his past, was the sort of person that *should* have been a *septembriseur*, even if he had not been. We do not know the outcome of the proceedings, but letters from the Ministers of Finance, *Contributions directes*, and from the *Domaines* addressed to the Minister, in Fructidor year IV, all suggest that, in the absence of an inventory, and given the impossibility of ever obtaining any witnesses, the case had to be dropped.

The turning point in Chartrey's previously mediocre career had come with 10 August. The new Revolution had set him on the road both to promotion and to apparent prosperity. As a member of the *Commune*, he had been appointed one of Roland's propaganda agents; and among his associates as *commissaires du pouvoir exécutif*, he had gained valuable contacts in the Ministry of War, and, possibly, in the Cordeliers. This had set him on the highroad to Belgium, a profitable, though dangerous (it had had fatal consequences for Danton, Lacroix, and Ronsin) direction from every point of view. For he had picked up an attractive young girl on his way north and had no doubt settled himself in her affections by the gift of fine clothing and by a life of apparent magnificence in Brussels. The former public letter-writer, as the result of the fortunes of Occupation, found himself in charge of the disposal of much of the loot of the Belgian Provinces, perhaps the most affluent area in Western Europe. He had been fortunate, too, in his immediate superiors; for, while it has never been suggested that Ronsin profited directly from his post as *commissaire ordonnateur* – such a charge was never made even at the time of his trial and the inventory drawn up at the request of his widow, after his execution, reveals only the bare, scattered possessions one would expect of a general often on the move and of a playwright who had never had much of a success[1] – there seems to have been little doubt that Danton and Lacroix were both engaged in extensive pillaging while in Belgium, and Delorme is by no means the first witness to have spoken of wagon-loads of loot

---

[1] *Les Armées révolutionnaires*, pp. 102 (102) and (103), and Arch. Seine DQ 10 436 (succession du général Ronsin).

arriving in Lille and then in Paris.[1] Chartrey may well have been attempting to make off with a consignment of his own when some of his transport fell into the hands of local peasants, at Alost, on the road from Ghent to Brussels.

In any case, after Neerwinden, he remained in the supply services of the Army. It may be that there was nothing against him; or it is possible that, after the dismissal of Beurnonville and the appointment of Bouchotte as Minister of War, he continued to have powerful protectors, especially in the *Bureaux de la Guerre*; while in Montpellier, we hear little about his *train de vie*, but in the course of the autumn and winter of 1793, and the spring of 1794, there is plenty to indicate that he continued to militate, as a propagandist and as an *homme de liaison*, putting new life into the local *société populaire*, preaching active dechristianization, while, in private letters, expressing his dislike and his contempt for those he regarded as mendacious, tricky, and cowardly southerners.[2]

He had in fact all the prejudices of the Parisian militant when precipitated into a provincial milieu, particularly a Mediterranean one. His behaviour, in the year II, is much more that of the archetypal Cordelier activist[3] than that of a scoundrel and a war-profiteer, though, of course, the two roles, though rarely combined, may not have been entirely incompatible. There is plenty to suggest that, even in the midst of his militancy, he continued to live on a fairly grand scale while in Montpellier, keeping open house, especially to the garrison, and displaying with the pride of a forty-year-old the visible charms of his young wife. It is likely that a man with such a marked political past would have had to leave the Midi in the course of the year III – indeed, he would have been suicidally foolish if he had not done so – and he may have been given a new appointment, either in another garrison town, or with the armies of Occupation, the refuge of so many militants of his type in the course of the difficult years of the Counter-Terror in France.

His trial, in the year IV, undoubtedly has political undertones, the prosecutor questioning him closely both on the September Massacres and on his mission in the Departments; he is eager, for instance, to prove that Chartrey had set up the principal instrument of the Terror in Auxerre. Furthermore, as a witness, Delorme is suspect; the eagerness with which he pursues his former superior and the haemorrhage of repetitive denunciations which he pours out on the Minister and on the public prosecutor indicate something more than a zeal for the pursuit of justice. It

---

[1] G. Lefebvre, 'Sur la fortune de Danton', *Études sur la Révolution française* (Paris, 1954).
[2] 'Dans ce pays, on ne sait à qui donner sa confiance, les hommes en général y sont autrement qu'ailleurs, c'est-à-dire menteurs, orgueilleux et beaucoup égoïstes' (Chartrey à Sijas, AAG, Class. gén. 683, Chartrey; and *Les Armées révolutionnaires*, p. 550).
[3] *Les Armées révolutionnaires*, p. 252 (74).

is, of course, possible that the tapestries, silverware, clocks, and damasks may have been put to good use, especially in the favourable conditions of the year III, when there was an immense revival of the international trade in furniture and *objets d'art*, for the purchase of a country property and of a substantial piece of land, in an area where Chartrey had previously had no contacts. The precautions he took, on coming to Paris, may have been merely those of any ex-terrorist, faced with the threats contained in a regime that proclaimed as its principle *le retour au règne des lois*; or they may indeed have been dictated by a desire to conceal his identity, to break with the past, and to cover up the evidence of a change of fortune too apparent to be healthy. These are matters that will have to be left to the judiciary; and we do not in fact know whether Chartrey was to have further encounters with the courts.

The interest of his career to the historian of the Revolution lies else-where; and, as the historiography of Danton has so abundantly indicated, the endless pursuit of charges of peculation can be a most unrewarding subject for historical research and historical judgement. It is as an example of a 'career under the Revolution', within the framework of war and Terror, a combination that enabled so many other *commissaires du pouvoir exécutif* temporarily to better themselves, as *hommes de liaison*, though most, unlike Chartrey, were to pay dearly for their promotion, either in the spring of 1794 or in the course of the Counter-Terror. Chartrey used the Revolution; and he was used by the Revolution. The bargain seems to have been advantageous to both sides, though, one suspects, the *commissaire* did the better out of it. One of his assets is visible: a new, attractive, apparently well-dressed, and, no doubt, loving young wife. He also acquired a mother-in-law, who may have served a rather different purpose, if he did in fact purchase a *domaine* in her name. Unlike Guénot and Cochon, we have to part company with Chartrey at the time of his inconclusive and possibly unfinished trial, in the summer of 1796. One would indeed like to think that, if cleared at the end of that year, he retired to those mysterious estates, to live in cultivated peace, with his wife, his mother-in-law (she would have been too dangerous to dispose of) and his daughter. Certainly, he seems to have used the favourable cir-cumstances created by Revolution and war, to cover his traces, efface all evidence of his previous career, and make it impossible for his first wife, if she still existed and felt so inclined – and she might have been more interested in a husband enriched by striking clocks and brocades than by one who had been a struggling public writer – to trace him. His one mistake, in what we know of his revolutionary career between 1792 and 1796, was to have forgotten that Paris was, and is, a village, and that, sooner or later, on returning there, someone was bound to recognize him. He was, in a matter of days.

THE ULTRA-TERRORIST

The careers of Guénot, Cochon, and Chartrey are all, in their different ways, indicative of certain general themes in respect of the impact of a revolutionary crisis on the life of the individual. A fourth example – the career of Louis-Michel Musquinet-Lapagne, dit *Constantin*, is difficult to fit into any standard mould, Musquinet being the type of extreme individualist who defies any attempt at generalization. His case history is both more dramatic and more tragic than any of those that we have dealt with; it might be taken to illustrate the progression from crime to ultra-revolutionism – a progression that was certainly not uncommon in the favourable circumstances of the autumn of 1793, circumstances that so often put a premium on violence and adventurism, more especially through the medium of the extremer forms of dechristianization. It also indicates the persistence of violence in the temperament of what can best be described as a *grand exaspéré* over a period of fifteen years.

Musquinet-Lapagne emerges for the first time in the history of the *ancien régime* in 1777, when he was convicted of the murder of Jean-Baptiste Berthault, *cavalier de la maréchaussée*, during the night of 11–12 May, in the course of a burglary committed in the town house of Mlle de Juvigny, place Saint-Maurille, in Angers. Judgement was given by the *sénéchaussée criminelle* of Angers, on 9 April 1778:

[Il] (Musquinet) est convaincu d'avoir enlevé des plats, couverts, flambeaux, écuelles à oreilles, salières, huilliers, et autres pièces d'argenterie, une somme de 421 livres, linges, vêtements, certains de ces effets ont été trouvés sur lui ainsi que dans une malle attachée à son cabriolet; il a tiré sur Berthault, tué net, ainsi que sur deux autres cavaliers de la maréchaussée; il est également convaincu ... d'avoir pendant l'instruction du procès tenu aux prisonniers des propos séditieux & tendans à exciter la révolte, & d'avoir commis plusieurs violences & insultes graves aux juges. Pour réparation de quoi nous avons condamné le dit [Musquinet] ... de faire amende honorable à la porte et principale entrée du Palais de cette ville, où il sera conduit nud en chemise la corde au cou, portant dans les mains une torche de cire ardente du poids de 2 livres ... & là étant à nue tête et à genoux, dire & déclarer à haute & intelligible voix que méchamment & témérairement il a commis rébellion à la justice & tué d'un coup de pistolet ledit Berthault ... qu'il s'en repent & en demande pardon à Dieu, au Roy et à Justice, ce fait, le condamnons à être rompu vif sur un échafaud qui sera à cet effet dressé sur la place publique des halles.

He was further condemned to pay damages of 3,000 *livres* to the widow and children of the unfortunate Berthault.

Despite the apparent ferocity of the sentence, despite the deliberately terrifying language of the law, the sentence was never carried out. It is possible that Musquinet, who seems to have been well-connected – he was related to a *parlementaire* family from Pontoise, in the Vexin – may have been saved as the result of the personal intervention of some highly-placed official. In any case, he was eventually imprisoned in the Bastille, in Paris. He succeeded in obtaining his release on an appeal accepted by the *tribunal du 1er arrondissement* of Paris dated 18 March 1791, after a protracted campaign both on the part of his counsel with the new courts, and through a series of pamphlets written by himself and by his brother and issuing from the print shops of the Palais-Royal from the beginning of the revolutionary crisis up to the spring of 1791. At the time of his release, Peyre was his defence counsel. In this document, he is described as *avocat au Parlement de Paris*. He was at once given an unconditional release from the Conciergerie, to which he had been transferred, after thirteen years in various prisons. He was to enjoy three years of liberty and of intense political activity, before being arrested once more, on 15 Brumaire year II (5 November 1793), on the orders of the Committee of General Security, and after having been denounced as an ultra-revolutionary by Lacroix and Legendre, who, in the autumn of that year, had been sent on a mission to the Seine-Inférieure. He was condemned to death by the Paris Revolutionary Tribunal on 26 Ventôse year II (Sunday, 16 March 1794) at the height of the *hébertiste* crisis, and was guillotined on the same day. The unfortunate *cavalier de la maréchaussée* was thus avenged, seventeen years after his murder; his alleged assassin was, however, condemned to death by a political court and for a political crime, and was executed as an 'ultra-revolutionary' and a demagogue, though his past was also brought up in the course of his trial.

On his release, although draped in the prestigious clothes of a former *embastillé*, Musquinet appears not to have lingered in Paris. Not unnaturally, he also kept clear of Angers, though, in the course of the summer and autumn of 1793, his brother, Musquinet-Saint-Félix, was to carry out important repressive functions there, as president of the *commission militaire*. Nor did he emerge at all in Pontoise. At some stage in 1792, possibly in July, he took up residence in the *commune* of Ingouville – a place on the heights overlooking le Havre that figures more than once in the present study. Apparently he very rapidly ingratiated himself with the inhabitants, for, in December 1792, they elected him *maire*. It was his activities in this capacity that were to be the cause of his eventual undoing.

One of Fouquier's police spies reports on the *maire* of Ingouville, in Frimaire year II (November 1793), from the Luxembourg, to Lacroix and Legendre: 'Je m'empresse de vous marquer que le fameux Musquinet de Lapagne ... est un intrigant, pour ne pas dire un scélérat ... Il est connu d'un nommé Roussiale, habitant de Pontoise, pour avoir volé une somme considérable à une personne dont il étoit le commis. Il demeuroit pour lors à Angers.' On 3 Brumaire (24 October 1793), Alexandre and Canuet, two leading members of the le Havre club, draw up a report which was later to be the basis of the official indictment against this violent, and perhaps unfortunate, man:

On dira que Lapagne est dangereux, que la société doit s'en garantir parce qu'il n'est qu'un Prothée, qui prend toutes les formes pour séduire plus artificieusement l'homme faible, l'égarer et l'attirer dans son parti; Lapagne, à le bien prendre, est un factieux, et n'est autre chose qu'un brigand ... Dès son enfance il fut mauvais fils ... Lapagne a été mal jugé, les portes de son cachot doivent lui être ouvertes; si elles l'ont été en effet, a-t-il pour cela cessé d'être criminel? Non: son délit subsiste toujours parce qu'il n'a point été acquitté ... Un meurtrier est donc redoutable et dangereux ... il arriva là [à Ingouville] vers le mois de juillet 1792, il a répandu quelqu'argent, il en a beaucoup promis, mais il a peu tenu; la rareté des subsistances lui a fourni matière à se faire inspirer quelque confiance.

He is further accused, in this report, of having threatened the *curé* of Ingouville if he did not subscribe to a fund raised for the relief of the poor, and of having taken in an escaped convict.

Musquinet's own account of himself is naturally in a very different tone. In a letter to his brother, dated 22 Pluviôse year II (10 February 1794), he appeals to Musquinet-Saint-Félix:

Ne perds pas de tems, mon frère, il n'y a ni parens, ni frères, ni amis, ni pères, ni enfans qui tiennent, il faut que le salut public passe avant tout. [Musquinet, like many other ultra-revolutionaries, tended to confuse public safety with his own private fortune.] L'imagination du républicain le plus exalté ne pourra jamais concevoir avec quel courage et quelle fermeté j'ai combattu pendant 18 mois toute l'aristocratie du département de la Seine-Inférieure, qui n'a cessé d'être en pleine Contre-Révolution depuis 89 ... tous les monstres réunis aux Cristina, aux Humbert, aux Foache, Boullogne, Begouin de Meaux, Viale, Pouler, La Haye, les Grégoire, les Duval, des Escallier [the ship-owners, grain-traders and slave-traders of the *Grand Quai* of le Havre[1]], tous les négotiants et leurs commis ont cousu un vaste plan de conspiration pour livrer tout le Département à l'ennemi, et sont tous ligués contre la ville de Paris ... Je n'ai pas donné un quart-d'heure à mes plaisirs depuis 3 ans, je n'ai pas trouvé d'autre jouissance, après 22 ans de prison [more accurately, 13], que de servir la révolution avec passion. Tous les conspirateurs ne pouvoient rien sans moi, parce que les batteries nationales qui défendent l'entrée du port sont sur le territoire d'Ingouville sous ma responsabilité. J'ai fait de cette commune un poste d'ob-

---

[1] Robert Richard, 'Le Grand Quai', in *La Porte Océane*, published by the Chambre de Commerce du Havre (Le Havre, 1952).

servation ... J'ai fondé une société populaire qui m'a bien servi,[1] j'ai éclaré le peuple pendant 18 mois, j'étois adoré de tous les habitans des campagnes, j'étois regardé comme le sauveur du pays ... j'ai vécu sous le poignard 18 mois, on est venu chez moi pour m'assassiner, j'ai reçu un coup de fusil au milieu de la nuit, rien ne m'a effrayé ... Legendre me cherchait querelle parce que la municipalité d'Ingouville avoit fait arrêter deux contre-révolutionnaires qui demandaient un roi et appelloient les Anglais, il m'a traité de despote et de voleur, il m'a donné un soufflet, un coup de poing et m'a provoqué pour me battre avec lui dans la rue ... un magistrat incorruptible ... qui, dans le moment que les Anglais étoient dans notre rade, qu'ils envoyaient pendant la nuit dans la ville des signaux avec des fusées, qu'on leur renvoyait les mêmes signaux, qu'on avoit éteint les phanaux [*sic*], que le bruit étoit général que la commune d'Ingouville alloit être incendiée, que je serois la première victime – un magistrat qui ne voit que le danger de la patrie, qui assemble ses concitoyens dans la société populaire ... La contre-révolution a été faite dans le moment, les patriotes ont été écrasés.

The day after writing this confused narrative to his brother, he asked him to intercede on his behalf with Collot-d'Herbois, Deville, Prieur de la Côte-d'Or, Maure ('mon ami'), Montant, Reverchon, Frémanger, Dufourny, David, Vadier, Sergent, and Laloi. He was to remind them of the praise bestowed upon him in his paper by Marat. Perhaps a long habit of petitioning sundry authorities – judicial, political, criminal, *ancien régime*, and revolutionary – and the many years he had spent in prison had given the bewildered man the belief in the efficacity of vast *démarches* of this kind, or perhaps he was merely getting desperate, in the knowledge that *Représentants* like Legendre and Lacroix were in every way a match for the *maire* of a poor village on the outskirts of le Havre – for he can have hardly been known to quite such a huge assembly of revolutionary leaders (one is surprised at the absence of Robespierre in such a *palmarès*). He was, on the other hand, certainly well-inspired to denounce the doubtful Legendre. Such appeals were, however, to no avail. No doubt on instructions from the two Committees of Government, the Revolutionary Tribunal adopted the thesis that Musquinet was a counter-revolutionary disguised as an ultra-patriot (Fouquier was at the time preparing the indictment of the so-called *hébertistes*). The *acte d'accusation*, drawn up on 26 Ventôse (16 March 1794) states:

Il en résulte que ledit Musquinet est un de ces hommes profondément scélérats, lesquels cachés sous le masque du patriotisme, ne s'occupent qu'à ourdir les trames les plus funestes au salut du peuple ... on les voit se remuer en tous sens pour égarer et tromper les bons citoyens, les animer les uns contre les autres, et

---

[1] On the subject of this *société*, see my article, 'La campagne pour l'envoi de l'armée révolutionnaire dans la Seine-Inférieure (septembre 1793–frimaire an II)', republished in *Terreur et subsistances*, p. 104.

les amener ... à s'entre-égorger et par ce moyen faire détruire le peuple par le peuple ... par les moyens des cabales et des intrigues il est parvenu à capter pour un instant la confiance du peuple, et à se faire nommer maire de la commune d'Ingouville ... il en a lâchement abusé pour exercer toute sorte de brigandage et vexations, il a fait des visites domiciliaires chez des citoyens de sa commune ... il a fait arrêter et incarcérer arbitrairement des citoyens ... il a employé tous les moyens pour exciter les citoyens de la commune d'Ingouville ... contre ceux du Havre, et surtout en répandant les calomnies les plus infâmes contre cette dernière commune.

He had made against the municipality and the other authorities of le Havre the classic accusation of having organized a local famine, by arranging for the illegal export of grain from the District de Montivilliers to the southern counties of England; these accusations had been readily accredited among his own *administrés*, who, thus prepared, had descended in force upon the port, in March 1793, in search of the allegedly 'hidden grain supplies', an incident that had, of course, not endeared the *maire* to either the authorities or the *sociétaires* of le Havre.

What is the historian to make of this bitter career, so heavily and constantly marked by violence, by the threat of violence, by the evocation of *coups*, as well as by an inexhaustible belief in 'plots' and 'counter-plots'? Musquinet belonged clearly to the family of the *grands exaspérés* who, in the course of French history, have so often been thrown up by periods of violence and by conditions of suspicion, uncertainty, and insecurity. He is closely related, by temperament, to many of the leading figures of the Counter-Revolution in the south-east; and, indeed, he might have lived longer had he opted for the other side, instead of establishing himself as a self-appointed Cerberus, on the heights overlooking le Havre, as the scourge of the merchants and artisans of that port. His real crime, one feels, was to have obtained such a ready hearing among the numerous poor and violent of that dangerous faubourg, to have campaigned so lustily in favour of a population both disinherited and mobile. We do not know in what circumstances he had arrived in Ingouville in the first place; but there is no doubt that, within a few months, he had built himself up a considerable following in the place; and, as we shall see, he was to be remembered with affection in Ingouville many years after his execution.

His career is at least an exercise in exaltation and in a continuity of violence. Violence the former murderer seemed to attract, as if he could never settle down and live in a settled and peaceful atmosphere. He enjoyed in fact only three years of freedom; and these seem to have been largely devoted to denunciation, to fiery oratory, and to incitement. It is likely that he believed in the plots that he so readily denounced; and it is not surprising that he had no difficulty in gaining the credence of his *administrés*, for whom le Havre had always been an object of loathing and jealousy. Musquinet was brave as well as violent and wildly imprudent; he had even spoken ill of Vadier and had complained of the difficulty of ever obtaining the ear of the Committee of General Security. He was certainly lacking in any political sense and he does not seem even to have had the vaguest notion why a bureaucratic Revolutionary Government should have struck him down with so little hesitation. Was he not a patriot of the purest? And had he not saved his little corner of the French coast from the English (who, literally, seem to have haunted his nights, as he watched out for signals, red and green, from the sea, just as, more understandably, Legendre haunted his days)? The tragic career of this strange man, well-connected, well-born, and occasionally, almost unexplainably criminal, obviously accessible to the grievances of the very poor – perhaps he had both learnt his social history and acquired his bitter sense of social oppression during his many years in prison – indeed, able to speak their language and capture their trust – violent in act and in speech, restless and fiery, is above all an example of the dangers of extreme individualism. Musquinet would not be acceptable to any administered regime; and a revolutionary one had no intention of forgiving a man who had shot a member of the *maréchaussée*. Though briefly enjoying the prestige of a former *embastillé*, Musquinet would not have to wait long before once more experiencing persecution at the hands of a society that he had defied and that he continued so openly to defy. Rather than indulge in a one-man war against le Havre and its inhabitants, he would have done better enlisted in a group of bandits. Crime would perhaps have given him more chance than politics; it was the switch from the one to the other that probably brought about his destruction. But Musquinet, one feels, is not the sort of person to survive, under any regime. He seems to have slipped into crime by accident, and in a panic. Perhaps he had always been the black sheep of his family; certainly, his brother, who had much the same political views as himself, made quite a successful career out of ultra-revolutionary attitudes, using the Revolution, and above all the enveloping demands of repression, as a platform for a successful later career in the Army and on its fringes. But then his brother had not killed a member of the mounted police. The moral of this sad, dramatic story would seem to be that, if one has a past, it is wiser to avoid the politics of *l'exagération* and prudent not to take on, at the head of a small army of shipwrights, smugglers, fishermen, sailors, and prostitutes, the powerful and very united community of one of France's leading Channel ports. Musquinet had succeeded in the first part of an operation often carried out, somewhat hastily, by men such as himself who had a past to live down: *se refaire une virginité républicaine (et judiciaire) en se faisant parachuter dans une commune nouvelle*. But having done this, he proceeded, without delay, on the dangerous path of seeking public appointment and of using his position to disturb a very large number of entrenched interests. What is quite certain about his story is that it can only witness for itself. If Guénot, Cochon, and Chartrey can all exemplify certain general traits regarding careers under and through the Revolution, Musquinet can only be a witness for extreme human folly, both in personal and political terms. He may, of course, have been a class victim of *le Grand Quai* and its allies; but, it should be recalled, he had attacked them too in class terms.[1]

*

In the previous section, we have attempted to describe the emergence of a terrorist mentality and to illustrate both the progression from private life to public militancy and the exploitation of revolutionary chance to private advantage, through the medium of four individual careers within the Revolution, and three beyond the Revolution, a period far more revealing of individual motivations, mentalities, and personalities than that of the Terror, as it no longer put such a premium on the public expression of orthodoxy and on the ostentatious display of fashionable attitudes. The Thermidorian reaction and above all the Directory are such interesting periods for the historian concerned with individuals, because, in both, there are no longer any widely held public assumptions, the recognition signals have been lost, without being replaced by others, so that people had to grope along a narrow ledge, uncertain of the direction in which they were going or of what they might meet round the corner. In short, it was a period in which people were left very much to their own devices and in which personal choice might be a matter of life or death.

None of these careers is entirely representative. Guénot was a semi-criminal, while Chartrey, in his political attitudes and in the sort of posts he obtained in succession, was very much a run-of-the-mill *hébertiste* (or at least that is what he would have been called by his opponents, or by those anxious to have his job in his place); in his deviousness, on the other hand, he represents a special case. Few of his former colleagues and fellow-militants would have been either so anxious, or so well placed, to

---

[1] On Musquinet-Lapagne, see AN, W 338 (601) (Tribunaux révolutionnaires) and F7 4774 55 pl. 4 (Musquinet-Lapagne). See also *Terreur et subsistances*, pp. 97, 105, 226, 231 (18), *Les Armées révolutionnaires*, pp. 100, 651 (42), 823 (57), and 'La mission de Siblot au Havre-Marat', *Annales de Normandie*, May 1953. Musquinet and his brother, Saint-Félix, who was to enjoy a much longer career, would be admirable subjects for a biographical approach to the study of the fringe elements of French society before and during the Revolution. Both brothers owed much to the Revolution – Lapagne, his freedom, and, later, his death – both adopted ultra-revolutionary attitudes. But there the parallel between them ends. Saint-Félix, apart from ambition, clearly had a great deal of sense.

cover up their traces. The secret of his success was a mobility that enabled him to escape from the needling memory, the jealousy and the confining meanness of a quarter, a small town, or a village. Mobility, too, enabled Musquinet-Lapagne to acquire a new identity, to separate himself from a compromising past and to establish himself as a champion of the people's rights in a *commune* in which he had been completely unknown even in the early years of the Revolution. But his very success, in his new role as a public figure and as an ultra-revolutionary, was to be his undoing. If, like Guénot, he had operated, as a terrorist, *en coulisse*, there is a reasonable chance that he might have survived, even as a less combative *maire* of Ingouville. Cochon, as we have seen, could witness for many of those bureaucrats who administered terror at a high level. The only claims that we can make for any of the four is that their careers tell us quite a lot about the impact of the Revolution, at its various stages – and it was the rapid succession of these stages that made the revolutionary period such a lottery in terms of individual opportunity or collapse – on the lives of persons who are both private and public. In Guénot, the private and the public persons are indistinguishable; much the same could be said of Musquinet, a career so bizarre as to be *hors concours*, but in which the element of continuity is extreme violence. He *could* not, one feels, have survived. It so happens that he was cut down by the *robespierriste* Terror; had he not been, he would inevitably have been arrested under the Thermidorian reaction, mild though it was in Upper Normandy, and he is the sort of intransigent enthusiast who would then no doubt have become enmeshed in inane *babouviste* commitments. In Chartrey, lurking behind the public militant and the Occupation official, we can obtain convincing, and not unattractive, glimpses of the private person beyond. Cochon, at a very different level, is never a private person.

So much for people, private and public, within the context of their careers. It is now time to approach the terrorist, both through his more personal traits, and, above all, in the collective context of prevailing orthodoxy, class and social origin, and professional expertise. It would certainly be unwise, in pursuit of any of these investigations, to make too much of conscious decision, deliberate ambition, clearly felt ideological conviction, or mere desire for power, as the only sources of revolutionary commitment. As a number of case histories of the unfortunate members of the *Commune robespierriste* show, only too clearly and tragically, it was often very easy to be caught in the enveloping machinery of the Terror – *dans l'engrenage de la Révolution* – as the result of a single, or of a series of minor resolutions, none of them in the least important or decisive in itself. One man was eventually to be engulfed in the barbaric collective proscription of all the members of Fleuriot-Lescot's *Conseil général* because he had been sufficiently well thought of by his fellow-citizens to have been proposed for, and – after much hesitation and many calls to his sense of duty – reluctantly to have accepted, a post as *administrateur des hôpitaux*. The rest had followed, with dreadful momentum, from the apparently innocuous decision, dictated by a sense of duty and by a commitment to charity. The road to the guillotine had led eventually from this acceptance of a position of no apparent political importance. It did, however, mean that the poor man came under the aegis of the *maire* and the *Conseil général*. Furthermore, it was difficult to refuse office, when thus offered, in a time of public emergency. Refusal could indicate a selfish indifference to the welfare of one's fellow-citizens, or even worse. In the conditions of the year II, *any* public office, save perhaps one so completely apolitical as *juge de paix*, could expose its occupant to a political affiliation that he had never sought and of which he might be completely unaware. It is very unlikely that any members of the last *Commune* of the revolutionary period ever thought of themselves, for instance, as *robespierristes*; and by the time official opinion, closely imitated by a sedulous echo from the *grand public*, had bestowed that fateful title upon them, they would be either dead, or outlaws, on the run, generally not for long; for these men, all well known in their Sections – a fact to which they owed their fatal eminence – were the last people to be able to go into hiding or even to think of doing so. They were all *hommes de quartier*, enclosed in a warm, but compromising, family network. Often it was as easy to become a terrorist as to be picked for a jury. The Terror had a way of enveloping people in its dangerous tentacles, however slight the origin of a hesitant commitment. For many, it was impossible to keep out of sight; this was a luxury often denied the man who was well set up in his own quarter. It was only the totally obscure or the very wily who might achieve this merciful state.

A return to the individual terrorist is, in any case, long overdue. For we have supped too long and too well of *les sans-culottes*, of *la sans-culotterie*, of *le sans-culottisme*, until we are sick and tired of the lot of them. We have seen them drilled, marched up and down, and dismissed, responding with alacrity to the orders of their commanders. It is altogether too well rehearsed, too much of a set fairground piece; and, in some cases, their movements, like a film run at speed, become increasingly staccato, as, in even shorter books on exactly the same theme, the *sans-culottes*, reduced now to derisory proportions in which no human features are any more perceptible, automata, responding to concepts, rush through their prepared drill. Historians are so much given to placing unsophisticated and primitive protesters inside a 'movement', as if they had been bought up by a football team, or were holding cards indicating that Citizen X was 'No. 3223 of the Paris *sans-culotte* movement'. They may have heard of the word, for they used it of themselves, just as their enemies had used it of them, but of the 'movement' it is likely that they had not the slightest notion. They were not, after all, readers of *Past & Present*.

Indeed, it would be difficult to imagine a more disparate group than the so-called *sans-culottes*, a mere *agglomérat* of negative attitudes and prejudices, of crude fears, of collective antipathies, of shared and accepted habits of violence, and of violent solutions, of a range of personalities extending from the semi-literate Breton market porter or Aveyronnais water-carrier, to the sophisticated, but embittered *clerc de procureur*, the self-satisfied, domineering building contractor, the successful grocer, and the much respected, wise doctor – finally, of a range of vision – and ambition – that hardly took in more than a single street, at most, a small complex of streets in a well-defined quarter, clearly differentiated topographically from all its neighbours. The *sans-culottes* are only definable collectively in terms of what they were against – and they were against an awful lot of people, an awful lot of attitudes, and an awful lot of institutions. They are never definable in terms of class and social origins, nor, indeed, of provincial origins.

The Paris *sans-culotte* might opt for the Republic of the year II, or rather, for his own peculiar, highly localized version of it – the Republic of the Gravilliers or of the Arcis would be something very different from the Republic of the Montagne or of Lepeletier; the Republic of the Section Finistère or of the Panthéon-Français were miniature Genevas, unique, proud and suspicious of all that surrounded them – his Lyon equivalent, at least in attitude, temperament, and relative lack of wealth and luxury, would massively opt for Lyon, that is, against the Republic, or at least the Republic of Paris. His Marseille equivalent would do what his better-educated fellow-citizens told him he should do; if he was told that the best way to 'defend the Republic', to 'obey the Convention', to 'déjouer les intrigues des ennemis de la Révolution' was to enlist in a *compagnie du centre*, or in some other federalist force, he was likely so to enlist, in the belief that he was doing the right thing. Later, even repressive commissions were prepared to give him the benefit of the doubt: *il avait cru bien faire*. How could he know *which* Republic to defend, when, apparently, there were so many of them, all of them, so it seemed, respectable and desirable? The best thing he could do was to take advice from where he had always taken advice: his neighbour, the grocer or the godlike *notaire*, or the big ship-owner, who brought employment and prosperity to his city. His Bordeaux equivalent would, if living in or near the Chartrons, opt for the autonomy of Bordeaux; but if he squatted in the untidy shacks and hutments of one of the new working-class quarters on the edge of the city, he would be more prone to listen to the *Représentants*, encamped at la Réole or Libourne. If again he lived in the old heart of the city, near Sainte-Croix, he might at first opt for Bordeaux Mark 1 (that is the acting municipality, the Bordeaux of the wine-growers, wine merchants, shipping merchants, and slavers), then, after a few weeks, a certain amount of observation, and a bit of persuasion – both from within and from outside, for one of the peculiarities of this ghostly and somewhat unreal crisis was that petitions and addresses, both from federalist municipalities and from authorities that had decided to remain faithful to Paris, reached the Bordeaux Sections indiscriminately, often by the same courier – veer over to Bordeaux Mark 2 (a jumble of peripheral and central Sections and some of the authorities outside the city).

In Toulouse, *sans-culotte* opinion, based on the Sections on the south bank of the Garonne, took its cue from the municipality, composed largely of merchants and *parlementaire* hangers-on from the well-to-do Sections on the north bank – putting, first, a timid toe into federalist commitment, then, after only a few days' hesitation, hastily withdrawing from an attitude so positive, and draping itself in prudent, somewhat tepid loyalty to the Convention. The important thing, one feels, for all the Toulousains, *sans-culottes* or *notables*, was to present a solid front to the outside world, prevent the 'strangers' – Chabot and the other *Représentants*, the garrison commanders, and so on – from having any good pretext to interfere in the private affairs of the *capitale du Midi* (for Toulouse too was a pretender to this coveted title). In Toulouse, too, the proximity of the armies of the King of Spain helped all the inhabitants to get their priorities right; with the *fanatiques espagnols* at the gates of Perpignan, polarizations dictated from as far away as Lyon, Marseille, Avallon, and Paris, might appear above all irrelevant. It was easier to discover some form at least of acceptable unanimity with the enemy almost at the gates. What must also have helped the Toulousains eventually to make up their mind on which side to stand was the fact that the authorities of Bordeaux had apparently come out so strongly in favour of federalism. To do the opposite to what the Bordelais did was an ancient rule of Toulousain conduct and was also flattering to local pride. It was also in accordance with the interests of the city as the principal centre of the grain trade of the Lauragais plain; for the municipal authorities would then have a good excuse to cut off the supplies of corn, via the canal du Midi and the valley of the Garonne, normally destined to the markets of the 'rebel' port. It was no doubt significant, in this respect, that places like Tonneins and Moissac, situated on the supply routes to Bordeaux, likewise plumped for the Convention.

In Toulouse, perhaps more than anywhere else, municipal solidarity took precedence over any distinctions, in terms of class interests, between *sans-culottes*, merchants, clergy and the hangers-on of the former *Parlement*. It was not only the Spaniards who had been instrumental in achieving this apparent miracle. Throughout the revolutionary period, including the Thermidorian reaction, despite the fulminations of the newspaper, *L'Anti-Terroriste*, against the former terrorist personnel, politics remained those of moderation. The year 1795 went by without any large-scale prison massacres in the city. Even during the troubled years of the Directory, despite the existence of an active neo-terrorist cell around Destrem and that of ultra-royalist groups, the White Terror never took the violent form it was to take in the Ariège or in the Rhône valley. The bells, it was stated with some pride, were rung in the Haute-Garonne, but there were no killings during their period.[1] There was a royalist-inspired peasant rising, in the neighbourhood of Revel, in the year VII, but it received only tepid support from the prudent Toulouse ultras. If the city fathers were eventually to welcome in, with such demonstrations of enthusiasm, the advancing armies of General Beresford, it was not only because the English troops were well-disciplined and paid for everything in cash, it was above all because their arrival preserved the city from the horrors of war and guaranteed the population a safe transition to the new regime. Despite the murder of General Ramel, the second White Terror was a mild affair here, although, in the early years of the Restoration, the town was to be one of the principal strongholds, thanks to the political influence of Villèle, of southern brands of ultra-royalism.[2] In the revolutionary period, despite the stresses of federalism and Terror, the *sans-culottes* from the south of the river would have subscribed, like everyone else, to the old cry of *Viva Tolosa*. And, in the old centre of the *Jeux Floraux*, couplets, both patriotic and ultra-royalist, were sung, in strong tenor voices, in the cafés bordering on the place du Capitole, *moderato cantabile*, in dialect, a further protection from interference from the north and the north-west and an additional guarantee of local solidarity.

Nor indeed are the *sans-culottes* even definable in terms of the institutions through which they operated and which, for a time, gave them a very loose collective identity. For the so-called *mouvement sectionnaire* could be similarly differentiated in political terms. The 29 May revolt in Lyon was an operation carried out by the thirty-two Sections against a municipality dominated by a Jacobin minority; and, thenceforth, till the end of the siege, Lyon federalism operated primarily through the *assemblées sectionnaires* and the *comités révolutionnaires* of the Sections. The same was true of Marseille. In the end, *la sans-culotterie* is revealed as almost as useless a term of collective identification as that old, battered favourite, once respectable, now completely sunk in public esteem, a

---

[1] *The Police and the People.*
[2] Daniel Resnick, *The White Terror and the Political Reaction after Waterloo* (Princeton, 1966).

leering, toothless *péripatéticienne*, the last on the rue Quincampoix beat, *la bourgeoisie révolutionnaire*.

In this respect, Colin Lucas, in a recent, remarkably sensitive and imaginative thesis,[1] has proposed collective definitions and groupings that are far more sophisticated than the crude jumble sale of Soboul's *mouvement de masse* or Rudé's wearisomely repetitive *Crowd* (always 'tending' to do something or other, spending all its time 'tending', whether to riot on a Monday, or to get drunk in a wine-shop, or to destroy a threshing machine if it did not like a threshing machine, or to riot on or near a market, if there were a market day, or on or near a grain port, if there were a lot of grain coming through). Referring to the militants of Montbrison, Dr Lucas suggests connections derived from school days, the fraternity of the classroom, the frequentation of the same café, shared habits of leisure, indoors or out of doors: bowls, fishing, hunting, walking, pigeon-fancying, cockfighting, dominoes, cards, *Tarot*-reading, conundrums, gossip, malice, amorous adventures, boasting of amorous adventures, visits to the local establishment – the range is infinitely expandable – family relationships, the fact that two men married cousins, the fact that two men were neighbours, lived in the same street, the fact that two men were roughly of the same age, had fought in the Seven Years' War in the same sectors or in the American War, the fact that two men had done their *Tour de France* together, the fact that a certain quarter specialized in a given trade – tanners generally lived together, if only because, owing to the smell, no one else would ever live near them – the fact of belonging to a religious minority, the fact of a shared deformity or of a common illness, the simple fact that two men liked each other. One of the Roannais militants speaks out in favour of an ex-terrorist, threatened by the Counter-Terror, under the Thermidorian reaction, because, as he says, *C'était mon ami, je ne partageais point ses opinions, mais on a été amis depuis notre enfance.* Friendship is no doubt difficult to record historically, for it is much less likely to leave written records than long-standing animosities and personal feuds, so many of which could be revealed either in litigation, or in the even more favourable circumstances of the Terror, in the *livres des dénonces* kept up-to-date by revolutionary committees. Comments like the above are rare; but we cannot of course reckon without the ties of friendship and affection, even if they so often defy any form of documentation.

In most towns divided by rivers, there would be a right and a wrong side of the river on which to live – both Toulouse and Lyon are good examples of this type of differentiation by quarter and *rive*. Those who lived on the wrong side would be likely to have a greater sense of solidar-

---

[1] Since published as *The Structure of the Terror: the Case of Javogues and the Loire* (1973).

ity and, consequently, a readier proneness to collective action than the more privileged, but also more supine, inhabitants of the right side. In this respect, it was better to be on high ground than on marshy and easily flooded areas caught inside a bend in the river; but those who were thus caught in the bend and who were regularly exposed both to natural disasters and to unpleasant and unhygienic smells and vapours would derive from their relative misfortune a sense of identity.

Finally, leisure is a more lasting reality than militancy, a temporary, peculiar, abnormal state of tension; and – and this is the rather reassuring lesson of the first French Revolution – leisure outlives militancy, is, indeed, the inner rot that will destroy it in the end. Perhaps one should not, however, make too much of this distinction, for, no doubt, in many other instances beside those so dramatically provided by the example of the Loire, militancy itself may merely have been the means by which a power élite succeeded in perpetuating itself, even during this difficult period. Nor does militant commitment take into account the equally important interconnections and relationships, services mutually rendered, mutual dependence, or unequal dependence, of work and employment. If it does, then it will simply reproduce a collectivity already existing; and, in that case, *la sans-culotterie* will merely be a disguised trade union, an assemblage of building labourers and building contractors, a close corporation of *mariniers* (it was the river that held the *égorgeurs*, the counter-revolutionaries of Condrieu, so closely together), a freemasonry of barbers, surgeons, and wigmakers, a proud oligarchy of watch-makers and jewellers and goldsmiths (as in the Section du Pont-Neuf, in Paris). In Bordeaux, almost every inhabitant had a vested interest, direct or indirect, in the slave and sugar trade with the Antilles; and this shared interest commanded political alignments and took precedence over any other form of militancy, indeed, largely prevented any other form of militancy from emerging at all, save among the fringe elements of the population: itinerant tinsmiths, pedlars, wandering children, those who could look outside, those who had come from the Gers and the Landes and from the poorest areas of the Pyrenees to seek perhaps seasonal employment in the city, the sort of sturdy mountaineers from the Pyrenees who, in the course of the first half of the following century, sold their bodies to the *agences de remplacement*, so as to relieve the Bordelais and, indeed, the peasantry of the Gironde, from the burden of military service.[1] In a community like Bordeaux, the chimney-sweep was as dependent on the wine trade as the governess, the seamstress, the domestic servant, or the sedan-chair carrier.

Finally, of course, there are the time-servers. *Sans-culotte* was a con-

[1] Bernard Schnapper, *Le Remplacement militaire en France. Quelques aspects politiques, économiques et sociaux du recrutement au XIXme siècle* (Paris, 1968).

temporary expression. It meant a number of things, all of them desirable in the conditions of 1793 and the year II. It was, therefore, a good thing to be; and a great many people rapidly discovered that they were. It was, after all, a title very much for the taking; a few adjustments in dress and in speech might be all that was needed. And as it was as much in the mind as anywhere else, it was often enough to think that one was a *sans-culotte* to become one. When a certain external way of life, when given loudly-expressed attitudes become fashionable, there will always be a great many takers, a rapid army of converts. In Rouen – and in how many other places – the so-called *sans-culottes* of the year II are the *notables* of 1789, the *monarchiens* of 1790, the moderates of 1792, and the Thermidorians of 1795. In some places, they are the *patriotes de 89*, in others, the *patriotes de 93*, the old-stagers or the late-comers. It was a question of chance, of local power groups, of where one stood in the queue, of at what stage ambitions had been satisfied, of how to leap-frog over those in front. This is where external events could be usefully exploited; the Paris political labels, when stuck on provincial backs, could mean something quite different. They were above all useful as a means of toppling existing power groups and of taking their place. *On a chacun son hébertiste; on est toujours le dantoniste de quelqu'un.* These were, all at once, bad things to be; they could then be used to clear the decks. The labels might not even come from Paris; they could be of more local origin. In the Loire, 'federalism' was brought in from outside, by groups of armed men riding in from Lyon. But the experience of 'federalism' and the subsequent repression directed against those who had collaborated with it, enabled one power group – of almost exactly the same social standing and wealth – to oust another in those towns that had been most affected by the crisis. In those that 'federalism' had bypassed, there was scarcely any change at all in the power structures, either at District or municipal level. Both those who had been exercising authority ever since the beginning of the Revolution, and, in some instances, ever since the assemblies of 1787, and those who were thus able to come in on the backs of the 'federalists' in the autumn of 1793, would call themselves *sans-culottes* and would be considered as such. But we do not hear the word *sans-culotte* any more much after the spring of 1794; in 1795, it completely goes out of existence, even as a term of abuse. It was probably best forgotten, for, at one time, so many people had taken it as their own that it would have been embarrassing when, in the year III, *sous le règne des honnêtes gens*, the *notaire*, walking on the *mail* with his family, on the way back from Mass, met the *procureur*, with his family, on the way back from Mass, and recognized in him *son frère sans-culotte* to whom, on one of those lacrimose and effusive *tutoiement* occasions, he had given *le baiser fraternel*, in the presence of hundreds, at a meeting at the local *société populaire*. Such things were best forgotten, it was in the interest of a great many people to do so. A number of former *sans-culottes*, it is true, were to perish physically, in the violent anarchy of the White Terror. Others were driven into exile, or went into prudent hiding. But most merely faded away.

What then is left? One can hear the protests: all the signposts have gone, all the charts of collective identities have been destroyed. How is one to find one's way amidst the confused and, often, one suspects, deliberately created complexity of French provincial life, during the Revolution and beyond, when no generalizations as to groups and group motivations will stand up to a close scrutiny? How can anyone ever again write anything about the French Revolution on the national level when, apparently, every place is a law to itself and nothing is quite what it seemed to be at first sight?

Such qualifications do of course make the history of this recalcitrant period and diversified country very difficult. But then it was a grave error, even a fraud perpetrated on the reader or the student, ever to suggest that it could be easy and could be confined within the framework of easily assimilated general laws. All that we have proposed, in the first place, is to emphasize some of the difficulties, to suggest some new lines of approach, and, above all, to insist on the urgent necessity of rediscovering the individual – not, of course, the unrelated individual, for, unhappily, such a being does not exist – but the individual caught up in environment – Ingouville, for instance, must have affected Musquinet, almost as much, no doubt, as Musquinet affected Ingouville – or collective commitment, the man drawn into *l'engrenage de la Révolution*, as the result of an initial, hesitant step, or the individual attempting to escape from both environment and commitment, or, finally, the individual struggling to exist at both levels at once. One of the common themes is the interaction of public catastrophe and private fortune, the exploitation of national emergency, either for personal advantage, or simply as a means of survival. This, above all, is the theme that I intend to take a stage further, in the context of those who *vivent en marge* (there is no adequate English equivalent for this admirably expressive phrase), whether in lonely squalor, at the top of a tall house, or in a hut in the woods, or in the closed confines of mental illness and madness, or, on the contrary, in proud and open defiance, in an anti-society, rejecting the Revolution and all its works, replacing it, as irrelevant – and it is reassuring to think of a great Revolution as a magnificent irrelevance – with its own codes, its own hierarchy, its own language, its own sense of time, and its own calendar. I have taken as my example the *bande d'Orgères*; some other groups of highwaymen and bandits might have done equally well, for there are plenty to choose from, especially during the Directory. The *bande d'Orgères*, however, has certain advantages for the illustration of my principal theme: it is well documented, it extended over a period longer than the Revolution, at both ends, existing, as it were, *en marge de la Révolution*, and it was limited, both in scope of activities and in recruitment, to a definable geographical area, thus offering, like Lyon as a centre of Counter-Terror, Counter-Revolution, and crime, an example of the conditioning of individual and collective conduct by environment – in this case, a very intractable one. But the *bande* is not merely a collectivity, a criminal version of Rudé's *Crowd*, though its components can be cut down to a certain number of trade and occupation categories. It is composed too of individuals, of personalities who come to life, even through a documentation largely collective and the work of magistrates and policemen, and who have their own standards of comfort, discipline, pleasure, honour, and ambition. As Eric Hobsbawm has said, bandits (unlike Babeufs) are never boring; and these particular bandits cannot be said either to have influenced, or been influenced by, the course of the Revolution, though, as a result of the great famine of 1795 and the consequent enormously increased wretchedness of an overcrowded rural population, in an area of rich farmland and visible, and recent, wealth, contrasting with dramatic poverty, they may have been the more readily supplied with a steady supply of recruits.

Another aim is to emphasize the importance of the angle of vision. To employ a truism, things look different, depending on the level from which they are viewed. I am proposing angles which are not those of the Convention or of the other seats of political power. One angle is as good as another; and the serving girl knew rather more about authority than a *physiocrate*. Restif's calendar is marked by memory, rather than by revolutionary *journées*; it is a calendar both more reassuring and showing an acuter sense of priorities. So, after a brief excursion into biographical method, a method proposed not as an exclusive approach, but rather in an effort to supplement other less conventional, but, recently, more well-tried approaches, and the illustration of the experience of the Revolution as witnessed by four very different individual lives, we are embarking on a groping, tentative journey, into a secret world of closed rooms, of hidden doors, the abodes of the humble, the anonymous, the fearful, the prudent, the unambitious, the indifferent, the superstitious, the wicked, the cynical, the blind, the deaf and the dumb, the very mad, the half mad, the sinned against and the raped, the trackless world of servant girls, daughters, and seamstresses, governesses and laundrywomen, *bouquetières* and *revendeuses*, the very poor, the very lonely, and the very sick.

Juxtapositions such as Revolution and birth, Revolution and love, and Revolution and sex have no doubt little meaning, in eighteenth-century terms, save to illustrate the irrelevance of the Revolution to some of the most important human activities. Are they then worth proposing, if they merely confirm what must, from the start, have been self-evident to any observer endowed with common sense? The objection is perhaps valid; but it is no doubt helpful, even so, to suggest some of the more obvious limits to revolutionary action, as far as the life of the individual or of the couple were concerned. Indeed a combination such as Revolution and birth is in fact not entirely irrelevant to two of the principal themes of this book: continuity and survival. A steady succession of childbirths, from, let us say, 1787 to 1795 – and we can produce instances of this kind, more especially in the families of those who were to be the most directly affected by the political course of the Revolution, the victims of White or of Counter-Terror – is as good an argument in favour of continuity and, indeed, of survival of a sort, as the private calendars proposed by Restif and by other extreme individualists. A child conceived in 1787 hardly reflects on the *assemblée des notables*; a conception of 1795 has little to tell us about the Thermidorian reaction, though if a marked decline in conceptions can be proved for that year, we have obtained a valuable commentary on the extent of the famine crisis of the year III. Sex and love may have been recalcitrant to most of the efforts undertaken by the revolutionary authorities to organize them in the service of the Republic; it is none the less interesting to recall that they did attempt so to organize them.

Revolution and death is, on the other hand, a juxtaposition that is always meaningful, in a society in which murder is so frequently the ultimate answer in a political dispute and in which the politics of vengeance take on new forms, increased bitterness and a greater degree of impunity, with each year of the revolutionary period, each successive year providing yet more to avenge, as the corpses of the recently slain pile up in shallow graves, in the extensions of the old cemeteries, or simply disappear downstream, towards the sea.

It is, I think, on the whole, a reassuring, even a hope-giving exercise, if one can take one's eyes off so much random killing and forget the cost, in personal and family terms, of murder and maiming.[1] For it illustrates the limitless capacity of the individual to live out of reach of terrible and dangerous events and to shut the door on the shouting, the screams, the roars, the howls, the ugly surge of collective commitment and of vengeful lust (just as, on hearing repeated appeals of *au secours, au secours*, the wiser, the more prudent citizens, in the Saône and Rhône valleys at least, would close their ears, and, when confronted with the spectacle of a stab-

[1] AN, BB 18 687 (Rhône, Merlin au Ministre, 13 frimaire an VIII): 'Merlin demeure à Lyon, rue de la Barre, no. 192, expose qu'ayant été blessé le 25 frimaire an VII [Saturday 15 December 1798] d'un coup de stilet triangulaire par une bande d'assassins royaux, il en résulte un œil tiré, et le second très endommagé, enfin myope à un degré très inférieur pour la vue, l'exposant, ami de la liberté, avoit un sort avant la Révolution, il lui restoit plus de 5,000 livres, il s'est vu fatalement forcé de la manger dans sa maladie et [il] se trouve au dépourvu de tout.'

bing, would turn the other way, closing the shutters and bolting the doors). For every single man who listened with rapture to the impetuous notes of the *trompette guerrière*, there were ten who closed their ears to this dangerous music; and there were many more who did not even faintly perceive the strident roar of Unanimity. Unanimity was a moral concept that had little to offer the provincial artisan or tradesman who had always had to fend for himself and to keep his head above water in a small, fiercely competitive, world.

9

La Vie en Marge: *Living on the Fringe of the Revolution**

'Imaginez des êtres sans morale, sans idées, ni de l'honnêteté, ni de la religion, ni de la droiture, en un mot, d'aucune loi sociale ... Rarement ces filles sont corrigibles; elles naissent, meurent et vivent dans Paris ... sans en avoir jamais eu plus d'idées que si elles étoient nées parmi les Hottentots ... Toute leur politique est à la Grève, c'est là seulement qu'elles voient un acte d'autorité publique; le Guet est pour elles tout le Gouvernement et le Commissaire est le seul Magistrat.'

> Restif de la Bretonne,
> *Tableaux de la vie et des mœurs du XVIIIme siècle*

'... répond que la Révolution, sans lui plaire, ne l'a pas fatigué au point de rien entreprendre contre elle ...'

> Cross-examination of a madman by a Grenoble doctor,
> in Ventôse year VI (February–March 1798)

'Ils sont étrangers à tout ce qui dépasse hors du cercle de leurs plaisirs.'

> Restif de la Bretonne, *Monsieur Nicolas*, VI, 1797, p. 3252

'Je m'écartais des Groupes ... et je suivais tantôt Victorette, tantôt Septimanète, Sérafine, Extelle-Henriette, Cécile, Rosette, Lutine, Frédérique, Sofiette, Eléonorine, Yvette, Céleste, Dorotée, Nina, Reine, Alcazette, Issine ...'

> Ibid., 1789, p. 3197

THERE ARE, OF course, many possible approaches to the problem of the relationship between Revolution and private life. One could multiply endlessly both the 'angles of vision', the private calendars, and the use of an ever-wider extent of personal case histories. It is unlikely, however, that one's conclusions would be any less tentative. In this frontier zone of history, much will remain unstated, a great deal has to be guessed at, often on very thin evidence, something may even have to be

---

* From *Reactions to the French Revolution*, pp. 128–79.

348

invented. People who are afraid are not loquacious; and a great many people were afraid, at least in the conditions of 1793–4, for both the Thermidorian reaction and the confused years of the Directory echo a clamour of vituperation, argument, denunciation, self-justification, and verbal incitement; that is why, as we have suggested in another context, it is much easier to pin down the lonely individual, the private man, after 1795 than before. Many more were above all anxious to escape attention. The study of the first or great Terror, especially in the Norman Departments, is often reassuring, for it reveals the ability both of individuals and of whole communities to keep pace with political change, by constantly adapting their language to the needs of orthodoxy, while retaining their private lives and living much as before. *Attentisme* has always been one of the most admirable political virtues of the French, particularly in the countryside; and, in an agrarian economy of this kind, the countryman is eventually likely to have the last word. The Counter-Terror was, we have seen, primarily a rural phenomenon, though it might at times invade towns, even inhabit them. It did not mean that the rural counter-terrorist rejected the Revolution *in toto*, that he was a counter-revolutionary. He was generally nothing at all of the kind. But what he had objected to was the Terror of the year II and to those who had served it with indecent zeal. 1795 was his opportunity to turn the tables; 1796 and 1797 were better opportunities still. For the countryman's chance came with the virtual disappearance of a centralized State during these troubled years. It was not as if he wished to put anything in its place, he did not even think, as some gentlefolk did, in terms of a mythical *royaume du Midi* or of an Arthurian West, he merely wanted to be left alone; and this he did achieve, to some extent, once the crisis of the year II, with its terrible pressures, had passed. He wanted to be free of Paris, indeed of every other *chef-lieu*. So that Thermidor and the Directory constitute brief oases of extreme individualism and of un-government, a trough of anarchy, between the rigid, terrifying, uniform systems of the year II and of the Empire. Whatever may be said about their weaknesses, their incoherence, there is no doubt that they met the unstated needs of a large section of the rural population.

The other danger of pursuing the individual further into the elusive secrets of his private life is that one might end up writing, yet again, in the wake of so many Hachette historians, an 'Everyday Life [under the Terror, the Thermidorian Reaction, and the Directory]' and fall into the profitable, but footling trap of anecdotal history. I do not intend to eavesdrop, even at the door of the servant's attic or of the apprentice's cupboard-bedroom. My purpose is to study elements that tend to hover on the fringes of any society and that, for a number of personal reasons, seek to shun the glaring light of publicity and avoid the dangerous race of collective ambition, power, and responsibility over others. My other purpose in the present section is to attempt to illustrate that, for many, it was possible almost to live outside the Revolution, to opt out of collective commitment altogether, and, that for a few, it was even possible to ignore it, caged as they were in an obsessive and all-embracing mental prison (though it would appear that the Revolution did sometimes penetrate, albeit in a very garbled form, or in a confusion of myth and deranged historical memory, into the minds of the very mad). For some, this 'opting out' was not even a matter of choice; they did not reject the Revolution, the Revolution rejected *them*. The Revolution, if it were not for the few – though in many of its aspects it was entirely élitist – was never, at any point, for the *many*. It had nothing to offer the vast body of the poor, of vagrants, beggars, the sick, the old, the cold, abandoned children, ill-treated children, save worse conditions, better repression, and an additional opprobrium that saw in the petty thief – the child that stole a log off a wood port, the servant girl who stole a sheet – an 'enemy of the Republic'. Was not, in the conditions of the year II, *everything* the property of the Republic? Human beings, animals, the woods, the rivers, the produce of the land? The poacher, the inhabitants of the villages in the great bend of the Seine that enclosed Paris, who fished the river illegally at night and with prohibited tackle, they too were 'enemies of the Republic'. They too were driven out of and against the Revolution.

I am seeking to depict individuals, swimming desperately in collective currents, attempting to keep their heads above stormy waters and to reach the other shore. This is perhaps an over-dramatic view of events. For we can witness other people who merely turn their backs on the public scene, shutting the window to drown the cries of *à mort* or *à la lanterne*, not merely as dreadful and threatening, but also as irrelevant; they did not care, it was no concern of theirs. They wished to preserve their apartness. Restif was by no means the only obsessive egotist of this kind. And we will see too individuals exposed to ancient, predatory violence. The rape of a rural servant girl in the Pays de Caux in the year VII bears no relation to the Revolution and its aftermath. It is an act of private war. So are a number of murders to which I have already referred. It is not always possible, or even desirable from the point of view of historical method, to bring out the pointers and to establish the relationship between public and private acts. Sometimes, the only relationship in fact is one of contemporaneity, or simultaneity, like the seduction of a Lorraine servant girl, on her second night in Paris, 9–10 Thermidor. This is why I shall deal at some length on the importance, to individuals, of private calendars and of dates that are unworthy of historical textbooks and of educational drilling. When all the usual recognition signals have been destroyed, as was the case in the years 1794–1804 or so, people will naturally tend to fall back on family and village memory or on personal reminiscence. The past – the familiar past – will appear some sort of guarantee of the future, when the present is utterly uncertain.

Some may object that this is a singularly ungenerous and therefore incomplete account of human conduct, allowing so little place as it does for revolutionary enthusiasm, disinterestedness, and patriotic sincerity. There is no intention of denying the strength of these more conventional, public emotions. Nor do I intend to cut down the poor *sans-culotte* to the dimensions of an articulated puppet, jerked into movement by envy, malice, rancour, and low ambition. There is little place for martyrs in this account, because it is not particularly concerned with martyrs, or with persons in any way admirable or exceptional. This is a chronicle of ordinariness, of privacy, representing as it does an attempt, in revolutionary terms, to re-create a collective *Diary of a Nobody*, not necessarily drab, occasionally picturesque, but certainly not always edifying. There are many levels at which people can, and do, live and at which they can be depicted. In this book, the emphasis has at all times been on the lowest, most private, and most obscure of them. Save for the counter-revolutionary, especially in the Lyon setting, and for the counter-terrorist, in Lyon and elsewhere, this is not intended to be a public group photograph. I hope at least that I have made some of these obscure individuals, caught for a moment in the 'still' of an attitude, bending in rapt concentration over a table of dominoes, or eating a melon with a stiletto, used a few hours previously for the murder of a *commissaire général*, or ironing the shirt of a ruffian sleeping upstairs, after a highway robbery, or running for cover towards the Rhône, a boat, and the safety of the far bank, 'statufied' in the secrecy of a private act, convincing, living persons, not mere chronicles of names and nicknames, places of birth, age, and appearance, nor pawns in some vast enterprise of social structure mechanics. At least, whenever possible, I will allow them to witness for themselves, in their own language. For the Revolution exists as much through their narrow, unremarkable lives, or in their violent and bloody enterprises, as in the lives of the great.

POPULAR CULTURE

The Revolution was not all-embracing and totally invasive. There were some sectors of private life that must have escaped it altogether. It is doubtful, for instance, that love marched readily to the dictates of the year II and that the General Will invaded the attic of the servant girl and the apprentice. The Terror might destroy the sleep of the unworthy with the 4 a.m. *visite domiciliaire* of the man with the arrest warrants; but the vast majority of the innumerable furnished rooms on seventh floors were never visited (and, when they were, it was on the part of the *commissaire*, come to establish the facts of a suicide or an accident, or to carry out a search for stolen goods or to draw up an inventory of the scanty posses- sions of a dead seamstress).

Nor of course did sex respond to the dictates of the revolutionary war trumpet and to the *rousseauite* visions of a prissy Robespierre. Young people might walk hand in hand down avenues of poplars, garlanded with flags and tricolour ribbons, listening to the massed choirs of revolution- ary feast days, their hearts brimming with fraternity; but they did not live in revolutionary dormitories, and, once they had gone home, they could shut the door on the year II. Saint-Just's dreadful Sparta was happily the nightmare project of a cruel, relentless, and humourless twenty-seven- year-old, the *phalanstères* are nineteenth-century models in collective crankiness.

Suicide, on the other hand, appears, for a time, to march to the revolu- tionary overtures and to respond as much to public as to private pressures. At this period, it would always be credited with political connotations, even if in fact it had been a purely private gesture of despair. In Chalon- sur-Saône, in the year VI, a suicide was at once subjected to political exploitation, on this occasion against the *concierge* of the local prison. In a petition drawn up by the poor man and his friends and addressed to the local magistrates, 22 Vendémiaire year VI (13 October 1797), we read:

> Le citoyen Baroin étoit concierge de la maison de correction de Chalon … jouissant de la confiance de l'administration … lorsque la rumeur le prononça coupable d'un grand crime … Voici le fait. Un homme fut arrêté sous le titre de mendiant et vagabond, conduit à la maison de correction. Cet homme étoit un maniaque furieux qui, par l'effet de sa bizarrerie, vivoit séquestré des autres prisonniers, il étoit dans un tel état de misère qu'à peine il avoit les vêtements du premier besoin. Ainsi que le concierge le répète dans son récit: 'Un des prisonniers m'avertit que ce maniaque travailloit sous son lit aux moyens de s'évader et que déjà il avoit creusé le mur à 2 pieds et ½ de progrès, j'étois donc averti, et pour le déconcerter mieux, je voulois le prendre sur le fait; arrivé à l'heure de minuit, j'entre au dortoir, je vois ce prisonnier insensé fouillant le mur … je me bornai à de vifs reproches et à quelques coups sur les cuisses avec le fourreau de mon sabre, bref, je le tirai du lieu de son travail et l'obligeai à se mettre au lit, cet homme déconcerté ne quitta son travail et ne se mit au lit qu'avec toutes les démonstrations de la fureur et du désespoir, il se heurta rude- ment la tête, donna enfin tout à augurer du suicide; heureux si je l'eûsse enchaîné! je me retire en le menaçant du cachot, mais cet homme redoublant de fureur, parvient à se détruire en mon absence, à la vue du suicide commis j'aver- tis l'administration, elle me répond avec indifférence, je fais mon devoir, je demande les chirurgiens, depuis 33 jours ils n'avoient paru à la maison, je vais 5 fois les chercher … cet homme fut 11 jours souffrant enfin il expira – je fais

la déclaration de sa mort à la municipalité, elle me donna une permission d'in-humation et cet homme fut enterré après toutes les formalités légales.

'A peine fut-il enterré que la rumeur qui s'accrédite en proportion de sa malice me prononça un assassin. Elle dit que ce mendiant ... avoit 25 louis doubles et que la cupidité m'avoit décidé à l'immoler, que je l'avois donc homi-cidé, qu'enfin pour couvrir mon crime, je l'avois enterré tout chaud! toutes ces assertions diverses sont démenties par les débats du procès, il n'est resté de l'ac-cusation que l'homicide, mais pour le prouver l'on s'est prévalu du rapport de quelques propos insignifians que j'avois tenus, et surtout de la déposition des prisonniers, comme s'ils ne devoient pas être réputés suspects, contre leur concierge, qu'ils regardent comme leur tyran ... Tel est le résultat étonnant du malheur d'un Républicain que l'on se plut à condamner sous le nom de terror-iste, d'un fils pieux qui nourrit sa mère.'[1]

In the year II, on the other hand, elderly, aristocratic ladies of the faubourg, abandoned by their children, who had emigrated, and living in the maids' attics of their former palaces, requisitioned for the expanding needs of a revolutionary bureaucracy, committed suicide by throwing themselves out of high windows, after leaving notes for the *commissaire de police*, asking him to provide for a pet lap-dog or for a canary, left behind from the general wreck of a way of life. But a great many others saw it out, as governesses in the families of the new rich, and putting to commercial use skills in embroidery and crochet-work acquired from the nuns. In 1795–6, suicide takes a further toll, but this time of poor women, driven desperate by hunger and seeking an end for themselves and for their children in a conveniently-placed Seine.

The crisis of 1795 undoubtedly brought a massive increase in prostitu-tion, both urban and rural, an increase that appears to have been main-tained in the course of the following two years. More and more country girls were driven into prostitution 'pour avoir du pain' and in order to feed their children.

Exposent des malheureuses victimes des vicissitudes des événements de la Révolution et des misères qu'elle a occasionnées, sans ressources de travail et dénuées d'en pouvoir espérer, vu que toutes les branches de commerce et autres étoient anéanties, comme elles le sont encore actuellement, ce qui les a con-traintes à se manquer à elles-mêmes par la prostitution et sans autres crimes ... Dans tous les ci-devant règnes l'on [n'] a jamais sévi avec de telles violences, ni rigueurs à leurs égards.[2]

---

[1] AN, BB 18 721 (Justice, Saône-et-Loire, les soussignés aux Magistrats de Chalon, 22 vendémiaire an VI).

[2] AN, BB 18 807 (les détenues de la maison d'arrêt du Havre au Ministre de l'Intérieur, 1er ventôse an V: Hélène Carpentier, Marie Gillet, Legendre, Marie Brumant, Marie-Anne Petit).

This eloquent plea, made by Hélène Carpentier and a number of other female prisoners, to the public prosecutor of le Havre, in February 1797, could have been repeated, word for word, in most other cities of the north of France. On 7 Nivôse year VI (27 December 1798), the *Ministre de la Police générale* reported to his colleague:

> Je suis informé ... que les délits contre les bonnes mœurs se multiplient d'une manière qui devient de plus en plus affligeante, plusieurs commissaires du Pouvoir exécutif de cette commune [Paris] m'observent qu'on ne veut pas faire droit sur les procès-verbaux concernant les filles publiques et sur toutes celles qui affichent la prostitution sur les boulevards, dans les jardins et autres lieux publics, qu'on exige des preuves testimoniales, mais que les témoins sont difficiles à trouver et ne veulent point déposer.[1]

The second-in-command at the Hôtel des Invalides, faced persistently with the same problem, had a more direct approach to it, acting with that violence that characterizes masculine attitudes towards women throughout the revolutionary period and to which we will return later in this section. We hear of his initiative in a shocked letter from the *juge de paix* of the Division des Invalides, addressed to the Minister on 7 Pluviôse (26 January 1799) of the same year:

> Ce sont de ces mesures prises par ce commandant [en-second] que je dois vous rendre compte; le 3 de ce mois une fille, trouvée dans une salle de 27 lits couchée avec un invalide me fut amenée par le garde de l'hôtel après y avoir eu les cheveux coupés, la figure noircie et ayant un écriteau en gros caractères portant ces mots: *FEMME LIBERTINE*; cette scène d'un genre nouveau n'a point manqué de spectateurs et j'avoue que j'ai été également surpris que le public ... j'ai envoyé cette fille aux Madelonnettes.[2]

The Minister, a less merciful man, wrote back to tell him to mind his own business. Apparently the normal processes of law were not to apply to prostitutes, who, in any case, seem to have had little love either for the Revolution or for the regimes that followed it. In Lyon and in le Havre, they appear in fact to have been closely allied both to crime and to the exponents of the Counter-Terror. There is an interesting case history from Chalon, again in the year VI, on the subject of two girls of no fixed address, one a tailor, the other unable to account for herself who, having arrived in the town in the coach from Lyon, appear to have associated with the local royalist leaders and to have been fêted by them. The account given by the municipal authorities has a threefold interest. It illustrates, in

---

[1] AN, BB 18 756 (Justice, Seine, an VI).
[2] AN, BB 18 759 (ibid.).

a particularly dramatic form, the dangers, in terms of crime and potential political violence, of one of the great annual fairs. It is a further example of the fascination exercised by Lyon on the republican authorities of the Saône valley, in the conditions of the White Terror. Finally, it reveals the complicity, so often denounced in this area, of the judicial authorities, both with crime and with the Counter-Terror:

> Je m'appelle Marguerite Mallet, native d'Avignon, âgée de 20 ans, je n'ai jamais eu de profession, femme du C. Chauvel, marchand à Avignon, domiciliée à Lyon depuis environ 8 mois ... Depuis quel tems êtes-vous à Chalon? Je suis arrivée en cette commune le 22 [prairial an VI (10 June 1798)]. Où logez-vous? Le jour de notre arrivée, je suis descendue dans une auberge, je la quittai le lendemain pour aller prendre un logement chez le C. Solest, traiteur à Chalon. Quel est le motif de votre venue en cette commune? Je suis partie de Lyon dans le dessein de me rendre à Mâcon pour y voir une personne de ma connoissance, ne l'ayant point trouvée, j'ai poursuivi jusqu'à Chalon où je croyois la rencontrer; et j'y ai été arrêtée.

Her companion, Louise Bougrat, *tailleuse*, aged eighteen, is likewise a resident of Lyon. The municipal authorities were evidently unprepared to accept their explanations, believing that they were prostitutes, with connections with the Lyon and the Chalon royalists. As a result, on 3 Messidor (21 June 1798) following, the municipality wrote to the Minister of Justice:

> Deux filles ou femmes arrivées dans cette commune sans passeports, y affichant dès le moment de leur arrivée la prostitution et la débauche, arrêtées par nos ordres et renvoyées devant le directeur du jury qui les a fait mettre en liberté, arrêtées de nouveau par nous, puis remises en liberté par le même directeur et enfin arrêtées une troisième fois ... Le 27 prairial ... un des commissaires de police nous informa qu'il est arrivé à Chalon 2 jeunes personnes qui paroissoient n'avoir d'autre occupation en cette commune que celle de courir les ramparts et d'y recevoir les hommages et l'argent des dupes qui s'adressaient à elles ... elles répondirent qu'elles étoient venues pour attendre quelqu'un qui à la vérité n'étoit pas leur mari, mais leurs *bons amis* ... Nous apprenions la mise-en-liberté des 2 femmes, et si l'on en croit la chronique, en sortant de la maison d'arrêt elles allèrent partager un repas splendide dans un jardin où se trouvoient, dit-on, quelques-uns de leurs juges avec la jeunesse qui les avoient défendues ... L'administration, sentant la nécessité dans la circonstance particulière où elle se trouve à l'occasion de la plus forte foire de l'année, où elle a plus de 50 passeports à viser par jour ... d'autre part, c'est la déclaration qu'elles ont faite qu'elles devaient être suivies à Chalon de plusieurs hommes qui viendroient de Lyon et qui n'étoient point *leurs maris*, mais leurs *bons amis*, et l'administration qui dans tous les tems redoute par l'expérience qu'elle a acquise l'arrivée de certains hommes sortant de Lyon, a dû concevoir de plus vives inquiétudes encore lorsqu'on lui a annoncé qu'il devait en arriver qui ne seraient

attirés que par l'esprit de débauche, et ce dans un moment où ils pourroient plus facilement échapper à la surveillance au milieu des tourbillons que doit entraîner la foire …

The two girls must have had a most enjoyable outdoor meal. It is also consoling to learn that further attempts on the part of the municipal authorities to have them arrested and expelled from the town were equally unsuccessful, thanks to the sympathetic attitude displayed towards them by the *juges de paix* and by the other judicial authorities. Chalon had long been notorious in local Directorial circles as one of the principal centres of the White Terror and Counter-Revolution. The conflict in fact is of more than purely anecdotal interest; around the fate of the two young girls there took place the type of confrontation that was particularly common in this part of the world throughout the year V, between republican municipalities attached to the Directory and a judiciary openly royalist. As a result of Fructidor and legislation enacted in Nivôse year VI (January 1798), there was a vast purge of unreliable judges; but it does not seem to have affected Chalon by the summer of that year.[1]

Nor was there any diminution in the clientele of the trade. It merely changed. The *Gardes Françaises* had disappeared, but the police spies had not, the Princes had emigrated, but had been succeeded by middle-class customers and by the military, of whom there were more than ever. 9 Thermidor represented, in this important respect, a decisive victory for libertinage and vice. It was also, in a more indirect way, a victory for private life, for privacy, for individualism, and for all the fantasies of imaginative selfishness. Whatever might be said of the turpitudes of the Thermidorian regime and of Thermidorian society, they were infinitely varied. Private fantasy once more dictated a wide range of enjoyment; and, in 1795, the first foreign tourists – Swiss, Prussian, and Dutch – began to be seen once more in Paris, adding further recruits to the custom of the Palais-Royal.

Gambling went on unabated, much to the distress of the revolutionary authorities of the year II who saw in it a major source of political indifference and absenteeism (and as a realm of purely private pleasure). The gamblers did not mind if they played with Kings and Queens and Knaves, or with playing cards bearing the new revolutionary devices. The *imagerie de Chartres* continued to prosper, the old Saints' calendars continued to be published and read, the old catechisms, published under the imprimatur of the Primate of the Gauls and with prayers for the royal family, were still circulating in the Lyon area seven or eight years after the execu-

[1] AN, BB 18 722 (extrait du greffe de la municipalité de Chalon, prairial–messidor an VI).

tion of the King and Queen, six or seven years after the death of Louis XVII – they merely had to be printed in Lausanne and brought in from there[1] – there was no great change in the contents of the *bibliothèques de colportage* (no wonder *colporteurs* were an object of such extreme suspicion to the political and ordinary police), popular culture remained unaffected. The old military nicknames denoting physical courage, physical strength, ability to kill, success in love as well as in war, sexual expertise or provincial origin: *le Gros Bâton, l'Effrayant, les Gros Yeux, Brin-d'Amour, Darius, Bande-Toujours, le Renard, le Piqueur, le Sérineur, le Lorrain, le Normand, le Marseillais, le Provençal, le Picard, l'Impérial, le Kaiserlicche* (*sic*) were still proudly displayed by revolutionary soldiers and royalist *égorgeurs* alike. There were no revolutionary nicknames, save for those, very numerous, evocative and ingenious, applied, not without love, but always with a certain familiar respect, to the new machine of death. It would have been flying in the face of Providence to have spoken lightly of *la Veuve*, a demanding, stiff-necked lady, very touchy on the point of good manners and etiquette. But the instrument of the People's Vengeance, so long the principal hero of Hébert's fulminations, once reduced to a more familiar, less exalted role, with the loss of an exceptional clientele, continued, long after the Terror, to be the subject of similar verbal inventiveness, both on the part of its potential customers – and they had a certain pride in seeing themselves as such, even if, despite all sorts of verbal provocation, they might not eventually make the much-evoked journey – of its definite customers – monks of a strange order – and of a much wider public, the usual spectators of such collective occasions. Indeed, the guillotine, so often evoked as the principal instrument of the Terror, survived that period without the slightest difficulty, producing, at each new generation, new excursions into popular verbal fantasy. The instrument of death survived through two more centuries as an inspiration to the fullest scope of the popular vocabulary. Nor were there any other revolutionary diminutives, apart from *la petite fenêtre*; and the survival of diminutives and the invention of new ones are the surest signposts to the durability of popular affection. Only bandits, as some always had, at least within living memory, were to continue to have a claim on the adjective: *le petit. Le petit Beauceron*, and others of his kind, went back to the beginning of time, before the Revolution had ever been thought of.

Cartouche, Mandrin, Hullin remained far more popular, reassuring heroes than the newly established boys and girls who perished, holding the bridge, pierced with a thousand lances, or standing on burning decks. Even the rather obscure *Poulailler*, apparently a very ordinary sort of thief, and hardly a Bandit Hero, much to the loudly expressed concern of

---

[1] AN, BB 18 687 (Justice, Rhône).

the police and the judicial authorities of Paris, as late as 1797, thirty years or more after his execution, was still the subject of crudely coloured popular prints and of ballads, sung and sold by an itinerant *marchand de chansons*, before an appreciative audience, place Maubert, a dangerous place, in any case, for evocations even of such vaguely remembered exploits – and he was described in the song as Captain of 500 Bandits (he would have been lucky if he had ever had five at his command). The Criminal Hero outlasted the Revolutionary Martyr, Damien was remembered long after Marat and Lepeletier had been forgotten; the militants of the year II undoubtedly understood the significance of the *dépanthéonisation* of the former – an operation that cut much too near the bone for them not to feel alarm for themselves – but there is no evidence that the general mass of the population was even aware of the intended significance of that bizarre ceremony. It is doubtful in fact whether Marat and Lepeletier had ever caught on at all, outside the rather narrow, parochial confines of the Paris *sans-culottes*. One would have to look very far indeed to discover one of Soboul's patiently recorded *saintes patriotiques*,[1] a freak of nature that no doubt represented a gesture to the prevailing orthodoxy, on the part of a former constitutional priest anxious to curry favour with his local revolutionary authorities. One suspects that the *saintes patriotiques*, like the bleeding heart of Marat, never achieved a wide acceptance and that they had been given the rather grudging, weary recognition that so many local authorities offered to the new calendar: one would make a show of using it, it was a revolutionary way of going through the motions, of displaying an orthodoxy that one did not feel but that one knew was expected, that did not matter very much in any case, and that one frequently got wrong. Even the best-intentioned local *comités* and *sociétés* were liable to confuse Ventôse with Germinal, Frimaire with Brumaire, or get them in the wrong sequence; and they were frequently shown up in their ignorance, in the revelation that their homework had been ill-prepared, by repetitive relapses back into the old calendar, the evil of evils, the visible daily, weekly, monthly, yearly sign that nothing had really changed, covering themselves as best they could by the qualification, in brackets, of the letters *v.s.* (*vieux style*). The lower one reaches down in the records, the commoner *v.s.* becomes. The new calendar, one suspects, only really took on with the bureaucrats. It is true that there were more of these than ever before, especially from the autumn of 1793 and the spring of 1794. It could also be used to confuse, to evangelize, and, above all, to defraud, the new citizens of the Republic, as it expanded after the conquests of 1795, while leaving the French with their old saints. Contracts and hirings continue to be dated from Trinity or

---

[1] A.-M. Soboul, *Paysans, jacobins et sans-culottes* (Paris, 1966).

Michaelmas even under the year XII of the Republic, for these were things that mattered to private individuals; and so they had to be got right. It was safe to leave the new calendar to the official commemoration of revolutionary *journées* the significance of which many people had forgotten. The ultimate irony played on the revolutionary calendar is that it should have survived to this day, in a small, medieval, fortress town in the Hurepoix, on the edge of the Île-de-France, in the most traditional, most popular of all institutions, that of a great and ancient annual fair, the *foire de Ventôse*, early in March each year, in Dourdan.

THE ANGLE OF VISION

The important thing, then, was the angle of vision, especially if one went down far enough. What would *la fille de la populace*, as described by Restif, know of the Revolution, much less care about it? For her, previously, authority had figured physically as the public execution, after all the appropriate appetizers – *amende honorable*, holding a candle, clad only in a red shirt, and so on – on the place de Grève, Government and power, as the chief magistrate, the *guet*, the *commissaire*, the *exempt*, the *archer*, and the *Lieutenant criminel*.

> Les Filles de la populace ... les Crieuses des rues, les Marchandes ambulantes de poisson, de fruits, d'amadous, de vieux chapeaux, &ca ... Imaginez des êtres sans morale, sans idées, ni de l'honnêteté, ni de la religion, ni de la droiture, en un mot, d'aucune loi sociale ... Rarement ces filles sont corrigibles; elles naissent, meurent et vivent dans Paris ... sans en avoir jamais eu plus d'idées que si elles étoient nées parmi les Hottentots ... Toute leur politique est à la Grève, c'est là seulement qu'elles voient un acte d'autorité publique; le Guet est pour elles tout le Gouvernement et le Commissaire est le seul Magistrat.[1]

For such as these, the Revolution would merely mean a change in the geographical location of the place of punishment, and the substitution of the instrument of death – the gibbet, the rack, and the wheel – for the guillotine. In Lyon, their equivalent would not even have to adjust themselves to the former change, the guillotine merely replacing the gibbet where it had always stood, place des Terreaux. It was only in the early days of the Directory that the Lyon authorities decided to move the instrument of

---

[1] *Tableaux de la vie et des mœurs*. He placed in a slightly higher category 'Les Filles des Manœuvres, c'est à dire des gens sans profession, qui travaillent à la journée: elles sont marchandes de fruits, filles-de-peine, blanchisseuses, etc. – les individus qui composent [cette classe], voyant moins les autres classes, en sont moins connues; d'ailleurs, comme elles ne sont pas mises en Demoiselles, & que leur vêtir tranche absolument, les petites Bourgeoises ne les jalousent pas.'

justice to the heights of Saint-Just, in order to make a visible break with an only too well-remembered past. But it was too far from the centre and could not even be reached by road. In 1812, the Prefect and the judicial authorities therefore decided to return to the Terreaux, opposite the Hôtel-de-Ville.[1]

What again would *les ouvrières* make of the Republic of Virtue? Would they even be aware of its existence and of its aims?

> Les couturières, les tailleuses, les brocheuses, les gazières, &ca ... la plupart de ces infortunées gagnent si peu qu'il leur est presqu'impossible d'être sages ... La plupart sont des dévergondées qui ne rougissent pas de tenir les propos les plus sales, qui fréquentent les cabarets comme les hommes, et les endroits pernicieux où l'on danse le soir, comme les tabagies du Port-au-bled ... J'ai connu des filles-brocheuses qui valaient moins que les soldats-aux-gardes, pour la retenue, la décence, la sobriété, la pudeur.[2]

For them, the Revolution would merely mean a certain loss of custom, as a result of emigration, and the replacement of the brutal and lecherous *Gardes Françaises* by the equally brutal and lecherous troops of the Republic. For them too, as for all those who lived somewhat *en marge*, or had nothing to hope for and everything to fear from the repressive authorities, the new regime would spell a great deal more power both to the *commissaire de police* and, above all, to the *juges de paix* who, in a period of mounting crime (especially after 1793) had, in addition to their functions as conciliators and as civil law officers, been made responsible for the initial stages of actions involving the *police judiciaire*. They complained bitterly, and at great length, of thus being overworked, going on to point out that the functions of a *juge de paix*, with the emphasis on conciliation and persuasion, were in fact incompatible with those of a prosecutor, whose duty was to mete out punishment. But there can be little doubt that, for *les ouvrières* and their like, such an accumulation of functions in the hands of men well acquainted with even the humblest residents of their Sections, must have made repression, rather than conciliation, far more effective, even if it further retarded the course of justice and greatly increased the periods of detention incurred even by minor offenders while they awaited trial. The *juges de paix*, in this new, unfamiliar role, would certainly enforce

---

[1] AN, BB 18 693 (Rhône, procureur-général impérial au Grand Juge, 5 juillet 1812): 'Avant la révolution et de tems immémorial les exécutions s'étaient faites à Lyon sur la place des Terreaux vis-à-vis l'hôtel-de-ville ... Après la révolution, et parce que cette place avait été le théâtre de toutes les exécutions révolutionnaires ... les exécutions ont été faites sur la montagne de Saint-Just, lieu très élevé, d'un accès difficile et fort éloigné du centre de la ville ... Il convient de revenir à l'ancien usage.' The Prefect had in any case published an *arrêté* ordering that executions should once more take place on the place des Terreaux.
[2] Restif, *Tableaux de la vie et des mœurs*.

a stricter regulation of dance halls and *guinguettes*.[1] They only joys of this class of girls described by Restif would continue to be the noisy dances in the weekend, open-air establishments, in the nightly carters' balls in the suburbs, or in the rivermen's rough dances on the port. But much of the spontaneous fun would have gone out of life, as the result of a regime which, largely owing to the special demands of the Terror, with its increasing emphasis on crimes against the State – absence from work, the theft of wood lying on the quays of the wood ports, any crime or misdemeanour, in fact, involving the interests of the Republic – had brought the administration of justice down to a level much closer to the common people. All that the *ouvrière* might know of the Revolution was that it appeared to be much more oppressive and interfering, as far as she was concerned, than the *Lieutenant criminel* and his army of spies had ever been.

MASCULINE VIOLENCE

The Revolution did nothing to alter masculine violence in relation to women; it brought no diminution to the repetitive *déclarations de grossesse* that form such a volume of the daily reports of the *commissaires de police*. Rape and seduction did not march to the new tunes of the year II, and a Revolution that formulated the Rights of Man never had even a passing thought for the virginity of women. Girls continued to be kicked in the stomach, beaten, whipped, tarred, and feathered, dragged by the hair across the room, made love to on the tables of wine-shops, on the ramparts or in rural ditches, their clothes torn, their skirts pulled up, even in the middle of a Paris street,[2] as joyfully and with about as much impunity as under the old regime. And revolutionary soldiers were no change in this respect; nor were they any less prone to the accidents that were likely to follow such activities. There was no decline in the regular clientele of Saint-Louis and similar establishments.[3] A *sans-culotte* shop-

---

[1] *Monsieur Nicolas*, VII, 1774, p. 3799: '*Rosalie-Prudhomme*, fille d'un chantre de Saint-Séverin, d'abord Couturière, ensuite Décoratrice aux Italiens, puis Entretenue, Danseuse de Guinguette, & Catin. Je la trouve, un jour, rue des Prouvaires ... Si loin de notre Quartier! ma Jolie Voisine! (lui dis-je) Pour toute réponse, elle me prit le bras, en me disant – Allons aux Porcherons?'

[2] AN, BB 18 744 (Ministère de la Justice, Seine, Maisoncelle, 194, rue du Petit Carreau, au Ministre, 10 pluviôse an IV).

[3] *Monsieur Nicolas*, VII, 1774, p. 3768, *Agatine*: 'Je découvris bientôt que cette Infortunée était une Fille publique ... Je lui dis ... vous serez bientôt prise, mise à l'Hôpital, et dépouillée au profit de l'Inspecteur, du peu que vous avez amassé. Comment faire? Redevenir honnête ... Elle était indécise; son métier de Couturière est si peu lucratif! Elle y mourait de faim.' See also ibid., VI, 1789, p. 3260: 'Quelle situation que celle des Femmes de Paris, durant la cruelle époque de la disette! Combien de jeunes personnes y ont trouvé la mort, ou la perte de leur innocence? Tant de poitrines délicates que donne le régime de Paris.'

keeper, a militant in his Section, perhaps one of the leaders of left-wing extremism, and so qualifying for the attentions of historians as a pre-socialist, as a person already groping his way towards *babouviste* solutions, would not hesitate to break into the mezzanine bedroom of his female servant. Varlet had a private income; what he got out of the Revolution was a mistress; Leclerc de Lyon did not have a private income, but he acquired, as a result of the politics of extremism, a wife. That was the end of his political rage; he calmed down and, from having been a public figure, became a private one.[1] For the country girl up to Paris, nothing would have changed; *la Paysanne Pervertie* of 1775 would remain *la Paysanne Pervertie* of 1794, though her chances eventually of being abducted by a Duke would have been considerably diminished and the range of promotion open to her greatly narrowed. But, in 1795, Dukes could be conveniently replaced by the Thermidorian new rich and by avid and ambitious young generals. Marguerite Barrois, a country girl from the east of France, arrived in Paris, with a letter of introduction to a watch-maker from the same village as herself, on 6 Thermidor year II (25 July 1794); on the night of the 9th to the 10th, she succumbed to the insistence of an apprentice, likewise from her village, who slept in a cupboard opposite to her bedroom, employing, as a clinching argument: 'Next winter, we will go back to our village and get married.' A month later, she was pregnant; she would remember the night of 9–10 Thermidor, but not for the reason it is commemorated in history books.[2] Equally characteristic is the account given of herself, since her arrival in Paris, by a Norman girl from Gaillon, Catherine Robillard, in a petition addressed from prison to the Minister of Justice, on 15 Prairial year IV (3 May 1796):

Je suis née de parens honnêtes, mais peu accommodés des biens de la fortune, quoi qu'il en soit, mon père a donné à tous ses enfans une bonne éducation, mes 2 frères embrassèrent l'état ecclésiastique en n'ayant pas voulu le serment que la loi exigeoit d'eux, ils furent obligés de quitter le territoire de la République; mon pauvre père n'ayant pu survivre à cette disgrâce est mort de chagrin. Me voyant sans appui et réduite à vivre avec des parens que la différence d'opinion me rendoit la vie fort dure, je résolus de venir à Paris pour jouir de cette aimable liberté. J'entrai chez un marchand de papier, rue André-des-Arts. J'y tins ses livres pendant 10 mois ... Sans aucune expérience, je fis connoissance d'un jeune homme, je puis le traiter de scélérat puisqu'il a trompé ma bonne foi, il m'a dissipé tout ce que j'avois et m'a réduite dans la plus affreuse misère. Un moment de désespoir m'a fait commettre une bassesse; je pris donc un drap du lit de la chambre où je demeurois et je le vendis 35 livres. Voilà mon fait et je suis jugée à huit années de détention. Je verse des larmes de sang sur mon

[1] *A Second Identity*, pp. 168–76 ('The Enragés').
[2] *The Police and the People*, pp. 224, 294.

malheur, je suis privée de tout, n'ayant pas osé écrire à mes parens ce qui est arrivé … La malheureuse détenue Catherine Robillard.[1]

Or let us take the case, in the first year of the Directory, of another country girl, this time from Upper Normandy, Thérèse Créseau, *fille majeure*, daughter of François Créseau, a farmer from the village of Guilmécourt, in the canton of Envermeu, near Dieppe. Thérèse recounts her misfortunes, in terms similar to those employed by Catherine Robillard, to the Minister of Justice, in a letter dated 19 Floréal year IV (8 May 1796):

Il me suffira de vous dire que les mauvais traitements que j'ai éprouvés dans la maison paternelle m'ont contrainte de l'abandonner à l'âge de 27 ans. Cependant, avec l'approbation de mon père, je me suis donc retirée à Dieppe chez les citoyennes Maquinhau, marchandes d'indiennes. Là je n'ai pu éviter de travailler à devenir mère, aussitôt que je me suis aperçue de ma grossesse, je suis sortie de chez les citoyennes Maquinhau et je me suis confiée … aux soins du Citoyen Trouard-Riolle, officier de santé et accoucheur … Ce fut le 23 pluviôse dernier [12 February 1796] … je suis maintenant au sixième mois de ma grossesse et âgée de 28 ans. Depuis mon entrée chez le C. Trouard-Riolle, voulant éviter les sarcasmes du public, je n'en suis nullement sortie. Mais le jour d'hier, 18 floréal, sur les environs des 11 heures du matin,[2] le citoyen Riolle étant parti à la campagne pour voir un malade, une femme que je ne connois pas, sous le prétexte de lui parler, est venue frapper à la porte; le jeune homme ayant été lui ouvrir, cette femme tenant la porte ouverte, tout-à-coup sont entrés deux de mes frères, savoir l'aîné et le quatrième puîné, lesquels se sont rendus de suite dans l'appartement, se sont forcément emparés de moi, m'ont arrachée de la maison, là j'ai trouvé mon père avec une multitude de peuple, auquel j'ai été donné en spectacle et dont j'ai supporté toutes les invectives. J'ai eu beau réclamer la justice contre l'oppression, mes cris ont été étouffés, mon père et mes frères, triomphant de mon humiliation, et de ma douleur, sans respecter mon état, ni être émus d'aucune sensibilité pour le malheureux fruit que je renferme dans mon sein, m'ont traînée jusqu'à leur auberge, place du marché aux veaux, et ayant pour enseigne les trois maures, là j'ai été beau implorer la clémence de mon père et de mes frères, leur représentant qu'étant ma maîtresse, et ne leur demandant aucun secours, ils ne pouvoient me forcer de suivre leur volonté, tout a été inutile, sur les 2 heures [that is, one hour before the after-

---

[1] AN, BB 18 748 and 755.
[2] This was a Saturday, 7 May 1796, a fact that may explain both the presence of her father and her brothers – it was unlikely that Cauchois farmers would absent themselves from work on a weekday – and that of such a large and appreciative crowd, come to witness the girl's public humiliation. The affair has all the characteristics of a community's collective weekend summer vengeance. In the Midi, it would have been an excellent occasion for an exemplary lynching, on a sunny square. In Dieppe in admirable early afternoon conditions, it would offer the numerous population of le Pollet the benefit of a free spectacle, a little before mealtime, when people would be standing outside their houses.

noon meal, at a time when people would be still outside their cottages], ils m'ont
fait traverser tout le faubourg du Pollet, et toujours à la bonne compagnie de
huées, et ensuite m'ont placée dans une charette pour me mener à leur domicile,
où je suis enfermée jusqu'à ce qu'il leur plaise de me transférer dans un autre,
afin d'ôter tous les moyens que pourroient employer mes amis à me réclamer
. . . Je vous en préviens, j'ai tout à craindre de mon père et de mes frères.[1]

This happened in the year IV of Liberty and Equality, neither of which,
it is clear, would apply to the twenty-eight-year-old daughter of a
Norman peasant, kidnapped by her father and by her four brothers, no
doubt in an effort to re-establish, in the eyes of a cruel rural community,
the family honour. The Minister expressed characteristic caution, showing
a marked reluctance to support the unhappy girl in her legal rights.
Writing, three weeks later (7 Prairial), to the public prosecutor of Dieppe,
he comments, guardedly:

> Il est possible que ses plaintes soient fondées puisqu'il n'est pas sans exemple
> qu'un père aît abusé de son autorité à l'égard de ses enfans. Je vous invite à
> vérifier s'il y a oppression et attentat contre la liberté individuelle. Vous devez
> mettre beaucoup de sagesse et de prudence dans vos démarches. S'il est juste de
> venir au secours d'une infortunée qui est peut-être victime d'un excès de
> sévérité [a masterful understatement in the circumstances] de la part de sa
> famille, il faut aussi se garder d'intervenir trop légèrement dans des contesta-
> tions de ce genre. Vous ne devez donc agir que dans le cas d'un attentat à la
> liberté individuelle bien avérée.[2]

The public prosecutor no doubt took the hint that was so clearly suggested to him, for this is the last one hears of the poor girl's complaint. A
daughter would have little chance, under the Directory, when faced with
the collective reprobation of all the menfolk of her family. The scene as the
girl is dragged through the fishermen's faubourg of le Pollet recalls the
persistence of the cruel, cowardly tribalism of other women, when gratified with the spectacle of the misfortunes of one of their number who,
having sinned against the orthodoxy of the group, was displayed as an
object of public derision,[3] as well as it illustrates the guffawing, perhaps
slightly embarrassed complicity of the men, anxious to display their
participation in this hideous manifestation of collective brutality. The
Revolution might have changed many things, but it had had no effect on
the *mores* of collectivities, on the cruelty and moral violence of small
towns and villages and on the terror inspired in female children by brutal

---

[1] AN, BB 18 806 (Seine-Inférieure, Thérèse Créseau, au Ministre, 19 floréal an IV).
[2] Ibid. (Ministre au commissaire près le tribunal du Département, 7 prairial an IV).
[3] On feminine incitement and verbal and physical violence, see *The Police and the People*,
p. 351 (2L).

fathers and brothers.[1] Indeed, by stifling compassion and by drying up the sources of charity, in the name of Indivisibility and Unanimity, as well as by giving an added, more strident premium to every form of collective sentiment: orthodoxy, enthusiasm, hate, fear and panic, social resentment and jealousy, it had made the fate of the individual member of society – the girl pregnant before marriage, the homosexual who had sinned against recognized social conventions – infinitely more disagreeable. Under the old regime, Thérèse might at least have expected a little mercy and a little understanding from the priest or the nun; the Revolution left her, alone in dock, in the face of a pitiless secular public.

It was a natural step from this that the sheer cruelty of the Revolution should have been directed, in part at least, against the most vulnerable, least protected members of society and that anti-feminism and brutality towards women should have been given new, unexpected proportions, despite legislation that, nominally at least, improved the conditions of the daughter, the sister,[2] the wife, and the unmarried mother. There are many references, not only in petitions addressed to the Minister from female prisoners during the Directory, to the insulting attitudes adopted by the *commissaires de police* of the year II towards female delinquents of humble origin – it was a different matter if they were girls of good family who had been accused of political crimes[3] and, in Ventôse year V (March 1797), there is a revealing exchange between the *commissaire* attached to

---

[1] For a particularly pathetic example of the effects of parental terrorism on a teenage country girl, see AN, BB 18 126 (Ardèche, Préfet de l'Ardèche au Ministre, 26 prairial an XII): 'J'ai l'honneur de vous prévenir que Marie Malègue, âgée d'environ 14 ans, fille à Jacques Malègue, meunier, habitant à Malandines, commune de Saint-Fortunat, ayant été chercher de l'eau à la fontaine, le dimanche 23 floréal dernier [13 May 1804], vers les 11 heures du matin, est tombée ou s'est suicidée en se jettant dans la rivière de Boyon ... On présume que la cause de cet événement est provenu de quelques reproches que son père lui avait faits pour avoir laissé porter ses bestiaux qui lui avaient échappé, dans la vigne d'un particulier qui leur en avait porté plainte à tous les deux.'

[2] 'Je suis artiste en peinture ... le 11 août dernier j'ai été arrêtée revenant de la manufacture de Sèvres ... je fus par mon triste vêtement deux fois arrêtée et renvoyée une troisième fois ... j'ai été ... renvoyée au Bureau Central pour être conduite dans mon Département d'Orléans [*sic*] de brigade en brigade sans aucun délit que vengeance de frères. Je suis dans cette Capitale depuis 36 ans, âgée de 45 ans' (femme Émilie Léveilly au Ministre de la Justice, le 5 germinal an VII, AN, BB 18 763); a note from the *Bureau Central* accompanies this petition: 'Cette femme a des frères à Paris qui ne l'estiment pas assez pour vouloir s'occuper d'elle.' So much for the legal rights of a sister!

[3] Madeleine Poirée, femme Paul, demeurant 48, rue Saint-Denis, complains to the Minister, in a letter dated 28 Frimaire year IV (19 December 1795), 'que le 19 de ce mois elle fut arrêtée chez elle par le commissaire de police de sa Section [Bonne-Nouvelle], qui, *se croyant encore dans le tems du Gouvernement révolutionnaire*, lui fit déposer ses boucles d'oreilles et autres objets, et, au mépris des lois et du respect qui est dû au malheur, lui dit qu'elle n'avoit besoin de rien, que ce qu'elle avoit étoit encore trop bon pour elle' (AN, BB 18 741, femme Paul au Ministre, 28 frimaire an IV). See also my *Quelques aspects de la criminalité parisienne*.

the *tribunal de police du canton de Paris* and the Minister: the former writes:

> L'intérêt de la société exige que je vous dénonce un délit qui ne me paroît point reprimé, faute de connoître la loi qui en détermine les peines. Cette loi, qui étoit en pleine vigueur sous l'ancien régime, semble être tombée en désuétude, ses conséquences sont trop majeures pour ne pas la provoquer, si elle n'existoit pas: c'est celle qui astreint les filles enceintes à faire la déclaration de leur grossesse. Déjà le commissaire de police de la Division du Mont-Blanc a constaté l'accouchement d'enfants morts-nés de la part de 2 filles sans déclaration préalable. Je n'ai pu donner connoissance d'un pareil délit à qui de droit, ne me rappellant point la date de la loi, ni ses dispositions.

The reaction of the Minister was abrupt and, for once, unexpectedly liberal. 'Vous sollicitez, Citoyen,' he replied, on 21 Ventôse (11 March 1797), 'une loi qui assujetisse les filles enceintes à la déclaration de leur grossesse, vous voyez dans cette mesure de grands avantages, mais vous n'en calculez pas les inconvéniens nombreux. Vous voulez faire revivre l'édit de Henry III! cet édit barbare ...'[1] The Minister's liberalism on this occasion hardly conforms to the general climate of the revolutionary period, highly unfavourable, in practice, to the female offender against the social *mores*, as well as to the female delinquent, guilty generally of some minor theft.

Restif, always highly sensitive to any change of climate that might affect the condition of women in a brutal and predatory masculine society, had few illusions as to the effects of the Revolution in this respect. Indeed, he believed that, by destroying so many of the old collective taboos and, after Thermidor, by giving an added incentive to vice, libertinage, and social greed, it was about to inaugurate a period of unprecedented oppression. Whereas others, in more recent times, have seen in the Marquis de Sade the complete revolutionary, the man who preached total liberation from all constraints, Restif, his contemporary, sensed that he had facilitated the approach of a new era of brutality, slavery, and oppression. Writing, with unusual prophetic vision, in 1797, he was to comment:

> J'y ai trouvé la source de la cruauté des exécrables Ouvrages composés depuis la Révolucion, *Justine, Aline, le Boudoir, La Théorie du Libertinage* ... Si jamais *la Théorie du Libertinage* vient à paraître (comme je m'y attends dans ce siècle démoralisé) elle fera frissonner les plus scélérats ... O Gouvernement! préviens ce Scélérat, qui peut donner une mort cruelle à 20,000 femmes, s'il est lu par les soldats.[2]

---

[1] AN, BB 18 751 (commissaire du Pouvoir Exécutif près la deuxième administration municipale du canton de Paris au Ministre, 14 ventôse an V).
[2] *Monsieur Nicolas*, VI, 1797, p. 3240.

He could have added, from the dreadful experience of his own niece, that the combination of Revolution and war would leave women exposed to the ancient, medieval horrors inflicted by a conquering army on the female population as a whole.[1] In his advocacy of true equality, Restif was out of step with all of his contemporaries, whether revolutionary or counter-revolutionary; none could have added, as he was justified in doing, at the conclusion of his immense, meandering book: 'J'en suis à 1797; je dois terminer ma IXme Époque … je peins l'amour, & jamais la débauche, encore moins la cruauté … Je n'ai jamais profané la Femme que j'ai possédée … Pourquoi vivons-nous dans un siècle, & avec des Hommes, qu'on puisse, qu'on doive se faire un mérite d'être, non pas tendre, mais humain, avec les Femmes …'[2]

THE PRIVATE CALENDAR

Restif also, at frequent intervals, in 1789, 1790, 1791, 1792, 1793, 1794, 1795, 1796, and 1797, as he writes, then prints the immensely wordy *Monsieur Nicolas*, establishes his own private calendar, or, rather, a whole series of private calendars, relating occasionally to the state of his health, but more often to the memory of women and girls, and sometimes to a cycle of private misfortunes that have only the most indirect relationship to the course of public events. Here, for instance, is a cycle that could be described as *mes dix ans de malheur*, in a nineteenth-century 'social' novel:

Une triste réfléxion que je fais aujourd'hui [1797], c'est qu'il ne s'est pas écoulé une année, un mois, depuis le retour d'Agnès-L. [his wife], en septembre 1778, où ma situation n'ait empiré … En 1786, je connus *Félicité* & je manquai le mariage de ma Fille cadette … En 1787, je commençai *les Nuits de Paris* … En 1788, je perdis mon ami Guillebert-de-Préval … En 1789 commença ma ruine. En 1790, une banqueroute l'accéléra: je fus obligé d'interrompre l'impression de mes *Provinciales*. En 1791, je commençai sans moyens l'impression de ce *Cœur Humain*, sous une promesse de fonds qu'on a tenue trop peu de tems. En 1792, je fis une association désavantageuse. En 1793, je la rompis avec perte; ma Fille-aînée me quitta. En 1794, je n'eus plus les fonds promis; la Terreur cessa.

---

[1] Ibid., VI, 1797, p. 3036: 'Ce qui confirmera ceci, c'est que je ne vais pas taire ce qui m'est arrivé, en 1793, avec une de mes Nièces, fille de ma sœur Catherine … J'appris de ma fille Agnès que cette infortunée, âgée de 16 ans, s'était prostituée … Elle céda, et vint avec moi. La Leblanc cadette me promit d'en avoir soin, & m'a tenu parole, jusqu'à Chaumette [who, as *procureur de la Commune* in 1793, attempted to extirpate Paris prostitution, having many of the girls rounded up, sent to hospital, or driven from the city]. Alors, mon infortunée nièce alla aux Armées. Elle y a péri, malheureusement, ayant été massacrée par les Ennemis, après qu'ils se furent assouvis sur elle. Qui avait perdu cet Enfant? Moi …'
[2] *Monsieur Nicolas*, VI, 1797, p. 3256, Fin de la IXme Époque.

En 1795, je descendis aux portes du tombeau, et j'allai prendre un lit et 25 bains aux Écoles-de-Santé. En 1796, je suis ruiné, ayant été payé en Assignats ce qui me restait dû …[1]

Elsewhere, always preoccupied with his health, he proposes another calendar, covering a much longer cycle, and corresponding, in a curious manner, to the recurrent dearth crises of eighteenth-century France. It is that of the return of what he calls, rather prudishly, *la maladie haïtienne*, which he experienced for the first time, as the result of an imprudent encounter in Paris, in 1757, returning in 1770, 1776, 1785, and 1795, a time schedule that omits to take into account the Revolution altogether.[2] More reassuringly, he notes down that such-and-such a date was the fortieth or forty-fifth anniversary of a successful seduction or of a first meeting with a girl whose memory he cherishes. For him, 31 May 1793 is not an important date in its own right, but an occasion to recall an outing with Toinette that ended up in the hayloft in the middle years of the century, and, in March–April 1794, at a time when the *hébertistes* were being tried and the *dantonistes* were about to be and the Republic was being tossed in the high seas of what historians have described as *la crise de ventôse*, he is harking back to a spring night on an island in the middle of the Yonne, with Fanchette, in 1753.[3] The same year, as Robespierre's Red Summer gathers momentum, he recollects that it is the fortieth anniversary of the unhappiest day of his life, the death of Madame Parangon, his beloved Colette. Referring to his first love, Jeannette Rousseau, he notes: 'Je lui consacre le 1er mars depuis 47 ans. C'est le 4 juin 1788 que j'ai appris qu'elle ne s'est jamais mariée … En 1794, devenu libre, par mon divorce … j'écrivis à mes sœurs … J'écrirai au Curé de K. qui vit encore en mars 1797 … Jeannette aura 66 ans, étant née le 19 décembre 1731. *Fiat!*'[4] Referring to the year 1767, and writing in 1796, he recalls: 'Je marchai quelque tems à pied,

[1] *Monsieur Nicolas*, VI, p. 3671.
[2] Ibid., VI, pp. 3233–5, 3238: 'J'eus une Hernie & le flux hemorroïdal en 1786. Je suis menacé de la Pierre … Depuis ma maladie de 1795, toujours prête à revenir … j'attends la mort en travaillant …'
[3] *Monsieur Nicolas*, II, p. 1266, III, p. 1444, p. 1559, p. 1601: 'Elle est donc finie, cette terrible année du 26 mars [1754]! Elle est finie! Elle roule dans le fleuve immense des temps – je la vois, je la vois encore … au bout de 40 années [jeudi 3 avril 1794, à ma case] … je vois Colette … Colette, l'âme de ma vie …' In the revolutionary calendar, this was 14 Germinal year II. See also, on the subject of Toinette: 'Elle le verra, au bout de 40 ans [10 juin 1794] et cette lecture ne la flattera pas; elle lira la NOTE que je place ici …' This time, the recollection coincides with 22 Prairial year II, the date of the most sinister piece of legislation of the whole of the Terror period.
[4] See also ibid., VII, p. 3622, mars 1748, Jeannette Rousseau. See also ibid., V, p. 2455: 'Le Curé de Kourgis vit encore aujourd'hui 5 septembre 1796 … et l'abbé Tomas est mort le 12 février 1786. Le Curé avait été chassé de sa Cure par les Robespierristes, en février 1794; il fut incarcéré aux Urselines d'Aucerre; le député Maure [who was to commit suicide during

cueillant des fleurettes, que je mettais dans un livre, en disant: "Je vous conserverai toute ma vie, en me ressouvenant du jour où j'ai vu Sofie, que je crois Edmée-Colette, ma fille ... O fleurette! je ne vous reverrai jamais sans verser des larmes!" Et j'en versais en les cueillant; et j'en verse encore, en les renvoyant aujourd'hui (1796)'[1] – a preoccupation that one would not normally associate with the year IV, the second year of famine and the beginnings of the Directory. The next year, there is the commentary: 'O Fanchette! peut-être le 1er mai 1797 a été la 42me et dernière fois que j'aurai célébré votre fête...'[2]

Very occasionally, public events intrude briefly on his tenderly nurtured private world of memory, sensibility, preoccupation with illness, and worry about money; but they never do so entirely in their own right. 'Pendant les douloureuses années de la Révolucion, 90, 91; durant les années terribles 92, 93, 94; celles de la famine 95 et demi-96, je goûtais le plaisir inexprimable de voir journellement et de recevoir les caresses d'une Fille adorée (Alanette); mais, hélas, depuis le milieu de vendémiaire, je ne l'ai plus!'[3] The year 1796 is compared, as a year of utter disaster, with that of 1757, but, in each case, the disaster is mainly private. Germinal year III (April 1795), a month which for most historians would recall the great popular risings in Paris and in the other towns of the north of France, is for Restif the month in which he nearly died as the result of a prostate.[4] He was in hospital throughout the following month and the Prairial Days bypassed him there. For him, 1789 is the year he had to move his lodging,

---

the Thermidorian reaction] durant son séjour dans le Métropole du département de l'Yonne, étant tombé sur son nom dans la liste des Incarcérés, s'écria – Quoi! vous incarcérez la Vertu! – et il l'a fait mettre en liberté.'

[1] Ibid., V, 1797, p. 2700.

[2] Ibid., VII, 1755, p. 3645.

[3] Ibid., VI, 1789, p. 3158. Restif constantly harps back to a calendar recalling past and present feminine encounters and it is clear that, for him at least – and no doubt for many others of his contemporaries – the continuity represented by the life of a single individual had much more reality than the apparent hiatus in the development of society by the advent of the revolutionary crisis. See, for instance, VII, p. 3775: *Maguelone*: 'Je n'ai fait que l'entrevoir depuis, au Palais-Royal en 1788, où elle me dit: – Si tu savais qui tu as eu à ma place chez la Sévreuse! Blonde – Une de tes lectrices – Tu serois bien fier! – En 93, au mois d'Auguste, je la revis encore. Enfin, en 1794, elle me dit en passant, & sans s'arrêter: Elle est morte.' Ibid., VII, p. 3776: *Aline*: 'Aline eut un Fils en 1772, et, depuis, elle m'a refusé constamment ses faveurs. Elle est morte en 1790, le 25 du mois d'octobre. Son Fils est Jockei du Prince de ****, actuellement à Turin.' Ibid., VII, 1771, p. 3800: *Julie-d'Étange*: 'Je la rencontrai pour la première fois en 72 ... Julie est encore jolie en 92.' Even in 1797, he has not quite given up hope: 'Il faut dire cependant qu'au milieu de Fructidor an IV, ayant vu sortir d'une boutique de la rue de Thionville une femme de 32 ans, je ne pus m'empêcher de l'admirer. Elle marcha devant moi, se retroussa, & montra une jambe parfaite' (VI, 1797, p. 3242).

[4] He fell ill on 27 Germinal year III (16 April 1795) and had to take health baths till 1 Prairial (20 May) of the same year. 'J'étais donc â l'Hôpital. J'y ai passé le beau mois Floréal tout-entier' (VI, p. 3223).

losing, as a result, most of his books. 'Mon *Aristophane* s'est perdu, lors
de mon déménagement pendant le cruel hiver 1788–9, de chez Pointcloud,
procureur au Parlement, rue des Bernardins, no 10. Ce scélérat me donna
congé dans le tems où j'étois embarrassé de toute l'édition des *Nuits de
Paris* . . . Depuis sept ans (6 mars 1795) je ne puis rétablir l'ordre parce que
je suis logé plus étroitement! retrouver mes livres, mes pensées éparses
. . .!'[1] It is a calendar far more reassuring than that of the bloody *journées*
marked by barricades and squares and forecourts strewn with the corpses
of men who will no longer make love and of boys who have never done
so. The Revolution might destroy the external vestiges of the past, might
abolish the old calendar; but it could not destroy memory. So it was not
safe with people like Restif, of the older generation. It was not only his
age that made Restif so immune; it was also his splendid egotism.

There are other examples, however, of a more direct relationship
between public and private calendars, though, in two instances at least, the
former did not represent those of *ancien régime* or of revolutionary
France. After his desertion, at the time of the American War, it may be
recalled, Guillaume Bienassis had made his way to Danzig, where he had
entered the services of a Polish gentleman. From there he had gone on to
Vienna, an unfortunate choice, for this deserter from the regiment d'Aunis
soon found himself caught up in another monarch's wars, being enlisted,
in 1789, in the Emperor's wars against the Turks. Similarly, 'vous expose
humblement Nicolas Lamesme Granbois', in a petition addressed to the
Minister of Justice from Hesse-Cassel, 30 December 1797 – he was not
even aware of the new republican calendar, nor could he have been
expected to have been, as we shall see:

> originaire de Coulanges-sur-Yonne, généralité d'Auxerre et Dijon, en
> Bourgogne, âgé de 64 ans, ancien militaire pendant la guerre d'Hanovre et celles
> de Corse, dans le régiment d'Auvergne, en dernier lieu en celui de Soubise,
> couvert de blessures, qu'ayant eu le malheur d'avoir eu une rencontre en 1761
> le 27 d'aoust étant en recrue après la bataille de Clostercampe, il auroit eu celui
> de tuer Valentin Lemaire, dragon au régiment d'Autichamp, ce qui ne l'em-
> pêcha pas de continuer son service jusqu'à la paix conclue à la prise de l'isle de

---

[1] *Monsieur Nicolas*, IV, 1758, p. 2120. Another private calendar frequently employed by
Restif is that of the printing of his innumerable works. 'L'impression de ces IV excellens
volumes n'était pas achevée au commencement de 1787, que ma tête fermentait déjà pour
Les Nuits de Paris, qui ont remplacé *le Hibou-Spectateur Nocturne* . . . *L'An* 2000 a le défaut
d'être fait avant la Révolucion; mais il la suppose faite, & présente les mœurs qu'on aura
dans 200 ans . . . Dans ma *Dramomanie*, qui me tint de 1784 à 1791 j'allai jusqu'à faire un
Drame en V Volumes. C'est *Tout le Cœur Humain Dévoilé* . . . Il a été imprimé en 1792–3
. . . A la veille de la Révolucion, en 89, j'imprimai *le Thesmographe* . . . J'avais imprimé *les
Filles-du-Palais-Royal* en 89 . . . *Les Provinciales* . . . furent imprimées en 90, 91, 92, 93, 94
. . . Enfin, j'imprimai cet Ouvrage-ci' (ibid., VI, 1787, p. 3130).

Corse: que le suppléant rentra en France, où il ne put demeurer, ce qui le contraignit de passer en Espagne qu'il quitta pour solliciter sa grâce, à l'effet de quoi toutes contumaces et décrets n'eurent plus lieu, puisque son emprisonnement fut commencé à la ville d'Auxerre où il fut condamné à perdre la vie, par une sentence qui intervint et dont le suppléant appella au Parlement de Paris qui le trouva digne de lettres de rémission qu'on obtint et fut autorisé après une prison de 4 ans, les peines et les souffrances du suppléant devoient avoir la fin heureuse qu'il espéroit depuis si longtems. Mais il fut trompé dans son espérance puisqu'il fut encore mis en tournelle criminelle et condamné à un banissement perpétuel par le parlement dont Sauvigny étoit président; pendant l'exil de celui d'auparavant, c'est en 1777, et depuis ce tems le suppléant n'a plus paru en France, en 1781 il passa en Russie d'où il n'a pu sortir qu'au commencement du règne de l'Empereur d'aujourd'hui [Paul] ayant été forcé au serment sous le règne précédent, c'est avec les passeports que le suppléant a obtenus dans le courant du mois d'aoust dernier qu'il a passé les mers et qu'il s'est présenté à tous les Ministres de la République françoise, sans pouvoir obtenir aucun passeport, excepté celui du général Olivier à Cologne, pays conquis, pour aller à la première municipalité y faire viser le sus-dit passeport lequel visa eut lieu à Erf, en passant à Liège la municipalité de ladite ville s'est emparée de tous les passeports et extraits baptistaires du suppléant ... ce qui a obligé l'infortuné de venir à Cassel implorer les bontés du C. Simond, chargé de la légation de la République près S. A. le Landgrave de Hesse-Cassel.

After this reference to His Highness, he signs his petition and once more he is out of date – 'salut et fraternité'. These examples are not, however, entirely characteristic, the soldier, especially the deserter in foreign service, being exposed to an abnormally wide variety of other people's public calendars.

One is reminded too of the country people, mentioned also by Restif, who, in the rigorous winter of 1754–5, put on the clothes – furs, sheepskins, goatskin – made by their parents or their grandparents, to withstand the fearful winter of 1709 – clothes that had since remained hanging, in huge peasant wardrobes, awaiting a disaster of similar proportions. One is reminded, too, of those inmates of the Maubeuge workhouse who went right through the revolutionary period without a change of clothing and who, in the year III, were shivering in what was left of the uniforms provided by an exiguous ecclesiastical charity.[1] One is reminded, indeed, in

---

[1] AN, F 15 254 (Hospices et secours, Conseil général de la commune de Maubeuge, à la commission des secours, 12 fructidor an III): 'Le nombre des pauvres s'accroît tous les jours au lieu de diminuer; le prix exorbitant des denrées, le discrédit de nos assignats dont les habitans des campagnes ne veulent plus absolument et ce à l'exemple de *nos prétendus amis belges*, mettent l'indigent dans l'impossibilité de se procurer ce qu'il a besoin journellement pour vivre ... Les indigens faisant partie de l'hospice de charité sont sans vêtemens; depuis 5 à 6 ans ils n'ont point été habillés, de manière que, presque nuds, ils présentent le tableau de la plus affreuse misère.'

this respect, of Restif himself, who boasted, for he was clearly proud of the fact: 'Depuis 1773, jusqu'à ce jour 6 décembre 1796, je n'ai point acheté d'habits. Je manque de chemises. Une vieille redingote bleue, aînée de mes habits, me couvre journellement, parce que mon avoir entier va aux impressions.'[1] In the countryside, above all, the old calendar, the old anniversaries would outlast the new. The members of the *bande d'Orgères* were as sensitive as Restif, though for quite different reasons, to the annual recurrence of the old feast days: Saint-Jean, Saint-Pierre, the Trinity, Michaelmas. For Restif, they were memories of encounters with girls; for the bandits, they offered the unique opportunity of a great fair. The complaints, on this subject, of the public prosecutor of Dieppe, writing to the Minister of Justice on 18 Germinal year V (7 April 1797), could be multiplied up and down the country. 'Dans la nuit du 13 au 14 pluviôse dernier, répondant à celle du 1er au 2 février, fête de la vierge dans le culte catholique, deux ministres de ce culte, dont l'un réfractaire ... occasionnèrent un rassemblement de 2 à 300 personnes dans une ci-devant église de la commune de Lammerville près Bacqueville-en-Caux.'[2] A paltry victory indeed to call the church 'ci-devant'! and a small enough concession to the new orthodoxy.

Restif may have been a crank, a sexual boaster, a shoe fetishist – he was much put out, in this respect, by republican low heels and by the resulting muddy bottoms of skirts: it was, one suspects, one of his main grievances against the regime of the year II[3] – a night bird, a hypochondriac, a spelling reformer, an individualist of extreme introspection, an autodidact, a man of immense family conceit, the author of some immensely boring novels; but he is as good an historian as Barère, Choudieu, Paganel, and the energetic Montagnard Levasseur de la Sarthe. But he is informing at a different level; he, not Barère and his colleagues, is able to get into the furnished room, into the attic, into the tiny bedroom of the dying seamstress, in the wake of the non-juror priest, as, in the midst of the year II, he carries her the consolation of extreme unction.

He at least is aware too of *Démophile* and *Démocrate*, his *seigneurs-populaires*, the one a former Duke, who profits from the Revolution to

---

[1] Monsieur *Nicolas*, V, 1782, p. 2884.

[2] AN, BB 18 807 (Seine-Inférieure, directeur du jury de Dieppe au Ministre, 18 germinal an V).

[3] *Monsieur Nicolas*, VI, 1782, p. 3059: 'Ce fut le 25 octobre 1782 que j'éprouvai la dernière impression faite par une chaussure élevée. Depuis ce tems, les pieds-plats de nos Républicaines, leur jambe nerveuse, leur derrière crotté m'ont toujours repoussé.' Restif was not, however, totally opposed to the new fashions introduced by the Revolution. 'La mise de 1792 était délicieuse, surtout pour l'Adolescence; un fourreau, dégageant une taille fine, svelte, joncée; une longue jupe cachant la turpitude des pieds-plats ou n'en laissant voir que la pointe agréable; une coiffure *capricieuse*, c'est-à-dire, volontaire & non-sujète ...' (VI, 1790, p. 3212).

marry the pretty daughter of a shopkeeper of Restif's beloved Île-Saint-Louis, the other an *ex-marquis* who effects the even more difficult transfer by getting himself accepted by a butcher's family from the rue Saint-Denis and marrying the daughter of the house. The *seigneurs-populaires* were not figments of the novelist's imagination, but realities of his observation. There were those who used the revolutionary crisis to climb out of the straitjacket of class convention and social condition, those who owed to the Revolution the opportunity to move down in society, as well as to move up. There is no place for such people – perhaps not numerous – in the calculations of historians of social structures, who, like the contemporary police, do not like people to step out of turn or disturb the movements of their class-graphs.

He is thus the first historian to have understood the attraction of social exploration, through sexual experience. Jallez, in *Les Hommes de bonne volonté*, would take the experiment a stage further, with a bed awaiting him and occupied by a national product, in every capital in Europe – a typically masculine fantasy.[1] But Restif's *seigneurs-populaires* were seeking happiness, not just the brief excitement of a change of milieu. There is no doubt that the Revolution, by greatly adding to the picaresque elements in eighteenth-century life, and by enormously extending both the range and the depth of mobility, must have made such love matches much more frequently possible.[2] In the general spectacle of carnage, violence, vengeance, and intransigence, one would at least like to think that this was so.

FRINGE OCCUPATIONS

We have no means of knowing how the Republic of the year II may have appeared to little boys and girls of five, born with the Revolution, other than possibly as a good time, as a period of marvellous anarchical freedom, when they did not have to go to school, as most of the schools were closed, at least up to 1795, when there was a limited resumption of primary education. We do not know how this lack of formal education in their early years may have affected the later lives of those who were twenty-six in 1815. The little boy might have to learn the Rights of Man rather than the

---

[1] Jules Romains, *Les Hommes de bonne volonté* (Paris, 1936–40).
[2] This was as true of the *émigrés* as of those who stayed in France throughout the Revolution. Many of the *émigrés* not only discovered, under the stress of hardship, vocations and skills that had previously remained unsuspected, or that, for reasons of dignity, they had been unable to indulge – one became a celebrated London book-binder, another an antiquarian book-seller, others again entered the service of the Empress or made fortunes in the United States – they also acquired foreign wives or mistresses and greatly extended the area, in terms of class and nationality, of their sexual experience and of their personal happiness. One of them married an Irish prostitute in London (Jean Vidalenc, *Les Émigrés français*).

Pater and, if his parents beat him, he could always denounce them as bad republicans and might indeed get a hearing. But his sister would still have to do her embroidery, run errands for her mother, eke out a few *sous* selling flowers on street corners, carrying love notes to wealthy ladies, or distributing bundles of firewood from house to house; and she was still in as great a danger as ever of being kidnapped, if she were pretty, neat, and well-dressed (the theft would be as much for her clothes as for herself). The reports of the *commissaires* for the years II and III are full of detailed descriptions: last seen wearing a nankeen shirt in blue and white stripes, white stockings, buckle shoes, velvet bodice; and the same source, as later, under the Directory, the reports to the Minister of the *Bureau Central*, reveals the sad, nightly haul of runaway children and adolescents, found sleeping in entrances to houses, under the arcades or on the pavement, above the ovens of bakers, clinging together, often brother and sister – and come to the city in order to escape parental brutality or lack of love. The Revolution might make a cult of child martyrs; but it did not lighten the heavy hand of unloving parents. And, if anything, it witnessed a steady increase in children's crimes – generally petty theft, often accompanied by breaking-in – committed especially by such runaways, often on their second or third day in Paris, no doubt as a result of the pressing needs of hunger.

Here, for instance, is part of the haul for Vendémiaire year VI (October 1797), at a period when crimes of theft are at their highest point in Paris:

Alexandre Pierre Jarry, 15 ans et ½, natif de Paris, marchand de brochures, demeurant à Paris, rue des Filles-Dieu chez le C. Duval, logeur, division de Bonne-Nouvelle; Alexandre Cresson, 15 ans, natif de Jouarre (S-et-M), marchand de brochures, même demeure; Jean-François Michel, 13 ans, marchand de brochures, à Paris depuis l'âge de six ans, ignorant le nom de l'endroit de sa naissance, le croyant situé dans le département du Cantal, demeurant à Paris, rue au Lard, division des Marchés, chez le C. Lebrun, logeur … 3 jeunes gens de 15 ans et ½, de 15 ans et de 13 ans, tous trois se disant marchands de brochures au Palais-Égalité, lieu où la jeunesse peut sous tous les rapports (ne) recevoir que de mauvais exemples.

They are accused of having stolen a silver fork from the kitchen of a flat off the arcades that they had entered on the pretext of selling their pamphlets and news-sheets.

A more detailed list established a month later, in November 1797, gives further details as to the length of stay in Paris, the place of origin, the address – or lack of it – and the alleged trades of these small unfortunates:

Lous Portier, 12 ans et ½, natif d'Argenteuil, vendeur de journaux, sans domicile fixe; Jean-Louis-Marie Lambert, 13 à 14 ans, natif de Paris, sans état, demeurant à la Pitié – prévenus d'avoir volé des bonnets de police; François Blanchard, 15 ans, natif de Versailles, commissionnaire, demeurant rue des Martyrs, dans une auberge [theft of a silver coffee spoon]... Étienne Thévenot, 15 ans, natif de Paris, sans domicile depuis deux jours et sans état [theft of a man's leather belt]... Antoine Mégnot, 14 ans, natif de Versailles, demeurant ordinairement audit Versailles, chez son père, marchand de tabac, rue de la Loi, et, lors de son arrestation, à Paris, rue de la Sonnerie depuis 3 jours... Jean-Baptiste Vérien, 15 ans, orphelin élevé à l'hospice des Enfans-Trouvés, sans état, ci-devant mousse sur le vaisseau *la Menaçante*, arrivant du Havre et sans asile à Paris; Antoine Maurisse, 16 ans et ½, natif de Nancy, commissionnaire, et avant, novice matelot employé sur la corvette *le Vulcain*, au Havre [theft of a jacket]... Jean-Pierre Renaud, 14 ans, natif de Lyon, demeurant rue Saint-Éloi, chez une logeuse [theft of a knife and of several silver forks]... Jean-Jacques Mercier, 19 ans, natif d'Auxerre, servant les maçons, arrivant à Paris lors de son arrestation, sans domicile [theft of three handkerchiefs]... Jean-Baptiste Bénoire, 13 ans, natif de Paris, rue Sainte-Marguerite, faubourg Saint-Antoine, chez la citoyenne Coperon, logeuse, commissionnaire [theft of three pieces of lard]...

Several had only recently arrived in Paris. Those who were not homeless were living in lodging-houses, which was almost as bad. These, in any case, far from being homes, constituted almost ideal schools for crime, these lonely boys often being driven into theft at the behest of the *logeuse* herself. A few, however, on these lists, lived at home, with parents who may have been unaware of their children's brief descent into petty theft; or, at least, that was the rather improbable claim most would make when faced with the evidence supplied by the *commissaire*.

Such instances are even commoner with young girls and women in their late teens, partly because they were more exposed than boys to the numerous hazards of the city, but also no doubt because, as servants, waitresses, serving maids, laundresses, *bouquetières*, *marchandes de falourdes*, and so on, they had readier access to premises normally closed (girls are commonly accused of having committed a theft 'dans un endroit fermé où elle a reçu l'hospitalité' or equally 'où elle a eu un travail salarié'). The widow Blanchot petitions the Minister, in the summer of 1796:

Si j'osois vous prier de prêter une oreille de compassion sur ma fille, âgée de 10 ans, étant jugée à 5 années de réclusion pour soi-disant avoir pris un goblet d'argent à la citoyenne Dernis, marchande de vin, faubourg Martin, la pauvre enfant étant innocente de ce délit, la Dernis l'a conduite chez le commissaire Morlet, moi ne sachant ce qu'était devenue ma fille... Je me jette entre les bras de votre humanité.

There is a similar petition, dated December 1795, from a widow living in a lodging-house, near the Pavillon de Flore, quai des Tuileries:

Citoyen Ministre, je suis une pauvre femme accablée d'infirmités et de malheurs et les plus grandes peines que je ressens dans cette misérable vie . . . c'est la priva-tion de ma fille, qui depuis trop longtems gémit dans la prison de Saint-Lazare pour un égarement de jeunesse . . . Enfin, on peut le dire, sans favoriser le vice, c'est pour une bagatelle de la valeur de 20 sols que ma pauvre fille éprouve une captivité sans exemple à un âge capable de m'aider dans mon infortunée et déplorable situation où je suis incapable de pourvoir à mes besoins dans ces tems malheureux où la vie du pauvre est aussi souffrante.

Nor did the Revolution bring any halt to masculine lubricity so far as female children were concerned. Police reports for the Terror period and petitions to the Minister for that of the Directory reveal a litany, almost as sad as that of petty theft, on the subject of the rape of girls between the ages of nine and twelve, often on the part of *sans-culotte* employers, shopkeepers, revolutionary militants, artisans and schoolteachers and private tutors. Gauché, *compagnon charpentier*, rue des Prêtres, No 7, division du Panthéon, in a letter dated October 1796: '. . . vous expose que la vindicte publique et lui se trouvent attaqués par le viol que vient d'éprouver le 9 de ce mois sa fille âgée de 9 ans et qui la retient au lit depuis cette époque par un citoyen de la section du Panthéon qui lui servoit d'instituteur (et) contre lequel il a rendu plainte . . .'

The old penal code had, no doubt, been far more brutal in its relations with the petty thief. But, like all the authorities of the old regime, it had also been more unpredictable. The revolutionary penal code dealt out a justice both inexorable and automatic; most of these children received minimum sentences of eight years, though it was possible for boys of under sixteen, if they were medically fit, to earn a remission by being taken on as cabin boys in the war fleet. Everything considered, it cannot be denied that the Revolution had made things much worse for the occa-sional law-breaker and petty thief, especially for those who had been driven into crime out of hunger and desperation, both by making retribu-tion more severe and repression more effective. There seems to have been little thought of educating these unfortunate children into becoming better citizens; on the contrary, especially in the conditions of the year II, the theft even of an article of clothing from a private individual seems to have been regarded as a 'crime against the Republic'; the child who had committed it had proved himself 'unworthy' of being a republican; he had to be punished, not regenerated. The old Châtelet, like the old clergy, had no doubt been more merciful. But then it was not attempting to set up such high standards; and it had behind it a long experience of mis-fortune, tempered by a considerable degree of compassion. In this respect at least, the Directory represented some improvement on the system of the year II. The judicial authorities of the Directory were doing their best to bring society back to a respect for legality, and, although, in the political sense, they failed very largely in this commendable enterprise, they certainly did succeed in tempering justice with mercy. They did in fact mean what they said quite literally, when they spoke of 'le retour au règne des lois'. They might be very hard ones. But for the occasionally delinquent child, the regime was considerably less arbitrary than that of the year II,[1] despite the latter's idealization of republican child martyrs and the dewy-eyed reception given by *sans-culotte sociétaires* to eight-year-olds trundled in to recite, in their monotonous and parrot-like voices, the *Déclaration des Droits de l'Homme* or some similar piece of republican moral uplift. It was, it would appear, little more than going through the motions. And it was a painless way of acquiring an agreeable sense of virtue as a model parent, even if one was in the habit of beating one's apprentices and errand boys. Uriah Heep would have done well as a popular militant at the level of the Section.

*

A regime which, in its suspiciousness, multiplied the paper checks on the movement and actions of ordinary citizens, gave additional opportunities to the numerous and ingenious people who, by trade or by necessity, were capable of circumventing them. Under the Directory, Lyonnais royalists, we have seen, were seldom at a loss to obtain the necessary papers, whether *certificats de non-émigration*, or exemption, on medical grounds, from military service. After theft, the commonest crime in the statistics for Paris, from 1795 to 1798, is that of *faux en écritures*. The *juge de paix* of the First Division of Rouen, writing to the *commissaire* attached to the criminal court, refers to a hardened customer of this type:

> Le nommé Martin, qui se dit avoir descendu dans sa conscience et y avoir trouvé le calme et la paix ... que son cœur assure qu'il est innocent, &ca, est déjà convaincu d'avoir fabriqué un faux extrait de naissance, un faux passeport, un faux certificat de civisme [very nearly a grand slam in revolutionary terms] ... il est aussi à peu près convaincu d'avoir essayé de violer une jeune fille de 5 ans et de lui avoir donné la maladie vénérienne, il est de plus soupçonné d'avoir embauché pour nos ennemis et d'avoir fait des escroqueries ...

in short, an all-round talent.[2]

---

[1] See, for instance, in AN, BB 18 752 (*Projet de message du Directoire Exécutif aux 500*, s.d., prairial an V): 'De grands motifs de justice et d'humanité ont fait admettre dans les lois pénales une distinction entre les individus qui se livrent au crime sans distinction de l'âge, avec la réflexion et la connoissance dont ils sont alors susceptibles et ceux qui n'y ont été entraînés que parce qu'ils n'ont pas le discernement d'en calculer l'horreur et les suites.'
[2] AN, BB 18 809 (Justice, Seine-Inférieure, juge de paix de la deuxième Division du canton de Rouen, au commissaire près le tribunal criminel du Département, 2 messidor an VII).

We have already referred to Gillet, the man who passed himself off alternately as Casenave, as Dupont, and as Boissy-d'Anglas, all leading Thermidorian personalities, in the course of the year III. A few months later, in Nivôse year IV (January 1796), the Rouen public prosecutor tells of another form of embezzlement even more directly related to the political events of the Revolution.

> Un nommé Goudier, condamné à la peine de mort pour cause de vol et d'assinat, a reçu en un mois plus de 20,000 livres au moyen de ces sortes de lettres où il se peignoit comme détenu à cause de révolution, il a reçu entre autres 600 livres en deux fois, d'un fabricant de ——? auquel il avoit promis part à un trésor par lui caché appartenant à feu Lepeletier de Saint-Fargeau.[1]

In this area, war and Revolution had largely brought to a halt the activities of the fishing fleets of le Havre, Honfleur, Fécamp, and Dieppe, no longer allowed out at night – that is, in the most favourable conditions for herring or mackerel fishing.[2] But, after Thermidor, the Revolution had also brought the fishermen, and all those associated with the coastal trade, new, lucrative, but dangerous opportunities as *passeurs* of the numerous *émigrés* and English agents who, throughout the Directory, were plying regularly between England, the Channel Islands, and the Normandy ports. A letter from an *émigré* to a friend in London, dated August 1796, outlines the system to be followed:

> Je me suis embarqué à Deal le 18 ct. à 10 h. du matin, et le lendemain samedi 19 nous étions en rade à 10 heures du matin, à 9 heures du soir nous étions tous débarqués ... Qu'il vous suffise de savoir que le Havre passe pour la meilleure ville ... Si par hasard quelques personnes de votre société veulent rentrer, et plus particulièrement ceux de cette province, voilà la marche qu'ils doivent tenir: s'habiller en matelot, chercher un capitaine américain qui puisse vous prendre comme homme d'équipage, ne pas se montrer beaucoup aux autres passagers de peur d'être reconnu ... Une fois dans le bassin du Havre vous travaillez aux cordages et le soir vous descendez avec vos effets sans rien craindre. Si l'on connait la ville, l'on se rend chez un ami, on le peut, rien de plus aisé.

Further details as to this profitable trade in passengers, organized by French or American merchantmen and Norman fishermen, could be obtained, one gathers, from 'Mr Booth, taylor, No. 86 Little Tower Hill,

---

[1] AN, BB 18 806 (commissaire au Ministre, 13 nivôse an IV).
[2] R.C. Cobb, 'Politique et subsistances en l'an III. L'exemple du Havre', in *Terreur et subsistances*, p. 229. See also 'Problèmes de subsistances en l'an II et en l'an III: l'exemple d'un petit port normand: Honfleur', *Mémoires du Congrès des Sociétés Savantes de Rouen* (Imprimerie nationale, Paris, 1953).

six doors from the minories'.[1] It was with some reason that the revolutionary authorities eyed sailors with particular suspicion. In these parts, it was clearly easy to come by a sailor's uniform, and sailors, real or false, are frequently described as having taken part, with the *bandes* of *chauffeurs*, in attacks on farms in the Pays de Caux during the years IV to VIII. Others are stated to be living in places like Ingouville, on the immoral earnings of prostitutes and laundrywomen, another trade that, thanks to its easy entry into the houses of the well-to-do, would be a valuable ally to those whom the Revolution had driven into the more recently formed ranks of crime.

*

Of course, others were ruined, or had to look elsewhere. The fencing-master sought employment with the *Garde nationale*: there would always be something for that loud-mouthed, prickly man, in the new, uncertain, yet more extensive hierarchies of revolutionary honour; for, if, under the old regime, personal honour had been the guiding light of the minority, the Revolution had the effect of opening the ranks of honour to all. In this, there was no break with the past; on the contrary, the habit of avenging an insult in blood, by drawing on a sword or a sabre, in a society in which nearly every adult male was able to express the pride of his recently acquired citizenship, was likely to be followed even by the commonest. Honour now became the treasured jewel of the butcher and the grocer, as the military virtues of an archaic, semi-medieval society were adopted by the population as a whole – a very considerable step backwards from the comparative enlightenment of the educated classes at the end of the eighteenth century and from the revulsion felt by them for this brutal, cruel, bloody exercise of masculine pride. The fencing-master would not be short of pupils; and it is probable, though as yet it has not been proved, in the absence of detailed research in the judicial records, that crimes of honour greatly increased during the revolutionary years.

Many a *garde française* must have followed Guénot's example and graduated into informing, surveillance, and procuring; it was an easy step for soldiers who had already been very close both to police and to crime. The music-master, previously so well placed to capture the immature hearts of his feminine pupils – it was, therefore, a trade apparently much favoured by the habitual seducer – must have lost most of his more desirable clientele; but he may have replaced them, like poor *Jean-Christophe*,

---

[1] AN, BB 18 807 (Seine-Inférieure, anon. to anon., 27 August 1796). The writer of the letter adds: 'Il faut qu'il s'informe s'il y a un capitaine qui doit aller en France, et surtout demander après William Cotton, qui est le capitaine avec lequel je suis passé.'

with butchers' daughters, or, after the year II, with those of farmers who had profiteered from the famine. The governesses often starved, no one knows what became of the *chaisière* and the organist.

THE IRRELEVANCE OF THE REVOLUTION

Some of the mad seem to have been unaware that there had been a Revolution at all. (Two had got out, when the Bastille was pulled down, but they were both back behind bars, and chained to the wall, in Charenton, within ten days.[1]) One of them, Alexandre Fortunat Meccoud, aged twenty-six and described as living with his father, was to tell a doctor attached to the Grenoble prison that he was Gratian II, an eleventh-century bishop of Grenoble. When asked about the Revolution, 'répond que la Révolution, sans lui plaire, ne l'a pas fatigué au point de rien entreprendre contre elle'. Asked why, in a letter to a girl, he had offered her a golden throne, covered in diamonds and rubies, imperial robes and a crown, and why he had signed this letter 'Imperator', 'répond qu'il vaut mieux prendre la grande place que la petite, quand cela ne coûte pas davantage'. His main complaints, at the time of his cross-examination, in Ventôse year VI (March 1798), were that the raucous crowing of the rooks outside the windows of his cell interrupted the flow of his medita-tions on the subject of his imminent beatification, and that his mother, when she came to see him in prison, was in the habit of wearing red and black ribbons in her hair, 'qu'il vouloit prendre une hache pour les couper ... qu'il attribuoit à ces couleurs des idées sinistres et qu'elles lui présentoient l'image du sang et de la mort, ce qui le tourmentoit en les voyant ...' The Revolution had clearly left the poor young man aside. 'Peu de choses l'inquiètent,' he explained, 'dans la situation d'esprit où il est depuis longtemps.' An *officier de santé* was to certify him totally insane. The Revolution had, however, vaguely impinged on his disordered brain; what had upset him most was the prohibition of clerical garb. He himself had wished to put on, like his purely imaginary fiancée, a robe of gold with mauve trimmings, like the Sibyl, in her strange communications with the Holy Roman Emperor, in one of Roger de la Pasture's paintings in the Musée de Dijon. The poor young man was living in a fantasy world all of his own and in which the eleventh century had a much greater rel-evance than the events going on around him in the late eighteenth.[2]

Another undoubted madman, however, seems to have had a better

[1] Jacques Godechot, *La Prise de la Bastille* (Paris, 1965), p. 221. One of them was an Englishman.
[2] AN, BB 18 394 (Isère, interrogatoire à la prison de Grenoble, 15 ventôse an VI).

grasp at least of the contemporary situation, though, as far as the Revolution was concerned, he might be said to have subscribed to 'the plot theory of history'. His version of events is really no more bizarre than that proposed, at much the same time, by the abbé Barruel. Under the title: *Crimes énormes et sans Exemple!*, in a petition addressed to the Minister of Justice – it was in the nature of his functions that he was frequently in receipt of missives of this kind – an anonymous citizen pours out his confused grievances, in May 1797:

> Quand on m'a enlevé, en juin 1788, pour me mettre à la prison de la Force où j'ai resté 2 mois et ½, il y avoit une infinité de dépôts de poison, établis depuis 4 ans chez des limonadiers, des marchands de vin, des traiteurs, des aubergistes, brasseurs, marchands de cidre, &ca, pour mettre dans le boire et manger qu'ils me vendoient afin de me faire boire jusqu'à perdre connoissance, m'efféminer et me faire passer pour fou . . . Le C. Longchamps, brasseur, faubourg Marceau, m'a vendu un quart de bière empoisonné, par ordre de police, ainsi que le C. Leroy, *à la loge verte*, port Nicolas, un quart de cidre empoisonné . . . Les traiteurs, les aubergistes &ca chez qui les Lieutenants de Police Le Noir et de Crosne avoient établi, pendant 4 ans, des dépôts de poison, doivent en avoir bien parlé au commencement de la Révolution dans les Districts . . .[1]

And there are several pages more of similar divagations. He was right at least – as we shall see – about the quality of drink sold by most *marchands de vin* and *brasseurs*. But he was quite wrong to think that he had been picked out for special treatment at their hands. Most of them poisoned *all* who came their way.

Sade had not yet been sent to Charenton (he *enjoyed* the Revolution, save for a brief period of confinement, as a moderate, in the year II[2]), wandering madmen, dressed in skins and muttering at street corners, confused the Revolution with the end of the world, while evoking the Wars of Religion of the sixteenth century. (These, it is true, were in many people's minds, especially after the September Massacres.) The wandering blind man may likewise have been largely unaware of a change in society that would be likely, as far as he was concerned, to transform the small round *liards* of alms into pieces of paper the value of which could not be calculated by touch, so that he would now have to be accompanied by a child, if only to calculate the value of street-corner charity. Those more fortunate of the blind – the elderly and the infirm – who had been admitted, during the last decade of the old regime or in the course of the Revolution to the hospital especially set aside for their welfare, would, like all inmates of charitable establishments, feel the added pinch of deprivation, above all

---

[1] AN, BB 18 757 (Ministère de la Justice, Seine, anonyme au Ministre, s.d. floréal an VI).
[2] *Les Armées revolutionnaires*, pp. 1, 45, 46.

after a law of Messidor year II (July 1794) – it was perhaps characteristic of Robespierre's Republic of Virtues that, while talking so much of the claims on the State of the very poor, it should thus have deprived that section of citizenhood least able to defend itself, of its wherewithal – had cut them off, as former ecclesiastical bodies, from the sources of their income. By the year III, the blind of the Quinze-Vingts were subsisting in desperate conditions.[1] The deaf-and-dumb were even worse off, their benefactor, the abbé de l'Épée, the beloved founder of their school, in the parish of Saint-Jacques-du-Haut-Pas, having been arrested, in the winter of 1793, as a *fanatique* and a suspect, so that the education of these unfortunates was interrupted throughout the rest of the Terror. The *abbé*, it seems, had inculcated in his pupils fanatical views out of harmony with the new order. Until his release in the course of the Thermidorian reaction, those who had been entrusted to his charge were to subsist, as a special category of non-citizens, totally cut off from the prevailing orthodoxy surrounding them. Like the very mad, they may have been the only sector of the population, save for the very young and the desperately ill, to have been totally unaware of the appeals of Unanimity and Indivisibility. When they were made once more aware of the music of the outside world, with the return of their teacher, it was to the old tunes – the catechism, religious instruction – that they were reintroduced, as if the Revolution had never taken place at all. The Thermidorians, so anti-clerical when it was a matter of preserving the revolutionary land settlement or of checking the progress of the White Terror in the south-east, were sensible enough to leave the *abbé* alone, as the only expert in his field.

The various institutions set aside by pious and charitable women for the care of orphan girls, during their first few months in the capital, were similarly hit by lack of funds, especially after Messidor year II. The personnel that had run them had, in most instances, already left, as a result of the disappearance of the various orders of nuns. Most had been closed by the year III. Many of the girls who, during the most dangerous part of their stay in the city, had thus been preserved from the street, were, consequently, the more readily driven on to it. It was not only that the Revolution had deprived charitable institutions of their financial support; it had done something worse still, killing the very spirit of charity itself. In this respect, the report made to the Minister of Justice, in July 1806, on the conditions of the prisons in Napoleonic France, might witness for this general change of attitude, expressed in the prevailing class selfishness of revolutionary and post-revolutionary society.

---

[1] AN, F 15 256 (caissier de l'hospice des 15/20 aux commissaires des secours publics, 11 pluviôse an III): 'La rigueur et la longueur de la saison ont absorbé la provision de bois que j'avais faite, et qui devait me conduire naturellement à la fin de l'hiver. Je me vois réduit en ce moment à une demie voie de bois.'

Les prisons que l'exposant vient de parcourir, depuis Strasbourg jusques ici [Penne-d'Agenais, Lot-et-Garonne] sont en général mal tenues et mal administrées, manquant de paille, tantôt bon pain, tantôt mauvais, mauvais cachots pour coucher, remplis de vermine et de galle, mauvaise eau, point de chemises ni d'habits pour changer … aussi en meurt-il beaucoup de faim et de misère tous les ans, dans lesdites prisons, sans secours ni visite de personne, *comme n'ayant plus de foi, ni charité, il semble* … Le prisonnier préféreroit avoir moins du pain tous les jours, pour avoir un peu de soupe, mais vivre avec du pain sec et de l'eau si longtems, les chiens ne pourroient tenir à une pareille existence.[1]

Already, in the spring of 1796, the *concierge* of Bicêtre had made a similarly dismal report on conditions then prevailing in certain provincial prisons and on the state of health of those who had been rounded up and sent on to Paris, before being marched to one of the penal establishments, at Rochefort, Brest, and Toulon, as part of the *chaîne*:

Quantité de condamnés aux fers [the official reports to the Minister of Justice] … de Rouen, d'Évreux et Dourdan, pendant les opérations de la formation de la chaîne [meurent en cours de transfert] … je me suis occupé de concert avec les officiers de santé … des causes qui ont mis ces condamnés dans cet état déplorable et tous nous ont appris que la première cause étoit la misère dans laquelle ils avoient été dans leurs prisons, manquant de tout, couchés sur le carreau, n'étant changés de paille qu'une fois par mois, n'ayant rien pour se couvrir, ayant pour la plupart les fers aux pieds, ne faisant aucune exercice, étant couchés jusqu'à 30 et 34 dans des salles d'environ 30 pieds carrés et n'en sortant jamais.

Ajoutons à ces défauts de secours la dureté des chefs comme des employés de prisons où ils étoient renfermés, notamment à Rouen [the infamous *Tour aux Fers*, dreaded by the criminal population of the whole of the north of France, had, three centuries earlier, housed Joan of Arc, while she was awaiting execution] où lorsqu'un prisonnier vouloit se plaindre du sort qu'il éprouvoit … on le maltraita et on le chargeoit de fers … le nombre des condamnés en total étoit de 484 et il auroit pu en partir environ 400 … Pour rétablir autant que faire se pourra la santé d'une partie des condamnés aux fers venus de Rouen et d'Évreux, dont un de ces derniers est mort le lendemain de son entrée à Bicêtre, les officiers de santé ont résolu qu'il falloit leur faire prendre des bains … j'y ai conduit les condamnés … cette opération s'est passé sans aucun événement.[2]

Between these two reports there are ten years of worsening conditions, imposed in part by the financial difficulties of the Thermidorian regime and the Directory, but due also, without doubt, to the increasing indifference to the normal demands of charity and to the traditional hold of mercy and compassion.

[1] AN, BB 18 692 (Ministère de la Justice, Rhône, P. A. Sarrasin au Ministre, 15 juillet 1806).
[2] AN, BB 18 745 (concierge de Bicêtre au Ministre, 3 germinal an IV).

Children[1] continued to beg in enormous numbers, often sent out, with suitable sores, by their parents or their alleged such, though they temporarily abandoned church steps in favour of the forecourt of the Tuileries and the entrances to clubs (many of them were former churches in any case). The new legislation of the revolutionary period greatly increased the penalties for all forms of vagrancy, and especially for the crime of *mendier avec menaces*, while it imposed further paper checks on itinerants and *gens sans aveu*, subjecting all those who were unable to make a good account of themselves, by producing a certificate of good conduct from four citizens of their *commune* of origin, to expulsion from Paris and from the other large cities on the order of the police, and later of the *Ministre de la Police générale*. Under the Directory, the Minister of Justice attempted to put a stop to this last practice, which he rightly denounced as completely illegal and as recalling the arbitrary nature of the legislation of the Terror period, which had assimilated vagrants to the category of political *suspects*. But he was unable to overcome the attachment of his colleague and of the police authorities generally to administrative orders that enabled them to dispose of persons against whom no legal case could be made out. As in so many other spheres, the judicial authorities of the Directory were full of good intentions; but they were seldom in a position to enable these good intentions to bear practical results. There was at least an awareness that it was utterly unjust to treat those who, for one reason or another, were unable to produce witnesses to their legal existence and respectability, as political suspects. In this respect, the occasional or the professional beggar, whether adult or child, was slightly better off than he or she had been at the height of the Terror. The Directory was, as we have so often asserted, a regime reasonably favourable to individualism; and there could be no greater individualist than the wandering *vagabond errant*.[2]

Babies continued to be left at night on church steps, even when the churches had become stables, powder magazines, and arsenals. Infanticide was probably commoner than before the Revolution, though it still

---

[1] And not only children. A list dated Messidor year V (June–July 1797) and drawn up by the *commission des secours publics*, lists as authorized beggars, in receipt of relief: Panthéon-Français, 91; Bonnet-de-la-Liberté, 45; Bonne-Nouvelle, 34; Champs-Élysées, 25; Observatoire, 23; Temple, 19; Homme-Armé, 18; Amis-de-la-Patrie, 15; Muséum, 15; Poissonnière, 11; Thermes, 10; Montblanc, 9; Gravilliers, 8; Théâtre-Français, 6; Lepeletier, 6 (AN, F 15 1870, Hospices et secours). This is only the tip of the iceberg. Only sixteen Sections are listed and only officially authorized beggars recognized as such by the *commission* and the police authorities as incapable of any other form of activity to gain a living are included.

[2] For a fuller discussion of the various legal aspects of the definition and problems of vagrancy and the processes of administrative orders, see my *Quelques aspects de la criminalité parisienne*.

remained primarily a rural crime. We find only a dozen convictions for infanticide in Paris for the whole period 1796–9, though there are hints on the part of the *Bureau Central* that a number of other cases may have gone undetected, in the absence of a proper post-mortem. A commoner form of urban crime is the failure to report a birth. Infanticide appears likewise to have been punished with a correspondingly greater severity in the new courts. An improved police, far greater opportunities for delation, an increased inter-correspondence between the various repressive author-ities, certainly made detection much easier, especially in the conditions of the years II to X, when, it might be said, everyone was watching everyone else; and nothing could be more visible than the contours of a country girl's stomach or of those of some poor laundress or seamstress, housed, in Paris, *chez une logeuse*, rue Saint-Merri, rue Sainte-Avoye, rue des Lombards, and who, three or four times a day, had to pass before the vig-ilant door of one of these ill-natured, inquisitive police spies. Farm girls and domestic servants, constantly exposed to the malevolent gaze of rancid spinsters and of ladies of good position, were of course much worse off in this respect than the daughters of the well-to-do, who stood a reas-onable chance of disposing of the fruits of their errings in a manner that might defy detection. In Paris, the dozen or so women convicted of this crime appear in any case to have belonged to the criminal fringe, as they nearly all have nicknames; and this no doubt made them more noticeable to the police authorities.[1]

But even country girls could sometimes get away with it. We hear, for instance, of such a case, in the canton de Vienne, in Messidor year VIII (June 1800):

> Une fille, âgée de 18 à 19 ans, accouche au milieu d'un champ et étouffe son fruit; cette action est cachée, elle enterre son enfant au moment de sa naissance – le juge de paix, 8 à 9 jours après, est prévenu qu'un chiot a déterré le cadavre d'un enfant mâle, la fille, qui avait été remarquée ayant le ventre gros, est aus-sitôt soupçonnée, elle était d'ailleurs malade, et son ventre avoit repris son volume ordinaire ... la fille, devant moi [the public prosecutor of Vienne] convient d'être accouchée, mais elle dit avoir fait son enfant mort et qu'elle l'a enterré de suite.[2]

And that was the end of the matter. The girl had been exceptionally lucky. But we hear of a similar instance, this time from Paris:

> La nommé Flore, fille au service de la citoyenne Monnet, marchande de modes, rue des Bons-Enfans, No 3, est violemment soupçonnée d'avoir détruit l'enfant

---

[1] One of those so convicted in Paris had the rather unsuitable nickname of *Chère-Mère*. For a fuller discussion of the whole problem of infanticide, see my *Quelques aspects ...*

[2] AN, BB 18 395 (Isère, directeur du jury de Vienne, au Ministre, 3 messidor an VIII).

dont elle s'est accouchée elle-même, sa fuite depuis son accouchement et aussitôt qu'on en a eu connoissance, l'attention de n'employer aucun secours étranger dans ce moment si critique et dangereux, le corps de l'enfant trouvé dans la fosse d'aisance, que le juge de paix a fait vider ... la déclaration de l'officier de santé qui constate que l'enfant est venu à terme et a vécu: tout porte à croire que cette fille a sacrifié à l'opinion les droits sacrés de la nature, à moins, et j'aime à le penser, qu'en s'accouchant elle-même, elle n'aît involontairement donné la mort à son enfant et qu'embarrassée sur le parti qu'elle avait à prendre, elle n'aît cru faire tout disparaître en le précipitant dans les latrines. Le juge de paix de la division de la Butte des Moulins est chargé de l'instruction de cette affaire.[1]

We do not know the outcome of this particular affair; but it seems likely that this girl too was given the benefit of the doubt. So much then for those for whom the Revolution was either an irrelevance or a source of aggravation of a condition already deplorable. It would perhaps be unfair to indict the revolutionary authorities for having either totally neglected the fate of many of those who have formed the subject of this section or even for having made their conditions worse, for, living through an intense emergency, they undoubtedly felt that they had more urgent priorities than these ancient problems.

CLEANLINESS AND DRUNKENNESS

The Revolution, in its later stages, was a particularly arduous time for all those, especially the old and the infirm, who suffered from the cold. In the year II, partly owing to the enormous needs of the naval building programme, partly to those of arms factories, wood became almost unobtainable, outside the black market, and while wood merchants and speculators made enormous fortunes, the poor shivered[2] and many people were reduced to unemployment, as they were unable to heat their furnaces or ovens. It was the same with soap and candles; the shortage of these brought temporary unemployment to night-workers, to laundrywomen, and to starchers. It was not surprising that so many *blanchisseuses* were reduced to petty crime or to prostitution. Skin diseases increased correspondingly; their proliferation was further encouraged by the depleting stocks of sheets and blankets in the miserably run-down hospitals and *hospices*. In the spring of 1795, the *directeur des maisons de bienfaisance* of Mézières, in the Ardennes, was to report to the District de Libreville (Charleville):

---

[1] AN, BB 18 751 (commissaire près l'administration municipale du 2nd arrondissement, au Ministre, 26 germinal an V).

[2] See above, the letter from the *caissier* of the 15/20 (AN, F 15 256).

Le linge étant presque tout consommé par la grande affluence de malades depuis plusieurs années, il n'y reste plus que 111 paires de draps de 300 paires qu'il y avoit autrefois, parmi les 111 paires restantes, 31 seulement sont en bon état, 40 passablement bons, et les 40 autres absolument hors de service; il y a cependant 80 lits à couvrir, lesquels n'ont point été reblanchis depuis plus de 4 mois . . .[1]

The same official, in an earlier report in the course of the terrible winter of 1795, complained of the spread of *la galle* in conditions such as these:

C'est une grande peine pour les âmes sensibles d'être obligées de refuser l'entrée de cette maison aux malheureux détenus attaqués de la galle, et à qui on ne peut pas procurer la guérison, pourquoi? parce qu'elle n'a pas de local séparé pour traiter cette maladie communicative, les malades de cette espèce étant confondus avec les autres et dans la même salle, à coup sûr ne manqueroient pas malgré toutes les précautions de la communiquer à ceux surtout qui sont d'un âge tendre.[2]

Drunkenness was as much as ever a source of popular violence and ferocity. In July 1789, a generous distribution of wine, no doubt by the *marchands de vin*, had given force to the arms of those who pulled down the *barrières*[3] and there is plenty of evidence that the *massacreurs* of September 1792 had been wildly drunk throughout the horrible proceedings.[4] According to an inquiry carried out by the *Commune*, in Germinal year II (March 1794), at the time of the great political trials, there were a total of 1,685 cafés and wine-shops in Paris (as compared to 724 bakers' shops, 562 butchers' shops, and 1,091 groceries). The largest number – 87 – were concentrated in the Section des Lombards; there were 69 in the Amis de la Patrie, 61 in the Butte-des-Moulins (which was also the principal centre for prostitution and gambling), 60 each in the Tuileries, the Halle au bled and the Théâtre-Français, 58 in the Bonnet-rouge, 55 in Unité, 52 in the Gravilliers, 51 in the Temple, 50 in the Quinze-Vingts, and only 46 in the Panthéon-Français, the most heavily populated Section in the city.[5] There was thus a very heavy concentration of drinking establishments in the central Sections of the right bank, particularly in those bordering on the river, from the Tuileries to beyond the Hôtel-de-Ville.

The common people of Paris were in the habit of drinking local wines

[1] AN, F 15 261 (directeur au district, 10 pluviôse an III).
[2] AN, F 15 261 (directeur au district, nivôse an III).
[3] George Rudé, 'La composition sociale des insurrections parisiennes de 1789 à 1791', *AHRF*, July–September 1952.
[4] R. C. Cobb, 'Un témoignage inédit sur le massacre des Carmes', *AHRF*, April–June 1949.
[5] AN, F 7 3688–4.

– *vins de Choisy, vin de Suresnes*, and so on – from the vineyards on the slopes above Issy and Meudon. These were not high in alcoholic content[1] – but they were seldom served pure, by the time they reached the wine-shop, and bore only a nominal relationship to the juice of the grape. An inquiry carried out, a month earlier, in Ventôse year II (24 February 1794), on the orders of the *comité de surveillance du Département de Paris*, by a group of municipal chemists and wine-tasters, is particularly damning in this respect. 'Vous avez fait déguster et décomposer du vin de différentes espèces chez 68 marchands différens. A peine s'en est-il trouvé 8 chez lesquels on puisse attester qu'il se vendoit du vin,' runs the report.

> Les uns, mêlant le cidre, le poiré et l'eau à des couleurs factices et toujours per-nicieuses, vendoient cette boisson à 12 et 15 sols. D'autres voulant donner aux mêmes mélanges plus de feu et de piquant, pour en augmenter le prix, y ajou-toient encore de l'eau-de-vie et faisoient payer cette drogue 15 à 20 sols ... Il en est un citoyen dans le vin duquel la décomposition prouve qu'il entroit du *plomb* ... il en est qui met l'*alun* à cette boisson malfaisante ...

Better still, 'dans le vin de Legage il n'entre pas de vin, c'est un de ceux qui ont le talent merveilleux de faire le vin avec de l'eau'. Legage, who was fol-lowing an illustrious precedent, was ordered to be sent before the *tribunal de police correctionnelle*. The report concludes by drawing attention to what was clearly an exceptional situation: 'Beauvalet, rue de la Juiverie, vend du vin naturel et de bonne qualité.'[2] A month earlier, in Pluviôse (January 1794), the inspectors had examined the wine sold by Polissus, 57, rue Vieille du Temple, Section des Droits de l'Homme: 'La première qualité de vin à 12 sols est un mélange de vin blanc et de poiré coloré avec la betterave, ne contenant que peu de tartre.'[3] But the mixtures most com-monly employed were *poiré*, coloured wood, and alum. Lead was found in the wine of six out of the sixty-odd merchants that had been the object of inquiry.[4]

There is every likelihood that, had the inspectors, rather than thus taking a random check among sixty-eight *marchands de vin*, extended the scope of their inquiry to include their fifteen hundred or so colleagues, the results would have been similar and that people like Beauvalet would have been revealed as extremely rare, not to say perversely eccentric. One can imagine the possible effects of such lethal mixtures, described, without exaggeration, as a *drogue*, on people with empty stomachs or suffering

---

[1] Robert Dauvergne, 'Vignerons d'Ivry-sur-Seine au XVIIIme siècle', *Mémoires, Paris et Île-de-France* (1949).
[2] AN, BB, 3 75, rapport sur les marchands de vin, 6 ventôse an II.
[3] AN, BB 3 63, pluviôse an II.
[4] R. C. Cobb, 'Une enquête de ventôse an II sur le vin', *AHRF*, 1964, pp. 222–5.

from habitual malnutrition. The Revolution multiplied the occasions for collective inebriation, adding its own commemorative dates to an already overloaded Saints' calendar. *Décadi* were observed, but so were Sundays. Fairs were, of course, further occasions for violence arising out of drunkenness, as well as for crimes of every description.

THE FAMILY

Démocrate and *Démophile* owed to the Revolution the opportunity to extend the range of their social exchanges and to marry, as it would be said in a more stable order, 'beneath them'. Other members of their caste would likewise welcome a change in society that released them from parental or fraternal oppression. This would be particularly the case of younger brothers, especially in Normandy and other areas of *droit coutumier*, who welcomed the Civil Code and who, quite often, denounced to the local authorities their eldest, either as an *émigré* or as an *émigré rentré*. The Terror of the year II in particular owed much of its efficacity to allies from within the family citadel of this kind. And, in the year III, when there were persistent rumours of an imminent counter-offensive, led by the first-born, now more confident of their position in a once more hierarchical society, there is a stream of petitions to the *comité de législation* on the part of the *puînés de Normandie*, a sort of trade union with a vested interest in the preservation of the very liberal, individualistic revolutionary family code.[1] Sisters too would have motivations similar to those of younger brothers. It is no doubt characteristic that, faced with the spread of crime and violence and the breakdown of all authority, especially that of the centralized State, in the early years of the Directory, a former magistrate should have called both for a complete reassertion of the authority of the father, and for a divorce much less easily obtainable.[2]

He rightly confounded the authority of the family with that of the collectivity and, thus, of the State. The Directory, despite its faults, fortunately remained attached to the concept of individualism; younger sons

---

[1] Many of these petitions, from younger brothers and from unmarried sisters, are to be found in AN, D III 269 (Dieppe), 270 (Fécamp), 270 (Le Havre), 272-3-4 (Rouen). I am unable to quote them other than from memory, having mislaid my notes of this series from the papers of the *comité de législation*.

[2] AN, BB 18 756 (anon. au Directoire, s.d. pluviôse an VI): '*Quelques observations sur les moyens de réprimer l'assassinat et le vol ... Titre des Mœurs ...* Il faut pour la gloire des Mœurs qu'on arrête ce torrent corrupteur du divorce. L'inconstance française n'avait pas besoin de ce nouvel appât ... Il ne faut pas qu'on assimile les enfants naturels aux légitimes. C'est une nouvelle porte ajoutée aux cent portes du libertinage. Il faut pour la prospérité des mœurs qu'on se hâte de rétablir la puissance paternelle, puisque rien ne soulage le magistrat comme la bonne organisation des familles, comme le bon fils fait le bon citoyen.'

and daughters would be duly sacrificed, on the altar of parental authoritarianism, under the next regime.

A similar interest group, likewise won over to the Revolution, following the new legislation, would be illegitimate children of both sexes;[1] these again we sometimes find in the middle ranks of terrorism and among the petitioners of the year III, when, in a reactionary society more favourable to the collective interests of the family as a unit, they saw their newly acquired rights threatened by a return of the forces of tradition. There is undoubtedly a certain connection between illegitimacy and terrorism, especially at the level of the château and the manor house. The career of Louise Michel, in the course of the following century, may serve as a reminder of this,[2] though it would be unwise to make too much of such accidents of birth, save as a source of social humiliation. At a very different level, natural children are to be found numerous in the ranks of the *bande d'Orgères*; but their presence merely reflects the fact that the *bande* itself constituted a sort of counter-society, with family relationships none the less strong for having been developed outside wedlock. The *bande* rejected the normal family unit, just as it rejected conventional morals, while establishing its own forms of a looser family network – it was, as we shall see, a sort of extended family – and imposing upon each of its members its own code of honour, assumptions, obligations, rewards, punishments, and formalities. Illegitimate children could more readily find acceptance, affection, and friendship in a loose federation of courage, brutality, and daring of this kind. Equally, those raised in Bicêtre or la Pitié would be hardly likely to eye existing authority and organized social patterns with anything but bitter rejection.

> Si les maisons de correction n'étoient pas des asiles où les enfans qui ont le malheur d'y entrer y puisent plutôt les leçons du crime que des principes de vertu, je serois beaucoup moins alarmé; mais nous savons tous qu'en sortant de ces maisons, les enfans, au lieu d'y être corrigés, deviennent ordinairement le fléau de la société … Je suis père de 5 enfans, je ne suis point riche; mais, en travaillant, je me trouve dans une honnête aisance, j'ai fait donner à mes enfans l'éducation nécessaire, ils ont tous des états et celui dont il est question alloit entrer en apprentissage au moment où il a été arrêté.[3]

Thus writes a father to the Minister of Justice, in the summer of the year IV. Crime so often begins with the rejection of the family, better still, with

---

[1] AN, BB 18 756 (ibid.).
[2] Edith Thomas, *Louise Michel* (Paris, 1971).
[3] AN, BB 18 748 (Bernard Mouchotte, employé ci-devant à la commission des approvisionnements, en qualité de commis, actuellement marchand forain, domicilié à Paris, rue des Cordiers, no 602, 11me arrondissement, au Citoyen Ministre de l'Intérieur, 27 prairial an IV).

rejection by the family. Catherine Robillard had come to Paris after her father's death; from prison, she did not dare to write to her relatives to inform them of her fate. In so many petitions to the Minister, there is a Jansenist-toned insistence on the honourability of the family background and on the excellence of the education of the petitioners. This may, of course, constitute little more than a groping after respectability, in order to catch the eye of the Minister; but it probably represents the persistence of family influence well beyond adolescence. The family unit was so important that, as we have seen, it often constituted the principal basis for the organization of a criminal gang. *On volait en famille; on tuait en famille*. This only brings out more dramatically the terrible isolation of the foundling, brought up in an institution and subjected to the terrible Jansenist discipline of Bicêtre. There was, after all, a solidarity in crime.[1]

There are other zones that must, for the time being, remain mysterious. It is doubtful whether there would be any profit in pursuing, through the revolutionary period, the confirmed homosexual or the lesbian, for, generally, they are too elusive ever to be recorded, especially by singularly innocent *sans-culotte* militants, who took the minutes at popular assemblies and who were only dimly aware of such Gothic horrors – and that only in a purely historical context: *Henri III et ses mignons*. It would hardly have occurred to them that, by looking over their shoulders, they might still perceive the survival of Valois vices. And yet homosexuals too must have formed closed and shuttered worlds, well protected from the collective *mores* of revolutionary rejoicing. Relationships of this kind were entirely inward-looking. Nor indeed would there be much profit in proceeding any further into this very tentative exploration of individual attitudes and motivations. In the present chapter, we have merely attempted to suggest some of the limits imposed, at least in eighteenth-century terms, on the margin of revolutionary – or counter-revolutionary – intervention, as far as the individual was concerned, as well as to insist on the irrelevance of the Revolution itself to certain marginal elements of society.

The picture that emerges must, in the last resort, appear incomplete, confused, and highly fractionalized, for we are not dealing with any form of coherent or even organized opinion, openly expressed, or with attitudes that are in any way particularly conscious. Those who 'lived outside the Revolution' would often hardly be aware that they were doing so – if

---

[1] AN, BB 18 125 (Ardèche, commissaire près le tribunal criminel d'Aubenas, au Ministre, 4 prairial an IX): 'Le 29 [floréal] au matin le tribunal spécial a jugé la nommée *Adélaïde*. Cette fille était un enfant trouvé qui avait été élevée à l'hôpital de Nice, d'où elle sortit lorsque les Français s'emparèrent de cette ville. Elle se livre au vagabondage et à la débauche; il n'y avait pas d'autre délit à lui reprocher que celui d'une mauvaise vie; le tribunal ... a ordonné qu'elle serait reconduite dans l'hôpital de Nice.'

only because they had previously 'lived outside the *ancien régime*' (and would, no doubt, though this was likely to be much more difficult, in a regime so minutely regulated, continue to 'live outside the Empire'); and they would be even harder put to explain, if asked, *why* they were doing so. Probably, most had never given the matter a thought. There had never been any place for them inside any established, legalized society. Where, for instance, would the wandering communities of gypsies fit into either the old or the revolutionary orders? And what did the old monarchy or the Republic have to offer the habitual poacher, the man – or the woman – who lived off the pillaging of forest and woodland, the riverman who subsisted off the proceeds of the illegal night-fishing of the Seine and the Marne and the Oise? They would only differentiate between one system and another in the crudest, physical terms of relatively effective repression; and, in this respect, they would be likely to conclude against the Revolution, as a system both more severe and more effectively punitive. At least they would have known their way through the intricacies of *ancien régime* repressive institutions. People at this level, unlike political theorists, are not given to speculate on the origins of the State, on Natural Rights and Original Compacts. For them, as for Restif's *fille de la populace*, any regime can only be personalized in the form of the *sergent de la maréchaussée* or the *gendarme*. The best they could expect was a system of government that was largely ineffective and that left them to their own devices. In this respect at least, the Directory must have had a very wide, though negative, and generally unstated, appeal. For it could never be claimed that it was a particularly invasive form of government.

At best, the more self-aware, if hard-pressed, might have been prepared to admit that they were quite capable consciously of putting the series of revolutionary crises to their own private advantage. This was, after all, not particularly difficult either to think of or to do, when the amnesty of Brumaire year IV (October 1795), and similar legislation in the year VII and the year VIII invited the private citizen – yes, positively *invited* him – to give as extended an interpretation as he chose to actions under the enormously convenient blanket of events arising 'des faits de la Révolution'. This might, as we have seen, cover a husband-slaying, even a parricide,[1] as well as the suppression of a business partner or a creditor. It

---

[1] AN, BB 18 754 (l'accusateur public près le tribunal de Cahors, au Ministre, 9 frimaire an VI): 'J'ose joindre la déclaration qu'un jury spécial a donnée, le 3 du courant, en faveur d'un individu accusé de parricide. Je pensois qu'il seroit convaincu de ce crime; le commissaire près le tribunal a cédé au cri général et à l'indignation publique en se pourvoyant en cassation du jugement qui acquitte cet accusé. Je puis cependant affirmer que l'esprit de parti n'a point dicté cette déclaration; c'est la philanthropie, quelques jurés ont cru que la société n'a pas droit de retrancher de son sein certains membres. Ce système est peut-être fondé sur *la loi du 4 brumaire an IV*, la peine de mort doit cesser à la paix; je suis sûr que le jury croyoit

was too good an opportunity to be missed; and, as the political evolution of the Republic became increasingly more incoherent and *staccato*, from the advent of Thermidor till the proclamation of the Empire, such opportunities would constantly recur, at regular intervals of from three to six months. Such candour would, however, be rare. People are not prone to own up to the pull of naked self-interest, and, throughout the Revolution, there would always be a natural temptation, unless one were an *émigré*, to equate pure selfishness with the salvation of whatever one imagined France to be; and one could always find, such was the extent of the range, *une France à sa taille*. For a time at least, when all appeared equally threatened by the military menace from outside, it must also have been quite easy to identify oneself with a Republic that seemed the best guarantee of personal security. After 1795, however, it would be quite another matter.

To admit that one had totally opted out of the Revolution would also have little sense in historical terms. For it would imply an awareness of the confused narrative of events that few, other than the top political leaders of the revolutionary movement – and many of these became overtaken by events – can ever possibly have possessed. For the revolutionary crisis is anything but a coherent whole; on the contrary it can only be seen as an endless clash of discordant voices and confused infighting. It is even difficult to establish just when it *began*; if historians are still arguing about it, how could contemporaries have been sure? How could they say, as they looked at their calendar, in 1787, or 1788, or 1789, or 1792: 'The Revolutionary Crisis has begun today. What am I going to do about it?' More important, perhaps, because the awareness of the fact might have important consequences in terms of individual physical survival, was to be able to decide when the revolutionary crisis really *ended*. Not even the members of the Committee of Public Safety could have told, at the time, where 9 Thermidor would lead them, in a matter of only six or seven weeks. And when Thermidorians and Directorials talked in terms of *le retour au règne des lois*, it was an expression of intent, rather than a sober appraisal of an utterly confusing political scene. They certainly *wanted* the revolutionary crisis to end, because they were hankering after security and a minimum of order. But they were as unaware as almost the humblest of citizens of what might be just round the corner. There was a certain logic in the position of the members of the *bande d'Orgères* and of many other similar groups, in deciding to create their own history (and myth), in a narrative of violence, pillage, and murder. They at least were,

---

l'accusé coupable et qu'on eût vu avec plaisir qu'il eût subi les peines qui seront substituées à celle de mort. Ce jugement m'afflige d'autant plus que le 1er du courant la peine de mort a été prononcée contre un homme contre lequel il existoit moins de preuves et dont le crime étoit moins horrible.'

for a time, masters both of the present and of the immediate future; and no one can lightly dismiss a narrative, however anarchical and violent that, thanks to their efforts, to the fears that they inspired, and to the wide extent of complicity that they enjoyed, they succeeded in keeping going for nearly ten years, an existence longer than that of any of the current revolutionary regimes. For the private individual, more humble, less ambitious than these bold bandits, in the conditions of 1795 and the Directory, *Tarot*, a soothsayer, a reader in cards would all offer a more reliable guide to the political present and the immediate political future, than the gazettes and the newspapers. The horoscope seemed a better measurement of time than repetitive *coups*, the ripples of which ran out, every few months, from the capital, to be felt in varying degrees of violence and vengeance through every *commune*. This was probably why so much was made at the time of beautiful hands, emerging from a black lake, holding a book printed in indecipherable characters, of *lettres d'or*, couched in apocalyptic terms, showered down from dark and thundery skies, on to the receptive hills and mountains of the Massif Central. Even if, from the late summer of 1794, there would be a fairly general awareness that a certain form of Terror was at an end – for every person released from *robespierriste* prisons there would be a score of people – relatives and friends – who would be quick to draw the conclusion from this happy state of affairs – it soon became apparent that there would be no diminution of violence and that life would continue to be highly dangerous. The position of the individual, in a period when all the normal beacons had been removed, was much that of the figures in Gauguin's allegorical painting: *Que sommes-nous? Où allons-nous?* Where indeed? At best, there might be a vague consciousness of 'muddling through', the peasant's and the countryman's dream of seeing it out and coming through to the end of the tunnel. We can perceive this clearly in Restif. But he is not a good example; his self-awareness as an utterly unrepentant egotist places him *hors concours*. We are not dealing with people endowed with his own splendid singleness of purpose. Restif was anything but humble.

So like the variegated subjects of this chapter, we are indeed groping in a *zone d'ombre*, into which we may at best have allowed to penetrate very occasional shafts of light – seldom the light of evidence or of concrete fact – more often that of tentative, inventive perception, or, to put it more baldly, historical guessing. 'It must have been like this', 'he must have thought like that', 'they must have seen it this way', 'he must have regretted marrying into such a family', and so on. Historical guesswork can be made to look more respectable and more impressive in the looser expressions of French than in the cold light of English. *Parions que* ... can cover a multitude of suggestions, while leaving all channels conveniently open. There is no all-purpose phrase quite like it in English. Even if they owed much to Bonnington, the Impressionists owed more to the light of the Seine Estuary, and they were, mostly, French. The present chapter, more than any in this study, has been a very tentative, very hesitant exercise in historical impressionism. Whatever it may be, it certainly is *not* the Tables of the Law, handed down through a thick cloud, to the combined sound of thunder and organ music. Its purpose is merely to be a contribution to the study of lost attitudes, presuppositions, assumptions, and submerged mentalities, though, whenever possible, we have attempted to give body to these from concrete examples taken from contemporary reports, petitions, and letters.

10

A View on the Street: Seduction and Pregnancy in Revolutionary Lyon*

Les diamans, les bijous, un ameublement superbe, un carrosse du dernier goût, tout cela est prêt: un mot, & une bourse de mille louis va précéder.

Restif de la Bretonne, *La Paysanne pervertie*

Le jeune Page hardi comme un Page, en vérité! & il n'y a rien de solide là-dedans: ça est trop-jeune, & ça n'a pas d'état, ça sera un fréluquet, qui laisserait là une Femme un-jour, pour aller courir de garnison en garnison, commes les Officiers des cazernes de Joigni, & d'ailleurs.

Restif de la Bretonne, *Monsieur Nicolas*

... si vous n'avez Personne, je suis bien-sûr de vous faire un-jour Comtesse. Le malheur, c'est que je n'ai que 16 ans! mais je suis orfelin, & les droits des Tuteurs cessent plutôt [*sic*] que ceux des Pères.

Restif de la Bretonne, *La Paysanne pervertie*

Pour plaire à la fille
qui est si gentille
c'est à la maman
qu'il faut faire le baratin.

Parisian rhyme, XXth century

Dans toutes ses visites Pierre Dusurgey fit à la remontrante des promesses de mariage, auxquelles elle crut d'autant plus facilement qu'il n'y avait aucune disproportion dans leurs professions et leurs âges, la remontrante est âgée de 23 ans, et Pierre Dusurgey, de 24; l'un et l'autre travaillaient pour la chapellerie ... il avait pour elle des complaisances marquées; chaque jour, après la journée de travail, il venait la chercher, pour l'accompagner à la promenade, il en faisait autant les

---

* From *A Sense of Place*, pp. 77–135.

fêtes et dimanches, enfin il disait publiquement et à leurs connaissances mutuelles qu'il la recherchait en mariage.

> Déclaration de grossesse faite par Benoîte Bonnard, coupeuse
> de poils pour la chapellerie, devant le tribunal de Lyon-Ville
> 15 February 1791, Archives départementales du Rhône, 36 L 52

Il y a environ un an elle fit la connoissance du Sr. Jaivry, voyageur de
commerce pour cette ville à Bordeaux, et habitant alternativement
dans l'une ou l'autre de ces deux villes ... il lui fit des propositions de
mariage, il n'attendait, disait-il, que le moment où il auroit pu parvenir à arranger des affaires de manière à pouvoir se fixer absolument
à Lyon. Le Sr. Jaivry se ménageait de tems à autre des entrevues avec
la comparante à l'insu de ses parents, il l'entretenait du BONHEUR
qu'il disait se promettre du mariage qu'il contracterait *incessamment*
avec elle.

> Déclaration de grossesse faite par Annette Dementhon, fille du
> Sr. Dementhon, marchand de dorures fausses, demeurant à Lyon,
> rue Saint-Dominique, âgée de 17 ans, 21 April 1791

Dlle. Jeanne Planet, ouvrière en soie, demeurant à Lyon chez
Monsieur son père, rue Bourgchanin, fille mineure ... qu'il y a
environ un an qu'elle fit la connaissance du Sr. François Nicq, serrurier à Lyon ... rue Désirée; que ce dernier, charmé de la conduite de
la remontrante, *demanda à ses père et mère l'entrée de la maison* et
promit d'épouser leur fille. Les père et mère ... furent d'autant plus
faciles à croire cette promesse que le Sr. Nicq, sans père ni mère, peut
disposer de lui et est absolument libre, il venoit donc assidûment chez
eux.

> Déclaration de grossesse faite par Jeanne Planet, ouvrière en soie,
> 25 May 1791

Le Sr. Brigand ... s'est fait un jeu de tromper son innocence, *peu
accoutumée au séjour de la ville*, le Sr. Brigand a profité de son inex-
périence et de sa crédulité, et lui a fait entrevoir l'avenir le plus
heureux si elle se livrait à lui.

> Déclaration de grossesse faite par Pierrette Blanc, brodeuse,
> Petite rue Tramassac, âgée de 21 ans

... depuis plus d'une année le Sr. Bavet venait la voir assidûment dans
son domicile où elle demeuroit alors, allée des Images, *il entretenait
même avec elle une correspondance lorsqu'il était absent*, ou que ses
moments ne lui permettaient pas de se rendre auprès d'elle.

> Déclaration de grossesse faite par Françoise Dueure, brodeuse,
> quai de Saône, 28 June 1791

THE ARGUMENTS, LIKE the promised rewards, may vary, but the *langage du cœur*, however phrased, seeks always the same capitulation, and the extracts quoted above spell out, in varied forms, the same sad, sad story. Restif clearly has in mind seduction at a high, or at least, an ascending, social level, and diamonds, jewels, magnificent furniture, a carriage in the very latest style, even a purse containing a thousand *louis* are hardly inducements that will speak to the tender heart of the Lyon *brodeuse* or *ouvrière en soie*, her feet relatively firmly on the ground. For her such promises would appear so improbable as totally to undermine the credibility of the persuader, of what in Parisian cynical parlance would be described as *le baratineur*. It would be necessary to adjust language to the economic expectations and the strongly held social conventions of the addressee. For the working girl, a similar, or very slightly superior economic status would act as a powerful argument. The facts of neighbourhood would likewise count, as would old acquaintance, which would appear as a sort of guarantee. The receipt of a letter, or of several letters, proudly displayed to workmates, and no doubt read out loud by one of them, would be much more convincing than a purse of gold. A man without parents would hold a powerful card; similar ages, with the man perhaps two or three years older, would argue in favour of rapid capitulation. To ask parents entry to their house would be the surest of all guarantees. Absence likewise *parle au cœur*, if at least it eventually came to an end. A similar provincial origin, especially a village one, would be a sort of reassurance, as if the closely scrutinized orthodoxies and standards of behaviour imposed by the rural collectivity would be likely to be retained even in the city. We will return later to these conventions and, in more detail, to the analysis of those conventions of language, the nuances of emphasis, the delicately shaded promises of happiness (*il m'a fait entrevoir le bonheur*, like a curtain pulled aside to reveal a table groaning with food and foreign wines), or the cruder material arguments, because they tell the historian a great deal more about eighteenth-century *mores*, in an urban or recently urban setting, than they would have told the girls themselves, who, however naïve – and they are naturally primarily concerned to emphasize their naïveté and inexperience – would at least have had a pretty good idea as to what it was all about, just as much as the prudish and *jansénisante Présidente* must eventually have guessed what was the final purpose of Valmont's long-drawn-out and carefully conducted siege. Valmont may not have been an artillery officer, but Laclos was.

Let us then, first of all, discuss our principal source and attempt to assess its reliability, its more obvious traps and falsities, and its eventual value to the social historian concerned to reconstruct the often unstated assumptions of people both very poor, very ignorant, and generally unable to express themselves in reasoned tones. Under an ordinance of Henri III, pregnant girls or women were required to come before a public official at some stage of their pregnancy, generally before the eighth month, in order to make a *déclaration de grossesse*. This obligatory declaration had no doubt not been conceived in the interest of the declarant, though, of course, it might help her to make a paternity claim. What seems much more likely is that the requirement had been imposed in the interest of Authority, in order at least to place some impediment on infanticide, clearly much easier to check in a city than in a rural community, although Olwen Hufton has demonstrated that, given the widespread complicity of certain collectivities, this commonest form of female crime of violence could often be committed with almost complete impunity, and sometimes on a vast scale, in both.[1] The *déclaration de grossesse* remained obligatory in the early years of the Revolution, until the introduction of the penal and civil Codes in 1790–1 removed the obligatory character of the statement, converting it into a voluntary one at the choice of the declarant. We find, for instance, one of the declarants, Barbe Condamine, 'fille domestique à Sainte-Julie-en-Beaujolais, demeurant actuellement en cette ville, rue Bourgneuf, chez le Sr. Antoine, cabaretier', in fact the country girl exposed to the dangerous location of a *cabaret*, 'laquelle *pour satisfaire aux ordonnances du royaume* ... a déclaré qu'elle est enceinte d'environ 6 mois et ½ des œuvres de Jean-Baptiste Perrachon, travailleur de terre, demeurant en ladite paroisse de Julie' (my italics). (Barbe, far from fitting into that much-favoured eighteenth-century literary convention of *les dangers de la ville*, of *la paysanne pervertie*, had lost her virginity before coming to town, had, indeed, no doubt come to town for that very reason; we will return in due course to this important category of country girls who had come to Lyon in order to conceal their shame.) This was on 4 December 1790, right at the beginning of the period of two years covered by our documents. Most such statements would then not have been obligatory, and were made on the initiative of the girls and women, for a variety of reasons, but all primarily for the purpose of identifying the seducer (and it would of course be up to the girl to suggest that there had in fact only been one, while it was commonly argued by each man thus named that, if he had indeed had carnal relations with the declarant, he had been but one of several). After Thermidor and during the Directory a number of judicial authorities, apparently alarmed at the dramatic increase in infanticide both during the revolutionary years, which were also years of considerable libertinage, and during the years of extreme hardship that followed immediately on the Terror, were to put pressure on the Garde des Sceaux in order to induce him to bring in legislation to

---

[1] Olwen Hufton, *The Poor of Eighteenth-century France 1750–1789* (Oxford, 1974).

make the *déclarations* once more obligatory. But the Minister, Merlin de
Douai, strongly and successfully resisted such demands, which he rightly
described as utterly oppressive, reminiscent of the worst abuses of the old
order and smacking of feudal barbarity. At least until the end of the First
Republic, such statements were to remain voluntary. Even when they had
been obligatory, they would primarily have affected members of the
feminine poor: working girls, domestic servants, girls living in lodging-
houses, their stomachs closely observed for any hint of *rondeurs* by
logeuses and *concierges* anxious to keep in the good books of the *police des
garnis*. For a girl protected in the cocoon of the family unit, as for the girl
with affluent parents, it would no doubt have been relatively easy, at least
in late eighteenth-century conditions, not only to avoid making an official
declaration, but also to dispose of an unwanted pregnancy in some discreet urban establishment. Mercier, with his usual bold jump at figures,
and with his usual impudent inaccuracy, was to count 223 such establishments for Paris in the 1780s.

We possess fifty-four such statements, from fifty-two women and girls,
two of them, decidedly accident-prone, having turned up twice within
periods of eighteen months. All of them are living, at the time, in the area
covered by Lyon-Ville (as opposed to Lyon-Campagne, which contained
the faubourgs and independent *communes* outside the fortifications, as yet
intact). Most of the declarants in fact give addresses in the central area,
entre Rhône et Saône, either in les Terreaux, in Bellecordière or on the
quays. The statements run from 4 December 1790 to 27 November 1792,
that is for a period during which the impact of war would scarcely have
been felt. It is important to bear this fact in mind, for war and revolution
have always been firm allies of masculine designs on women, owing both
to the prestige attached to uniforms, especially among female silk-
workers, in a garrison town, and to the extra facilities that they would
afford to the possibilities of escape on the part of the seducer. On the other
hand, thanks to the creation of the National Guard and the expansion of
the army, as well as the normal movements of troops – as we shall see, a
number of the girls were to claim that they had been seduced by soldiers
from the Régiment de la Marck, which had been quartered in the city in
1790 – many of the wartime conditions favourable to increased masculine
mobility and irresponsibility might be said already to have existed. The
figures themselves, month by month, do not appear to have any particular significance, not being sufficiently numerous to bear witness to any
sudden increase or decrease: two statements date from December 1790;
there are thirty-four for 1791, the most numerous being in March (six) and
August (five). There are fifteen *déclarations* for 1792. As, in each case, the
duration of the pregnancy is given (*enceinte de six mois, enceinte de huit
mois*, and so on), it would no doubt be possible for historians concerned

with the degree that religious discipline still prevailed with the poorer elements of the female population to use this kind of source; for, by calculating the dates of conception, the researcher, on the basis of information of this kind, would be in a position, when in possession of a larger body of evidence, stretching over a longer period, to establish to what extent official religious prohibitions of sexual intercourse during the period of Advent were still respected. In this instance, the declarations are not numerous enough to offer any significant clues. But, clearly, this is the sort of problem on which a more extensive use of this type of documentation, over a longer period, and in a number of localities, might offer useful indications as to the relative survival, in one area or another, of the restraints of religious discipline.

Most of the fifty or so girls in the Lyon *dossier* were extremely young, and may indeed have been as innocent and as inexperienced as so many of them were to claim in their statements. Four were seventeen or seventeen and a few months; there were three eighteen-year-olds, three again of nineteen; one gave her age as twenty, one as twenty-one; three were twenty-two. There was one woman of thirty; four were simply described as *filles majeures*, and two as *filles mineures*. Thus most of those – a minority – whose ages were given, were minors. Thirty-one were completely illiterate, being unable to sign their names; twenty-one could at least do this, though the spelling was often erratic (for instance, *Marte* for *Marthe*). As might be expected of women and girls living and working in Lyon, the commonest professional status was employment in some form of silk manufacture: a mass of *ouvrières en soie* and of *brodeuses* and *fileuses*, individual *tireuses*, *dévideuses*, *gazières*, *metteuses en mains*, *apprêteuses*, *ourdisseuses de rubans*, *coupeuses*, *chapelières*, *faiseuses de bourses en soie*: in all, about half the group. Equally predictably, we encounter twelve domestic servants or the sadly eloquent *ex-domestique*. There were two *blanchisseuses*, a *lingère*, an *épicière*, an *ex-cuisinière* (no doubt likewise dismissed as a result of her condition), a *fripière*, a *fille de marchand*, and a *comédienne*, a Lyonnaise who had gone to Marseille to train as an actress and who, according to her account, had succumbed to the attentions of a merchant from that city who had attempted to point out to her the dangers inherent in such a profession: to take a leaf out of Fourier's celebrated *Dictionnaire des Cocus* and to attempt a similar enterprise for the many categories of seducer, one might range this gentleman as *le séducteur moralisateur*, a line of approach that seems to have been particularly paying. With the exception of the *fille de marchand*, who seems to have lost the expectation of a considerable sum of money from an aunt, as the result of the shame that she had brought on her family, and the *marchande de modes*, who employed several female apprentices (these came to the court to witness in her favour and to identify her seducer as a man whom they had frequently seen coming up the staircase at dusk, or disappearing down it, 'carrying a packet under his arm', in the early hour at which these girls got up), none of the girls could be said to have had any prospects, other than a marriage that might slightly better their condition (an *ouvrière chapelière*, for instance, seems to have been in hopes of marrying a *marchand chapelier* from her own village, until the young man's parents intervened to point out that he would be marrying beneath him) and a tenuous existence based on very long working hours, followed by a few febrile hours of leisure. For all, a pregnancy would have been an unmitigated disaster. Indeed, one of the themes that emerges most persistently from these sad statements is the humility and the lack of expectancy of most of the declarants; those, for instance, who seem to have faced up to the fact that they were unlikely ever to see their seducers again, because they had gone away, because they were soldiers, pedlars, commercial travellers, hairdressers, medical or veterinary students (the whole range in fact of the more persistent, better-placed eighteenth-century seducer), merely made their statements in order to solicit a place in the foundling hospital for their unborn children (*a demandé un billet pour la Charité*, a phrase that recurs with distressing regularity). There was indeed not much to be expected of a soldier, often only known to the girl under his nickname, nor even of a hairdresser who went under the unhelpful name of *Provençal*.

DEPARTURE FROM HOME AND CHANGE OF ADDRESS

A very common accompaniment of a seduction resulting in a pregnancy, the visible sign of having *fauté*, once it had become visible, would be either departure from home, in order to flee the wrath of parents, or, worse still, of brothers, and to escape from the cruel gaze of a tight rural community (*parties de chez elles* – and for such, even the warning of what might befall them in the city, on the favourite ecclesiastical theme among country *curés* of *les dangers de la ville*, might not deter them), or, less dramatic, but equally eloquent, a change of address which, from our documents, can so often be dated from the third or fourth month of pregnancy: sometimes it was only a matter of moving a couple of streets, within the same quarter; more often the girl would take the trouble to move out of the quarter altogether, let us say from one of the narrow streets of les Terreaux to one of the quays. Such changes of address would presumably spell out a dismissal: for instance, a domestic servant, who had been seduced by her employer, or by his son, or by both, would nearly always have been thrown out of the house in which she occupied some wretched attic or cupboard. Her mere presence in her visible condition would have been taken as a form of moral blackmail on the part of her former employers. Barbe Condamine, whom we have already mentioned as having been seduced by a *pays* from her own village in the Beaujolais, would clearly belong to the former category: she had come to Lyon, when she was six and a half months pregnant, in order perhaps to seek anonymity, and, possibly, to obtain a place for her child. Marianne Motte, 'demeurant ci-devant au Bourg-Argental, de présent à Lyon chez le Sr. Duperrin, son beaufrère, arquebusier, demeurant rue de la Boucherie des Terreaux', who had been seduced by another inhabitant of Bourg-Argental, described as a *bourgeois*, had come to Lyon for a similar purpose, using, like so many provincials of both sexes when first in the city, the family network. There are a great many cases of changes of address within the city, some of them quite explicit: thus 'Françoise André, native de la paroisse de Montluel, fille domestique au service du Sr. Charretier, rue de Trion [her alleged seducer], demeurant actuellement chez la veuve Mathéra, garde-malade, rue de la Barre'. Marie Dangle, *brodeuse*, at the time of her declaration was living with, and working for, her sister, rue de l'Enfant-qui-pisse. Previously 'elle consentit à aller habiter avec le Sr. Flandrin dans un appartement qu'il loua pour elle, place Neuve des Carmes, et elle y a demeuré pendant environ 5 mois'. When she had told Flandrin about her condition, he had thrown her out, and she had then turned to her sister. Marie was luckier than a great many of the *déclarantes* in thus having a close relative in the city. Marie Chirat, the daughter of an inhabitant of la Guillotière, had moved, as a result of her pregnancy, to a room near the porte Saint-Clair, on the road to Geneva, taking the precaution to place the Rhône between herself and her family. Jeanne Rouzon, *lingère*, rue Confort, stated that 'il y a environ un an qu'elle était en apprentissage de sa profession chez la femme du Sr. Canot, tonnelier, demeurant en la paroisse de Caluire'. Canot had seduced her, and she had then moved to the nearby city. Claudine Poncet, 'ouvrière, demeurant chez Mlle Royer, marchande de modes . . . rue Mercière . . . [states that] depuis environ une année et demie elle demeuroit dans la pension où logeoit le Sr. Antoine d'Audiffret', her alleged seducer. Much the same had happened to a girl who had come from the country, with her mother, to Lyon, where they had taken a room in a lodging-house:

> Pierrette Blanc . . . demeurant rue Saint-Jean (en avril 1791) [states that] . . . au commencement de l'année dernière elles quittèrent Grézieu-la-Varenne, qu'elles avaient toujours habité, et vinrent se fixer en cette ville, elles prirent un logement dans la maison du Sr. Brigand.

The following year, after having had a child by Brigand, she had moved to la petite rue Tramassac. Anne Burtin, 'ci-devant cuisinière, demeurant chez les demoiselles Reynaud, marchandes de modes, place de la Comédie [se déclare] actuellement logée chez le Sr. Bonneton, ouvrier en soie, place de l'Homme de la Roche'. Benoîte Marduel, who had been a domestic servant of a tradesman, grande rue Mercière, was living in July 1791, rue Tupin. The case of Marie Perrichon, 'dévideuse de soie', is even more explicit:

> Demeurant rue Saint-Georges … son père compagnon maçon à Neuville … [elle] entra au service du Sr. Quet, marchand fabricant … place de la Croix-Paquet … pendant 4 [mois] et demi qu'elle est restée dans la maison dont elle ne sortit que lorsqu'elle fut convaincue qu'elle était enceinte.

Jeanne Rey, who had gone to Marseille to take up the theatre, and had there met her seducer (*le moralisateur*), who had set her up in a room there, and who had, on learning that she was pregnant, told her that he would be unable to marry her owing to opposition from his family, had returned to Lyon, where she was 'logée en chambre garnie, rue Basse-Ville'. Benoîte Bonnard, living at the time of her statement 'porte Sablet, paroisse Saint-Georges', had had an address in the previous year in the rue Raisin.

Most of these moves can only have been for the worse. For many of these girls, while employed, were likely to have also been housed. Now, in so many of the cases that we have mentioned, they were thrown on to the insecurity, the discomforts and the manifold dangers of a *chambre garnie*, almost certainly shared with several other girls, who, as we shall see from individual examples, would take it in turns to leave the room, on Sundays or feast days, or in the evening, when one of them was receiving her lover. In Lyon, no doubt as an example of the quirks of popular humour, a great many *chambres garnies* were situated at this time either in the rue des Vertus or in the equally inappropriately-styled rue Confort (which is still one of the principal centres of the city's prostitution). And this, then, was likely to be the first of a whole series of changes of addresses, whether as a result of further pregnancies, or of failure to pay the rent. Even the fact of a single change of address may indicate, to the attentive social historian, the principal outward manifestation of a personal tragedy of momentous consequences to the girl concerned. It was a matter of being as it were cast into the outer darkness, removed from the comforting embrace of the family unit, and from the satisfactions of neighbourliness, one of the few compensations of the very poor. It would take little imagination to depict the increasingly desperate journey across the city of a girl thus sent on an ever more rapid quest. Changes of address are certainly more eloquent in *déclarations de grossesse* than in almost any other form of contemporary documentation.

A great many of the country girls who had come to Lyon for one reason or another, once they had discovered their condition, would have been seduced by *pays*, by men from their own localities. In such cases, it would have been quite impossible to conceal what had happened both from the family and from the majority of the locals. For instance, Marianne Faye, 'ouvrière papetière, demeurant ordinairement à Rives (Isère)', where she had worked in a paper mill, had, so she claimed, been seduced by her employer; she adds: 'La comparante a été obligée de quitter sa famille pour venir cacher son malheur et sa honte en cette ville.' Marie Pierry, the daughter of a peasant from Villeurbanne, said that she had been seduced by a gardener, from la Montée de Balmont, paroisse Saint-Didier, in Lyon itself; though he could hardly be described as a *pays*, the girl is likely first to have met him because, like her father, he worked on the land, and was a rustic within the urban community. Even more interesting is the case of Françoise Dubessy, who, on 16 February 1792, says that she was:

> domestique à Lyon, y demeurant, rue Tramassac, âgée de 27 ans ... que depuis son enfance elle était liée avec Jean Biolay, marchand de vin, habitant à Pouilly-le-Monial, ils étaient du même pays, il venait voir la comparante en cette ville, il a profité de l'intimité qui régnait entr'eux depuis si longtems pour ... la séduire ... [elle est] enceinte depuis environ 6 mois de ses œuvres.

We learn from another source that the wine merchant had been in the habit of walking the very considerable distance from Pouilly-le-Monial to Lyon to see Françoise every other Sunday. The girl, who clearly had had her eye on such an advantageous match for a very long time – they had known each other for over ten years – took this assiduity as a guarantee of the seriousness of the man's intentions. What is more, her workmates had met him on a number of these occasions.

Jeanne Rouzon, whom we have already mentioned, stated, in May 1791, that while working in Caluire, her birthplace,

> elle y a fit la connoissance du nommé François Bergeron, garçon cordonnier, demeurant actuellement en ce bourg, chez le Sr. Laurent, marchand cordonnier ... que cependant voilà près de 8 jours qu'il a cessé de la voir, sans aucun sujet de mécontentement si ce n'est que sa position ne lui permettant de rester plus longtems sans terminer la promesse qu'il lui a si souvent réiterée, elle le pressoit vivement à ses fins, ce qui peut peut-être l'en avoir éloigné.

The poor girl, though illiterate, was clearly no fool.

There are two further instances of alleged seduction by *pays* from two localities much nearer Lyon, indeed on the very outskirts of the city. The first concerns 'Dlle. Isabelle Collonge, fille mineure, apprentie gazière, demeurant en ce canton [Cuire] chez le Sr. Germain Poisson, laquelle a dit que ce dernier, chez lequel elle est apprentie, l'a séduite'. The other is that of a girl from the *commune* of la Guillotière, a place which, owing to the number of its *guinguettes* and its popularity with the inhabitants of the central peninsula as a weekend resort and as a centre for Saturday and Sunday *bals*, must have accounted for a very large number of pregnancies:

> Marguerite Terrier, tailleuse, demeurant au faubourg de la Guillotière, chez Sr. François Terrier, son père, chirurgien juré [déclare] ... qu'elle a eu le malheur de se lier avec Pierre Landouard, élève de l'école royale vétérinaire établie aud. faubourg ... à peine la remontrante était-elle enceinte qu'il est parti de ce pays promettant, il est vrai, de bientôt revenir, mais bien résolu cependant de fuir à jamais celle qu'il avait séduite.

This is perhaps not quite the case of a girl succumbing to the usual arguments of a compatriot, arguments which would normally go much as follows: 'A Pâques (ou à Noël) on retournera au pays pour s'y marier et pour s'y fixer.' For her seducer was only a *casual* inhabitant of la Guillotière, and was thus better protected than most more stationary male seducers. But it is fairly clear that the two must have met both as a result of the presence of the school in the faubourg and because her father would no doubt have had many acquaintances in medical circles.

Both the victims themselves and what might be described as accepted popular opinion, and the sort of parallel popular justice that would operate as a form of community pressure in such matters and that was often more effective than the official system of rewards and penalties, were particularly severe on men who were seen to have profited from the fact that they had been from the same village in order to capture the confidence of the object of their lust. They had, in some way, sinned against the collectivity, as well as against the girl. Indeed, their force of persuasion would if anything have increased in the alien setting of a large city, in which people from the same village would naturally tend to be thrown together – and there was every likelihood in a city as geographically localized by quarter, trade and provincial origin as Lyon that they would in fact often be living in close proximity, in the same street or even in the same lodging-house – and in which links *entre gens du pays* would become all the more insistent as a form of self-defence and mutual help. Seductions of this type seem to have been regarded as a particularly obnoxious form of *escroquerie morale*, in that the girl's defences would be down almost before the operation had been undertaken.

MASCULINE MOBILITY AND FLIGHT

For the man, on the other hand, especially if unattached, there would always be an easy way out of a situation in which he was being asked to accept responsibility for paternity: he merely had to leave the city, generally after a long string of promises, including that of a forwarding address which, in most cases, would never be forwarded. Any exceptional external factors, such as war or revolution, that would increase masculine mobility would be likely both to render the potential seducer more enterprising, more indifferent to the inevitable fate of the girl, and to offer him a number of socially acceptable channels of escape, the most acceptable, at *any* period, being enlistment. And there was not much that a girl could do about a seducer who was already in the army, or who was a medical or veterinary student, or, equally, who travelled for his living. The Lyon *déclarations de grossesse* offer a sad, repetitive, but indeed predictable chronicle of departure, *absent de la ville*, and so on, in this respect, very much on the old, old theme of *parti sans laisser d'adresse*, save that, in most instances, they had indeed promised the girl to send one on, once they had found a settled abode.

> Le Sr. Tournachon (marchand libraire, Grande Rue Mercière) prétexta qu'il avait un voyage et qu'il ne pouvait être en cette ville que vers la fin de mai dernier [and we are now in mid-July] ... Depuis, la comparante est instruite que le Sr. Tournachon est en cette ville, quoiqu'il fasse dire qu'il est encore absent.

Tournachon was of course *bound* to come back, attached as he was to les Terreaux by the possession of a prosperous business in books and stationery. He had, in this instance, only gained a temporary respite; and he must have been singularly thoughtless, or equally careless, to have believed that his return would pass unnoticed by his former servant, Benoîte Marduel, whom he had allegedly seduced, and who, at the time of his unheralded return, was living a few doors away from the rue Mercière, in the rue Tupin. In this closed community of les Terreaux, the steep, narrow streets turning in on one another in a confused jumble of *montées* and *descentes*, steps, *traboules*, slopes so steep as to necessitate the provision of chains for the pedestrian to hold on to, nothing would pass unnoticed, especially the return of an important tradesman. Tournachon in fact decided in the end to sit it out and to deny everything. It was his word against that of his former servant. And would not the mere fact that he had dismissed her (had *had* to dismiss her, he would add) have witnessed against her, with its suggestion of moral turpitude or professional incompetence? Le Sr. Tournachon, a man of standing in his quarter, would not have much to fear from a discharged servant, save perhaps the occasional embarrassing encounter, rue Tupin, and strident insults coming from a seventh storey, or from the black entry to a *traboule*, rue Mercière or rue Bouteille, delivered by the Dlle. Marduel herself or by one of her numerous workmates. But this is in fact an exceptional case, in that the man *did* come back. In most instances, the men did not, though they had left saying that they would – *incessamment, en peu de tems quand il sera établi, quand il aura terminé ses affaires, quand il aura visité sa famille, quand il aura l'accord de ses parents, quand il aura mis de côté une somme suffisante*, the formal rigmarole of *escroquerie sur l'avenir*, a sort of masculine *fuite en avant*, merely to gain time – a few weeks or a few months – a pathetic example of masculine cowardice, or of a sense of guilt in which the main concern is to hide a few blushes.

Here is Virginie Bergeon, naturally *ci-devant domestique*, because she belongs as by right to that class of almost professional candour:

> demeurant à présent à l'hôtel de Provence ... 22 ans ... [déclare] qu'elle est enceinte d'environ 5 mois des œuvres du nommé *Joseph*, soldat qui a été en semestre en cette Ville pendant 5 mois, et qui s'est absenté de cette Ville depuis Pâques [and it is now 18 May], led. Joseph devant revenir dans quelques tems en cette Ville, la comparante ne doit rien négliger pour assurer l'état de son enfant.

The poor girl does not even know the fellow's full name. She is not likely ever to see him again; and she would do as well to ask for a ticket for *la Charité*.

Louise Verchère, *blanchisseuse de bas*, aged twenty-five, domiciled place du Change, is less optimistic, or, perhaps, more realistic, for she at least knows that *her* seducer is unlikely ever to show his face again in Lyon: '[déclare] qu'elle est enceinte de 8 mois et ½ des œuvres d'un garçon perruquier nommé *Provençal*, actuellement absent de cette ville, et qu'elle est dans l'intention de se procurer un billet de l'hôpital de la Charité pour y placer l'enfant', clearly the only possible solution when the alleged seducer was known to the girl only under the name of *Provençal*.

Then there is the case of Annette Dementhon, 'fille du Sr. Dementhon, marchand de dorures fausses, demeurant à Lyon, âgée de 17 ans', a girl who had been unlucky enough to have taken up with a commercial traveller:

> ... qu'il y a environ un an elle fit la connoissance du Sr. Jaivry, voyageur de commerce pour cette ville à Bordeaux, et habitant alternativement dans l'une ou l'autre de ces deux villes ... il lui fit des propositions de mariage, il n'attendait, disait-il, que le moment où il auroit pu parvenir à arranger des affaires de manière à pouvoir se fixer absolument à Lyon. Le Sr. Jaivry se ménageant de tems à autres des entrevues avec la comparante à l'insu de ses parens ... il lui a annoncé qu'il retournoit à Bordeaux pour arranger ses affaires et revenir immédiatement demander sa main à ses parens.
>
> Le Sr. Jaivry, en partant, annonça à la comparante qu'elle recevrait incessamment de ses nouvelles, et qu'il lui donneroit des adresses sûres pour qu'elle pût lui écrire; cependant deux mois se sont écoulés et elle est encore dans l'attente,

le Sr. Jaivry a gardé le plus profond silence. La comparante a lieu d'être étonnée, mais il lui importe d'assurer l'existence de l'enfant.

Of all the men mentioned in this repetitious chronicle of departures, Jaivry was perhaps the best placed professionally thus to opt out, without any material damage to himself.

There are one or two examples of the man persuading the girl to leave, promising to follow on at a later date. This is what happened to the would-be actress, after she had met her *séducteur moralisateur*:

Jeanne Rey, de présent à Lyon, logée en chambre garnie, rue Basse Ville ... qu'au mois d'août 1789, elle partit de cette ville pour se rendre à Marseille dans l'intention d'y jouer la comédie, arrivée dans cette dernière ville, elle se disposoit à exécuter le projet qu'elle avait formé lorsqu'un Sr. Pierre François Plurnel Laguille, négociant en ladite ville ... fit connoissance de la comparante dans une maison à laquelle elle étoit recommandée ... à force de sollicitations il parvint à la dégoûter de son état et à la recevoir habituellement dans un appartement qu'il lui a loué à Marseille aux fêtes de Pâques 1789 [1790?] ... il lui a témoigné que des raisons de famille et des intérêts de commerce exigeaient qu'elle vînt faire ses couches en cette ville [de Lyon].

Plurnel Laguille, no doubt a man of substance, once he had learnt of his mistress's condition, was almost indecently anxious to see her out of the way, and on the road north. There was absolutely no likelihood that he would ever be following her there.

And so it goes on: 'Marie Faton, blanchisseuse ... demeurant rue des Forges ... 19 ans ... enceinte d'environ 7 mois des œuvres du Sr. François Revelain, crocheteur, absent de cette ville'; 'Françoise Perchon, apprentie tailleuse ... demeurant chez la femme Genon, rue Longue ... 20 ans ... enceinte d'environ 4 mois et ½ des œuvres du Sr. Pinjon, perruquier, actuellement absent de cette ville' (she does not insist but asks for a *billet pour l'hôpital*); 'Louise Nardy, tireuse de soie à Lyon, y demeurant, rue Mercière ... enceinte depuis près de 6 mois des faits & œuvres du Sr. Grégoire, Sergent au Régiment de la Marck', who, by February 1791, had left Lyon; 'Pernon Prévôt, brodeuse ... demeurant rue Sainte-Catherine ... âgée de 18 ans ... qu'il y a environ 8 mois qu'elle fit la connoissance d'un Sr. Enstremanny, marchand suisse, pour lors en cette ville ... il est absent de cette ville, elle espère qu'il ne l'abandonnera pas.' But it is unlikely that the *marchand helvète* will be seen in Lyon again, or at least rue Sainte-Catherine, right in the middle of les Terreaux, where everything is at once known and in which his presence would at once be spotted by dozens of Pernon's workmates in silk. 'Anne Burtin, ci-devant cuisinière ... demeurant chez les Dlles Reynaud, marchandes de modes, place de la Comédie, actuellement logée chez le Sr. Bonneton, ouvrier en

soie, place de l'Homme de la roche ... enceinte depuis environ 5 mois et
½ des œuvres de Jean Lespinasse, garçon perruquier, engagé dans les
volontaires nationaux et absent de cette ville' (*billet pour l'hôpital*).

The alleged seducer of Françoise Dueure, *brodeuse*, Bavet, 'marchand
drapier, associé du Sr. Gaillard ... rue de Saint-Nizier', a man whom we
have already encountered in his category as *séducteur correspondant*, has
this to say:

> il lui dit qu'il partoit pour voyage et qu'à son retour qui devoit être prochain, il
> lui donneroit sa main ... de retour en cette ville depuis 8 jours, lorsqu'elle l'a
> pressé de nouveau de tenir la parole ... il a pris le parti de faire sur le champ un
> nouveau voyage.

Françoise, who was a *brodeuse*, must have had illusions of grandeur if she
had really believed that a *marchand drapier* would marry her in order to
regularize her situation. But Bavet must also have been extremely imprudent if he believed that his return would pass unnoticed: for he lived in the
rue Saint-Nizier, while Françoise had an address, quai de Saône, just
round the corner.

Jeanne Caillot, *brodeuse*, living rue Plat-d'Argent, and the oldest of the
women in this group – she was thirty – had been ready to believe that her
age would in fact argue in her favour with the man who had shown a persistent interest in her over a period of years, and who seems to have played
a waiting game, till finally cornered:

> ... qu'il y a nombre d'années que le commerce de broderies a amené dans son
> domicile le Sr. Claude-Marie Desvernai, commis chez le Sr. Sonnet, marchand
> brodeur ... led. Desvernai a depuis longtems proposé à la comparante de
> l'épouser, comme l'état et l'âge de ce dernier, qui est âgé de quarante ans, étaient
> très sortables, la comparante a cru aux promesses dud. Desvernai ... le Sr.
> Desvernai, loin de tenir sa parole, s'est absenté ...

though, as a *commis brodeur*, he cannot have gone very far. Perhaps he
merely moved up the hill to la Croix-Rousse, where he might have
expected to obtain employment in his trade.

Benoîte Bonnard, *coupeuse de poils pour la chapellerie*, appears to have
driven her alleged seducer away, back to his village, by being too pressing,
and by setting her workmates on to him to remind him of his duties:

> La grossesse s'avançant la remontrante a été plus pressante pour l'engager à
> tenir ses promesses, mais Pierre Dusurgey a abandonné la ville et est allé
> s'établir maître chapelier à Mornant. Alors la reclamante lui a fait écrire [for she
> was illiterate] et a fait faire auprès de lui différentes démarches. Pierre Dusurgey
> a été sourd à ses sollicitations.

However, this was not quite the end of this liaison. For we learn from one of the witnesses, Brossard, *cordonnier*, who had gone for walks with the couple,

que Pierre Dusurgey étoit très lié avec la plaignante, au point que lorsque led. Dusurgey s'est retiré à Mornant, sa patrie, il venoit tous les 15 jours voir la plaignante, que sur la fin de novembre dernier [and it is now mid-February] sachant que la plaignante étoit enceinte, lui témoin en parla aud. Dusurgey, que ce dernier sembloit douter que ce fût de ses œuvres, disant cependant qu'il épouseroit volontiers la plaignante si ses parents de lui Dusurgey ne s'y opposoient pas.

It was perhaps an easy and rather cowardly way out, for it is evident that the parents of a *maître chapelier* would be unlikely to favour their son's marriage to a girl working as a mere *coupeuse de poils*. It was on occasions such as these that the pull of the native village might become irresistible. Dusurgey was fortunate in thus possessing a line of retreat to the nearby village of Mornant, within walking distance of Lyon, though there was the possible danger that Benoîte might be tempted to do the journey in the opposite direction and go and seek him out there, and confront his parents and relatives with the spectacle of her condition.

La Dlle. Chirat, metteuse en mains ... demeurant près de la porte Saint-Clair ... [se porte] en déclaration de grossesse contre le Sr. Bouillier, natif de la ville de Lons-le-Saunier ... commis facteur chez le Sr. Talon fils & Mollière négotiants de cette ville ... Le Sr. Bouillier [she adds enviously] est déjà riche par le décès de son père et de son oncle ... [She herself] fille mineure de défunt Sr. Chirat, bourgeois à la Guillotière ... enceinte depuis environ 8 mois ... état qui l'a brouillée (avec assez de raison) avec sa famille, et principalement avec une tante de laquelle elle a beaucoup à espérer.

She has an apprentice of eighteen who witnesses to Bouillier's assiduities, adding that he had not come to see her since January; and it was now March. He had in fact gone back to Lons. La Dlle. Chirat, who was in the trade, should perhaps have known better than to have taken up with the travelling representative of an important firm based on Lons, because it should have been clear to her that his regular employment offered him an easy line of retreat back to the Jura. The nature of his work would indeed have made it very likely that he only came to Lyon for limited periods, to contact manufacturers for his employers. Marie Chirat may also have felt that her prospects would be improved by the fact that, like her alleged seducer, she was fatherless and that, having a female apprentice, she was far from representing a losing proposition.

Gasparde Latour, *brodeuse*, certainly has no cause for hope; for, a year previously, she had taken up with a *perruquier*, and as so often happens to those in that highly mobile trade, he had gone long since on his way.

> Dlle. Claudine Poncet, ouvrière demeurant chez Mlle Royer, marchande de modes … rue Mercière [déclare] que depuis environ une année et ½ la déclarante demeuroit dans la pension où logeoit le Sr. Antoine d'Audiffret … depuis quelques tems il a quitté la ville, cependant la remontrante, âgée à peine de 17 ans, n'a perdu son honneur que faute d'expérience.

There is not much hope for her either. The case of Louise Perenne is likewise sadly straightforward, witnessing as it does both for the likeliest inception of a liaison and the most probable outcome of its course, once she was pregnant. She was a domestic servant who worked for the *maître des postes aux chevaux* of Villefranche-sur-Saône, on the highroad from Lyon to Paris. Her father was a *vigneron* in the same town. Nine or ten months before her statement, she had become acquainted, in the course of her work, with 'Sr. Joseph Castaing, maître tailleur du régiment appellé ci-devant Guyenne, en garnison à Villefranche'. The poor girl was likely to be fair game for any passing soldier, for to be the servant of a *maître des postes* would be almost as perilous as to be a *fille de salle* in an inn on one of the great military highroads. Nor would she ever be likely to catch up with Castaing, and with the *régiment ci-devant Guyenne*, which by this time, in late December 1791, would have long since left Villefranche, a town which, in any case, never had a permanent garrison, being, unlike Lyon, merely a *lieu d'étape*.

The statement made by Dlle. Marie Maillot, *fille épicière*, 'demeurant rue du Puits de Sel', is likewise of more general interest, as it illustrates not only the by now only too familiar theme of masculine *dérobage*, villainy, cowardice, or selfishness, in the usual forms of departure or going to earth; it also suggests a compensatory solidarity among the poor and the humble; for Marie, in her efforts to bring her lover to accept his responsibilities, enlists the support of a female witness, no doubt a workmate, certainly a neighbour, as she appears to be very much aware of the previous comings and goings of the couple, and who agrees to go and see the man, on Marie's behalf, in an effort to appeal to what sense of duty he may have possessed. Marie herself says

> que depuis environ 8 mois, un Sr. Benoît Bergoz, compagnon charpentier chez le Sr. Bœuf, place Saint-Jean … est parvenu à la séduire et a habité son domicile avec assiduité, mais lorsque la remontrante est devenue enceinte … celui-ci a cessé ses fréquentes visites, et depuis peu il l'a entièrement abandonnée.

It is at this point that the witness takes up the account:

que la veille de Noël [we are now in February 1792] dernière la dlle. Maillot vint chez la déposante où elle resta pendant trois semaines, c'est-à-dire jusqu'au milieu de janvier dernier, que pendant ce tems elle a vu venir trois fois le Sr. Bergoz qui s'entretenait avec lad. Maillot, que cette dernière dit à la déposante qu'elle devait se marier à Pâques avec led. Bergoz, qu'elle déposante est depuis allée chez led. Bergoz de la part de la dlle. Maillot pour l'engager à venir parler à cette dernière, qu'il lui répondit qu'il alloit s'y rendre et que lad. Maillot n'avoit qu'à l'attendre chez la déposante, mais led. Bergoz ne s'y rendit point.

It would have been rather astonishing, having himself fixed the meeting place, and knowing that he would have to face both girls, if he *had* indeed turned up.

The remaining chronicle of woe, injured innocence and hopelessness is entirely predictable. Pierrette Carret, 'tailleuse, enceinte depuis environ 7 mois des œuvres du Sr. Gochon, officier dans les volontaires, actuellement absent', asks for *un billet pour la Charité*. Marie Béatrix, 'demeurant rue des Trois Écuries', names as her seducer Philippe Gandin, 'ci-devant domicilié à Lyon, demeurant actuellement à Montagny'. Another obliging female workmate comes to the aid of Dlle. Marie Persan 'fille majeure, dévideuse ... demeurant rue Saint-Cosme', who had succumbed to the arguments of Laurent Giret, 'ouvrier en soie, demeurant rue Ferrandière'; she states

qu'il y a environ deux mois, se trouvant chez la fille Persan sur environ 7 heures du soir, elle vit entrer Laurent Giret, que la fille Persan fit sortir une ouvrière [for, at this level of society, to be alone with someone is something of a luxury that needs to be planned and that is dependent on the goodwill of other workmates] et quand elle se trouva seule avec la déposante et Laurent Giret, elle dit en pleurant à ce dernier qu'il étoit bien tems de prendre des arrangemens relativement à l'enfant dont elle était enceinte par ses faits, que Laurent Giret répondit qu'elle étoit folle, qu'elle n'était sûrement pas enceinte, que led. Giret paraissant vouloir s'en aller, la fille Persan chercha à la retenir, mais il la poussa avec brutalité sur des fagots, que la déposante lui observa qu'un honnête homme ne se conduisit pas ainsi avec une fille dont il avait joui, à quoi led. Giret ne répondit rien et se retira.

– a case, by no means rare in this brutal world of masculine violence, of employing force as well as escape tactics. Claudine Gariot, *dévideuse de soie*, states that she is pregnant 'des œuvres du nommé Vivien, garçon chapelier, duquel elle ignore la demeure'. Having no illusions, she asks for her ticket. Catherine Sapin, another *dévideuse*, 'demeurant rue Henri, chez le Sr. Solary, maître fabricant en étoffes de soie, [se déclare] enceinte des œuvres de Jean Robin, cordonnier, absent'. Jeanne Rey, *brodeuse*, accuses a former *commis aux octrois*, 'actuellement absent de cette ville'; Marie Pierrette Blanc, habitante de la Guillotière, dépendante de l'autorité de son père, enceinte des œuvres de François Antoine Haley fils cadet, demeurant rue de la Monnaie, ce jeune homme avoit promis de l'épouser, il a reçu de Pierre Blanc [the girl's father] une somme considérable pour fournir à la dot . . . ce jeune homme paraît vouloir tromper lad. Marie Pierrette Blanc, car il s'est absenté.

He had indeed a double reason for disappearing from the scene, once he had laid hands on the money.

Perhaps the last word on the subject of masculine mobility should come from a document of a different nature, and from a different city, in the form of a *certificat d'indigence* delivered by the *comité de bienfaisance* of the Section des Arcis, in Paris, on 22 Thermidor year III (9 August 1795), in favour of a former nun who had married:

> . . . [déclare] avoir délivré le présent certificat d'indigence à la citoyenne *Anne-Louise Droz*, ex-religieuse, âgée de 32 ans environ, et depuis 18 mois femme du citoyen Charles Mollet, *perruquier chambrelant* [perhaps only an ex-nun in her innocence and inexperience of the ways of the world could have joined forces with an itinerant hairdresser, whose trade took him from house to house, allowing him, any moment, a convincing excuse for absence!] demeurant rue de la Poterie No. 6 . . . mais dont le chagrin causé tant par le défaut de pratiques que par la circonstance des temps difficiles, a fortement [?] porté led. C. Mollet à délaisser sa femme enceinte de six mois avec un enfant d'un an environ, pour s'en aller courir le pays, après avoir vendu jusqu'aux cendres du feu, ce qui composait leur petit ménage, et de plus avoir contraint son épouse à consentir à l'engagement du brevet de pension de 500 livres qui lui avait été délivrée par l'État, pour l'indemniser des avantages qu'elle [*sic*] jouissait en conventualité . . . ladite citoyenne . . . véritablement malheureuse, tant par son inexpérience et bonhomie que par le délaissement de son époux . . . n'ayant même de quoi coucher ni son enfant, elle est réléguée dans un cabinet garni, rue de la Verrerie, 100.[1]

Such was the lot of an ex-nun, living in a sort of cupboard – in one of the worst lodging-houses of the rue de la Verrerie, a street which, with its prolongation of the rue des Lombards, was notorious for these flea-pits and for the rapid turn-over of population that they contained – abandoned by her husband 'pour s'en aller courir le pays, après avoir vendu jusqu'aux cendres du feu', while she had to look after a child of one and face up to an immediate future in which there would soon be a second one, and that to be born in the bitter month of November 1795: and even she could not have foreseen, from the depth of her misery and pessimism, just how bitter that winter was going to be. Perhaps the most surprising thing about this statement on the subject of the double standard is the ex-nun's

---

[1] AN, F 15 2820 (comité de bienfaisance de la Section des Arcis, attestation datée du 22 thermidor an III).

resignation. There is scarcely a hint of criticism of her husband's conduct towards her, and she seems to take his departure, to enjoy the freedom and adventure of the open road, almost as a matter of course. Or perhaps it is not so surprising after all. Aged thirty-two, and presumably released from her vows in her late twenties, she had had a long schooling in self-abnegation. And, in the famine year of 1795, and in the absence of *les pratiques*, what else remained for a *perruquier chambrelant* to do, other than to enlist or to take to the roads, the usual alternatives that Swift reserves for his discharged footman butler?[1] For Mollet, rather than walking from house to house, with his brush, his razor, his bowl and his towel, it would now be a matter of trying his luck on the highroads, perhaps on the fringes of army service – *transports militaires, habillement*, or even in his own profession, in the wake of the *armée du Nord*. One way or another, and with the prospect opening out before him of endless encounters with *filles de salle*, as he headed towards the old borders, he would no doubt soon have forgotten his wife and child and future offspring, and the damp and wretched rue de la Verrerie. War, famine and cold formed a trinity that, in eighteenth-century conditions, offered the most persuasive incentive to masculine selfishness and opting out.

✳

I have not yet quite finished with this theme of escape: *absent de cette ville, parti sans laisser d'adresse, actuellement dans les volontaires nationaux.* For of course, it was not *always* the man who was at fault – the girls who made their statements had to name a man, *one* man, but he would not necessarily be the right one. And they would, if in the slightest bit calculating, be more likely to name a man of some substance than a workmate who could hardly be expected to do anything very much for them in their present condition. There was a masculine point of view, too; and it was not necessarily a false or selfish one. 'Why pick on me,' the man might ask, 'when it is well known that la Dlle. in question accorded her favours to a whole quarter?' And flight was not always accomplished alone. The most agreeable form of travel would not be flight at all, but *à deux*, at a stage of the relationship before pregnancy had reduced the girl's mobility and had given the man a powerful motive to get right away. It is these two subjects that we should now consider, before moving on to the strategy and language of seduction as employed by the male.

---

[1] 'To grow old in the office of a footman, is the highest of all indignities ... I directly advise you to go upon the road, which is the only post of honour left you: there you will meet many of your old comrades, and live a short life and a merry one, and make a figure at your exit, wherein I will give you some instructions.

'The last advice I give you, relates to your behaviour when you are going to be hanged; which ... may very probably be your lot.' Jonathan Swift, *Directions to Servants* (1731).

Even the judicial authorities, who had so often been in a position to transcribe the sad monologues of these ill-used women, were not always entirely sympathetic to the *déclarantes*. When for instance, Marie Dangle, *brodeuse*, aged seventeen and a half and nine months pregnant, accuses the Sr. Flandrin, whom, characteristically, she had met at her sister's, a girl older than herself, the judge points out to her: 'A elle représenté qu'il paraît qu'elle a été séduite bien facilement, puisqu'il n'y a eu que peu d'intervalle entre la connaissance qu'elle a faite du Sr. Flandrin et l'époque de sa grossesse'. She had met Flandrin at her sister's ten months previously, so that what she calls her *première imprudence* must have occurred very soon after this meeting; and she admits that, soon afterwards, she allowed Flandrin, who seems to have been a man of some substance, to set her up in a room of her own, the rent of which he paid, and where he came regularly to see her. Her reply to the judge's remarks was: 'Répond que la promesse que le Sr. Flandrin lui avait faite de l'épouser, et surtout l'amitié qu'il était parvenue à lui inspirer ont causé sa faiblesse.' Flandrin had certainly been a fast operator. But the judge was perhaps being rather hard on a girl not yet eighteen.

The commonest masculine point of view is best expressed by Clémence Bonnenfant, 'boulanger à Lyon, y demeurant, rue Groslée . . . 24 ans':

> . . . qu'il ne disconvient pas d'avoir eu des familiarités, avec Pierrette Chapuis (domestique), mais nous assure qu'il ne lui a jamais promis de l'épouser, qu'il y a entr'eux une trop grande différence d'âge pour penser à un établissement aussi malassorti puisque lad. Chapuis a au moins 10 ans de plus que lui [she is one of the few girls who does not give her age in her statement] . . . qu'il serait injuste de le déclarer père de l'enfant de cette fille, puisqu'elle lui est convenue avoir eu des liaisons avec d'autres que lui.

Bonnenfant was being ungallant, but if la Chapuis was indeed thirty-four, she may well have had designs on the young man.

We have an obvious case in which a former servant attempted to saddle her one-time employer with the paternity of a child who seems to have been fathered in fact by the man with whom she was living at the time of her statement:

> Jean-Marie Morel, demeurant à Lyon, place des Cordeliers, paroisse Saint-Nizier . . . [dépose] qu'il vient d'apprendre qu'une fille qui demeuroit chez lui il y a environ 5 ans en qualité de domestique nommée *Josèphe* dont il ignore le nom de famille, a rendu contre lui une plainte en paternité de l'enfant dont elle se dit enceinte.
>
> Cette accusation n'est qu'une pure calomnie machinée entre cette fille et le nommé Duret, matelassier, avec lequel elle habite, et d'autres personnes, leurs fauteurs et adhérens. En effet, le suppliant vient d'apprendre que cette fille loge

dans une chambre, rue Neuve, qu'elle se fait nommer femme Duret, et qu'en effet led. Duret vit logé et couché avec elle.

And another witness is even more precise:

François Martin, colporteur ... 50 ... ans ... rue Neuve ... dépose qu'il ne sait autre chose ... si ce n'est que la fille *Josèphe* habite une chambre dans la maison Poirat, rue Neuve, depuis environ 2 mois, que lui témoin habitant dans la même maison et porte à porte sur le même palier, il a vu presque tous les jours le nommé Duret, matelassier, venir chez lad. fille *Josèphe*, ne sait le témoin si led. Duret couchait dans l'appartement où il venoit ordinairement sur les 10 heures du soir ... ajoute ... que la fille *Josèphe* se faisoit appeler femme Duret, que depuis 8 jours la fille *Josèphe* n'a pas couché dans son appartement.

Martin is followed by his wife and two daughters; all prove very unsympathetic witnesses to the girl Josèphe, showing her up as a pretentious liar and an impostor, whom they appear to have regarded as a disgrace to the neighbourhood. There is certainly very little they seem to have missed about the girl's habits and statements, and there is a certain glee in their eagerness to unmask her. *La femme* Martin, *brodeuse*, also aged fifty, states

qu'il y a environ 2 mois que la fille désignée ... de *Josèphe* est venue habiter une chambre ... que le nommé Duret ... s'est aidé au transport des meubles de cette fille, elle déposante l'ayant rencontré dans l'escalier portant un matelas, qu'il est à la connoissance de la déposante que led. Duret mangeait souvent avec la fille *Josèphe*, lui apportait du pain et y couchait fréquemment, que la déposante ayant quelques fois exprimé sa surprise à la fille *Josèphe* sur ce que le Sr. Duret, son mari, couchait quelques fois hors de chez elle [this is rather more than neighbourly concern], la fille *Josèphe* lui observait que son mari, en raison de son état de matelassier, étoit souvent obligé de coucher chez les maîtres qui l'occupaient, et la déposante a appris depuis environ 3 semaines que led. Duret n'est point le mari de la fille *Josèphe*, ayant ouï dire que led. Duret a femme et enfant, et qu'il demeure rue Téraille, ajoute la déposante avoir vu une femme boîteuse et d'un âge avancé qu'on lui a dit être la véritable femme Duret et une jeune fille âgée de 10 à 11 ans ... en le désignant sous la qualification de son père.

The two daughters of the Martin family back up their mother's testimony with evident satisfaction and plenty of malice. Françoise, also a *brodeuse*, aged twenty-three, states

que lad. fille ... s'y est annoncée comme femme mariée, et sous le nom de femme Duret, que sur l'observation faite par la déposante à lad. femme Duret qu'elle n'avoit point de bague de mariage, cette dernière lui répondit qu'elle était mariée depuis un an, mais qu'elle avait été obligée de vendre sa bague par nécessité.

The elder daughter, Claudine, twenty-four, likewise *brodeuse*, backs up her sister's statement, adding the interesting piece of information 'qu'elle a même ouï dire que led. Duret avait une loquetière de la porte d'allée', that is, that he could open the wooden door of the *traboule* leading to the staircase that gave access to the storey, so that he would have been able to let himself in at any time, day or night.

Finally, yet another inhabitant of the house, Marie Piard, a twenty-four-year-old *dévideuse de soie* – there is a solidarity among the four silk workers who are witnesses that seems best to express itself in scarcely concealed hostility to the so-called *femme* Duret, who, it seems clear, was not in the trade – makes her contribution to the demolition of Josèphe:

> que la fille *Josèphe* habite une chambre au 5me étage ... ayant vu led. Duret entrer le soir et sortir le matin, ajoute la déposante que s'étant liée en raison du voisinage avec la fille *Josèphe*, cette dernière lui a fait ses confidences, et lui a dit qu'elle n'était pas mariée avec led. Duret, qu'étant enceinte depuis plusieurs mois, elle devait faire sa déclaration sur un inconnu, mais que quelques tems après la fille *Josèphe* lui fit part du projet qu'elle avait de désigner dans sa plainte le Sr. Morel.

One cannot help feeling rather sorry for Josèphe, so completely caught up in her web of lies and contradictions, her pathetic inventions (why, one might ask, would a *matelassier*, of all people, be expected to work at night, *chez les maîtres*, who would presumably be using their own mattresses to get a bit of sleep? He might, of course, have been expected to deliver mattresses, according to need, at nightfall, but this would hardly account for his absence throughout the night), her unconvincing suggestion that she had pawned her ring, an old, old fable on the part of girls in her situation; and harried with such sustained questioning and close observation by the three women in the Martin family – the father seems to have been rather more indulgent and rather less observant, but then he would have had less inclination to stand around, *sur le palier*, and gossip with the imprudent girl – and by the other *brodeuse*. One suspects that the women at least had spotted from the start that there was something irregular in the girl's situation, and had then decided to play her along, in an effort to find out more, and to trap her in her contradictory statements. *La femme* Martin, in particular, must have gone to considerable trouble to identify the deformed woman and her ten-year-old daughter, asking her workmates, or making inquiries in this or other quarters, as she delivered half-finished goods, or went out to take orders from *marchands de soie*. It is possible, too, that the Martins worked as a family unit. *La femme* Duret, the real one, who was said to be antique, and who walked with a limp, would have been a figure widely identified in this heavily populated, close-packed, and closely observed area, each of the long black windows hacked out of the tall ochre-coloured seven- or eight-storey buildings acting as so many observatories for what went on in the dark gulleys of the street, far below, as well as offering an excellent *vue plongeante* into shadowy interiors, at the level of the storey, or a little below it. Lyon was not a shuttered town, and only in the hot months would the interiors be partly hidden from indiscreet gaze by brightly striped awnings. Perhaps the principal interest to us of the doings of *la fille Josèphe*, as observed by the Martins, is not whether she was out to ensnare her former employer, the no doubt substantial Morel. That would be her concern, not ours. But the episode abundantly illustrates several themes to which we will return later: the community of the staircase and the promiscuity of *le palier* – how often, in these statements, do we hear witnesses who live opposite a room, on the same landing, and who, getting up very early, or returning from work in the evening, are able to observe all the comings and goings of their neighbours, even to such details as a table laid for two places *pour le souper*; the solidarity within a given trade, a solidarity that would often be transformed into suspicion or hostility when facing outwards; the fact that women are generally more severe than men in their judgements on sexual irregularity, especially when the sinner is herself a woman; the pattern, through the day, of occasional conversation, during a pause *sur le palier*; the ability to read much into apparently simple acts – that, for instance, of carrying a mattress upstairs to a certain room, taken to indicate that the occupant had a sleeping companion. Lyon has often been described as *la ville secrète*; and that is certainly the hermetic face that the city has always liked to affect towards strangers. But there cannot have been much secret about life in the rue Neuve or the rue Confort.

Let us now turn our attention to a *voyage à deux* that had some of the characteristics of an abduction – we do not know whether it was followed by pregnancy – and that should have terminated in Marseille, but did in fact end, miserably, in Perrache. On 12 March 1791,

Sr. Jean-Baptiste Ducret, compagnon imprimeur à Lyon, y demeurant, rue Saint-Jean … employé à l'imprimerie du Sr. Faucheux [déclare] qu'il vient vous dénoncer un rapt de séduction, une action considérée par les loix comme un crime capital. Le Sr. Vagenay, fils du Sr. Vagenay, marchand tripier à la boucherie des Terreaux, a fait la connaissance de Marie Ducret, fille du suppliant. Après avoir tout mis en usage pour la séduire, il a eu recours aux promesses de mariage; âgée de 15 ans et ½ Marie Ducret crut Vagenay; elle consentit de l'épouser mais avec le consentement de son père et de sa mère. Vagenay … lui persuada qu'il est de leur intérêt respectif de taire ce mariage et qu'il doit être fait secrètement ... Vagenay parvint à l'engager à fuir avec lui à Marseille, l'assurant que c'est là qu'il veut et peut l'épouser. On profite d'un instant où la fille est seule, Vagenay, pour mieux la tromper, lui aide à faire un paquet des hardes dont elle croit avoir besoin; ils s'échappent, les voilà en route. Ils n'allèrent pas loin, la nuit approchoit; ils s'arrêtèrent dans l'allée Perrache à *l'auberge des Deux Amants*; ils y soupèrent; Vagenay présenta la jeune Ducret comme étant sa femme, ils furent accueillis, couchèrent ensemble ...

Les ayant découverts dans *l'auberge des Deux Amants*, le suppliant y entra accompagné d'une escouade de la garde nationale et des soldats de La Marck ... on les trouva couchés ensemble ... Vagenay eut l'adresse de s'évader [what he did was to tell the soldiers that he had to go outside in order to discharge a pressing need, they had let him out, and he had fled through the night, presumably eventually turning up again at home, in les Terreaux] ... Cette scène affligeante eut lieu le 5 novembre dernier ... Vagenay père, homme riche, ne veut pas que son fils épouse une fille qui a, selon lui, deux grands défauts, l'une de n'être encore qu'une enfant, l'autre, d'être sans fortune.

It was a wretched ending to a journey that, for the young couple, had started under such excellent auspices, including the inviting roof of an inn so suitably named *l'auberge des deux amants* – and no doubt the name was both an invitation and an indication of the sort of travellers who would be welcomed in an establishment so conveniently placed just beyond the city walls, and on the highroad south. Vagenay probably knew of the place already, as the result of a weekend excursion; or he may have consulted one of his workmates about an accommodating address of this kind, within walking distance of Lyon on a winter's night. He had also shown considerable flair in suggesting to the girl that Marseille would be their chosen Eldorado, that there they would be able to get everything arranged, before coming back to face both lots of parents with the *fait accompli*. A *Lyonnaise* of fifteen would have been aware of Marseille, in a way in which she would not have been aware of Paris, too far away, too foreign ever to have impinged on her imagination. *Marseillais* were familiar figures in eighteenth-century Lyon, the route south was both inviting and facilitated by the Rhône, the principal channel of communication. She would have been prepared to believe that in Marseille there would be no difficulties, no questions asked. Perhaps Vagenay had never intended to go to Marseille at all. But it was the sort of destination to appeal to a teenage girl from Saint-Jean. He may merely have been concerned in getting the girl to bed as quickly as possible, and in a place where they would be likely to escape detection. If this were the case, he must have been singularly inept; for the couple had told several friends and neighbours that they were heading for Marseille, so that the *allée de Perrache* would be the first place anyone would have looked for them, if their departure had been noticed only after nightfall; it was known that they had left on foot, for the parents would have checked, in the first place, with the *bureau des diligences* and the *coche d'eau*. It does then seem that the abductor may have been almost as naïve as the abducted. It was certainly a humiliating end to a trip so full of promise. The night, so brutally interrupted, may have left a more permanent memorial already visible, nearly five months later, in March. If this had not been the case, it is difficult to see why the father should have gone to the trouble and expense of going to court and lodging a formal complaint for abduction against the son of a rich man. For this would hardly have been the best way of persuading Vagenay to allow his son to marry the girl.

As in the matter of *la fille Josèphe*, the episode of the interrupted night, of the young couple caught already in bed, after what must have been an extremely pleasant supper at the inn, is not merely of anecdotal interest. Nor can Marie be seen as a victim; she appears to have been only too willing to be persuaded. The episode is above all yet another reminder of the extent to which aristocratic values and *mores* had penetrated downwards, to permeate even this comparatively humble level of society. For here we have the very classical theme of *l'enlèvement* played out with its principal actors the son of a tripe merchant and the daughter of a companion printer. It is true that here was no closed carriage, no coachman wrapped up to the eyes so that he would not be easily recognized, nor would his livery be visible. At the end of the road, there would be no *pavillon* in the neo-classic manner, its lights faintly seen at the far end of a misty park, its approaches flanked by sphinxes and marine monsters; inside there would be no beautifully adorned bedroom, approached, with a negro page holding up the candles and leading the way, as the lover pressed secret mechanisms that released panels in concealed doors; there would be no superb collation, accompanied by *vins capiteux*, laid out on a Louis XVI side-table, its feet the gilded claws of lions. The young couple would have made their preparations on their own, without the intervention of an army of servants: footmen, coachmen, lady's maids, *bouquetières*. All Vagenay had had to do was to hang about the quartier Saint-Jean, waiting for an opportunity to see the girl on her own, when her parents were out. And, at the end of a road, walked, there would be a carters' inn, probably of no very good repute, and regularly visited by the police. But all these were merely props. In either case, there would be a bed at the end of the journey.

SEDUCTION: MASCULINE LANGUAGE AND TACTICS

In the earlier stages of a developing relationship between a young man and a girl of much the same age and condition, and living in the same city, sometimes, as we have seen, both strangers there, having come from the same village, or originating from the same quarter, or contiguous quarters, the language and tactics likely to be followed, in a series of prudent and searching moves, by both parties, will generally follow an almost conventional, formalized pattern, a sort of moral *gavotte*, the steps of which bring the partners now so close as almost to be touching, now distant from each other, feigning indifference or slights, a dance that in fact, though stepped out in the tender or mocking intimacy of *à deux*, would never be lacking an appreciative, critical or disapproving audience, there primarily to see that the rules were observed by both sides. For in the conditions of eighteenth-century Lyon, the only thing of which one could be quite certain would be that such tentative gropings would be watched by large numbers of people: workmates, brothers, sisters, room-mates – and the presence of these might at an early stage prove a valuable insurance, though, later, it would be necessary to persuade him or her to go – employers, and, indeed, employees, neighbours, much of the street, the idlers and *badauds* on the quays, *sur la Promenade*, on the *cours*, place Bellecour, in the marshy woodlands and scrub of les Brotteaux, in the *guinguettes* of la Guillotière, or those high up on the two hills: Fourvière and Saint-Just, and la Croix-Rousse. For, in Lyon, there is an established geography of leisure, of walking, idling, gaping, and wild jigging and frenetic dancing, so often the point of departure, the opening of the Tunnel of Love, before the rattling train disappears into the screaming, dusty darkness, with its characteristic smell of dust and gunpowder. And perhaps the fairground is no bad metaphor for an exercise closely governed by leisure, by the open spaces, and by feast days, weekends, and festivals. It would be as easy to draw up, from the evidence of the girls' statements, an urban or 'faubourienne' *carte du tendre*, as it would be to illustrate the distribution through the city of *ateliers* and *entrepôts*. In short, seduction would be as formalized at this level of society as it was in Valmont's protracted tactics to bring down the prudish and virtuous *Présidente*.

It will follow a predictable pattern, imposed by collective conventions and unstated assumptions, the collective honour of a family, the fear of parental disapproval, the solidarity of workmates, of those who follow a similar trade, a moral solidarity, based on friendship and mutual preservation, rather than an embryonic trade union, the opinions and prejudices of neighbours, the observations of those who live on the same storey, and who watch every time a door is opened, and of those whom one passes on the stairs, late at night or early in the morning. The receipt of a letter, then read out loud *en petit comité*, by a literate friend or workmate, thus becomes a pledge, almost as binding as a formal demand to parents. A regular visit to a girl on Sundays or feast days has a similar force of promise, especially if the girl, when the man, for some good reason, is unable to come, stays alone in her room all Sunday.[1] *Demander l'entrée de la maison* is of course an even more traditional pledge on the future, both in urban and rural communities; and to go back on it would be a severe assault on popular morality. Even to be seen regularly on *la Promenade*, on the arm of a young man, but accompanied too by one's friends and mates of both sexes, is considered as a form of pledge, perhaps not entirely binding, but none the less a clear statement of intention; and the larger the number of witnesses, of those who have gone out together with the couple, the more powerful will be the message for the future. To take a girl out to eat *chez un traiteur*, to display her thus to the public of the long tables, at which are seated people who will almost certainly know both the girl and her host, is also a step towards formalizing a relationship. Sometimes the *traiteur* himself will step forward to congratulate the couple, or, equally, to banter with them on their good fortune, with crude allusions to future joys, the whole thing played out to a loud, appreciative and guffawing audience, coarse, but not unkindly. Needless to say, there may also be the more formal, clearly-stated bid on the future, the *promesse de mariage*.

The run-up to seduction will take different forms in different places. Much depends on geography and climate. In Paris it is likely to be a more secretive and intimate affair than in Lyon, where each stage, save the ultimate one, will generally be played out in the open, in the street, in the tavern, in the wide empty space offered by the quays, by a huge square, the monument to the conceit of monarchs, but used appreciatively by those with very different, homelier aspirations. It will be a sunny business, as full of light and airiness as one of Goya's colourful and dusty fair scenes in eighteenth-century Madrid. So *la gavotte* will be closely related to the principal compensation, one would be tempted to say, wealth, of the poor of both sexes, the freedom of the street, the escape from dark, miasmic *cours* and cellars, from fifth-storey rooms containing five or six mattresses, from the sweat and heat of the *atelier*, from the acrid smell of raw silk, feathers and stuffs, from the steaming humidity of the laundry, from the noisy ground-floor forge of a *maréchal* and the terrible stink of a *triperie* off les Terreaux.

The *déclarations* often seem to suggest bright sunlight, open spaces, the

---

[1] André Charpenet, a witness for Marguerite Gulon, 'matelassier, à Lyon, y demeurant place Saint-Georges ... 39 ans ... nous observe seulement qu'allant fréquemment voir quelqu'un qui demeure dans le même corps de logis que la plaignante, il a eu occasion de rencontrer le nommé Bonhomme avec la plaignante.' Another witness, Anne Coilier, *brodeuse*, rue de la Ruelle-Renversée, aged 24½, states 'qu'elle demeure porte à porte avec la plaignante ... elle a vu fréquemment et presque tous les jours le Sr. Bonhomme chez la plaignante, qu'ils alloient souvent à la promenade ensemble, que quand il ne venait pas la chercher le dimanche, elle ne sortoit pas de son domicile.'

yellowy dust of the *Promenade* blown to and fro in a gusty southern wind, the dark shadows thrown by the tall façades of the rue Mercière, the rue Bouteille, the rue Terraille and the rue Sainte-Catherine as it creeps timidly uphill, a study of ochre, deep black, brilliant blue, with stems of tender green peeping over grey-yellow walls on the *montées*, the alarming, tumultuous greenish-grey of the Rhône, a river without the least hint of amiability, offering no invitation to dawdle, to bathe, or to wash out clothing (though this might be done in some of its calmer, more pacific pools, among the sandbanks near the porte de Saint-Clair), and not even an attraction to fishermen, merely a permanent threat and a visible frontier. No wonder 'la Guille' and les Brotteaux enjoyed such a detestable reputation with *Lyonnais* and *Lyonnaises*, especially the latter, of all conditions. They would think of them as others might refer to 'outre-Rhin', 'outre-Quiévrain', or 'outre-Manche'. La Guillotière was not a safe place for innocent girls; and we will encounter one whose downfall dated from a weekend christening party held there. It was perhaps the first time that she had crossed the river. And even at this period, the bridges; pont de la Boucle, pont de la porte Saint-Clair, pont de la Guillotière, form the no-man's-land between the relative safety and predictability of the central quarters, and the sinister marshlands beyond, the terrain of duels and casual murders, long before the conditions created by terror and repression had made them the favoured killing grounds of the White Terror. Perhaps it is not mere chance that so many of our *déclarations* – over two-thirds of them, made between five and eight and a half months from conception – should have dated from the winter months, and especially from November, December, January and February, visible and unwelcome reminders of happy spring excursions, of summer walks and explorations, among the hills or in the woodlands and sandbanks on the other side of the Rhône, of warm nights along the quays. The spring and summer would count among the poor girl's inalienable luxuries. But the memory of them would be doubly bitter when carrying a winter stomach.

Indeed, what the statements reveal most strikingly with the passage of time, as the date of lying-in approaches inexorably, is an increasing and fundamental difference in the very definition of time itself. For the girl, six or seven months gone, too late for the intervention of a *faiseuse d'ange*, even assuming that she had ever been able to hear of the existence of one through one of her older female employers, or from another *brodeuse*, time is running out. The future can be counted in weeks, and the often-promised marriage becomes more and more imperative: 'Let us decide on a date.' But for the man, the future above all is not thus boldly to be defined, pinned down to a fixed date; it must be endlessly and vaguely extendable, best expressed in that conveniently vague and much-used adverb *incessamment*, which may mean anything; it will always be just round the corner, just out of sight, a desperate bid to gain time, a little more time, in the hope that something will turn up, that an escape route will suddenly present itself, that a second seducer will be discovered, even that a man ready to take on a pregnant girl may be found. When it is not *incessamment*, then it is the old calendar, the old feast days, always safely away in the future. If it is November, there will not be much harm in saying 'on se mariera à Pâques'; if it is April, 'on se mariera à la Trinité' will still give plenty of time. There are any number of excuses to be found to justify an ever-later date: parents to be consulted, financial arrangements to be made, a necessary journey first to be gone on, lodgings to be found, furniture to be acquired, a mattress to be paid for, money to be borrowed, a place in the country, *en nourrice*, to be secured. Thus time can only increase the fundamental divergence that may have started, on the part of both participants, in affection, tenderness, friendship, and thoughtlessness, especially about the future. Now, as acidity begins to corrode the relationship, the girl's insistence on the subject of the future will become increasingly strident and unwelcome; the weaker, more easygoing man will attempt to keep away, the more brutal one may take to blows. Whatever her previous weaknesses or even encouragements, the girl will now harp on her innocence and naïveté. It had all been a calculated piece of masculine villainy, a sort of reasoned *escroquerie sur l'avenir* calculated, from the very start, to break down the girl's defences, and give preferably rapid satisfaction to masculine lust. But, in some of the cases quoted, we hear of couples who have known each other, *se fréquentant*, in the innocent sense of going out together, spending their leisure together, as much as six or ten years. In retrospect, when the girl makes her *déclaration*, she will see this long time-lag as an additional manifestation of masculine calculation and selfishness, the sinister tactics of a Fabius, the cruel deliberation of a person who, for years and years, has dealt out kind words, kisses, and warm smiles, concealing, all the time, his fell purpose. Yet, how often could this delay have in fact pleaded in the man's favour, suggesting the solidity of his affections and the seriousness of his purpose? They must not rush headlong into marriage; but must wait till, economically, they are both reasonably well set up. And then all such deeply laid plans can be undermined in the course of a summer night. The girls *have* to put all the blame on the men, *have* to argue convincingly that they have been seduced, as many, but by no means all, undoubtedly have. It does not really matter to us whether they have, or have not been. We are not the judges who received these statements and who had to try to decide whether there was a convincing case for a paternity order. But we must constantly bear in mind this widening divergence of interest between male and female, if we are correctly to interpret these documents, and to attempt to reach behind the girl's version of the story, of necessity designed to suggest that it has been the man who, from start to finish, has made all the running, and that she has merely been over-trusting, candid, and innocent. We should not make too much of these professions of candour, for even the most ignorant *brodeuse* will have had impressed upon her, from childhood, both by her parents, and in church, the moral and economic value of virginity. Indeed, the reluctance of many of these girls to face their families is a clear indication that, in most cases, the lesson had made a deep imprint.

There are other assumptions that we may safely make, without attempting to press our material too far, to make it testify for what it in fact conceals or leaves vague. In the master–servant context, indeed, in the employer–employee one, it is reasonable to assume that the man's intentions are entirely dishonourable, especially when he is already married. But it does not follow that, for instance, the servant has been all that wide-eyed and defenceless. The female domestic of a rich man did not have to have read Swift to have seen her opportunity, especially if with child, to set her cap, if not at the master (the father of the child), then at least, in a rich house, at his steward.[1] Masters had, it is true, what might be described as the advantages of *les lieux*, that is, of the choice of the most propitious time and place. He could call the girl down to the cellar to help him with the wine; or he could ask her to accompany him to his place in the country, in the Monts du Lyonnais or the Beaujolais, to do some washing. Any girl who ventured into such dangerous places would have been asking for trouble. It is also reasonable to suppose that a girl who accuses a man ten years younger than herself may be using her condition in an attempt to secure herself a husband. This is of course what young men thus accused would be the first to claim. Finally, some of the girls may indeed have been as easy conquests as their alleged seducers were likely to suggest. There was probably not much to be said for girls who picked up with soldiers, medical students, or *garçons perruquiers*, whereas a *brodeuse* who had been seduced by a man in the same trade might indeed have been as inno-cent and trusting as both she herself and her workmates, sometimes too her female employer, *marchande brodeuse*, *marchande chapelière*, were to come forward and affirm. There is even the case of a *marchande* being wit-nessed for by one of her *apprenties*, though the testimony of the latter may not have been entirely voluntary and disinterested. Clearly, within a trade, there exist unstated rules of the game, and when these have been infringed,

---

[1] 'In such a family, if you are handsome, you will have the choice of three lovers; the chap-lain, the steward, and my lord's gentleman. I would first advise you to chuse the steward; but if you happen to be young with child by my lord, you must take up with the chaplain. I like my lord's gentleman the least of the three, for he is usually vain and saucy from the time he throws off his livery; and if he misseth a pair of colours, or a tide-waiter's place, he hath no remedy but the highway.' (Swift, 'Directions to the *Waiting-maid*'.)

there will be a general rallying-round the aggrieved party, even on the part of masculine workmates and neighbours.

Perhaps there is no need to labour any of these points further, as we have already heard a number of detailed versions offered by the girls and have been made insistently aware of the importance of the *promesse de mariage*, preferably at a named season, as an inducement to compliance with masculine demands. At this stage it would perhaps be best to allow some of the girls to tell their own stories, in their own words, or, rather, in the rather formalized and much more educated and reasoned words put in their mouths by judge or *greffier*, who took down their statements and who tended to standardize them into set formulae that lend to the loss of virginity and the beginnings of pregnancy, both events of tragic proportions to the victim, much of the banality and inhumanity of the language of French law. After reading fifty or more of these statements, the historian has to remind himself that this was not an inventory of stock in a bankruptcy suit, nor the dull litany of objects read out in a sing-song voice by a *notaire* at the drawing up of a marriage contract, but a statement revealing the most intimate, and often tragic, aspects of a girl's present and bleak immediate future, and that *la comparante, la déposante, la plaignante*, or whatever other semi-neutered description she was arbitrarily placed under, disguised the reality of the living, and often no doubt attractive and appetizing Pernon, Thérèse, Françoise, Marianne, Annette, Gasparde, Suzanne, Virginie, Benoîte, Louise, Jeanne, Marthe (signed *Marte*), Pierrette, Catherine, Isabelle, Marguerite, Claudine, Antoinette, Martine, Constantine, Denise, Barbe, Philippe: *Lyonnaises*, or girls from the region, who had been given these names by their parents or guardians, or by the parish priest. Nor, when describing a decision that would account for her presence before the judge, would the girl herself have said that 'elle lui accorda les dernières faveurs', 'elle céda à ses instances pressantes', 'elle porte aujourd'hui les marques visibles de cet excès de confiance', and so on and so forth. What the girl herself would have said would have been expressed in terms more direct, cruder, and less circumlocutory. The language of the law is so disguised, so allusive, that, at times, one is liable to forget what these statements are in fact about. It is true that eighteenth-century language, possibly even at this level, often affects an indirect and metaphorical approach to this ancient and oft-described activity, and that Cleland succeeds in describing the act a hundred or more times without ever using the word 'copulation'. But we should make allowances for the pithy directness of popular language; and it does not seem probable that a *Lyonnaise* would be any less inclined to call a spade a spade than a *dame de la Halle*, from Paris.

It would then be appropriate, at this stage, to begin with the most familiar, commonest theme of master–servant, or employer–employee seduction, for this was the easiest form of seduction to carry out, as it placed the man from the outset in a position of tremendous strength, and the girl at a complete disadvantage, both at the time, and later, when, so often, it would be her word against that of her former master, who had the advantage of being able to prove his case by the mere fact of dismissal. A domestic servant who had been dismissed must be presumed to have 'mené une mauvaise vie'. The unequal relationship is generally emphasized in the girls' own statements, in the standard expression: 'profitant de l'ascendant qu'il avait sur moi', 'le Sr. Tamisier a profité de l'ascendant qu'un maître a sur ses ouvriers', or, in this case, referring to the master's son, always as much a threat as the master himself: 'le Sr. Jean-Marie Peclet, son fils, voulut abuser de l'ascendant que sa qualité lui donnoit sur elle pour la séduire.' Indeed many masters seem to think that to seduce their servants was not merely an opportunity, but a right. For instance here is the case of Françoise Baroud, 'demeurante à Lyon, rue de l'Enfant-qui-pisse,' who states

> que sur la fin de l'année 1789 la plaignante entra en qualité de domestique chez le Sr. Ferrand, marchand culottier ... à peine deux mois, furent-ils expirés qu'il reconnut quelques bonnes qualités dans la plaignante & lui proposa de l'épouser.
>
> Cette dernière, qu'un avenir heureux flattoit, consentit volontiers à cet engagement ... aussitôt qu'elle s'est aperçue enceinte, elle en a fait part à son ravisseur, qui, voulant cacher sa conduite, s'éloigna de son domicile au mois de juillet dernier.

In January 1791, she is eight months pregnant.

The master, Jacques Ferrand, forty-three, *marchand culottier, en peau*, rue Puits de sel, questioned by the judge,

> répond qu'elle a été à son service, mais qu'il l'a mise hors de chez lui il y a environ 10 mois, parce qu'il s'est aperçu qu'elle menait une mauvaise vie.
>
> A lui représenté que la mauvaise vie qu'a pu mener cette fille n'excuserait pas lui répondant d'avoir eu un mauvais commerce avec elle ... Répond que cette fille demeurant chez lui en qualité de Domestique, il n'a eu d'autre rapport avec elle que le service qu'elle faisait dans son ménage.
>
> Interpellé de convenir que les rapports qu'il a eus avec cette fille ne sont pas seulement ceux d'un maître avec son domestique, qu'il est accusé d'avoir fait avec elle des parties de plaisir qui annonçoient une liaison plus suspecte, qu'il l'a menée dans des cabarets, qu'il y a demandé une chambre en particulier, qu'il y a mangé avec elle, et qu'ils paraissaient tellement familiers que le maître du cabaret demanda à cette fille si lui répondant étoit son amoureux.
>
> Répond et dénie tout le contenu.

But the judge, well used to the professional *morgue* of masters, when accused of having misused one of their servants, would have none of this:

A lui demandé si lors du temps de la fédération, il n'a pas été plusieurs fois se promener avec la plaignante dans l'enceinte dud. Camp [Even the Revolution could thus serve the very private designs of lovers and seducers!]
Répond ... qu'il n'est jamais allé se promener avec elle.

Ferrand decided to take legal advice. He further insinuated that, before entering his service, Françoise had already had at least one child and several lovers, and that she was attempting to wreak vengeance on him for having sacked her. In order to clinch his argument, he added the detail that during the period in question, he could not have had sexual relations with the girl, 'étant malade et n'étant pas capable de copulation'. Perhaps he was overdoing it, for he was unable to produce a medical certificate to this effect. Anyhow, another witness seems to have been of a very different opinion. François Dumas, *compagnon cordonnier*, twenty-six,

dépose que le 15 ou 16 juin dernier [1790], allant porter une paire de souliers à Françoise Baroud ... il entra dans la boutique ... n'y ayant trouvé personne, il pénétra plus avant et dans une espèce de cabinet à main droite il vit la plaignante et le Sr. Ferrand sur un lit étant dans led. cabinet, que ce dernier descendit aussitôt dud. lit et remit sa culotte qui était à bas.

Ferrand had evidently recovered his powers. It might be emphasized, too, that with the constant to-ing and fro-ing that are necessary accompaniments and indeed one of the principal consolations of life in a pre-industrial urban society, seduction during working hours was relatively easy and was no doubt as often observed by the unexpected visitor or intruder.
A further witness, Claudine Péronnat, aged thirty,

dépose qu'aux environs de la Saint-Jean dernier, restant pour lors rue Pierre-Scise et près la rue Puits du sel, passant au-devant de la boutique du Sr. Ferrand ... sur environ 9 heures du soir, elle vit led. Sr. Ferrand qui embrassait la plaignante, et avait avec elle des familiarités qui fixèrent l'attention de plusieurs personnes qui passaient dans la rue au-devant de la boutique.

Lyon, if not strictly speaking a southern town, either in language, more akin to *dauphinois*, or in *mores*, in the sense of the extended family, the tribalism and violence of *les méridionaux*, and of southern brutality where children were concerned, was, like Marseille, a city in which the street, as much as *Guignol* himself, constituted a sort of open, permanent and free theatre for the benefit of the passer-by, with the best performances scheduled for the evening hours, when the windows were wide open to capture a little of the cool creeping in from the Rhône or from the Monts du Lyonnais, and when there would be plenty of people, couples, families, lonely *voyeurs*, *badauds*, out and about, in search of free entertainment: a drunken brawl, a shouting match between two women, a fracas outside a *cabaret*, or, perhaps, best of all, the spectacle so generously and regularly offered, rue Confort, by a *marchande fripière* whose odyssey will concern us later. This is why in Lyon 'the freedom of the street' would probably be more valued than in Paris, a city in which one would perhaps be disinclined to dawdle. *Entre Rhône et Saône*, with its tall, narrow streets trapping the heat, would force people out of doors, towards the windy quays of the Rhône, towards the pont la Feuillée, to watch the east–west traffic. And Lyon had a double bonus, possessing two rivers, rather than one.

   Similar to the experience of Françoise Baroud, though it concerns the relationship between employer and employee in silk manufacture, and not that between master and domestic, is that of Marie Perrichon, *dévideuse de soie, demeurant rue Saint-Georges*,

> procédante à cause de sa minorité de l'autorité de Philippe Perrichon, son père, compagnon maçon à Neuville ... que le 15 avril 1791, âgée de 18 ans, elle entra au service du Sr. Quet, marchand fabricant d'étoffes de soie ... place de la Croix-Paquet, en qualité de dévideuse. Celui, âgé d'environ 50 ans, et marié, commença par alléguer le poids des services qu'il devait attendre de son ouvrière; il eut pour elle sur les autres certains égards, certaine préférence en toutes choses; bientôt elle s'attacha naïvement aux intérêts et à la personne de son maître, sans soupçonner qu'il avoit des vues criminelles ... de coutume, c'est Quet qui va chercher dans sa cave le vin et quelques autres denrées dont son ménage a besoin. Cet endroit est extrêmement sombre, il est impossible d'y pénétrer sans une lumière, sous le prétexte de la lui porter ... Quet y invita une première fois la plaignante, qui obéit. Là il commença la séduction par des promesses de bien-être, il la caressa et se permit même des licences qui cependant n'attaquaient point la pudeur.

But this was merely the softening-up process:

> La plaignante succomba et ce commerce charnel dura 3 mois et ½ consécutifs pendant 4 et ½ qu'elle est restée dans la maison dont elle ne sortit que lorsqu'elle fut convaincue qu'elle était enceinte.

   Such an extreme disproportion between the ages of master and servant, employer and employee, is characteristic of eighteenth-century urban society, when it would be common for a girl barely nubile to be in the service of a master already middle-aged. Much of the sexual attraction of domestic servants to their masters and employers can certainly be attributed to the fact that they were both so young and so inexperienced (or, better still, *apparently* inexperienced, for it is the uncertainty that arouses the man well advanced in life). Quet was a married man of fifty, his wife was probably not very much younger, and the master may have hinted to his employee, in the course of the sessions in the cellar, at the possibility of a divorce, for the new Codes had by then been introduced. The possibility of exchanging places legally, as well as physically, with the master's wife may have been a powerful inducement to Marie to comply with Quet's desires. Such great reversals of fortune did in fact happen, as Swift reminds us.

Quet, like most people, had a cellar. The next seducer, in the master–servant category, had a house in the country, a convenient base, especially for a married man, from which to operate a discreet seduction, the bourgeois equivalent of Valmont's use of his country château, and of the château season, to further his designs on *la Présidente*:

Françoise André, native de la paroisse de Montluel, fille domestique ci-devant au service du Sr. Charretier, aubergiste, rue de Trion, demeurant actuellement chez la veuve Mathéra, garde-malade, rue de la Barre … [dépose] qu'elle a demeuré au service du Sr. Charretier pendant 22 mois, dans les derniers tems le Sr. Charretier, qui avait conçu le dessein de la séduire, sous le prétexte de lui aider à faire une lessive dans une maison de campagne à la Tour-de-Salvagny où il étoit pour lors, lui fit l'ordre d'aller l'y rejoindre.

This is perhaps the crudest example of masculine lust in our collection. No compliments, no promises, no efforts to impress the poor girl, no drawing aside of the curtain of the future to reveal the marriage bed, *le bonheur*, or a journey to a distant part of the kingdom, no dinner *en tête à tête*, no *partie fine*, no *promenade*, just an order. Domestic servants, especially those of innkeepers, are mere *bêtes à séduction*; they do not even merit the dubious effort of 'chatting up', they are ordered into bed, or whatever it may be, as they are ordered to wash the floor, clean out the kitchen, or do the week's washing. If Françoise had refused to report for duty at La Tour-de-Salvagny – where her employer had presumably gone to be unobserved by his wife – she would have been sacked. So she went, and was sacked anyway.[1]

---

[1] It would hardly be an exaggeration to suggest that eighteenth-century female domestics often lived in a veritable terror of their masters, not merely because there was always the danger of seduction, but because they feared that they might be dismissed for some trivial failure: oversleeping, failure to respond immediately to the imperious summons of a bell, a breakage. There is a pathetic example from Paris of the atmosphere of terror in which a young girl in service, especially if recently taken on, might be living. The *commissaire de police* of the Section de la Butte des Moulins, the quarter of the Palais-Royal, received a statement from a girl's employer, Jacques Geoffroy, *peintre doreur*, who came to report, on 4 Frimaire year III (25 November 1795) that the girl had been discovered unconscious in the courtyard of his house, rue des Moulins, after falling out of the window of her attic room: 'que Marie-Anne Lâche était sa fille de confiance depuis 3 jours et que les deux premiers jours qu'elle a été chez lui, s'est levée longtems avant le jour et est venue sonner & frapper à sa porte pour demander ce qu'elle avait à faire, et qu'il lui répondit qu'il falloit

It may be presumed that female domestics had fewer illusions than *brodeuses* or others in the silk trade, for, when not subjected to the assiduities of *le fils du patron*, they would be at the disposition of innkeepers, perhaps even of their customers, their anatomy would have been much commented on by drinkers, as, *filles de salle*, they bent down, washing the floor; they might, before ultimate degradation, have passed through many hands, and received few expressions of friendship or affection. And in large establishments, the houses of the rich, the *hôtels particuliers* of the *soyeurs* of Ainay, they would be further exposed to the predatory assaults of male domestics, *la valetaille*, dressed in the master's discarded clothes, and adopting the young master's cavalier attitudes to women. A footman, perhaps more than anyone, would be anxious to assert his position below stairs by seducing the kitchen maid. But girls in other occupations appear to have few illusions about what to expect from a manservant.

> Philippe Montagne, dévideuse de soie à Lyon ... Petite rue Thomassin ... [dépose] qu'elle est enceinte de près de 9 mois des œuvres du nommé Cortey, domestique, et qu'elle a pris des arrangements avec l'hôpital général de la charité pour y placer l'enfant dont elle doit accoucher.

And that is that, and quite right too; for she cannot even give the man a Christian name.

Jeanne Coton has moved from domestic service to the trade of *dévideuse*, 'dans la maison du Sr. Chatard, rue Pareille, quartier ... Saint-Vincent'. She explains the reasons for this change of occupation:

> Il y a environ 6 années qu'elle est entrée au service du Sr. Jean Peclet, bourgeois de cette ville, demeurant sur le quai Saint-Vincent [she has not moved away very far, no doubt to the annoyance of the Peclet family, remaining in the parish, near the houses of the wealthy inhabitants of this quay of the Saône], elle ne fut pas plus tôt dans cette maison que le Sr. Jean-Marie Peclet, son fils, voulut abuser de l'ascendant que sa qualité donnoit sur elle pour la séduire, après 18 mois elle

---

qu'elle se couchât, qu'il n'était pas tems de se lever, qu'il croit que cette fille avait toujours peur de ne pas faire son devoir, car elle s'est levée toutes les nuits qu'elle est chez lui, qu'elle était seule dans sa chambre.' The doctor believed that she must have fallen out of the window in her sleep. Fortunately, she got away with nothing worse than a broken leg, though even that would be a major disaster for a serving maid, as it would incapacitate her for a time at least. Questioned at the Hôtel-Dieu, she could not remember how she had come to fall (APP, A/A 95, commissaire de police de la Section de la Butte des Moulins, procès-verbal en date du 4 frimaire an III). The extent of the girl's anxiety is a terrifying reminder of the extreme fragility of the status of a female domestic in eighteenth-century urban society. Dismissal would be a constant threat; and, after dismissal, what then? Prostitution, the humiliation of a return home, exposure to cold, starvation, or employment in some even more wretched capacity, such as laundress or *marchande de fagots*. Domestics, after all, were at least housed and, above all *fed*, and sometimes even *clothed*.

quitta le service du Sr. Peclet et ne fut pas pour cela délivrée des sollicitations du Sr. Jean-Marie Peclet qui n'en fut que plus assidu auprès de la remontrante qui est devenue *deux fois* enceinte, elle a d'abord fait un garçon qui n'a vécu que 11 mois, elle en a fait un autre qui est âgé de 19 mois, elle est en ce moment enceinte pour la *troisième fois*, toujours des œuvres du Sr. Jean-Marie Peclet, de plus de 8 mois et ½ ... Le Sr. Peclet vient, par un procédé atroce, d'abandonner la remontrante sans secours, sans moyens de fournir à ses besoins à l'instant d'accoucher.

Jeanne produces a witness, presumably a workmate, and judging from her address, either her room-mate as well, or living in the same lodging-house:

Marie Besson, dévideuse de soie ... rue Pareille ... 27 ans ... [dépose] qu'à une de ces époques elle vit led. Sr. Peclet sortir de table, qu'elle comprit qu'il avait dîné avec la plaignante, parce qu'il y avoit encore deux couverts sur la table.

A second witness, also a *dévideuse*, and giving the same address, is equally observant – and equally damning: 'Il y a environ 2 mois elle vit entrer le Sr. Peclet chez la plaignante, et que led. Sr. Peclet avait un paquet sous le bras.' The implication presumably being that the parcel contained some of his clothing, and that he was going to spend the night, or, equally, that he had recognized his paternal responsibilities, and was bringing clothing for the surviving boy. What seems established is his insistence in pursuing the girl, years after her departure from his parents' home.

What is equally apparent is her determination – and who can blame her, with a third pregnancy at the hands of Peclet – not to let matters rest; and in this respect, her attitude is much in contrast to the humble resignation and fatalism of most of the *déclarantes*. For she produces a third witness – she must have drummed up pretty well all the girls on her storey – also from the rue Pareille, describing herself as 'une ouvrière en étoffes de soie, âgée de 30 ans', who states that 'comme la fenêtre de sa chambre donnait sur l'escalier, elle voyoit monter fréquemment le Sr. Jean-Marie Peclet fils'.

He was indeed closely observed, and no doubt much commented upon by these girls, no longer young, by eighteenth-century standards – and Jeanne herself must have been nearing thirty, as she had known Peclet for over six years – and thus probably more aware than most that time was running out for their companion as far as marriage prospects were concerned. Peclet too gives his age as twenty-eight. The judge clearly thought the case unusually important, for he took some trouble to question him closely, making much of the meal or meals that they had had together, and asking him why he had been seen coming *out* of the house with a parcel under his arm. (The witness had said that she had seen him coming *in* with it, a less damaging assertion, because if he still had it on leaving, it would have been clear that he had spent the night in Jeanne's room.) Peclet denied everything, or as much as he could, replying

> qu'il a été attiré dans le domicile de cette fille par des parents de cette dernière pour faire un arrangement sur l'accusation qu'on méditait de porter contre lui, qu'à cette époque il a en effet mangé chez cette fille avec lesdits parents, et en est sorti avec eux sans faire aucun arrangement, n'étant point l'auteur de la grossesse.

His denial of responsibility, underlined by his sneering reference to Jeanne as *cette fille*, is entirely predictable on the part of a *fils de famille* who lived on the affluent Quai Saint-Vincent, the principal base of the *notariat* of Lyon. The girl was being a persistent nuisance, insisting on haunting the quarter, wandering around displaying her stomach. Peclet's story about being trapped into accepting a meal, in order to meet her family – and this is the only time that we hear of Jeanne's relatives – is hardly convincing. At least, none of the witnesses could remember having seen any other visitors coming in or going out of the girl's room. Of course, it is just possible that Jeanne was telling a pack of lies, for Peclet's son would have been a good catch for a former servant who was only a *dévideuse*. Her female neighbours and workmates would have been likely to stand by her in any case, through thick and thin. But it seems much more likely that Peclet *fils* was unable to break with her entirely.

*

The abuse of the position of master or employer was obviously the commonest instrument of seduction, in a society in which domestic servants would constitute 15 per cent of the feminine labour force in most cities (this was the figure for Paris at this time; for Toulouse it was a little lower, 12 per cent), and in which, in Lyon, *brodeuses*, *dévideuses* and so on would have accounted for as much as 25 per cent. This was simply a matter of exploiting a position of total power. But there was a more sophisticated, less naked approach that seems to have been used by the potential seducer and to have been accepted as a point in his favour by a number of girls: the insistence on the similarity of age and condition. Benoîte Bonnard had thought that she could eventually count on Pierre Dusurgey, it will be recalled, because they were both much of an age, and both worked in the hat trade, she as a *coupeuse de poils*, he as a *compagnon chapelier*. Marie Pierry, too, had listened favourably to the pleas of Louis Guichon, because 'la plaignante, jeune et sans expérience, devait compter sur ce mariage, puisque Louis Guichon est un jardinier dont la fortune n'est pas au-dessus de la sienne'. In this case, there was a triple tie, because, while the girl lived in Villeurbanne, the gardener lived nearby, montée de

Balmont. Jeanne Caillot, 'brodeuse à Lyon, demeurant rue Plat-d'Argent, âgée de 30 ans', states similarly

> qu'il y a nombre d'années que le commerce de broderies a amené dans son domicile le Sr. Claude-Marie Desvernai, commis chez le Sr. Sonnet, marchand brodeur … led. Desvernai a depuis longtems proposé à la comparante de l'épouser, comme l'état et l'âge de ce dernier, qui est âgé de 40 ans, étaient très sortables, la comparante a cru aux promesses dud. Desvernai … le Sr. Desvernai, loin de tenir sa parole, s'est absenté.

Equally, Marie Madeleine Martin, *faiseuse de bourses de cheveux*, aged twenty-two, rue des Missionnaires, was to explain

> que depuis 5 ans le Sr. André Colombet, maître ferblantier, lui rend des soins assidus, que depuis ce tems il a parlé souvent à la comparante du dessein où il était de l'épouser, la conformité d'état et d'âge, led. Sr. Colombet ayant environ 26 ans, a fait croire à la comparante que les promesses … étoient sincères, elle a cédé … le Sr. Colombet paraît avoir des motifs pour éloigner de quelque tems leur union … comme le sort de l'enfant dont elle est enceinte lui est cher.

In both these cases, the sheer length of the relationship – in the former, several years, in the latter, they had known one another for five years – must have seemed to the two girls a further guarantee of the men's serious intentions, though, reading these statements, one often has occasion to be surprised by the number of girls who claim to have been made pregnant by men whom they had known and with whom they had been going out for anything up to the last ten or eleven years.[1] It is difficult to know what we should make of this. In some cases, it might have been that the couple had decided on a long engagement to enable them to save up enough to set themselves up in an establishment, and that their calculations had been thrown out of joint by an unexpected and unwelcome pregnancy that had caused the man to think again. For a woman of thirty and a man of forty can hardly have been sexually inexperienced, and such long periods of voluntary abstention seem extremely improbable. This is, however, not the sort of thing that is likely to be revealed by a *déclaration de grossesse*. Another, less charitable explanation might be that the girls mentioned, having become pregnant as the result of other contacts, had fallen back on long-standing men friends, in the hope that they would regularize the situation.

---

[1] 'Marthe Villard, tailleuse à Lyon, demeurant rue Saint-Pierre-le-Vieux … 19 ans … [déclare] qu'il y a 6 ans qu'elle fit la connaissance du nommé Simon Picard, domestique de la veuve Ferrier.' If we are to believe her, Ferrier must have met her when she was only thirteen. Perhaps they had been childhood friends; or perhaps he was merely a skilled exponent of the waiting game.

Just as age, trade, quarter and contiguity may prove to be valuable allies of seduction, so can certain days, certain occasions, certain periods of the year, and certain places favour such enterprises. The role of physical proximity (*voisinage*) is an obvious one, for, in any relationship between male and female, there has to be a starting point: where to meet? And how to meet? There is a statement, for instance, to the *commissaire de police* of the Section Popincourt, in Paris, that spells this out very clearly:

> La citoyenne Nicole Moricard, âgée de 25 ans, demeurant à Paris, cul de sac Sébastien No 2, fille de Edme Moricard et de femme Françoise Palois, de la paroisse de Sauvigny-le-Bois [near Avallon], demeurant à Paris depuis environ 4 ans ... pendant près de 3 ans elle a travaillé en qualité de journalière chez le C. Driancourt, jardinier, rue Popincourt ... pendant tout ce tems, et avant, elle a vécu d'une manière irréprochable [we have her word for it] ... à la sollicita-tion du C. Nicolas Langrand, alors porteur d'eau, et actuellement voiturier sur le port, *demeurant cul de sac Sébastien No 2*, elle a été demeurer chez lui le 1er janvier 1794, et que pour l'engager d'y entrer, il lui offrit moitié plus de gages qu'elle ne gagnoit chez le C. Driancourt, ce qui l'a déterminé d'y entrer ... à l'époque de cette entrée l'épouse du C. Langrand existoit et est depuis décédée ... pendant l'espace de 5 mois après la mort de son épouse, il s'est comporté en galant homme ... quelque tems après il a commencé à faire des propositions ... il couchait dans une chambre servant de cuisine & ladite citoyenne ... dans l'écurie, au bout de lad. chambre communiquant dans la surd. écurie ... [il] a eu le premier de la déclarante ... [elle est] enceinte de 8 mois et de quelques jours.[1]

All one can say is that the country girl, employed in a country trade in Paris – the Section Popincourt had a great many gardens – and coming from the same part of the world as Restif's *la paysanne*, seems to have gone into this with her eyes open. Perhaps she thought that the presence of Langrand's wife offered a guarantee of her virtue, as indeed it seems to have done. But she was surely asking for trouble, staying on in her stable room, after the wife had died. Or perhaps she had calculated that she was well placed to succeed her in every sense; Langrand, at least, knew how to play the waiting game. The episode reveals another theme: that of loneli-ness. The country girl in Paris for the first time will be extremely grateful for company, and will be likely to take up with the first man who takes the trouble to talk to her and to take an interest in her. Langrand, who had been a *porteur d'eau*, would himself have been a provincial, almost cer-tainly from the Aveyron. But, of course, the important thing about this document is that Nicole and Langrand were living at the same address!

Marguerite Terrier, *tailleuse*, the daughter of a *chirurgien* from la Guillotière, met her seducer who was a student at the École Royale

---

[1] APP, A/A 219 (commissaire de police de la Section Popincourt, déclaration faite par Nicole Moricard, le 22 ventôse an III) (12 March 1795).

Vétérinaire, which was also in this *commune*, just over the bridge from Lyon. It is much the same story with 'Dlle. Antoinette Bally, dévideuse de soie à Lyon, y demeurant, maison de l'Oratoire, quai du Rhône, [qui] expose qu'elle a eu le malheur de faire la connaissance depuis plusieurs années du Sr. Pellorin fils ... [qui] demeure chez son père, maître boulanger à la Guillotière'. It is easy enough to see how they must have met in the first place; the pont de la Guillotière was the physical link between them, an invitation in stone to bring them eventually together. Perhaps Pellorin met the girl on the Lyon side, quai du Rhône, on one of his visits to the city; or perhaps Antoinette had come across to la Guillotière on a weekend outing. What seems pretty certain is that the man's intentions were not serious; even though he had known the girl for several years, the son of a *maître boulanger* was unlikely to think of a *dévideuse* as a future wife. The chances are that he had been in the habit of crossing over, quai du Rhône, in the pursuit of pleasure.

Marie Dangle, *brodeuse*, had, we may remember, met her alleged seducer 'venant habituellement chez la sœur de la comparante où elle travaillait de son état de brodeuse'. Sisters are not always a protection, especially elder ones; they can be extremely dangerous. We will return later to the special case of Thérèse Bonnard, a woman undoubtedly *généreuse de sa personne*; but a *marchande fripière*, with her establishment in the rue Confort, would be likely to have a constant stream of visitors, as an old-clothes shop would be almost as much in demand, at this level of society, as the *Mont de Piété* (which must also have been the point of departure of a great many romances, happy or unhappy, although it is never mentioned in the statements that we have used). Benoîte Bonnard met her man when she was 'demeurant rue Raisin, et près du domicile de Pierre Dusurgey, compagnon chapelier, ce voisinage donna lieu à ce dernier de faire connaissance avec elle; il lui faisait des visites fréquentes' (for he only had to cross the street). Marguerite Gulon, with an address 'à la Pierre Percée', would soon have come across Dominique Bonhomme, who lived in the rue Saint-Georges. According to Bonhomme, he had first met the girl, who was a *brodeuse*, when he had brought her one of his waistcoats to be embroidered. Jeanne Rouzon, a year before her statement, had been apprenticed to a *tonnelier* of Caluire, and it was there that she had met François Bergeron, *garçon cordonnier*, who likewise lodged with his master. Bavet, *marchand drapier*, rue Saint-Nizier, was a neighbour of Françoise Dueure, *brodeuse*, who, when they first met, lived in the allée des Images, where 'il venait la voir assidûment dans son domicile'. 'Dlle. Claudine Poncet, ouvrière demeurant chez Mlle. Royer, marchande de modes ... rue Mercière' stated 'que depuis environ une année et ½ la démontrante demeuroit dans la pension où logeoit le Sr. Antoine d'Audiffret', who had taken advantage of her youth – she was seventeen –

to seduce her. Françoise Dubessy and Jean Biolay, as we have seen, had
known each other in Pouilly-le-Monial; and the girl, on coming to Lyon,
had sought him out: the usual story in fact of the lonely provincial girl in
the big city. 'Catherine Marcel, fille domestique, demeurant à Lyon chez
M. Dubour, place de la Charité . . . a eu le malheur d'écouter les promesses
séduisantes du Sr. François Bourdonneau, cuisinier chez M. Dubour.'
Isabelle Collonge, *apprentie gazière*, apprenticed to a *gazier* of Cuire,
states that she had been seduced by her master.

> Antoinette Guillot, veuve Blanc, et Pierrette Blanc, sa fille, âgée de 20 ans . . .
> dévideuse à Lyon, y demeurant rue Saint-Jean [déclarent] qu'au commence-
> ment de l'année dernière [1790] elles quittèrent Grézieu-la-Varenne, qu'elles
> avaient toujours habité, et vinrent se fixer en cette ville, elles prirent un loge-
> ment dans la maison du Sr. Brigand, avocat, et elles passèrent bail pour 6 années.
> Le Sr. Brigand, profitant de sa qualité de locataire, en a abusé pour s'introduire
> dans le domicile des comparantes.

Clearly there was as much danger in being a tenant, as of taking up an
abode in a lodging-house.

In most instances, the two would have met because they either lived in
the same house, or were neighbours, or had met through work. Men obviously did not have to go very far to find a suitable companion. *On séduit
de près plutôt que de loin*, or, to put it less grandly, one took the first
opportunity that happened to turn up. So much for places, for the very
obvious geography of 'where to meet'. Then there is the matter of timing,
and this would obviously be dictated by weekends, feast days, and public
or private occasions. One of the witnesses for a *déclarante*, who was also
her employee, after stating that 'la plaignante travaille chez elle, témoin,
en qualité d'ouvrière depuis environ 6 années', was able to recall 'qu'elle
a appris que la plaignante a fait la connaissance de P.D. le jour du mardi
gras de l'année 1790'.

> Anne Lassalle, brodeuse à Saint-Just, y demeurant chez son père, citoyen de
> Lyon, résidant Rue de Trion, paroisse de Saint-Just . . . [déclare] qu'au mois
> d'octobre 1788 elle fut invitée pour assister à la cérémonie du baptême de
> l'enfant de Charlotte Grely, mariée à Jean-François Armanet, limonadier à la
> Guillotière, elle y fit connaissance de Louis Armanet, frère du père de l'enfant,
> elle était à peine âgée de 17 ans, Louis Armanet la combla de politesses et d'hon-
> nêtetés, abusant de son inexpérience, il la persuada que bientôt elle serait son
> épouse, il était âgé de 32 ans . . . Quelques jours après, il lui fit chez son père une
> visite dans laquelle il lui exprima les mêmes sentimens, il continua et bientôt il
> lui tendit des pièges, il convenoit, suivant lui, d'avoir des entrevues particu-
> lières, il prétextoit la sévérité du père et de la mère de l'exposante . . . la plaig-
> nante se rendoit dans les endroits qu'il lui indiquoit. Elle est devenue enceinte.
> Pendant sa grossesse il a montré tant d'empressement qu'elle ne pouvait le

soupçonner de la tromper. Elle accoucha le 4 décembre 1790 d'une fille baptisée sous le nom de Marie, née d'elle et d'un père inconnu, elle a conservé son enfant, elle l'a allaitée et continue à l'allaiter dans la maison et sous les yeux de son père et de sa mère. Ils ont eu soin d'elle pendant sa grossesse. Il semble que le malheur qu'elle a éprouvé la leur a rendue plus chère ... Mais elle vient de s'apercevoir que son séducteur est un monstre ... il a tenté de lui faire arracher son enfant, pour y parvenir, il a recours à différentes personnes. Le Sr. Pupier, l'un des frères de l'hôpital, est venu le lui demander en lui exposant que Louis Armanet avait payé entre les mains du recteur les droits d'entrée, il a fait l'impossible pour l'engager à le lui céder.

The only consoling, indeed unusual, feature in Anne's sad yet predictable narrative is the humanity and compassion displayed by her father and mother, both during her confinement and after the birth of Marie, an attitude that stands in marked contrast to those displayed, in similar circumstances, by most families (Dlle. Chirat: 'état qui l'a brouillée (avec assez de raison) avec sa famille, et principalement avec une tante'; Dlle. Faye: 'la comparante a été obligée de quitter sa famille pour venir cacher son malheur et sa honte en cette ville', and so on). The rest reads very much like a set piece. As the child was born in December, the fatal christening party must have taken place in March or April, at the beginning of spring, a season always favourable to enterprises of this kind. Armanet, who, we learn, was a blacksmith, was obviously an old hand at the game, but he had quite unusual advantages. For instance, having a brother who was a *limonadier* in la Guillotière would offer him at all times, but especially at weekends and feast days during *la belle saison*, a particularly favourable terrain on which to operate, presumably as a single man, thanks to the presence, on such occasions, of large numbers of *brodeuses, dévideuses*, female domestics, and so on, coming either in parties of two – there might be some protection in this, but, more likely, two girls were better placed to play up a man or a couple of men – or in groups of four: two girls and two men – and most of these girls, making up for lost time in the sort of febrile pleasure that characterizes the short hours of leisure of the very poor, would be likely to become very drunk in no time, thanks to the solicitude of the men friends whom they had brought with them or whom they had met at the *guinguette*. Then it might be a matter of retiring, there and then, into the conveniently enveloping shrubbery. But a *family* occasion, such as a christening, would offer even better opportunities, for it would cut down on the time devoted to the preliminary skirmishes – to the formalized *ballet d'amour* as stepped out, in a group of four, by two girls and two men: 'who are you?' 'you *would* like to know, wouldn't you?', 'can we have a guess?' and so on – as it would offer a perfect excuse for formal mutual introductions. The host would see to it that the two *brodeuses*, one of whom was possibly a friend of his wife's, should meet his brother, unattached and available – this would be pointed out by the *limonadier* or the hostess – who could then go right ahead, ply the girl with (free) drink and plenty of attention, charm her with his solicitude, tell her of his work and of his loneliness, prepare the ground for another meeting. Family affairs would always be the most dangerous. The only other aspect of Anne's story that seems somewhat atypical is the insistence of the blacksmith to have the child placed in a foundling hospital.

Spring and summer weekends and feast days were certainly the most dangerous, apart from these family reunions. A witness, passing in the street, 'aux environs de la Saint-Jean dernier', recalls a couple glimpsed kissing and engaged in other *familiarités*. But February was likewise perilous, as can be illustrated from a case of rape, reported to the Minister of Justice, in March–April 1807, by the judicial authorities of Mons, at that time the *chef-lieu* of the Département de Jemappes:

> Un viol s'étant commis en la ville de Soignies … ayant appris que 2 desd. prévenus avaient pris la fuite, et la rumeur publique m'ayant instruit qu'ils s'étaient enrôlés dans le régiment des Chevaux-légers Belges qui se formait à Liège, je me suis adressé à mon collègue en cette ville.[1]

And from a second letter we learn the following details:

> Il s'est commis un viol la nuit du 8 au 9 février dernier en la ville de Soignies sur une jeune fille honnête qui se trouvait dans une auberge où on donnait bal à cause du carnaval et qui est devenue la victime de la brutalité de plusieurs libertins. Il importe à la société que les coupables soient punis, un exemple devient d'autant plus nécessaire que déjà une jeune fille a été horriblement maltraitée en la même ville.[2]

This is not, of course, to suggest that there existed an open or a closed season for the satisfaction of masculine lust, feminine desire, or mutual tenderness and affection expressed in the physical act of love. That would be nonsense, as the only seasonal variations would be those imposed by the monthly advent of what the French, rather unfairly, for we have not invaded that country all *that* frequently, describe as *les anglaises*. Otherwise, there would be no restrictions, apart from those imposed by space and opportunity: hence, as we have seen, the utility of a cellar, or a *maison de campagne*. What is revealed to us is only, of course, what, in one way or another, went wrong. The *déclarantes* are being forced out into the open by sheer need, coming forward, no doubt bashful and humiliated –

---

[1] AN, BB 18 402 (Justice, Jemappes, directeur du jury d'accusation de Mons, au Grand Juge, le 7 avril 1807).
[2] AN, BB 18 402 (Justice, Jemappes, directeur du jury d'accusation de Mons, au Grand Juge, le 11 mars 1807).

so that many of them bring along with them workmates and employers, not just as witnesses, but for moral support – to be questioned by male judges, *greffiers*, or *commissaires de police* who generally show scant respect for their feelings, are not above giving them moral lectures on their conduct, and who often express scepticism as to their claims of innocence and inexperience.

Our material, it is perfectly clear, has no statistical value whatever; it is the product of chance, unlucky chance at that. *Le secret du boudoir, le langage de l'oreiller* do not obligingly speak to the inquiring social historian, and, perhaps in a majority of cases, we are dealing with an act between two people only and that takes place in intimacy, in a closed place, and in the absence of witnesses. Of such an act, it goes without saying, there is no written record, and even verbal recollection is generally to be discounted as solid evidence, owing to masculine habits of boastfulness. It is not the purpose of the historian to draw aside the curtains, and reveal *la Marquise* with her fine company of *quatre-vingts chasseurs*; we can leave that sort of thing to the old-fashioned *commissaire de police*, at a period when French divorce proceedings were less liberal and far more prying and indiscreet than at present. Nor are we attempting to render an act of mystery, tenderness and beauty a mere boon to the avid researcher, scrabbling for evidence. All this happened a very long time ago; and we are not insulting Pernon, Philippe, Victoire, and others, in thus revealing their ill-expressed secrets. Nor are we even particularly concerned, as they naturally would have been, with the physical consequences of the act itself, or with the name of the seducer. It is perhaps a little hard on these dead girls that we should seek profit from their terrible misfortunes and personal disasters; but, in this half-explored field of research, we have to clutch at any little hint that is going. We are searching for the fringe evidence, for the peripheral remarks that reveal, often quite unconsciously, generally accepted popular assumptions, the conventions of collective behaviour, *les politesses et les pudeurs* of the very poor and the very underprivileged, as much concerned with such externals as those at the top end of society (it might be noted, *en passant*, that the key word *l'honneur* recurs insistently in these documents, and that the honour of a *brodeuse* is potentially of greater value and of much more importance than that of a Duke, because it is all that she has got); public views as to what constitute a definitive commitment, made *au vu du monde* (and it is the fact of publicity that makes it so binding); the likeliest channels of movement within a city, the probable forms of the employment of leisure, the sociability and solidarity of the poor, even such physical matters as the number of people to a room, even to a bed, or where people meet. And it is for these reasons that we have placed so much emphasis on the collective, almost public aspects of what, in the end, would, in most cases, be the most private of all acts, though, in Lyon at least, it often seems to have commanded, *sauf votre respect*, a large, amused, and noisily appreciative audience.

THE FREEDOM OF THE STREET

What must stand out emphatically from much of this peripheral, almost incidental evidence that we have collected in support of the girls' statements (much of it a confused mumbling, a word spoken in parenthesis, a sudden slip of the tongue, or a heartfelt expression of prejudice, or the warming appeal of solidarity), at least to anyone not conversant with the tiny compensations of life as it presented itself to the working population and the lower orders in an eighteenth-century city, is the relative freedom of movement, outside, in the street, from street to street, enjoyed by all those with whom we have been concerned. The *brodeuse*, the *dévideuse*, the *coupeuse*, the *tailleuse*, the *blanchisseuse*, the *apprêteuse*, the *marchande de modes*, even the domestic servant, like their various masculine equivalents, are constantly walking the city, especially within the central peninsula, and bearing the handy and visible pretext of some errand[1] – a half-finished waistcoat, a three-cornered hat awaiting its trimmings and plumes, a dress that still needs to be embroidered, a woman's hat that has still to be ironed into shape, a basket of wet linen, a bouquet containing a note, a dozen bottles of wine, a tray containing a meal prepared by a *gargotier*, a tray containing cakes and pastries, a brace of pheasants, a box of tools, a sack full of old clothes – the tell-tale passports to the freedom of outside during working hours. Mobility within the city, the pretext to wander the streets in daytime, the freedom of movement of the female artisan, servant and shopgirl were the minor, but appreciable privileges enjoyed by the hard-worked and the exploited, and that often distinguished them from girls of superior social status and economic resources whose valuable virtue could not thus be exposed to the manifold hazards of the street-corner and the doorstep conversation and encounter. Restif and Mercier were quick to point out that, in this respect, *la fille de l'artisan*, *l'ouvrière*, *la grisette*, even *la fille de salle*, enjoyed a measure of freedom, often within the whole length and breadth of Paris,

---

[1] The wisdom in thus carrying, as visibly as possible, the external symbols of a legitimate occupation, at all times, was not confined to eighteenth-century France. When I was employed as a sanitary orderly, in the British Army, at one stage of the Second World War, emptying lavatories and cleaning out urinals on Chepstow Race Course, it was impressed upon me most succinctly, by a Welsh corporal, my colleague and mentor: 'Always have a hard brush and pail to hand, bach, in case the sarge comes by; he won't come *too* close, owing to the stink. Believe me, bach, you are in a safe billet in a job like this which makes you stink. They won't interfere with you.' And they didn't. But I always had the pail and hard brush to hand.

that would have been totally denied to *la fille du marchand*, and the girl of high condition. It was perhaps a minor compensation for terribly long working hours, frightful working conditions, and overcrowded lodgings, bad food, and only occasional drink, and that of poor quality. But it offered in return a wealth of gossip, information, sociability, amusement, contact, friendship and humour. The 'freedom of the street' was not to be disdained merely as a few moments gained, surreptitiously, from the monotony and extreme fatigue of the working day.

For one thing, many of these female trades were by nature peripatetic. The marvellous mobility of the *blanchisseuse* has often been remarked upon, both by contemporaries and by historians; and because she commanded her small continents of streets, quays and bridges, because she spent much of her time walking from quarter to quarter, and because she possessed, in her basket, the passport to the interior, albeit to the servants' quarters, of the houses of the great, her services were also much in demand with those who were criminally inclined. It is perhaps less often realized that even a silk worker will spend much of her working hours outside the workshop or the shop, taking samples, picking up materials, taking hats to be finished; for at this level of *l'artisanat*, production would not be confined to a single workshop, to the room of a single *maître-tailleuse*, there will be a whole range of finishers, *apprêteurs* and *apprêteuses*, *fourbisseurs* and *fourbisseuses*, so that the completed article would be likely to have passed through half a dozen different hands, and to have travelled, on an apparently meaningless course, doubling back on its tracks, climbing *montées*, even crossing one of the rivers, half across the city, before at last reaching the shop of the *marchande de modes*; and even that will not be its final destination; for the servant of the eventual purchaser, who was possibly also the *commanditaire*, would be sent to pick it up and bring it back to a grimly shuttered, fortress-like *hôtel particulier* in Ainay or Perrache, its prison-like walls blind to the excitements and activities of the streets. The *soyeurs* and the *bons bourgeois de Lyon* must have paid heavily for their constant search for privacy and security in a great deal of boredom; *ennui* has never been an ailment of the common people.

This would apply particularly to a luxury industry like silk, almost every article of which would have been made to order and according to very strict specifications. The *commanditaire* would thus want to see the progress of the article at each stage, and, in the case of clothing of any kind, there would be a whole series of fittings, each of which would be an occasion for one of the junior *apprenties brodeuses* or *fileuses* to cross the quarter, or several quarters, carrying the dress, the coat, the hat, or the skirt. As these hand-made articles were of considerable and lasting value, they would have to be handled with great care, protected from the elements, especially from rain or snow, or from the glare of the summer sun.

So the elements too could be allies of a walking girl's outside leisure: a pause in a covered entry during a shower, a pause in the shade of a *traboule* so as to protect the bright colours from the midday sun; and each pause would be put to profit in the form of conversation. In Paris, during the revolutionary period, Fouquier-Tinville and his like received a great deal of valuable information from working and walking women – as well as from stationary ones like portresses and *concierges* – who knew how to use their eyes and ears, and who could report on anything unusual, anything out of place, whether a gathering on the Pont-Neuf, or a bigger crowd than customary at the *café Chrétien*. Much of the immense body of papers of the former Public Prosecutor consists of information derived from this type of observant source. So in Lyon, at a later stage of the revolutionary period, the semi-secret armies of the White Terror were in receipt of copious, often hour by hour information regarding the *faits et gestes* of members of the garrison, hated strangers in the city, the object of uniform opprobrium, who could not even set foot beyond the safety of the barracks, in pairs, or in larger groups, without being designated, in advance, as they walked down from la Croix-Rousse or crossed over from la Guillotière, by female scouts, standing in doorways or apparently going about their normal business, by prostitutes, on their usual beats, by girls looking out of upper windows. The social solidarity of a city population engaged largely in a single trade would now be further reinforced by an even stronger bond of *political* solidarity, taking the form of bitter hostility to Paris, a carefully nurtured sense of local grievance, and feeding on the terrible memories of the Siege and the *mitraillades*.

Mobility within the city – one would be tempted to call it the freedom of the city within working hours; the easy, friendly and mocking sociability of the street, of the open-doored wine-shop, *échoppe*, *gargote*, shoemaker's shop, indeed, all of those artisans and tradesmen who lived open-doored on to the street, as if not to miss anything of the passing theatre; the bustle, noise and gossip of the main markets – the *salons* of the poor, the parlour of *la Mère Duchesne* and her kind (but, in Lyon, *la Mère Duchesne* would entertain very different political views from those stridently stated by her *cousine* in Paris); the brief respite offered by *la Promenade* and by the quays, the availability of the network of the *traboules*, which, as well as furnishing ready escape routes to the swift-footed malefactor or political assassin, offered a convenient covering, a brief extra tunnel of illicit leisure, to the dawdling apprentice, the whistling child *commissionnaire*, or the pretty *tailleuse*, happily aware of the attention of which she was the moving object – all constituted one of the principal compensations for those obliged to spend long hours indoors, in dark and airless cellars or ground-floor rooms, using up their eyesight on minute embroidery or on complicated stitching, in a city in which most houses would have as many as seven storeys. It is as if the many errands that could legitimately be fitted into working hours, discreetly prolonged, even repeated – it was so easy to forget some small object, a thimble might be the excuse to return over three streets – formed the preparation for the much greater, exhilarating, almost limitless freedom of the weekend, when joyful little bands of workmates, two girls, two men, headed for *la Promenade* or *le champ de la Fédération*. One can picture the *brodeuse*, as, on her way, she takes in a small, shaded square, a cool fountain, a wine-shop, its entry covered with a trellis of roses or cool ivy, or a handsome butcher's apprentice, standing proudly in his bloody apron, and makes mental notes to return there longer, to investigate here further, on the longed-for free afternoon, or in the coolness of a summer evening. For the life of the urban poor is probably at its worst indoors, where it would be subjected to constant scrutiny on the part of the *marchande de modes* or of the *tailleuse*. The view from within was a window on to freedom, the promise of adventure. How often, in our statements, do we encounter such phrases: 'que le 15 ou 16 juin dernier, allant porter une paire de souliers à Françoise Baroud, il entra dans la boutique' (this of a *compagnon cordonnier*); 'elle a eu la visite du Sr. V., maître tailleur ... sous prétexte d'acheter des marchandises' (this of a *marchande fripière*, whose adventures will concern us shortly); 'ajoute que ladite Bonnard vient habituellement chercher du pain chez lui' (this of a *maître boulanger*, and, as Henri Béraud reminds us, in his marvellous *La Gerbe d'or*, the *boulangerie-pâtisserie* is the people's forum for the whole of les Terreaux, receiving as it does the more leisurely Sunday trade as well as that of the week with less time to waste in talk); 'elle ... est allée plusieurs fois chez la plaignante ... pour lui rendre du linge' (this of a *blanchisseuse*). Jeanne Caillot, *brodeuse*, states: 'il y a nombre d'années que le commerce de broderies a amené dans son domicile le Sr. .... commis chez le Sr. .... marchand brodeur' (for *brodeuses* generally worked in the house in which they slept: the seventh floor for much-needed sleep, the ground floor for the long hours of work, so that it was an easy ascent from the latter to the former for the man who made regular visits to the workshop).

What emerges from these snippets of information is that the companions of leisure had often been recruited, in the course of the working week, in the *camaraderie* of the street, in the hoped-for hazards of errands. 'Can I come and fetch you on Sunday?' 'Shall we all go to *la Promenade* together at the weekend?' And this will end us up with some statement such as this: 'Marguerite Pagot, coupeuse de poils à Lyon, y demeurant, rue Raisin, âgée de 24 ans ... [déclare] qu'elle a habité avec la plaignante, avec laquelle elle couchait chez la veuve Anciau ... qu'elle ... a même été souvent de leur promenade', while another witness, Jean-Baptiste Brossard, *cordonnier*, living rue du Cornet, and aged twenty-three, also adds the information 'qu'il s'est souvent promené avec eux' – a foursome of twenty-three- and twenty-four-year-olds, resulting in the pregnancy of one of the girls. In other words, leisure could be more dangerous than work, because it carried a relationship begun during working-hours a stage further, bearing the girl, as on an invisible stream, that much nearer to the perils of seduction. And, ultimately, there is perhaps no great safety in numbers, save to provide the ill-used girl with ready witnesses in her hour of need. Even so, at least at the tentative stage of the relationship, the couple chooses to be accompanied by another couple, even by two more couples. Six can make more noise and have more boisterous fun than four, *on partage*, so that the money will go further, and, with a reserve of two other men to dance with, or to flirt with, the girl has an extra hold over the young man who is attempting to make the running.

Of course, as far as women and girls are concerned, this freedom of movement should not be exaggerated, especially in revolutionary terms. The Revolution gave *men* a greater passport to the freedom of the road, as well as to the freedom of the night. (We will hear of a man who states 'lorsqu'il venait passer la nuit avec la plaignante, il faisait entendre à sa femme qu'il allait passer la nuit au piquet de garde'; but a woman had no guard duties, and the National Guard would thus offer her no alibi.) Women, especially in the silk industry, could cadge the odd half-hour of freedom here and there, in the course of the day, but their mobility would hardly extend beyond the bounds of the city. *Le retour au pays* would be the worst, because the most humiliating, of all solutions, while pregnancy, above all, will severely restrict the possibilities of escape from an urban environment and from the relentless search for alternative employment following dismissal. It is the male who holds all the cards in this respect; if the worst comes to the worst, he can always opt out altogether by volunteering. And he will not be ill thought of, save by the girl whom he has abandoned.

THE DAYS AND THE NIGHTS OF THE RUE CONFORT

On 14 January 1791, Dlle. Thérèse Bonnard, giving her profession as *marchande fripière*, rue Confort, came before the judge. In her statement, she said that seven months previously 'elle a eu la visite du Sr. Vermillière, maître-tailleur, rue Bourgchanin, sous prétexte d'acheter des marchandises, il est resté longtems, est revenu, disant qu'il était libre tandis qu'il était marié . . . [il] lui a fait des promesses de mariage'. Giving her age as twenty-six, she added that she was now six months pregnant.

The judge was not impressed, for he had taken the trouble to inform himself from other, and as it turned out, numerous and loquacious sources. Dlle. Bonnard's ground-floor abode facing on to the rue Confort might have been described as 'a room with a view', but one that looked inwards, rather than outwards; and a majority of the inhabitants of her street, as well as plenty of passers-by, by day or in the middle of the night – for, during the previous summer, plenty of them seem to have been still up and about well after midnight – had taken to looking inward, while almost as many had indeed 'looked in'. Yet it is clear from the numerous witnesses heard by the judge that the girl, though apparently extremely accommodating to a succession of male visitors, was not popular, either with those who had enjoyed her favours or with the other inhabitants of the street and the quarter. But a popular *marchande fripière* would be something of a phenomenon in eighteenth-century conditions; for hers was an occupation that preyed on poverty, debt and improvidence. The *fripière* was the pawnbroker of those in desperate straits for the next meal. It was the last resort: after pots and pans and cooking utensils, would come clothes, first those that were not immediately needed by the requirements of the season, then pretty well the whole wardrobe, save what actually covered one's nakedness.

The first witness to be heard is François Prime, *fabricant de bas*, aged thirty-five, living rue Bourgchanin, who

> dépose que Thérèse Bonnard est connue dans tout le canton pour une fille de mauvaise vie, que lui témoin ayant été appellé plusieurs fois par lad. Bonnard, a eu la faiblesse d'avoir des habitudes avec elle, que chaque fois qu'il est allé la voir, il lui en a coûté son argent, qu'elle fit confidence au témoin il y a environ 3 mois et ½ qu'elle étoit enceinte des œuvres du nommé Ragoût, marchand, toilier, qu'il a su qu'elle couchoit habituellement pendant l'automne dernier avec un Sr. Rimbaud, chirurgien ... que lui a cessé d'aller chez elle, parce qu'il craignoit qu'elle ne lui mît le paquet sur le corps.

So much for the not very gallant Prime. Then there is the picturesque Jean Fleury Font, who, as well as describing himself as 'tambour du canton de [la] rue Bellecordière et de la place Neuve', aged thirty-eight, is something of a humourist out of *Guignol*'s repertoire:

> ... dépose que la fille Bonnard lui a fait confidence d'avoir eu des habitudes avec un marchand de violons, et avec un nommé Ragoût, marchand toilier, qu'elle était fiancée avec le marchand de violons, que c'étoient 2 drôles qui cherchoient à lui jouer des tours orduriers en plaçant à sa porte mille choses indécentes, accompagnées de lettres remplies d'infamies, qu'ils l'avaient mise dans la peine, mais qu'elle préférait garder ce qu'elle avait et ne les plus revoir, qu'elle proposa à lui témoin de surveiller led. Ragoût et le marchand de violons pour les surprendre lorsqu'ils viendroient déposer à la porte de lad. Bonnard les objets indécens dont elle se plaignait, que lui témoin a en conséquence fait le guet avec un nommé Gilet, tambour du Plâtre, pendant 2 nuits après le piquet [de la garde] retiré, que la 3me nuit entre minuit et une heure il rencontra lad.

Bonnard, assise avec le nommé Ragoût sur le Quai Monsieur, qu'étonné lui témoin dit à la fille Bonnard, *il ne valait pas la peine de nous faire passer deux nuits pour arrêter des personnes avec qui vous êtes si bien d'accord*, que lad. Bonnard s'en fut avec led. Ragoût, que depuis ce moment il ne lui a pas parlé.

The next in line is Augustin Rimbaud, *chirurgien*, 'greffier de la municipalité de Saint-Martin-la-Plaine, y demeurant ... 32 ans', who states

qu'il a travaillé en qualité de clerc chez le Sr. Achard, chirurgien en cette ville, place Grenouille,[1] que la tante de Thérèse Bonnard, demeurante porte à porte avec le Sr. Achard, lui témoin y fit la connaissance de lad. Bonnard avec laquelle il eut des habitudes dès les premiers instants, ce qui lui donna fort mauvaise idée de la vertu de cette fille ... dans le courant de l'été dernier, étant allé demeurer chez le Sr. Pointe, chirurgien en cette ville ... il eut occasion de passer sous les fenêtres de lad. Bonnard ... que cette fille l'appella et l'engagea à la visiter pour savoir si elle était enceinte, que lui témoin confirma lad. Bonnard dans ses soupçons ... depuis son séjour chez led. Sr. Pointe, il a joui encore à plusieurs reprises de lad. Bonnard ... qu'elle vouloit que le témoin lui administrât des remèdes pour la faire avorter, mais qu'il s'y est refusé.

Rimbaud seems to have had a little professional conscience, but not much else. Although in the medical profession, and knowing the risks, he continues to enjoy the perilous favours of la Bonnard while at the same time blackening her morally. The next witness is a woman, Marie Chise,

femme d'Antoine Duplan, blanchisseuse à Lyon, y demeurant, rue Ferrandière, âgée de 62 ans ... qu'étant plusieurs fois chez la plaignante et notamment dans le commencement de ce mois pour lui rendre du linge ... elle y a vu ... le Sr. Vermillière ... cette dernière racontait au Sr. Vermillière que sa femme étoit venue chez elle lui faire des reproches de ce qu'elle voyoit son mari, à quoi led. Vermillière répondit qu'il étoit fâché de donner du chagrin à sa femme, qu'il ne croyoit pas qu'elle eût pu découvrir leur liaison, parce que lorsqu'il venait passer la nuit avec la plaignante, il faisait entendre à sa femme qu'il alloit passer la nuit au piquet de garde, cherchant led. Vermillière à consoler la plaignante en lui promettant quelques écus de tems en tems.

François Thévenon merely states 'qu'il étoit voisin de la demeure de la plaignante, il a vu un particulier vêtu de gris frapper sur le contrevent de la fenêtre de la plaignante, qui habite au rez-de-chaussée.' The last witness is René Cordonnier, *portefaix*, who states

seulement que passant dans le courant du mois d'août dernier entre 10 heures et 11 heures du soir au-devant de la boutique de la plaignante ... il vit le Sr.

---

[1] On Jacques-Joseph Achard, born in Lyon, parish of Saint-Nizier, 29 May 1765, see Dr Jean Rousset, 'Un chirurgien Jacobin: "L'Infernal Achard"', *Albums du Crocodile*, No. 1 (Lyon, 1964).

Vermillière qui frappait avec son chapeau contre la fenêtre de la plaignante, qu'il se suspendit même à lad. fenêtre qui est au rez-de-chaussée, que lad. Bonnard ouvrit sa fenêtre et appella ce particulier par son nom, qu'elle vint ensuite lui ouvrir la porte de l'allée et il entra.

Unfortunately, that is all that we know about Thérèse Bonnard and her matrimonial affairs. Clearly, in view of her trade, she was likely to have had some money of her own, and Vermillière, although married, as a *maître tailleur,* would have been a better proposition for her than a *marchand toilier,* a *marchand de violons,* or even a *chirurgien.* Nor is one concerned to decide whether the girl, so much abused by the testimony of men who made no difficulty about admitting that they had enjoyed her favours, not merely once, but on a number of occasions, with or without payment, deserved the reputation that she had obviously acquired with many of her neighbours of both sexes and of different ages, and with the inhabitants as a whole of the *canton* of the rue de la Bellecordière. The rue Confort is a microcosm of life, at all hours by day and by night, *entre Rhône-et-Saône,* very near the quays of both rivers, but nearer to the Saône. On a hot August night a *tambour* encounters the so-called lovers, quai Monsieur; and, on other summer nights, there are plenty of witnesses, even after midnight, to the muted life of the narrow street; living on the ground floor, Dlle. Bonnard might as well have been living on a stage, her every movement and gesture watched by sleepless or merely inquisitive neighbours, one of whom can hear her call Vermillière by name as he attempts to climb up to window level. After the night watch has passed, there seem still to be plenty of people in the street, and they are certainly not minding their own business; some, on their own admission, take the opportunity to place unpleasant objects – either excrement or primitive contraceptives – as well as insulting notes and messages, at the girl's door. Those who observe her and those who enjoy her favours belong to the whole range of the local population of the *canton,* from *portefaix* and *blanchisseuses,* to master-craftsmen, shopkeepers, merchants, doctors and apprentices. Her case is a dramatic, and therefore perhaps somewhat untypical example of the sociability of a collectivity that is still perpendicular rather than horizontal, a unit in which the passer-by will look upwards, rather than to the front. And although all these people would have had a very hard day's work, many seem still to have had the energy and the inclination to fool about at night, whether to tap at Thérèse's window, or to watch at her door. The two *tambours,* for instance, were eager to accept her challenge, though they had no particular reason to act on her behalf; but she was fooling *them.* At least this is what Font must have thought when he met her with her lover (her alleged persecutor) on the quay, well after midnight, on his third successive night keeping watch. Restif seems to have had plenty of imitators in this almost southern city, in which, in August at least, there would have been much more to satisfy their impudent curiosity than in Paris.

CONCLUSION

We have been engaged on an excursion into the hidden life and assumptions of a pre-industrial society, the principal characteristic of which is perhaps the very shadowy frontier between work and leisure. It is a pattern of life that is not governed by the stop-watch or the factory whistle, and which, owing to the many successive stages that brings a piece of raw material to the final, completed article, allows the artisan a certain freedom of movement, limited perhaps in time, none the less difficult fully to control or to check. The picture that emerges, though one of extremely long working hours, in unhealthy conditions, and dominated, in the case of women, by the constant fear of summary dismissal, as a result of pregnancy, is not one of an existence entirely heartless, devoid of compassion, enjoyment, fun, and rowdy pleasure. There are the compensations of companionship, mutual help, and the gusty enjoyments of the very poor, of those who are prepared to make a little go a long way, of those who will eagerly pick up anything that is going for nothing, from a piece of fruit lying in the street, to a cool breeze over the Rhône, from the music of a street band of *Savoyards*, with their dancing bear and their monkey, from the hard-hitting puppets of *Guignol*, to the massed choirs of *la fête de la Fédération*, from the pomp, awe, excitement, majesty and naïveté of a religious procession, to the pleasure of sitting in the sun, with a male friend, on the quays, from the quite exceptional, rumbustious, and dangerous excitement of a christening or a wedding, to the calmer pattern of a Sunday spent at home, over an unambitious *ragoût*, followed by a stroll, from the enjoyment of a street dispute, to a brief conversation with a young man standing outside a shop. There is in fact a considerable range of wealth and experience in these unsophisticated and often unexpected enjoyments, and one can, from the material that we have employed, appreciate the gusto and vigour with which the common people threw themselves into leisure, despite, or perhaps because of, the very precariousness and discomfort of their daily existence. Gwynne Lewis has elsewhere remarked upon this apparent disparity between wretchedness and rumbustiousness,[1] and it has been our intention to illustrate it further and in depth,

---

[1] Gwynne Lewis, *Life in Revolutionary France* (London, 1971), p. 112: 'Yet, when one has tabulated the misery provoked by a fairly heartless society, produced graphs to show the high incidence of suicide in 1796 or deaths from cholera and typhus during the last years of

even to suggest that, far from there being a contradiction between the realities of life and the breezy optimism so often displayed towards them, the one produced the other. One does not have the impression that this was a society that was sad or sick. It was certainly very uncomfortable; but it could also rise to simple, even ecstatic joy, and to a completely uninhibited enjoyment of the passing moment, without a thought for what would follow. What would follow, of course, was the early rise in the morning, and the prospect of another long working day. But even that would not be entirely predictable, it would contain elements of uncertainty, the possibility of a chance encounter, the promise of a brief escape into the swirling freedom of the open street. Indeed, *nothing* would ever be entirely predictable, save that, inexorable, of the advance of a pregnancy. And even that might not be the unmitigated disaster it would appear to have been at first sight: a number of these girls seem to have been eager to keep their children, a few of them were fortunate enough to have had parents who were understanding and helpful.[1]

We have also sought, by exploring behind the formal words of standard legal phraseology, to penetrate a language rich in hidden assumptions, and hinting at the elements of a popular collective morality, of an alternative system of justice, even of a popular religiosity, all of which were parallel to, and not necessarily hostile to, official morality, official religion, and the carefully defined rights and wrongs of the new Codes. In this sense, our task has been in the nature of an *explication de textes*, of a close examination of the wording of our *déclarations*, not so much in an effort to put a name to the seducer – a matter of indifference to the historian – as to pick up the hints. Thus, we have been concerned primarily with a study of language; and language and history are so closely tied that even translation is likely, by forcing the former through an artificial and diluting filter, to dull the full impact of meaning and emphasis, tone and half-tone, vigour and reticence (not that we can find very much reticence either in the *milieu* we have been examining, or in the language in which it is expressed). Even so it is not the direct language of the girl, as she poured out her woes to the judge or the *commissaire*, in that unmistakable, rather slow, rather hesitant speech, as if feeling its way, careful to avoid a southern gabble of

---

the Empire, one is still confronted with a residual enjoyment of life among the *classes populaires* which appears, at first glance, inexplicable. There were times, however, when "joy was unconfined"; for example, the Sunday visits to the small, crowded inns on the outskirts of Paris ...'

[1] It is interesting, for instance, to note, that of the fifty-odd *déclarations* that we have used, only one, that of Thérèse Bonnard, mentions the possibility of an abortion. According to one of the young *chirurgiens* quoted, she had called down from her window, asking him if he could conduct one for her himself. She did not even make any secret of her intentions, shouted out to the young man as he went by, *en pleine rue*.

words, or the cheeky impudence of the Parisian accent, apparently rather
lazy, as if the speaker were only half awake, in fact very careful, always
with the listener in mind, always ready to beat an instant retreat in the face
of the slightest sign, even a visible one, of offence or objection: in short,
l'accent lyonnais, a manner of speech and a tone of voice unique, like
everything about that city, indicative itself of a careful, prudent, watchful
vigilance, even perhaps of a fundamental pessimism, though thoughtless
optimism seems to have been what guided the leisure of most of the
déclarantes. To reconstruct their speech and their accent requires an effort
of imagination, though not an insuperable one, as one attempts to hear
through the muffling blanket set upon the girls' voices by the formality
and toneless monotony of legal language. If, at times, we have succeeded
at least in this: in allowing the girls to explain themselves in their own
simple, often tragic, words, then we have indeed achieved what we set out
to do: to view, from the level of these *brodeuses* and *dévideuses*, *la vie
lyonnaise* of the early 1790s – the date would have had little meaning for
people in their condition, though it might reach down to them through
the fluctuations and eventual slump in the silk trade and manufacture – the
predictable pattern of the day, the equally predictable and grim prospect
of the immediate future, at the stage at which we leave them, to their
uncertain, often dangerous fate, just this side of conception, and before
the advent of a further generation of witnesses to the continuity of that
life, witnesses born, so often as an indirect result of *la Promenade*, in the
early 1790s, most of whom would thus be likely to experience the very
different quality of life and public events in the Lyon of the 1830s.

Appendix I

SELECTED LIST OF REVOLUTIONARY FIGURES, FACTIONS AND HISTORIANS

Babeuf, François-Noël (1760–97), egalitarian journalist and revolutionary on the extreme left, executed after the betrayal of the 'Babeuf Plot' against the Directory.

Bailly, Jean-Sylvain (1736–93), astronomer, president of the Third Estate (1789) and mayor of Paris who was held responsible for the Champs de Mars 'massacre' of 1791 and was guillotined by the Revolutionary Tribunal.

Barère de Vieuzac, Bertrand (1755–1841), hard-line Jacobin and a founder of the Committee of Public Safety who survived the purge of Robespierre's followers in 1794.

Barras, Paul-François-Jean-Nicolas, Vicomte de (1755–1829), a Provençal nobleman, member of the Committee of Public Safety, prominent in the downfall of Robespierre and later the most powerful figure in the Directory; overthrown by Napoleon after 18 Brumaire.

Beurnonville, Pierre Riel, Marquis de (1752–1821), minister for war for two months at the beginning of 1793 until captured by the Austrians.

Billaud-Varenne, Jean-Nicolas (1756–1819), violent republican and member of the Committee of Public Safety who played a role in the overthrow of the Girondins and Danton.

Bouchotte, Jean-Baptiste Noël (1754–1840), successor to Beurnonville as minister for war from April 1793 to April 1794.

Brinton, Crane (1898–1968), American historian of the Enlightenment and the French Revolution; author of, among many other works, *The Jacobins* (1930).

Brissot, Jacques-Pierre (1754–93), Girondin leader and advocate of war as a means of consolidating Revolution; enemy of Robespierre; guillotined in the Terror.

Buonarroti, Philippe (1761–1837), Italian-born revolutionary who popularized the theories of Babeuf after the latter's execution.

Cadroy, Paul (1751–1813), politician who survived the defeat of the Girondins to play an active role in the anti-Jacobin repression after Thermidor.

Carnot, Lazare (1753–1823), military engineer and administrator, known as the 'Organizer of Victory' for his reform and mobilization of the revolutionary armed forces.

Caute, David (1936–), historian of the European Left and author of *Communism and the French Intellectuals* (1964).

Cendrars, Blaise (1887–1961), French-speaking poet and essayist of Swiss origin.

Choudieu, Pierre-René (1761–1838), president of the Parisian Jacobins' Club (1792), campaigned in the Vendée, was arrested after Thermidor.

Cochon de Lapparent, Charles (1750–1825), minister of police 1796–7 and a senator under the Empire.

Collot d'Herbois, Jean-Marie (1749–96), extremist Jacobin agitator and member of the Committee of Public Safety partly responsible for the sanguinary repression in Lyon at the end of 1793.

Constant de Rebecque, Benjamin (1767–1830), Franco-Swiss novelist and liberal politician, author of *Adolphe* (1816).

Cordeliers, Club of the, founded in 1790 and dominated for a time by Marat and Danton before coming under the sway of the *hébertiste* faction.

Custine, Adam-Philippe, Comte de (1740–93), general commanding the Army of the Rhine (1792–3), denounced as a traitor by Robespierre and executed.

Danton, Georges (1759–94), a dominant figure in the revolutionary government in 1792–3, later an opponent of the Terror and victim of Robespierre's purge of March 1794.

Desmoulins, Camille (1760–94), influential journalist and moderate Jacobin, an ally of Danton, executed by Robespierre.

Dumouriez, Charles-François du Périer (1739–1823), revolutionary minister and general, victorious against Prussian and Austrian armies in 1792; defeated the following year, he defected to the Austrians.

Fouché, Joseph (1758–1820), political intriguer and survivor who served in, or advised, every government from 1792 to 1815, usually as police minister.

Fouquier-Tinville, Antoine-Quentin (1746–95), public prosecutor of the Revolutionary Tribunal and a leader of the Terror, executed by the Thermidorians.

Fréron, Louis (1754–1802), Jacobin journalist who directed the Terror in Marseille and Toulon but changed sides and participated in the conspiracy which brought about Robespierre's downfall.

Germain, Charles-Antoine-Guillaume (1770–1835), officer of the

Republican Army, vehement critic of the Directory and close associate of Babeuf.

Girondins, members of a political group prominent in the Legislative Assembly in 1791–2 and the Convention in 1792–3, rivals of the Jacobin Montagnards who defeated them and executed many of their leaders after June 1793.

Godechot, Jacques (1907–), historian, author of *La Grande Nation* (1956) and defender of traditional French interpretations of the Revolution.

Goupilleau de Montaigu, Philippe-Charles-Aimé (1749–1823), extremist member of the Convention who survived the fall of Robespierre and joined the Thermidorians.

Guizot, François (1787–1874), French historian and statesman, the dominant minister of the July Monarchy from 1840 until 1848.

Hanriot, François (1759–94), commander of the Paris National Guard (1793) responsible for the arrest of the Girondin leaders; executed with Robespierre.

Hébert, Jacques-René (1757–94), demagogic journalist and leader of an extremist Jacobin faction demanding a state-controlled economy; defeated by Robespierre and executed with nineteen of his followers in March 1794.

Isnard, Maximin (1751–1830), Girondin politician who became president of the Convention and managed to survive the Terror.

Jacobins, members of the most influential revolutionary club, who demanded the execution of Louis XVI and the overthrow of the Girondins; from the summer of 1793 they supported Robespierre and the Terror.

Lafayette, Marie-Joseph-Paul-Yves-Roch-Gilbert du Motier, Marquis de (1757–1834), French nobleman who fought against Britain in the American War of Independence and at the start of the Revolution became commander of the National Guard in Paris; abandoned the French army after the overthrow of Louis XVI. A leader of the 1830 revolution.

Le Bas, Philippe-François-Joseph (1765–94), member of the Convention, friend and disciple of Robespierre.

Lefebvre, Georges (1874–1959), pro-Jacobin Marxist historian, admirer of Robespierre and author of, among many other works, *Les Paysans du nord* (1924).

Lepeletier, Félix (1769–1837), brother of Michel Lepeletier, who was assassinated in 1793 after voting for the execution of Louis XVI.

Marat, Jean-Paul (1743–93), radical journalist, editor of *L'Ami du Peuple* and Montagnard leader who called for the execution of the Revolution's enemies; assassinated in his bath by Charlotte Corday.

Mercier, Louis-Sebastien (1740–1814), successful journalist and playwright and moderate revolutionary politician who opposed the death penalty for Louis XVI; imprisoned during the Terror but released after the death of Robespierre.

Montagnards, hard-line revolutionary group closely associated with the Parisian Jacobin Club who, after destroying the Girondins, dominated the Convention during the Terror of 1793–4.

Paganel, Pierre (1745–1826), moderate politician, member of the Legislative Assembly and the Convention.

Palmer, Robert Roswell (1909–), American historian famous for his view that the American and French revolutions belonged (like lesser European upheavals) to a single wave of late eighteenth-century democratic revolution.

Parein, Pierre-Mathieu (1755–1831), one of the most intelligent of the revolutionary generals, public prosecutor in the Vendée in 1793.

Ramel, Jean-Pierre (1768–1815), soldier who fought successively in the royalist, republican and imperial armies and was lynched at Toulouse during the White Terror.

Restif de la Bretonne, Nicolas-Edmé (1734–1806), prolific French novelist and author of *Monsieur Nicolas*, an autobiography set largely in the Parisian underworld.

Robespierre, Maximilien de (1758–94), Jacobin leader, principal spokesman of the Montagnards in the Convention and, as the dominant figure of the Committee of Public Safety, chief director of the Terror in 1793–4; overthrown and executed in the Thermidorian coup.

Roland, Jean-Marie (1734–93), Girondin leader who became minister of the interior in 1792 and tried to prevent Louis XVI's execution; escaped from Paris during the purge of the Girondins but committed suicide after learning of his wife's execution.

Ronsin, Charles-Philippe (1752–94), republican general who became one of the *hébertistes* and was executed with them.

Roux, Jacques (d. 1794), priest, leader of the *sans-culotte* crowds and chief of the democratic extremists called *Enragés*; expelled from the Cordeliers Club and arrested, he committed suicide in prison.

Rudé, George (1910–93), English Marxist historian of 'the Crowd'; author of *The Crowd in the French Revolution* (1959).

Saint-Just, Louis de (1767–94), an ideologue and colleague of Robespierre, a leading figure of the Terror and the member of the Committee of Public Safety who oversaw the revolutionary armed forces; executed after Thermidor.

Soboul, Albert-Marius (1914–82), Marxist historian of the Revolution, famous for his studies of the peasantry and the Parisian *sans-culottes*.

Tallien, Jean-Lambert (1767–1820), Montagnard, regicide and supporter of the Committee of Public Safety until his denunciation by

Robespierre in June 1794; thereafter he changed sides and became one of the Thermidorian leaders, a supporter in turn of the Directory, Napoleon, the first Bourbon restoration and the Hundred Days.

Talmon, Jacob Lieb (1916–80), Israeli historian, author of *The Origins of Totalitarian Democracy* (1952).

Vincent, François-Nicolas (1767–94), general secretary at the Ministry of War (1793), a sanguinary orator guillotined with the other *hébertistes* in March 1794.

Appendix II

THE REPUBLICAN AND GREGORIAN CALENDARS: TABLE OF CORRESPONDENCE YEAR II

Year II	*1793–4*
1 Vendémiaire	22 September 1793
10	1 October 1793
20	11
1 Brumaire	22
10	31
20	10 November 1793
1 Frimaire	21
10	30
20	10 December 1793
1 Nivôse	2
10	30
20	9 January 1794
1 Pluviôse	20
10	29
20	8 February 1794
1 Ventôse	19
10	28
20	10 March 1794
1 Germinal	21
10	30
20	9 April 1794
1 Floréal	20
10	29
20	9 May 1794
1 Prairial	20
10	29
20	8 June 1794
1 Messidor	19

10	28
20	8 July 1794
1 Thermidor	19
10	28
20	7 August 1794
1 Fructidor	18
10	27
20	6 September 1794
1er jour complémentaire	17
5e	21

Index